HAROLD LASKI

HAROLD LASKI

A Life on the Left

ISAAC KRAMNICK AND
BARRY SHEERMAN

ALLEN LANE

THE PENGUIN PRESS

ALLEN LANE   THE PENGUIN PRESS

Published by the Penguin Group

Penguin Books USA Inc., 375 Hudson Street, New York, New York 10014, U.S.A.

Penguin Books Ltd, 27 Wrights Lane, London W8 5TZ, England

Penguin Books Australia Ltd, Ringwood, Victoria, Australia

Penguin Books Canada Ltd, 10 Alcorn Avenue, Toronto, Ontario, Canada M4V 3B2

Penguin Books (NZ) Ltd, 182–190 Wairau Road, Auckland 10, N.Z.

Penguin Books Ltd, Registered Offices: Harmondsworth, Middlesex, England

First American edition

Published in 1993 by Allen Lane The Penguin Press,

an imprint of Viking Penguin, a division of Penguin Books USA Inc.

1 3 5 7 9 10 8 6 4 2

Printed in England by Clays Ltd, St Ives plc

0-7139-9106-2

CIP data available

To Miriam Brody and Pamela Sheerman,
with all our love

Contents

PART III

THE 'AGE OF LASKI': THE 1930s

PART IV

DISILLUSION: THE 1940s

Acknowledgements

For the socialist Laski writing was a private enterprise. In preparing his books he worked alone, sharing with no one his ideas or his drafts, and using no one to help with research. We, on the other hand, readily acknowledge that writing a book has its collective side and that many people have helped us in the course of our work. Those who graciously spoke or wrote to us about their memories of Laski are listed appreciatively in the bibliography. Norman MacKenzie, Ralph Miliband and John Saville shared with us at the very start of our work their recollections of and insights into their former teacher and encouraged us to push on. John Saville also provided for our use the treasure trove of Laski's lifelong correspondence with his wife, Frida. Anne Bohm masterfully guided us through the politics and personalities of Laski's LSE, and John Ashworth, the school's current Director, gave us access to Laski's personnel file. Andrew Mathewson, Laski's grandson, found and allowed us to use his grandmother's autobiographical typescript, Laski's never published *The Chosen People*, and many splendid family pictures. Pat Mathewson and her husband, Laski's grandson Roger Mathewson, gave us family stories and pictures as well. Bill Williams introduced us to the fascinating history of Manchester Jewry and Gabi Scheffer helped immensely with research in Israel. Jerry Howard and Richard Polenberg deserve our deepest thanks for having seen so early how fitting it would be for Viking to be once again connected with Laski. Michael Millman and Paul Slovak have been superb as our Viking men in New York, and Andrew Franklin has been a dear friend and master editor for Hamish Hamilton in London. Thanks also to his able colleagues Sally Abbey, Keith Taylor, Karen Geary and Charlie Hartley.

We owe a special debt to the many dedicated archivists and librarians who assisted us with the wealth of Laski material scattered in the numerous collections we consulted, which are listed below in the bibliography. Thanks are due the staff at the House of Commons Library and most particularly the reference librarians and the circulation and inter-library loan staff of Cornell's Olin Library. Without their dedicated and patient help this project would not have been possible. Larry Moore and Miriam Brody read the entire manuscript and made valuable suggestions. Glenn Altschuler deserves special thanks. He not only read the manuscript, but his sensitive historical and literary skills made it much improved. Cindy Sedlacek deserves praise for her technical wizardry in turning nearly a thousand hand-written pages into a typed and readable text.

We also thank the number of students and young people who have helped us with research over the last five years. With us virtually through all these years was Vivienne Hemmingway, to whom we are deeply grateful. Thanks also to Rachel Calvo, Jennifer Condry, Paul Davies, David Folkenflick, Loren Gatch, Martin Gammon, Dan Gintner, Matt Goldberg, Jonathan Brody Kramnick, Leah Kramnick, Rebecca Kramnick, Russ Lamotte, David Lytel, Lucy Sheerman, Madlin Sheerman and Seth Wilson.

A final word about the authorial division of labour. The original idea for the book was Barry Sheerman's in 1986. For most of the next five years the project was very much a joint enterprise, with Barry Sheerman and Isaac Kramnick both mapping research strategies and evolving interpretive perspectives. Barry Sheerman did most of the digging and interviewing in Britain and Isaac Kramnick in America. By 1991 most of the burden for research fell to Isaac Kramnick and it was also he who actually wrote the manuscript. So much of the final book reflects our earlier common endeavours, however, that we see it in a general sense as jointly authored.

The Public Intellectual

Harold Laski was everyone's favourite socialist. For decades nearly everyone made use, for good or ill, of his name and reputation. When H. G. Wells created a 'utopian' character in his 1922 novel *Men Like Gods*, he called him Laski. When Ayn Rand needed a model for her evil anti-individualist in her 1943 novel *The Fountainhead*, she 'saw Laski' as 'the soul of Ellsworth Toohey in the flesh'. When George Orwell sought in 1946 to ridicule political writing that mangled the English language, his first example was a passage from Professor Harold Laski. When William Buckley in *God and Man at Yale* needed in 1951 a list of authors that he felt no teacher should refrain from refuting, he came up with 'Marx or Hitler, Laski or the Webbs, Huxley or Dewey'. And as recently as 1968, when Saul Bellow had to illustrate in *Mosby's Memoirs* how well his hero understood the landmarks of the 1930s, he wrote, '"I shall never forget Mosby's observations on Harold Laski." "On packing the Supreme Court." "On the Russia purge trials." "On Hitler."'

Harold Laski, who came so easily to mind, was a Professor of Political Science who taught at the London School of Economics from 1920 to 1950. He was a prodigious writer who published over twenty books and thousands of essays. The range of his writings was enormous, and while the impact of his books varied, some like his *Grammar of Politics* (1925), *Liberty in the Modern State* (1930), *Reflections on the Revolution of Our Time* (1943) and *The American Democracy* (1948) were landmark studies in their day. Laski was also a Labour Party activist, elected to its National Executive Committee from 1937 to 1949, who during the election year of 1945 served as the party's chairman. Laski spent nearly one third of his teaching career in America, where he became friends with Oliver Wendell Holmes, Jr, Louis Brandeis, Felix Frankfurter, Franklin Roosevelt, Edward R. Murrow and Max Lerner. A warm and gregarious person, Laski cultivated friendships with important people, whether they were revolutionaries or heads of state.

Not only did Laski's life and career stand monumentally astride the first half of the twentieth century, so much so that the Oxford historian Max Beloff labelled inter-war England 'The Age of Laski', but the life itself was a moving narrative of rebellion, recognition and repudiation. His marriage at eighteen to a woman eight years older caused a break with his family that led him to forge his career on his own under constant financial pressure. With his books and his contacts Laski made it to the pinnacles of influence and fame in the 1920s and 1930s, often becoming himself the centre of attention. Four times in his life Laski was the focus of widespread public controversy. A speech on behalf of striking policemen in 1919 created an academic freedom crisis at Harvard. Lectures in Moscow in 1934 raised a civil liberties fuss in Britain. His statements during the general election in 1945 became the focus of Churchill's campaign strategy. And in 1946 his sensational libel trial in London was reported by the world press. Sadly, in his last years the rebuke and repudiation by his own party, governing in its own right for the first time, left him deeply disillusioned.

For a time Laski was the most important socialist intellectual in the English-speaking world. He tempered the abstractions of continental Marxism with his own mixture of Anglo-American pragmatism and faith in democracy to become in the 1930s and 1940s the principal theorist of a democratic socialism indelibly identified with the British Labour Party, the London School of Economics and Laski. He was also a legendary teacher, convinced that youth would break the age-old cycle of exploitation and suffering and, if he could assist that process in the lecture or seminar room, there were no limits to the time and interest he would give.

The influence of Laski's ideas went far beyond the college classroom. He was one of the twentieth century's principal public intellectuals. As a publicist for socialism he wrote not only more than twenty books, but hundreds of articles for the 'weeklies', like Britain's *New Statesman* and America's *Nation* and *New Republic*. He also served long stints as a newspaper columnist for mass circulation newspapers and was constantly lecturing the public, on the BBC, at army bases, at Boston's Ford Hall or on worker education weekends, trying to teach the politics of democratic socialism to anyone who would pay attention.

Laski was also a political activist who devoted much of his time to the nitty-gritty of party politics. It was not unusual then for intellectuals to move easily in the world of practical politics, but what makes Laski different is the paradox of styling himself as an alienated, radical outsider, demanding a fundamental transformation of society to end class oppression, while delighting in playing the political insider influencing a marginal change here and an incremental policy development there. This was paralleled by his thundering against the ruling elite as he sought an egalitarian socialist brotherhood, while at the same time cultivating the very same Great and Good people his ideas sought to topple. Almost as important to him as attacking the privileged was dining with them. Even when his membership on Labour's National Executive Committee brought him within the party's leadership, he thought himself free to continue the role of outside critic, which in turn led to well-publicized rebukes of him by Attlee, Bevin and Dalton. In the course of Laski's life much energy would go to the delicate management of this outsider/insider ambivalence, so basic to his self-identity.

As an activist and writer, Laski's career represents the odyssey of many on the left in the first half of the twentieth century. He began as a direct-action suffragist and syndicalist before the First World War, even engaging in violent politics. Abandoning the 'cult of the deed' during the war, he turned to an intellectual exposition of a trade-union-focused socialism, which he called pluralism. In the 1920s he was gradually won over by the Webbs to their variety of Fabian socialism, and in the 'red decade' of the 1930s, unemployment, Spain and the rise of fascism moved him further leftwards to overt Marxism. But Laski's Marxism always had to accommodate his liberal commitment to civil liberties and his democratic revulsion of any form of extra-parliamentary or non-electoral political methods. As much as he praised the Soviet Union in the 1930s as the bastion of anti-fascism and the embodiment of socialist potential, Laski denounced its repressive, anti-democratic politics. He criticized the treason trials and was infuriated by the Hitler–Stalin Pact. In the 1940s he was as critical of the Soviet Union as of the United States in parcelling out blame for the Cold War.

Throughout his odyssey on the left he never wavered, however, in his commitment to the ideals of true socialism, the replacement of economic individualism and the profit motive by an egalitarian society based on cooperation and public service. His was the enduring conscience of the British left. Others in the labour movement would sacrifice principle for power, but in the 1930s and 1940s Laski's writings and activism always stressed the importance of these socialist principles, often lost sight of by his colleagues in their eagerness to govern.

In contrast to the universalism of Laski's socialist ideals was always the parochialism of his Jewishness, not that unusual among the many Jewish leftists in Europe and America, but rare in Britain. As Laski worked with other English socialists to realize William Blake's dream of building Jerusalem 'in England's green and pleasant land', he was conscious that he was one of the few Jews among the labour movement's earnest Christians. His Jewishness and his attitude to it were central issues in his life. They shaped the events of his early adulthood and many of his American friendships, and featured in his recurring involvements in the politics of Palestine and Zionism. As aloof as Laski tried to remain from personal identity as a Jew in his allegiance to socialist internationalism, Hitler's Holocaust contributed to a wartime crisis that turned Laski into an outspoken advocate of Jewish rights and led to bitter confrontations with Bevin over Palestine after the war. Throughout his career anti-Semites in England and America on the right and even on the left would not let him forget his ethnic origins.

Laski's was an Anglo-American career. He was almost as well known in America as in Britain. His closest friends were Americans. He moved as easily in political and cultural circles in America as in Britain and played a principal role in shaping the ideas of democratic socialism in America in the inter-war period. He was the quintessential socialist for many Americans and was just as likely in the 1930s and 1940s to be written about (and attacked) in the American press as in the British. No one else in public life in the first half of this century had a comparable dual career in both countries.

No small part in explaining Laski's successful career was his personality. World-class scholar, indefatigable socialist publicist, consummate insider and political operative, he also possessed an ebullience and charm that won people over. He was open, generous and kind. People liked to be with him, fascinated by his learning, his humour and his marvellous conversation. He enjoyed important and interesting friends, and they were drawn to him, to his mind, his wit and his stories.

Laski knew nearly everyone of note, or so he claimed, which presents a serious difficulty for his biographer. In addition to everything that Laski did in his life, there is even more that he said he did. The fundamental

'Laski problem' is that he boasted and exaggerated about achievements and acquaintances, which we refer to as his myth-making. Margaret Cole, an important socialist contemporary of Laski's, warned in 1978 that 'historians can never rely on any incident communicated by Laski ... unless it is confirmed by some other authority'; and Edmund Wilson, the literary critic and friend of Laski, wrote in the *New Yorker* that Laski 'left traps for his biographers'. Laski was, in fact, less unreliable than conventionally described, but one must still be wary of the traps.

Laski's life speaks to a lost world. If we are now living through what some see as the twilight of socialism, then Laski's life speaks to its morning. The Russian Revolution and the Bolsheviks' success had much less appeal to the left in Britain and America than it did on the European continent, so the promise of socialism's new day and the building of Jerusalem anew in a community of equals were best captured in the English-speaking world by Laski in his steady stream of books and articles on democratic socialism. Progressives have now lost that morning of promise: it was a victim of the Cold War, in which ideological excess by the Stalinist left and the anti-communist right allowed no breathing space for the democratic socialist alternative. Laski saw this late in his life. In the grim disillusion of his last years he provided his most enduring achievement, his penetrating critique of the Cold War. As world power shifted from his Britain to America and the Soviet Union, he saw this promise of a democratic socialist *via media* doomed by the irrational stupidity of superpower rivalry.

Though Laski was a professional intellectual, this book is not an intellectual biography focused exclusively on tracing and analysing his ideas and insights through their evolution in his voluminous corpus. As important parts of his life, his writings and ideas will be integrated into the description of his career to play the crucial role they must in the portrait of a public intellectual. The book's ambition is a broader one, however: it seeks to fill what Kenneth O. Morgan described in 1987 as a massive Laski historiographical gap. He hoped then that 'a proper biography will do justice to this unassuming little Titan whose monuments still lie all around us, landmarks of the revolution of our time'.

PART I

APPRENTICESHIP:

1893–1920

CHAPTER ONE

'Manchester Born and Manchester Bred'

Harold Laski and his socialism were 'history's revenge on the city of Manchester', *Time* magazine pontificated in its obituary of Laski in 1950. Seat of the Industrial Revolution, Manchester had given its name to the school of economic thought that to this day preaches the virtue of *laissez-faire* capitalism. Free trade and cotton made and sustained Manchester in the nineteenth century. From Calcutta and Bombay in India, from Alexandria in Egypt and from New Orleans, Mobile and Charleston in America, cotton came by boat to the nearby port of Liverpool, from where it went by rail or water to Manchester's factories. Out of those factories came the world's cloth, making their owners like Laski's father among the richest men in Britain.

Lecturing once at the University of Manchester, Laski proudly proclaimed that he was 'Manchester born and Manchester bred'. It was a particular Manchester, however, that nurtured him, Jewish Manchester. Jews had lived in tolerant nonconformist Manchester since the late eighteenth century and in 1895 the Jewish population was about 10,000. Manchester's Jewish population rose to 35,000 during the period between 1875 and 1910, when the great migration of Eastern European Jews to Britain increased the total number of Jews in the country fourfold from 60,500 to 250,000. Jews at that time constituted one half of 1 per cent of the total British population, the vast majority of them living in the capital. Manchester, already in 1870 the largest provincial Jewish community in Britain, remained so in 1910, followed by Leeds with a community of 25,000 Jews and Glasgow with 15,000.

Many of Manchester's Jews flourished in the cotton trade, the garment industry, and in chemicals or engineering. Charles Dreyfus in chemicals, Nathan Laski in cotton and Simon Marks and Israel Sieff, the pioneers in retail trade, lived lives of comfort and wealth which distanced them from the thousands of poor Jewish tailors, pressers, cap-makers, and pedlars who made up the bulk of the Manchester Jewish community. But the Jewish merchant princes of Manchester never achieved the riches of the Anglo-Jewish banking families, the intermarried 'cousinhood' of Rothschilds, Montefiores, Samuels and Sassoons.

The leadership of these merchant entrepreneurs, combined with the generally liberal atmosphere of Christian Manchester, produced a particularly thriving and influential Jewish community. Education was a critical factor. Manchester Grammar School, highly regarded nationally, was completely open to Jewish boys. The city's university brimmed with new scientific ideas. This, together with Manchester's diversity, helped to produce a community that one historian has described as 'perhaps more cosmopolitan in texture than any other Jewish community in Western Europe'. To it would come the chemist Chaim Weizmann in 1904 and from it would come not only Harold Laski but novelists, the likes of Louis Golding, one of Britain's most popular authors in the 1930s, and Laski's own niece Marghanita Laski. Indeed, the anonymous author of Marghanita's obituary in the *Guardian* noted in 1989:

> Hampstead (where she lived most of her adult life) cannot claim Marghanita's roots. She belonged to that intellectual, aesthetic and moneyed ghetto in Manchester that gave more to British culture than any other community between the arrival of the Huguenots and Hitler's refugees.

The families in that 'moneyed ghetto' maintained their distinctive culture derived from Jewish tradition and religious practices. They did not remain aloof from English life, however. They followed the advice of the *Jewish Chronicle*, London's widely read Jewish paper, that encouraged provincial Jewry to 'iron out the ghetto bend' and to 'turn Polish into English Jews'. The Laskis were themselves an example of this measured assimilation to English culture, with the parents Nathan and Sarah choosing to name their children Neville, Harold and Mabel. The names of the children notwithstanding, the Laski household remained a traditional Jewish home where the dietary laws of Kashrut, as well as the sanctity of the Jewish Sabbath, were strictly observed. An indication of Nathan's commitment to traditional Jewishness was his stubborn refusal to leave his twenty-room house on Smedley Lane in the predominantly Jewish area of Cheetham Hill in north Manchester when it became fashionable and more 'English' for well-to-do Jews to move to the genteel southern suburbs.

Nathan Laski was a tough act for any son to follow. He was born in 1863 in Middlesbrough, on Teesside, his father having emigrated from Poland in 1831 as a small child. Nathan had no formal schooling and in 1876 at the age of thirteen went to work as an office boy for the cotton merchants G. P. Gunnis and Co. He rose eventually to be senior partner in the business, and then G. P. Gunnis was absorbed into Laski and Laski, the company Nathan formed with his brother Noah which became one of Lancashire's largest and best-known cotton goods export houses. The basis for Laski's phenomenal success in business was his India connection. In 1885 he was sent by G. P. Gunnis and Co. on the first of what would be forty-four business trips to India. He was the first Manchester entrepreneur to realize the potential of doing business directly with native merchants in India, and he assiduously cultivated these personal contacts. The specific source of his fortune was his recognition of the enormous market in India for fabric remnants and left-over ends of bolts.

Nathan was the oldest of four siblings. The second oldest was Noah, the silent partner in the company that Nathan built. While Nathan's energy fuelled the company's growth, Noah devoted most of his time to good deeds, earning him the title 'King of Schnorrers', or master collector for charities. Noah's only child, Norman, was the one cousin Harold remained close to throughout his life. Norman married Simon Marks's daughter Elaine and became a director of Marks & Spencer's when it moved from Manchester to London, a position he retained even after the two were divorced and he remarried. Nathan's sister Rachel, the next oldest sibling, was married to Simon Blond, who was in business on his own. Nathan's youngest brother, Morris, worked for Laski and Laski. He too was well known for his charitable work, running sunshine camps and collecting money for poor Jewish children to spend holidays at Blackpool.

Among the three brothers Nathan's was clearly the dominant personality. He was a handsome man who stood tall and erect. It was said that 'if you saw him on the street you would think he was a Guardsman'. He was well dressed, neat and always had a cigar in his mouth. His granddaughter Diana, Harold's only child, remembered him as 'a great big, handsome man'. She also remembered that she was 'scared stiff' of him. He was, indeed, short-tempered and, as his daughter-in-law Cissie Laski put it, 'couldn't bear to be crossed in anything'. Popular, friendly, 'hail-fellow-well-met', she added, but nevertheless a tough-minded man of strong convictions.

Nathan Laski was the acknowledged leader of Manchester Jews, described informally as 'Jewry's Communal King' and by the press as the 'lay head of the powerful Manchester Jewish Community'. In 1896 he became the youngest President of Manchester's elite synagogue, the Great Synagogue. He served as President of the Manchester–Salford Jewish Board of Guardians, the paternalistic communal body that supervised the distribution of charitable services to less fortunate Jews, for many years. For many years too he held the ritually powerful position of Chairman of the Board of Kosher Butchers in Manchester. He was also the first provincial Jew to serve as an officer of the Board of Deputies of British Jews, the lay governing body of British Jewry. He served as Treasurer on this Board when the other officers included Lord Rothschild and also while his elder son, Neville, was President of that important body. Finally, Nathan was one of the seven English representatives on the Jewish Agency which worked with the British government to carry out the mandate in Palestine.

As well known for secular service and good citizenship, Nathan served twenty-eight years as magistrate, having been made a Justice of the Peace in 1906. He was proudest of his many years' involvement with the Victoria Memorial Jewish Hospital, founded at the turn of the century and eventually to become one of the great hospitals of northern England. He had opposed its building at first for fear it would encourage an image of the Jewish community as overly exclusive, but when it became a clearly non-sectarian hospital, supported principally by Jewish charity, he converted to its support and was for many years the zealous Chairman of its Board. When he retired in 1934, a grateful city honoured him. He was awarded an honorary degree from the University of Manchester and friends collected £8,000 with which they founded a colony, the Kfar Nathan Laski, in Palestine. He in turn donated several thousand pounds to Jewish and non-Jewish charities.

There were two sides to Nathan Laski's benevolence as 'King' of Manchester Jews. There were occasional lapses into tyranny, as with most rulers. He would put down a speaker at Board of Guardians meetings with a peremptory 'Sit down, young man; when I want to hear from you I'll call on you.' When a ritual slaughterer refused to join the Board of

Slaughterers over which he presided, Nathan called him in and is alleged to have said, 'If you don't join I'll have you deported.' When the man took Nathan to court for threatening him, Nathan was represented by his barrister son Neville, who argued that what, in fact, his father had said was, 'I'll have you reported.' Nathan won the case. There was also another side to his power. He was a man of immense generosity who personally distributed matzo to the poor on Passover and gave large amounts of money to teach new Jewish immigrants trades. He also financed hostels for them to live in. In his years as magistrate it was not uncommon for Nathan to pay the fines for many who appeared before him. By far the most unusual dimension of this generous side, however, was his twin reputation as mediator and resolver of private disputes and as giver of advice and solver of problems. It was claimed at his retirement that he settled fifteen disputes a day and perhaps 70,000 in his lifetime. Like a rabbi in a medieval shtetl, he would 'hold court' for the Manchester Jewish community. A part of each day would find him in the morning room at Smedley House with an almost continuous procession of 'petitioners' asking for advice, for help, for aid in righting wrongs.

Smedley House was an appropriate setting for this uncrowned 'monarch'. It was close and accessible to the largest concentration of Jews in the Cheetham Hill area. The large house had four live-in servants: cook, parlourmaid, nurse and undernurse. There was an impressive library on the first floor. Nathan purchased many books, mainly on Jewish themes, and Neville and Harold acquired many more as they were growing up. Nathan liked to give the impression of being a well-read man, even writing a short book of Indian impressions himself. In truth he had little time to read. Constantly at meetings for his causes, he always reserved two evenings at home, Wednesday for bridge and Friday for the family Sabbath meal. He did not work on Saturday, but after synagogue he visited the sick at the Jewish Hospital.

Presiding over Smedley House, the servants, the Sabbath meals and the three children was Sarah Laski. Six years younger than Nathan, she was born in 1869 in Manchester, the daughter of Philip and Anne Frankenstein. The Frankenstein family was in the waterproofing business, but her father, a gentle and pious man, spent most of his time as gabai (beadle) of the Great Synagogue. Small and diminutive, the much more likely source of Harold's physique, she married Nathan when she was twenty. She was traditional in her Judaism, but she pursued an active life outside Smedley House as well. At first there were the good works for Jewish charities, the Ladies' Visiting Committee and the soup kitchen. Then came non-Jewish charities, the War Pensions Committee and the National Council of Women. But then came the unusual. She served on the Poor Law Authority from 1919 to 1928 and, in an even more surprising departure from the norm, she stood in 1925 for the Manchester City Council and was elected. She continued to represent Cheetham ward, the ward she was born in, as a Liberal until her death in 1945. On the council she was involved with libraries, education and public health.

While she lived an unusually public life, Sarah held to traditional views about women. She was uninterested in the suffrage movement, and when she gave a talk to 'the girls attending the Sabbath Services at the Jews' School Manchester' in 1916 on what they could do for the war effort her message was conventional. 'We must put away for ever all frivolous and self-centred thoughts that sap away all that is good in us,' she urged. 'There is nothing better to promote real happiness than by doing one's best for others. This is peculiarly the lot of our sex.' And she certainly did her share. Like Nathan, she was widely known for her generosity and her concern for the poor. She was called 'the Beloved Lady of Smedley House'. It was said that few in Manchester cared more for others than she. She insisted that they should receive no gifts for their golden wedding anniversary in 1939, but that contributions be given to Manchester hospitals, which produced a fund of £10,000.

Her daughter, Mabel, demanded a good deal of Sarah's care. Harold's older brother by two years, Neville, would figure prominently in the course of Harold's life, but Mabel would be relatively unimportant and features principally in his early years in Manchester. She never left home. Only after Nathan and Sarah had died and the big house became first a hostel for refugee children and then a home for handicapped children did Mabel move out to a rooming house near by. The exact nature of Mabel's condition seems not to have been discussed with Harold or Neville and was not passed down in family lore. She led a sheltered existence, was kept at home through her school years and received a modicum of education from tutors and governesses. Whatever the nature of her mental disability, she was certainly able to mingle in the world. A regular commitment was a Sunday and Tuesday visit to the Jewish Hospital to wrap bandages, and she attended communal parties regularly. Her parents were in fact so devoted to Mabel that if there was a community affair the invitation had to read 'Mr and Mrs Laski and Miss Laski'; otherwise, the parents wouldn't attend. The brothers were less solicitous. Neville told friends that 'something was wrong with her bone structure', and Harold wrote to his wife from family visits that she was 'obstinate as a mule, and utterly helpless', and years later that she was 'a pathetic little creature . . . completely unaware of the world around her'. Nevertheless, she filled the house with her piano playing and was always present when the Laskis entertained, joyfully agreeing when asked by Nathan to 'go up and get your dad a cigar'.

The Laskis liked to entertain, and were socially ambitious. If Nathan held court during the day at Smedley House, Sarah took over on Saturday evenings. Ensconced on a large carved armchair in the breakfast room, she received relatives, local merchants like the very rich Sam Cohen or Simon Marks, or local dignitaries like the Tory Lord Mayor, John Louis Paton, the High Master of the Manchester Grammar School, C. P. Scott of the *Guardian* or the Jewish philosopher Professor Samuel Alexander. Their evenings at home also attracted people from far beyond Manchester as well. Neville reminisced in a newspaper piece many years later about the guests at these Saturday soirées: the Governor-General of Sierre Leone, generals of the Indian army, presidents of the Board of Deputies and even London actresses. Nathan was particularly proud of his ready access to important people. In the course of his trips to India he had audiences with every viceroy from Lord Dufferin to Lord Halifax. He loved to regale listeners with tales of his having shared three trips to India with Lord Kitchener. He enjoyed public exposure and seeing his name in the Jewish press.

Such was the family into which Harold Joseph Laski was born on 30 June 1893, when his father was thirty and his mother twenty-four. In his early years, as throughout the rest of his life, Laski was sickly and frail. His heart seemed weak and he suffered from recurring chest congestion, flu and pneumonia. His brother, Neville, with whom Harold would carry on a lifelong rivalry, was robust and healthy as well as an excellent student. Harold was studious as a boy and through long patches in bed became a voracious reader. The novelist Louis Golding has provided one of the few images that exist of Harold as a boy. It is the familiar depiction of Laski as a prodigy:

At the top of every form, more knowledgeable than his masters, striding on thin shanks along Cheetham Hill Road loaded with books like a ship with barnacles.

Harold spent his bar mitzvah year, 1906, almost entirely in bed, although he was still able to have the service at the Great Synagogue, where Nathan was President, and the reception at Smedley House. With gifts of money he purchased what would be the beginning of his book collection. While his relationship to Judaism would be a central issue in his adult life, as a boy in the house of Nathan and Sarah he was an observant Jew. Norman MacKenzie, a former student of Laski's, a distinguished social scientist and biographer of the Webbs, Shaw and Wells, recounts Laski years later telling of his early fear of a vengeful Hebrew God. He was sixteen and sitting for entrance exams at Oxford. The exams were held on a Friday and he stayed the weekend with Neville, already at Oxford in Corpus Christi. Harold's story has him standing outside the Ashmolean Museum but unable to enter in dread that divine retribution over such a frivolous excursion on the holy Sabbath day would lead the examiners to fail him. Kingsley Martin, editor for many years of the *New Statesman* and one of Laski's closest English friends, writes of Harold always retaining through his emancipated adulthood a revulsion at the smell of pork. Indeed, years later, in the dark days of Second World War shortages, Harold, in writing to his wife about how limited the available food was, made the point by noting that he had no choice but to eat a ham sandwich.

Laski's early education took place at the Temple School, an elementary school near his home, where precocious Harold seems to have occasionally read editorials from the *Manchester Guardian* to his perhaps less than interested classmates. From there he went in 1904 to the Manchester Grammar School and it is at this point that Laski's life takes on specificity, for here the written record of his life begins, with his school file. The Manchester Grammar School was one of the finest schools in the country, its sixth form collecting more Oxford and Cambridge scholarships than virtually any other in England.

Laski was active in the school. He thought it unfair that boys in the lower forms had to wait until they were in the upper school to debate, so he organized a junior debating society. He was secretary to the regular debating society and secretary to the school's literary society, which was given the special privilege of having its meetings in the High Master's study, where tea would be taken while boys and masters read papers. (Neville, meanwhile, though a pupil at Clifton College in Bristol, was still a rivalling presence, managing in his summers to be made President of the Manchester Union of Jewish Youth Literary Societies.) One of the papers Harold read to the MGS Literary Society exists as the first in a long career of publications. Published in the school magazine, *Ulula*, his essay on Macaulay is littered with casually dropped names of historical scholars.

What is truly surprising about Laski's six years at MGS are his poor grades. Prodigy he may have been, perhaps more knowledgeable than his masters, but Golding's recollection in 1955 that Laski was 'top of every form' is untrue. For example, in two terms of second form Laski was ranked twentieth out of twenty-nine and twenty-first out of thirty-one, and in his two terms in the sixth form he was twenty-fifth and fifteenth out of twenty-six. Equally striking is the number of terms he received no ranking because of the number of absences due to illness. He invariably did better in divinity and English and in French than in physics or chemistry (often at the bottom), better in classics than in mathematics. His schoolmasters, to their credit, were not put off by Laski's form rankings. They recognized both his precocious mind and the effect on his test performances of his repeated illness and absences. They encouraged him to read and often sent assignments and work to Smedley House. The High Master, Paton, was especially struck by young Laski's wide reading, his verbal facility, his argumentative and debating zeal and his general erudition. Paton soon became a family friend of the Laskis, often appearing at Sarah's Saturday nights, and as one of two formative intellectual influences on Laski in his Manchester boyhood he would become a lifelong friend.

Paton began as High Master of the MGS the year before Laski joined, and he presided over the school for the next twenty-one years until, in 1925, he left for Newfoundland, where he established the Memorial College of St John's. He was thirty-nine when he arrived at the MGS fresh from having been the sixth-form master at Rugby. His style was unorthodox and democratic. He didn't dress like a traditional High or Head Master; indeed, his dishevelled untidiness was legendary. Paton knew the names of all his students and he familiarized himself with their family backgrounds. He allowed the Jewish students to miss school on Jewish holidays without accruing an absence and to eat special lunches. The general spirit he passed on to his boys was egalitarian. He talked often of 'the need for increased educational opportunities to enable every citizen to become one and to do the best that is within him'. He practised what he preached, giving a good deal of his out-of-school time to helping Albert Mansbridge create the Workers' Education Association in the first decade of the century.

Paton saw a young Harold Laski that the form rankings did not reveal. He realized that Laski had a virtually photographic memory and he trained it by setting him to memorize a quota of twelve lines of Latin or Greek a day. He noticed that Laski could read and comprehend over two hundred pages an hour by pulling his eyes down the printed page instead of across, and he fed this ability by providing young Harold with a constant supply of books on history, politics and literature. When Laski was ill for long stretches, Paton visited and talked for hours about books, ideas and politics. Laski had warm memories of the MGS and the concern of its masters in his sickly boyhood. Years later he relished returning to speak as a successful old boy.

When Paton came to Smedley House on Saturdays for a family visit, he was likely to meet the other formative intellectual influence of Harold's boyhood, Professor Samuel Alexander. Alexander was a fabled figure in Jewish Manchester. An Australian Jew born in 1858, he came to Balliol and the great Jowett in the Oxford of the late 1870s, and he never went home. He was the first Jew to be a fellow of an Oxbridge college and a distinguished philosopher whose *Moral Order and Progress* was considered one of the best general treatises on ethics in its day and whose *Time, Space and Deity* made him a founder of the school of process philosophy. He was given the Chair in Philosophy at the University of Manchester in 1893 and remained in Manchester until his death in 1938. Alexander, who never married, became a familiar figure in Manchester riding his bicycle to and from the university. No surprise, then, that he became a regular at Smedley House, often to pursue his one recreation, bridge. His close friend Chaim Weizmann, also of the University of Manchester, wrote of Alexander that 'he looked like some ancient Jewish prophet' with his very tall frame and his long white beard. Years later Harold Laski wrote of visiting Alexander, 'whom I have known and loved since I was a boy', whenever he visited his parents in Smedley House. An evening chat with Alexander, whom Laski introduced to Felix Frankfurter in 1934 as 'the greatest living English philosopher', was always part of Laski's trips back to Manchester in the 1920s and 1930s. In turn the elderly Alexander wrote to the successful Laski in the 1930s, 'Your affection is one of the things I prize most.'

Like Paton, but unlike Nathan Laski and his brothers, Alexander was an example of an older man committed to a life of the mind; and like Paton, Alexander helped to shape young Harold's political consciousness, weaning it from the family's Gladstonian Liberalism. Alexander was an ethical socialist not terribly interested in party politics, but willing to devote a good deal of his time to worker education projects in the Manchester area. His main political passion during Laski's school years was the suffragette movement. He chaired crowded public meetings in Manchester's Alexandra Park and walked behind banners in suffragette processions. He championed the position of women at the University of Manchester, which had admitted females since 1883. He was described as 'a sort of godfather of the women's side. No one would have dreamt of taking any important step in that connection without first consulting him' – and this in the university where Christabel Pankhurst was a student of law.

That Laski's political ideals were being forged in these schoolboy years is clear. Both in 1939, in his contribution to a collection edited by Clifton Fadiman, *I Believe: The Personal Philosophies of Certain Eminent Men and Women of Our Time* (reprinted in the *Nation* 14 January 1939 as 'Why I am a Marxist'), and in his 1948 article 'What Socialism Means to Me', written for the *Labour Forum*, a Labour Party quarterly review, Laski cited his 'great schoolmaster' J. L. Paton as having made him 'feel the sickness of an acquisitive society'. Paton advised Laski in his bedridden year of 1906 to read the book that the adult Laski saw as the source of his socialism, William Morris's *News from Nowhere*. In his boyhood he also read books by the Webbs, which led him to 'realize that a whole class of human beings was overlooked in the traditional liberalism of the family to which I belonged'. Laski remembered lunches while at school at Manchester's leftist Clarion Café, named after Robert Blatchford's inspirational socialist journal, where he heard the fiery W. C. Anderson, the head of the Independent Labour Party (ILP), speak. Here, too, young Laski heard a speech by Keir Hardie on the efforts of the Scottish miners to form a trade union, which left him able 'at least dimly to understand the price the workers have to pay for the social reform they achieve'.

Laski indicated in these adult credos that his early awareness of politics also evolved in a context of Judaism. His socialism was 'the outcome of a Jewish upbringing, the sense it conferred of being treated differently from other people and for no assignable cause'. In the confined world of his Manchester boyhood the 'Jewish question', so formative an issue for young Laski, played a prominent role in local politics, and at its centre were his father and Smedley House. Here at home, Laski's life became intertwined for the first time with Winston Churchill's. Nathan Laski rescued Churchill at an early crisis in his career, and centrally involved in this was the 'Jewish question'. Churchill had entered the House of Commons in 1900 at the age of twenty-five as Tory MP for Oldham, near Manchester. In 1903, however, when Joseph Chamberlain, the Unionist ally of the Tories, introduced proposals for protectionist tariffs, Churchill, a committed free-trader, crossed the floor and joined the Liberals. He needed a parliamentary constituency in which to stand as a Liberal at the next election, and here appeared Nathan Laski, who at the time was a powerful, if not the dominant figure in Liberal North-West Manchester. Nathan, enamoured of Gladstone and the Manchester gospel of free trade, was predisposed to be impressed by Churchill's principled act. What led Nathan to write to Churchill in 1904 offering to use his influence to help him become the Liberal candidate for North-West Manchester, however, was Churchill's brave stand on the Aliens Bill.

Harold's childhood saw a level of public anti-Semitism in Britain equalled or surpassed only by the Mosley years of the British Union of Fascists in the mid-1930s, a hostility towards people perceived as non-British that forged Laski's sense of outsiderness. The prominence of Jewish capitalists and financiers like Barney Barnato and Alfred Beit in the economic life of South Africa led many opponents of Britain's role in the Boer War, like the Marxist Henry Hyndman or the trade-union MP John Burns, to exploit anti-Semitism. Burns declared in the House of Commons in 1900 that 'wherever we examine, there is the financial Jew, operating, directing, inspiring the agencies that have led to this war'. The British army, he went on, traditionally 'the Sir Galahad of History', had become in Africa the 'janissary of the Jews'. Even more worrisome to Jews like Nathan Laski, however, was the public concern over the increasing number of foreigners in Britain. This had the potential for unifying trade-union resentment and traditional xenophobic attitudes of Tory politicians like Major William Evans-Gordon, whose British Brothers' League was the major force behind the anti-alien legislation proposed in the Parliament of 1904. The law forbade the immigration into Britain of anyone 'of extreme poverty', or who had engaged 'in violent crime' or had 'a contagious disease'. Jews were not specified in the legislation, but as by far the largest group of recent newcomers they personified the alien.

Newspapers and contemporary writers were, in fact, much more direct than parliamentary statute writers about whom they meant. 'The aliens will not conform to our ideas and, above all, they have no sort of neighbourly feeling,' offered one observer, who quickly turned to his real concerns. 'A foreign Jew will take a house, and he moves in on a Sunday morning . . . his habits are different.' Most shocking was that he wouldn't garden, he'd store smelly things in his yard 'until the neighbours all round get into a most terrible state over it . . . most extraordinary sights are seen'. Jewish workers were accused of accepting low pay and miserable working conditions, undercutting the livelihood of native workers. Singled out by the anti-alien forces were cities like Manchester. The *London Standard* in March 1903 wrote:

> The last two decades have seen the formation and spread of a careful series of provincial Jewries in the great trading and industrial centres of the kingdom, characterized by all the dirt and nastiness, the squalor and crime, the superstition and vice, which are the salient features of the Hebraic settlements in the Russian and Polish frontier districts.

Churchill vigorously opposed the Aliens Bill of 1904. He spoke in Parliament about the pogroms which since 1881 had brought death to some and economic chaos to most of the five million Jews living in Russia's Pale of Settlement. Nathan Laski wrote to Churchill in May 1904 offering historical material and statistical data about the Jewish community in Britain. Churchill thanked him in a letter of 30 May 1904, noting that what had surprised him most in studying the papers Nathan had sent was 'how few aliens there are in Great Britain. To judge by the talk there has been, one would have imagined we were being overrun by the swarming invasion and ousted from our island.' Laski's figures allowed Churchill to claim that 'all the aliens of Great Britain do not amount to a one hundred and fortieth part' of the total population. Churchill's letter to Nathan Laski also praised the tradition of asylum from which Britain had so often benefited. He ended the letter by criticizing Balfour's Tory government for stirring up 'patriotism at other people's expense' and for appealing 'to insular prejudice against foreigners, to racial prejudice against Jews'.

Churchill sent a copy of his letter to Laski to the *Manchester Guardian*. The Manchester Jews were pleased, as they were again in June and July, when he spoke passionately against the Bill in committee. On 14 July 1904, as his son Randolph put it, 'Churchill received good news from Manchester.' He had found his rescuers. Nathan Laski, thanking Churchill for his efforts 'for freedom and religious tolerance', wrote that he had been able to secure for him the Liberal candidacy for North-West Manchester. He promised him 'a body of splendid workers' and the support of Charles Dreyfus, the well-to-do Jewish chemical manufacturer who intended to desert the Tory Party for Churchill. Nathan Laski ended his letter:

> I have had over twenty years' experience in elections in Manchester and without flattery I tell you candidly there has not been a single man able to arouse the interest that you have already done – thus I am sure of your future success.

Meanwhile Balfour, the Prime Minister, who later would become one of the twentieth century's great heroes to Jews, answered opponents of the Aliens Bill with parliamentary speeches that infuriated and frightened English Jews and fuelled Harold Laski's adult feeling that the anti-Semitism of his youth, 'being treated differently from other people and for no assignable reason', was an important source of his socialism. Balfour told the House of Commons:

> It would not be to the advantage of the civilization of the country that there should be an immense body of persons who ... by their own action, remained a people apart, and not merely held a religion differing from the vast majority of their fellow country-men but only intermarried among themselves ... Some of the undoubted evils which had fallen upon portions of the country from an alien immigration which was largely Jewish gave ... some reason to fear that this country might be ... in danger of following the evil example set by some other countries.

Churchill 'nursed' the North-West Manchester constituency from July 1904 to the next general election in January 1906. The constituency had never returned a Liberal. Its Conservative MP, Sir William Houldsworth, a leading cotton merchant of the city, had been in Parliament for twenty years through six elections and declared he would not stand again. Churchill appeared in the constituency often in this period, and when he did he usually stayed the night with Nathan at Smedley House. On one such occasion, well covered in the press, Churchill spoke at a meeting called to protest the Kishinev massacre of Jews in Russia. If there was any doubt that the domestic 'Jewish question' was going to be a central issue in the 1906 election campaign, the Tory choice of William Joynson-Hicks (known to all by his nickname Jix) as their candidate made it certain. Jix was a staunch supporter of legislation limiting aliens which, in a watered-down version, had made its way through Parliament. Churchill, on the other hand, with Nathan Laski at his side, courted the Jewish vote. He respected Saturday as a day free from campaigning and addressed meetings on Sunday. Jix, meanwhile, refused to attend Sunday meetings, and to the accusations that he insulted Jews by such behaviour he replied, 'You respect your Sabbath. I respect my Sunday. I will never go electioneering on a Sunday – no, not to gain all the Jewish votes in the world.'

There were six constituencies in the city of Manchester and in 1900 five had gone to the Tories, including North-East Manchester, whose MP, Balfour, became in 1902 Prime Minster. Balfour's vigorous campaigning for Jix in the neighbouring constituency, together with Churchill's candidacy as a convert to the Liberal Party, focused national attention on North-West Manchester. Churchill was victorious by 1,241 votes. In fact, all six Manchester seats went to the Liberals; even Balfour was defeated. The general election of 1906 was, it turned out, the biggest landslide since 1832, the Tory split over the tariff issue giving the Liberals 400 seats, as opposed to their 184 in the election of 1900. The dimensions of the Liberals' national victory could not, however, diminish Nathan Laski's sense of himself as kingmaker.

But very soon there was a replay. Asquith succeeded the ailing Campbell-Bannerman as Liberal Prime Minister in 1908 and promoted the rising Liberal star Churchill to his Cabinet as President of the Board of Trade. The convention then existed that mid-session promotions to Cabinet rank required a by-election. Churchill had to resign his seat and seek re-election. So it was that in April 1908 Churchill and Jix squared off again. Once again Nathan Laski mobilized the Jewish community for Churchill and once again the nation was absorbed by the election in North-West Manchester. Lloyd George, Chancellor of the Exchequer, visited and spoke for Churchill. An ailing Balfour and a young Stanley Baldwin appeared for Jix.

It was a bruising battle and once again the 'Jewish question' was central. Churchill apologized to the Jewish voters for his inability to move his party to repeal the Aliens Act. Jix, on the other hand, told the *Manchester Guardian* that 'he was not going to pander for the Jewish vote. He would treat those who were Englishmen as Englishmen, but as to those who put their Jewish or foreign nationality before their English nationality, let them vote for Mr Churchill.' Churchill responded to this comment with direct charges of anti-Semitism.

> I do not think that in his anti-Semitic views Mr Joynson-Hicks really represents the Conservative Party which, after all, once had as its great leader Mr Disraeli . . . but last week Mr Joynson-Hicks distinguished himself by putting himself altogether adrift from the interests and aspirations of the Jewish community. [Cheers]

Throughout the campaign Jix was heckled by Jews. According to the *Manchester Guardian* of 17 April 1908, he apologized to one audience for having a weak voice, because earlier in the day he had been faced by 'vociferous Jews and it was very difficult to shout them down'.

Nathan Laski's problem, and therefore Churchill's problem, was Jewish defection, however. In August 1907 Churchill as local MP had intervened in a cap-makers' strike which produced a settlement generally seen as harsh to the owners. Thirteen of the leading immigrant cap-manufacturers, together with two important waterproofing entrepreneurs and a calico printer, deserted Nathan Laski and supported Joynson-Hicks. Jix won by 432 votes, with 90 per cent of the electors having voted. It was a spectacular reversal. The national Tory press gloated that the turncoat Churchill had been repudiated.

Very shortly after this humiliation, on 11 May, the Liberal Party found Churchill a safe seat at Dundee, and he would be back in the House of Commons as a Liberal until he returned to the Tory fold in 1924. Jix would also move on to become the controversial anti-Semitic Home Secretary in the Tory government of 1924, when he would clash with Nathan's son Harold. But now he was unrepentant. Even if a significant set of prosperous Jews had supported him in 1908, he was in no mood to make peace with Nathan Laski and the Manchester Jewish establishment. He chose an address shortly after his election, on 19 May, to the Maccabeans, a Manchester Jewish dining society, to let them know. Nathan Laski and the others were astonished as Jix, their new MP, berated them.

> If they liked he could say smooth things. He could say that they were a delightful people, that the Jews were delightful opponents, that he was very pleased to receive the opposition of the Jewish community, and that, in spite of all, he was their very humble and obedient servant. He could say that if they liked, but it would not be true in the slightest degree. He very strongly deprecated the position taken up by the great bulk of the Jewish community in Manchester . . . He had beaten them thoroughly and soundly, and he was no longer their servant.

The Laski–Churchill–Jix confrontations in the years between 1904 and 1908 were Harold Laski's introduction to politics. In those four years young Harold progressed from mere recipient of affectionate pats on the head to accompanying Churchill on his electoral rounds. Harold's wife wrote years later that he had confided to her of a youthful hero-worship in those years as he 'stood and gaped at Churchill rehearsing his speeches in front of the bedroom mirror'. Laski's more favoured students were even treated in the 1940s, when he and Churchill were bitter political foes, to Laski imitations of Churchill practising those speeches in his father's house. In 'What Socialism Means to Me' Harold Laski credited Churchill with a vital part of his early political education for speaking out 'with moving eloquence at a great meeting over which my father presided' in protest of 'the Kishinev massacres and other similar anti-Semitic excesses'. But the Laski of 1948 was quick to insist that Churchill also provided negative lessons in those early years. He was vigorous in his condemnation of pogroms, but 'he saw no reason to protest against the alliance of the Liberal government in which he served with the Czarist dictatorship which patronized and welcomed the pogroms'. Laski also suggested in 1948 that equally formative for him was the disjuncture between hearing Churchill at meetings and at Smedley House talk of 'the superiority of Liberalism over Socialism' because of its commitment to 'the individuality and dignity of the citizen', and the reality of Manchester's slums that he passed daily.

While Harold Laski's and Churchill's future paths would soon diverge so dramatically, to intersect only in periodic clashes – the General Strike in 1926, India policy in the 1930s, the peace aims of the Second World War coalition, and most memorably the election of June–July 1945 – Nathan Laski would remain a loyal supporter and distant friend of Churchill over the years. When Churchill returned to the Conservative Party, the senior Laski remained a Liberal or, in the 1930s, a supporter of the National Government; but Nathan was still drawn to Churchill's maverick views such as his opposition to softening imperial rule in India. Nathan wrote to Churchill in 1937 acknowledging that he was mistaken to have supported Chamberlain's India Bill, since 'our trade [with India] is dwindling every year as the figures recently made public show'. Nathan and 'hundreds of thousands of people in this country like myself' could not understand why Churchill was not a member of the new government announced that May. Two years later Nathan congratulated Churchill for 'the great and statesman-like speech you made on the Palestine question last night'. Churchill and a small handful of Tories had voted against Chamberlain's 1939 White Paper restricting Jewish immigration to Palestine. 'I think it is not exaggerating to say,' Nathan added, 'that you will get the blessings of Jews all over the world.' Once again Nathan lamented that Churchill was not 'in charge of the affairs of this country'. Churchill, in turn, always remembered Nathan Laski's significant role at a very difficult moment in his career. Laski's wedding present of an Indian carpet to Winston and Clementine in 1908 was given a place of honour in Winston's dressing-room of their London house in Eccleston Square, and in 1935 Churchill sent Nathan a copy of his book *Great Contemporaries*, inscribed 'For Nathan Laski and his wife and daughter. Keep the flag of freedom flying.' When Nathan died in 1941, Churchill wrote to Harold:

> He was a very good man whose heart overflowed with human feeling and whose energies were tirelessly used for other people and large causes. I have lost a friend and all my memories of Manchester and Cheetham are veiled in mourning.

These years of Harold's boyhood in Cheetham were witness to one final feature of his father's public life that introduced young Harold to yet another person destined to be a central figure of twentieth-century history as well as to an issue which would play a major role in virtually every stage of Laski's career: the person was Chaim Weizmann and the issue the politics of Palestine. Weizmann, a leading disciple of Theodor Herzl, emigrated to England at the age of thirty in 1904, the year Herzl died in

Vienna. He settled in Manchester and immediately became involved in the Jewish politics of the city. Before he received his appointment in chemistry at the university, Weizmann was employed by Charles Dreyfus, the proprietor of the Clayton Aniline Company, Manchester's largest chemical firm, and the political co-leader, along with Nathan Laski, of Manchester Jewry. Though he would quietly help Churchill's candidacy in 1906, Dreyfus was a Tory member of the city council and Chairman of the Manchester Conservative Party and as such, he was the major Jewish patron of Balfour in the North-East Manchester constituency. Despite the fundamental gulf between them, Dreyfus and Nathan Laski agreed on Jewish politics. They were both, with Nathan Laski characteristically the louder, avid believers not in the recreation of a Jewish state in Palestine but in the 'African solution' to the 'Jewish question'.

The vision of an African Zion had emerged in 1903 when Herzl, seeking desperately to find a place of refuge for the victims of the Kishinev pogrom, negotiated an arrangement with Lord Lansdowne for the settlement of Russian Jews in the British African colony of Uganda. For Herzl this was meant to be an intermediate stage on the ultimate journey to, and the settlement of, Palestine as a Jewish state. The Uganda proposal was ultimately rejected by the Seventh International Zionist Conference in 1905, but it had already split world Jewry into two opposing camps: those who saw the resettlement of Palestine as the ultimate dream, and those who sought a resettlement of oppressed Russian Jewry elsewhere, usually in Africa. The leader of the African faction was Israel Zangwill, the distinguished English Jewish novelist, who had seceded from the Zionist organization and founded the Jewish Territorial Organization (JTO) to seek the establishment of a Jewish homeland in Africa. In Manchester his staunchest supporter was Nathan Laski.

Weizmann's dramatic emergence as a presence in the English Zionist debate occurred on 3 April 1905, and Nathan Laski was its cause and its victim. Laski had arranged and chaired a meeting for the local JTO group to hear the case for African settlement be put by Barrow Belisha, a transplanted Australian Jew who had lived in Manchester for many years. After politely listening to Laski and Belisha, Weizmann rose and ridiculed the idea of an African Zion. Writing to Moses Gaster in London, the rabbinical head of English Sephardic Jewry and perhaps the leading English Zionist, Weizmann described the meeting.

I told the gentlemen emphatically that their enterprises were doomed in advance, as they know neither the people nor their needs. 'The poor Jews of the East', having waited 2,000 years for Laski and Belisha to call a meeting to render aid, will go on waiting without being unduly bothered by the resolutions adopted at the session. This struck the meeting like lightning, and covered it with ridicule. Professor Alexander, who attended the meeting, clapped furiously for me, and immediately afterwards invited me to his home. I shall go tomorrow. I have of course made myself 'unpopular' with this pack, but I'd rather be an object of hostility to these people than be liked by them.

Samuel Alexander, then forty-six, became Weizmann's closest friend in Manchester, which is not surprising since Weizmann at first had little use for Manchester Jewry, non-Zionist or Zionist. He disliked the materialism of provincial commercial Jews, their 'ignorance, rudeness, and triviality'. 'The Cheethamites,' he wrote to a friend, 'who consider themselves the betters of "our poor ghetto brothers", are in fact worse. Their Zionism is empty, a mere amusement.' As Weizmann's authority in Zionist circles increased, the Cheethamites, more eager to fraternize with 'the Great and the Good' than bear a grudge, tried to incorporate him into their circles. Nathan Laski invited Weizmann to Smedley House to dinner, where he met Churchill for the first time, on the night of Churchill's moving condemnation of Russian pogroms. Nathan then tried unsuccessfully to enlist Weizmann's support for Churchill in the general election of 1906. Weizmann also chose to stay aloof from the efforts of his employer, Charles Dreyfus, to have him endorse Balfour in North-East Manchester in 1906.

The relationships first formed in Manchester and often witnessed by young Harold in Smedley House or on the campaign trail during this Cheetham period would prove crucial in the years to come. In the First World War Weizmann worked on explosives, and in the coalition government headed by Lloyd George Churchill was Secretary of State for War and Balfour the Foreign Secretary, all of whom played some role in the Balfour Declaration of November 1917. Churchill and Weizmann would become good friends and collaborators, as would ultimately Harold and Weizmann. Nathan, interestingly enough, would never befriend Weizmann and would only reluctantly in the 1930s become a Zionist; for although Nathan Laski served as an English representative to the Jewish Agency in the 1920s, it was as a non-Zionist. Nathan stuck to his principles, never contemplating the reassembling of diaspora Judaism in the historic homeland of Israel. Like most anti-Zionists, he saw Zionism as a form of religious or national separatism. He argued that Jews should live within other nations and still maintain their communal uniqueness. He refused to deviate from these convictions even after his son Neville married Cissie Gaster in 1915, the daughter of the man who shared the Zionist leadership in Britain with Weizmann.

Nathan Laski was a strong man, a dominating figure, wedded to a traditional Jewish life-style, who nevertheless saw himself as a worldly figure in public secular life, an insider mixing easily with important people of consequence. Still, through all the wheeling and dealing he stood steadfast for his principles. Among all the models for Harold's adult male life (teachers, politicians, businessmen), his father may have been the most important, with his fidelity to a national, religious identity and utter immersion in worldly affairs. Young Harold had no idea how truly powerful a figure, committed to his convictions, his father could be. He learned soon enough.

CHAPTER TWO

Frida and Eugenics

Shortly after his eighteenth birthday Laski married Frida Kerry, who later described herself as 'the first non-Jewish girl of his acquaintance'. They had met when he was a schoolboy of sixteen during the Christmas holidays of 1909 at Halesowen, a town outside Birmingham where country house resorts catered to guests of a certain class, many of whom were recovering from illness or operations. Harold, in the autumn of 1909, his first term in the sixth form, had had an appendectomy which contributed to his disastrous ranking of second from bottom at the end of term. Weakened by the operation, he was allowed by his parents to accompany Neville, and Frida Kerry, masseuse and occasional lecturer on eugenics, was there at the end of a longer and more fascinating odyssey.

Frida, eight years older than Harold, was born on 12 August 1884 as Winifred Mary to a comfortable Suffolk farming family. Called Frida as long as she could remember, she was the oldest of four children born to Kate Ellen Lord, who at the age of eighteen had married the 43-year-old Francis John Kerry. Kate was deeply religious and Frida recalled the rhythm of childhood bound up with the feasts and festivals of the Church of England's calendar with two visits to church every Sunday. There was ease and abundance, her father having inherited four farms, and her childhood was shared with three house-servants and large numbers of farm workers who lived in the thatched cottages that went with their jobs.

Frida was aware of tension between her parents. In addition to the great disparity in age, the two had totally different temperaments. Frida's mother was lively, outspoken and ambitious. Her father was easy-going, lacking initiative and generally submissive to Kate's dominance in the household. He was also a poor businessman: while he often boasted of being able to trace the Kerrys back to 1189, he seems to have amiably and incompetently presided over the failure of the family farms and was eventually forced to sell out and retire. Frida remembered being much closer to and fonder of her assertive mother, though it would be with her that the young adult Frida, equally strong-willed, would ultimately clash.

When they met in 1909 Frida, not Harold, was the rebel. Harold was the not unusual scholarly offspring of first-generation Jewish commercial success. While perhaps more open to the left than his parents, he was still firmly in their traditional cultural and religious fold. By 1909 Frida was the embodiment of the new woman, emancipated herself and in touch with every liberating fashion of the age. To all this she would introduce the sixteen-year-old Harold and he would be forever transformed.

Frida's early years were conventional enough, with a governess until she was eleven, when she went away to boarding school. At sixteen she was sent to be 'finished' at a college for young ladies in Belgium, where she learned to speak perfect French, to play the piano and to dance with grace. She also became passionately interested in gymnastics and physical education. Frida's announcement of her intention to pursue a teacher-training course in gymnastics in Sweden produced a hysterical response from her mother. Such a life was too vulgar for a Kerry. Frida was rescued, however, by the headmistress of the Belgian school and her gymnastics teacher, for they knew of a scholarship programme at the Swedish Royal College of Gymnastics and put Frida's name forward. She was accepted and in 1904, aged eighteen, she went off to Stockholm. Her furious mother wrote: 'You are a rebellious, wilful girl . . . how dare you go against my wishes . . . from now onwards the door of my heart will be closed to you.' So, too, was her purse. Only her amiable father, unbeknown to his wife, gave Frida thirty pounds' spending money.

In Sweden Frida specialized in medical gymnastics (physiotherapy today) and massage. She learned anatomy, physiology and biology. Outside class she discovered a world of freedom and politics. Nude bathing seemed natural and ordinary. Her Swedish women friends smoked and so did she (as she would for the rest of her life). Her class-mates talked of sexual relations for pleasure's sake, unrelated to procreation. She learned of birth control and of women who wanted the vote. She learned of trade unions and of socialism. The cause she would most commit herself to in Sweden, however, was eugenics, which brought together her interests in bodies, health, sexuality and birth control, all tied together with the worship of science which seemed to underwrite all advanced ideals. This passion transformed her life and Harold's. Many years later Frida wrote:

Just at the right moment came the opportunity for me to attend a lecture in eugenics and I was captivated. From then on I became a fervent disciple, attending lectures whenever I could and reading widely on the subject . . . I dwell on it here . . . for the simple reason that it played such a major part in my destiny, turning the tide of events for me which otherwise might have been completely humdrum.

When Frida finished her course in Stockholm in 1906, she intended to return to England to seek a teaching position while living at home. Her mother was not pleased. In much reduced circumstances the family had moved to Mill Hill in outer London, where an ill brother was 'costing them a fortune' and her mother 'did not want me there to add to her troubles'. Frida returned instead to Belgium, where for two years she worked as a teacher of gymnastics in a school at Antwerp and gave private massages to augment her income. In autumn 1908 Frida returned to England to take up a teaching position in the Anstey Physical Training College in Erdington, Birmingham. Four years of separation came to an end as Frida's mother accepted her daughter if not with warmth, at least without anger or recrimination. Frida soon came to appreciate her mother's burdens: her husband's failing strength and 'sweet ineffectuality', the son's illness, the financial worries. The two women, in fact, became quite close again. At Anstey College Frida taught anatomy, physiology, gymnastics (medical and practical) and massage. She also threw herself into politics. She joined the Fabian Society and became an ardent suffragette and tireless missionary for the eugenics movement. Whenever she could she lectured on eugenics, and to supplement her income she again practised as a private masseuse, working during the school holidays in resorts around Birmingham, which brought her to Halesowen at Christmas in 1909.

There can be few young couples more dissimilar than Harold and Frida. He was a frail, sickly, bookish, bespectacled, dark, verbal, intensely intellectual boy of sixteen, and she a strong, fair, strikingly beautiful, athletic, healthy, political and social activist woman of twenty-four. He was from an urban Jewish commercial family but two generations from Poland, and she from rural Christian farmers, eight centuries Englishmen. He was away from home only under the watchful eye of his older brother, she was the free woman who had rebelled and was author of her own self. All the same, in Frida's words years later, 'from the word go Harold exercised a strong power over me'. They met at one of her informal evening lectures on eugenics. Harold walked into the lecture room and took a prominent position in the front. When she finished speaking he remained to discuss the subject more deeply. She took him for twenty; he said he was eighteen. He was, of course, sixteen. Frida at first thought Harold was intrigued by her non-Jewishness, or perhaps by her presentation of herself as a 'self-confessed rebel', but then she realized he actually wanted to talk, about eugenics or about anything. Frida's description of Harold, albeit written years later, provides an interesting picture of him well before his emergence into prominence.

> I remember noticing the intensity of his expression and was struck by the intellectual prominence of his forehead and an overall delicateness which puzzled me ... He was constantly there, hovering around for a chance to converse with me. That, I must say, was the basis of our relationship ... talking, always talking. He was the most articulate person I ever knew ... What talks those were! We took in every conceivable subject; the pet ones were eugenics, physical education, the human species, women, people and politics, reform, Victorian inventions, the Electoral Reform Bill of 1832 and the Suffrage Movement. I might have been talking to a boy but what I heard was the voice of a man seeking the spark that would kindle the fires within him. I believe I was that spark. Harold's challenging mind and intense interest acted as a perfect foil for my progressive ideas and the militant streak in my nature.

It was a surprising relationship. That Laski, so young, so relatively sheltered and sexually inexperienced, should respond so quickly to this older, worldly Christian woman whose ideas dazzled him suggests he was running away from home in some sense. Frida, on the other hand, having earlier abandoned home, found a boy and a mind to nurture and train. She was, indeed, very much 'that spark'. Harold returned to his final term at Manchester Grammar School in January and began an intense reading programme in biology, Darwinism and eugenics. He wrote on 28 March 1910 to 'Miss Kerry', telling her of arguments with the High Master over Plato's eugenic schemes. A vigorous correspondence ensued with his most recent thoughts about eugenics always the central focus. Harold convinced his parents he could use a fortnight's rest in Halesowen in early summer and once again Harold and Frida talked endlessly. On 1 September 1910

Harold wrote, now to 'my dear Frida', that 'all the reading and thinking I have done during the last nine months' was intended to have 'placed me more or less on an intellectual level with you'. He still had far to go, but it was 'a privilege to be treated by you essentially as a colleague and a fellow-worker'. In his awkward way the recently turned seventeen-year-old went on:

> It is essentially a woman characterized by your own ability and charm that I should be proud to have as my wife ... I think you should remember too that you belong to the small band of women who make for the progress of the race. I am proud to remember the change that has come over me since I knew you; how you have broadened my outlook and vivified my ideals; and I can honestly say that I know no one for whom I have a greater affection or respect than yourself.

A great change had occurred in Harold's life. Not only was he falling in love, but, inspired by and seeking to impress Frida, he had with that characteristic combination of brazen ambition and brash self-promotion which would become his trademark emerged that summer as a published author in no less a place than the eminent literary and political journal the *Westminster Review*. The fruits of his reading, of his correspondence and of all that talk with Frida came together in an article, 'The Scope of Eugenics', submitted to John Stuart Mill's old journal and published just after his seventeenth birthday in July 1910. Laski had wanted both his and Frida's names to appear on the title-page, but Frida demurred. It was, she said, principally his work.

To read Laski's first published work is to encounter a mature and self-confident essayist who wrote so well and with such command, who was so familiar with the genre and its codes, that he seemed an established author, not a seventeen-year-old sixth-former. The great scientist Francis Galton, founder and namer of eugenics, then eighty-eight, was so deeply impressed with the article that he wrote to the author, whose name he did not recognize, care of the editor, and was incredulous to discover 'this morning in a very nice, modest letter that he is a schoolboy at Manchester, aged 17!! It is long since I have been so much astonished.' Galton invited Harold to call on him in London, and in August he described the visit to his niece Milly Lethbridge.

My wonderful boy Jew, Laski by name, came here with his brother to tea
. . . the boy is simply beautiful . . . He is perfectly nice and quiet in his
manners. Many prodigies fade, but this one seems to have stamina and
purpose, and is not excitable, so he ought to make a mark.

Well might Galton have been so astonished, for in 'The Scope of
Eugenics' Laski lyrically sang the praises of Galton himself and the new
science of eugenics which Galton had single-handedly brought into being
with his publications in 1869 of *Hereditary Genesis* and in 1889 of *Natural
Inheritances*. Laski argued that Galton and his cousin Charles Darwin had
provided science as the principal tool by which twentieth-century statesmen
could solve national problems. Man, not divinity, was master of his own
fate. Eugenics, the study of 'the mysterious working of heredity' and the
method of improving the mental and physical characteristics of the race,
put social problems, like pauperism and unemployment, into a biological
context, and thus rendered them manageable. The time had arrived, Laski
proclaimed, 'when man can consciously undertake the duties that have
heretofore been performed by nature'. Darwin's teachings on natural
selection had been supplemented by Galton's great insights into the much
greater importance of nature over nurture. Galton had made it abundantly
clear, Laski wrote, that just as men inherited physical characteristics, so they
inherited psychical and social qualities. Society, then, could encourage or
discourage social behaviour by the regulation of marriage and mating.
'Natural selection must be supplemented by reproductive selection.'

Sounding much like Herbert Spencer, Laski argued that 'kindly but
thoughtless humanitarianism' mitigated against the force of natural selection. National perfectibility and the survival of the fittest had not occurred
because 'we could not let our weaker brethren go to the wall'. Indeed, an
apparently heartless Laski saw everywhere the unfit 'increasing at the
expense of the fit'. The fitter classes, statistics revealed, produced much
smaller families, while the feeble-minded and the mentally defective prolifer-
ated. If the nation was not to decline, then 'marriages should be selective'
and 'the propagation of the unfit must be prevented'. To those who
insisted that marriage was entirely a private affair and that the state had no
authority to interfere, Laski suggested that 'whatever action is fraught with
national consequences rightly comes within the cognizance of the state'.
Laski recoiled, however, from a vision of 'state-offices established to

dispose of individuals in marriage'. He preferred the state to rely mainly on influencing public opinion and to propagate the eugenic ideal of parenthood 'with the fervour of a new religion'. It would persuade society through education to regard 'the production of a weakling as a crime against itself'.

The state should discourage reproduction of the unfit through birth control and encourage reproduction of the fit by exhortations on the public value of the healthier classes producing more children. Laski refused to follow Spencer's social Darwinist disciples in their *laissez-faire* calls for repeal of social legislation despite their 'distinctly anti-eugenic' aspects. No one, he insisted, with 'ordinary feelings of humanity' could ever contemplate a 'return to the days before those Acts were passed'. A real appreciation of the true needs of the working class would in fact link interventionist state actions to the biological support of fitter children through, for example, enhanced public health facilities and a minimum wage, especially for the fitter parents of healthy children. Such legislation would then 'understand the essential dependence of economics on biology'.

However easily the internal consistency of its argumentation might unravel when pressed, 'The Scope of Eugenics' was a dazzling début for a schoolboy. Nor is its significance diminished because Laski would quite soon drop eugenics – except for the interest throughout his career in the cause of birth control – and move into quite different areas of scholarship. Already apparent in this love-inspired schoolboy work are stylistic and substantive characteristics which would always be found in Laski's writing. Patterns of sweeping historical tendencies are revealed producing near-apocalyptic crisis, the solution to which is always found in one of two options, only one of which a truly rational people would choose. The not overly original argument serves a strongly felt political preference, but its articulation reads like the wisdom of a disinterested wise man, stoical in his recognition that despite human frailty reason will triumph. The rhythm and inspirational patterning of his concluding sentences anticipate the characteristic cadences of his adult prose.

> The advance of modern science, and the insight it has given us into life, make us realize more vividly, and with greater truth, the possibilities and limitations of our civilization. Upon the framework, with which genetics provides us, we build a strong political superstructure. We see the necessity of a radical reform in the basis of our life, we have realized that the science

which enables us to elevate it lies ready to our hand. Society will work out its own destiny without eugenics; but with its aid it can accomplish its salvation.

Many of the essay's substantive themes would stay with Laski. Throughout his career he tried, as here, to balance intervention by the state with respect for the autonomy of individuals. He never lost his faith in the benevolent purpose of science or in the capacity of expert scientific minds to shape society. He would forever vacillate between images of the poor as either unfit and ignorant or exploited and oppressed.

But first Laski had to go to university. He took his entrance exams for Oxford in the autumn of 1910 and received word in December from H. A. L. Fisher, the history tutor at New College, that he had won an exhibition to read modern history. A proud Nathan declined the financial award for his son. But Harold had to occupy himself for nine months before going up to Oxford. He had seen a good deal of Frida during the summer, at Halesowen, and they also arranged simultaneous trips to London to visit Galton as well as several jaunts to festivities connected with George V's coronation. Frida was now far away, however, having taken a new job in the autumn of 1910 as physical training instructress in the secondary schools, and supervisor of physical training in the primary schools, in Lanarkshire. She lived in Glasgow and travelled to her different schools by train. In Frida's words, 'by now very much in love' they had succeeded in causing no alarm in Smedley House; even Neville had no sense of the depths of their feelings. Staying in or frequently travelling to Glasgow was, therefore, impossible, so Harold convinced his father that he would profit from studies at University College London in the winter and spring to prepare him better for Oxford. Nathan agreed and paid for Harold to live at the Strand Palace Hotel from January to July 1911.

Once in London, Harold took a temporary job with the university's Eugenics Institute. Out of his love for Frida he had, in fact, decided to scrap history and read biology. With Francis Galton's exuberant praise he had no trouble being invited to join the laboratory of the eugenics circle's leader designate, Karl Pearson. That Laski at seventeen had embraced the 'new religion' of eugenics was for its time not that extraordinary, for in 1910 and 1911 eugenics 'fervour' was widespread in English intellectual and

political circles, even among progressive liberals and socialists. The ideas of
Galton had become the venerated text, and late in his life he gave
institutional structure to the spread of his gospel by establishing the
Eugenics Education Society in 1908, by founding the Laboratory of
National Eugenics at the University of London in 1906, and by endowing
a research fellowship in national eugenics in 1904 and then a chair in
eugenics in 1911 at the university.

Galton distinguished the public policy implications of the new creed as
either 'positive eugenics', the encouragement of breeding among superiors,
or 'negative eugenics', the discouragement of breeding among the socially
disadvantaged, those whom he labelled 'the residuum'. Most of his energy
and that of his followers went into the former, and while he occasionally
mentioned 'stern compulsion', he assumed inferiors would be generally
discouraged from marrying simply by the weight of an informed public
opinion. The creation of that public opinion was dramatically encouraged
in Galton's last years by his new journal *Biometrika*, by the Eugenics
Education Society and by the national soul-searching that followed the
Boer War. This last was a reflection of the dramatic reports from recruitment officers that, for example, 403 of every 1,000 recruits in Manchester
were rejected as physically unfit for military service. They were made
much of in the press and great concern emerged about 'national degenera-
tion' or 'race deterioration'. In 1902 the Inspector-General of Recruiting
wrote that a great cause of anxiety 'as regards recruiting is the gradual
deterioration of the physique of the working classes, from which the bulk
of the recruits must always be drawn'. In these last years of Edwardian
England a campaign for 'national efficiency', the phrase that signified a
revitalized race, pervaded English life. Galton used the term frequently,
noting, for example, the need to encourage 'a more virile sentiment, based
on the desire of promoting the natural gifts and the national efficiency of
future generations'. Frida's vocation was centrally involved in the campaign.
A Royal Commission on Physical Training had studied Scottish
schoolchildren and in 1902 recommended systematic school exercises, and
in 1903 the National League for Physical Education and Improvement was
established. Politicians in the Liberal Party, especially in the Liberal imperialist wing – Limps, as they were called, like Haldane and Asquith – were
leaders in the campaign for national efficiency. Imperialists and new state
Liberals joined socialists in calling for greater state concern with health,

with education and with eliminating grinding poverty. Philanthropic and egalitarian motives mixed with concern for strength, military preparedness and imperial power. A Liberal MP apologizing for his defence of free meals and free baths for schoolchildren captured the ideological confusion inherent in the efficiency campaign:

> All this sounds terribly like rank socialism. I'm afraid it is . . . because I know it also to be first-rate Imperialism, because I know Empire cannot be built on rickety and flat-chested citizens.

The preoccupation with a restored national efficiency coincided with the early years of the eugenics movement, and 'positive eugenics' became a focus for halting racial deterioration. Karl Pearson had early on seen the linkage between all these sensitive national concerns. In his *National Life from the Standpoint of Science* he worried about England's rivalry with Germany, and he offered what he called his 'scientific view of a nation' informed by a pure Darwinian sense of efficient natural selection.

> An organized whole, kept up to a high pitch of internal efficiency by ensuring that its numbers are substantially recruited from the better stocks, and kept up to a high pitch of external efficiency by contest, chiefly by way of war with inferior races, and with equal races by the struggle for trade routes and for the sources of raw material and of food supply. This is the natural history of mankind.

In this context anti-alien legislation emerges as a form of 'negative eugenics'. Far more threatening to 'internal efficiency' than the Jews, however, was the larger issue of what was referred to neutrally as 'differential fertility' or, more bluntly, as 'the fecundity of the degenerates'. Concern with birth rates brought one to the heart of the eugenics agenda, as it had in Laski's essay.

Not only Liberals but many further to the left like Sidney Webb were caught up in this racist–eugenicist–imperialist nexus. Webb, who like Galton had written earlier of 'degenerate hordes of a demoralized residuum unfit for social life', lamented in 1901 'the stunted, anaemic, demoralized denizens of the slum tenements of our great cities'. One solution lay in a collectivist programme of health, welfare and education measures, but eugenics were equally important. In his 1907 Fabian Tract *The Decline in the Birth Rate*, Webb concluded that the source of Britain's declining rate was the voluntary decision by the sections of the population who practised 'thrift and foresight' to have smaller families. Meanwhile,

> children are being freely born to the Irish Roman Catholics and the Polish, Russians and Jews on the one hand and to the thriftless and irresponsible – largely the casual labourers and other denizens of the one-roomed tenements of our great cities – on the other . . . This can hardly result in anything but national deterioration; or as an alternative, in this country gradually falling to the Irish and Jews.

Socialism and eugenics sat easily together. They shared the conviction that life and society could be rationally planned, that science and reason could tame chance, evil, greed and ignorance. For Sidney Webb it was self-evident: 'No consistent eugenicist can be a *laissez-faire* individualist,' he wrote, 'unless he throws up the game in despair. He must interfere, interfere, interfere.' He, too, popularized the phrase 'National Efficiency' in a famous article of 1901 when he urged Lord Rosebery, a leading figure in the Limps, to turn the Liberal Party into a party of National Efficiency which would clear the slums and reform housing, sanitation and education, all 'to insure the rearing of an imperial race'. The Fabian socialists also shared the Limps' commitment to imperialism. In his *Fabianism and Empire* George Bernard Shaw argued that a well-managed British empire needed trained scientific administrators and a healthy population who could serve in the military and carry on further colonization. The source of Laski's major policy recommendation in his 'Scope of Eugenics' was clearly in this 1900 essay by Shaw, who insisted that to produce a healthy population a national minimum wage was essential, since it alone could improve the quality and efficiency of the national stock:

> We contrive to raise a handsome revenue by income tax; and we should reap a much handsomer one in national soundness and reduced disease bills, crime bills, and inefficiency bills by a Legal Minimum Wage.

The year of Laski's decision to commit his life to science and to begin at Pearson's eugenics laboratory, 1910, saw two milestones in the marriage of eugenics and socialism. The first was the publication by the physician Sidney Herbert of 'Eugenics and Socialism' in the *Eugenics Review*. Herbert, the most prominent Jew in English eugenics circles, praised eugenics teachings as 'essentially communistic in spirit', because they emphasized 'the common interest of each social unit with the whole'. Much more important in 1910 was the publication of Sidney Webb's minority report to the Royal Commission studying the Poor Law. One chapter of his dissent was entitled 'Eugenics and the Poor Law', and it was in his characteristic phrase a plea to 'interfere, interfere, interfere'. Britain 'cannot afford to leave ... bad environment alone', he wrote, for an environment unfavourable to progress would mean 'the survival of the lowest parasite'. The solution was clear. It was 'our business as eugenicists deliberately to manipulate the environment so that the survivors may be of the type which we regard as the highest'. The specific manipulation Webb offered was his National Minimum, first described in 1901: a national standard of life, guaranteeing to all in society a minimum level of health, education, wages and employment, which would 'ensure the rearing of an imperial race'.

The socialist literary flank was also caught up in the eugenics movement. Shaw's *Man and Superman* in 1905 depicts John Tanner as the servant of a vital Life Force zealously and relentlessly pursuing the cultivation of rational brain power by selective breeding of national leadership. Shaw's preface to the play ridicules those who scoff at eugenicist planned breeding 'under cover of delicacy and morality'. While no such scruples prevented the killing of millions in warfare, 'we have never deliberately called a human being into existence for the sake of civilization'. Shaw called for

freedom to breed the race, without being hampered by the mass of irrelevant conditions implied in the institutions of marriage ... What we need is freedom for people who have never seen each other before and never intend to see one another again to produce children under certain definite public conditions, without loss of honour.

In his novels of the first decade of the century H. G. Wells developed similar eugenic theories. He shared the Webbs' approach to the eugenic encouragement of children in the fitter classes. In both *A Modern Utopia* and *The New Machiavelli* Wells depicted societies with generous family allowance schemes to encourage 'desirable' parents. Motherhood was 'a service to the state', Wells wrote, and 'it must be provided for like any public service ... it must be sustained, rewarded and controlled'. This control might well even require a dose of 'negative eugenics'. He ruled out forced breeding as well as the compulsory prohibition of pairing in his 1905 *Utopia*, but he still insisted that

> the state is justified in saying, before you may add children to the community ... you must be above a certain minimum of personal efficiency ... and a certain minimum of physical development, and free of any transmissible disease ... Failing these simple qualifications, if you and some person conspire [i.e. propagation as a crime] and add to the population of the state, we will, for the sake of humanity, take over the innocent victim of your passions, but we shall insist that you are under a debt to the state of a peculiarly urgent sort, and one you will certainly pay, even if it is necessary to get the payment out of you.

In their writings both Shaw and Wells were landmark prophets of a 'new woman'. Here, too, they spoke for the powerful place of eugenics in the current of progressive ideals before the First World War. While it might be caricatured as demeaning women as merely better or worse breeders, essential to the eugenic ideal was the separation of reproduction from sexual gratification. The pioneer American feminist and free-love advocate, Victoria Woodhull, was one of the first to make this connection. She was a convinced eugenicist who preached that 'if superior people are desired, they must be bred; and if imbeciles, criminals, paupers and otherwise unfit are undesirable citizens, they must not be bred'. She insisted in her lectures that the 'scientific propagation of the human race' would lead to greater scientific sexual understanding and education as well as to the emancipation of women. The English eugenicist who brought together these same themes in this period was Havelock Ellis, the great sex pioneer. 'The question of eugenics,' he wrote, 'is to a great extent one with the women question.' Eugenics was, Ellis noted, 'constantly misunderstood, ridiculed, regarded as a fad', when in fact it was essential in allowing women to control their own lives. Mechanical control of birth through reliable devices, Ellis added, left sexual life a matter of personal pleasure, for which women were as capable as men, and separated private sexual acts from procreation in which one expressed a civic transpersonal obligation to the race.

Laski's political and emotional coming of age, from meeting Frida in late 1909 to his graduation from New College in 1914, was shaped by this conceptual cluster of feminism, socialism, birth control and eugenics. Frida, who had joined the Fabians in 1907, opened the horizons of Laski's concerns in politics far beyond those of Smedley House, though they would pointedly intersect on the 'Jewish question'. Frida appeared to Harold to embody the new woman of Shaw's *Man and Superman*, with a mystical, elemental Life Force serving 'a purpose that is not their purpose, but that of the whole universe'. Through their choice of a mate such women naturally served the improvement of the race. Harold's letters to Frida see her 'always in the van of progress', destined 'to win a great victory'. She showed Harold 'the rule of life to follow' replete with 'glorious possibilities'. Indeed, 'nine-tenths of eugenic progress rests with you – you can make or mar the future', he wrote to Frida. There is a suggestion in Laski's letters to Frida in 1910 and 1911 that they believed their relationship transcended their private lives, that they were select trustees of a better future who were destined to mate and to serve the higher aspirations of civilization with their offspring. This sense of destiny may well be a romantic fantasy not unknown to other people in love, but in the context of eugenic frenzy it assumed heroic proportions for them.

Frida, meanwhile, was in Glasgow and in January 1911 Harold settled into working with Karl Pearson in London. He was widely recognized as the leading academic eugenicist and his laboratory the premier source of scholarly studies in the new discipline. It was a distinct honour, then, for Laski to accept Pearson's invitation to join his laboratory. In turn, it is understandable that in the seventeen-year-old Laski, Pearson, then fifty-seven, saw the potential disciple he had become to Galton. That Laski's essay suggested the progressive eugenics politics more characteristic of the socialism of Pearson's own youth, which he had thoroughly repudiated by 1911, was apparently irrelevant; it was service to the science of eugenics that attracted them to each other. Nor should one underestimate the common elitism that characterized both the Liberal–Fabian interventionist eugenicists and the far more *laissez-faire* Spencerian attitude of Pearson in 1911, a theme to be encountered often as Laski's life unfolds.

Another reason for Pearson's interest in Laski, Galton's 'beautiful' and 'wonderful boy Jew', was his value for a study Pearson had begun in 1908. Pearson's Biometric Laboratory published hundreds of statistical studies in the first two decades of the century on the correlation of intelligence to physique, the impact of parental occupation on children's ability and health, and on the inheritability of everything from genius to cleft palates, hermaphroditism, insanity and mental deficiency. One study particularly absorbed Pearson's interest from 1908 on: a major comparison of the intelligence, cleanliness and physique of a group of Jewish boys and girls and a group of Gentile boys and girls. Pearson had undertaken the study, he later wrote, specifically to apply rigorous academic and scientific statistical analysis to the claims made during the debates over the anti-alien legislation. Were Polish and Russian Jewish immigrants 'fully up to the level of the English workman in physique and intelligence' or were they as 'painted in lurid colours . . . weaklings, persons with a low standard of life and cleanliness'? It was to this study that Laski devoted a good deal of his six months with Pearson. Letters exist in Pearson's papers at University College showing him using Laski to write to Jewish officials and agencies for data needed in the study.

In Pearson's laboratory, then, Laski found himself directly involved with the close nexus that had clearly emerged between eugenics and 'the Jewish question'. Fresh from the formative involvement with Jewish issues and politics that had permeated Smedley House from 1904 to 1908, Laski was now deeply immersed in studies that touched the anti-Semitism of immigration opponents as well as the anti-Semitism evident in the general racist views of progressive eugenicists like the Webbs. Not that Laski had any reason in 1911 to doubt Pearson's objectivity. Pearson was committed publicly to a rigorous testing of rhetorically inflamed claims and he had, after all, wanted Laski, a Jew, to work with him. The conclusions of Pearson's study would not be published for the first time until 1925, many years after Laski had any connections with Pearson. His findings were that 'taken on the average, and regarding both sexes, the alien Jewish population is somewhat inferior physically and mentally to the native population'. On the third area of comparison there was a much clearer distinction. In the matter of 'personal cleanliness', the standard of Jewish alien children was 'substantially below that of even the poor Gentile children'. Pearson and his co-author, Margaret Moul, offered in 1925 what they considered a scientifically justified eugenic recommendation to their countrymen on Jewish immigration. A standard should be set '25 per cent higher than the mental and physical averages of the native population . . . let us allow none to enter who fail to reach this standard'.

Laski published the results of his small related study in the January 1912 issue of *Biometrika*. 'A Mendelian View of Racial Heredity', his second article, appeared four months after he had gone up to New College and it offered a very different perspective on Jewish themes than would be found in the larger study when it was published years later. While ostensibly rejecting because of its lack of quantitative analysis Dr Radcliffe Salaman's claim that Jewish facial expression was a recessive character subject to the Mendelian Law of Heredity, Laski brashly took on as well 'the loose and worthless categories' that the eminent biologist had used in his *Journal of Genetics* article. Even at eighteen Laski knew how to use the pen to ridicule and conquer. Salaman made claims about noses, chins and jaws, Laski wrote; yet

> when we ask what 'Jewishness' is, we are told that it is the quality of looking Jewish, and to the question of what it means to look Jewish Dr Salaman would doubtless reply that it is to possess the quality of Jewishness. So vicious a circle of reasoning seems, scientifically, almost ludicrous, and it can hardly have value from the standpoint of anthropology.

Laski worked on another project with Pearson in 1911, a multi-city study of 'the correlation of fertility with social value'; in other words, a statistical verification of the claim that the 'more intellectual and energetic, the more prudent and well-to-do classes in this country have a lower fertility'. Other researchers studied Blackburn, Preston and Birmingham, and Laski, no fool, wrote on Glasgow. The study was published in 1913 in the *Eugenics Laboratory Memoirs* with Laski's data from Glasgow as Section III of the paper. He had done some of the work on correlating his four variables – size of family, age of mother, wages of father and rent of house – on visits to Frida and during his first year at New College. But by the time the study appeared in 1913 with its principal Pearsonian recommendation that 'wages ought to be directly proportional to social value as measured by physique and mentality', Laski was no longer interested in eugenics or science, and his politics had dramatically changed.

While working with Pearson in the first few months of 1911 Laski corresponded with Frida frequently. Only his letters survive, but it is clear from them that Frida had immersed herself actively in Fabian and women's suffrage circles in Glasgow. Laski wrote to her of his commitment to the vote for women and of his general admiration for the 'new woman' that Frida represented. He sent her books as tokens of his love, like *The Poems of*

Omar Khayyám, and because he claimed that she was a 'mere babe in book buying' he also sent her books that he thought she should read.

Harold visited Frida in Glasgow in late March, taking a room for the weekend at Mrs Brownlie's rooming house where Frida lived. It would be their first night together. His letters after his return to the Strand Palace Hotel are more openly amorous and begin to talk of marriage, albeit in the not too near future. The Manchester Laskis were certainly aware of their friendship; Neville would not have kept it secret. They also knew from J. L. Paton, who, after a meeting with Harold in London in the spring, wrote to Nathan to say 'what a great thing Harold's Glasgow friend has done for him; he does his new work with a zest that shows it his true work'.

By early summer Laski's letters refer to a more imminent marriage and to the anticipated response of their parents. Harold writes that his parents will be angry, 'but I don't mind that'. He will say to them, 'Here is my wife, as you loved me, love her – if you cannot accept her, reject me also.' 'His people', he thinks, will be 'tremendously mad for a year or two', but they would soon come around because 'they can't do without me and once they know you how could they help loving you'. Nor does Harold think the Kerrys will be too pleased. 'I suppose,' he writes to Frida, 'your mother and the rest of them won't like the idea of your marrying a Jew.' His religion is clearly no issue for Frida, Harold senses, as he writes that, 'I've met in you the only one in the world who understands that underneath the cloak of the Jew there can beat a really human heart and that he, too, knows how to love.' He joyously shares his Judaism, sending Frida a Passover Haggadah and suggesting, 'We must read it together one day so that I can explain to you all the little Jewish bits particularly in that last one, Chad Gadya.'

It was in fact Mrs Kerry, living in London, who first discovered in late July 1911 the intensity and seriousness of the relationship, and she was not pleased. Frida remembers her mother's outrage 'at what she called my cradle-snatching and betrayal of my Christian upbringing'. Mrs Kerry's only recourse if they continued to see each other was the threat to expose the couple to the Manchester Laskis. This was Harold and Frida's greatest fear, since they assumed Smedley House would require them to part for ever. Harold's response was a hasty application for a marriage licence, and on 1 August 1911 Harold, recently turned eighteen, and 26-year-old Frida were married in Glasgow Town Hall between the drunkards queuing up to pay their fines. The newly-weds were in the third day of their honeymoon at the Central Hotel in Birmingham when they were descended upon by Uncle Noah Laski and brother Neville who had been sent to find and fetch the couple by Nathan and Sarah upon receipt of their telegram announcing the marriage. They were immediately brought to Manchester.

At Smedley House Harold and Frida were brought upstairs to Nathan's bedroom, where he lay complaining of a heart attack brought on by their treachery. Frida remembered Sarah 'tight-lipped and agitated', throwing up her hands in despair and rushing out of the room. Uncle Noah spoke for the family. They had done an unforgivable thing. Harold was under age, a schoolboy. His academic career was in jeopardy. How could he go to Oxford? Noah offered a deal. Frida first had to promise not to use the name Laski and the marriage must remain a secret. They could not cohabit nor could they meet while Harold was at Oxford until the Laskis gave their permission, and then only under close supervision. If Frida agreed to these terms, the family would pay Harold an allowance of £200 per year for expenses and the Oxford fees necessitated by their earlier rejection of the exhibition grant. Should this arrangement in itself not wreck the marriage, no further allowance would be given after Oxford if they remained together unless Frida converted to Judaism. Frida felt the couple had no choice but to agree, and Harold concurred. He was required to spend the night in an attic room and she to share Mabel's bedroom. The next morning Neville and Noah put Frida on the train for Scotland.

Harold's acceptance of the terms while refusing to repudiate the marriage infuriated Nathan. Much more grievous than his marrying a woman six years his senior was his marrying a Gentile. Nathan immediately took from Harold the many books he had purchased with his bar mitzvah gift money and until his trip to India that autumn Nathan dealt with Harold as if he were a dead son. Mrs Kerry, on the other hand, after realizing that she had hastened the elopement by her ill-timed threat, accepted their marriage and eventually welcomed the couple in her Battersea home. For the remainder of the summer and until the beginning of the Oxford term in the second week of October Harold was a virtual captive in Smedley House. Pearson, meanwhile, heard what had happened and wrote to Harold suggesting he might give way to his parents' wishes and perhaps reconsider the marriage. Harold rejected the advice. 'It seems to me wrong to go back on what I have done.'

Harold's letters to Frida in this waiting period are a poignant blend of a lover's longing, unabashed excitement at the expectation of Oxford, and continuing eugenic enthusiasm. In one letter he wrote of packing his photographs of Frida along with those of Galton, Darwin and Pearson and that to see her 'amongst them makes me feel that their great ideals will find their realization in our children'. In another he proclaimed triumphantly that all was set, having established that in nearly three years' time his exams would end on 21 June. 'I shall come for you on the 22nd. So now you have it all beautifully fixed and arranged.' That was to be, for now on 12 October 1911 Laski arrived in Oxford, still determined to read science and with a severe sore throat. He carried with him a letter of paternal advice not from Nathan, then in India, but from Karl Pearson in London. Pearson intuited quite correctly what lay ahead.

> You are now going up to Oxford with three or four years before you. You will see things on a bigger scale and learn to know a great variety of workers at all sorts of branches of learning. Give your whole heart to your work there and to your new university. If at the end of that time you still desire to take up biometrical or eugenics work, I shall only be too glad. But don't look upon your Oxford work as secondary to something else. It will be quite engrossing enough and needs all your thought and undivided attention ... you will very likely find that ... other branches of knowledge claim your attention.

CHAPTER THREE

Oxford, Feminism and Syndicalism

Laski arrived at university a married man and a published author. He kept his marriage secret but told everyone about his articles. Laski flourished at Oxford, even if in later years he was fond of suggesting it taught one only how 'to command people gracefully to do for you what you ought to be able to do for yourself'. His college, New College, founded in 1379 by William of Wykeham, traditionally received large numbers of boys from Winchester, also founded by William, as well as from the Manchester Grammar School. New College instilled in its students a strong obligation to public service. Though not as single-mindedly dedicated to this mission as Jowett's Balliol College, New College would, for example, be the Oxford college most closely associated with the Workers' Educational Association that Albert Mansbridge founded in 1903. It was a leader among Oxford colleges, even if not always considered the best.

Laski's rooms were in Robinson Tower and his first-year tutor was Geoffrey Smith, a scientist who specialized in cytology. During his first year Laski read physiology, chemistry, botany and comparative zoology. Luckily for Laski, Smith was an admirer of Pearson who disliked Mendelism and they got on well. Laski's letters to Frida, sometimes two a day, are full of detailed descriptions of laboratory experiments and small-animal dissection. Eugenics was still his passion, however. Shortly after he arrived he founded a Galton Club at the college for the discussion of eugenics, which exists to this day. He remained in close contact with Pearson, sending him work on his Glasgow cases and receiving encouraging responses in turn. In the spring of 1912 Laski invited the great man to New College to give a talk at Laski's 'little eugenics club'.

His passion for eugenics also helped to determine Laski's friendships in his first year. One classmate was spurned as a potential friend because his cousin was doing research with Bateson and 'we fought just like cats and I went for him all I knew'. More happily, it was eugenics which sealed Laski's friendship with J. B. S. Haldane, son of the great Victorian physiologist John Scott Haldane, and, more importantly for the future course of Laski's life, nephew of Richard Burdon Haldane, lawyer, philosopher and Liberal Party luminary. J. B. S. Haldane, destined to become one of twentieth-century Britain's leading geneticists, while also in the 1930s and 1940s a leading member of the Communist Party, was as passionately interested in Darwin and eugenics as Laski and already much more eccentric and unconventional. Haldane thought nothing of barging into Laski's room at any hour to talk over his work, whether it was his tutorials or, as on one occasion, a paper he and his father were writing on haemoglobin in the blood. Laski wrote to Frida that one night he was able to get rid of Haldane only by literally throwing cold water on him, and in the spring of 1912 it took the angry refusal of their tutor to thwart the plans of Laski and Haldane to raise and keep guinea-pigs in the college.

Although his first year was devoted principally to science, Laski did go to H. A. L. Fisher's lectures. Fisher, the historian who had written on behalf of the College accepting Laski to read history, was tolerant of Laski's redirected studies and, like Paton, Alexander, Galton and Pearson, he discerned in Laski the marks of a prodigy. Laski, in turn, found in Fisher not only a friend, but a model of the active and committed intellectual that he would ultimately seek to be. Tutor at New College for twenty years, Fisher was brother-in-law of the great medieval historian Maitland and nephew of that most eminent of Victorian scholars Leslie Stephen; Virginia Woolf and Vanessa Bell were thus his cousins. Fisher had studied under the philosopher T. H. Green at Balliol and passed on to his students Green's Hegelian conviction that a moral life required disinterested service to the state. This meant that as a historian he not only trained others to be civil servants but like Green, who had sat on the Oxford city council, he also actively participated in public life. Fisher entered the House of Commons in 1916, where he sat as a Liberal until 1925. He served in Lloyd George's wartime government as President of the Board of Education and in 1918 was the author of the Liberals' great Educational Reform Bill that lifted the school leaving age, without exception, to fourteen. He was also responsible for making teachers' salaries uniform throughout England and establishing for the first time a pension system for teachers. Fisher returned to New College in 1925 to be Spooner's successor as Warden, and stayed until 1940, turning out New College men in the generation after Laski, like Richard Crossman and Hugh Gaitskell, to progressive careers in public life, as well. Laski, the teacher of politics and history for thirty-six years, would in turn pass on Fisher's conviction that scholarship and political commitment went hand in hand. He would also acquire from Fisher the latter's preoccupation with the immorality of Britain's rule in India and his rationalist suspicion of and disdain for religion, two themes of great significance to Laski throughout his life.

Fisher's profound impact on him notwithstanding, Laski was still in his first year committed to a career in science and he had little doubt it would be a distinguished and important career. From his arrival at Oxford Laski's letters to Frida reveal little of the self-doubt or questioning of worth so typical in a new undergraduate comparing himself for the first time with so large a pool of talented peers. On the contrary, Laski displayed a cocky air of self-confidence and self-importance, images of self that throughout his life would be at the core of his personality. Two and a half weeks after his arrival at New College he wrote to Frida that a fellow student had

> told me one or two things which I don't repeat from egoism but because perhaps they will please you a little. He heard that Fisher thinks that I am easily the most brilliant man of this year and that the college likes me very much though they are a little frightened of me. I'm awfully bucked at this because Neville swore I was going to be awfully hated up here and it rather disproves his point.

When his tutor asked Laski's opinion on a new paper he had written, Laski 'showed him some misinterpretations of the statistics'. Laski decided to give a talk to the Galton Club, and then to Frida's eugenics society, in which he would 'show exactly what the difference between nature and nurture means because I don't think that even K. P. has done that quite satisfactorily'. He also planned an assault on one of John Scott Haldane's papers and then 'my God, there is going to be a rumpus in the physiological world'. At the end of November he wrote to Frida about wanting to be President of the Junior Scientific Club so that he could 'have disposal of the Boyle lectures for one year'. He let Frida know that he would write the definitive book on eugenics and win the Weldon Prize. He was ambitious, he confided to Frida, 'because I want you to be proud of me'. In these letters to Frida only once did Harold's confidence slip and a note of conventional undergraduate self-doubt appear.

> This man Haldane is remarkable. He was captain of Eton, he's a maths scholar, he knows enough practical zoology to take the advanced course and he is going to do maths, mods, then greats and then physiology and he seems awfully well up in everything. It's rather remarkable I think and what he does know he knows really well. . .You see I don't know all these things.

Laski's self-confidence, his assumption of control and mastery, was shaped in part by his sense of being already a married man with a firm vision of family and career. He wrote again and again, surprisingly given both his and Frida's advanced feminist perspective, of returning home at the end of a day teaching or at the lab. Frida would tell him what the children had done; there would be four, one named Frida, another Karl, the other two as yet unnamed. She would be as proud of him 'as K. P.'s wife is of him'. Laski was freed of the uncertainty which exacts so much from young adults, and able to devote all of his time and energy to his studies and to self-promotion. He had his Frida and his emotional life set. Liberated from the rituals of undergraduate sexual exploration, he was able single-mindedly to try and 'know all these things' and, like Haldane, be 'awfully well up in everything'.

Not that the separation was easy. It was, he wrote, 'a thousand times harder than I thought it would be'. His letters in the first year count off the months and days till holidays and until the second honeymoon of spring 1914. Not surprisingly, his letters have long passages describing intense sexual longing, complete with vivid erotic depictions of past and future intimacies. But even here a confident self-control is at work. They are eugenicists, after all, and so their separation becomes itself exemplary of the rational control of sexuality. How wonderful, Laski wrote to Frida, 'that because of our love of what is pure this great compelling instinct is under our control'. It literally was, for the married couple refrained from actual intercourse, reserving it solely for the creation of their child. True to their eugenic convictions, sexual pleasure was a different matter. Frida seems clearly to have initiated Laski into mutual fondling and masturbation and his letters contain long fantasy scenarios about the doings of 'Dickie' and 'Topsy'. Uninterested in using birth control, they made the decision not to have intercourse the supreme expression of their rationalist ideals. Their separation became for them both a testing and a facilitator of their intellectual commitments. Laski's father unknowingly had put them to the fire, and young Laski was, here too, self-confident in his sense of mastery.

> Each day I seem to long more and more for the three years to pass because I long for that intercourse so much, dearest, because ... the ecstasy of that moment will be so intense we shall hardly know we are alive when Dickie creeps very softly into Topsy. It will be gorgeous then to throw right away all restraint and control and to make myself part of you ... Because we can wait and yet hunger for it ... with us intercourse has assumed a spiritual loveliness that has been absent from all other love just because we are the pioneers in a great movement that one day will free the world from so much of the pain of now because it will make it so much more pure and sacred.

Laski's ability to transform his separation from Frida into a heroic trial may help to account for the absence in his letters of any sense of rage at his family, especially his father and his almost biblical patriarchal pronouncement that thou shalt live apart from thy wife for three years. On several occasions Laski did write of his anger 'at my people', of not being able to ask for money for a microscope since it would put him over the £200. It is also clear, however, that Laski wrote fairly regularly to his mother about life at Oxford and on occasion even to his father in India. Letters were exchanged between Frida and Sarah, who in general seemed more cooperative and less upset than Nathan. Laski suggested to Frida in one letter that his parents no longer had any objections to her except her not being Jewish. He was quite pleased how proud they would be in Manchester when they heard how well he was thought of by Fisher. The relationship continued to be strained, but there was also a quality of business as usual. Laski saw Neville almost weekly in their overlapping year, playing tennis on occasion or accompanying him to meetings or Sabbath services at synagogue. One of Laski's first chores at New College had been to get himself released from Chapel, but even this, he wrote to Frida, was really designed to please his parents. Next year, he assured her, he would have nothing to do with the synagogue because Neville would have gone down 'and there won't be any appearances to be saved'. Even Laski's charged rivalry with Neville was absorbed by this need for the prodigal son to impress his parents. Laski's letters to Frida reveal that it was he who wrote most of Neville's essay which won Oxford's Beit Prize in 1912, an honour which would appear prominently in any future list of Neville's achievements. Laski hoped that Neville's essay would win 'because I want very much to hear what they say to me because father and mother know that he really has not done very much more than provide the substratum of fact in it'.

Laski found an even more interesting vehicle with which to express and work through his complicated feelings towards his father's response to Frida and to the religion of his father's fathers. During the January 1912 holiday, most of which he spent in Manchester, Laski shared with Frida what he variously described as his 'wee book', his 'little essays' or his set of 'small tales'. Only Frida would see them when they were done. He would try twice to publish these 148 pages as *The Chosen People: Essays Toward an Interpretation*. It was rejected both times and in 1915 he 'put it away in a drawer'. The manuscript, recently discovered, still remains unpublished. It provides a fascinating glimpse of eighteen-year-old Laski's views on religion, science, Judaism, women and his father.

One idea dominates *The Chosen People*. Judaism is a rigid and intolerant religion unable to cope with a modernist scientific world-view. All religious tenets must be tested 'as a fact in chemistry, in mathematics, in zoology is tested', and Judaism in particular must 'remove from itself relics of barbarism alien from the spirit of today'. This is rendered especially difficult for Judaism, Laski argues, because the hatred of others, which isolated Jews in ghettos, produced a ghetto mentality. The Jews felt safer clinging to the traditions of the past than in embracing modernity and the world outside the ghetto. Their quest to remain a separate people is embodied in their resistance to intermarriage, an attitude which unites Orthodox and Liberal Jews. A totally separate existence as a national identity, the Zionist vision, 'the dream of a rejuvenated Palestine', is, according to Laski, where such particularism leads. But Zionism is a futile dream. Like his father in these years, Laski argues that Jewish solidarity and the continuity of Jewish history rest solely on a belief in religion, not on territorial or communal proximity. Better for the Jew dispersed in other people's lands to leave the ghetto and embrace modernity, to replace isolation with assimilation.

Each of the remaining chapters in *The Chosen People* restates this theme in a fictional 'tale', reminiscent of extended Chasidic legends, the autobiographical referents of each but thinly disguised. Chapter 2, for example, is the story of a son and a father. The son, a sensitive and lonely scholar, of poor health, has a wonderful memory, does scientific research and has 'an intensely Jewish spirit'. He has little belief in the Jewish religion or its rituals; 'it was rather in the nation itself that he believed'. He could identify not with its dogmas, 'as a religion it is a code of cooking utensils', but with the spirit of the Jewish nation, 'its intense determination to achieve a mighty end . . . a great mission'. This intensely Jewish son sought to marry a Gentile woman. The father is 'generous to a fault – save upon this issue'. The son is torn; on the one hand, his parents 'have loved and cared for me and thought no sacrifice too great did it but bend towards my well-being'. On the other hand,

> they bid you weigh the sadness of your people and your race. You are made to understand how their neighbours will point a finger of scorn at them, shun them a little, because you have deserted the tradition. Their social prestige will be threatened.

The son chooses the woman and in two years he is dead of tuberculosis.

The third chapter tells of a conversation between an old rabbi and a young Jewish man. In this dialogue between the traditional past and the future of science, Laski reveals a thorough knowledge of Jewish history and religious texts. He understands the appeal of a ritual and a literature that inspires with its faith so much enthusiasm. But the rabbi goes too far when he claims that the spirit of modern science is dangerously producing only 'ceaseless self-torture and eternal unrest'. The fear of the Lord, not a pitiless searching, is the beginning of wisdom, the rabbi insists. After a long silence the young modernist respectfully replies, 'We can hold nothing true save that which science has shown.' The proper guide is experience not faith, 'our prophets Darwin and Newton, not Moses and Isaiah'. Laski gives the old rabbi the last word in this tale as he had the rebellious son in the previous one.

> You say I am to replace Moses by Darwin, Isaiah by Newton. Yet shall the law of the struggle for existence hold in my heart the same place as the Ten Commandments and a mathematical law of motion have the same sanctity as those God-inspired thunderings of old?

There is an enduring Jewish spirit, the rabbi concludes, a 'mingled sadness and splendour with the promise of triumph in the end'. The rhetorical victory in this tale goes to particularism and the ghetto over universalism and reason.

In the third and final story *The Chosen People* resolves its ambivalence and comes down solidly for assimilation over isolation. It is a tale of a father and a daughter and for its time it is a surprisingly advanced Jewish feminist tract. The father had as a youth been a political revolutionary in Russia and a free-thinker full of the knowledge of English science. Fleeing the tsarist authorities, he had settled in England. Forty years passed and he became a wealthy financier who had returned to Judaism, but as an English Jew, fully a member of the English community. When his daughter became a doctor he had not objected, because it 'had seemed to mark his own truly English tolerance, his distinction from the old ghetto ideas of a woman's place and function'. Eventually the daughter's total transformation to the 'new woman', her infection 'with the virus of feminism', bothered the father, as did rumours that she wished to marry a Christian. The father discovered that as English as he felt himself to be, he could not contemplate the 'union of the flesh, the thought that his daughter would give birth to children who could never be Jewish as he himself was a Jew'.

Smitten with curiosity about her views, the father read one of his daughter's feminist pamphlets. Women, she wrote, are more than mere bearers of children. 'Her domestic labour and her sexual labour are as economically productive as that of a man.' Jews sanctify motherhood, but only as breeders of the race. Women are the equals of men and the chivalry that degrades them must be replaced by comradeship that ennobles. 'I do not wonder that the Jews have a prayer thanking heaven that the lot of women was not theirs,' the pamphlet announced. 'Their lot is subjective because it has made acquiescence and obedience virtuous.' The father was shocked at the pamphlet and its spirit of revolt against women's traditional place in Judaism. He saw nothing wrong with Judaism's exclusion of women from membership in the religious community. It was fit, he believed, that 'religion, for her, contained not so much ethics as a series of dietetic laws without explanation, often without reason'.

When his daughter finds him reading the pamphlet the father turns on her for rejecting the Jewish ideal of womanhood, 'the wife who bears her husband's children, who is his right hand and to whom his word is law'. She retorts that her father's Judaism is outdated, that 'what was invented for a half-civilized tribe cannot be true of us today'. When he complains of

her intention to marry a Christian, the daughter complains that Jewish men
have 'an instinctive feeling that man must be master of the world, and that
to share his dominion with woman is the lowliest degradation'. She has
found a non-Jewish man who treats her as an equal and why shouldn't she
marry him?

> You teach us to understand that there is no Jewish nation, only Jewish
> Englishmen. When the Russian Jew comes to England, you Anglicize him
> with all the rapidity that comes of a process rapidly approaching perfection.
> Religion apart, there is no department of our daily life not thoroughly
> permeated with English ideas.

Having filled me with English ideas, the daughter pleads, you now tell
me that to marry an Englishman is 'to break the Jewish tradition which has
been our glorious heritage for nearly six thousand years'. You cannot have
it both ways. 'The alternative is isolation or assimilation.' Before her father
can reply the daughter tells him of a dream she had. She was high on a
mountain and around her were all the women yet to be born. Most were
chained to rocks, their chains 'a badge of the servitude that will be our lot
on earth'. They were destined 'to be but ministers to men's pleasures or his
beast of domestic burden'. Then a woman appeared in the dream to
announce a new age of freedom when 'man then will be not my lord, but
my comrade; not my master but my equal'. The father, moved by the
daughter's dream, remembers his conviction in Russia that he could not
live a life of ease if others suffered, and his belief in equality between
Christian, Jew and Moslem and between men and women. His memories
tempt him but he resists their seductive appeal. He rejects his daughter's
arguments both for assimilation and for sexual equality. The daughter
leaves her father, with whom there is only darkness, to follow the gleam of
light beyond the door to the new age of freedom. The manuscript of *The
Chosen People* ends with the daughter walking out of her father's house
and, as in Ibsen's *A Doll's House*, 'the door closed behind her noisily with a
thud that seemed to shut him out from a new civilization'.

Laski shared *The Chosen People* and its unabashed feminist message with
Frida at the end of his first Christmas holiday from New College. Though
he never returned to these themes directly in his future writings, its issues
and concerns would not be lost. Some have suggested, in fact, that his
attitudes to his father explain in some way his political writings and

political career. His ambivalence over and preoccupation with the nature of his Judaism would recur throughout his life, and his feminism would very soon find activist expression. One wonders why in later years, when Laski could easily have published his reflections on anything, he never sought to have *The Chosen People* put in print. Perhaps it was its very private significance for him and for Frida that kept it for ever in the drawer, or perhaps it was that the purpose of writing it at the time was achieved, the displacement of the anger he couldn't as a dependent level directly against his father. Then there is the possibility that by the 1930s German anti-Semitism had so overtaken him that naïve choices between assimilation and stagnation may have seemed archaic and *The Chosen People* less relevant, erroneously so, to be sure.

By the end of the 'long vac' which followed his first year at Oxford Laski had abandoned his nearly three-year-long fascination with science. In his remaining two years at university he returned to his original intention, the study of history and politics, the interests around which the rest of his life and career would be centred. One of the puzzles of his Oxford years is how and why he made this abrupt shift, so determinative of his adult being, and a family myth has emerged to help to explain it. Laski realized, so the story goes, that he was inept at practical, mechanical and physical tasks and thus abandoned science. Frida wrote of his 'ham-handedness all his life' which left him helpless to make scientific slides. His daughter Diana would refer to his inability to dissect earthworms or to draw the circulatory system of the frog. Kingsley Martin, one of his closest friends, adds that these evident difficulties caused Laski not to sit for his first-year science exams. Laski was, indeed, mechanically inept and sloppy with laboratory work, but more important in explaining his shift is that he did sit for his exams but flunked them. 'The Warden and Tutors' minutes' in the New College archives report in 1912 that 'Mr Laski failed for a third time in the science prelims'. It was suggested that he change his course 'or not be allowed to reside further'. Embarrassed by the exam disaster, Laski apparently never mentioned it to Frida or in later years to anyone. But he was not devastated by the failure. He took it in his stride, self-confidently turning to history and in two years mastering a three-year course that culminated in his winning the Beit Prize, this time for himself, and in receiving a First in his exams. It was a total and decisive break from his first year. The New College Library borrowing register shows that from

October 1912 until he left in July 1914 he did not borrow one science book.

Fisher had left New College for a position on an Indian Commission simultaneously with Laski's shift to history, so Laski turned to two new mentors. Gilbert Murray, Fisher's closest friend at New College, took over Fisher's avuncular interest in Laski. One of the twentieth century's greatest classicists, Murray was also deeply involved in contemporary politics. He was an outspoken advocate of women's suffrage and in later years their lives would intersect in the service of civil liberties, the League of Nation's Union (whose founder and chairman Murray was from 1923 to 1938), Nazi refugee work and pro-Indian causes. Murray, like Fisher, stayed a Liberal and never shared Laski's socialism, but they remained friends, Laski even suggesting to Felix Frankfurter in 1929 that Murray be appointed ambassador to the United States. Both Murray and Fisher played a significant role in Laski's writing career as well. They were editors of the immensely successful Home University Library of Modern Knowledge series which published two of Laski's most widely read books in the 1920s, his *Political Thought from Locke to Bentham* in 1920 and his very important *Communism* in 1927.

Much more significant for Laski's training as a scholar of history and politics while he was at Oxford was his new tutor, Ernest Barker (later Sir Ernest). Barker, like Laski, was from Manchester. The son of a coal-miner, he too had gone to Manchester Grammar School, though on a scholarship. Twenty years older than Laski, Barker became one of England's most distinguished historians of political thought in a long career that after New College saw him Principal of King's College, London, and then Professor of Political Science at Cambridge University. At New College Barker gave extra tutorials to the eager Laski to help him catch up and, significantly for Laski's future scholarship, set him to read the works of the great triumvirate of medieval historians, the German Gierke and the Englishmen Maitland and Figgis. Laski wrote to Frida often of 'dearest Barker' who is 'so splendid' and who thinks 'I do my work so thoroughly'. Not surprisingly, Laski found occasional fault with his tutor and was convinced 'the evidence is in my favour'. Barker in turn provided a rare portrait of Laski the undergraduate in his 1953 autobiography.

He was just turned twenty when I met him; but he was a plant of early and rapid growth, and he had already a large range of knowledge and a quick (at times, indeed, too quick) intelligence. He seemed to me much beyond his years . . . he sometimes made me shy by the warmth of his appreciation of what I said or wrote. He was too quick to be always accurate; he was a musketeer rather than a rifleman; and some of his shots went astray . . . But if he could be erratic, he could also be incisive, and he was certainly encyclopedic. He had already, even at the age of twenty, a remarkable knowledge of bibliography; and he had a flair for discovering rare books.

Laski remained a respectful friend of Fisher and of Murray in later years, but his relationship with Barker was more complicated. Barker had trouble with Laski's flattery, which often trod a thin line between generosity and self-service. Laski's dedication of his first book, *Studies in the Problem of Sovereignty*, in 1917 to Fisher and Barker with effusive praise for both was clearly difficult for Barker to accept. He wrote to Laski that he made too much of him. Over the years they would review each other's books, with Barker criticizing Laski's socialism and Laski criticizing his old tutor's attacks on Marxists and socialists. It was clearly more than politics, however. Laski could easily accept Barker's membership in the Liberal 'Next Five Years Group' in 1935 and even Attlee's well-publicized comment that Barker had been his favourite teacher years earlier when he had been at Oxford. There was sometimes a surprising pettiness in Laski's later attitude to Barker that pointed to other sources of the problem, as when in 1931 Laski wrote to Frida that Barker had been at the University of Minnesota two years earlier and had 'done his best to decry me and completely failed'. What lay behind this was a pattern that repeated itself throughout Laski's career. He often had personal difficulty with those whose work and writings were closest to his, who might be rivals for his reputation and fame as a political theorist. This pattern transcended political affinity; it was professional proximity. Murray and Fisher proved no problem, Barker did; R. H. Tawney did not, G. D. H. Cole did. George Catlin, Barker's student at New College just after Laski, proved this rule. A socialist and a distinguished political theorist like Laski in both America and Britain, Catlin, the father of Shirley Williams, found in his relationship with Laski a streak of pettiness which he too ascribed to rivalry.

A major arena for Laski's combative and self-confident personality in his years at New College was the Oxford Union, where so many other leaders of British public life were schooled in public speaking, wit and verbal retorts. Having apprenticed at the Manchester Grammar School's junior and senior debating societies, Laski was ready for both New College's own society, the Twenty Club, and the Oxford Union, then dominated by Balliol and New College men. Three weeks after he arrived in Oxford, Laski wrote to Frida of his rising to speak at the Union on 'the racial question' and of having been invited to speak as a principal the following week, a distinction usually confined to second-year men. He was thrilled, he wrote, 'because I can gloat to Neville'. By late November Laski was a featured speaker at the Union, even opening debates. When he told this to Neville, Laski wrote to Frida, 'he stared open-mouthed, as if he had a fit'. Others were impressed, if not quite as much as Laski, by his Union début. The December issue of *Isis* evaluated the year's new crop of debaters.

> Who is not dull at the Union? Firstly, there are three New College speakers who have treated the House to some genuine oratory – Mr Raju, Mr Laski and Mr Gollancz. All these are naturally fanatic, and the two latter have a rather exaggerated idea of their own importance. But anyway, they remain as the only three (and the third is doubtful) who really can move the House.

Laski spoke at the Union in favour of women's suffrage, against Zionism and in favour of a eugenics motion. He met Harold Macmillan there, then of Balliol, whose politics in those years were much like Laski's. The two never became close, but two Union speakers from New College did become lifelong friends. Douglas Jerrold, the future military writer, High Tory editor of the *New English Review* and frequent debater with Laski on the BBC in the 1930s and 1940s, was even then on the other side. In writing of his Oxford days Jerrold remembered Laski as 'the first and last leader of the feminists'. People sought him out, he recounts, as the opponent of Laski, 'then, as now [1938], debonair, eloquent, charming and wholly detached from the stream of life', in an endless series of debates on feminism. Much more likely to be on Laski's side was the other New College debater, Victor Gollancz, Jewish and the future socialist publisher who would play an important part in Laski's life in the late 1930s. Like Laski, Gollancz was a serious feminist, having written a play on this theme at New College. He was also famous for staging play-readings. On occasion Laski borrowed plays from him to read and Gollancz remembered that 'he came round one evening and told me he had been working very hard: "I want to slack a bit," he said. "I should like to read one of your plays."' Gollancz asked him whether he wanted a light or heavy play. '"I don't care in the least,"' Laski replied. Gollancz, recalling this years later, was still rather miffed at Laski's response to the play Gollancz handed him. 'He glanced at it hurriedly and asked for three more. "I'll bring them all back in the morning," he said.'

Laski seems not to have been a favourite of his fellow undergraduates. One remembered him as 'a devastating critic of almost everything and very nearly everybody'. He was also apparently a prankster who took delight in tripping up his artistic friends by getting them excited with the pictures hanging in his room, which were in fact scraps he had cut out of posters and framed. A habit of his which won him few friends at the Oxford Union or the Twenty Club was his annoying practice of passing pieces of paper to the speaker with appropriate quotations spontaneously culled from his prodigious memory. He was also notorious for interrupting speakers with aggressive questions. On one such occasion a motion was entertained 'that domes of silence be attached to Mr Laski'.

Fellow students and even his close friends must have wondered why Laski took so many mysterious trips to London in his last two years at New College, for a second important change in Laski's Oxford career had occurred in the autumn of 1912. Frida accepted a post teaching gymnastics in London and moved in with her parents at 50 Overstrand Mansions, Prince of Wales Drive, Battersea, and Laski often went down for the weekend. He never explained the real nature of these trips to friends or to the college authorities when asking permission to leave, often citing research visits to the British Museum, nor with Neville having graduated did word get back to Smedley House. Frida's move not only brought them closer together, it also dramatically increased Harold's actual involvement in politics, especially the women's movement, in which Frida was an important activist.

Frida's feminism was shaped generally by her career conflicts with her parents and more particularly, she recalled years later, by her fury as a young adult reading somewhere that 'a woman, a cat and a chimney should never leave the house'. Only the suffrage, she thought, would end the role of women as 'underdogs in a man's world. God made men. Men made laws. Women obeyed.' On her return to Britain in 1908 she became a suffragette, the term coined in January 1906 by the *Daily Mail* to describe militant suffragists. Frida was much more than a private but not quite a general in the suffragette war waged 'shoulder to shoulder' for four years against the British state after the 'Black Friday' in November 1910 when hundreds of women and policemen, disguised as East-Enders, fought outside the House of Commons. Within the suffragette movement and its internecine feuds she was a follower of the moderate militants, the 'Peths', and not the more militant militants, the 'Panks', as *Punch* mockingly chose to label them. For a time the two groups had together dominated the Women's Social and Political Union (WSPU), founded in 1903 by Mrs Emmeline Pankhurst and her daughter Christabel, the 'Panks'. By 1910 the founders of the WSPU had been joined at the head of the movement by the Pethick-Lawrences, the 'Peths'. Frederick Lawrence was a wealthy Eton- and Cambridge-educated lawyer who had joined his name to his wife's maiden name after their marriage. Emmeline Pethick had been educated at a Quaker boarding school and was an early recruit to the WSPU. The Pethick-Lawrences were together business manager and editor of the union's 20,000-circulation weekly newspaper, *Votes for Women*, published at its two-room headquarters at 4 Clement's Inn, the Strand. In October 1912 Mrs Pankhurst and Christabel, angered by the Pethick-Lawrences' criticism of the escalating violence of the movement, purged them from the WSPU and established their own 'official paper', *The Suffragette*, at a much larger office in nearby Lincoln's Inn. Also dividing the two camps was the increasing separatism of the 'Panks', their eagerness to rid the movement of male allies. *Votes for Women* continued to be published by the 'Peths', and Frida, recently arrived in London, became indispensable to its production. Helping to compile and distribute the paper, she became a close friend of the Pethick-Lawrences and critic of the 'Panks', who she felt were 'anti-sex and anti-men'.

Even closer was Frida's relationship to Sylvia Pankhurst, Mrs Pankhurst's younger daughter, who, after graduating from the Royal College of Art, took the movement in yet a third direction, more compatible as it turned out with 'Peths' like Frida than with 'Panks'. Sylvia had forged a close alliance of suffragettes and the Labour movement, moving to London's East End and joining forces with trade-union and socialist activists. Frida shared Sylvia's commitment to the entire set of original WSPU aims, which, in addition to votes for women and equality of the sexes, had pledged 'to promote the social and industrial well-being of the community'.

More significant for Frida's close relationship with Sylvia was that they looked alike and it became clear that the resemblance could be put to tactical use. Police and detectives tried hard to arrest suffragette leaders at their rallies, marches and demonstrations. Sylvia was arrested six times between July 1913 and March 1914 alone. To the traditional strategy developed to foil such arrests, a tight ring of sympathizers surrounding the speaker, there was added in Sylvia's case the use of Frida as a decoy to assist her in fast get-aways. The two women became firm friends as a result of this unique relationship, with Sylvia occasionally putting up Harold and Frida at her artist's studio at 45 Park Walk, Chelsea.

It was through her friendship with Sylvia Pankhurst that first Frida and then Harold met George Lansbury. Lansbury, whom Laski described in his 1939 'Why I am a Marxist' as one of the two 'greatest men I have ever known', gave Laski his first job after Oxford and was one of two godfathers chosen by the Laskis for their only child. Lansbury, a charismatic Christian socialist who continued the Keir Hardie role as soul and heart of the labour movement, was the darling of the East End poor who sent him to Parliament as their MP in 1910. Caught up in the suffrage movement (as was Hardie, who unsuccessfully introduced a bill for women's suffrage in 1906) and Sylvia Pankhurst's efforts to join the workers' and the women's causes, he became an overnight hero to the latter in 1912 as a result of a passionate parliamentary outburst. In March 1912 Mrs Pankhurst and Mr and Mrs Pethick-Lawrence were arrested for conspiracy. They were released in June after all three went on a hunger strike. Asquith, the Liberal Prime Minister, answered a parliamentary question on 25 June with a claim that suffragette leaders could walk out of prison if they pledged no further militant action. Lansbury rose from his seat and rushed forward to the government's front bench, shaking his fist at Asquith and screaming:

> You are beneath contempt . . . you drive women mad and then tell them to walk out. Who are you to talk of principle? . . . you ought to be driven out of public life. These women are showing you what principle is. You should honour them, instead of laughing at them.

Lansbury resigned from the Labour Party in October 1912 when it refused to endorse the vote for women and ran again for Parliament as a women's suffrage candidate. He lost and for the next several years devoted himself entirely to the women's and the workers' causes with Sylvia

Pankhurst at his side. Lansbury was arrested in April 1913 after a speech at the Albert Hall under an obscure medieval statute that was originally passed to control the behaviour of disorderly soldiers returning from wars in France. He too went on a hunger strike in prison and was released though not rearrested as were Sylvia and others under the provisions of the 'Cat and Mouse Act', which discharged prisoners for 'ill-health' and then rearrested them upon recovery. One of Lansbury's daughters (he had twelve children), Dorothy, was a good friend of Frida's and through her as well as Sylvia Harold and Frida came to be part of Lansbury's radical East End circle.

Frida marched in the great suffragette coronation procession in a group of several hundred gymnastic teachers wearing the purple, white and green tricolour sashes that became the suffragettes' trademark. She marched in the funeral procession for Emily Wilding Davison, who in June 1913 had thrown herself before the King's horse, Anmer, in the Derby at Epsom Downs. She was also one of the women beaten in the famous suffragette deputation to George V in May 1914. Harold, who had also hoped to go to Buckingham Palace that day, couldn't because it required a special mid-week leave permission from New College. He cautioned Frida that if she went and was arrested she should try to go to prison with her famous friends 'so as not to get a long sentence'. Frida did much more than march. When arson became the order of the day in January 1913, she popped lighted fireworks into letter-boxes, and at other times she poured chemicals into them. She disrupted a service at St Paul's Cathedral with a group of suffragettes; as the litany was intoned, they stood up and chanted prayers for the release of detained suffragettes. When the churchwardens approached the group they fled, with the wardens giving chase. Frida was banged on the head with a long staff topped by a crucifix.

Meanwhile, at Oxford Laski threw himself into the suffragette cause. In his last two years at university it replaced eugenics as his great passion. He was indeed, as Jerrold wrote years later, 'the first and last leader' of Oxford's feminists, as his unpublished Chosen People makes clear. His letters to Frida told of his anger at undergraduates who joked about women and of meetings where 'we were all militants, and talked suffrage for hours'. He would support no Fabian for Union committees who did not declare support for the suffrage, and continued to insist that 'men must be educated to appreciate a newer conception of womanhood'. Harold saw himself a

'Peth', not a 'Pank', and as with Frida it was less over the issue of militancy than separatism, as well as sympathy with Sylvia's interests in linking gender issues to class issues. 'Sylvia's work,' he wrote, is a thousand times more important than Christabel's.' He had no sympathy for 'Christabel's sex war against men'. Dismissing men or their world-view, he wrote to Frida, 'is something I can't stand in the suffragette movement'. There is, he concluded, 'something seriously wrong with Christabel'.

At Union debates Laski and the cause of women became synonymous. When Sir Austen Chamberlain came to speak about Tory politics, Laski berated the politician for his opposition to suffrage. Like Frida, moreover, Laski took his militancy beyond mere speech. In 1914 he and Gollancz disrupted Oxford's premier spring social event, Race Week. They chartered a small launch and while the races were in progress steamed up and down the river shouting 'Votes for women' through a megaphone. They barely avoided a severe beating by angered undergraduates. Rebecca West, the distinguished writer and early lover of H. G. Wells, reminisced thirty-four years later about another example of the student Laski's 'political guerrilla warfare' in 1912. She too was nineteen at the time and like Laski was a delegate at a conference on non-militant methods of achieving women's suffrage. She recalled him standing up and

> sweeping away the elderly and experienced chairman of the meeting, persuaded the meeting to cross the road from the hall where it was being held and convert itself into a raid on the House of Commons, which was one of the most militant forms of suffragist action conceivable.

Rebecca West didn't know the half of Laski's militancy, or of his 'guerilla warfare'. No one did. On the rainy night of 3 April 1913 in the Surrey village of Oxted, Laski and a friend placed an explosive device in the men's lavatory of the railway station. Triggered by an alarm clock and wrapped in a cardboard box, the device detonated but the damage was slight, since the gunpowder fuse had failed to ignite the petrol in it. Laski was, it seems, truly clumsy and mechanically inept in manual skills. The *Caterham and Purley Weekly Press and County Post* on Saturday 5 April linked the 'Oxted Station Outrage' to the by then four-month-long arson campaign that had followed Mrs Pankhurst's arrest at Plymouth in December. The paper quoted a local livery-stable proprietor who had been awakened by two men at 4.30 a.m. (the blast occurred at 3.00) asking to be driven to nearby Croydon. He described the two as 'of gentlemanly appearance, apparently well educated. One man was about 5'8", of fair complexion, and wearing a hat. The other man, '5'6"in height, dark complexion, slight black moustache, wore a dark overcoat, but no hat.' The press account of the bombing also told of how narrowly the station had escaped serious damage because the men's lavatory adjoined an oil storage area. The next week's edition of 12 April had more information on the two suspects. They had claimed to be Oxford students lost on a walking tour and 'the shorter man, who had no hat and did all the talking . . . bore resemblance to a foreigner'.

Surrey county police records indicate that a gent's soft felt hat was found in the urinal. The hat bore a shop's name inside it: 'A. Pellet, Cross St and Market St Manchester'. A pistol with a single cartridge loaded with lycopodium and pepper, designed to stupefy the person shot, was also found. To complete the bonanza of clues police recovered some brown paper used to wrap parts of the bomb with the address 'Mrs Watkins, Sea Park Road'. Scotland Yard reported that the hat, a popular model, could not be traced to a specific individual, nor could they trace the pistol. They were more successful with the paper, however. It was from a watchmaker's shop on Battersea Park Road, London. The proprietor identified it as part of a parcel ordered and delivered to a 'Mrs F. J. Kerry, 50 Overstrand Mansions, Prince of Wales Drive, Battersea', and received at the door by a man who signed for it with the name L. B. Lion. Mrs Kerry was interviewed and, according to the County Police Records.

> she flatly refuses to say who the man was that received the package from Mr Watkins the jeweller, but states that the paper was subsequently used to cover a WSPU collecting box that was sent to Lincoln's Inn the same afternoon. This woman, and her parents, with whom she resides, are connected with the suffragette movement, and, of course, are antagonistic to our inquiries.

Having reached a dead end, the Surrey county constabulary never solved the 'Oxted Station Outrage' and file case GC98/11/2 is still labelled unsolved.

Laski, the future Chairman of the British Labour Party, was meanwhile hiding in Paris. Frida had borrowed some money and a friend's car and driven Laski, covered with a rug in the back seat, to Dover. Once in Paris he coolly acted as a tourist guide for four days and made enough money from showing Americans around the city to pay back what Frida had borrowed. On the boat crossing the Channel to France Laski wrote to Frida of his 'wee exile'. What he had done was 'the realization of the big ideals you have taught me to love'. Militant direct action was ennobling. Two months later Laski described Emily Wilding Davison's martyrdom as 'wonderfully, almost madly brave'. From the boat on 5 April 1913 he wrote to Frida:

> Dearest it is splendidly worth it and now I feel that we are truly soldiers in the liberation war of humanity dear lover and we can feel that we have done just a little to help on the fight. And sweetheart your share in it all is so big because all my understanding comes solely from what your love has taught me.

Laski never told anyone nor did he ever write a word about the Oxted bombing for the rest of his life. It is told here reconstructed from Frida's autobiographical fragment, Laski's letters to her, police and press reports. So well kept was the secret that his closest English friend and first biographer, Kingsley Martin, wrote that in this period Laski avoided militant suffragette activity, choosing 'more or less constitutional types of agitation'.

Laski, however, would not have repudiated this Oxted action. On several occasions during his career Laski would defend suffragette militancy in surprisingly outspoken terms, while making no reference to his own experience. In May 1919 in the American literary journal *Dial* he argued that in the exceptional case of extension of the suffrage militant, even violent, activity was justified. The extension of the suffrage to the middle class in 1832, to workers in 1867 and to women, finally, were not 'peaceful surrenders to logic' but 'ungrateful yielding to militancy'. Again in November 1932 Laski defended suffragette militancy, even if violent. In a lecture, 'The Militant Temper in Politics', given at Caxton Hall in Westminster, Laski argued, still only with respect to the right to vote, that on occasion it was 'necessary to give it a kick from behind'. Urgent and angry clamour that insisted on an extension of the right to vote was always answered with 'You cannot yield to violence.' When the right to vote was granted, Laski noted, violence was never given its due credit because people had been 'intellectually convinced that the perspective of events has changed'.

These two later references are but faint intellectual echoes of his Oxford militancy. With the Oxted railway incident successfully buried, the writer and activist Laski saw himself throughout his career profoundly committed to peaceful constitutional processes. While it is true that this early act of political violence, albeit by a teenager, looms all the more fascinating given the libel case which would capture world attention in 1946, the Oxford militancy remains significant even without that intriguing connection. Personally it involved a risk-taking erotic bonding with Frida and a dramatic repudiation of his father's politics, decisively differentiating him from the Jewish bourgeoisie. In any case, there can be few such clear-cut overt acts of political violence buried in the political pasts of major players in twentieth-century British parliamentary politics.

Several examples of Laski's verbal militancy on the suffrage issue that occurred after Oxted can be found in the historical record. The first is a Laski confrontation with Lloyd George, then the Chancellor of the Exchequer in the Liberal government. Lloyd George came to Oxford on 21 November 1913 for a debate at the Union on Liberal land and farming policy. Because of Tory animosity to his 'People's Budget' of 1909 with its supertax and pioneering social welfare schemes, and because of general Establishment disdain for him as an elementary school graduate and populist 'champion of the people', university officials feared for his safety and sent decoy cars to the Union while he arrived by a roundabout route. The Union was packed and Lloyd George, a consummate orator, charmed the students, his motion carrying by 654 votes to 500.

Before the Union debate began, Laski asked the Chancellor if the following day he would meet a deputation of Oxford men, graduates and undergraduates, who were sympathetic to the suffragettes. Lloyd George agreed on condition that the group of men refrained from breaking into his speech at the Union. They remained silent and he saw them the next day at Christ Church Deanery. He was much less successful with this deputation of seven men than he had been at the Union. According to the summary account in *The Times* and the verbatim report in *Votes for Women*, they criticized him principally for his opposition the previous year to the Conciliation Bill, at that time the principal hope of the suffragettes. It would have granted the suffrage to all women householders, and Lloyd George, claiming to be a supporter of total suffrage, opposed the legislation as simply swelling Tory Party ranks. He wanted 'working men's wives on the register as well as spinsters and widows, or . . . no female franchise at all.' The Oxford men accused him of going back on previous pledges. He was also criticized for his support for forced feeding of hunger strikers and for dismissing suffrage enthusiasts at his speeches as paid provocateurs seeking only to create a newsworthy confrontation. *Votes for Women* described the assault by Laski.

> Mr H. S. [*sic*] Laski (New College) made a spirited attack upon the Cabinet's policy with regard to the women, saying that the teaching of history should have warned them of the impossibility of stamping out the movement by repression, and demanding that they should remove the stain on their honour by an immediate measure for woman suffrage . . . I want to end with this word of personal challenge . . . I have been thrown out of your meetings and thrown out with personal violence . . . I ask you to make that assertion against myself, that I go and get thrown out because I am paid by the Suffrage Party . . . We hoped to have something to do with your Party because it stood for ideals we admired, but it is only now by either leaving this government which is a stain upon your reputation and honour, or else by bringing in a suffrage bill, that we can see the possibility of associating with you or changing the policy which we believe will lead to this goal.

After Laski's attack Lloyd George noted somewhat appreciatively that he could now better understand why the group felt a 'certain measure of indignation which I think has driven you all beyond what is judicious'. He would not change any of his positions, however. This prompted the senior scholar and head of the deputation, Henry W. Nevinson from Christ Church, to pledge the continuation of militancy. Nevinson vividly remembered the event in his autobiography, *More Changes, More Chances*, describing how 'Harold Laski, still a scholar of New, set upon the unhappy minister with the fury of a gamecock, and a passion of indignation far surpassing the careful restraint of us older men.' This Lloyd George episode not only provides evidence of Laski's political activism in his Oxford years but also addresses the issue that haunts Laski's career and daunts those who would chronicle it. In later years while boasting of his many encounters with the Great and the Good Laski often made mention of having told off Lloyd George to his face. To many listeners in America or in Britain, sensitive to Laski's fatal character flaw of exaggeration and invention, this seemed a dubious claim. One is alerted here, as in stories about 'Churchill often being a guest in my father's house when I was a child', to the realization that often, though by no means always, Laski's stories were based in fact.

The Lloyd George incident provided a further opportunity for Laski to dazzle yet another famous older man who would play an important part in his life. Henry W. Nevinson, born in 1856, was one of Britain's most famous journalists. He was a passionate liberal and author in 1909 of *Essays in Freedom*. That same year he was converted to the suffragette cause and resigned his position on the London *Daily News* because his paper supported the government's policy of forced feeding. From 1909 to 1923 Nevinson wrote for Massingham's liberal London journal, the *Nation*, to which he introduced Laski, a connection which proved important in the early 1920s. Nevinson is the second of the two 'greatest men I have ever known' that Laski recalled meeting at Oxford in his 'Why I am a Marxist'. From Lansbury it was equality, from Nevinson he learned 'the meaning and importance of liberty'. At Nevinson's death in 1941 Laski wrote to Nevinson's second wife, Evelyn Sharp, the former suffragette and political writer. 'We loved him and were proud of him; when we were on his side we knew we were on the right side. Frida and I became a part of his army of freedom when we first knew one another, and ever since, over thirty years, our road has followed the star he pointed out to us.'

Nevinson was a national leader of the Men's Political Union for Political Suffrage (MPU), founded in 1910, and through him Laski became secretary of its Oxford branch. His letters to Frida as well as his correspondence with Nevinson are full of MPU business. Much of this activity was focused on Nevinson's writings, tracts and articles in *Votes for Women*, for whose distribution in Oxford Laski was responsible. Laski also had a small piece of his own writing published as correspondence in the 13 February 1914 edition of *Votes for Women* of which, his letters to Frida indicate, he was extremely proud. In it Laski complained that the principals of Oxford's women's colleges had refused to allow the Women's Debating Society to have anything to do with the Oxford MPU because of its militant politics. Laski concluded with a plea for women graduates of Oxford to write to their principals 'to protest against this unfair censorship of discussion'.

Laski was as involved in his last two years at Oxford with the workers' cause as he was with the women's cause. He had been interested at Oxford in labour movement politics, he wrote in his 1948 'What Socialism Means to Me', from the first talk he had heard G. D. H. Cole give at a Fabian Society meeting in the autumn of 1911. Cole graduated from Balliol in 1912, but from 1912 to 1919 he was a fellow at Magdalen College and led the university's socialists in support of the striking Oxford tram-drivers in the spring of 1913. Laski did not participate in the strike, for he was preoccupied those same weeks with the women's cause and Oxted. He did join the Fabian Society at Oxford, however, but like Cole, who at the time was a guild socialist, Laski was losing interest in the state socialism of the Webbs and was quickly converted to the direct action socialism of George Lansbury and Sylvia Pankhurst.

As Laski's busy college years coincided with the pre-war period of women's unrest and violence, so too they coincided with one of the twentieth century's most dramatic periods of labour unrest and violence in Britain. In the first decade of the century a typical year saw four million working days lost in strike activity. In 1911 the figure reached ten million, in 1912 forty-one million and in 1913 twelve million. Unemployment rates were low, inflation was high, and the proportion of national income going to manual workers declined dramatically. The coal-miners in south Wales went on strike in 1910, prompting Churchill, now the Liberal government's Home Secretary, to send troops to the town of Tonypandy to assist local police. Tonypandy became a part of labour movement mythology, clouding Churchill's reputation throughout his career and, indeed, to be recalled often in the 1940s by his critic Laski. The nation's dockers struck in 1911, as did railwaymen throughout Britain. The most serious strike in the period was the national coal strike in 1912 over demands for the '5 and 2', a minimum wage of five shillings for adults and two shillings for boys. By early 1914 the Triple Alliance had been formed, an agreement to coordinate strike activity by the railway, miners' and transport workers' unions. Until the outbreak of the world war that summer it looked like Britain might face a syndicalist general strike.

Informing this fear was the realization that these great strikes were not the products of a moderate trade-union leadership but reflections of the influence of syndicalist ideas, including use of the strike as a political weapon and industrial action as the revolutionary tool of a self-reliant working class. The theory of syndicalism was articulated for intellectuals by the Frenchman Georges Sorel in his *Reflections on Violence* in 1908, and in Laski's years at Oxford it offered a much more romantic action-oriented vision of socialism than Fabianism did. For labour movement activists in this period, on the other hand, much more influential than Sorel was the American syndicalist writer Daniel De Leon, whose ideas were popularized in Britain by the great Irish revolutionary James Connolly. Connolly, in turn, was a follower of the English labour activist and syndicalist theorist Tom Mann. In their speeches and writings Mann and Connolly preached that socialism would never come from state intervention on behalf of workers carried out by intellectuals, bureaucrats or politicians. The process of parliamentary politics advocated by the nascent Labour Party was also rejected. Mann and Connolly argued that economic struggle at the factory level, at the point of production, not political tactics, general strikes or socialist pamphlets, produced social change. Worker-owned and self-governing units of economic production, not the authoritarian state, would be the focus of politics. This syndicalist vision was picked up by two other charismatic labour revolutionaries in Britain: Ben Tillet of the dockers, and James Larkin, like Connolly an Irish trade unionist. In turn their leadership percolated down to activist shop stewards who were the key people in translating militant syndicalism into strike action.

The appeal of the syndicalist vision to intellectuals and trade unionists alike required its popularization and mass dissemination, which was accomplished by a vitally important player in the politics of Laski's Oxford years, the *Daily Herald*. This new paper was born in January 1911 as a short-term strike sheet put out by striking London printers. It was refounded in April 1912 as a national Labour daily, its principal supporter being Ben Tillet. George Lansbury, out of Parliament since November 1912, became its editor in 1913 and made the paper the organ of revolutionary syndicalism, attracting syndicalist activists opposed to the state-sponsored social reform of the Liberal government as well as the state socialism preached by the Fabians. The *Daily Herald* championed James Larkin, the industrial militant who lashed out at conciliatory trade unionism and advocated the strike weapon as the principal means of achieving what he called 'industrial solidarity'. Larkin organized a great wave of transport strikes in Ireland in 1913 and British militants sent supplies of food to Dublin. Larkin had hoped to foment sympathetic strikes in Britain as a prelude to a general strike. But even with the massive support of the *Daily Herald* Larkin's direct action assault on the British state was unsuccessful, mainly because of the opposition to sympathy strikes of the Trades Union

Congress's moderate leadership. Still, by 1914 labour militancy had acquired its holy trinity in the cry 'We Believe in the *Daily Herald*, Jim Larkin and Direct Action.'

Lansbury, as one might expect, also made the *Daily Herald* an outlet for suffragette ideas and strategy, announcing in the edition of 6 November 1913 the formation of a 'People's Army'. Every day, Lansbury wrote, 'the industrial rebels and suffrage rebels march nearer together'. (Only Sylvia marched, of course; Christabel, then in exile in Paris, sent word that she had no use for 'aid from male allies'.) A common theme ran through suffragette militancy and trade-union militancy: the cult of the deed and the exultation in direct self-reliant action, as opposed to mediated intellectual theorizing or protracted political organizing. It was a politics, as Laski put it, that was 'wonderfully, almost madly brave'. In its preoccupation with action – disruptive, often violent, action – it was a direct repudiation of what historian George Dangerfield quite rightly has pointed out was 'Liberal England's' obsession with security, respectability and the virtue of political compromise.

Laski was introduced to syndicalism at New College by a fellow student, Alec Herron. Herron was in Laski's year and shared with J. B. S. Haldane the distinction of being the only other classmate Laski thought might be cleverer than he. Ernest Barker thought Herron was, in fact, the best in the class despite his militant politics. Herron's fate was symbolic of syndicalism's. He put aside his politics to go to war, and in defence of his state he fell at Givenchy in the war's first year. Laski's first book, the anti-statist *Studies in the Problem of Sovereignty*, draws attention to that irony in a moving invocation of Herron's memory.

Syndicalism was almost as important a theme as the suffragette cause in Laski's Oxford letters to Frida. There were as many references to the *Daily Herald* as to *Votes for Women*. Laski was instrumental in getting Lansbury to give a talk at the university. In several letters he pleaded with Frida to use her connections with Sylvia and Lansbury 'to get Larkin to speak here, if you can'. It would be, he added, 'a splendid piece of propaganda'. If she were able to talk to him, Laski suggested she tell him that he would make a lot of money for his cause at Oxford. He, in turn, was sure he could get Gilbert Murray to take the chair at a Larkin Oxford appearance. Frida succeeded. Larkin came to speak at Oxford in February 1914.

Laski graduated from Oxford a convert to syndicalism, abandoning the statist Fabianism associated with the eugenics with which he had arrived. It informed his dislike of Lloyd George as much as his feminism did. Now Laski criticized the Chancellor's ameliorative social reforms, most particularly the National Insurance Act of 1911, as did most syndicalists, for its paternalism, its extension of the state's size, reach and power with labour exchanges and payroll deductions, its general intrusion into trade-union autonomy. Syndicalism was, in fact, the theme of the letter to Frida in which Laski provided the first detailed written statement of his political views since his schoolboy essay of 1910. He was convinced, he informed Frida, that 'the root evil of today is the regarding of labour as a commodity that can be bought and sold'. Once you granted this, you gave power to the capitalist either as personal power in the man himself or in the impersonal power of trusts or states. Since, Laski wrote, 'political power follows economic power', the worker's vote is useless.

> The change I would advocate would be one in the point of view about labour that it is not a commodity the workman has to sell sweetheart, but absolutely his life. Then one sees what a change must come and how futile even collectivism is as a remedy just because you see darling it is really only substituting one master for many and not touching the heart of the evil.

How appropriate, then, given his passionate commitment to syndicalism and the suffragette cause, that Laski's first job after graduating from Oxford should have been with the *Daily Herald*. On 17 July 1914 Laski received a letter from Lansbury, which years later Laski framed and hung on his study wall.

> My Dear Laski,
> How would you like to come and lend me a hand, more or less as my own personal kind of right hand, till you go to Oxford again; it would be good experience, and you could help me quite a lot.
> Best of good wishes to you both.

Having no fixed plans for the future, Laski was thrilled to be offered work so like that of the two men, Nevinson and Lansbury, who were then his idols. He accepted the offer and he and Frida moved into a house outside London owned by the Countess De la Warr, a suffragette friend of Lansbury's. It was the first time they had lived together as a married couple and, as Frida noted, 'it was wonderful to have each other's company part of every day'.

Laski's assignment was to write the unsigned editorials for the newspaper. His distinctive prose style with its irreverent radical message buttressed by the occasional learned historical citation and delivered repetitively, often in sentences far too convoluted, appeared for the first time on 21 July. 'King George and King Carson' is both an essay on the constitutional powers of the British monarch and a slashing indictment of the conference on the Irish Home Rule crisis convened by King George at Buckingham Palace that month. The King should stay out of political affairs, the editorial proclaimed, but if he does interfere why does he choose only this issue? 'The Irish question is not more important than the suffrage question, or more important than the industrial question. Why was no conference called on these?' Perhaps it is because women and strikers have been militant, and the King cannot condone crime. In that case, what about Sir Edward Carson's treasonous actions in Ireland? Beside Carson's activities the conspiracy of Mrs Pankhurst and the sedition of Jim Larkin 'pale into insignificance'.

This first editorial and several others he wrote that summer on the Protestant revolt in Ulster over Irish Home Rule show Laski's career intersecting, albeit only in writing, with the third of the three rebellions that Dangerfield saw auguring 'the strange death of Liberal England'. Sir Edward Carson, a Dublin-born lawyer, Member of Parliament and charismatic leader of Irish Protestants, had mounted a virtual military opposition to the Irish Home Rule policy of Asquith's Liberal government in 1913 and 1914. Carson, organizer of the Ulster Volunteers, drilled troops, landed guns and openly flouted government orders by urging British army officers to resign their commissions if ordered to coerce Ulster to accept participation in a Home Rule scheme. Some politicians railed at Carson. Churchill, then First Lord of the Admiralty, sent a battle squadron to Ireland in the spring of 1914 and spoke of Carson's 'treasonable conspiracy'. But even after 'the Mutiny at the Curragh', when fifty-seven officers were dismissed because they refused to move north to Ulster, nothing was done to Carson. In fact, he soon served in the Liberal Cabinet as Attorney-General in 1915 and as First Lord of the Admiralty in 1916–17.

Carson's Ulster 'rebellion' and its success in temporarily derailing Irish Home Rule, aided, of course, by House of Lords opposition and the outbreak of world war, had an enduring influence on Laski's political consciousness. He returned to it often in his writings and speeches, as proof of the unconstitutional lengths to which the rulers of Britain would go to enforce their will. The Establishment took care of its own. Laski's editorial voice, characteristically repetitive, is powerful evidence of the unravelling of Liberal England in the summer of 1914.

> The law is a class law. It is one thing for the poor and another for the rich. It is one thing for Jim Larkin and Sylvia Pankhurst when they speak their minds, and another thing for Sir Edward Carson when he is moved to utterance. It is one thing for Mrs Pankhurst and her friends, and another thing for Sir Edward Carson and his army.

Laski's stint as editorial writer for the *Daily Herald* coincided with the outbreak of war, and on 29 July Laski's editorial called upon the trade unionists of Europe and Britain to declare a general strike to prevent war and bring about 'the commencement of a new era in history', when armies would cease to be tools of ruling classes and when 'workers will decide the problems for the decision of which they must bear the cost'. By 3 August Germany was already at war with Russia and Laski called on Britain to stay out of the conflict and for all workers in all countries to declare their 'brotherhood and solidarity'. Two days later, in an editorial 'The Die is Cast', Laski acknowledged the 'calamity and the disaster' which was Britain's entry into the war. All industrial and social progress would be pushed aside. This and subsequent editorials no longer called upon the workers of the belligerent countries to strike in repudiation of the war. Though Ramsay MacDonald was praised for his resignation from the Labour Party because of his opposition to the war, the *Daily Herald*, like the European labour movement in general and the British Labour Party, unhappily accepted the war and refused to call for its subversion. It turned to what would be its major wartime theme, protecting the poor 'against the machinations of the plunderers' who would exploit the war to the advantage of their own wallets.

Laski's unsigned editorials introduced a voice that would often be heard over the next thirty-six years. Few professional academics would write as much for the popular press as he. Also introduced in this *Daily Herald* summer was Laski the indefatigable book reviewer. Ten signed Laski reviews appear, including two of biographical interest. A short though very favourable review of Graham Wallas's *The Great Society* is an intimation of things to come, for six years later Wallas would seek to bring Laski to the London School of Economics as his colleague. A longer review on 12 August of Volume One of Karl Pearson's *Life of Francis Galton* served as a final leave-taking of a part of Laski's already extraordinary career. It was a generous review with much praise of both Galton and Pearson as pioneers in understanding the role of heredity. But Laski made perfectly clear that eugenics was behind him.

> This is not wholly to neglect the sphere of environment. Ample leisure, valuable friends, private means, intellectual opportunity – these must count for not a little; far more, perhaps, than Professor Pearson in his enthusiasm is ready to admit. Many of us cannot fail to have met trade unionists whose intellectual powers have been stunted by the hardships of the lives they have led. Close, unremitting physical toil does not make for the occasion to show great mental powers.

Shortly after starting work at the *Daily Herald*, Laski returned to Manchester hopeful that at last his parents would recognize his marriage. He was bitterly disappointed. Nathan and Sarah had assumed that after Oxford Harold would give up his marriage. They knew nothing about the frequency of the weekend visits over the last two years and were, therefore, devastated at his decision to remain with Frida and live in London. Moreover, they were indignant that Harold was working for the *Daily Herald*, an association which they assured him would forever hurt his chances of a respectable career. His Oxford allowance was ended and the young couple were left totally on their own. Frida wrote, 'His parents had refused to recognize the marriage or accept me. As far as they were concerned a certain Frida Laski did not exist.'

The outbreak of war unexpectedly presented the couple with an opportunity to forge their own lives and fortunes. H. A. L. Fisher, back from India, wrote to ask if Laski was interested in a position as Lecturer in History at McGill University in Montreal, Canada. G. N. Clarke, a student of Fisher's, had accepted the position but wished to be released from the obligation in order to join the army. McGill would not agree to his request until he found a replacement. The idea of an ocean between them and Manchester seemed very appealing to Harold and Frida.

Laski had himself tried to enlist and was rejected for his weak heart and flat feet. It is perhaps less difficult to imagine the syndicalist, anti-war editorial writer of the *Daily Herald* enlisting if one remembers that concern over 'slackers' was widespread in Britain during the First World War, especially the belief that many of the educated and well-to-do were not carrying out their patriotic responsibilities. It is quite possible that Laski and his fellow syndicalist Herron in fact felt an obligation to enlist so that the war would not be fought just by the poor. It is also quite probable, whatever his motive in trying to enlist – even instinctive patriotism – that Laski thought it likely he would be turned down. After all, from his eugenics past he was familiar with the data on physique and health requirements in recruitment.

Meanwhile, there was a serious problem of paying for the passage to Montreal. He was to be reimbursed for travel expenses upon arrival but had to raise the money to buy the tickets. Harold swallowed his pride and went to Manchester. It was a painful visit, for by now a clear pattern was emerging of Harold as the bad son. Harold was working for the *Daily Herald* and Neville was training for the Bar. Harold was rejected by the army and Neville had been accepted by the Lancashire Fusiliers with the rank of captain. Most important of all, while Harold had married a Gentile, Neville was engaged to be married in January before going to France to a woman who was not only Jewish but was the daughter of Moses Gaster, the esteemed Sephardic Chief Rabbi of all Britain. To Laski's amazement, however, Nathan and Sarah came up with the passage money, on the condition it be paid back as soon as they arrived in Montreal. They also asked the couple not to visit again for any kind of a farewell call. Frida's autobiographical fragment records the unexpected success of Harold's visit: 'He sensed their relief at our decision to put the high seas between them and us. Apparently they would not have to lose face now in the eyes of their Jewish friends.'

Sylvia Pankhurst threw a huge party for Frida and Harold, inviting all their London and Oxford friends, and in early September they set sail from Liverpool. There were some wistful thoughts about Neville and Frida's brother Francis going to war, and of mother Kerry and the senior Laskis already talking of volunteer war work. 'It seemed as if we were the only ones to be running away,' Frida wrote. But the romance of the ocean voyage overtook them and they saw it as the continuation of their interrupted honeymoon of August 1911. 'Flat feet or not I soon got Harold on the floor and we danced. How we danced, cheek to cheek under the stars, all night till the first pearly streaks of morning drove us, dog-tired, to our beds.'

CHAPTER FOUR

Montreal and Making Connections

Montreal defined the adult Laski. He arrived a political activist of a scholarly bent, given to spontaneous militancy. He left two years later a professional academic with little interest in 'madly brave' deeds. Whether this transformation was shaped by intellectual commitment alone or the pressures of domestic and family responsibility, the sense of self that emerged in Montreal would remain with Laski for the rest of his life. He would be Professor Laski, a scholar and teacher. However, this retreat to the ivory tower would never be complete. Laski's irrepressible need to be at the centre of things would propel him eventually to an activist role in the less brave world of parliamentary politics. But that would wait. For now Laski withdrew to the academy which for some years would be the main arena for the expression of his ambition. Montreal would help both worlds, since this was a period of his life in which he formed the important friendships that would maintain him in a position of influence.

The Laskis were on their own. They knew no one in Montreal, and as if to drive home their sense of isolation, they arrived in Montreal to find a telegram from Manchester reminding them that the arrangements called for immediate return of the passage money. Their social lives were very much focused on their flat at 854 Dome Crescent, and luckily the couple discovered that they liked living with each other. Harold immersed himself in lecture preparation and historical research. Frida set herself the task of becoming pregnant. By the time the shock of the cold and the snow hit them, Frida had conceived and Montreal seemed bearable. But their euphoria was dashed in March 1915 when Frida had a miscarriage, and the loss of blood left her seriously ill. The rest of the harsh winter was gloomy for both of them after the excitement of comradely London.

Laski had one friend in North America and it is from his correspondence with Ben Huebsch, who lived in New York City, that we know the details of life in Montreal. Like all of Laski's American friends, Huebsch brought Laski professional and career benefits. They had met in August when Huebsch, a small independent publisher, was in Europe looking for manuscripts. He had been in Germany when war broke out, and on his arrival in London shortly thereafter he was interviewed by Laski for the *Daily Herald* to comment on the state of public opinion in Germany. Huebsch's politics were decidedly leftist and he and Laski enjoyed talking about politics and books. The two men saw a good deal of each other in Huebsch's remaining time in London, and were joined on some of those occasions by Francis Meynell, a radical friend of Laski's in both his syndicalist and suffragette circles who also worked at the *Daily Herald*. When Huebsch left London he insisted that Laski promise to look him up in America. Whenever Laski went to New York in the next two years, he would stay with his first American friend.

A close professional relationship also developed. Huebsch was a small publisher with an uncanny ability to pick his books carefully and to do well by them. On his August visit to Britain, for example, he acquired a collection of short stories by a new writer, *The Dubliners* by James Joyce. By 1914 he had already published H. G. Wells's *Discovery of the Future*, Maxim Gorky's *The Spy* and Eduard Bernstein's *Evolutionary Socialism*, and books by Thorsten Veblen, Van Wyck Brooks, Sherwood Anderson and D. H. Lawrence. He found in Laski an insatiable reader of history and politics whose speed-reading abilities made him a walking reference file. Huebsch called on Laski frequently for advice on manuscripts or reprints of European books. Their correspondence suggests that Laski was hardly ever without one of Huebsch's manuscripts to read and that Huebsch was thrilled to have the advice of one so aware of current developments in British and continental scholarship. This professional relationship would persist. In 1925 Huebsch merged his business with the new company founded by Harold Guinzberg and George Oppenheimer: Viking Press was born. As vice-president and editor-in-chief of Viking Press, Huebsch became the American publisher for most of Laski's books.

Like most of Laski's future American friends, Huebsch was Jewish. The son of a rabbi, he too was a secular Jew who had abandoned his father's ways, but whose Jewishness was still an important part of his sense of self, and their shared sense of Jewishness played an important part in their bonding. There is a light banter in their letters around Jewish topics. When

Laski jokingly suggested that his extensive reading for Huebsch merited his being a partner in the company, he drew the logo of the joint venture as a menorah. Frida, Harold related in another letter, would not be able to add her customary few lines since it was Yom Kippur and she didn't like to write on the holiday. When Frida did add her lines to a letter written close to the day she was due to give birth, she joked to Huebsch about preparation for 'pydanaben', the Yiddish word for the ceremonial redemption of a first-born son thirty days after birth. Huebsch in his letters applauded the good deeds, or mitzvahs, Laski had performed.

But there was also serious talk of Jewishness. In January 1915 Laski sent Huebsch his *Chosen People* to look at, telling him that it had been turned down once but that he didn't want it published out of politeness. Huebsch liked the manuscript but found it too short and suggested it be elaborated. Laski never did and 'put it away in a drawer' for life, but he did ask Huebsch for his 'attitudes to Jews and the kind of future you forecast'. For his part, Laski told Huebsch of his more recent thoughts on Montreal Jewry and the themes raised in *The Chosen People*. He had recently given a lecture 'to an enormous Jewish audience' and what impressed him

> was their crude attempt at Anglicization. It was very pathetic and very futile too; for they have a real ghetto here and they try to live two lives simultaneously.

Huebsch proved helpful with Laski's most pressing problem in his Montreal years: money. Laski's salary was $1,500 in his first year at McGill, and the last week of each month, Frida recalled, was a 'financial nightmare'. Pregnant twice and very ill with her miscarriage, Frida didn't work. In the spring of 1915 they had to choose between the doctor's bill and their rent. On one occasion they coped by wiring Frida's mother to sell an etching by Seymour Haden which Laski had left with her. Frida suggested that his constant worries over money, especially after being turned down by McGill in a request for a salary rise, turned Laski into a smoker. She smoked moderately, but he smoked 'like a chimney'. Indeed, after Montreal it was a rare moment when Laski was awake and not teaching that he was without a Craven A cigarette in his mouth. To make matters worse, their dog bit a neighbour and they were sued, which led to unexpected legal fees just before Diana was born. Harold tried to augment his income by giving a set of lectures in Toronto, and another in Winnipeg. But none of this was enough and he had to borrow money from Ben Huebsch. Frida wrote with evident contrast to Manchester:

> Harold had to borrow the cash from a Jewish colleague in New York and that was the first time I encountered the generosity of Jew towards Jew – a quality I grew to love and admire in my husband's people. But a debt is a debt and it was only years later in England that we were able to pay back the loan.

Huebsch was also a central actor in Laski's most ambitious Montreal scheme to add to his income, ghost-writing a book that Huebsch published in 1916. Like his first prize history essay, Laski's first published book was written under someone else's name, Mary Fels. The book was the biography of her husband, Joseph Fels, who had died in February 1914. Fels was a close friend of George Lansbury and it was he who brought Fels's widow and Laski together. Fels was a man whose life was so much the stuff of fables that one assumes only a novelist could have dreamed it up. The son of German Jews who had emigrated to the American South, he was born in Halifax County, Virginia, and grew to own one of the largest soap companies in the world, Fels-Naphtha. He ran the European branch of the business from London while his brother Sam ran the American branch from Philadelphia. Fels was a socialist who told his critics, 'I shall go on making as much money as I can and I will use it to prevent people like you and me being allowed to do so any longer.' Fels helped to take the Fabian Society out of debt in 1904, but his most spectacular act of socialist philanthropy occurred in 1907. The Russian Social Democratic Party conference was taking place in London, but the organization had run out of money. Lansbury talked Fels into providing £500 to pay for the remainder of the meetings and the passage home to Russia of the delegates. Thus on the conference's last day Lenin and his Bolsheviks were able to carry the debate against Martov's Mensheviks and to return to Russia with a vote for revolution.

Laski spent some time in Philadelphia with Mrs Fels in May 1915 to plan the book, and Frida joined him during the summer while he was writing it. There were, of course, some problems. He wrote to Huebsch, the book's publisher, 'She's too aesthetic to mind dates, and I as a damned historian believe in them, confound it.' The published book, *Joseph Fels: His Life-Work* by Mary Fels, did not mention Laski. Long passages on land tax policy in Denmark, Sweden and Belgium, and learned discussions of physiocratic economic policy in eighteenth-century France, were interspersed with details of Fels's domestic life. Laski was particularly qualified to write about Fels's role in Jewish politics, his support for Zangwill's Jewish Territorial Organization and its quest for Jewish settlement in South America or Africa. His discussion of Fels's involvement at Lansbury's side in the suffragette movement allowed Laski to lift whole sentences from his *Chosen People* to debunk male claims of superiority over women. Mary Fels's description of her husband has Laski's *Daily Herald* voice.

> Joseph Fels was never able to see that humanity beneath a greasy engineer's suit was essentially different from his own. He could never bring himself to believe that it did not matter whether poor children were fed or not. He knew that if these people had their due there would be no great fortunes to expend on carriages, flunkies, great houses, expensive dress and charitable subscriptions.

Laski never ghosted a book again, but another of the ways he made money in his days of debt was something he did over and over again throughout his lifetime, even when he no longer had money problems. Frida was quite candid about it: 'Looking for a way to increase his income, Harold began in Montreal to write articles for the American papers – especially the *New Republic* and the *Nation* – and it turned out to be a thoroughly lucrative occupation.' He was paid two cents per word for writing these pieces, which added up to between $20 and $60 per article. Writing for these magazines did more than allow bills to be paid. According to Frida, it offered him 'an outlet as well for his political thinking and his verbosity'. Seeing himself in these magazines catered to his vanity too, Frida noted. Writing for the literate left allowed him 'to hold centre stage in whatever he said or did'.

Whatever he was earning and whatever his status, the indefatigable Laski gave freely of his time throughout his career to non-remunerated or low-paying lecturing to workers. Always the intellectual with his polished paragraphs, he was nevertheless effective with working-class audiences who were moved by his enthusiasm as well as by his eloquence. As early as November 1914 he ran a tutorial class in economics for the mainly Scottish workers from Montreal's Angus Railway Shops. He also held a weekly evening class at his home for men and women trade unionists to study history and politics. While he was teaching for money at Winnipeg Laski lectured for free at a trade-union college run by the Cooperative Commonwealth Federation, the forerunner of the New Democratic Party (NDP), Canada's present Socialist Party. Laski also spoke at union rallies, and one such speech to a group of munitions workers in November 1915 was followed by a letter to Montreal's *Daily Mail* from some workers 'much struck to think that such an eloquent professor should speak on behalf of the working classes'.

Laski described his labour movement activity to Lansbury in letters written from Montreal. He told him that it was 'really Frida's enthusiasm' that started him on the idea of giving workers' courses. In these letters, as in others of this period, Laski's worry that he appeared to have run away from the war often surfaced. Despite his financial concerns he berated his own comfort, observing that two of his cousins had died in the war, as had Herron, 'his best friend from Oxford'. He wrote of 'longing to be in France', of 'aching' to be there 'fighting'. He poignantly told Lansbury that 'half the men you met in my room at Oxford have been killed and I wonder in my soul where we shall get the intellect for the next generation'.

Laski wanted England to negotiate peace with Germany and suggested to Lansbury that the *Daily Herald* lead a campaign 'advocating a definite peace plan'. Lansbury, 'the only one who can lead us', should push a post-war reconstruction movement that would retain wartime taxation levels and nationalize monopoly services such as shipping, or at least achieve the 'fixation of the conditions of employment by law'. Laski went public with his war views in a letter to the *New Republic* published in December 1915. Though convinced 'of the moral rightness of the Allied cause', he was also certain that it was futile to discuss the origins of the war. More crucial were a negotiated peace with Germany and, in anticipation of John Maynard Keynes's later argument, a peace settlement that would not punish Germany too severely. If such a position was called 'pro-Germanism', Laski informed the American public not yet at war, so be it and 'one most sincerely hopes that Mr Asquith is pro-German to the last degree'.

Laski's views on a negotiated settlement of the war provide the background to the controversial speech he gave at Montreal's Canadian Club in his second year at McGill. No text of the speech survives, but in 1939 Laski referred to his attack on Lloyd George in the speech for the latter's 'bitter-endism'. To his dislike of Lloyd George's suffrage waffling and his syndicalist opposition to the National Insurance Act, Laski now added Lloyd George's conversion as newly appointed Minister of Munitions to a strategy of all-out victory over Germany. After Laski's speech many present at the Canadian Club demanded he be fired from McGill. According to the *Montreal Star*, Sir William Peterson, the Principal of McGill, 'stood by Professor Laski' and 'the urgent demands for [his] dismissal' were ignored.

Though Laski gave the impression in 1939 that the controversy was an important reason in convincing him to leave McGill, in fact he had been seeking to leave long before the Canadian Club furore. Despite his promotion in the second year to an assistant professorship and his salary rise from $1,500 to $2,000, Laski had decided in his first year that he didn't like McGill. In the February of his first winter in Montreal, Laski wrote to Huebsch that he couldn't 'stand my colleagues'. The students were taught poorly and learned little that was important. 'Fancy a Canadian university without a single course attempting to deal with American history.' It was clear to him that he must move on, for 'the job doesn't ask, and largely doesn't want, the best I can give'. But how to find a place that was worthy of his best? The answer, Laski knew quite well from his boyhood in Manchester and his years in London and Oxford, was a judicious combination of who you knew, what you knew and how well you knew it. In meeting these requirements Laski was, in Montreal as throughout most of his life, consummately successful.

In his first months at McGill Laski came to the attention of Norman Hapgood, President Woodrow Wilson's ambassador to Denmark who was in Montreal on government business. An attorney who had also served as editor of *Collier's* and then *Harper's*, Hapgood was a close friend of Louis Denbitz Brandeis, the famous progressive lawyer then practising in Boston, and of Felix Frankfurter, who in 1914 had begun a distinguished career at Harvard Law School. Hapgood wrote to Frankfurter about meeting the 'most extraordinary young man I've ever come across anywhere', and early that spring in 1915 Frankfurter, who was then visiting Ottawa, made the journey to Montreal to meet Laski.

> Everything that Hapgood said about his extraordinary qualities was verified
> within an hour. I was charmed by his manner. His quickness, his eagerness,

his liveliness, his range of interests – all wholly apart from the learning I was told he professed – made me realize I was in the presence of a very unusual person.

They talked the next day of public law – Frankfurter's field – and of the history of political theory – Laski's. Frankfurter was struck that Laski 'wasn't interested in agreement, that he was interested in the exchange of ideas'. So began the friendship between the 'frail stripling' who looked to Frankfurter as if he didn't weigh 100 pounds, and the man destined to be one of the most influential advisers to Franklin Roosevelt's New Deal presidency as well as one of America's most distinguished Supreme Court justices. Their long and intimate friendship survived long after Frankfurter's politics sharply diverged from Laski's in the 1930s.

When Frankfurter returned to Harvard he told the Dean of the Graduate School, Charles Haskins, a distinguished medieval historian, that Harvard should try to get the extraordinary Laski. Laski came for a day and met Haskins, his new friend Frankfurter and, as he wrote to Huebsch, 'a wonderful man named Roscoe Pound', as well as 'Lowell, the President, who is very impressive'. Pound was one of America's leading legal theorists and Lowell had written *The Government of England* in 1908. Laski, who knew the work of both men, had found the place that could bring out the best he could give. When he returned to Montreal he wrote to Huebsch: 'My God! I want to be with these men, they make life quite different.' He had an important book to write and 'one can only begin it in the Canadian backwoods'. He confided in Huebsch that 'I do really want the chance of teaching my curious political ideas at Harvard.'

Laski was committed to teach at McGill a second year and no formal offer was made by Harvard, though Haskins did ask that he be notified if Laski planned to leave McGill. All the same, Laski was confident. 'There is a first-rate chance of my going there next year,' he wrote to Huebsch. He let Frankfurter know throughout the summer of 1915 that his ambition was one day to be his colleague. Meanwhile, he asked for Frankfurter's outlines on administrative law and urged him to make sure Pound saw a review he had done of a book on Bracton, the British medieval legal writer, in the *Nation*. Laski was thrilled to hear that 'the greatest authority in America' liked it. In these first of what would eventually be hundreds of letters exchanged between Laski and Frankfurter, Laski played his characteristic chord of flattery. 'By the way,' he wrote, 'Pound said to me (entre nous) he was more proud of you than any other member of the university.' Laski then added, 'I hope I shall say that one day.'

Morris Cohen, philosophy professor at City College, New York, and Frankfurter's room-mate in 1905–6 at Harvard, invited Laski in the autumn of 1915 to give a paper at the Fourth Annual Conference on Legal and Social Philosophy held at Columbia University. 'Heaven knows why they have asked me,' Laski wrote to Huebsch, and claimed modestly that 'it is rather absurd for me to talk to such people'. Nevertheless, 'I am keen to do it for a world of reasons'. Laski read his paper, 'The Sovereignty of the State', in front of one of the most illustrious and influential groups of scholars in America. Cohen was the conference secretary and the chairman was John Dewey. Also listening to Laski's paper were Brandeis, Pound and Frankfurter, and the historians Arthur Lovejoy of Johns Hopkins and James Harvey Robinson of Columbia.

On 28 November, immediately after the conference, Laski began writing to Pound. Harvard invited Laski for an extended visit in December, and in January Frankfurter wrote that Pound was to be the new Dean of the Law School. Laski's letter to Pound knew no bounds in its flattery: only Harvard was worthy of Pound, and he hoped that 'you will pay a visit to Montreal and teach us the functions of a law school'. An article of Pound's, 'Common Law and Legislation', which Laski claimed he had read five years earlier, should be compared only to Maitland and Gierke. These were no mere formal congratulations, but 'rather the inner satisfaction that comes from right being done'. In early February Harvard did right again: an offer was sent to Laski. Laski had made it to the 'centre stage' that Frida saw as his constant need. He wrote to Huebsch:

> I am coming to Harvard next year, that is practically settled. I am to have six hours' work, my present salary and time to take an LL.B in the Law School … Felix Frankfurter arranged it all and we are nearly off our heads with delight. A few more b—y months here and then Elysium.

There is still more impressive evidence of Laski's skills in who he knew. Not only did he write extensively for the *New Republic* in 1915 and 1916, but he became a member of its influential inner circle, spending a small amount of time at its offices in the summer of 1915 and virtually the entire summer of 1916 working in an editorial capacity at its New York offices on 23rd Street. Through his *New Republic* activities Laski became a part of a bright and influential collection of political writers centred on the progressive movement, Frankfurter once again providing the introduction. He was a close friend of Herbert Croly, the magazine's editor, and while he never officially took a title he was a frequent contributor and member of the editorial board. The magazine was founded in the autumn of 1914 as a progressive weekly by Willard Straight with the money of his socially conscious heiress wife, Dorothy Whitney Straight, daughter of William L. Whitney, one of America's rubber barons. In addition to Croly, the initial set of editors included Walter Lippmann, who graduated from Harvard in 1910 and who had recently published his first book, *A Preface to Politics*. Alvin Johnson, the *New Republic*'s resident economist and social scientist, was recruited from Willard Straight's Alma Mater, Cornell. The magazine was modelled on the *New Statesman*, launched by the Webbs in 1913: it too welcomed conventional liberal as well as socialist writers, committed to 'progressive reform'. The magazine attracted a distinguished set of writers: John Dewey, Charles Beard, Thorsten Veblen and many of Morris Cohen's conference group. A large number of British writers, including Shaw, Wells, Keynes, the Webbs, Brailsford, Nevinson and Gilbert Murray, could be found in its pages. The Labour Party in Britain and its amalgam of liberal and socialist ideas was particularly appealing to the *New Republic* set, most of whom were inveterate Anglophiles. Laski fitted in beautifully, then. He was able to write on anything with facility and verve. Like the rest of them he was youthfully irreverent and passionate in his optimistic commitment to reform. And he was fun to have around, a dazzlingly articulate young man with devastating English wit.

Laski succeeded, however, not only because of who he knew, but because what he knew was an important expression of the general mind-set characteristic of the American progressives. In other words, his was both a world-view and a mind to be reckoned with. Virtually all the important people Laski knew through his *New Republic* and Conference on Legal and Social Philosophy connections shared a set of intellectual convictions that had at its centre the philosophy of pragmatism and the politics of democratic political and economic reform, both of which were informed by a faith in science.

Pragmatism in the influential writings of William James and John Dewey insisted that truth and morality were inherent not in logic, definitions or first principles of abstract thought but in the actuality of factual results in the real world of experience. Formal inquiry which sought single unifying truths that were abstract, fixed and objective overlooked the true nature of reality, which was uncertain, evolving and contingent. The role of the philosopher and the social theorist was not to weave formal definitions of truth or good in moralistic or intellectual terms, but to look at the facts, the experience of people and institutions and the consequences of beliefs and actions on their lives. The pragmatic thinker was, then, as the American philosopher Morton White characterized it, always in 'revolt against formalism'.

Such a pragmatic approach, it was assumed, led the philosopher inexorably to progressive politics. Elites and ruling classes hid behind abstractions and formalism and cloaked their self-interests with mystery and pieties about the social neutrality of intellectual concepts like truth and good. The focus of progressive legal thought captured this close connection of pragmatism and reform. Law was not a set of abstract general principles applied to concrete cases. It was not applied to everyone in the same objective way, unrelated to the status or the power of particular individuals. Oliver Wendell Holmes's conviction in his famous essay *The Common Law* pervaded progressive legal theory: 'The life of the law has not been logic, but experience. The law . . . cannot be dealt with as if it contained only the actions and corollaries of a book of mathematics.' Justice Holmes's famous dissent in the 1905 Lochner case – insisting that it was not legal abstractions like 'due process' and the sanctity of contracts, but Herbert Spencer's social philosophy and the class interest of industrialists that lay behind the majority decision overturning New York's statute regulating the hours of bakery workers – was a flash of realism that appealed to progressives. Cases like Lochner were decided by the formal application of concepts and not by 'scientific investigations' and 'social necessity'. The *New Republic* frequently repeated this linkage of reform with science and the scientific method; science was the pragmatic method in action. Life, Darwin had shown, was not given in certain and fixed truths but was shaped by new experiences that questioned certainty and undermined the axioms that were yesterday's truths.

What Cohen and his conference group and Lippmann and his *New*

Republic colleagues discovered was that Laski in 1915 and 1916 was taking their common 'revolt against formalism' to that most sacred citadel of politics, the state, and he was doing it with an impatient disregard for received wisdom. In Montreal Laski had added American philosophy and legal theory to his reading and research and began offering in preliminary pieces his critique of the state. The German idealist tradition absorbed by English liberals like T. H. Green had described the state as a formal unity and source of neutral moral principle that existed apart from the world of experience. Laski's mission was to wield the pragmatic and Darwinian spirit in an effort to demystify that state and to suggest that it was not an absolute source of transcendent justice or law. Behind its mystical façade were real people, a collection of officials and their specific actions. And these real officials usually did what served the ends of powerful economic interests.

Laski wrote numerous book reviews in 1915 and 1916 that attracted attention to his erudition and wit, but it was his first two published articles and his lecture to Cohen's conference that announced his presence to the progressive intellectual community. In 'The Personality of the State', published in July 1915 in the *Nation*, 'The Sovereignty of the State', delivered in November as his paper at Columbia, and 'The Apotheosis of the State', which appeared in the *New Republic* in July 1916, Laski joined the American pragmatic 'revolt against formalism' to his syndicalist anti-statism in the first iterations of what he called 'pluralism'. He urged the abandonment of the German theory of the state with its 'mystic monism'. William James, after all, had said that 'nothing includes everything or dominates everything'. Laski rejected the argument that one's obligations were primarily to the state because it was 'sovereign' and only secondarily to unions, churches or clubs. Those associations, he argued, have real wills and personalities just as the state does. Moreover, people feel real and pressing obligations to these corporate entities that compete with loyalty to the state and often override it. This pluralist vision, Laski insisted, 'fits the facts of life' and 'starts from the concrete world we know'.

What this meant, according to Laski, was that the much-touted sovereignty of the state, understood as the sole source of authority, did not exist. The state was obeyed when its will was consented to against the other wills that competed with it and when, 'Darwin-wise', its will had survived by better providing what people wanted. It was therefore sovereign not from any formal or defining features but only when it was assented to. It enjoyed no 'necessary pre-eminence for its commands'. The state deserved no special worship, nor any special respect. It was not a first principle of truth or good in its own right: it received respect and loyalty only when it achieved its purpose.

Political allegiance is, then, experimental. It is impermanent and tentative. The state claims to seek the common purposes and the general good of all, but the 'analysis of hard facts' demonstrates that the only good achieved is that 'of a certain section of the state, not the community as a whole'. The trade unionist sees 'nothing absolute or unqualified' about his obligations to the state. On the contrary, Laski insisted, it is not 'right' for him to obey the state when it serves only the capitalist's good. For what 'I mean by right is something the pragmatist will understand. It is something the individual ought to concede because experience has proved it to be good.' Laski's early worship of Darwin hovers over his vision of the state competing with other private associations for individual loyalty. His pluralist theory of the state, he writes, 'sets group competing against group in a ceaseless striving of progressive expansion'. All the while the framework is pragmatic and instrumental. At the Columbia conference Laski concluded his paper:

> The pluralistic theory of the state . . . is what Professor Dewey calls 'consistently experimentalist' in form and content. It denies the rightness of force. It dissolves – what the facts themselves dissolve – the inherent claims of the state to obedience. It insists that the state, like every other association, shall prove itself by what it achieves . . . It does not try to work out with tedious elaboration the respective spheres of state or group or individual. It leaves that to the rest of the event. It predicates no certainty.

It was obviously, then, not only who he knew but what he knew that explains Laski's call to Harvard. The progressive philosophers, historians, legal and political scholars, and journalists were dazzled, as others had been before, by the brilliance of this 23-year-old professor from McGill, this 'frail stripling'. He excited them with his capacity to wed the concerns of European historical and legal erudition to their own 'revolt against formalism'. As iconoclastic as many of the progressive intellectuals saw themselves, they had to admit that Laski outdid even them, for his pluralist theory of the state contained, as he proudly admitted, 'a hint of anarchy'. His message was, he proclaimed, an indictment of those who 'prostrate themselves in speechless admiration before the state'. His scholarly attack on 'a certain grim Hegalianism' evoked the tone of his not-so-distant *Daily Herald* editorials as he repudiated those who saw the state as 'a kind of modern Baal, to which the citizen must, unheeding, bow a willing knee'.

It is to the credit of the *New Republic* set that they accepted Laski so enthusiastically, for they were much more sympathetic to the state and state authority than he was. They were by no means state worshippers, but the magazine fairly faithfully reflected Croly's opinion, outlined in his *The Promise of American Life* and *Progressive Democracy*, that progressive and democratic reform required America to abandon Jefferson's 'suspicion of authority' and accept Hamilton's vision of a vigorous and powerful national government. A positive and active state, Croly believed, would serve Jeffersonian ideals of equality by curbing with its strength and in the name of the majority the power of industrial and monied minorities. It would superintend a moderate redistribution of wealth through progressive taxation policies and the nationalization of monopolistic enterprises like the railways and the telegraph system. Croly's views and the *New Republic*'s position were not unlike the reform liberalism of the Liberal Party of Asquith and Lloyd George. Croly's conviction that progressive reform required a powerful national government not only attracted Theodore Roosevelt but saw the *New Republic* welcome the centralization of authority in Washington and the revitalization of a sense of national purpose brought about by the war, which America entered in 1917.

The practical and institutional implications of Laski's pluralism also ran counter to the *New Republic*'s efforts to increase the power of the American state. Laski emphasized federalism, localism, decentralization of power, and checks and balances as powerful antidotes to an overbearing state. Croly, on the other hand, was critical of federalism and suspicious of the separation of power. Laski's pluralism was actually much more compatible with the other powerful tendency in the progressive movement associated with Brandeis and Wilson, the anti-trusters, who saw industrial capital best tamed by breaking up large institutions and large aggregations of power. Despite these cross-currents, Laski, the *New Republic* and Brandeis, as well, had much in common. On the great issue of the day, the industrial question, they were all unabashedly pro-labour, bent on eliminating exploitive working conditions and unfair wages. They shared a faith in science, expertise and professionalism which could on occasion conflict with their democratic and egalitarian ideals. Finally, they shared the pragmatic sense of society, its institutions and its social policies, as being constantly in flux, impermanent, tentative and experimental.

Appropriately enough, Laski's pluralism was not his final vision, nor did he regard his decentralized anti-statist politics with any finality. These tentative efforts to combine thought with action would eventually be discarded for other experiments which in turn would be judged by their consequences. What some call the inconsistencies or the contradictions of his changing political ideology in the next thirty-five years, Laski might well have called at this stage in his career the healthy process of instrumental experimentation in the never-ending, always evolving, engagement with social life.

Despite Laski's attitudes to the state, Croly championed his work. He visited Laski in Montreal for a day in March and encouraged him to join the staff of the *New Republic*. He also urged him to turn his articles and papers into a book. Yale University Press showed interest in the project and in June 1916 sent Laski a contract to publish the as yet unfinished manuscript of Laski's first book, *Studies in the Problem of Sovereignty*. He had told Huebsch that it wasn't appropriate for his company because it was too academic, nonchalantly adding 'that it was the work of a genius. (This of course strictly between ourselves.)'

The day after the letter from Yale University Press arrived, Laski became a father. The child, so anticipated and glorified in the Oxford years of eugenic self-control, was born on 3 June. Had it been a boy it was to have been Michael, no longer Karl. But it was a girl and she was named Diana Maitland, the middle name that of the great medieval historian, whose works Laski was poring over for his book and who had recently died. She was given two godfathers, George Lansbury and Ben Huebsch. Several days after her birth Diana became ill from an obstruction in her intestine. Laski, writing daily to Huebsch, telegrammed 'Afraid no hope', but she recovered and remained in the hospital for three weeks. Frida, who had had a protracted labour and was left weak by the delivery, was, in general, fit. After the crisis passed the baby experienced many weeks of stomach distress until she began to gain weight. Frida recalled Diana as 'dark and wide-eyed and pert like her father' and Harold as 'ham-handed' and unable to hold her properly. These few months were complicated even more by their poor finances, made worse by Diana's illness, requiring Harold to go off to New York and do his summer stint for the *New Republic*. He was clearly torn. He needed the money desperately and he certainly thrived at the magazine; but he was genuinely upset at not being able to be more helpful with Diana. He enjoyed being a father, and his letters to Huebsch are exuberant as he describes the baby with her long fingers, 'clearly another Beethoven', with 'amazing abilities' as befits 'her distinguished parents'. It was a 'wonderful joy just to watch her . . . If it is possible it has brought us even more closely than before together.'

There were few people in Montreal to share their excitement. Their one friend, Stephen Leacock, the head of McGill's Political Science Department and famous humorist and comic writer, sent them a delightful letter on the pitfalls of parenting. For more reaction they had to depend on their distant families. Laski telegrammed the news of Diana's arrival to London and Manchester. Mrs Kerry, by then a volunteer nurse, wrote of her joy at becoming a grandmother amidst all the pain of the war. Mrs Laski, who had earlier accused the couple of 'a shameful lack of responsibility' in having a child before they 'had fallen on their feet', did congratulate them and asked whether Diana was going to be brought up Jewish. Harold and Frida were insulted and wrote, as they told Huebsch, that 'the reply in any case is a flat negative'. Paton, the beloved High Master of Manchester Grammar School, sent a letter full of splendid sentiments about 'something in the face of a child that prevents one from holding or accepting the diabolist view of the universe', adding that he had seen Neville at Smedley House the night before and that he was improving. Neville was home from the war after being wounded in the leg at the Dardanelles the previous October. When he received word about the injury Harold had been 'very upset', he told Huebsch, even though ten months earlier he had written to him with dripping sarcasm about Neville's wedding and its 500 guests. Whatever the sarcasm, whatever the acclaim of university presses or professors, 'my people' still mattered to Laski. And now in the 'good son, bad son' reckoning, as if it was not enough that his parents had only one interest in his child, Neville, who had gone off to fight while he went off to Canada, was a decorated war hero, to boot, receiving visitors at Smedley House.

CHAPTER FIVE

Cambridge, Massachusetts and Pluralism

Four years at Harvard completed Laski's transformation to professional scholar. They also established the contradictory pattern that characterized his public persona for the rest of his career. In his writings and teaching he was the rebel, the irreverent and mischievous *enfant terrible* constantly critical of those with power. In his professional and social connections he was driven, as Frida put it, to 'centre stage', to friendship with the Great and the Good. He moved easily from working on anarcho-syndicalist books to having lunch with the powers that be. Teaching at an elite university facilitated such a double life. The Establishment permitted its young exposure to the free play of ideas, even to the radical critique of its own privilege and power. On the other hand, the teacher at Harvard was naturally assumed to be a part of the ruling elite, respected and socially welcomed by the powerful parents of their students. By 1920, when Laski left Harvard after having been Instructor and Lecturer in History and Tutor in the Division of History, Government and Economics, he was the friend of two of the nine justices of the United States Supreme Court and a name on a political subversives file in J. Edgar Hoover's new Bureau of Investigation.

In another way, Laski's four years at Harvard were an augury of the years to come. He evolved a work regimen of intense busyness and productivity which seemed to defy the limited hours of the day. No matter a new home in a new country, a new job with new lectures, let alone a new baby, in the autumn of 1916 Laski was also writing books, learned articles, weekly journalism and book reviews. He was lecturing and doing tutorials while he himself was enrolled as a student in Harvard Law School. Not only had he begun his lifelong habit of frequent and lengthy correspondence, he was also making his mark in the political and social world of Cambridge and Boston. No wonder Laski's new friend, the 77-year-old

Oliver Wendell Holmes, Jr, urged him to slow down and not 'turn out so much' lest he 'run his machine too hard'. But Laski didn't know how to slow down unless he were ill, and then he would read voraciously as he had in Manchester. What slowing down in normal times meant to Laski was nicely described in a letter he wrote in 1918 while on his summer holiday at Rockport, Massachusetts.

> I've been superbly lazy – reading, catching fish and writing a paper on administrative areas. I have also finished a piece for your Law Review.

Laski's preoccupation with work almost botched up his arrival in Cambridge. Frida had decided that in late August Harold should go directly from his summer work at the *New Republic* in New York City to Cambridge to find accommodation, while she and Diana remained in Montreal. Her instructions were that he use 'the money he earned from his article writing to buy furniture and get everything shipshape' before she and the still sickly Diana arrived. She had forgotten Harold's utter impracticality, however. Carrying Diana and with their dog at her heels, Frida arrived in early September at 1697 Cambridge Street, the address he had sent her, 'to find Harold delighted to see me, blissfully enmeshed in writing' and looking 'lost like a small boy' in an apartment empty but for one bed 'and a desk with reams of writing paper'. Frida took charge and purchased all their furniture. Her initial anger had given way, as she put it, to her realization that Harold was 'the most impractical of creatures, half-man, half-child and maddeningly dependent on me'.

Serious money problems persisted in Cambridge. The Kerrys were unable to help and the Laskis unwilling, not that Harold even bothered to ask, for his relationship with his parents remained strained. He heard nothing from Nathan or Sarah and only occasionally from Neville. Frida was tempted by her anger with Manchester to have Diana baptized, but she desisted at the last moment out of deference to Harold. This estrangement from Smedley House clearly bothered Laski, who, whatever sophisticated indifference to roots he might affect, was constantly pulled by deep bonds of loyalty and love. He was overjoyed when his peripatetic Uncle Noah and Aunt Sarah, visiting America in 1919, got in touch with him. After a warm reunion in New York City Laski wrote to them that being with them gave him a glimpse 'of dreams I have often had in the last eight years' of sharing his happiness 'fully with my people'. He asked that when they returned his love be given to all in Manchester, 'especially to father and mother'. Noah and Sarah should report to his parents, he added, that he had become 'a seriously introspective scholar with pedantic interests', but also that 'scholarship is not incompatible with affection'. All the same, no financial help came from Manchester during the Cambridge years.

Complicating the money crisis in Cambridge were constant doctor's bills. Harold was sick each winter with bouts of influenza or pneumonia, as he would be for virtually his whole life. Diana was ill again in the autumn of 1917 and required an operation in January 1918. Though his persistent illnesses provided Laski with what he described as 'vacations', time to read, they also meant not only unexpected expenses but that Frida, the only strong and healthy Laski, could not earn money from massage patients because of all the nursing she had to do for her husband and daughter. For his part, Laski was driven to more and more supplemental work. He read manuscripts for Huebsch and wrote articles and book reviews for the *New Republic*, *Bookman* and *Dial* magazines. According to Frida, he also discovered in Cambridge yet another 'new way to add to our income', accepting invitations to lecture at other universities. Not that paying for furniture and health care was the only source of financial pressure between 1916 and 1920: there was also the cost of maintaining the proper life-style. Just as in Laski's boyhood when Nathan and Sarah took a house during the summer in a Jewish seaside community, so now Laski moved his little family in the summers of 1917, 1918 and 1919 to the fashionable coastal resort and artist colony Rockport, on Boston's North Shore.

Laski's Harvard salary of $2,950 wasn't enough to pay for all of this, nor were the manuscripts, articles and reviews. In 1917 he taught summer school at Harvard and also put in some time with the *New Republic* editorial staff in New York, as he did again in the summer of 1918. He tried to borrow money as well. Ben Huebsch obliged with a second loan, but surprisingly Laski unashamedly went beyond personal friends in efforts that seem rather forward and gauche. In the spring of 1918 Laski wrote to President Lowell of Harvard requesting a $245 advance on his autumn salary to pay for a summer rental of a cottage by the sea. When Lowell replied that this was never done, Laski wrote to Roscoe Pound, Dean of the Law School, for a loan of $300. He had saved $300 for a summer holiday, he wrote to Pound, but it had disappeared to pay for his child's operation. He would pay back half in November and the rest in January when he was paid by Radcliffe, Harvard's sister campus, where he, like many Harvard faculty, taught for extra wages. There is no record of Pound's reply, though it is clear that the Laskis did spend the summer of 1918 at Rockport. Laski also tried to borrow money from the richest people he knew, Dorothy and Willard Straight, the progressive patrons of the *New Republic*. His letter in February 1917 suggested that he needed the $200 loan not for himself but for a friend who worked at a Cambridge bookshop while writing a history of American astronomy. The friend had come from the West Coast and needed the money to ship his books east. This letter and others to Mrs Straight in this period were vintage Laski. The line between truth and fiction is unclear. Laski, for example, had himself told Huebsch the previous year that he had been unable to afford to bring most of his books across the Atlantic. But there is also the heavy-handed flattery, praise of Willard as 'one of a half-dozen men of distinction in America', and the dropped names of the great, the 'entre nous, Justice Holmes the other day said wonderful things about the *New Republic*'. Again, only Laski's request for his friend's loan survives. All we do know is that years later when Laski's American friends were trying to raise money to purchase his library for the London School of Economics, mention was made of approaching Michael Straight, then publisher of the *New Republic* and former student of Laski's, since 'his mother . . . loved Laski'.

Laski's appetite for work knew few limits. His enrolment as a full-time student at the Law School had been prompted by reading Maitland at Oxford and by his recent connection with Morris Cohen's legal circle. He took easily to his Law School studies, writing to Pound: 'I am loving every hour of the School. It is a time to discover how hopelessly ignorant I really am and how many things there are besides churches and sovereignty and corporations.' Untroubled by his friendships with its dean and its distinguished professor Frankfurter, who was judge in one of Laski's student moot court cases, he was, however, daunted by the burden of his teaching, his poor health that winter and by the confinement of again being a student 'after two years of freedom'. At the end of the first semester he admitted, as he seldom would in his career, that he had tried too much, and so he gave up his law studies, deciding that his future lay in political and historical scholarship. One of the things he regretted about this decision was no longer being able to experience the thrill of fellow first-year law students discovering that he was the author of *Law Review* articles himself. Just before he resigned as a student, Laski wrote:

> I have written a long paper in the *Yale Law Journal* . . . on vicarious liability. A fellow who sits next to me in torts reads it and comments to me thus: 'I didn't know your father was a lawyer.' 'He isn't? Oh! but I read his article in the *Yale L. J.*'

Laski had, in fact, already published a piece in the *Harvard Law Review* before he came to Harvard, 'The Personality of Associations'. By the time he left Harvard he had published three more articles or notes for the *Harvard Law Review* and one for the *Michigan Law Review*. These articles all focused on the legal implications of his pluralist argument, the insistence on the real existence and, therefore, legal liabilities of corporate bodies. The *Yale Law Journal* piece that impressed his fellow student, 'The Basis of Vicarious Liability', is still cited in the 1990s in torts law-case books.

The entrance of the United States into the war in April 1917 had depleted the ranks of the entire university, and the board of the *Harvard Law Review* badly needed help, and so from November 1917 until June 1919 Laski served as book review editor of the *Harvard Law Review*, the only editor in the history of the *Harvard Law Review* who was not a registered student in the Harvard Law School. His tenure was important for the *Review*, the Law School, and American law in general. He brought to the book reviews of America's premier legal journal a heightened sensitivity in American legal studies to the relationship between law and the social sciences. Pound, a pioneer of the sociological approach to law, wrote to Laski that he had done wonders for the journal's book review department. Years later he was credited with opening 'the eyes of American lawyers to a new range of books' and 'a new kind of reviewer'. He featured books by European, especially French and German, legal scholars and historians; he invited reviewers who were philosophers, historians and theologians. Looking back at Laski's two years at the *Harvard Law Review* after Laski's death in 1950, Zechariah Chafee wrote:

> There are few men with whom I have disagreed so often, and fewer still with whom I have passed so many happy hours and from who I have learned so much.

What an even more wonderful memory of the Harvard Law School Laski might have had if, instead of dropping his studies in January 1917, he had stayed on but two more months. Then he could have had the thrill of his fellow students marvelling not at a piece in the *Yale Law Journal* but at his book. In March 1917 the first of Laski's twenty-five (authored, many more were edited) books, *Studies in the Problem of Sovereignty*, was published by Yale University Press. Only twenty-three years old, and a mere four and a half years since his conversion from science to historical studies, Laski published what would prove to be one of his most influential works. He dedicated the book to his New College tutors, H. A. L. Fisher and Ernest Barker, beginning a practice he would continue throughout his career of dedications to important acquaintances and friends. It was fittingly done in this instance, for the book reinforced Laski's case for a pluralist theory of the state with learned historical arguments from early modern and nineteenth-century political and church history. The book was a marriage of New College historical erudition with Darwinian-informed American pragmatism.

Laski's strategy in the book was to view the state factually and realistically, not as a metaphysical entity, and to contrast its real and contingent authority with that of voluntary associations like trade unions. The surprising move he made from his earlier argumentation was to concentrate much more in the book on the claims of churches in the face of overweaning state power. One reason for this was that there was much richer historical documentation of the state as enemy of plural religions and religious freedom than of state sovereignty confrontations with the more recent phenomenon of trade unions. Another was surely the broader audience sympathetic to his attack on the state that this strategy would produce. He wrote as such to Bertrand Russell, whose own *Political Ideals* (1911) was a similar attack on the state. Not only had Laski come to realize that the church and the state had changed places since the Reformation and that the evils of unified ecclesiastical control had become the tactics of the modern state, but, as he informed Russell, 'it then struck me that the evil of this sovereignty could be shown fairly easily in the sphere of religion in its state-connection where men might still hesitate to admit it in the economic sphere'.

Politics, indeed, makes strange bedfellows, for four of the book's chapters find the secular leftist Laski allying himself with historical episodes of church resistance to state sovereignty. Packaging much of the book's attack on the sovereign state in rapturous praise of Catholic and medieval theory illustrated not only the political calculation Laski revealed to Russell, but the general ideological confusion surrounding pluralist attacks on the state before and during the First World War. Laski admitted, in fact, that most clerical critics of unitary state sovereignty wouldn't 'care a damn about freedom for any of its rivals' if they were in control of state power. The problem was that the pluralist assault on the state was a movement that came from all ideological directions. The 'medieval' defence of autonomous and overlapping communities uncorrupted by the vision of the unified sovereign state gave Laski not only 'guild socialists' like G. D. H. Cole as bedfellows, who built a socialist future on the re-creation of pre-industrial guild-centred modes of production, but also fully fledged 'medieval' reactionaries like Hilaire Belloc and G. K. Chesterton. In the journal *New Age* as well as in the *Daily Herald*, where all varieties of anti-statist sentiment were welcome, Belloc and Chesterton published anti-socialist libertarian pleas to leave the poor alone and 'free' in the countryside, as well as anti-Semitic visions of Jewish financiers as evil state-builders.

There was a common anti-statist language, however, that ran through all the diverse strains of pluralism, and Laski's book speaks it well with his insistence that 'we have been perhaps too frankly worshippers of the state', for the state 'like man ceases to be human when it is exalted into godhead'. But there is no mistaking that it is neither churches nor the medieval corporate *communitas* that prompted the critical, argumentative and angry tone that constantly breaks the learned calm of historical and textual erudition in Laski's book. It is his concern for the interests of labour and trade unions. Much is made in the scholarly literature on Laski's political thought of his abandoning an early anti-statist pluralism through a later embrace first of Fabian and then of Marxist centralizing ideas. Overlooked is the consistency of Laski's concern for labour's interests, the changes occurring only in the ways that could best achieve them. Laski's pluralist assault on the state was premised on the conviction, not yet informed by any Marxist theory or language, that the beneficiaries of state worship were the forces of capital. Citizens are told that the state embodies the ethical will and the good of all, yet pragmatist Laski wrote: 'When we come to the analysis of the hard facts, it becomes painfully apparent that the good actually maintained is that of a certain section, not the community as a whole.' The state will win the allegiance of groups like trade unions when its actions produce results and consequences good for everyone, not just for the privileged.

Laski cited the actions of the miners in south Wales in the summer of 1915 as paradigmatic of his argument. In early July the Munitions of War Act declared restriction of war-related industrial output a criminal offence, safety regulations in abeyance till the end of the war, and strikes illegal. Two hundred thousand miners in the south Wales fields went on strike for higher wages on 21 July in a direct challenge to the law, their stoppage clearly threatening supplies of vital naval coal. Lloyd George could not implement the Munitions Act and imprison so many strikers; instead, he successfully pressured owners to accede to some of the demands. Laski conjured up 'retired colonels on half-pay writing from the comfortable seclusion of a London club that the working classes must be compelled' to do their work, because 'the existence of the state is threatened'. This, Laski insisted, was to confuse legal sovereignty with moral sovereignty, might with right. 'The state is only one of the associations to which he [the worker] happens to belong' and he will give it whatever pre-eminence it deserves. Laski's reply to the retired colonel anticipated the argument he made to Churchill in the even darker days of the next war:

> The state may ask the workers for their aid; but the conditions must assuredly be that when it fights, their good, no less than its own, is bound up with victory.

One final theme in his first book deserves notice: his praise of America, whose federal political structure is the pluralist state in the flesh. He lauds its dispersal of power between federal and state governments as more 'consonant with political facts than the unitary theory so favoured by the majority of European observers'. He compares the self-sufficient power of Wisconsin with the impotence of Liverpool. Laski is lyrical in his enthusiasm for America's 'diversity', 'variety' and 'plurality'. Sounding like de Tocqueville before him and the academic pluralist social scientists of America's 1950s and 1960s after him, Laski praises American localism, voluntarism and 'the variety of its group life, and the wide distribution of its sovereign powers'. As America was de Tocqueville's foil to the centralized governments of Bourbon monarchy and Jacobin revolutionary rule, and the academic pluralists' foil to Nazi and Soviet totalitarianism, it was for Laski in 1917 the foil to Germany and 'its consistent uniformity of outlook'. In America, interests must be balanced and opinions combined, which is so much better than when 'real authority is single'. 'We prefer a country,' Laski wrote, 'where the sovereignty is distributed, where the richness of corporate lives is insurance against such sterility of outlook.' Laski's appreciation of the pluralism of American life and politics lasted throughout his career, even after he identified with the more statist approaches of Roosevelt's New Deal and his own Labour Party. The very fact of regional, ethnic and religious diversity in America, together with its intrinsic egalitarian spirit as well as its greater opportunity for social mobility, always led Laski to admire America, even in the periods of his most Marxist-inspired denunciations of her as the quintessential repressive regime of big business. Few English socialists in the twentieth century would be as fond of America as he, and behind this attatchment clearly lay, in part, his own personal experience. European repressiveness must have been crystallized for him in the domineering Nathan Laski, demanding he keep to the ways of his father; in contrast, democratic America – the land of opportunity and independence from fathers – and its most prestigious institutions welcomed and rewarded this Jewish foreigner with recognition and influence.

Laski's pluralist hymn to America in 1917 also speaks across the decades to the 1980s and 1990s. His praise of the vitality of American civil society as opposed to her state apparatus sounds much like the pluralists of eastern Europe, with their theoretical and actual rehabilitation of intermediary bodies – voluntary associations like churches, trade unions and trade associations, and even regional and local entities – freed from an all-absorptive state. It could be pluralist Václav Havel in 1990 who insists in the words of Laski that 'there can be no servility in a state that divides its governance'. The ideological motives that inform their pluralism certainly differ, but the continuity of the pluralist vision in this century is clear when Laski praises America in words that could be Havel's:

> Certain local groups have a life of their own that is not merely delegated to them by the state. They are capable of directing their own concerns. Their interest in themselves is revivified and inspired by the responsibility for such direction.

By the time reviews of Laski's book began to appear, America had entered the war. The totality of the First World War had enlarged the state's presence in people's lives to unprecedented dimensions in Britain. The entire economy was run by the state, War Socialism doing what non-syndicalists on the left had been advocating for years. With the American state gearing up quickly for war, Laski's anti-statist book became the focus for anguished soul-searching at the *New Republic*. Walter Lippmann, friend and dinner companion of Laski on his periodic visits to New York, saw Laski's book and the war forcing American scholars to reorient their research and specialization around a completely new set of questions. Laski's 'courageous assertion that the state is not absolute but plural and that allegiance . . . is necessarily experimental and federal', he wrote, would topple simplistic dogmas 'of archaic political theory' and pose a set of intellectual problems which were 'certain to preoccupy the next generation'. Lippmann, whose brilliant book *A Preface to Politics* was the first to apply Freudian notions to politics, wondered whether human beings were as psychologically capable of pluralist loyalties as Laski blithely assumed. In a perceptive anticipation of a good deal of later writings on Nazism, Lippmann suggested the need for 'political science in the next few years to examine the psychic sources of this political monism'.

Croly made Laski's book the focus of his lead article, 'The Future of the State', in the 15 September edition of *New Republic*. He ignored Laski's lyricism about American dispersal of power, a topic not very compatible with his progressive agenda, and focused on Laski's attack on those who 'beatify' the state. Interestingly enough, he used Laski's arguments to bolster his own statist vision. Croly acknowledged that the state was too much 'an unnecessarily powerful and dangerous servant and an unnecessarily jealous master', but this was because, as Laski himself had suggested, the modern state simply attributed moral sovereignty to its physical force without any concern that its power be used for the 'genuinely social purpose' of all its citizens. Justifiably, then, many 'considered the state to be essentially a middle-class organization' undeserving of 'the undivided allegiance of the wage-earners'. The war would end this, Croly suggested. The moral purpose sought by the state in the war, as well as the pervasive institutional controls and commitments to the general welfare required by the state at war, would lead, as Laski wanted, to the state earning the consensual allegiance of all its citizens through the moral consequences of its actions rather than by force.

Elsewhere in America, the book's reception was more mixed. For the professionals at the *American Historical Review* it was 'painstaking and rather brilliant historical writing', even if its discussion of the contemporary state was 'less happy'. The *American Political Science Review* described Laski as one of a new 'brilliant school of political writers' forging a new theory of the state. Other reviewers suggested it was tough going for American readers, written in 'an unduly allusive style'. While the book was perhaps marked 'by a certain agreeable scholarship', there was no doubt for one reviewer that 'his practical teaching would destroy itself through its very absurdity'.

Its reception in Britain was generally more critical. Sir Frederick Pollock, the leading legal scholar, wrote to his friend Oliver Wendell Holmes that Laski was confused, his mind 'often loose and sometimes erroneous' and definitely 'un-legal'. Alfred Zimmern, the New College Oxford classicist and historian whose immensely influential *The Greek Commonwealth* had been published in 1912, and whose lectures Laski had attended, wrote a critical letter about the book to the *New Republic* in answer to Lippmann's piece. Lippmann, Zimmern suggested, had fallen for Laski's 'insidious syndicalism', which along with other arguments for divided allegiance, Zimmern feared, would weaken the sense of civic obligation to the state as *res publica*, the common thing, the commonwealth that binds all citizens in public 'righteousness'. By far the most important British commentary on the book, however, came in *The Times Literary Supplement*'s review of 17 May, which saw the book as 'disputable and even dangerous'. The *TLS* worried about its anarchic implications: the suggestion that the allegiance an individual owed to any group was no different than that which he owed the state, and that when they were in conflict he was 'morally justified in choosing between the two'. To illustrate the grave misgivings about Laski's trumpeting of a pluralist conception of the state, the *TLS* reviewer played on Laski's name. He is an Englishman 'but he bears a historic Polish name'; surely, then, 'he should study, from the point of view of that pragmatism to which he makes frequent appeal, the free veto of the old Polish Senate and its receipt for anarchy'.

Accusations of anarchist tendencies did not bother Laski. His letters in 1917 and 1918 describe reading that feeds 'my anarchist prejudices', and teaching his graduate students 'my anarchist gospel'. Indeed, in America at this time anti-statist syndicalism was seen and labelled, appropriately enough in some respects, as anarchism. No surprise, then, that Laski wrote on 20 November 1917 that 'I have had three lectures to prepare for a foundation at Smith College where I shall preach anarchism or rather polyarchism in the guise of political theory and pocket one hundred and fifty dollars.' (Polyarchism was the word invented by his teacher Ernest Barker in a 1914 essay, 'The Discredited State', to describe the pluralist rejection of the authoritarian state and its image of a dispersal of power in many hands, a word unknowingly reinvented decades later for the same purpose by the American pluralist political scientist Robert Dahl.)

Laski's anarchism and anti-authoritarianism during this period have led some observers to link his unusual private life to his public creed. The relatively unsympathetic fellow political theorist and Labour Party activist George Catlin has suggested that Laski's pluralist theory of the state 'was influenced and given dynamism by an Oedipus complex: when he said "the overbearing state" he really meant "my father Nathan".' The much more favourably disposed Kingsley Martin told the BBC Radio audience in 1962 that 'if his father was dominating, well, he was going to fight dominating people . . . Psychologically, he was always fighting his father.' This line of analysis, however, ignores the fact that Laski so easily abandoned his antipathy to the state later in his career, although a Catlin (who didn't) might point out that there just happened to be a parallel rapprochement with his father. Laski himself might have been sympathetic to such psycho-inquiry at this point in his life, when he was so supportive of Lippmann's pioneering adaptation of Freud to politics. After all, he did write in the *New Republic* in 1919 that 'we must take the overt acts of men as the index to the hidden or unconscious deeps [sic] beyond.' Even eight years later, when he was less under Lippmann's influence, Laski wrote in *Communism* that 'often enough, a man's political creed is born, not of an economic situation, but of an intense psychological dislike for the atmosphere of his family'. There is probably some truth to Catlin's claim, then, but such compatability between private resentment and public ideals is always only part of the story.

Anarchist he may have seen himself, but Laski left nothing to chance when it came to furthering his fame. He methodically sent copies of his book to anyone who mattered. *Studies in the Problem of Sovereignty* was sent to Wallas, Hobhouse and Webb at the London School of Economics, to Lord Haldane, Bertrand Russell, and, of course, Fisher and Barker. Massingham at the *Nation* in London and C. P. Scott at the *Manchester Guardian* got copies. In America Laski sent books to Brandeis and Holmes as well as to Dorothy and Willard Straight. Nor was this done without an occasional light touch. He notes with the Straights' copy, for example, that 'when you are unduly wakeful, you will find it possesses much admirable soporific quality'.

Singled out for thanks in the preface to *Studies in the Problem of Sovereignty* was 'my friend, Professor Frankfurter of the Harvard Law School'. In Felix Frankfurter Laski had a friendship with a man who would stand astride twentieth-century American history like a colossus. Born in Vienna in 1882, Frankfurter came to New York City with his parents when he was twelve. As for so many bright children of Jewish immigrants, an education at the City College opened the gates of opportunity for Frankfurter. From there he went to Harvard Law School, from which he graduated in 1906. Frankfurter's first legal job was for a prestigious New York firm which had never before hired a Jew. Eventually he moved from there to work as chief legal assistant in the New York City office of Henry C. Stimson, United States Attorney for the Southern District of New York. When the patrician Stimson, Frankfurter's mentor and patron, went to Washington in 1911 as Secretary of War, he took Frankfurter as special counsel. Meanwhile Frankfurter, who taught at Harvard Law School from 1914 to 1939 with periodic interruptions for service in Washington, had acquired an even more powerful friend in Washington, Franklin Roosevelt, whom he had known at Harvard. In the 1930s Frankfurter remained one of Roosevelt's closest advisers even after turning down an offer in 1932 from him to be the country's Solicitor-General. In 1939 he was appointed by Roosevelt to the United States Supreme Court, where he would sit as one of the court's most learned and eminent justices until 1962. Even while he sat in the High Court Frankfurter played the role of behind-the-scenes political power-broker in American national affairs as well as in American and world Zionist politics.

One of the reasons Laski and Frankfurter became such close friends was that they were so alike. Short, cocky and abrasive, they were both intensely verbal people who loved to talk and even more to argue. Though irredeemably Anglophilic, Frankfurter was decidedly un-British, as was Laski, in his openness, spontaneity and warmth, and seemingly incapable of quiet reserve or gentlemanly self-restraint. Laski wrote of Frankfurter: 'I don't know what I like more in Felix – his charming sauciness or his flashes of sudden coherence.' Frankfurter and Laski were also unabashed self-promoters who loved to wheel and deal in influence and power, and both of them loved attention. They were consummately skilful in the gamesmanship of political intrigue and in acquiring important friends. When Holmes wrote to Laski that Felix had 'an unimaginable gift of wriggling in wherever he wants to', he could have been describing Laski. Both of them had a wide circle of devoted friends throughout their lives (Mrs Frankfurter used to say that her husband had '200 best friends') and almost as many enemies. They were intensely loyal to these friends and bitterly dismissive of enemies. Both were extraordinary teachers, inspired by an almost religious calling to prepare young people for careers in public service. Frankfurter and Laski were also non-observant secular Jews who were intensely conscious and proud of their Jewishness. A crucial aspect of Frankfurter's self-identity was that he was a Jewish immigrant who had made it to the pinnacles of success in Protestant America. It was the profoundest glory of America that this could happen and it reinforced Frankfurter's (as well as Laski's) pride both in his Jewishness and in America. Finally, Frankfurter and Laski shared a deep ambivalence between public egalitarianism and private elitism, a not uncommon contradiction among progressive and leftist intellectuals. Laski could have been describing himself when he wrote to Holmes in 1925.

> What else have I done! Taken two friends of Felix round London to show them pieces of history and explained Felix to them. 'Why is he a democrat, Mr Laski?' 'Because he is an aristocrat with an infinite sense of pity.' 'Why does he not want to make money?' 'Because most people who have it are vulgar.'

Frankfurter had no children, and one biographer, who knew him well, has speculated that he 'loved Laski as if he were his own son, and Laski, of course, loved Frankfurter far more than his own father'. Love each other they certainly did, but less in paternal–filial terms than as brothers. Their correspondence over the years is full of open and uncharacteristically masculine expression of feeling and affection for each other. Laski could write to Frankfurter in 1929 that, Frida apart, 'you have a place in my life that no other human being has ever occupied. Our friendship gives to things a colour and quality inexpressibly precious to me.' Frankfurter, in turn, remained fastly loyal, even after his politics had diverged dramatically from Laski's (and when his friendship with a far-left Laski proved personally difficult for him, as in his Senate confirmation hearings for his nomination to the Supreme Court). A legacy of their intense friendship is one of the

fullest portraits extant of Laski as a young adult in a 1916 letter from
Frankfurter to Marion Denman, his wife-to-be.

> There is Harold Laski – there ain't nobody like that youth – undersized,
> sparse-looking, Oxford all over and under, not twenty-three, head teeming
> with ideas, heart brimful of generosity and aspirations, kid and man, married
> five years, broken with his family (a stern father who discovered he was tied
> to the old tradition when his son married a Gentile), as philosophically droll
> about it as can be (there are funny incidents in connection with it), and
> withal a scholar of the first rank ... Poor President Lowell doesn't know
> what a rebel we concealed in the Trojan horse when we voted Laski in.

Denman herself offers yet a different glimpse of Laski in these Cambridge
years. In a letter to Frankfurter discussing Laski she wrote of 'the languorous
beauty of him, the deftness of his imagination and speech, the intriguing
sense he starts in one's imagination, his capacity for romantic myth and
romantic briefness, adding to the tribute of his devotion, his recognition of
the fleeting character of all beauty'.

Laski became involved in the romantic entanglements of Frankfurter and
Denman, which were not unlike a replay of his own travails. Denman, the
daughter of a Congregational minister from western Massachusetts, and
Frankfurter had been friends since 1913. He had contemplated marriage but
backed off in 1917 after his recently widowed mother, Emma, objected to
a Gentile bride. Laski encouraged him to rethink this sacrifice of personal
happiness to family and religious duty, offering the example of his own
actions and the resultant blissful happiness. Frankfurter resumed seeing
Denman and in December 1919 Laski and Frida were two of the four
people present when Judge Benjamin Cardoza of the New York Court of
Appeals (and later of the US Supreme Court) married the couple. Emma
Frankfurter refused to attend, though she ultimately accepted the marriage.
One version of how she came round actually attributes her change of mind
to the Laskis. She knew and was fond of Laski and of his wife too, having
no idea that Frida (a Jewish-sounding name) was Christian. When she
discovered that Frida was non-Jewish, so the story goes, she was sufficiently
embarrassed that she was won over to the idea that her son could also be
happy with a Christian wife.

Frankfurter was not in Cambridge for all of Laski's years at Harvard. In
1917 he served as Assistant to the Secretary of War and part of his

assignment involved going to Turkey with the American ambassador, Henry Morgenthau, to get Turkey out of the Axis camp. It was this experience that initially involved Frankfurter in the politics of Palestine. Once America was in the war, Frankfurter took on an even more important assignment for President Wilson as Chairman of the War Labor Policies Board, the mediation commission in Washington that investigated and resolved labour disputes in industries crucial to the war effort. Laski missed Frankfurter in Cambridge and visited him frequently in Washington. In turn, Frankfurter persuaded the board to hire Laski as a consultant to study topics related to British labour practices and economic and political conditions in Europe. It was perhaps an exaggeration for Laski two years later to put on his curriculum vitae at the London School of Economics 'Chief Research Assistant to the War Labor Policies Board – 1917–1918', but the piece he did for the *New Republic* on 7 January 1920 describing the board shows he knew its workings well.

When Frankfurter went to the Paris Peace Conference in March 1919 as an observer for American Zionist interests, Laski filled him in on details about English and European politics. At the conference Frankfurter, with the help of Lawrence of Arabia, negotiated with King Faisal a fundamental understanding of peaceful relations between Zionist settlers and Arabs in Palestine in the wake of the Balfour Declaration. Faisal's letter read: 'We Arabs, especially the educated among us, look with deep sympathy on the Zionist movement . . . We will wish the Jews a most hearty welcome home.' When he returned to America Frankfurter was urged by Justice Brandeis to enlist Laski for a small committee of academics to study the suddenly promising Zionist cause, but Laski left Harvard before anything came of that suggestion. Before leaving, however, Laski played a crucial role in Harvard Law School's retention of Frankfurter. Alumni grumblings about Frankfurter's politics, his continuing indecision over Marion Denman, and an offer from Croly to be chairman of the faculty at his planned New School for Social Research in New York combined in 1919 to make Frankfurter hesitant about returning to Cambridge. Laski campaigned vigorously as an intermediary between Pound and Frankfurter to keep his friend at Harvard. He succeeded and Frankfurter remained at Harvard Law School for two decades.

It was through Frankfurter that Laski met Oliver Wendell Holmes, Jr. Holmes had read Laski's 'Personality of Association' in the February 1916

Harvard Law Review and asked Frankfurter about its author. In July 1916 Frankfurter took Laski with him to visit the venerable Supreme Court Justice at his summer home in Beverly Farms, Massachusetts. Laski 'inadvertently' left his hairbrush behind, and his thank-you note for the visit and Holmes's letter accompanying the return of the brush began a friendship that lasted for nineteen years, until the latter's death at the age of ninety-four in 1935. When their hundreds of letters were published in 1953, Frankfurter wondered if a playwright 'could have contrived a more dramatic contrast than Laski and Holmes when their friendship began'. Laski became the unlikely friend and confidant of a veritable American institution in his twilight years, a man whose seventy-fifth birthday a few months earlier had been celebrated as a national event. The courtly, witty and scholarly Holmes was the archetypal civilized Yankee, a Brahmin whose family personified generations of professional Boston gentility and Harvard breeding. In his youth he had heard his grandmother talk of the British attack on Boston. Wounded three times in the Civil War, Holmes went not into medicine, his father's profession, but the law. His book of 1880, *The Common Law*, made him a major figure in Anglo-American legal circles, and from 1882 to 1902 he sat on the Massachusetts Supreme Court, the last three years as Chief Justice. In 1902 President Theodore Roosevelt appointed him to the United States Supreme Court.

Holmes, like Galton before him, was dazzled by Laski. Right after he met him Holmes wrote to Pollock in England asking if he knew 'Harold Laski, an astonishing young Jew, whom Frankfurter brought over the other day'. To Bryce, the British scholar who had served as ambassador to the United States, Holmes wrote in 1917 of his fascinating conversations with 'a wonderful young chap from Oxford ... Harold Laski – an unbelieving Jew with a specialty of Church History ... in his twenties and one of the most learned men I have ever known'. In 1917 Holmes described Laski as 'diabolically clever and omniscient'. He wrote to his close Irish friend Lady Castletown that Laski was

> a paragon who seems to have read everything and to have seen a great many of the people that are worth seeing. He has written a noticeable book and is writing another, at the same time contributing to the weekly *New Republic* articles that flabbergast me by their variety and knowledge.

Friendship with Holmes brought the ambitious Laski to the innermost circles of scholarship and politics in America. Through his jurisprudence the elderly justice had become an intellectual guru to progressive intellectuals. He taught them that the Constitution was an experiment, that all life was an experiment. Law was not a sacred code but a set of rules that reflected group needs and demands, not fundamental or inherent principles. But Holmes shared none of the social and economic radicalism of the younger men like Frankfurter, Cohen and Laski who lionized him. His dissent in the Lochner case with its bitter denunciation of constitutional status for Herbert Spencer's *laissez-faire* politics was not an endorsement of progressive or socialist policies but of the capacity of reasonable men in democratic legislatures to solve social problems. Holmes's fundamental conservatism emerged frequently in his criticism of Laski's politics. He had never read a socialist yet, he told Laski, 'that I didn't think talked drool'. The 'robbery of labour by capital is a humbug'. Any talk of 'exploitation of man by man' always 'gets my hair up'. Socialism is caused by 'bad manners', by people not treating their servants and employees well. Those who, like Laski and his friend and colleague Brandeis, wanted to improve the lot of labour, Holmes caricatured as 'upwards and onward-ers'. To be a 'socialist was to be intellectually doctrinaire', the pragmatist Holmes insisted, to be one 'who knows they know', one who has 'seen the future'. It reminded him of the Abolitionists and Christian Scientists of his youth.

Holmes's young disciples – Frankfurter, Laski, Morris Cohen and Walter Lippmann – knew about his social views. What attracted them to Holmes, however, was his intellectual contribution to the 'revolt against formalism', as well as his courageous dissent in economic regulation and free speech cases. In addition, Holmes represented to them, Jews all, the benevolent potential for America's traditional patrician elite to 'moderate the excesses of American capitalism, discipline the vulgar business classes, uplift the poor, and usher in the benign future of expanded social welfare and security', as one historian has put it. Holmes was the principled and cultivated Protestant statesman whose dignity, austerity and rectitude seemed to embody the sacrifice of private ease to public purpose that was itself the prophetic core of the Old Testament. Such men were by spirit and mind the natural elite. For the rest of his life Laski would balance a lingering faith in the leadership role of learned and cultivated gentlemen like Holmes with a democratic commitment to the 'upwards and onward-ers' types that Holmes disliked.

Nor is it difficult to understand why Holmes was attracted to Laski, even if he occasionally sensed some opportunism in the young man. He was genuinely taken by Laski's brilliance as one who 'writes books faster than I can read them'. Holmes, who had corresponded with the greats in the world for decades, told Laski that he was 'the best correspondent I've ever had. Each letter is an interesting and charming piece of art.' He was flattered by Laski's devotion and loyalty. In 1920 Laski edited a collection of Holmes's *Collected Legal Papers*, which the justice always referred to as 'our book', and he authored several essays in Holmes's remaining years on the justice and his place in the history of the Court. More importantly, for nineteen years Laski wrote to Holmes, first almost weekly and then seldom less than monthly. He gave Holmes, an Anglophile with numerous British connections, a sense of being in the middle of British academic, political and social life, as well as keeping him current on the latest books. He invigorated the ageing Holmes. 'You are a splendid young enthusiast and make me feel more alive,' Holmes wrote to Laski on one occasion. 'What a pleasure would depart from my life if I ceased to receive letters from you,' he wrote on another.

Holmes and his wife, Fanny, had no children and he assumed a paternal regard towards Laski and Frankfurter. 'You and Felix have worked deep into my heart,' Holmes wrote to Laski, and in his letters and in their meetings he took to referring to Laski as 'my son'. Edmund Wilson, the distinguished American writer and literary critic who worked for the *New Republic* in its early years and knew Laski and Holmes well, has made a strong case for this, with Laski, in turn, acquiring a courtly and patrician father-figure in Holmes. Wilson also suggests that Holmes's philo-Semitism predisposed him towards Laski, that, like many Boston Brahmins, Holmes was attracted to the moralism, prophetic zeal, intellectualism and, finally, commitment to public service of Jews like Laski. In fact, he often referred to his Jewish disciples as his 'young prophets'. Shortly after Laski returned to England, Holmes wrote to him about 'how many of the younger men that have warmed my heart have been Jews'. While some think, Holmes added, that the Jew is concerned only with himself, he found they are disposed to others. To him they are 'loveable' and offer 'spiritual companionship' and a 'kind of holiness'. Whatever its source – paternal urges, a common biblical culture or the pure relish of flattering attention – Holmes in his declining years was drawn particularly close to Laski. When he died in 1935 Holmes left his estate to the people of the United States. His own copy of *The Common Law*, the book that made his career, he bequeathed to Laski. Laski, fittingly enough, donated it to the Harvard Law School.

Through Frankfurter Laski also befriended Louis Dembitz Brandeis, who was appointed to the United States Supreme Court by President Wilson in 1916. Brandeis's life was a very different version of the American Jewish experience from Frankfurter's. His parents were German Jewish liberals who had come to the United States after the failed revolutions of 1848. The family settled in Louisville, Kentucky, where they were first in the grain and then the cotton business. Born in Louisville in 1856, Brandeis graduated from Harvard Law School with the highest scholastic record achieved to that day. He had a distinguished legal career in Boston, during which time he emerged as a central figure in national progressive and pro-labour political circles. Much less the product of a Jewish upbringing than Frankfurter or Laski, Brandeis became a committed Zionist in 1910 and thereafter the leading figure in American Zionist politics. Brandeis and Frankfurter met in the causes of progressive politics and they became close friends, with Brandeis also bringing Frankfurter into his Zionist activities. Frankfurter was a tireless champion of Brandeis's appointment to the Court in what proved to be a divisive nomination battle over the first seating of a Jew. Harvard's President Lowell, by then an officer of Boston's Immigration Restriction League, sided firmly with the opponents of Brandeis. When Brandeis was approved for the Court by the Senate, Frankfurter became his political surrogate in American and Zionist politics. Frankfurter also brought to the new justice's attention his brilliant English friend who had just joined the Harvard faculty. Laski and Brandeis began a friendship that lasted for the next two decades, though neither their friendship nor their correspondence was as intense and intimate as that of Holmes and Laski, or even that of Frankfurter and Laski.

Throughout his career Laski took inordinate interest in his students, especially if they were poor, but he also learned early on to cultivate the children of the famous and the well-to-do. So it was that when Laski discovered in his Radcliffe class one Elizabeth Brandeis, the eighteen-year-old daughter of the Supreme Court justice, he made the most of his opportunity. In the course of some correspondence about *Law Review* pieces in November 1916, Laski wrote to Justice Brandeis that he wanted 'to tell you a little bit about Elizabeth', for she 'interests me enormously'.

She needs to read more in order to push her fine mind. 'Do you think sometime,' he asked, 'that I might plan a course of reading for her outside her ordinary work? I'd like immensely to do that.' And then, as if this might sound suspicious coming from an instructor just three years older than the girl, Laski added, 'My wife is most keen about her and we want her to feel that this house is always at her aid when she wants to probe its curiosities.' Elizabeth clearly visited 1697 Cambridge Street that winter, for Brandeis later wrote that his daughter appreciated what she was learning from Laski's instruction and that she also spoke enthusiastically of Laski's wife and infant. Elizabeth ultimately went on to an academic career in economics at the University of Wisconsin and also helped to draft Wisconsin's 1930s unemployment legislation.

Laski's teaching impressed more than just Elizabeth Brandeis. In 1962 Frankfurter told a BBC Radio audience that Laski's 'infectious enthusiasm' had made him overnight a sensation on campus. He was a scintillating lecturer and his experience with Oxford tutorials made him much more at ease with individual or small groups of students than the typical Harvard instructor. Laski further endeared himself to Harvard and Radcliffe students by his frequent office hours and by his weekly 'at homes' to which many of them were invited. It was still relatively unusual for Harvard faculty to mix so freely with students, but the Laskis nevertheless began in Cambridge their practice of open houses which over the years became part of Laski lore. Frida described the beginnings:

> We threw our door open to Harold's students, thus establishing a social/ intellectual set of our own and creating at the same time a precedent at Harvard ... The students came to discuss, talk, think – not only on political lines but generally, on a wide variety of subjects introduced in the main by Harold ... Our gender, in truth, was well represented by the females of Radcliffe College – young vibrant girls who graced our 'At Homes' gener- ally, made a great fuss of the baby and enjoyed the liberty of a 'smoke' in mixed company at a time when smoking for women was not the 'in thing'.

The President of Radcliffe was less pleased than Frida and wrote to ask that the Laskis refrain from encouraging women students to smoke.

Laski was unconventional at Harvard in other ways as well. While he saw the value of being the mentor of an Elizabeth Brandeis, he also devoted a good deal of special attention to poor commuting students, who were often Jewish or Catholic. Samuel Rezneck later wrote of how 'kindly and friendly' Laski was to him, and of how 'his enthusiasm' and 'ebullient spirit' seemed so different from other faculty. Because of this 'We listened raptly to his fluent and eloquent discussions of English history and doctrines of freedom and individualism.' Meyer Israel, a pupil, later wrote of meeting Laski, 'a thin, sallow young man, a cigarette always between his lips', for tutorials at Laski's house. Often he would find him 'lying on a cot in a room thick with smoke, usually reading a book he was reviewing for the *New Republic*'. Richard Strout, who would become a distinguished reporter for the *Christian Science Monitor* and for many years the anonymous 'TRB' columnist for the *New Republic*, remembered trooping up the stairs of 1697 Cambridge Street for weekly meetings of the class Government 20-0. He also recalled Laski's magical effect on young people like himself as he casually dropped into the conversation that 'he had just heard this from Justice Holmes or had to go off to New York the next day to help get out the next issue of Croly's *New Republic*. After class wife Frida would serve tea and daughter Diana romp around.'

Not much older than many of his students and without a doctorate (he would always remain critical of the emergent American practice of seeing the PhD as the norm for university faculty), Laski was often mischievous in his lack of respect for university regulations. A Radcliffe student remembered him telling her class that 'the university requires me to give you an examination. The questions will be as follows . . .' Sometimes he would give standard essay examinations requiring insight and judgement and not tell the questions ahead of time, but he would provide alternative objective questions for the 'weak sisters', as he called them. Those who chose the latter option, he would also announce, were not eligible for top grades. Not that he was totally cavalier about classroom requirements: the Radcliffe presidential archives contain a letter from Laski asking that a student be removed from his class for complaining to him about her grade. Far more typical was his reputation for generosity to students which, like the weekly at-homes, became part of Laski lore. Not only did he give selflessly of his time, but occasionally even of his money and always of his influence. Rezneck and Strout both went to England after graduation laden with letters of introduction to journalists, politicians and academics which also enhanced their sense of Laski's importance.

In two other special ways Laski enriched the lives of his Harvard and

Radcliffe students. Beyond the books he assigned or that they read for their
research, Laski communicated his own infectious enthusiasm for collecting
books to them. The result, according to Frankfurter, was that Laski's
favourite Cambridge bookseller, Maurice Firuski, owner of the Dunster
Book Shop, acquired many of his lifelong customers from Laski's students.
Laski also arranged lectures and occasionally evenings at his home for
Britons visiting or passing through Harvard to meet students. He brought
Graham Wallas and W. H. Rivers, the distinguished Cambridge anthropologist, but his greatest coup was arranging a lecture for the poet Siegfried
Sassoon and the one man Harvard's resident poet Amy Lowell thought the
undergraduates should hear. The battlefield experience of Sassoon, a
member of the wealthy, Jewish banking family, had turned him to pacifism
and socialism. After the reading Laski and Sassoon were invited back to
Miss Lowell's library. Sassoon's memory of the evening provides another
fascinating portrait of Laski in his Cambridge years.

> Listening to her and Laski, I felt almost non-existent as a talker. They were a
> remarkably contrasted couple – he, small, boyishly brilliant, provocative in
> argument, and essentially generous and idealistic; she, stout and masculine,
> jocularly downright and dogmatic, smoking a long Manila cigar.

His increasing renown and his constant need for income found Laski
often teaching and lecturing at other schools, as well as at Harvard and
Radcliffe. Amherst's President Alexander Meikeljohn was English and
fond of inviting compatriots out to western Massachusetts. Laski taught
there for several weeks in 1917 and 1918. While there in 1917 Laski also
gave a set of lectures in the nearby women's college, Smith. In the autumn
term of 1919 he was made the annual 'Harvard lecturer' at Yale University,
which involved commuting weekly and, as Laski told Holmes, 'plenty of
money and little work'. Taking his course at Yale was Robert Hutchins,
then twenty-two, the future President of the University of Chicago, and
the twenty-year-old Henry Luce, the future founder of *Time* and *Life*
magazines. Luce was a very bright and well-read student who caught
Laski's attention and they often dined together after Laski's class. Though
they never resumed their earlier closeness, Laski liked to think years later
that it was those lunches with Luce in 1919 which accounted for *Time* and
Life magazines never being quite as critical of him as they might have been.
One Yale student from that semester eventually became a close friend of

Laski's in the 1930s, though they never met in 1919. Max Lerner, the American scholar and journalist, was a freshman at Yale who retained vivid memories of the irreverence and brashness of a brilliant speech by Laski and the audacity of Laski having begun the first sentence of his first book with the word 'Hegelianwise'.

From 1918 to 1920 Laski was also involved in both helping to create and lecturing at the New School for Social Research. The school grew out of discussions held at the *New Republic* offices in 1918 among progressive intellectuals unhappy with American higher education. Croly was the central mover, but Laski's stories of Oxford and of the Webbs' London School of Economics fed the group's desires for an institution 'not handicapped by mobs of beef-devouring alumni, passionate about football and contemptuous of scholarship'. Intended to embody progressive attitudes to science, public policy and education, the school would serve mature adults not pursuing degrees, and be staffed by faculty with no departments and no president. As Croly described it in the *New Republic*, it would train social experts, especially for trade unions, and public administrators and managers to participate actively in the life of society. 'Thus a school of social science becomes above everything else an instrumentality both of social purposes and of social research.'

Dorothy Straight, whose husband, Willard, had died of influenza in December 1918, put up most of the money for the New School and it opened its doors in New York in 1919. Laski was very much involved in its first year. He wrote to Pound in March that 'I am authorized to ask you to give twelve lectures on jurisprudence for $1,000.' He himself gave a lecture course there in the spring of 1919 and again the following spring. At the same time he was discouraging Frankfurter from leaving Harvard for the new venture and also corresponding with Wallas about the school's strengths and weaknesses. In 1923 the economist Alvin Johnson moved from the *New Republic* to become its director, a position he held until 1945. Laski remained close to Johnson's New School, reoriented principally as an adult education institution. A set of lectures there during his spring holidays helped to finance his annual trips to America in the mid-1930s. Laski remained close to Johnson's other enterprise, which also carried forward the scientific vision of progressive America to the next generation. Johnson was for many years the editor of *The Encyclopedia of the Social Sciences*, a number of whose entries Laski wrote in the years to come.

Laski was the major force involved in the founding of yet another educational institution during his time in Cambridge, the Boston Trade Union College, the first collegiate enterprise in America under the operation and control of a labour union. The faculty, volunteers from Harvard, Wellesley, Tufts and Simmons College, taught courses in English, economics, government, law, literature, science, parties and politics, cooperative movements, economics of industry and labour statistics. For the first year of the college, classes were held in the evenings in the High School of Practical Arts in Roxbury. Laski taught government and politics courses in 1919 and 1920 and convinced both Pound and Frankfurter to join the enterprise. The college's founding creed reflects Laski's syndicalist vision of trade unions as the self-sufficient focus of a new industrial order as well as the commitment to the cause of worker education.

> Organized labour must develop its intellectual resources if it is to realize its hopes in the coming social and industrial order. Its methods of learning are cooperative, the instructors contributing their specialized knowledge and the students their practical experience. Its aim is that wage-earners may in this way prepare themselves in their progress towards freedom and self-government.

Helping Laski and the Boston unions with the financial details involved in establishing the Trade Union College was Mrs Glendower Evans, the widow of a legal colleague of Holmes and Brandeis, and a good friend of Marion and Felix Frankfurter, who through her tireless work as well as her money led the long, unsuccessful fight that all three waged after 1920 to clear the Italian anarchists Sacco and Vanzetti. Elizabeth Evans also introduced Laski to other interests of the socially conscious Boston elite. There was Ford Hall Forum, for example, Boston's famed free lecture institute, where speakers on advanced and radical topics were given sympathetic hearings weekly. There was also the American Civil Liberties Union, on whose board of directors she and Frankfurter sat and to whose founder, Roger Baldwin, Mrs Evans introduced Laski. On the 1962 BBC programme devoted to Laski, Baldwin told how Laski's lifelong interest in civil liberties began in Cambridge and that 'as a matter of fact, he was the only foreigner whom we ever took into our counsels, and he frequently attended New York meetings of our board of directors and gave us his advice'.

Laski's interests in trade unions and in civil liberties came together most unexpectedly in the autumn of 1919 when he himself became a *cause célèbre*. He and his friend Mrs Evans had marched with the workers in the great Lawrence textile strike earlier that year, and Mrs Evans's protest against police brutality on the picket line was credited by one of the strike leaders with winning their victory. But, ironically, that October Laski became the centre of public controversy in Cambridge and Boston for proclaiming solidarity with policemen, traditionally labour's enemy.

CHAPTER SIX

The Boston Police Strike

Involvement in the Boston police strike was the first of four occasions in his career when Laski would be 'centre stage', the focus of a widely followed public event. His actions in the autumn of 1919 were perfectly consistent with positions found in his writing. Throughout his career, in fact, Laski's scholarly works and political activity went hand in hand. Whatever else he might discard from his American period, he retained the pragmatic linkage of thought and action, theory and practice. He had been wrestling in virtually all his writings with the issues the strike raised, and only six months before had published in his second book a discussion of the place of public service employees in the syndicalist theory of unions.

Laski assumed that the end of the First World War would usher in a new age in which fundamental changes would transform the capitalist system. Revolution was less the word that came to mind for him and others than 'reconstruction'. In the new order the trade union would be the core institution. The 'end of the bourgeois state', he wrote to Holmes, when economic and political power was transferred 'from the mercantile to the working-classes', would not come on the winds of 'the relentless bureaucracy involved in state socialism and its utter incompatibility with liberty'. State-focused social reform simply 'multiplied the number of clerks and teachers and dethroned spontaneity for paternalism'. Educated workers giving their allegiance to self-sufficient trade unions through which they democratically controlled their sites of production were the backbone of the new post-war order. When Holmes chided Laski for his bleak assessment of the capitalist class, Laski replied that Holmes 'come[s] into contact with men of property on their very best side', the articulate and intellectual lawyer, the philanthropic businessman with cultivated aesthetic taste. 'You don't see the obvious evils that one gets contact with among the trade unions – the blindness to pain, the hard obstinacy, the relentless pressure.' Having seen the Lawrence strike 'at first hand', Laski suggested in May 1919 'that almost any system must be better than one which gives some men economic power over others'. He was not a Marxian socialist, Laski assured Holmes, but he did 'believe there is a real class-war'.

Laski was always clear at this point in his career that the major intellectual influence shaping his vision of the future was not Marx but the French anarcho-syndicalist Proudhon. Laski wrote to Holmes in April 1917 about 'a new enthusiasm. I have discovered Proudhon and I want you to share the joy. Really he is immense and he has all the virtues . . . his theory of the state satisfies all my anarchist principles.' Moreover, Laski told Holmes, Proudhon 'anticipated most of Karl Marx and . . . said it better'. In a series of articles that appeared in the *New Republic*, the Chicago-based literary review the *Dial*, the *Bookman* and the *Yale Review* between 1917 and 1920 as well as in the introduction to the translation of Duguit's *Law in the Modern State*, which he and Frida published for Ben Huebsch in 1919, Laski depicted a set of formulaic triads: Marx, statism and the Webbs on the one hand, and Proudhon, pluralism and syndicalism, or guild socialism, on the other. Laski was torn between Mr Cole, 'whose guild socialism is the most significant development in English political thought in the last decade', and Mr Webb, with his vision of scientifically trained experts managing a state-sponsored reform of society. Usually, Proudhon's syndicalism and Cole's guild social-ism won out in his writings, with coordination defeating hierarchy, federal-ism triumphing over centralization and self-sufficiency over paternalism. Laski's earlier flirtation with Fabianism in his eugenics period raised its head occasionally, however, especially when it resonated with the social scientific statism of the *New Republic* or the New School circle's sponsorship of leftist scientific experts, and even more dramatically in 1920 after Laski joined the Webbs at their London School of Economics. Most of the time until 1920, however, Laski dismissed the Webbs along with Marx, somewhat less accurately, as statists who were to be applauded for their sensitivity to the indignity of exploitation, but who failed to see that workers had little faith in any benefit coming from government action. Rather it was Proudhon, whose *De Principe Fédératif* was 'one of the great books of the nineteenth century', who captured the desire for an economic federalism that allowed each industrial and professional union, group or association to make itself an autonomous self-governing unit, rendering the sovereign state superfluous.

When Laski discussed how the syndicalist order would be achieved, he introduced a theme that recurred throughout his career, whatever his political orientation at the time, Fabian, Marxist, socialist or, as here, pluralist. Ruling-class concession, not revolution, should bring about the new order, or, as he eventually phrased it, fundamental social change should involve 'a revolution by consent'. However, what was at stake, he wrote in the *New Republic*, was the existence of capitalism and

> its destruction by concession is infinitely better than its destruction by revolution. But it may be that a capitalism such as that of Sir Eric Geddes in England or of Judge Garry or Henry Frick in America is incapable of necessary concessions; and in that event the direct action of the trade unions is destined to be the necessary part of attainment.

Laski's second book, *Authority in the Modern State*, was published in March 1919, again by Yale University Press. Dedicated to 'Mr Justice Holmes and Felix Frankfurter, the two youngest of My Friends', the book was a veritable hymn of praise to the role of trade unions in the post-war reconstruction of society. Like his first book, it began with a theoretical discussion of the modern state which was then elucidated by learned chapters providing illustrative historical material, in this case writings of nineteenth-century Frenchmen. As Laski had written to Holmes in 1917, Proudhon 'fits gloriously into the scheme of my new book and I'll make him a peg for a bundle of observations'.

For Walter Lippmann in the *New Republic* this erudition was admirable, for Laski 'is one of those invaluable persons who ... remember that the latest controversy did not originate in yesterday morning's newspaper'. His 'enormous scholarship' enabled Laski to produce 'the most elaborate and sustained criticism of the orthodox theory of single, unlimited state sovereignty which anyone has ever written'. Other reviewers were less generous. For the *Saturday Review of Literature* it was 'too allusive and discursive and full of not very relevant quotations. It is verbose in parts and the writer seems to be pecking little grains of erudition from the ground instead of digesting his material into a whole.' The *North American Review* criticized Laski's tendency to repeat 'essentially the same thought in only a slightly different form'.

In its 5 July review the *Nation* uncannily anticipated the relevance of Laski's book (sent to the publisher the previous September) for the smouldering labour tensions in Boston. In the 'very bowels of the state organization itself', the issue thundered, witness the recent police strikes in Liverpool and London, the creation of a policemen's union in Portland, Oregon, and the struggles of postal workers seeking to unionize. Switching metaphors, the *Nation* urged the state to 'come down from its pedestal, and accept the facts'. It must allow its own employees to organize and provide the right of any 'independent voluntarily associated group to live out its own life'. Laski's book did, in fact, speak directly to the post-war surge in unionization efforts. 'The trade union', he wrote, is 'the single cell from which an entirely new industrial order is to be evolved'. In this new decentralized and functional democracy the trade union played a crucial role, and to get government itself to allow its own workers this participatory power was a Herculean task. 'The public character of the state', Laski noted, has 'a factitious popular support against which it is difficult to make headway'. Government, he suggested, even less than private enterprise, was not 'prepared to tolerate democratization of control'. Government acts were viewed differently from private acts. 'To sue the King in his own courts has about it an air of unreason.' But what if trade unions, even for public servants, became the norm? In Laski the Boston police, trying to organize in the summer of 1919, had a champion.

> To admit the trade union to an effective place in government . . . is to make the worker count in the world . . . It removes the main lever by which the worker is prevented from the attainment of self-expression . . . It thereby gives to him a training in the business of government which otherwise is painfully lacking . . . When his trade union is making decisions in which his own will is a part he is something more than a tender of machines. His very experience on this side of government will make him more valuable in his quality as citizen.

It is important to note that his *Authority in the Modern State* also spoke to a different set of real world events in 1919. Laski's pluralism, his anarcho-syndicalism, had two faces. There was his passionate pleading for trade unions and other voluntary associations, on the one hand, and his outspoken defence of the rights of individual conscience and of the freedom of thought and expression against the state, on the other. It was his civil libertarian face which was the real source of Laski's immense appeal to people like Holmes, Brandeis, Baldwin, Frankfurter, Huebsch and Chafee.

It was their shared commitment to free speech, not necessarily their sympathy with his substantive message, that brought them to his defence over the police strike. Laski's passionate liberal support of individual free expression would persist throughout his career, long after his adoption of statist or Marxist ideals. Observers in these later stages of his career delighted in pointing to the paradox of Laski the 'libertarian Marxist'. Early in his career, however, there was nothing contradictory in his commitments to civil liberty and to labour. They were consistent expressions of his overarching anti-statism.

Laski's writings and personal influence were among the many sources of Justice Holmes's ringing defence of free speech in his dissent in the *Abrams* case in the autumn of 1919, which involved a group of five Russian Jewish immigrants arrested in the summer of 1918 for distributing leaflets in New York City protesting against American intervention in the Russian Revolution. The five were convicted under the recently passed Sedition Act and given prison sentences of between fifteen and twenty years. The conviction was upheld by the Supreme Court with Holmes (joined by Brandeis) offering his influential dissent which was to shape much of future First Amendment adjudication of free speech. The fame of Holmes's dissent rests on two pillars: his presumption that the state could not restrict free expression unless 'a clear and present danger' threatening the country resulted from that speech; and his broad philosophical defence of 'free trade in ideas' with 'fighting faiths' surviving the 'best test of truth', which was 'the power of the thought to get itself accepted in the competition of the market', since 'all life is an experiment' and no truth is accepted for ever.

At the very time that Holmes was sorting through his ambivalent feelings about unlimited free speech, he was being bombarded with a radical civil liberties perspective from Laski, who wrote often to Holmes about how much there was to learn from John Stuart Mill about the decline of liberty and the increased power of the state. Laski's crusade, he wrote to Holmes, 'is to take away from the state the superior morality with which we have invested its activities and give them back to the individual conscience'. There was much in *Studies in the Problem of Sovereignty* to influence Holmes's views on free speech. The Darwinian vision of faiths and truths fighting it out in a struggle was spelled out there in Laski's claim that evolution undermined dogmas that claimed eternal truth. Laski railed against those who 'make a fetish of obedience. To everyone there comes a point where to bow the knee is worse than death.' The book was full of phrases that echo back in Holmes's *Abrams* dissent: 'Progress is born from disagreement and discussion', there is 'no immutability of political form'; 'the price of liberty is exactly divergence of opinion on fundamental questions'.

Even more directly influential on Holmes's *Abrams* dissent were the pleas for civil liberties found in Laski's *Authority in the Modern State*, dedicated to Holmes and read by him in the very months before he wrote his dissent. In this book Laski insisted that history's greatest truth was that the 'only real security for social well-being is the free exercise of men's minds'. There is a 'realm within', the individual conscience, where 'the state can have no rights and where it is well that it should have none.' No mind was free, Laski wrote, 'once a penalty is attached to thought'. The modern state must regard 'freedom of thought . . . as absolute . . . whether on the part of the individual or of a social group'. For that state to claim it knows the one truth was to claim an obnoxious 'centralized infallibility'. Holmes's magisterial defence of free speech in his dissent was almost verbatim Laski's own amalgam of J. S. Mill and Charles Darwin. Political ideas are adequate for the moment they were formulated, but since men are various and move in varied directions, no one single scheme of interpreting life ever lasts. 'Political good refuses the swaddling clothes of finality. It is a shifting conception,' Laski writes. It is 'in the clash of ideas that we shall find the means of truth. There is no other safeguard of progress.'

If Holmes borrowed from Laski, Laski was in turn deeply impressed by the *Abrams* dissent. None of Holmes's many decisions, he wrote to the justice, 'seems to me superior either in nobility, in outlook, in dignity . . . It is a fine and moving document for which I am deeply and happily grateful.' Laski paid it the additional tribute of passing it on to sympathetic civil libertarians in England. To Bertrand Russell, imprisoned during the war for his pacifism and for an article claiming that the United States entered the war so American troops could break British strikes, Laski wrote, 'Holmes and Brandeis wrote (through Holmes) a magnificent dissent in defence of freedom of speech in an espionage case. I've sent the two opinions to Massingham (at the *Nation*) and suggested he show them to you.' Several years later during the 1925 communist trial in London, Laski would urge that an *Abrams*-like 'clear and present danger' test replace the sedition rules used by British courts which had sanctioned the imprisonment of Russell in 1917 as well as the twelve communist leaders in Britain. He was unsuccessful.

In addition to this general intellectual influence of Laski, especially his *Authority in the Modern State*, on Holmes's *Abrams* dissent, Holmes was aware that at the very time he was deliberating about the limits of free speech his beloved ersatz sons, Frankfurter and Laski, were themselves under attack. They had both been caught up in the fury of America's first anti-Bolshevik witch-hunt. It began in May 1918, when Radcliffe's president, LeBaron R. Briggs, received a letter of complaint from a Mrs Margaret Robinson, who had been hearing for months 'of the astonishing growth of pacifist and socialist sentiments among Radcliffe girls'. She had made inquiries and learned 'that Mr Laski's classroom is the breeding place of much of this propaganda'. He is, she had found out, 'in full sympathy with the movement which has brought ruin to Russia', and she protested that the future teachers of America were being 'inculcated with these doctrines'. Part of Laski's problem was that he had given a talk at a church in Cambridge that spring, which might have gone unnoticed except that a fellow faculty member, Professor Edwin H. Hall, the Rumford Professor of Physics, was in the audience. Hall came away from the talk spreading the word to people like Mrs Robinson that Laski was exerting 'a vicious, poisonous influence', though luckily, 'rattlesnake' that he was, Laski was 'noisy enough' to warn 'those prepared to meet him vigorously'. Hall claimed that while Laski had not proposed 'the overturn of our national government', he had advocated 'disrespect for law' and the end of trade-union conservatism. President Briggs responded to Mrs Robinson:

> As Mr Laski is a Harvard instructor, I am turning your letter over to President Lowell. I had not known him to be a pacifist, or even a socialist, though he has written for the *New Republic* and the *New Republic* which I am taking this year for the first time, gives me considerable unease – rather from its attitude about society and labor than from the suspicion of pacifism.

Laski was certainly not pro-German. In the course of the war he wrote a series of pieces for the *Dial* which depicted Germany as the *reductio ad absurdum* of state worship, and Britain and America as defending all that was good in freedom. Nor was the *New Republic* any less supportive of the war effort. Laski and the magazine were both sympathetic to Keynes's call for a more lenient peace, but it was other aspects of the *New Republic* which were suspect and which in 1918 led the Bolshevik-bashing Post-Master General Burleson to consider adding the magazine to the growing list of publications he was bent on suppressing as seditious. Laski, meanwhile, was well aware that criticism of his politics depended on labels. He wrote to Bertrand Russell, 'I find that when one presents the student mind with syndicalism or socialism namelessly, they take it as reasonable and obvious; attach the name and they whisper to the parents that nameless abominations are being perpetrated.'

Soon Laski was tarnished further by his close association with Frankfurter. While the latter was in Paris an effort began in Harvard alumni circles to have him removed from the Law School faculty. Two famous cases at the War Labor Policies Board had saddled him with a reputation for political radicalism. The Bisbee incident involved authorities in Arizona who had rounded up over 1,000 miners, who were members of the International Workers of the World, as suspected subversives. They were put on a train for New Mexico and then stranded with no food or water. Frankfurter's commission harshly criticized the inhumanity of the treatment. In the Mooney case Frankfurter recommended a new trial for the San Francisco labour organizer who had been convicted for participating in a bombing that had killed ten people, because perjured testimony had been used in the trial. Mooney went free and a new trial never took place. In both cases, due process concerns, not substantive sympathy with radicalism, motivated Frankfurter; nevertheless, in the wartime mood of heightened patriotism, his actions were seen as aiding the radical cause.

The even more intense xenophobia of the post-armistice red hysteria added to Frankfurter's problem. Anti-Semitism was not far from the surface. Scars persisted from the bruising battle over Brandeis's appointment to the Supreme Court which had pitted Frankfurter against Lowell, who seemed bent on preventing Frankfurter from being appointed to a Chair at the Law School. Brandeis wrote of the episode to his wife in June 1919: 'Old Boston is unregenerate and I am not sorry to have escaped a struggle there that would have been as nasty as it is unending. F. F. is evidently considered by the elect as dangerous as I was.' While this was happening, Gilmore Collamore, Secretary of the Harvard Club of New York City, made inquiries to F. W. Hunnewell II, Secretary of the Harvard Corporation, about Laski. Laski had been proposed for membership, and since 'Mr Laski is a Jew . . . the members of my committee . . . should like an expression of opinion from some source other than his sponsors'. Hunnewell responded that yes, 'he is a Polish Jew' and 'his wife is a Gentile'. As of March 1919 he was 'considered one of the most prominent of the younger instructors . . . he would be a very interesting member of the Harvard Club of New York'. Soon that would be a different story.

Laski and Frankfurter were two of only five Jews on the Harvard faculty. Another was Harry Sheffer in Philosophy. In 1919 Laski became deeply involved in stopping an effort to get rid of Sheffer. Laski wrote for help in August to Bertrand Russell, whose *Introduction to Mathematical Logic* had referred favourably to Sheffer's work. 'He is a Jew and he has married someone of whom the university does not approve; moreover, he hasn't the social qualities that Harvard so highly prizes.' The department wanted only 'respectable neo-Christians'. He concluded that 'the whole thing is a combination of anti-Semitism and that curious university worship of social prestige which plays so large a part over here'. Russell sent cables to the Philosophy Department and President Lowell, informing them 'that Harvard would be eternally disgraced if it dismissed him either because he was a Jew or because it disliked his wife'. Sheffer was kept on.

Holmes was well aware of Laski's and Frankfurter's difficulties. In April 1919 he wrote to Laski that every once in a while 'I hear that you are dangerous men'. What does it mean? he asked. 'Have your writings . . . led people who don't read them to believe that you were opposed to law and order or what?' Laski's response suggested that anti-Semitism was at work as well as an effort by Boston 'State Street Lawyers' to get even with Felix and his friends for 'the Brandeis affair'. Laski too had 'enemies and to spare'. Worrying that Pound had enough trouble resisting the calls for Felix's neck, Laski offered to resign his book review position at the *Law Review*. 'You have all the criticism and opposition you need,' he noted. In June 1919 Laski did resign his editorship at the *Review*, though the return of students from the war must also have contributed to his action. In addition, Laski asked Holmes, as former President of the Harvard Law School Alumni Association, to commend Pound and Frankfurter to that body. Holmes not only did this, but he also wrote to Lowell about how important Pound and Frankfurter were to the Harvard Law School, and in May 1920 Frankfurter was appointed Bryne Professor of Law. Meanwhile, in the midst of the spring 1919 crisis, Holmes had written to his friend Pollock about 'Laski's new book *Authority in the Modern State*, which he dedicates to me and Frankfurter'.

People in Boston seem to have got the idea that he is a dangerous man (they used to think me one) . . . I have had the greatest pleasure in his conversation as he is a portent of knowledge though still very young. There is also a prejudice against Frankfurter; I think partly because he (as well as Laski) is a Jew . . . Boston is nothing if not critical. It never occurs to me until after the event that a man I like is a Jew, nor do I care when I realize it. If I had to choose I think I would rather see power in the hands of Jews than in the Catholics' – not that I wish to be run by either.

All America, Holmes included, seemed concerned with the power of Catholics and Jews in 1919. After decades of massive non-Protestant immigration, the First World War had produced a nativist frenzy that inspired the Espionage Act of 1917 and the Sedition Act of 1918, which had featured in the Abrams Case. The Russian Revolution and the renewal of labour strife after the armistice brought about the country's first 'Red scare'. In the wake of a general strike and bomb scares in Seattle, the American Legion, newly formed in St Louis, pledged itself to 'foster and perpetuate a 100 per cent Americanism'. Attorney-General A. Mitchell Palmer's raids shipped hundreds of aliens to Russia on 'Soviet arks'. In Albany, New York, the New York State legislature refused to allow five duly elected Jewish socialist assemblymen to sit.

Citizens of Massachusetts felt particularly threatened. Twenty thousand telephone operators went out on strike in April 1919. A strike call, sent out in twenty languages, silenced the textile mills in Lawrence, where Mrs Evans and Laski joined the picket lines. One can only imagine, then, the nightmarish fears of Brahmin Boston at the prospect that their policemen, front-line defenders of life and property, might themselves succumb to what was perceived as a Red-induced strike mania. The Boston police force was an unlikely locus for Bolshevik plotting. The overwhelmingly Irish police might vote Democratic, but they were hardly social revolutionaries. Still, their lot was not a happy one. Many in the force earned no more than twenty cents an hour and worked a weekly shift of eighty-three or ninety-eight hours. So it should not have been surprising when, on 1 August, the Boston policemen voted 940 to 9 (with numerous abstentions) to form a union and join the American Federation of Labor (AFL). Edwin Upton Curtis, the Republican Commissioner of Police, acted swiftly. Announcing that a police officer could not 'consistently belong to a union and perform his sworn duty', Curtis suspended nineteen of the police union's newly elected officers. The force threatened to strike, but Curtis was not moved. In late August he called for 'volunteers' to replace the police should they carry out their threat.

'Come back from your vacations, young men; there is sport and diversion for you right here in Boston,' read a letter in the *Boston Herald* of 27 August 1919 from Edwin H. Hall. The Professor of Physics urged his students to return to Cambridge early and volunteer to patrol Boston if the policemen went on strike. Laski's nemesis from the previous spring was the first person to volunteer to replace the strikers. Led by Professor Hall, more than four hundred Harvard 'volunteers', mainly students, rallied to the call. President Lowell urged that students 'in a time of crisis ... prepare themselves for such service', which would 'maintain order and support the laws of the Commonwealth'. An emergency headquarters for volunteer activity on the first floor of University Hall was open night and day. Posters displayed in the windows of the university tobacconists emphasized Lowell's assurance that students who missed registration or even classes would in no way suffer 'from their devotion to public service'. In the last days of August the mayor of Boston, Andrew James Peters, a Harvard graduate and a Democrat, appointed a blue-ribbon committee to settle the police crisis (years later it would be revealed from his diaries that this pillar of Establishment rectitude was at this time repeatedly etherizing and seducing his eleven-year-old cousin). At the committee's head he put James Jackson Storrow, a Harvard overseer and former president of General Motors.

Storrow and his committee recommended that the police receive higher wages and that they be allowed to form a union as long as it was not part of the AFL. Storrow urged that there be no recriminations against the police and that the nineteen suspended officers be reinstated if members of the force agreed to these terms. Mayor Peters endorsed the solution, and the police grudgingly agreed. But Curtis would not budge. On 8 September he refused to give in on the suspensions. That night the police voted 1,134 to 2 to strike.

Two days of rioting and looting followed. In the name of 'public service', Harvard men patrolled the streets. Godfrey Lowell Cabot, cousin and classmate of President Lowell, arrived with two pistols strapped to his coat. Bill Hoffman, a cousin of the Roosevelts, headed to his post in Scollay Square in his Stanley Steamer. Many an Irishman from South

Boston went after the Harvard volunteers and scores of students were hurt. No Harvards were among the eight people killed during the days of rioting, however, and soon they retreated back across the Charles River to Harvard Yard. Mayor Peters had activated the Massachusetts State Guard and by the end of the week they were policing Boston. The Guard patrolled the city for 102 days, the last soldiers leaving on 21 December. Although most of the strikers had disowned the strike by the middle of September, Curtis declared their positions vacant, and by December more than 1,500 new policemen had been hired. This hard-line response was reinforced by Calvin Coolidge, the Republican governor. Elected in 1918 by a majority of only 17,000 votes out of more than 400,000 cast, Coolidge, the shrewd Yankee, saw political capital to be earned in the strike. Apprehensive that Peters might urge Curtis to rehire the strikers, Coolidge took personal control of the Guard after the first week of the crisis. His simple, blunt pronouncement as he did so would make him famous: 'There is no right to strike against the public safety by anybody, anywhere, any time.' Coolidge became a national folk hero, the strike ultimately catapulting him into national politics and the presidency of the United States, notwithstanding Laski's description of him to Holmes in the midst of the strike as 'dull, illiterate, stupid and obstinate'.

Boston and Harvard congratulated themselves for having turned the 'Red tide'. The *Boston Herald* announced the end of the 'Russianizing' of America; the city had refused to 'submit to Soviet rule'. The *Boston Evening Transcript* applauded the defeat of those seeking 'to overthrow American-ism'. For the venerable Senator Henry Cabot Lodge, it was the 1770s all over again: Boston's fight was once again America's, but this time against 'Soviet government by labour unions'. Foreigners were singled out as the principal villains. The *Transcript*'s editorial, noting that 'Bolshevism in Boston will be nipped in the bud', added that Boston 'is an American city, not a polyglot boarding house'. Describing a pro-police demonstration, the *Transcript* observed that large numbers 'clearly belonged to the Hebrew trades'. Letter-writers urged that the new policemen being hired should be 'full-blooded American'; there were 'altogether too many Irishmen in these positions'. Curtis and Coolidge were instructed to 'go back in the country towns and get some husky Yankee boys to put in their places. Good Americans and Yankees do not strike.'

In the midst of this nativist self-congratulation Harold Laski, foreigner and Jew, shocked the Harvard that employed him. On 6 October the Harvard student newspaper, the *Crimson*, sought out Laski to comment on the strike. Laski supported the strikers, insisting that 'every man has a right to belong to any organization, or affiliate with any body to better his own condition'. The fault lay with Commissioner Curtis, he added, not the strikers. The following day a *Crimson* editorial agreed with Laski's criticism of 'the harshness of the Commissioner', but ridiculed his sympathy for the 'disgraceful strikers'. Even this was too generous a response for Professor Carver of the Government Department, however: the *Crimson* quoted him as dismissing 'the stand taken recently by another member of the instruction staff' as that of a 'boudoir Bolshevist [*sic*]'.

Two days later President Lowell received a letter from an alumnus in Cincinnati, Ohio, Charles B. Wilby, the first of scores of letters furious with Laski, and still a week before his most egregious affront to Brahmin sensibility. Wilby wrote of a friend's son 'who comes of an old Boston family and ought to know better, showing decided socialistic views, which he admits are the results of the teachings of Mr Laski'. Furthermore, this man who 'tells his classes that he is a syndicalist . . . is no gentleman'. Wilby informed Lowell that Radcliffe students were told to come to Laski's house and 'when they arrived there, he was lying at full length on a lounge, and he greeted them by saying – "Well, shoot." He remaining on his back during the interview, not even offering them chairs . . . the manners of a barbarian'.

What truly shocked Harvard, however, and what made Laski the talk of Cambridge and Boston was the address he gave on the night of 15 October at Fay Hall to a meeting of the wives and relatives of the striking policemen. According to Frida, Laski was an unscheduled visitor to the rally of over 2,500 women. He praised the police and ended his talk with the stirring conviction 'that labour is more unified than ever . . . labour will never surrender'. This was too much for the *Transcript*, which asked the next day whether Laski was 'an instructor in American government or Soviet government'. The newspaper suggested that parents of Harvard students urge the university to fire Laski.

The *Crimson* quickly rose to Laski's defence. On 17 October in an editorial called 'Attack on Academic Freedom', it lamented both Laski's remarks and his presence at the rally but resented 'any attack on the right of any member of the faculty to say what he wants'. The *Harvard Alumni*

Bulletin also defended Laski's privilege to speak out, though it added the sobering thought that 'the average American is inclined to be very resentful of aspersion that comes from alien lips'. Others were less charitable in their response. The redoubtable Professor Hall, recovered from his policing duties, wrote to the *Herald* comparing Laski once again to a 'rattlesnake' and denouncing his colleague's 'glorification of Bolshevism'. Laski described the firestorm in a letter to Bertrand Russell:

> I spoke for the striking police here the other day; one of those strikes which makes one equally wonder at the endurance of the men and the unimaginative stupidity of the officials. Two newspapers and two hundred alumni demanded my dismissal. I was charged with teaching Sovietism when I said that men who get 1,100 dollars and work seventy-three hours [a] week are justified in striking ... some papers have actually demanded that the Yale University Press withdraw my books from circulation because they preach 'anarchy'.

Laski was not exaggerating. President Lowell's papers in the Harvard archives contain nearly a hundred angry letters, most signed by several alumni. Particularly distressing was the timing. Harvard was in the midst of a then unprecedented and well-publicized campaign to raise $15,200,000 for its endowment fund. Rumours spread that a prominent alumnus had offered Lowell and Harvard a million dollars to dismiss Laski. Paul Tuckerman, a Wall Street millionaire from the class of 1878, told Lowell that the Laski affair would discourage donations to the fund. Lowell replied that while he disapproved of Laski's 'public posturing', academic freedom was sacred. Tuckerman wrote back:

> If Mr Laski were teaching mathematics, the argument of academic freedom would have some force ... but he teaches our sons not mathematics, but government, and what reverence for our government and institutions can a professed Bolshevik teach? Is it not, Mr President, like selecting an atheist to teach our boys religion?

W. H. Coolidge did not worry about the effect of Laski's teaching on those like his son, then at Harvard, 'whose ancestors for two or three hundred years have lived in America and become imbued with American ideals', but was fearful of Laski's impact on 'those boys whose parents, perhaps, have come to this country from Russia, Germany, Austria or

Italy'. John A. Ferguson, on the contrary, worried that his two sons at Harvard, one a freshman and the other a sophomore, 'were much impressed' by Laski's 'erratic teachings'. In fact, what really disturbed him was that this 'carrier, a sort of Typhoid Mary of governmental disease', was an even greater danger because he heard from his sons that Laski was such 'a damn good teacher'. 'Academic freedom, sir, is a dangerous fetish,' Waldo S. Kendall Barker, from the class of 1899, wrote to Lowell. 'Under its cover licence flourishes. Human society can be held together only by the bonds of discipline, mental as well as physical.' Equally blunt was Freeland Jewett, who wrote to Lowell that anyone like Laski 'who encourages any lawless-ness . . . should be deported from the country and consider himself fortunate in not being shot'.

The bottom line in most letters demanding that Laski be fired was money, the endowment drive. Frederick Wainwright Bradlee had intended to give $2,500 to the drive and had heard about 'a Russian Jew, a man named Laski . . . reported to be an out-and-out Bolshevik', who approved 'of the shameful attitude of the Boston police'. If such people remained on the faculty, he was unwilling to contribute to Harvard. Arthur Fuller, Harvard 1877, and four classmates wrote that if the university retained Laski, 'no young man with whom we have any influence will go to Harvard, nor will any "grown-up" whom we can influence contribute hereafter to any Harvard fund'. Benjamin Curtis, 1888, told Lowell that 'Laski's treason' had led one of his classmates to change his mind 'on a gift of one hundred thousand dollars just because of this sort of Laski stuff that is tolerated'.

Lowell was clearly annoyed with the whole affair, which he estimated lost Harvard about $300,000. He wrote to Dean Haskins of the Graduate School that while 'academic freedom is a very precious thing, sometimes it seems an expensive one. What irritates is the fact that this cost is due to a lack of tact and of a sense of propriety.' Still, Lowell answered every letter he received from alumni about Laski. Each response contained a standard defence of academic freedom to explain why Laski would not be fired and often an impressive individual response to points raised by the enraged alumnus. To Fuller he noted that a greater danger than Laski was the threat to liberty of speech, which 'reminds me much of the Alien and Sedition Laws' which destroyed the Federalist Party. There never was a time, he replied to Mr Wilby, when in its history 'Harvard University was not accused of being radical. When I was young, this charge was brought in matters of religion; later in matters of economics; and now in politics.' Throughout it all, he reminded Wilby, Harvard was pledged 'not to represent only one point of view; if it did, it would be stagnant'. To Paul Tuckerman, Lowell wrote that today 'the word "Bolshevist" is used as "atheist" was two generations ago to apply to anyone whose opinions one did not like'. Lowell's letter to Tuckerman is an extraordinary document, with the President of Harvard, a former Professor of Government, assuring the powerful Wall Street financier that he at least had read Laski's two books and

> although you may not agree with all his views, they are very far from Bolshevik. This term, I understand, describes a condition in which absolute authority is claimed by the working class. Now, the whole essence of Mr Laski's teaching in his books is that absolute authority does not, and ought not to, rest in any organ of the state. One of his chief examples is that the state has no right to suppress the church; and this he believes true of other organizations. Such a multiple form of authority may or may not have any practical application; but it is certainly exceedingly different from Bolshevism, which implies class tyranny, with unlimited authority.

Not that Lowell wasn't also receiving some mail (much less, to be sure) from alumni, some equally powerful, applauding his refusal to fire Laski. A. A. Berle, a Boston teacher whose son studied under Laski and, far from being radicalized, 'was rather made more conservative', wrote that while Laski was a 'bumptious young fool who does not know much about American life', the 'present madness to prosecute and persecute everybody who does not happen to believe what we believe is a worse form of Prussianism than the one we offered our sons to destroy'. Albert Sprague Coolidge wrote to Lowell that if Laski were ousted he would 'be a very sore man and a mortified son of Harvard'. He had heard that some alumni were threatening to cancel their gifts to the endowment fund if Laski was not dismissed; in that case, he both warned and reassured Lowell, 'I hereby threaten to cancel my subscription if Mr Laski is dismissed. I will also help to make up any loss which his retention may cause.' Thomas W. Lamont, Chair of the endowment campaign, owner of the *New York Evening Post*, banker, and later of J. P. Morgan and Co., published a letter in the *Crimson* from the endowment campaign committee supporting Lowell's actions in defending academic freedom. Even Professor Hall, Laski's most outspoken faculty critic, wrote to Lowell enclosing a contribution of $1,000 for the endowment fund. Though he 'differed radically and publicly' from Laski's views, he praised the university's refusal to dismiss him.

The most influential supportive intervention may well have been the letter from Judge Julian W. Mack on 29 October, which must have impressed Lowell not only by its accompanying cheque, but for the circles of power it reminded Lowell that Laski moved in. A Harvard graduate who sat on the Circuit Court of Appeals in Chicago, Mack was a member of the Harvard Board of Overseers and second only to Louis Brandeis, his close friend, as lay leader of American Jewry. Mack's letter never mentioned Laski's name and enclosed a letter and cheque from an old friend of Mack's, Max Epstein, President of the General American Tank Car Corporation. Epstein, Mack informed Lowell, had never gone to college, but had been persuaded by Mack, Frankfurter and Pound to give the endowment fund $50,000 for the Law School. Mack hoped that this gift 'will tend to check any discouragement that may come from the refusal of other wealthy men to subscribe to the fund except under the condition that Harvard forsake her fundamental principles of academic freedom'.

Lowell's learned summary of Laski's books had not quietened Tuckerman, however. He wrote to several friends on the Board of Overseers, including Franklin Roosevelt, then assistant secretary of the navy. To Tuckerman's 'Why not clean house and get rid of the foreign propagandist?' Roosevelt replied, with no particular sign of support, that the matter was in fact being taken up at the next overseers' meeting. The board's decision at that meeting on 27 October was for a committee of overseers to interview Laski at the Boston Harvard Club and then report to a full board meeting in January. Meanwhile, Lowell and Laski had met on 26 October. Lowell reported that while he would resist the demands for Laski's removal, Laski 'as a foreigner ought not to have criticized American public officers, and, indeed, ... the whole occasion was an inappropriate one for him to have expressed his opinions'. Laski wrote to Lowell the next day with his gratitude and offered to give a gift to the endowment fund. Lowell declined the offer.

'Lowell was magnificent', Laski wrote to Holmes. Later, however, he told friends that Lowell told him in confidence to restrict his speaking to classroom lectures and 'not to expect promotion from the university'. As for what transpired at the overseers' interview on 17 December – or his 'Harvard Inquisition', as he referred to it years later – we have only Laski's account:

> Nothing could be further from the Grand Inquisitor than poor George Wigglesworth ... He looked at me and said, 'Mr Laski, do you believe in bloody revolution?' I looked him straight in the eye and said, 'Mr Wigglesworth, do I look as if I did?' We all laughed and had a good dinner.

Laski later wrote to Frankfurter and described his answer to Wigglesworth's question as 'I believe in revolution in the same sense as Americans did in 1776.'

The Board of Overseers met on 12 January 1920 to consider the Laski affair. It was an ominous week: Attorney-General Palmer had several days earlier arrested nearly 5,000 socialists around the country with a view to deportation. The board's decision, however, was to take no further action. They were satisfied that Laski's statements had been 'misunderstood and misinterpreted'. President Lowell had stood his ground. 'If the overseers ask for Laski's resignation, they will get mine,' he is reported to have told friends. According to the *Nation*, Lowell 'has carried off the honors among all our college presidents for his insistence upon academic freedom of speech and thought'. Like other American progressives, the *Nation* was pleasantly surprised at Lowell's stand. His public positions had seldom found him on their side before. Not only had he sent students to the Lawrence and Boston strikes, he was also a long-time officer of the Immigration Restriction League, founded in 1894 to defend the 'superiority' of the Anglo-Saxon peoples. He had lent support to the opposition in 1916 to Brandeis's Supreme Court nomination and he had dragged his feet on Frankfurter's appointment to the chair. Soon he would rule that Negroes could not live in Harvard Yard and propose a quota on the number of Jewish students at Harvard; furthermore, to the everlasting anger of liberal opinion, he would head the committee that investigated the Sacco–Vanzetti trial and rule it fair. Upton Sinclair, the great muck-raker, suggested in letters to Laski and in his 1922 book *The Goose Step* that Lowell was less than genuine in his support of Laski. He was, Sinclair conjectured, interested principally in the ambassadorship to Great Britain and worried about Laski's connections at Oxford and in the world of London politics and journalism. Lowell knew, in addition, that Laski was a close friend of two Supreme Court justices, and had friends and friends of friends on the Board of Overseers; perhaps he even knew that Laski's close friend Huebsch had published the widely read exposé of Scott Nearing's dismissal from the University of Pennsylvania. None of this, however, need explain Lowell's stand in the Laski case. He was socially and politically a snob and a conservative. He disliked Laski, what he stood for and what he had done. But, like Professor Hall policing Boston and denouncing Bolshevik rattlesnakes, Lowell still believed in academic freedom and the university as a place where political views, however 'inappropriate', could be expressed.

The overseers' decision to do nothing seemed to end *l'affaire Laski* – until the *Harvard Lampoon*, which billed itself as 'the oldest and third largest comic publication in America', had its say. On 16 January 1920 the *Lampoon* devoted its entire issue to Laski. The *Boston Herald* saw it as 'one of the most scathing attacks ever directed against a college instructor in America, an attack that is causing all Harvard to stir with comment'. The 'Laski *Lampoon*', as it came to be called in Harvard lore, hoped that the 'time will come when Cambridge may be purged of this scum'. Sixteen pages of anti-Semitic poems, parodies, cartoons, caricatures, songs and drawings mocked Laski. A sham autobiography had Laski born in Poland, sighing always, 'Oi Gewalt! I was delicate . . . went through Oxford in twenty minutes . . . It took less time to get me out of the synagogue than it did to eject Spinoza'; a version of his syllabus recommended 'Hebrew notes to facilitate readings'. Laski was parodied as Professor Moses Smartelickoff and ridiculed as critical of those who ate without hats on. A constitution for Russia was proposed with the troika of Lenin, Trotsky and Laski in charge. Scurrilous poetry linked him to the events of the autumn.

> 'Twould be greatly to his liking
> If the whole world started striking,
> With himself established at the strikers' head;
> In the parlance of the ghetto,
> He would 'shake a mean stiletto'
> From the firstski to the Laski he's a Red.

The *Boston Transcript* applauded the *Lampoon*'s patriotism and its courage in setting the university right before the world so that the silence of the overseers 'would not be construed as Harvard acquiescence in those utterances expressed'. The *Crimson*, on the other hand, announced on 29 January that it had received so many letters critical of the *Lampoon* issue that it wished no more to be sent, since 'it agreed with the criticism'. 'The *Lampoon* has overstepped its bounds,' wrote a group of six students. Someone also wrote that the *Lampoon* 'is approached in vulgarity only by German war cartoons. It is not funny or caustic; it is merely contemptible.'

Lowell now had to resist requests that he discipline the student editors of the *Lampoon*. The president of the publication wrote to Lowell regretting that they might 'have been discourteous towards the college authorities' in their criticism of them for not firing Laski, but insisting that the rest of the issue expressed their heartfelt sentiments. Laski wrote to Lowell apologizing 'that you should again be troubled by an affair in which, however unwillingly, I have a part'. He asked Lowell that the *Lampoon* people not be disciplined. Frankfurter sent Lowell an excerpt from a letter he had received from Justice Holmes complaining about the rudeness and religious prejudice of the *Lampoon*. 'It is disquieting that so serious a scholar and thinker as Laski should be subjected to the trampling of swine.' Lowell once again stood firmly on the side of free expression: Harvard, he wrote, 'will not yield to popular clamor'. The attack on Laski 'was vulgar and altogether deplorable; but the only wise thing is to treat it with silence and contempt. Punishment in such a case would do no good and not a little harm.' Lowell did, however, write to Edward A. Bacon, the president of the *Lampoon*, in February with a stirring defence of free expression and reasoned debate which has lain unnoticed in the president's papers for seventy years.

> I cannot fail to recognize that the recent number of the *Lampoon* was in very bad taste. I regret this the more because the faculty has always allowed the freest latitude for satire in student publications. In fact, this is part of the general policy of freedom of speech within the university which the *Lampoon* attacks . . . From all ages it has been a common practice when the arguments of one's adversary could not be met, to attempt to overwhelm him with obloquy or ridicule; and it is not difficult by such means to work on popular prejudice against him or his views. Yet surely it is not for this that a university exists; but in order to discover and demonstrate truth. For that purpose humor is a perfectly proper instrument; but not in the form of personal attack on those who differ from us, for the only essential question is the truth, not the personality of him who argues.

Laski's friends were worried that the viciousness and the anti-Semitism of the *Lampoon*'s attack might lead Laski to leave Harvard. Brandeis wrote to him and expressed his hope that 'you and Frida are not much concerned about the *Lampoon* episode. It is really a great compliment, and has done good service to the cause of freedom.' Much the most ambitious effort along these lines was the suggestion of Laski's Law School friend, Zachariah Chafee, in a letter to Lowell that a dinner be held for Laski presided over by Lowell 'to convince him that Harvard feels very differently from the *Lampoon*'. Its ostensible purpose would be to mark the publication of his Duguit translation, but, Chafee suggested, notice in the press that such a dinner had taken place with a list of guests would counteract the impression given out by the *Lampoon* and the *Transcript*. The dinner would serve 'some amends for the pain' he has suffered, as recognition of his work, and indicate our earnest desire that he stay 'to give us more teaching and more books'. Lowell was not interested. A dinner noticed in the press, he replied to Chafee, 'would be a mistake'. In fact, it 'would inevitably provoke a lot more criticism by those people – and there are many – who do not approve of him or of his being at Harvard'. No dinner was held.

The issue was soon moot. Laski wrote to Lowell on 6 May to resign his Harvard appointment. Reporting in its 10 May 1920 issue that Laski was giving up his university position for a job at the London School of Economics, the *Crimson* editorialized that 'the place left empty by Mr Laski's resignation cannot be easily filled'. It regretted that 'Harvard should have lost so promising a teacher, a profound student of economics and an intellectual genius'. Students would miss him. 'While they could not always agree with his political principles, they nevertheless found his influence stimulating and inspiring.' The *Boston Post* reminded Bostonians, lest they be too satisfied, that 'he is but twenty-six years old and is considered by many to be one of the most brilliant young scholars who have come to teach at Harvard'.

Later in his career Laski frequently suggested that it was the furore over his role in the police strike that led him to leave Harvard, just as he linked his departure from McGill to unpopular public speech-making. 'I am heartily sick of America,' Laski wrote to Bertrand Russell in February. 'I am very eager to get away from this country' to a place 'where an ox does not tread upon the tongue'. Oxford and Cambridge seem impossible, he added, but Graham Wallas was hopeful about the London School of

Economics. Several weeks earlier Laski had told Holmes that he 'was eager to go home', assuming 'some English university will want me'. His political views were suspect, he explained to Holmes, and the faculty didn't like his 'Oxfordizing', his assumption that a professor shouldn't just lecture students but should 'build his life round his students'. This apparent decision of January and February, however, merely confirmed and intensified an earlier resolve to leave which Laski had, in fact, made substantially before the notoriety of the police strike.

He would have loved to return to Oxford. Sending his book to Gilbert Murray in 1917, Laski hoped that their political differences would not stand in the way of his 'one day dedicating his life to the service of Oxford'. Laski was more direct with Fisher, with whom he had been closer and who had in fact offered him a job in November 1916 at Sheffield University, where he had gone as Chancellor before joining Lloyd George's government. Laski turned down Sheffield but wrote to Fisher in 1917 that he hoped his *Studies in the Problem of Sovereignty* would be 'the first stone in a path that will lead back to New College one day'. Laski also let Alfred Zimmern at New College know his intentions. The two had struck up an amiable correspondence in 1918 over Zimmern's critical review of Laski's first book and over a review that Laski was doing for the *New Republic* of Zimmern's new book, *Nationality and Government*. Laski was no doubt encouraged in the correspondence by his awareness that Justice Brandeis admired Zimmern. In November Laski wrote to Zimmern that peace 'brings all kinds of dreams nearer' and that his was to 'return to England'. He hoped his second book 'would persuade some university to let me come back and teach. Above all I want to go to New College – but I suppose being a Jew is a bar,' he confided to Zimmern, who was himself half Jewish.

Laski's chances for a job in England were helped by the attention his books were attracting there. Even Pollock, who was unimpressed by them, wrote to Holmes in May 1919 that 'Laski seems to be a rather important rising author'. With this English visibility in mind Laski agreed early in 1919 to do a volume in the popular Home University Library series edited by Fisher and Murray. His *Political Thought in England: Locke to Bentham* was a kind of coming home for Laski; it was published several years after the companion volume in the series by his teacher Ernest Barker, *Political Thought in England: From Herbert Spencer to the Present Day*. Laski's third book was dedicated to 'my friend Walter Lippmann . . . though there is little that can repay such friendship as he gives'. Reprinted countless times, this lively and opinionated survey of 150 years of English political and social thought fully succeeded in keeping Laski's name known.

Short of New College, Laski set his hopes on the London School of Economics, and his 'friend Walter Lippmann' played a role in making this possible through his unique relationship with Graham Wallas, the LSE's Professor of Political Science. Throughout Laski's years at Harvard he assiduously cultivated Lippmann's former teacher. One of the original Fabians who had deserted the inner circle of Webb and Shaw, Wallas was the premier intellectual figure at the Webbs' LSE. His *Human Nature in Politics* (1908) and his *Great Society* (1914, also dedicated to Lippmann) described a socialism as moral as it was scientific, almost inspirational in its vision of a participatory citizenship among economic equals. From his earliest written review of Wallas in the *Daily Herald* Laski always spoke enthusiastically of him. He seems to have genuinely admired the power of Wallas's mind and spirit. Laski confided to one friend that in his readings he 'rarely met such natural wisdom' as Wallas's, and to a student he paid Wallas the supreme compliment of noting 'how Wallas makes me feel inferior'. He wrote to Holmes that 'Wallas is one of the best stimulants I know', and equally fulsome words of praise appeared in print. Laski described Wallas's biography of William Place in *Dial* as 'a masterpiece of political biography', and he stated in a *New Republic* piece in 1917 that in recent writings on politics 'no one has made more fundamental contributions than Mr Wallas'.

Wallas and Laski began corresponding in 1917 when Laski sent Wallas a copy of his first book. Wallas wrote back with praise and advice. Laski's letter, in turn, told Wallas how important his books had been for him and how they and the friendly advice in his letters made Wallas, along with Holmes and Pound, 'real landmarks in my life'. Their common involvement in the founding of the New School was a prominent topic in their letters, with Wallas ever thankful for Laski's candid assessment of its personnel. Throughout their letters, especially in 1918, the suggestion emerges about how nice it would be if Laski were at the LSE. For this to become a reality, however, the intervention of another infinitely more influential pillar of the intellectual and political Establishment was necessary, Lord Haldane of Cloan, the uncle of Laski's New College classmate and idol.

Haldane was a man of many distinguished parts, philosopher, lawyer and politician. He wrote books about Hegel; while in the House of Commons from 1885 he championed Liberal Imperialism. He served in the pre-war Cabinet as Minister of War, and during the early years of the war he was Asquith's Lord Chancellor. He was one of Justice Holmes's many English friends. He was also a governor, and perhaps the most important patron, of the London School of Economics, in charge of a large endowment legacy crucial for the school's financing. Laski sent Haldane all his publications while at Harvard. Haldane wrote letters back in May 1917 and in May, October and November 1919 thanking Laski and especially praising his pieces that appeared in *Law Reviews*. Haldane sent Laski a copy of his own *Before the War*, in which he answered accusations that he had been pro-German.

Laski did not rest content with the sponsorship of Haldane and Wallas; he sent his books to other faculty at the LSE: to R. H. Tawney, L. T. Hobhouse and Sidney Webb, as well. When Samuel Rezneck, one of Laski's favourite Harvard students, was travelling in England on a Harvard Sheldon Fellowship in the autumn of 1919, he visited the LSE and called on the faculty to whom Laski had given him letters of introduction. Amazed to find virtually all of them reading Laski's book, Rezneck wrote in his diary, 'Laski is certainly some pusher.' It worked. In December 1919 Graham Wallas, then teaching at Yale and the New School, wrote to Laski that W. H. Beveridge, the new Director of the LSE, had written to Wallas asking for references on Laski and that Sidney Webb had done the same shortly thereafter. Wallas returned to London, full of Laski's brilliance and his plight since mid-November. He wrote to Laski from the SS *Rotterdam* about how uncannily 'the Boston Police Strike is an admirable laboratory experiment in Authority in the Modern State'. Perhaps Laski and Harvard, he suggested, could run a seminar 'on the facts and ideas of the police strike', and even arrange 'to do field-work by taking down evidence day by day'. When he arrived back in London, Wallas pushed hard for Laski; according to Beveridge, 'Wallas pleaded with me urgently to rescue him [Laski] from trouble and I invited him to come to us . . . deepening our red colour in many eyes.'

The offer came from Beveridge in March and Laski accepted it immediately. Frida told Wallas that when the letter came Laski had rejoiced like a 'mad excited Indian'. He would be paid £650 per year, about the equivalent of his Harvard salary, but with much less teaching responsibility. Laski wrote to Wallas thanking him for all he had done and on 15 April Wallas replied, 'I suppose that if I had not known you, you would not have got the job, but I don't think that would have been enough without Haldane's help.' Laski didn't inform Lowell until May, but he told his close friends immediately. Brandeis wrote on 1 April that 'you are right to go home. America has gained much from your stay here and you will carry back to England much of value in the understanding of things American.' He assured Laski that he and his wife had contracted the 'London vacation habit' and that they looked forward to visits. Contact would continue with Frankfurter too, who had already planned a late honeymoon trip to England for the summer.

It was Holmes, nearly eighty and not about to do any travelling, for whom Laski's leaving was the most difficult. 'All my abiding love for you comes tumbling to the end of my pen,' Laski wrote on 28 March, as he thought of how knowing Holmes had 'lit up those last four years'. Though they would not see each other, he reassured Holmes that he would send him 'week by week comment and gossip and talk, but above all my love'. Holmes had become extremely fond of Laski, and his letters after hearing the news vibrate with wistful poignancy. Just a few weeks earlier in response to Laski's birthday greetings Holmes had written, 'I think you have seen the delight I have had in your companionship . . . It has made my work easier and happier. It is a great fortune for an old fellow to have such intimacy with a young one, and your gifts have made it full of suggestion and instruction.' Holmes wrote to Pollock that 'I shall miss Laski badly, I am much attached to him', and on 31 March he wrote movingly to Laski:

> Your decision sounds right to me . . . But oh, my dear lad, I shall miss you sadly. There is no other man I shall miss so much. Your intellectual companionship, your suggestiveness, your encouragement and affection have enriched life to me very greatly and it will be hard not to look forward to seeing you in bodily presence. However, I shall get your letters and that will be much. I shall do my best to hold up my end of that stick . . . If we should not meet again you will know that you have added much to the happiness of one fellow-being.

In his last weeks at Harvard Laski was honoured at numerous student dinners, he entertained his future colleague Tawney, who was lecturing at

Amherst, and he and Frida corresponded with Wallas about where to live in London. Laski found time, of course, to mark his American leave-taking with a reflective piece in the *New Republic*. 'The Temper of the Present Time' begins with a claim that is as true of Laski as of the years that were his topic: 'We have concentrated into the fury of the past five years a generation of eager experience.' The essay was Laski's farewell to the America of police strikes, *Lampoon* character assassination, as well as to the nation of immigrants and the Yankee Holmes. America will have to confront 'industrial freedom', the single great issue of the post-war age. It will have to realize that 'freedom to the starving striker in Pittsburgh will be different from its interpretation by the corporation lawyer who reads the third-hand condemnation of that same striker's thoughts as he rides to his office in the club-car of a suburban train'. America must understand that dissent does not produce disorder, that ideas 'too weak to stand the fires of criticism' ought not to survive. Holmes has taught us, Laski noted, 'that no social order is a final arrangement', yet for most Americans to admit 'that some grievances are real is to open the floodgates of revolution'. He recommended Macaulay to America as he would to Britain for the next thirty years, Macaulay who on the eve of the Great Reform Bill in 1832 urged his parliamentary colleagues to 'reform in order that you may preserve'. In his resounding answer to his critics, Laski evoked an America that was their worst fear, an America 'not imprisoned by its past' to one 'single experience' and a 'homogeneity of tradition', but enriched by the diverse and varied dreams and aspirations of its waves of immigrants. His final peroration to America is, fittingly enough, less syndicalist Laski than progressive and civil libertarian Laski.

The only safeguard of social structure is criticism; and we must therefore cease to think that wisdom is perpetually resident in any group of men or principles. That is the natural desire of a world tired after a great effort of will and terrified at the forces it has called into being. Truth, like art, is a matter of dirt and sweat. It comes only from the clash of innumerable men and countless opinions. Some fragments may come from a West Indian orphan who finds his way to the staff of a revolutionary army, or from a half-starved German Jew who is driven like a hunted deer from the capitals of Europe. The vision is never whole nor is it immediate. It never comes, even in the most inchoate form, save where the mind is free to play untrammelled with the facts of life.

If 'The Temper of the Present Time' was intended to prevent more 'Harvard inquisitions', it failed sadly, for several months later Laski's nightmare was revisited upon his close friend Zachariah Chafee, Jr. Chafee had led an effort, supported by Pound and Frankfurter, to have President Woodrow Wilson commute the Abrams sentences. As a result, a group of twenty Law School alumni demanded that the Harvard overseers evaluate Chafee's 'fitness to teach'. The overseers appointed a committee consisting of eleven lawyers and judges to hear the charges brought by Austen Fox, himself a Boston lawyer and member of the overseers. Once again Lowell stood by his faculty member and opposed both Chafee's ousting and censure. Chafee spoke on his own behalf at 'the trial at the Harvard Club', as it came to be known, and according to Frankfurter's account ended with 'what I always thought was one of the most impressive sentences I ever heard in my life', It was the American voice of a Holmes that so appealed to both Frankfurter and Laski, the fair-minded Yankee voice of the Puritan conscience at its best.

> I come of a family that have been in America from the beginning of time. My people have been business people for generations. My people have been people of substance. They have made money. My family is a family that has money. I believe in property and I believe in making money, but I want my crowd to fight fair.

Such was the mood of America that Chafee was found 'fit to teach' by only six votes to five.

Nor could Laski have known what other inquisitions lay in America's Red-baiting future. Three days after 'the Laski *Lampoon*' appeared the Bureau of Investigation of the United States Department of Justice assigned agent W. E. Hill to investigate an instructor and lecturer at Harvard named Laski who had caught the attention of J. Edgar Hoover, the 24-year-old recent Law School graduate who had just been appointed to carry out a crackdown on Bolsheviks, which Attorney-General Palmer hoped would set him on the road to the White House. Hoover led the mass round-ups (the 'Palmer Raids') of 1919 and 1920 which resulted in the deportations of Emma Goldman and other foreign-born revolutionaries. Fanatically precise, in 1919 Hoover began setting up an index system and files for every radical in America, a practice he would perfect when the Bureau of Investigation eventually became the Federal Bureau of Investigation (FBI), which he headed for decades. The large file which Hoover's FBI would ultimately compile on Laski began on 19 January 1920.

The opening report from Hill contained the characteristic bureaucratic inaccuracies, describing Laski, for example, as having failed to graduate from Oxford and having been a student at McGill. It also had the characteristic agency thoroughness, describing his work at the Trade Union College and his friendships with 'the foremost men of this country'. There is new information, too. President Lowell, who informed the agent that Laski was truly 'a very brilliant scholar . . . radically inclined . . . but not to a degree that would be termed objectionable to the college authorities', disclosed that Laski had come to Harvard with a letter of recommendation from H. A. L. Fisher, the British Minister of Education who was 'talked of as ambassador to the United States'. This first report in Laski's FBI file also provides a glimpse of what some of Laski's Harvard colleagues thought about him. Professor Monroe, according to agent Hill, regarded Laski as 'tremendously conceited' and conjectured that he was probably 'pleased with the notoriety and advertising he is getting through the *Lampoon*'. 'He has a swollen head and is not a gentleman, but he has a lot of brains,' Professor Merriman informed Hill, and 'he is eccentric in dress and manner'. Also clear from the report is that Laski's reputation for myth-making had already attracted attention. One informant reported that 'he claims an acquaintanceship with President Wilson and at dinner parties has remarked, "Wilson sent for me, and Wilson this and Wilson that".' The bulk of the FBI's nine-page report, however, consisted mainly of meticulously collected news clippings. At the time that Laski was deciding to end his American career, the United States government file *In re: Harold Joseph Laski* began: 'An English-Polish Jew . . . said to be extremely radically inclined . . . who in a public speech stated that the police of Boston were justified in striking.'

When Laski sailed for Europe on 21 June 1920 he had, at the age of twenty-seven and after only six years as an academic, accomplished as much as most scholars do in a lifetime. He had published three important books, half a dozen frequently cited articles in learned journals and law reviews, and over thirty short pieces (not counting book reviews) in political and literary magazines. He had also been the subject of a public controversy that resulted in bitter personal pain and a US government file for subversive activity that he knew nothing about. More importantly, he had moved in heady circles of power and influence and, like many an intellectual before him, he liked it, even if those circles seemed worlds removed from the egalitarian brotherhood envisioned in his syndicalist writings. The taste of power acquired through his Harvard connections had whetted his appetite, and he wrote to Holmes that returning to England 'brings (I dare to hope) some very real political influence within my grasp'.

PART II

MAKING IT:

THE 1920s

CHAPTER SEVEN

'Rapidly Shot Up into Prominence'

The pre-eminent figure in British politics at the time of Laski's return was Lloyd George, who had become the wartime Prime Minister after ousting Asquith from the Liberal Party leadership in late 1916, effectively sending Asquith into opposition. As dramatic as Lloyd George's splitting the Liberal Party in two was the parallel rise to prominence in the House of Commons of the Labour Party, born in 1900 at a conference called by the Trades Union Congress which established the Labour Representation Committee for the sole purpose of electing to Parliament workers and others sympathetic to trade-union interests. In the 'Khaki' election of 1900, so called because the guns of the Boer War were hardly still, the new Labour Party sponsored fifteen candidates for Parliament and elected one, Keir Hardie. Labour's numbers slowly increased, reaching twenty-nine MPs in the 1906 election, forty and forty-two in the 1910 elections, and fifty-seven in the 1918 election. In the 1922 election, the first in which Laski actively participated, a surprising total of 142 Labour MPs were returned.

At first the Labour Party was totally the servant of the trade-union movement, neither socialist nor militant. In 1918, however, Arthur Henderson and Sidney Webb wrote a new constitution that committed the party to the nationalization of the means of production. A second important innovation in the constitution was the creation in each parliamentary constituency of local Labour parties which individual members could join, thus providing middle-class professionals and intellectuals like Laski, many of whom were non-socialist radicals, with a home in the Labour Party alongside the trade unions, a sometimes uneasy coalition that remains to this day.

In the 1918 election Lloyd George had promised returning soldiers 'a country fit for heroes to live in'. What they in fact found was economic chaos and industrial unrest. When price controls and government supervision of industry were lifted in 1919, prices rose dramatically, wage demands followed and the result was an unprecedented number of strikes. By late 1920 wages had begun to fall and prices increased; when the Lloyd George government rolled back public expenditure, unemployment rose from 2·4 per cent in 1919 and 1920 to 14·8 per cent in 1921 and 15·2 per cent in 1922. The British economy was in a shambles.

With 45 per cent of the workforce unionized by 1920, the government passed the Emergency Powers Act, which gave it in peacetime the near-dictatorial powers it had enjoyed during the war should it deem industrial action a threat to the security of the state. Lloyd George used these powers in April 1921 to break a miners' strike which had followed his refusal to accept the recommendation from the Royal Commission headed by Sir John Sankey that the coal mines remain nationalized as they had been during the war. Despite his government's extension of unemployment insurance to virtually the entire working class in 1921, the almost mystical bond between Lloyd George and the working class came to a crashing end in 1920 and 1921.

The men and women of the British left after the war ran the spectrum from statist 'new Liberals' like Asquith and Haldane through a complex variety of socialist intellectuals to cocky, clever and tough union leaders like Ernest Bevin, the leader of the Transport Workers. Bevin, a chapel-going Baptist who had left school at the age of ten, emerged as a nationally known figure, first by threatening a strike to stop the government sending troops to aid Poland in its war against revolutionary Russia, and then for his dramatic testimony before a public court of inquiry on dock workers' salaries, where he ridiculed estimates on exactly how many calories sustained a working man. Bevin produced in court the exact portions of bacon, fish and bread that had been deemed adequate. Pointing to the scraps, Bevin asked if this were enough to eat, and then pulled out the menu of the Savoy Hotel restaurant and described the breakfast 'which an ordinary ship-owner, whom we are asking for a living wage, would go to the Savoy today to have' and who would not go on to carry '5-hundred weight bags on his back for eight hours continually'. The next day, pictures of Bevin's scraps were in all the papers above the caption 'A Docker's Breakfast'. The court of inquiry awarded the £6 minimum wage Bevin requested.

Laski, then, returned to a Britain with a reinvigorated Labour Party, committed officially to socialism, and with fifty-seven members in Parliament. Its dedication to a statist socialism focused around a Fabian vision of nationalized industries seemed to fly in the face of Laski's pluralist syndicalist convictions, but a political party committed to the workers had an irresistible appeal to him. Since Laski was himself middle-class and an intellectual, a part of him on his return was also pulled towards the Liberal Party, for decades home in one of its wings to intellectuals and radical attacks on privilege. The Liberal Winston Churchill, after all, had described the House of Lords in 1907 as 'a one-sided, hereditary, unprized, unrepresentative, irresponsible absentee'. A highlight of the Liberal attack upon privilege had been, of course, the much more common-bred Lloyd George, with his famous indictment of the House of Lords in a Newcastle speech in 1909:

> A fully equipped Duke costs as much to keep as two Dreadnoughts; and Dukes are just as great a terror and they last longer . . . the question will be asked whether 500 men [the House of Lords], ordinary men chosen accidentally from the unemployed, should override the judgement – the deliberate judgement – of millions of people who are engaged in the industry which makes the wealth of the country. Who made 10,000 people owners of the soil, and the rest of us trespassers in the land of our birth?

But, of course, the 'new Liberals' even at their most radical, and even with their people's taxes, Health Insurance Acts and Unemployment Benefit schemes, never sought to overturn capitalism, or redistribute wealth, so for many on the left, like Laski, the radical Liberal tradition was too reformist, seeking only 'patchwork' change when fundamental transformation of Britain was required.

Not that British socialists spoke in one tongue; theirs was a chorus of varied voices that were as often hurled at one another as at their ostensible common capitalist enemy. It was their very variety that in some respects would make Laski, the rather stereotypical cosmopolitan European-like socialist intellectual, stand out as unique in their midst. British socialism was riven from its origins and throughout the twentieth century by differences between intellectuals and workers, elitists and egalitarians, scientific planners and apostles of ethical community. One could, of course, share more than one of these perspectives, even contradictory ones, and one could move easily back and forth from one to another. Laski provides abundant proof of this protean potential. Still, it is the dramatic diversity of British socialism and socialists that commands attention.

What is striking in British socialism is the relative absence of Marxist influence. Marx, who spent so much of his adult life in Britain, ultimately had much less influence on British socialism than native British sources. Far more important was the Fabian socialism of Beatrice and Sidney Webb and of George Bernard Shaw, which rejected the Marxist theory that saw the state forever doomed to be the tool of ruling economic interests. The state, according to the Fabians, was neutral, and democratic elections could make it the servant of the workers. The Marxist theory of history was also ignored. No apocalyptic transformative moment of revolution would introduce socialism. The 'inevitability of gradualness', the military tactic of the patient Roman general Fabius, who surrounded his enemies and let them slowly expire instead of rashly rushing into battle, was the Fabian vision of social transformation. While Fabian socialists needed a parliamentary party, which originally they saw as the Liberals and after 1918 Labour, and while they envisioned socialism occurring as a result of democratic elections, they were by no means democratic by instinct. They foresaw a socialist Britain managed and planned by technocratic, scientifically trained experts.

Less troubled about capitalist society's indignity and inequity, Fabians worried about its waste and inefficiency. Wells, who toyed with Fabianism and then dramatically indicted the Webbs for their non-heroic vision of socialism, captured their mood. They were, he wrote, dismayed at the 'extraordinary confusion and waste and planlessness' of human life and would replace it with 'a great ideal of order and economy', which they 'called variously Science and Civilization ... and Socialism'. G. K. Chesterton, a firm anti-statist though no great egalitarian, was perhaps able to express best the elitist quality of the Fabians in his description of 'Mrs Webb ... settling things by the simple process of ordering about the citizens of a state, as she might the servants in a kitchen'. One should not exaggerate Fabian anti-egalitarianism, however. With rare exceptions, such as Shaw's fascination with Mussolini and the Webbs' blindness to Soviet brutality in the late 1930s, Fabian socialist intellectuals in Britain were never apologists for totalitarian social engineering. They certainly stressed scientific planning over fellowship and solidarity, but this always assumed the give-and-take of democratic elections and parliamentary politics.

Pre-war guild socialists like G. D. H. Cole ridiculed the Webbs as 'fact-collecting drudges' who had no rapport with real workers. Guild socialists did not see workers as interchangeable citizens in a social order presided over by experts but as the central focus of a transformed society who would have power and responsibility in their reorganized industries. Power would be moved from bureaucratic national and state institutions to local sites of production. The guild socialists' anti-statist vision, like its closely related though less intellectualist ally syndicalism, never flourished after the First World War. In one important respect, however, the guild socialist ideal survived. It informed the 'worker-control' movement, which in the 1930s and 1940s unsuccessfully urged that nationalizing industry should allow workers themselves to democratically manage industry, to control their own work and their own lives, thus restoring the dignity and self-respect which had been alienated under capitalism.

Fabianism acquired a vastly disproportionate leadership influence in the Labour Party in relation to the number of its actual adherents, for the bulk of British socialists and most of its early leaders were some variety of ethical or 'movement' socialists. If socialism for Fabians was planning, rational management and efficiency, many other English socialists, following the lead of William Morris, saw socialism as about community, fellowship and justice. They talked less of class struggle or state planning than of moral revulsion at exploitation and oppression. Socialism sought not simply statist reorganization of society or economic efficiency but a transformation of ethical values, the elimination of selfishness, greed and competitiveness, and their replacement by service, love and cooperation.

British ethical socialism enlisted a high degree of Christian imagery and genuine Christian passion. There is much truth to the conventional wisdom that British socialism was shaped more by the Nonconformist chapel than Das Kapital. Henderson was a former Methodist minister and Lansbury's pacificism was grounded in Christian socialist convictions. Keir Hardie talked constantly of the 'gospel of socialism' replacing the 'gospel of selfishness'. There was a strong Anglican stream in Christian socialism, as well. Service in Canon Barnett's Toynbee Hall, a Christian settlement house serving the poor in London's East End, was an important phase in many a distinguished middle-class socialist's life, as it was for the young Anglicans Clement Attlee and R. H. Tawney. Even the man who vies with Laski as the most militant figure in the 1930s Labour Party, Sir Stafford

Cripps, was a deeply religious Christian. Its heavy dose of ethical Christianity often gave British socialism the flavour of a religious crusade. Nothing short of a redeemed humanity was socialism's objective. The 'Red Flag' and 'The Internationale' vied with the musical rendering of Blake's 'Nor shall my sword sleep in my hand, till we have built Jerusalem in England's green and pleasant land' at many a labour movement function. Any of a number of important English socialists in this century could have said what Labour's first MP, Keir Hardie, said in the House of Commons on 23 April 1901 as he spoke futilely in support of his own motion 'calling for the establishment of a socialist commonwealth in Britain'.

> The pursuit of wealth corrupts the manhood of men. We are called upon at the beginning of the twentieth century to decide the question propounded in the Sermon on the Mount, as to whether or not we will worship God or mammon. The present day is a mammon-worshipping age. Socialism proposes to dethrone the brute god mammon and to lift humanity into its place.

Much of this Christian rhetoric gives British socialism an ascetic, anti-materialistic, self-denying flavour alongside its Christian ideals of love and service. Such an emphasis could and would easily come into conflict with bread-and-butter demands by trade unionists for bigger slices of the pie, just one more division in the labour movement on the road to Jerusalem.

Establishing himself with 'some very real political influence' was the 27-year-old Laski's ambition on his return to this England of Lloyd George, the Fabians and the Labour Party; and he did exactly that during the 1920s. In March 1922 Viscount Haldane described Laski in the *Nation* as 'a fresh figure among us here . . . rapidly shot up into prominence'. It was hard work. Acquiring influence meant writing countless magazine articles and Fabian tracts, attending endless meetings and doing the rounds of dinner parties, luncheons, teas and weekends in the country with Liberal grandees and even the occasional Tory aristocrat. It required the cultivation of the likes of Viscount Haldane, John Sankey, Ramsay MacDonald, Arthur Henderson, Lord Curzon, Lord Cecil, Lord and Lady Asquith, Lord Morley, Sidney and Beatrice Webb, H. W. Massingham, Bertrand Russell, H. G. Wells, Winston Churchill, Arthur Balfour and Oswald Mosley. Most of the people Laski particularly wanted to see were older than he was, many in the twilight of their careers, and most were intellectuals as well as politicians. His learning and intellect impressed them, his attention flattered them and his wit enlivened them. He brought to the dinner party or the socialist weekend not only word of his latest book or exciting tales of important Americans but something else quite rare in British Establishment circles, a touch of exoticism. Haldane told the *Nation*'s readers that young Laski 'has a racial quality which distinguishes him. Slav blood carries with it gifts of imagination that are rare among Anglo-Saxons and Saxons. These gifts bring fresh light.'

Respectable Laski was still rebellious Laski, however. His strategic efforts to acquire 'real political influence' in England in the 1920s solidified his ability, forged at Harvard, to deliver sustained and bitter criticism of the ruling class while seeking their embrace. It is, of course, not uncommon for the radical intellectual to take an outside and critical stance, often devastatingly so, like Wells or Shaw, while thriving on the company, support and applause of the very people one has mocked, satirized and sought to topple. Magnify the ambivalence and the marginality in the case of a radical Jewish intellectual in Britain, however, and one can see that while his life strategy was not perhaps unique, its intensity was.

The disjuncture between Laski's political writings and social behaviour, once he returned to Britain, reflects the chasm between the revolutionary intellectual and the activist revolutionary. For some intellectuals like Laski, printed words overthrow regimes cleanly, silently and, most important of all, impersonally. This revolutionary transformation occurs at a distance from the delightful occasions when one wines and dines with the elite agents of doomed regimes, who themselves seem to be in awe of the potent force wielded by men of words. Words are themselves so all-powerful an agent of social change that they take on a life of their own, separate from their authors. At perhaps the most militant moment in his career, in 1936, Laski lectured a group of cooperative societies in Manchester about their lack of socialist fervour. He urged them to work for a total transformation of British life. They must, he implored, 'go for the jugular'. This could be done, he suggested, if the Co-operative Union launched an 'organized effort' to produce 'a great periodical' and new 'learned treatises' on 'the spirit of cooperation'.

In these same militant 1930s Laski developed a particularly dramatic reading of his leaving America and his return to England in 1920, a reading then codified by his friend Kingsley Martin in his 1953 book on Laski.

Attorney-General Palmer's 'Red Scare', labour unrest, the Boston police strike and his own treatment at Harvard taught Laski; 'the significance of the struggle between capital and labour'. He returned to England radicalized and convinced that 'equality has no meaning unless the instruments of production are socially owned'. This 1930s reading of his return makes sense only if Laski's college years are disregarded. It also involved an overly liberal or anarchic memory of Laski's American pluralist writings and the neglect of their syndicalist–socialist nature. But the most serious flaw in this reconstruction of his return is its suggestion that Laski came back to England a militant rebel, when in fact he returned to respectability and to 'making it'.

Laski the LSE teacher did not return to his direct-action friends of the summer of 1914, nor did he approve of the conversion by many of them to Bolshevism, the new cause that had swept through the left while he was gone. A candid letter to Ben Huebsch in late 1921 reveals the new Laski. It was the first letter since his return to the friend he had made at the *Daily Herald* in 1914. Profuse apologies were linked to his 'immersion in a new life and the really tremendous effort it takes to realize where one is going'. And, where was that?

> We've had a wonderful year, and I feel mentally as though I had lived through a dozen earthquakes. Everyone has been most kind to us and the work couldn't have been more satisfactory. The special joys have been Morley, Haldane, Sankey, the Webbs and Massingham. The Asquiths I've seen a good deal and like, but always with the sense that they are in an intellectual backwater. George [Lansbury] I have seen but little. I don't love him the less, but I feel that he is astride a ruinous policy without wisdom or direction in his journeying. Francis Meynell I saw a little earlier in the year but blood and thunder communism irks me morally so much that it was difficult to talk. The *Herald* was made difficult for me by the fact that I dislike Ewer almost as intensely as he dislikes me. My gang is the *Nation* and I think them nearer the truth of things than any other paper.

So much for old friends. Lansbury's 'ruinous policy' was his romance with Moscow. He had been there in 1920 and temporarily fallen under Lenin's spell. He then dedicated himself and the *Herald* to persuading British socialist organizations to join the Communist International. Francis Meynell, the third of the group of 1914 friends, by now a director of the

Herald, had been involved in negotiations that led the Bolshevik government to offer £75,000 to the financially strapped *Daily Herald*, which after the generation of much controversy was ultimately declined. Lansbury (and Meynell) no longer showed the way. Laski would be a critic of the Establishment from within the Establishment. His letter to Huebsch makes clear how that was done.

> I'm busy with a host of things – Fabian Society, Society of Civil Servants, British Institute of Adult Education, Labour Party et al. I have just edited a jolly collection of Burke's letters for Oxford, and written a long pamphlet on Karl Marx for the Fabians. Now I am settling down to my book on representative government.

While the Boston police strike had not 'radicalized' Laski for his return to England, the incident continued to haunt him. A minor flap in 1921 threatened to reopen the whole affair. A Harvard graduate studying in London wrote to his faculty adviser in Cambridge (who sent it on to President Lowell) about a lecture, 'My Experiences in America', that Laski gave to the Fabian Society on 11 February 1921. His version of the talk had Laski being introduced by 'Mrs Webb as the man who was discharged from Harvard University for his action in the Boston police strike'. The graduate's second-hand story then told of Laski devoting his lecture to the details of the strike and of his discharge from Harvard.

Lowell was furious, writing of Laski to a friend that 'if he said what he is represented as saying – and it sounds like it – he is indeed a dastardly person'. Lowell wrote to Graham Wallas and Beatrice Webb to ascertain whether Laski had accepted this depiction as a 'sort of martyr for academic freedom'. Wallas replied that he knew nothing about the episode, but Mrs Webb wrote that Lowell's 'informant must have had a very lively imagination'. What she had in fact said was that 'he had got into trouble at Harvard for his action in the police strike' and that Laski then 'recounted the whole tale, including your extraordinary chivalrous behaviour'. Mrs Webb, no great friend of strikes herself, added that she agreed with Lowell's sense that Laski's speech to the strikers' wives was 'indiscreet'. But then, she went on, 'he is a very excitable person, but a very charming one, and he is a great favourite at the London School of Economics, more especially among the students who flock to his house to be stimulated'.

Laski heard about the charges in a letter from the ubiquitous Frankfurter and he immediately wrote to Lowell offering his version of the Fabian meeting. Mrs Webb had, he wrote, indeed introduced him as coming 'to the School of Economics after being dismissed from Harvard University. My first sentence was a denial of this as emphatic as I could make it.' Laski assured Lowell that there is 'not in my mind even the fragment of a sense that I was "martyred" when I was at Harvard'. He had only been happy there, acquiring precious friendships and valuable experience. All was well; he had been misinterpreted. If nothing else, the police strike revisited certainly shows a Laski making his presence known in London intellectual life.

In the first few years after his return Laski neither walked with angry workers on picket lines, as he had in Lawrence with Mrs Evans, nor did he address the wives of the striking coal-miners in 1921 about mammon or the Sermon on the Mount. Soon enough he would speak at election rallies, but for the most part Laski spent from 1920 to 1923 teaching, writing, speaking and going to dinner parties. We know the details of Laski's re-entry into British life and of his emergence 'into prominence' from the stream of gossipy letters he sent to America, to Frankfurter and Huebsch, and especially to Holmes. While the two younger friends occasionally travelled abroad, the elderly Holmes moved only between Washington and Beverly Farms, and Laski's letters to him are vivid re-creations of his weekly routines. They are seldom introspective, but are delightfully colourful accounts of his public comings and goings, his reading, his thoughts on current events, his travels and his insatiable book-collecting with precise details of his latest coup at the expense of an unsuspecting bookseller. For the early 1920s, the Holmes letters are almost diary-like in chronicling whom Laski saw and how he navigated through Liberal and Labour waters.

Holmes's old legal friend Haldane, uncle of Laski's college friend, opened the most doors for Laski. Within two weeks of his return Laski met Haldane for the first time, and for the next eight years until his death Laski would dine with him nearly weekly. Their friendship, which Laski described in 1923 as 'by far the most fruitful gift I have had since I came back to England', was not difficult to explain. There was, of course, their common friend Holmes, whom Haldane described in an eightieth-birthday tribute (written at Laski's suggestion) in the *New Republic* as the 'best representative of American achievement and aspiration', and there were deep currents of common intellectual interests as well. Haldane, lawyer and politician, was in addition 'one of the country's leading philosophers', a Hegelian scholar whose multi-volume translation of the German philosopher's *The Word as Will and Idea* in 1909 is still one of the standard editions in English. Haldane, also the author of books on John Dewey's philosophy and on Einstein's theory of relativity, had in fact been offered the Chair in Moral Philosophy at St Andrews University in 1905, which he declined.

Laski's friendship with Haldane had a solid political basis too. Haldane was moving left. He had been a member of Sidney Webb's Co-Efficiency Club in 1903, which had brought together Liberal Imperialists like Asquith and Fabian apostles of expertise like Bertrand Russell and H. G. Wells. Always close to the Fabians, Haldane was not a socialist. He simply saw in them a desire he shared to make Britain a more efficient, scientifically organized society, a conviction which enabled him to participate in the creation of the London School of Economics. His distinguished career in the Liberal Party foundered with Lloyd George's 'coup' in the middle of the war, and in a letter to Laski at Harvard he described the Liberal Party as 'moribund' and expressed his concern in finding 'a new outlook which will serve liberalism and labour equally'. Increasingly in sympathy with the goal of 'equality of chance in life', he was, as he later wrote, 'more and more driven by conviction in the direction of the Labour Party' and to collaboration with the likes of 'Harold Laski, a highly gifted writer and publicist'. In Ramsay MacDonald's minority Labour government of 1924 Haldane was rewarded with the Lord Chancellorship.

Nor should one overlook the sheer personal side of their friendship. A 65-year-old bachelor in 1920 and deeply devoted to his mother (who died at the age of 100 in 1925), Haldane found young Laski's intellect, wit and attention appealing. He invited him to the famous weekly parties in his London home at Queen Anne's Gate, where in the early 1920s Laski dined with scholars such as Bosanquet and Einstein, and with four Prime Ministers: Lloyd George, Bonar Law, Ramsay MacDonald and Arthur Balfour. With what Laski described as 'an insatiable curiosity for the inside of events', Haldane loved conversation, politics and ideas, and at his table the 'fresh figure among us', Laski, was an iconoclastic master of all three.

Haldane and Laski were not only frequent dinner companions, they were also involved in common causes and often exchanged public favours.

Haldane's testimony to the Sankey Commission in 1919, in which he called on his six years as Minister of War to draw an analogy between the responsibilities of officers to soldiers and owners to miners, was praised by Laski in the *New Republic* and published in its entirety with an introduction by Laski in 1921. For ten years Laski would work devotedly for the British Institute of Adult Education, which Haldane had founded. In turn, Haldane wrote the preface in 1922 to a collection of articles in *The Development of the Civil Service*, which singles out Laski's essay in the volume. Much the most important public notice of Laski by Haldane, however, was his favourable and well-timed review of Laski's third book on pluralism.

The Foundation of Sovereignty was the first Laski book published in both America and England. The publisher in America in 1921 was Harcourt, Brace and Co. and in Britain, in early 1922, George Allen and Unwin, the left-wing publisher who over the years would publish most of Laski's books in Britain. Dedicated 'to my friend Roscoe Pound, Dean of the Law School in Harvard University', a school which Laski described in the preface as 'the greatest educational experiment on the American continent', the book is principally a collection of Laski's juridical and historical essays which restate the fundamental themes of his critique of 'the morally inadequate and administratively inefficient' theory of 'monistic-state sovereignty'. In its place the book again offered a vision of a pluralistic state which substituted 'coordination for a hierarchical structure'. A new introductory chapter, which gave the book its title, introduced the British reader to the heart of his argument. The state, as a philosophical conception, ostensibly represents what is common to all, a universal 'identical citizen-ship'. In reality the heart of the state is its government and 'the unity it represents is not so much the interests of its subjects as a whole as of that part which dominates the economic life of its members . . . that social group which at any given historic movement happens to dominate the life of the state'.

By far the most original part of the book was the chapter 'The Problem of Administrative Areas', built upon a lecture given at Smith College. Here Laski offered his most concrete proposal to date for a 'pluralist society' and he did so in the specific context of recent British politics. 'Devolution', not 'revolution', was the key to post-war reconstruction. The Sankey Commis-sion's majority advocating nationalization of the mines was read not as promoting central 'collectivist' state control, but as calling for a devolution of authority to the miners who would run the mines themselves in a democraticized and decentralized pluralist society. The meaningless 'suggestion box' would be replaced by an empowered worker with 'a spiritual interest in his work'. Workers with a real voice in industrial management would experience the liberty understood (here Laski borrowed a phrase from Graham Wallas) as the 'capacity of continuous initiative', which hitherto had been restricted to a small governing class.

Such an extension of liberty required a fundamental rethinking of politics that traditionally saw geographical areas and individual inhabitants as the focus for representative and governing institutions and now required seeing functional economic activity as even more legitimately the core of politics. 'Anyone can see,' Laski insisted, 'that the railways are as real as Lancashire.' Laski was not convinced that there should be a second chamber in the legislature representing productive or functional interests, ideas that the guild socialist G. D. H. Cole was entertaining, but he was very taken with the government's report 'Reconstruction Committee on Relations Between Employers and Employees', drafted in 1917 by J. H. Whitley, later Speaker of the House of Commons, as a model of what pluralist Britain would look like. The report recommended the creation in every industry of joint industrial councils made up of 'employers and work people', trade associations and trade unions, that would govern the particular industry. Laski saw that under this kind of 'economic federalism' a kind of economic sovereignty for industry would slowly replace the legal sovereignty of Parliament. Trade unions, meanwhile, would be full partners, recognized by law, in directing the economy. The joint industrial councils, however, never took hold as the way to organize the British economy or even industrial relations, except in rare cases such as the civil service, and in any event Laski would eventually abandon pluralism and the hope that the Whitley Report held out for his *Foundations of Sovereignty*.

People read and responded to Laski's book according to what they wanted to find. Louis Brandeis was deeply impressed, construing it, not inappropriately, as complementary to his own philosophy of anti-bigness and the importance of individualism. He wrote to Laski that the book was a moving defence of those who would 'adjust our institutions to the wee size of man'. In February 1922 *The Times*, on the other hand, interpreted Laski's 'wish to substitute a pluralistic state for the unified sovereignty of the present social organization' as more revolutionary and destructive, again not inappropriately, than the ends sought by the Bolsheviks. *The Times* turned Laski's complaint about the state's 'beatification of order' against the author, insisting that social order presided over by a unified state sovereignty was essential in protecting a civilized life, especially from critics like Laski so 'wholly at odds with the historic process in England'.

One month later Haldane came to Laski's defence in a review of the book in the London *Nation*, an act of friendship since Laski's arguments were intellectually at odds with the moral statism of the Hegelian Haldane. Haldane indicated his theoretical disagreements with Laski, even criticizing what he described as the latter's too facile rejection of the potential reality of a truly common will among citizens, but devoted much of the review to a neutral summary of Laski's important and novel positions, and praise of an 'indefatigable writer, with a real gift of form', whose 'energy and acquisitive capacity are of a high order' and whose 'knowledge is remarkable in its range'. The book is 'a remarkable success', Haldane concluded, and part of the reason why 'Mr Laski . . . still a young man . . . has rapidly shot up into prominence'.

At a Queen Anne's Gate dinner in 1920 Haldane introduced Laski to Sir John Sankey and the two soon became friends. Sankey, aged fifty-four, was like Haldane an older bachelor when Laski befriended him, but he was politically and socially less eminent. He had been made a High Court judge in 1914 after a legal career specializing in workmen's compensation cases. Generally regarded as a moderate Tory, Sankey surprised many with the definitiveness of his tie-breaking recommendation as Chairman of the Coal Commission in 1919. As with Haldane, the 1920s found Sankey also moving towards Labour. In his extensive correspondence with Laski during these years Sankey described him as 'one of the best missionaries for the cause I have at heart'. He hoped one of Laski's books in 1925 'will become a text-book for our young men'. Once admitted into the inner circle of Labour as he was at the end of the decade, Sankey remained on the right of the party. Still, Laski stayed close to Sankey, dining with him frequently while often being consulted by Sir John on legal and political matters. Though one suspects some exaggeration in a Laski note suggesting that 'since I came home from America nothing has meant quite so much to me as your friendship', it is clear that Laski was genuinely fond of Sankey, the miners' hero of 1919.

Asquith was another older man that Laski met at Haldane's and befriended. His relationship with Asquith was more complicated. They met in early 1921. Elected to Parliament in 1886, Asquith was unseated in the election of 1918, re-elected in 1920 and defeated again in 1924. In February 1921, in a letter to a friend, Asquith gave a vivid sense of the impression Laski made on him.

> And a newcomer called Laski – a Polish Jew by origin, but educated at New College, Oxford, and since then for five years a lecturer at Harvard in America, and now at the London School of Economics. He is by way (ostensibly) of being attached to the Labour Party, but is not far from what you and I regard as the political kingdom of heaven. He is a really clever creature, and talked brilliantly ... of ... the Webbs: also of President Wilson of whom he saw a good deal, with eyes of ever-growing disillusion. He quoted a good remark of William James (brother of Henry) the Harvard philosopher, who said of Bryce: 'To him all facts alike are born free and equal.'

Laski saw a good deal of the Asquiths in the early 1920s at Haldane's and at Margot Asquith's dinner parties and luncheons. The former Prime Minister was then chairman of a Royal Commission studying Oxford and Cambridge, and he and Laski had long talks about American and English universities. Captivated by Asquith's charm, his love of old books and his zest for scholarship, Laski was increasingly exasperated, however, with both Asquith and his wife for their assumption that Liberals, angry and weary with Lloyd George, would 'drive the country back to them'. He wrote critically to Holmes of Asquith's lack of knowledge during the coal crisis. 'His faults are inertia and a tendency to dwell too much on the virtues of the past and too little on the dream of the future.' Laski dedicated no texts to Asquith.

The left-Liberals associated with the *Nation*, Laski's new 'gang' as he described them to Huebsch, were dreaming of the future. His intense connection with the *Nation* between 1920 and 1923 recreated in London Laski's earlier relationship with the *New Republic*. The magazines in fact shared an advanced liberalism with socialist leanings. There was even a weekly *Nation* lunch on Mondays at the National Liberal Club which Laski often attended. Interestingly enough, during these same years Laski did not publish in the *New Republic*; his American pieces appeared in other weeklies.

Not that he didn't try, for his letters to Frankfurter note several times with pique that his old friends at the *New Republic* seemed uninterested in publishing him. That old 'gang' had changed. Lippmann and Johnson had left the magazine and Croly was involved with New School politics and a turn to religion. Edmund Wilson, the new editor, knew Laski less well. It would not be until 1925 that Laski published again with his old 'gang'.

His *Nation* connection was not made through Haldane. The journalist Nevinson, his former Men's Political Union mentor, was a regular writer on the *Nation* and had introduced Laski to its editor in 1914. The other regulars in the *Nation* set were much like the progressive intellectuals and writers that Laski had found in New York. J. A. Hobson was a Liberal economist, author of the immensely influential *Imperialism*, who in the 1920s would school the left about the crucial role played by underconsumption in the crisis of capitalism. J. L. Hammond and his wife Barbara were journalists and distinguished economic historians. H. N. Brailsford who had been active in the suffrage movement was also a socialist journalist active in the Independent Labour Party and a scholar of the eighteenth century. Leonard Woolf, Virginia's husband, was a writer and Fabian socialist, particularly interested in foreign and colonial affairs who, along with John Maynard Keynes, the already distinguished Liberal economist, was the *Nation*'s link to Bloomsbury. Presiding over the set was Massingham, whose fearless moralism had, since he assumed the editorship in 1907, given the weekly what Leonard Woolf years later described as a 'particular brand of high-mindedness [that] seemed to be peculiar in those days to Liberals who lived in Hampstead and Golders Green'. Laski obviously fitted in well, since Massingham wrote to Frankfurter in 1923:

> I can't tell you what a godsend Laski has been to politics here, as well as to our association at the *Nation*. He's a wonderful being, bound to go far and fast, as well as to be a joy to his friends.

The *Nation* had resisted jingoism during the war and stood for a negotiated peace. After the war, following Keynes's lead, it hammered away at the peace settlement's harsh treatment of Germany. Laski addressed this theme himself in a *Nation* piece describing a spring 1922 visit to France, the first of many efforts that the cosmopolitan Laski would make in the next three decades to bring the French mind and mood to English readers –

an unusual occurrence in the British left. France 'does not understand that she has imposed a Carthaginian peace' which will haunt the future of Europe. Belgium was no different, Laski wrote to the Hammonds in 1923, adding that everyone wanted reparations and businessmen feared German competition. 'You meet with not an atom of sympathy for Germany.' In the 1920s the left in Britain built up a great deal of goodwill towards Germany that would be hard for many, though not for Laski, to discard in the 1930s.

What particularly fuelled the passion of the *Nation* set at the time of Laski's return was hatred of Lloyd George. There was fury at his government's repressive response to Irish unrest in 1920 and 1921. England, the *Nation* claimed, treated Ireland 'as a subject race'. Brutality was the new norm of politics, it lamented: 'Lenin has shown that in Russia; Mr Lloyd George has shown it in England.' No doubt some of the *Nation*'s animosity to Lloyd George came in part from an almost aesthetic revulsion at his aggressive non-intellectuality, his Baptist solicitor's commonness, untouched by even a veneer of Oxbridge. Added to that was his ungentlemanly treachery to Asquith and his demagogic pose as the people's tribune. His style was sordid as well, enriching himself as Prime Minister and living openly with his mistress. All this mattered, but Lloyd George's most grievous sin to the high-minded moralists at the *Nation* was his utter lack of principles. Laski's correspondence with American friends is full of references that capture the full range of the Prime Minister's faults. In a letter to Pound Lloyd George is compared to Machiavelli's Prince. In letters to Holmes he is ridiculed in turn as 'neo-Napoleonic', governing by 'momentary improvisations', 'thin-minded and uncultured', and 'dramatic and compelling humbug'. Laski even based his friendships on Lloyd George, ceasing for a while to see his former teacher H. A. L. Fisher because he remained too close to the unprincipled Machiavelli.

Indeed, it was a savage attack on Lloyd George that most immediately brought Laski to the attention of the British intelligentsia and the political elite in 1920. With the Oxford Union and the McGill speech far behind him, Laski dissected the Prime Minister in a series of four articles, 'Mr George and the Constitution', which ran in the *Nation* in October and November. The cruellest cut was the suggestion that Lloyd George had subverted traditional parliamentary practices, replacing collective Cabinet deliberation with personal rule. He was 'virtually the President of a state'.

But it was even worse than a presidency: 'For the man in the street British government means simply the will of the Prime Minister in a sense no different from the fashion in which the will of France under the Second Empire meant the will of Napoleon III.' No matter that such a comparison might elude the typical man in the street, Laski also felt no restraint in making equally exaggerated claims, tarring the Prime Minister with comparisons to George III and Henry VIII as well. 'Personal control is the essence of his ambition. Personal control is the law of his being.' When government is made 'the instrument of private ambition it ceases either to inspire or to instruct'. Even more was at stake, for these were times of great crisis when the 'capitalist system has largely broken down' and 'a new economic equilibrium must be discovered'. The bitter mood of industrial and political crisis stood behind Laski's final cut at the Prime Minister. Readers of the *Nation* on 20 November must have wondered who this merciless Harold J. Laski was, tearing into the head of the Coalition government. Only a very few could know how these views had, in fact, moderated from previously held ones.

> It is the tragedy of our present situation that Mr Lloyd George . . . has not only deserted principle, he has rendered ineffective the institutions by which principles are translated into substance. The result is the frank declaration by many of a disbelief in the process of reason, the announcement that violence is the path to attainment, the proclamation that all avenues of peace are to be suspected. Direct action is the only method left open for men to whom the channels of constitutional action are deliberately closed. Men to whom the uselessness of Parliament is so obviously proclaimed will not be easily induced to trust their prospects to its operations . . . Of such a policy the end, if it be consistently pursued, can only be revolution . . . The Prime Minister seeks to array against the forces of reasoned change all ignorance that is capable to seduction and all interests that admit of purchase. It is upon his shoulders that the responsibility for the outcome must lie . . . He seems determined to sacrifice upon the altar of his private ambition the whole spirit of our public life.

Sentiments such as these did not please the Rowntree family, the Quaker chocolate manufacturers who owned the *Nation*. In January 1923 they eased Massingham out of his editorship and sold the magazine to a group of non-leftist Liberal intellectuals headed by Keynes. The *Nation* carried on until 1930, when it was absorbed by the *New Statesman*. Laski and

Hammond remained loyal to Massingham and refused to have any more dealings with Keynes's *Nation*. Laski, in fact, worked throughout 1923 trying to launch a new left-wing weekly with Massingham as editor. H. G. Wells was enlisted for financial support, and unsuccessful efforts were made by Laski to purchase the *Clarion* and the *New Age*. Massingham died in 1924 and in 1926 Asquith resigned from his leadership of the Liberal Party, replaced by a rehabilitated Lloyd George. Most of the former *Nation* 'gang' found a home in the Labour Party while Keynes and the *Nation* supported a transformed, albeit tiny, Liberal Party, open to new ideas of economic planning. Laski, himself, moved into the Labour Party while noting the historic and personal moment of his Liberal phase with his ultimate compliment. He dedicated his 1924 edition of the famous sixteenth-century defence of liberty *Vindiciae Contra Tyrannos* 'to my colleagues on the *Nation* with thanks for three pleasant years of service in a great fellowship'.

Laski's permanent move to the Labour Party was facilitated by his parallel involvement with the Webbs and the Fabian Society. By 1920 the Webbs were no longer involved in the day-to-day operation of the LSE, which, along with the *New Statesman*, Beatrice Webb referred to as one of 'her children'. As he saw more of them Laski wrote to Holmes of how he liked their 'generosity, enthusiasm, and scholarship'. Few 'were so willing to do for others as they do'. In his letters he also described their eccentricities. Beatrice was a strange mixture of scientific commitment and religious mysticism. Sidney, very much like himself, could read and master several hundred pages an hour, yet, unlike Laski, he seemed devoid of emotional intensity and feeling. A cultural philistine who had never gone to university, Sidney Webb was the efficient civil servant and man of pure reason. Again unlike Laski, who was constantly sick and aware of his body, Sidney seemed to have no body, claiming never to have had a headache or indigestion in his life.

Sidney had been a member of the National Executive Committee of the Labour Party since 1915 and was elected to Parliament in 1922 at the age of sixty-three. Beatrice saw her role as being not only to write her books but to bring together and preside socially over the various strands of the younger generation of socialist intellectuals. She did this in London at evenings at home that were characterized by a fabled and nearly ascetic spareness of food and drink and an equally fabled abundance of talk. On country weekends the austere amenities and flowing talk were combined with obligatory hearty hikes. On these visits it was almost as if a great struggle took place for Laski's socialist soul. He was clearly being pulled to the Fabian ideal of expertise, reason, science, middle-class respectability and faith in bureaucracy and away from what G. D. H. Cole and his wife Margaret still represented at these gatherings, the counter-ideal of emotion, impulse, bohemianism, anarchism and suspicion of meritocracy and civil servants. Fabianism has recently been described by Maurice Cranston as having 'purged socialism of its romanticism', and in some respects the Webbs were helping to put a final end to the 'madly brave' Laski. Like so many others, the Webbs were immediately impressed with Laski, though not without a perceptive sense of his flaws. Beatrice wrote in her *Diary* that of all the young intellectuals who visited her

> Laski is the most brilliant ... He attracts me by his lively talk, witty epigrammatic gossip, not distinguished for accuracy, and his extraordinary range of intellectual interests and book knowledge. He knows, or says he knows, everyone of importance; his sympathies and likings are volatile; he scoffs at the Labour leaders, dismisses the Asquith–Grey combination with scorn and hates Lloyd George ... He is anti-Guild Socialist, dislikes the Cole set intensely, an antagonism which perhaps makes him sympathetic to our standpoint.

The Webbs became something of a set of patrons for Laski. They invited him to dinner early in 1923 to meet the leaders of the Labour Party, and when there was discussion of publishing a new set of *Fabian Essays* they insisted in a letter to Shaw that Laski 'had to be involved'. They relied on his judgement, too, at one point delaying a publishing decision until 'we will see what Laski says'. Beatrice showed him drafts of radio talks and books for his comments and Laski was frank in his appraisal. On one occasion she wrote in her *Diary* that he 'pricked the bubble', causing her to 'recover my sanity about the book'. Laski did other favours too. After the 1922 election, which had brought so many new Labour members to Parliament, the Webbs prevailed upon Laski to hold 'educational' lunches at the LSE for several trade-union MPs representing working-class Yorkshire constituencies who were 'very eager to learn'.

An important aspect of Laski's appeal to friends and colleagues in Britain was his American connections. He was forever introducing them to

American visitors or giving travellers letters of introduction to Holmes or Brandeis. One understands, then, the pleasure with which Sidney Webb wrote to Beatrice of a substantial donation to the Fabian Society arranged by 'Laski [who] has seen Mrs Elmhirst [who] has still 12 million dollars!' Mrs Elmhirst was Dorothy Straight, who had married an idealistic British graduate student at Cornell, Leonard Elmhirst, and with her new husband had moved to England, where the two of them founded Dartington Hall, soon to be the famous progressive coeducational boarding school. It was the second time Laski had asked her for money; there would be yet a third.

It was, in fact, Laski's indefatigable work for the Fabian Society, another of their 'children', that both endeared him to the Webbs and brought him early and important notice after his return. A study of the Fabian archives from the autumn of 1920 reveals clearly how Laski, as Haldane put it, 'shot up into prominence'. His name is everywhere. He served on virtually every Fabian sub-committee: the publishing committee, the educational committee, and from the spring of 1921 the executive committee, on which he sat, often as chairman, until 1936. He also participated in Fabian summer schools, serving as 'director' of various weeks in 1922 and 1924. In the early 1920s it was usually Laski who organized and chose the six programmes for the famous Fabian lecture series held at Kingsway Hall. The series, which had begun in 1911 when the Webbs organized a debate between G. K. Chesterton and George Bernard Shaw, continued until the early 1930s, producing both needed revenue and vital publicity. Laski was often himself the featured Fabian lecturer.

As important as his organizational work was within the Fabian Society, even more important, certainly for his visibility, were Laski's publications for the society, his 'Fabian tracts'. Here, too, he was tireless. Laski could always be counted on to do his share and more in his unique combination of selfless service to the left and putting himself forward to be at 'centre stage'. During the 1920s no one wrote more 'Fabian tracts' than Laski. *The State in the New Social Order* had the honour of being tract No. 200 in December 1922. It carried a commemorative preface and the notice that since 1884 over 2,775,000 tracts had been sold first for one penny and in recent years for two pence. *The State in the New Social Order* introduced the difficult balancing act that Laski would stick to throughout the decade, the integration of the Fabian statist model and a continued but modified pluralist emphasis on decentralization and federalism. He advocated the nationalization of coal, power, transport and land, to be achieved gradually through reasoned parliamentary deliberation. In the pamphlet Laski for the first time accepted the notion that the state need not always serve dominant economic interests. Sounding not unlike the hybrid of New-Liberalism and socialism out of which Fabianism grew, Laski wrote that a reformed state could even be a moral state providing a minimum basis for a civilized and secure well-being of all citizens, where a 'spirit of service' replaced a 'spirit of acquisitiveness'. The older pluralist focus remained in his argument for democratization of industrial control and for decentralization of political control. Parliament would legislate only fundamental rules and regulations that related to issues of general citizenship and foreign policy. Most of its power would devolve to territorial institutions of local government and functional institutions of economic authority. 'We must learn,' he wrote, reusing his earlier formulation, 'to think of railways, mines, cotton, and agriculture as areas of government just as real as London and Lancashire.' He did not, interestingly enough, mention Westminster.

In Fabian tract No. 216, *Socialism and Freedom*, Laski offered an argument he would make over and over again throughout his career, whatever his ideological shading was at the time. Socialism did not undermine freedom and would not replace it with a regimented state that denied individuality. It would not, he wrote, produce 'a world of robots', with uniformity replacing uniqueness. In a ringing phrase that could stand as the emblematic motto of his entire career, Laski concluded the tract by proclaiming that 'the true socialist is a libertarian, and not an authoritarian'. A third Laski Fabian tract of this period, No. 213, deserves notice, for it too set out a theme Laski would return to frequently in his career, often to the dismay of his less radical colleagues. In *The Problem of a Second Chamber* Laski argued that the House of Lords was undemocratic, representative only of privilege and should be abolished. To calm fears about a runaway democracy with no second body to check a unicameral legislature, he proposed that no fundamental constitutional change be allowed in the one House without a two-thirds majority. But Laski was a realist, and as a convert to Fabianism a gradualist as well. He therefore proposed an intermediate experiment in which each newly elected House of Commons would choose until the next election 100 people outside the Commons to constitute a Second Chamber, the membership to be exactly parallel to the party alignment in the Commons. The Second Chamber would then be amenable to the will of the popularly elected assembly and there would be 'no danger of its functioning as the safeguard of privilege'.

Laski's most important and widely read Fabian publication in the early 1920s and, according to Margaret Cole, 'the most important' single Fabian writing of the decade, was not a numbered tract but a 'booklet', a distinction reserved for longer publications. Laski had told Holmes in July 1921 that he was writing a Fabian 'pamphlet on Karl Marx and all the Marxists will rise up and call me cursed when it's finished'. And so they did when *Karl Marx: An Essay* appeared early in 1922. The essay, Laski's first real writing on Marx, was both sympathetic and devastatingly critical. He lauded Marx as 'the first thinker to expose in all its hollowness the moral inadequacy of commercial civilization' and also as someone who realized that a society dominated by businessmen and organized for their prosperity was intolerable. Marx was also credited with realizing that 'the real cause of revolution is the unworthiness of those who control the destinies of a people, their indifference to suffering, their selfishness and lack of moral elevation'. It was in what Marx chose to do with these insights that Laski faulted him.

Laski had serious problems in 1922 with Marx's economic determinism. To note the important role of economic motives in history is 'commonplace', Laski suggested, but to insist on it as the whole explanation 'is radically false'. The impulses of men were 'never referable to a single source; the love of power, the herd instinct, rivalry, desire for display are no less important than acquisitiveness'. But it was the Marxist theory of proletarian revolution that most disturbed Laski and evoked from him arguments which he would use for the rest of his life. A revolution in the twentieth century was very different from the days of the Paris barricades; 'The Marxist view of a securely armed minority assuming power at a single stroke is unthinkable in the modern state'. Were it possible, Laski feared the resulting dictatorship of the proletariat. Power was poisonous, he wrote, and there was every reason to assume that the workers' dictatorship would breed habits fatal to a regime of freedom. A dictatorship of the proletariat would have no compassion or remorse; it would terrorize its opponents, imprison and execute its enemies, and control thought and the press.

The Marxist revolutionary scenario, according to Laski, looked forward to a new order that was too rigorously centralized and too authoritarian, an order where the citizen's 'capacity of continuous initiative' would be thwarted. Where Marx was right, Laski concluded, was in his insight that the distribution of economic power in a capitalist state makes such truly free citizenship impossible for most people, 'but it does not seem any more likely to emerge in the successor to it that he [Marx] contemplated'. Justice Brandeis liked Laski's *Karl Marx: An Essay* and told him it was the best writing he had done.

Fabians were not the only socialists that Laski befriended in these years. He saw a good deal of Bertrand Russell, and the two of them discussed plans for a new intellectuals' club, patterned on the Webbs' earlier 'co-efficients' which they variously called 'our new Utilitarians' or the 'sociological club'. Nothing came of it. Laski described Russell as 'the best mind I ever met', and was pleased when Russell asked him to look over a draft of his *Education and the Great Society*. Nor were the Webbs' the only socialist gatherings Laski was invited to. He and Frida became regulars at H. G. Wells's literary and political weekends in the Essex countryside. Wells, by then author of nearly twenty books, had made his peace with the Labour Party. In 1905 he had sought to take over the Fabian Society and transform it from a small, cautious group of intellectuals seeking only to 'permeate' the Establishment with its ideas to an activist elite of socialist 'samurai' who would replace politics with science as they took over Britain. The Fabians were too dull and too stodgy, the romantic Wells claimed. By 1921 Wells had settled down and wanted to be in Parliament, and there was talk of him standing for Labour in the University of London seat. He let it be known to Laski, his new friend, that he was interested in contesting the seat. Laski, already playing power-broker, had unfortunately worked to get Rivers, the Cambridge anthropologist and psychologist, as the candidate. Rivers died, alas, before the 1922 election and Wells became the candidate. Laski campaigned vigorously for Wells, but to no avail. That same year Wells named a character Laski in his novel *Men Like Gods*, and the circle was closed when Laski dedicated his *Karl Marx* to Wells.

Wells's weekends were much more fun than the Webbs'. There was good food as well as talk. Laski wrote to his Cambridge bookseller Firuski that 'Wells is a perfect dear – quick, agile, irrepressible, quite reckless in personal judgement and as generous as you please . . . we talked and talked and talked'. Wells required visitors to play a game he invented, a form of indoor tennis, and in the evenings there were charades. Charles Chaplin was often there as well, and on one occasion Frida Laski played Noah's wife with Chaplin as Noah. Laski, said by many to look like Chaplin, remained friends with the actor.

Wells's country cottage in the north of Essex was owned by Frances, the 'Red Countess' of Warwick, who lived nearby in Great Easton Lodge. One of the most colourful characters in the cast of fascinating figures in which Laski moved, Lady Warwick was an aristocratic beauty who had been converted to socialism in 1895 by Robert Blatchford. She had also been the mistress to Edward VII in the 1890s when he was Prince of Wales. Now, as the well-to-do patron of socialism, she controlled the selection of the parish priest in the nearby town and from 1910 to 1942 Thaxted was led in prayer by the most militant Anglican socialist in Britain, 'Red Father' Conrad Noel. When she spoke for Labour candidates at election rallies she often arrived by train in her own railway car. By the 1920s Lady Warwick was a huge woman who surrounded herself on her estate with dogs, monkeys, peacocks and socialists. Laski became one of the regulars at her weekends too, marvelling on one occasion at her 'great eighteenth-century library and Reynolds and Romneys'. The 'Red Countess' let Wells live on the estate, and from 1923 it was also used by the Labour Party and the Fabians for conferences and the summer schools, parts of which Laski often directed.

The election of November 1922, in which Laski worked to elect Wells to Parliament, was a watershed for the Labour Party. Labour's ranks swelled from 59 to 142 MPs, and with the two Liberal factions electing a total of only 117 MPs Labour became His Majesty's Official Opposition. Equally significant was the transformed nature of the parliamentary Labour Party. While virtually all of the previous 59 Labour MPs had been trade-union officials, trade unionists were now only slightly more than half the total, the rest being middle-class Labour MPs, among them Sidney Webb and Clement Attlee, Oxford graduate and lecturer at the LSE. Laski had given some forty-five speeches in the three-week election campaign for Tawney, Webb and Russell as well as for Wells, but only Webb was returned.

Several constituency Labour parties had asked him to be their candidate, Laski told Holmes, but he turned them down because it was more important to be a teacher and thinker, more important to write than live a life of active politics. His explanations to Frankfurter also cited his inability to tolerate the physical strain of nursing a constituency and running a campaign. When his correspondence with Holmes was published thirty years later, more than one reviewer and political columnist took exception to Laski's claims about these offers and described them as characteristic Laski myth-making. However, as with many Laski boasts, there is some truth here, less lies than exaggeration. Sidney Webb did suggest he seek a parliamentary career and he assured him of easy adoption by a Labour constituency party. One heavily mining constituency, where Laski did a good deal of adult education work, also sounded him out as a possible candidate. Laski was, in fact, a very appealing prospect. The overwhelming number of potential Labour candidates were still trade unionists in the 1920s and the parliamentary party was hungry for talented middle-class professionals, especially good speakers who could hold their own in the House of Commons. No wonder, then, that in the intensely small and centralized political world that was (and is) the British party system Laski would have seemed so attractive a candidate for Parliament in the early 1920s. For the next three decades Laski continued to resist urgings that he enter Parliament. It was important for him, however much political influence he might seek or achieve, to maintain some sense of being an outsider. He wanted both worlds: the insider's thrill of influencing events, and the outsider's capacity to criticize and dissent. It was a dual posture that would endlessly irritate party regulars.

Laski continued to write for American publications about British politics, reinforcing a practice he had begun at Harvard, of interpreting Britain and its politics for the American intelligentsia and the American left. Between September 1920 and December 1921 alone, a period of great industrial unrest in Britain, Laski wrote three pieces for the American *Nation* and ten for the *Survey*, a Chicago-based progressive weekly, edited by Paul Kellogg and Jane Adams and devoted principally to articles on social service, social work and 'movements of our time'. His American articles repeated the same apocalyptic concerns with the same journalistic colour that he used in letters to Holmes, Huebsch, Firuski and Frankfurter. Revolution seemed imminent, he wrote in April 1921.

We count the hours until the outbreak of civil war. As I write I hear outside the steady pat-pat of horses' hoofs, as the cavalry rides down to Kensington Gardens. I have seen the machine guns in place in Whitehall; and the tanks collected at railway stations ready for action. The trade-union leaders all expect a great outbreak.

Laski's American writings allowed him to criticize the Labour Party and its heavy trade-union dependence in terms he did not use in his British writings until the 1930s. Trade-union MPs were ridiculed by Laski in his American articles as poor debaters who showed 'a lamentable indifference to the substantial questions of the hour'. Any trade-union official who had done fifteen or twenty years' service for a union 'is considered eligible for the House without regard to the vital question of general fitness'. Laski suggested that the party and the unions themselves desperately needed research agencies and leaders 'who are also economists'. His American readers were also provided first-rate political analysis from someone whose comparative knowledge of the Anglo-American left was surpassed by no one. In describing the higher degree of unity of purpose in the British labour movement, for example, Laski emphasized British labour's much greater homogeneity as compared to the national, ethnic, religious and racial cleavages that divided American workers. Early on he made clear to American readers that, unlike their labour movement, the British movement sought to capture the machinery of the state. British labour, he wrote in the *Nation*, sought a society where wealth was 'derived from service only and so distributed as at no point to confer power over the lives of other men', and the abolition of the 'impersonal power of capital' and its replacement 'by the common direction of those engaged in service'. Such a new order would not be ushered in at once by catastrophic revolution and violence as in Russia, but 'piecemeal' and 'by instalment' through parliamentary elections. In an almost uncannily prescient vision of the dilemmas and tensions of the 1930s and the Cold War, Laski wrote in 1921:

> We have tried the experiment of conquering Moscow by force of arms and not even alliance with every sinister and dishonourable element in Europe has proved successful. The reason is simple enough. Moscow represents an idea; and ideas can be destroyed only by ideas. The answer to Moscow is not the bayonet, but the proof that the present order is capable of adaptation to new hopes and new demands . . . 'Reform in order that you may preserve' is, as Macaulay said, 'the watchword of great events'. But reform does not mean protest; reform means innovation . . . The world, inevitably, is to be a different world. We shall not long be given the present opportunity to be the moulders of that difference.

In 1923 Laski was asked by Harvard Professor Archibald Gary Coolidge to write an article for Americans on Lenin and Mussolini (who had seized power the previous year) for the new journal he edited, *Foreign Affairs*, a platform mainly for the eastern and internationalist Republican establishment. Laski must have been pleased when his piece appeared in the September issue along with articles by Arnold Toynbee, Charles Evans Hughes, Henry Cabot Lodge and A. Lawrence Lowell. In his essay Laski lauded the noble ends Lenin's revolution sought, 'the idea of emancipating a people from economic servitude', while dismissing Mussolini's as the embodiment of 'the desire of the small property-owner for security against the advances of socialism'. But the main burden of the article was an indictment of both men: 'the overthrow of institutions by violent means' is never 'likely to serve its intended purpose'. Laski's message for Americans on recent developments in Europe was that 'the path of social change is a matter for deliberation and argument, not for violence and physical conflicts'.

Although there was no difference in their methods, Laski observed that Lenin was generally criticized and his regime internationally ostracized, while Mussolini 'has been the subject of widespread enthusiasm', decorated by foreign governments and praised by great writers as well as by great men of business. Several years later, George Bernard Shaw's claim to see in Mussolini his longed-for Superman and vital Life Force infuriated Laski so much that he wrote a contemptuous review of Shaw's *Intelligent Woman's Guide to Socialism and Capitalism* in the American literary weekly the *Saturday Review of Literature*. A first-class row ensued in socialist circles as the irrepressible 71-year-old Shaw in 'a devil of a temper' came to a Fabian meeting and denounced Laski and other younger members as 'a collection of dull dogs who could not write English and did not know what they were talking about'. Laski stood his ground and continued for the next two decades to denounce fascism and its British apologists on the left and right. Fabian intellectual elitism and anti-democratic worship of expertise was one thing, but the abrogation of elections and civil liberties was clearly another for 'dull dog' Laski.

Laski was convinced that the alternative to violence, unreason and intolerance in politics, even to revolution, was education. 'We are running a race between education and revolution,' he told Americans in the *Nation*. In the years after his return to England he devoted himself to the cause of worker education, so much so that it vied with his work for the Labour Party over the next thirty years, where he put most of his energy and time outside teaching and scholarship. Laski helped Haldane to found the British Institute for Adult Education (BIAE) in late 1920, and from 1921 to 1930 he served continuously as its sole vice-chairman. Haldane had been a patron of worker education since 1903, when his friend Albert Mansbridge established the Workers' Education Association (WEA), which brought university teachers to work-sites around Britain for tutorials and lecture series. The WEA flourished under Mansbridge and its two subsequent leaders, William Temple, the future Archbishop of Canterbury, and R. H. Tawney, Laski's LSE colleague who served as the WEA president from 1928 to 1943. Haldane's skills were administrative and when he was out of office during the war he conceived of the BIAE to handle the wider organizational and academic aspects of workers' education, sponsor annual conferences on worker education and publish a journal which became a clearing house for ideas and innovation in the field. Haldane's ability to raise money also made the BIAE the conduit through which both private and government funding flowed to worker education. Laski evolved into Haldane's right-hand man in the BIAE, helping to organize conferences, writing papers and doing studies on the state of worker education as well as its philosophy. In 1928, the year of Haldane's death, Laski was the principal figure behind a fund drive to raise £100,000 for worker education as a commemoration to Haldane. The pioneering work in worker education of Mansbridge, Temple, Tawney, Haldane, Sankey and Laski before and after the First World War produced a moving success story. The 26,400 workers participating in education courses in 1924 grew to 750,000 at the eve of the Second World War when a staggering 87 per cent of all British labourers had done some studies in their working career.

Laski was more than an administrator of and spokesman for workers' education: he did it. He worked tirelessly over the years in actually teaching tutorials and giving lectures to workers around the country. He made weekend teaching trips several times a year, but his favourite trip was taken every September for the better part of two decades to the mining community of Ashington in Northumberland. He gave four lectures and 'talked each night with them until the dawn came'. He became the miners' friend; 'The dozen fellows I know best are all around sixty . . . [who] every Friday for thirty-six years have met to read and discuss a book. They argue grimly with text and counter-text and you have to know your piece to get by them.' Laski was moved by the workers' eagerness to learn about politics, economics, history and even philosophy. 'If they are ready,' he once told an LSE student, 'to devote some of their limited leisure to study after they've done a day's work, I ought to be willing to do what I can to help them.' There were, of course, awkward moments when the professor visited miners' cottages. A student who once accompanied him told of an invitation to high tea by a miner whose wife would not join them for the meal she had prepared. Laski refused to eat until she, too, sat down. 'Of course it did no good; all he did was embarrass everyone beyond belief.'

Laski wrote a good deal about the ideals and philosophy of worker education in his long career and it is clear that at different times he shared each of its several and often conflicting objectives. He agreed with William Temple, who saw education ending the worker's 'spiritual and mental slavery'. As did many on the left in his day, Laski wanted workers to have access to, as he put it, all 'the spiritual riches life can offer, its art, its literature, its science, its music', the cultural heritage which 'gave life its grace, dignity and fullness'. On other occasions he described worker education in instrumental terms of acquiring skills and enabling self-improvement as well as self-realization. Moreover, since the working class through its representatives was eventually going to attain political power, it needed to be a class of educated and enlightened citizens.

Laski was thus committed to the empowerment aspects of workers' education. A favourite quotation that he used frequently was from a trade-union magazine of 1850: 'Get knowledge, and in getting knowledge you get power.' He was less at odds, then, with the 'Pleb League' and its National Council of Labour Colleges than were most of his middle-class colleagues in the WEA. and the BIAE. This more Marxist and truly working-class approach to workers' education refused to take any govern-ment, foundation or university funding as too tainted by capitalism and only accepted money from trade unions. Its vision of worker education was schooling in anti-capitalist economic and socialist strategy, in creating proletariat consciousness. While Laski taught at Pleb weekends and summer schools over the years, albeit infrequently, his heart and his efforts were focused on the more enrichment-oriented ideals of the WEA. On occasion, in fact, he spoke out vigorously against using worker education as an organ of propaganda, insisting on 'a maximum objectivity of outlook', for 'if working-class education ever becomes the servant of a theory its merits as a movement will be destroyed'.

Not that Laski assumed utter objectivity. He knew full well that he and his fellow tutors and lecturers were committed socialists who could not keep their ideology out of the books they chose or the talks they gave, but he was a professor and could not totally abandon the academic ideal of objectivity which the trade-unionist Pleb League dismissed out of hand. The socialist part of him envisioned an intelligent working class running Britain, while the intellectual in him saw in almost Burkean terms this being done not only peacefully but in a manner respectful of tradition and high culture. In a collection of essays, 'The Meaning and Purpose of Adult Education', published by the BIAE in 1923, Laski wrote:

> The political importance of adult education lies in the fact that it provides the one plane of discussion upon which social change can proceed in peaceful fashion . . . For where men understand the delicate complexity of civilization they will be careful of its mechanisms and its traditions. It is where they are ignorant of, and careless about, the long effort that has gone into its building that they are prepared in blind anger to destroy. Education and peace are necessary correlatives; and universal suffrage is ultimately incompatible with social peace save as education sweeps the electorate within its ambit.

Laski had an abiding respect for high culture and, more surprisingly for its traditional guardians, the gentlemen and aristocracy of Britain. Whatever awkwardness there might have been in his visits to miners' cottages, he was very much at ease when being entertained by the Great and the Good in the years after his return to Britain, despite his socialism, his sympathy for the workers, and his *enfant terrible* mischief-making and iconoclasm. He was fascinated by the aristocracy. His letters to America tell of Lord Grey 'with that faint aroma of the great Whig families clinging to him which I always find most attractive'. He couldn't quite reproduce in a letter the exact moral impression Lord Robert Cecil left with him 'except to say that I went out feeling cleaner by contact with him'. Patricians like Lord Curzon, whom he met at Haldane's, were the aristocracy at their best, 'generous, cultural and spacious-minded'. This fascination with the aristocracy certainly made it easier to comply with Beatrice Webb's request to him in 1923 that Laski should help to expedite the move from the Tory to the Labour Party of Lord Curzon's handsome and aristocratic son-in-law,

Oswald Mosley. Laski accepted his charge and became good friends with the 'clever and eloquent fellow' whose move across the floor in 1924 caused a memorable outburst from the Labour side.

Laski also found the aristocracy 'colossally ignorant'. Churchill, for example, had never heard of Port Royal or read any political philosophy other than Machiavelli, and all he could talk about were contemporary plays, knowing nothing about the classical theatre. Viscount Long, a friend of Curzon's and First Lord of the Admiralty from 1919 to 1921, was 'obviously a really stupid man' whose 'favourite book is the Stud Book', Laski wrote. Still, Laski was irresistibly drawn to the aristocracy as he was to the writings of Burke, whose 'wisdom' and name unexpectedly turn up more often in his writings than any other authority on politics. A part of Laski wished, like Disraeli, that the British aristocracy made common cause with the working class against the bourgeoisie and the true cultural and economic villain, the philistine businessman. 'I at least,' Laski wrote, 'would rather have been governed by Lord Shaftesbury than by Mr Cobden, by the gentlemen of England than by the Gradgrinds and Bounderbys of Coketown.' These Victorian alternatives were not the only choices in the twentieth century, however, and Laski would ultimately free himself from his fascination with his social betters and opt for a third alternative: government by the working class or at least government for them by their intellectual sponsors. This meant, in other words, government by people like himself, in whom he began to see all the best qualities of the aristocracy, charm and altruism, but mediated by a thoroughgoing twentieth-century scientific education. All of which makes it even more interesting that he chose to remain formally outside government.

CHAPTER EIGHT

Married Life

The most important development in Laski's private life after his return to Britain was his reconciliation with his parents. At first it seemed unlikely. According to Frida, Neville, 'the golden boy' with his war wound, his new barrister's practice and the rocky early years of his marriage, was claiming his parents' full attention, so that Harold, 'the black sheep', met only Mrs Kerry when he arrived. When Laski paid Sarah and Nathan a visit almost immediately after his return, he wrote to Holmes that they did not reciprocate the 'real eagerness on my part for the resumption of our relationship'. Laski had a warmer visit at his old school, seeing Paton, who observed that 'he looks frail but I think he is stronger than he was . . . he must have a good wife'. Paton expected 'great things of Harold'.

Laski had hoped that the early visit to Manchester would produce not only a reconciliation but also some financial help in getting settled in London. But it seemed hopeless; he told Holmes, 'They've become very wealthy and my income and prospects are not on the plane which interests them very greatly.' The key issue was less his prospects than religion. 'The religious barrier was fatal,' he wrote, suggesting that they would not relent 'until they feel that Diana and Frida can be palatable even though they were not born Jews'. That was in July; by early September the Laskis had come round. Sarah came to London with £800 for them to buy furniture on the condition they move from their flat in Onslow Gardens to a house. Nathan at first refused to visit, persisting, as Laski put it, 'in regarding my marriage as a crime, and Diana as an illegitimate child'. Even this quickly passed. In October Laski received back the 200 books purchased with his bar mitzvah money which had been 'fetched from me at the time of my marriage', and on 1 November Laski was writing to Holmes that 'my family and I have made up the ancient quarrel'. Nathan had himself come to London and offered to give Harold £1,000 a year. Harold declined politely, saying he would accept money for furniture and a car, but he was overjoyed with the reconciliation and his father went 'to India happier than he had been for years, full of almost extravagant delight in Frida and me, and with copies of my books in his trunk'.

Harold told Holmes that the reconciliation was 'largely due to Frida's common sense and courage'. They had had no idea of her true qualities. In a letter to Huebsch, he described Frida as 'the family heroine, wise, brave, firmly independent ... my father full of deference to her, my mother reverent'. What Laski did not know at the time is that much of this new respect for Frida was produced by her having informed Nathan and Sarah that she was converting to Judaism. She did this because she felt that the family feud 'for which her marriage with Harold was responsible had lasted long enough'. Frida herself insisted that it had been the Laskis who made the first peace overture and that her conversion was in gratitude for that.

> Not having a penny at the time other than what Harold earned at the LSE as lecturer, money was what we needed most to set up house and home. So my gratitude was altogether sincere. I felt a need to repay them and the only way I felt it could be done was by becoming a Jew.

Whichever version of her motivation is true, two things are certain: Harold was 'dead against it', but went ahead with it none the less. She took instruction in Judaism from a sympathetic rabbi and received conversion papers which she sent to Nathan, 'who received it with great delight'. Years later she regretted her action. 'At heart I am and will always be a Gentile – a fact that Harold accepted when he married me, and never tried to change.' But apart from Frida's conversion, Nathan had other reasons to abandon his anger, and in particular he was proud of his son returning as a famous man who mingled easily with the Great and the Good. And indeed, having won back his father in part by flaunting his connections, it was small wonder that Harold would make a lifelong pattern of letting people know that he knew and was admired by important people. The political differences between father and son never seem to have diminished Nathan's pride in Harold – in fact, Harold had periodically to resist his father's urgings that he run for Parliament.

The reconciliation was permanent, and for the better part of the next two decades Laski would see his family frequently, including an annual

September trip with Frida and Diana, usually timed for the Jewish high holidays. Nathan and Sarah visited in London, as well, and on at least one occasion Laski took his father with him while lecturing in Geneva. On their visits to Manchester Laski and Frida were 'treated like gods, with a deference and politeness quite beyond words'. He felt like a returned prodigal, Laski told Holmes, discovering that the butler had special instructions on the necessary courtesies, and that

> my trousers get pressed every night whether they need it or not; the extra chauffeur hardly lets me use my legs in the zeal with which he presses the car on me and, as Frida says, it only needs their entrance into our room backwards to produce in us the complete conviction that we are royalty.

Despite the initial warm acceptance of Frida and her conversion, problems persisted, however. On one occasion at a family party in Smedley House little Diana piped up, 'Mummy, is everybody here Jewish except us?' Her grandmother grabbed her and, according to Frida, Sarah 'muttered, "Yes, everybody except you and mummy" and packed her off to bed in disgrace.' Harold found the visits not without tension. He wrote to Holmes that 'the atmosphere is so strange to Frida that I have to be, so to say, on duty all the time to see that she is comfortable'. It was 'the meeting of two quite different worlds and my job is to be the medium of adjustment'. Nor was the religious issue ever totally resolved, especially as related to Diana. In 1927 when their car, with Frida at the wheel, skidded on a wet pavement and seemed to be heading for a stone wall, Harold saw certain death and various thoughts quickly went through his head. If Frida survived, had he left her enough to be comfortable? Who would succeed him at the LSE? Why had he not finished his book on French political ideas? But more important even than these questions was the consideration of whether there was any danger of Diana receiving a religious education from her grandparents.

As dutiful a son as he was whenever Laski visited Smedley House alone, which he did increasingly after Diana started school and after Frida had made her discomfort clear, he found it 'dull as hell'. All there was to do was play cards and go along with Nathan on his charitable rounds. He enjoyed seeing Uncle Noah and there were quick visits to old Alexander, but for the most part it was agony revisiting his roots. Describing his 'annual week with my people' to Holmes in 1928, Laski indicated that it was impossible to write, let alone think, at Smedley House.

> One lives in an atmosphere of such luxury there that the main feeling which arises in me is that of the poor relation who ought to crouch in a corner. The vital questions turn either on market movements in cotton, on which my stock of information is small, or on the comparative merits of Rolls-Royce against Daimler – upon which I probably know even less ... I feel woebegone, and count the hours until I return.

The return was to London and to Frida. For thirty-nine years, from their meeting until his death, Laski wrote to Frida whenever they were separated. The nearly 500 letters are a vital testimony to their close and adoring marriage. While more frequent during the Oxford years and his trips to America when Frida stayed behind in London, there are also many that he wrote on internal trips for the Labour Party, for worker education and, most poignantly, from Cambridge, where the LSE was moved during the Second World War. There are also letters from his visits to Smedley House, his book-buying binges in Paris during spring breaks, and from London to Frida when she herself was on holiday abroad or after 1935 at their country cottage. It was not in Laski's ebullient and open nature to hide his affection. The letters are variously written to 'my very dearest heart', 'my own wee darling' or 'my very dearest wee soul'. They are signed 'ever your own loving', 'devotedly your own', 'all the love in the world darling' and 'ever your husband who adores you'.

Laski's general correspondence is full of references to his deep love for Frida and of his marriage as a rare blessing. Nor did he keep his love for her from Frida herself. He wrote in 1930 on a trip to Manchester that 'I don't think anyone can ever have had a lover as sweet as mine. Every year you seem to give me more and to make me happier.' As he sailed for a semester at Yale the following year he wrote, 'I love you today so much more than nineteen years ago that it hurts more to leave you now than it would have done then.' Fourteen years later, when he was fifty-two, Laski was just as ardent:

> I leave my whole heart with you; for I exist as myself only in you and through you. When I was in Manchester last Sunday I realized so vividly what our life together has meant and what a glorious adventure your love opened to me. I do not know the words for it; I wish I did, for if I did, I

would be able to write a book that would live as long as life. I only want
you to know in your inmost self that all of me is bound up with you and
loving you, and that your love is the centre of all I ever think and do and
feel. There will not be a moment when you are not deeply in my heart.

Frida was equally in love, and despite her feminist convictions she
devoted her life to Laski in a fairly conventional way. She worked occasionally as a physiotherapist and masseuse and did intense periods of political
and volunteer service over the years, but after their return to London she
never developed an independent full-time career outside her family
concerns. She, who had initiated the younger Laski into social ideas and
political activism, sensed even at the outset that she was being eclipsed by
someone bent on being 'centre stage'. As early as 1911 she confided to
Laski that she felt inadequate next to him, while he insisted that she stop
depicting herself as a 'wee speck intellectually beside her husband'. To her
complaints that she was not good enough for him, nor worth his love, he
replied with conventional Victorian pieties: 'You give me your ideals' and
'You are pure and lovely.' Her sense of inadequacy persisted. Even in the
1940s Harold worried about 'the element in yourself which always doubts
yourself, hesitates and leads purdah-wise to believe you are less than you
are, a strong, sensitive mind, very proud, very introspective'. He wrote in
that same letter that Frida was, after thirty years, still his inspiration.

> Please think of me as your adoring lover, as eager in my devotion and
> respect for you as when you first opened the world to me, and ever
> conscious that if I ever get something real done I shall owe it to the love and
> inspiration you give me.

In the internal economy of their marriage, however, Frida was more
than inspiration, she was in charge of taking care of Laski. His constant
bouts of flu, pneumonia and bronchitis, plus his utter impracticality, left
Laski, according to Frida, 'maddeningly dependent on me'. The reason she
gave for their having no more children was the constant need to nurse
Laski. 'It seemed that every time we thought of an addition to the family
Harold fell prey to illness . . . In those years Harold, too, was my child.
And he came first.' Laski's household ineptness was legendary among
family and friends, his grandchildren insisting that not only couldn't he
drive a car, but that he wasn't very good at cutting bread either. Frida did
virtually everything for him at home, from typing his letters and

manuscripts to driving him about or helping him to find the front door in the fog, and cheering him up whenever he was passing through periods of depression.

Frida handled the insurance and the bills. She organized their outings and all their trips. She was strong and robust and carried his bags, always on guard to shield Laski from fatigue. Unlike Laski, Frida was brusque and matter of fact, unsentimental and not easy with small talk. Nor for that matter did she enjoy or participate in Laski's intellectual and theoretical talk. She was aggressively plain, unsnobbish and unaffected, much less in awe of the Great and the Good than he was. Her frugality was as legendary in family lore as was his impracticality. She never took taxis, nor understood why anyone would, and had to be coaxed by Laski into buying dresses. Her straightforwardness led her to play the family role of corrector and deflator. At parties or at their evenings at home she persistently and yet unaggressively put the record straight. If Laski said 'x happened,' she would say 'Oh, Harold don't you remember it was y.' If he claimed that when speaking at some American university two hundred police were needed to protect him, Frida would crisply add, 'Now you know, Harold, it was more like two or three.' She was also his social monitor. Laski might be holding forth on a book or an idea and Frida would pipe up, 'Harold, they don't want to hear that.' Laski apparently did not mind being sat on and friends noted how graciously he accepted her corrections and simply moved on to another story.

The one topic of conversation that Frida did warm to was family planning and in the memories of many who attended Laski's 'at homes' she was usually in a corner talking intently about birth control with a cluster of undergraduates. Birth control became her central concern after several years' work in the early 1920s as a physiotherapist with private patients obtained through local doctors. Her practice proved lucrative enough to enable her to buy her own car, without Manchester's help, which she used to visit her patients in their homes. The pressures of looking after Diana and Harold, as she put it, and of 'acting hostess to Harold's numerous students' was too much and she gave up her patients, a move made easier when Laski's salary jumped with his promotion to professor. It was then she turned her rather formidable energy to the Birth Control Movement.

Frida had read and been converted to the cause by Marie Stopes's *Married Love*, which appeared in 1918. Stopes opened her first birth-control clinic in Holloway Road, north London, in 1921, which catered mainly to fee-paying middle-class women. Frida's concern was that working-class women should have similar freedoms in non-paying welfare clinics, which led to her playing the central role in the creation of the Workers' Birth Control Group in 1923. Her major collaborators were Dora Russell, the emancipated and free-thinking wife of Bertrand Russell, and her old friend Dorothy Thurtle, daughter of Lansbury and wife of Ernest Thurtle, a Labour MP. The WBCG flourished in the 1920s, bringing literature and advice to unions and workers' clubs, and running conferences. Its office was Frida and Harold's home, and she was the secretary. Her work often took her to provincial cities, where she visited women's sections of the Labour Party and urged them to write to the government to allow birth control to be taught in welfare centres. In the Labour government of 1924 the Minister of Health, John Wheatley, was a Catholic who rejected the campaign of the WBCG to regard this as a government responsibility and who suggested that sufficient information was available at hospitals for women who wanted it. An angry Frida wrote to the *Daily Herald* that her group had looked into that possibility and discovered that hospitals 'were neither equipped nor willing to do this service'. Of Frida's work for family planning, Dora Russell wrote that she always demonstrated 'a forthright contempt for the smug and sanctimonious arguments of our religious opponents'.

Laski shared Frida's desire to convert the Labour Party to sponsorship of birth control. He lectured frequently on the subject even to the British Medical Association and included discussions of the topic in many of his books. In the 1920s he spoke only for parliamentary candidates who supported Frida's group. If birth control were accepted by twentieth-century men and women and the population were controlled, he wrote to Holmes, 'it would be the greatest event since the discovery of fire'. The apocalyptic utopianism of Harold and Frida's earlier eugenics and suffragette passions lived on even in these much more respectable years.

As for their own child, Frida was the principal figure responsible for Diana's upbringing, though Harold, not surprisingly, took great interest in her schoolwork and was quite close to her as she grew up. His letters in the 1920s always had several sentences especially for 'Dikey', as she was affectionately called, and he invariably brought her dolls or a frock from his trips. In her adult years Diana remembered that Frida was the strict parent and the often absent Harold was the soft touch. She also remembered his ability as a bedtime story-teller, refusing to read anyone else's tales and insisting on making up his own. She recalled the times when her dutiful father took her to visit her grandparents in Manchester when Frida could not cope with visiting Harold's 'people'.

Particularly upsetting to Frida was having to spend any time in Manchester with Neville and his wife Cissie. Harold and Frida were troubled by the tensions in Neville's marriage and the obvious intrusion of Nathan into these difficulties. Not love, but apparently Nathan's zeal for the honour of such a match with the daughter of the chief Sephardic rabbi, seems to have pushed Neville and Cissie into marriage. In these years Neville seems also to have acquired the drinking problem that would plague him for much of his life, and Nathan accused him of being the source of the problems in the marriage. Harold's letters to Frida on his visits fill her in on Neville's fights with his parents and even of his brother's 'disturbed and dissatisfied sex life'. Harold vacillated in his sympathies. After one fight between Neville and Nathan, Harold wrote that 'Neville is an incomparable ass . . . What he does and says is quite unthinkable.' In another letter he said that 'Cissie is a beast and Neville a fool.' Yet, after a different fight Harold told Frida that 'Neville is not so bad; he's a simple soul.' Nathan and Sarah, he suggested, ought to give him more sympathy: 'He's stupid, of course, and unintelligent of things, but he means well.'

It was more than his brother's unhappy marriage that helped Frida and Harold to define themselves as what Neville and Cissie were not. There was also their religiosity and involvement in Jewish civic affairs, Neville having been made a member of the Board of Deputies of British Jews the year he left Oxford. Neville and Cissie were socially ambitious; and their need for a grand house, Harold wrote to Frida, led Neville to suggest that his parents move to a smaller place and give him Smedley House. Cissie was, according to Harold, preoccupied with consumption, extravagance, money and status. She had 'grand plans' for a home with 'four entertaining rooms and a tennis court'. Not only was she materialistic, but she wore too much make-up and spent dull and boring evenings playing bridge.

One also gets a sense of how Frida and Harold defined themselves from distinctions they drew with people whom they found more congenial. An example is Bertrand and Dora Russell. Close to Dora Russell in their shared commitments to birth control, Frida distanced herself from Dora's advanced ideas about marriage. In an autobiographical fragment, Frida indicated that she disagreed 'so much with Dora's book that I don't want to get into trouble'. Bertrand Russell's open sexual relationships with other women as well as his educational theories of an undisciplined and free classroom were behind Harold's comment that 'the atmosphere of Bertie's school must be rotten. Do you think it natural for children to think in that way? He is so occupied in throwing off restraint that he doesn't know the value of self-restraint.' On another occasion Frida agreed to host a party at Bertrand Russell's request for members of the International Sexual Reform Congress, thinking its concern was birth control. Instead, both Laskis were horribly embarrassed to be bombarded with questions about 'who were the leading perverts among Labour politicians', did 'he find sexual intercourse monotonous' and 'Was Diana being brought up to appreciate the philosophy of nudity?' This was not their idea of an evening of good talk.

Despite their own liberated past the Laskis had little use for the life-style of Bloomsbury socialism. They liked Leonard Woolf and found him approachable, but Virginia seemed cold to them and to have 'a wicked tongue'. As Frida put it, 'Of course she was very much of the Bloomsbury set which I disliked mainly because of their Bohemian undertones. Harold and I had our own name for them. Bohementia!' Much the same feeling put Harold off the elegant and handsome G. D. H. Cole. He was 'obviously a most distinguished mind', Laski wrote, 'but his henchmen are rather like third-rate Greenwich villagers who echo him wonderingly'. H. G. Wells was another socialist friend whose love-affairs as well as his defence of sexual promiscuity for the 'new woman' troubled the much more strait-laced Laskis. On one occasion, as Frida tells it, they took charge 'of one of his many illegitimate children, whom he scattered like wild flowers all over the place'. The girl was a companion to Diana and went with them on a holiday abroad. 'One day H. G. asked Harold to tell the girl that he, H. G., was her father. Harold asked him do his own dirty work himself.' Finally, in the range of rejected socialist life-styles there was the convert Mosley. By the late 1920s, Laski had abandoned his initial fascination with Mosley, partly, he seems to have told Beatrice Webb, because of Mosley's 'luxurious and fast life'.

In their combination of intellectuality, plainness and puritanism the Laskis resembled many middle-class socialist intellectuals and in their circle were closest to the Webbs who believed, according to Beatrice, in 'abstemiousness from all harmful, if not unnecessary, physical indulgence and vain display'. Both couples found D. H. Lawrence's writings an inappropriate glorification of physical desire. Frida, devoting her life to caring for Harold, was not unlike Beatrice Webb and her commitment shortly after her marriage to what she described as 'an act of renunciation of self and not of indulgence of self'. This devotion to Sidney obviously inhibited Beatrice's independent creativity less than it did Frida's; but since Sidney apparently had no insides, he was never ill. Not that the Laskis were totally without extravagance: unable to face the spartan fare of weekends with the Webbs, Frida would 'pack the odd bar of chocolate or biscuits' in her handbag. Harold, who fancied on occasion a piece of chocolate, an ice-cream sundae or a glass of good sherry, had the couple's only really expensive indulgence, his book-collecting.

When they first arrived in London, the Laskis had found a flat at 40 Onslow Gardens, South Kensington, which Frida described as a 'thoroughly inconvenient place which meant thumping up endless stairs'. In 1921 the reconciliation with Laski's parents had made it possible for them to move to Warwick Gardens, off Kensington High Street. Then in 1926, the year of Laski's promotion to Wallas's Chair, they purchased Devon Lodge, 5 Addison Bridge Place, near Warwick Gardens and the huge Olympia Exhibition and Conference Hall; it was to be their home for twenty-four years. Reflecting the simplicity of their taste, it was a conventional, plain brown-brick three-storied building with no ornamentation. It and No. 7, a house in which Samuel Taylor Coleridge once lived, were part of a row of seven eighteenth-century houses sandwiched between two Victorian apartment houses of five storeys. The neighbourhood was plain and middle class, though the train tracks for Olympia station which ran alongside Addison Bridge Place caused visitors to the house to comment on the noise of the trains and the ordinariness of the surroundings. Behind No. 5 was a small garden tucked in behind a high stone wall. Inside, the house was equally plain, with no fancy furniture and books everywhere. Each of the three floors had a library, and the Laskis' bedroom was the only room in the house with no bookshelves. Frida insisted on that. Laski's study and sitting-rooms were covered with photographs of their famous friends. Here, too, Frida drew the line at their bedroom. It had but one picture, a pen drawing of Felix Frankfurter. A unique feature of the house that overnight guests marvelled at was the third-floor room entirely full of luggage, for Laski always returned from trips with extra luggage in which he carried the books he had bought.

The Laskis acquired a country cottage in 1935 which they rented on a permanent basis. Located in the village of Little Bardfield near Braintree in Essex, it was not far from H. G. Wells's in Little Easton. Kingsley Martin and John Strachey also had cottages in the nearby countryside. The Laskis employed the village postman as gardener-cum-caretaker and Frida saw to it that Harold had quiet weekend retreats here. His study at the cottage looked out on long vistas of gentle Essex countryside and Frida wrote, 'Harold produced some of his best work from within her walls.' Everyone knew Laski in the village and he was a regular at the Spread Eagle, the local pub, where, according to his LSE colleague Lance Beales, 'he never played the great man'.

Where he did loom large was at his weekly 'at homes' in London. In the 1920s and 1930s these were held on Sunday afternoons from 3.00 to 6.30. Few took place during the war, and after the war they were on Tuesday evenings from 6.30 to 8.00. Tea, coffee, biscuits and little snacks, but no alcohol would be served by Frida, and people generally stood. Virtually everyone who knew Laski, famous or not, student, friend or colleague, was at one of these. There were usually between ten and eighteen people there, favoured students at the moment and important political or academic figures, often from Europe or America. Laski's father loved to come if he were in London on Sunday, and the students at the LSE considered it a great honour to be invited. Laski held forth on these weekly occasions, regaling everyone with anecdotes of the mighty. The American writer and critic Alfred Kazin remembers one such evening with Laski talking about his friend 'Frank' Roosevelt. The Laski Kazin remembers was almost comic in the combination of his intense intellectuality, his tiny frame and his fastidious dress, his tightly fitted suit, and his formal opera pump-shoes with little bows.

As much as Laski may have seen himself as an important man, he was invariably perceived in physical terms, his smallness the first characteristic cited in contemporary notices and in later reminiscences. Edmund Wilson remembers Laski as 'elfishly small' and Denis Healey writes of him as 'a mousy little man'. Lord Soper recalls his 'aggressive littleness' and the Labour historian Kenneth Morgan writes of Laski as 'the pint-sized Colossus' or the 'unassuming little Titan'. To Kingsley Martin, Laski forever 'looked like a nineteen-year-old schoolboy', notwithstanding his weekly holding forth about his encounters with great men. His actual height is unclear. On his application for a United States visa in 1945 he described himself as 5 feet 8 inches tall and his weight as 117 pounds. Years earlier at Oxford, clearly responding to a letter from Frida complaining that he was too thin and didn't eat enough and asking him to gain twenty-one pounds, he wrote back that he ate enough, thank you very much, and was fine at 5 feet 7½ inches and 109 pounds. Then, of course, there was the police report at Oxted with the witnesses describing a short, moustached foreigner about 5 feet 6 inches.

However slight, Laski took great care with his appearance. Colleagues and students describe him as dapper, even elegant. With his straight hair, usually combed flat with great precision and parted down the middle, atop his high-domed forehead, his big, round spectacles and his precisely clipped small moustache, he reminded Norman MacKenzie of a precious Dutch china doll. His clothing was always pressed and clean, his study neatly ordered with no sign of messy piles of paper or books lying about, and his handwriting was tiny and precise in controlled tight straight lines. He liked clothes and unlike Frida, would spend money on suits almost as easily as on books. He usually lectured in dark suits, and often with red ties. His preference for fitted coats and jackets led some to compare him to tight-waisted dance-band leaders. Beatrice Webb, not surprisingly, said that Laski was 'just a trifle too smart [looking] for a professor of socialist opinions'. His shoes were always polished and despite his chain-smoking there were never traces of cigarette ash on his clothes or his desk. Those who knew him at the LSE contrasted him with his colleague Tawney, who is remembered for his messy clothes and scruffy house.

Laski's striking physical appearance was immortalized in the novelist Ayn Rand's *The Fountainhead*. The arch-enemy of socialists, Rand had been persuaded by friends to hear Laski lecture in New York at the New School for Social Research. She decided on the spot that Laski would be the model for her novel's nemesis, Ellsworth Toohey. She drew a rough sketch of him during the lecture and returned even again to get it right. She transferred her drawing into prose in the novel.

At a first glance upon Ellsworth Monkton Toohey one wished to offer him a heavy, well-padded overcoat – so frail and unprotected did his thin little body appear, like that of a chicken just emerging from the egg, in all the sorry fragility of unhardened bones. At a second glance one wished to be sure that the overcoat should be an exceedingly good one – so exquisite were the garments covering that body. The lines of the dark suit followed frankly the shape within it, apologizing for nothing: they sank with the concavity of the narrow chest, they slid down from the long, thin neck with the sharp slope of the shoulders. A great forehead dominated the body. The wedge-shaped face descended from the broad temples to a small, pointed chin. The hair was black, lacquered, divided into equal halves by a thin white line. This made the skull look tight and trim, but left too much emphasis to the ears that flared out in solitary nakedness, like the handles of a bouillon cup. The nose was long and thin, prolonged by the small dab of a black moustache. The eyes were dark and startling. They held such a wealth of intellect and of twinkling gaiety that his glasses seemed to be worn not to protect his eyes but to protect other men from their excessive brilliance.

If Laski didn't belong to the 'shabby left' school, he also disdained the 'hearty outdoors' school epitomized by Beatrice Webb and other left-wing, summer-school nature zealots. Diana told a 1962 BBC radio audience that her father 'abhorred walking and any other forms of exercise'. At the country cottage his only exercise was the 500-yard walk to the letter-box in Little Bardfield to post his voluminous correspondence and his latest manuscript or newspaper articles. Diana exaggerated somewhat, since he did play tennis most of his life and usually set aside an hour a day at the cottage or on holiday in Belgium and he was not uninterested in sports in general. He shared the not uncommon intellectual's fascination with the history, trivia and statistics of sport. His photographic memory left him able to recite long lists of bowling and batting records in English cricket since 1880, an ability he often used to put down athletes and conventional students who were disdainful of intellectuals and social-ists.

While Laski enjoyed the theatre and music occasionally, his only passion-ate diversion from academic or political work involved books, buying, selling and reading them. One of his students described Laski's compulsive book-collecting as 'bibliomania'. His personal letters and several published articles on book-collecting and booksellers often comment 'on the exquisite pleasure of finding a rare book', next to which even 'the pleasures of the table and of sex are negligible'. Despite the suggested delicacy and hedonism of the process, Laski actually pursued his passion under strict market principles. He sold books high to get money for purchasing low, all the while on the prowl for the killing, a rare book underpriced by an unknowing seller. Laski wrote to Holmes that books, his only listed hobby in his *Who's Who* entry, were the 'only thing I am acquisitive about . . . I would steal for them'.

Reading novels, along with book-collecting, was his main source of pleasure. He was disdainful of people who found joy in radios and cars: only books set people thinking and talking. His taste in literature was, in fact, not all that cerebral. He read lots of detective stories, especially those written by Agatha Christie, John Buchan and Philip MacDonald. He read widely in American literature, tending again to prefer the traditional: Melville, Hawthorne, Cather and Sinclair Lewis. But his favourite author was Trollope. Why this most traditional apologist for the organic and hierarchical order of gentlemanly Victorian England, anti-Semitic as well, was unclear, just as was Laski's fascination with Burke. Both preferences speak vividly, however, to his love–hate ambivalence towards the English ruling classes. His passion for Trollope also reflected his distaste for the modernist impulse. Laski found Joyce's *Ulysses* incomprehensible. Neither his taste nor his patience extended to any 'damn Joyceism or Eliotism or any of those new modern patterns which I find so abhorrent'. Laski had problems with Dos Passos's delight with 'too much fornication', and like many on the left he dismissed the modern novel's preoccupation with 'minute psychological analysis of the fantastic or the insignificant which I regard as a real waste of time'. Politically radical, Laski was socially and culturally conventional.

> I would not exchange his [Trollope's] quiet pokes at the life about him for all the psychoanalytic modernities that were ever written; and your Proust and Sherwood Anderson with men who want blue women or pass their lives in finding sexual explanations for every cough they utter aren't fit to hold a candle to him. Take D. H. Lawrence whom one is taught to call a genius and compare any novel of his with one of Trollope's.

Laski's patterns of work and habits were as precisely organized as Trollope's. From October to December his days were spent teaching, seeing students and attending academic or political meetings. Saturday afternoon was always for book-buying. Evenings were devoted to meetings again, or dinner parties. On free nights Laski and Frida might play the pianola or, much more likely, Laski would write in his study till about ten, not at his desk, but sitting in a soft chair with a special writing board surrounding him and resting on the arms of the chair. As he wrote he smoked, of course, and usually there would be a Benzedrine inhaler warming up near the gas fire for his asthma and other respiratory problems. At ten it was usually to bed with a novel. Late December and much of January were free with a week customarily spent in Manchester or Belgium or both. February and most of March were high university and political seasons, and April was usually free. In the 1920s April invariably found Laski in Paris, often with a group of LSE colleagues on book-buying binges. In the 1930s April was the month he usually went to America for his lectures at the New School and elsewhere. May, June and a good deal of July were devoted to teaching and politics, and then six or more weeks for holidays, sometimes abroad or in Cornwall or Essex. Holidays, of course, tended to be the time for serious writing, with breaks for tennis and his favourite game, Monopoly, and September normally involved worker-education lecturing and again a visit to Manchester or Belgium. Laski wrote with a pen on a large pad of paper and the prose flowed in what was usually the first and final draft. Often he wrote from no notes and with no books to help. Friends recall him excusing himself at parties or social weekends for half an hour and returning with a completed article for the American weeklies or the *Daily Herald*. Frankfurter remembers being with Laski when he wrote a piece for *Foreign Affairs* 'as fast as his pen could move across the page'. His lectures and public speeches, delivered in his unique accent shaped by Manchester, Oxford and America, were also precisely structured and beautifully organized with no rambling, no 'ers' and no 'ums'. Listeners marvelled that his speeches seemed to be delivered in perfect paragraphs.

Not everything about Laski's character and personality was consistent, however. While he could recite by heart the three leaders of the morning's *Times* or repeat flawlessly whole pages of texts or novels, he was forgetful and classically absent-minded in personal matters and legendary in his capacity to misplace things. To Huebsch he sheepishly admitted that he had lost the book contracts that Viking Press had sent him or, even worse, royalty statements and cheques. Anne Bohm, secretary of the LSE's Graduate School in the 1940s, remembers Laski frequently asking, 'Anne, did I really have a student so-and-so? Did I promise this or that? Did I have an appointment at such and such a time?'

A more fundamentally paradoxical aspect of Laski's personality was that this methodical man, so measured and controlled in many areas of his life, endeared himself to so many people with his spontaneity, ebullience, warmth, generosity and even flamboyance. For A. L. Rowse, the leftist historian and poet, Laski was 'as lively as a buzzing bee'. Rebecca West captured the consensus on Laski when she wrote that he was 'full of vitality' and 'not at all a stuffed shirt'. He was for her 'the kindest man alive'; indeed, 'one can warm one's hands at his heart'. Public Laski often annoyed and enraged people; private Laski endeared himself to virtually everyone his life touched. It was partly his very American irreverence and lack of pomposity. While he might have been overly impressed with the power and status of others, he seemed himself to be utterly free of pretentiousness and snobbery. His students during the war remember, for example, Laski having no problem sharing the one bathroom in their digs with student boarders. While newspapers and Labour Party colleagues often referred to him as Professor Laski, he aggressively insisted that people 'not put titles to my name'. The articles he wrote for the popular press, he insisted be merely bylined Harold J. Laski, with no Professor attached. Intellectual elitist he may have been in aspects of his social theory, but he was utterly egalitarian in his personal relations. Anne Bohm has observed that no one on the faculty at the LSE was as close to and beloved by the porters and the administrative staff as Laski.

Much the most important feature of his character that endeared Laski to others was his generosity. If anyone asked for help – for a cause, an article, an individual, money – Laski gave. Morgan Phillips, for many years the Secretary of the Labour Party, noted that all he had to do was call Laski on behalf of the party and 'in hours he did prodigious tasks of research and reporting'. From 1932 on Laski gave time, energy and a good deal of money to help to relocate academic victims of Nazism. Years later George Wolf, by then a chemistry professor at the Massachusetts Institute of Technology, would recount how Laski arranged weekly money for him in London to enable him to finish his degree. The £31 that Laski gave the mother of a gifted but poor Jewish student to purchase a uniform for the City of London School would be remembered as the turning-point in his rags-to-riches career. Laski's generosity could focus on eminence as well.

He gave as a gift to the National Library of France a large collection of eighteenth-century letters to honour the courage of his friend Léon Blum, the great socialist statesman, who had been interned in a Nazi concentration camp, and for ten years Laski gave the LSE £30 twice yearly for the purchase of library books in honour of Sidney and Beatrice Webb.

It was, in fact, the LSE that was the focus of much of his generosity. Tales abound about his financial gifts over the years to students, usually from India and Africa, or of his finding books on his Saturday forays to Charing Cross Road that were appropriate for the topic of a student working with him. Colleagues tell stories about Laski calling the parents of students when they were ill or depressed or of his exceptional kindness to the widow and family of Allyn Young, a brilliant young American economics lecturer at the School, who died suddenly in 1929. What Laski's colleagues didn't know is that his LSE personnel file contains copies of numerous letters to the college accountant committing himself to pay fees and charges for various students and usually requesting that the costs be deducted from his salary. Few colleagues knew anything of Laski's generosity to other LSE staff, either.

Not that everyone sang Laski's praises. He would have, of course, legions of public political critics in his career, but there were also some who found him vain, self-centred, jealous or arrogant. Over the years even some who were fond of him found serious flaws in his character, often, in fact, flaws produced by aspects of him they cherished. Ralph Miliband, distinguished political scholar and former student of Laski's, insists that his sympathetic nature blurred Laski's judgement, which thus too often reflected loyalty and too great personal involvement. Student criticism of Blum or Roosevelt or Eisenhower elicited from Laski a 'You mustn't say that about X . . . he's a wonderful man, a great friend of mine', and the argument would be closed. At another extreme, according to Miliband, no one took seriously job recommendations from Laski: 'Everyone was a swan, or a combination of Marx, Freud and Einstein.' Anne Bohm insists that Laski 'could never say no to students and would promise everyone everything. He loved to be loved.' Norman MacKenzie, the biographer and another former student, is also torn in his assessment of Laski's personality. Laski was for him 'a very generous man, immensely kind and thoughtful and the cleverest man of his generation', but also the 'vainest man I ever knew, in his appearance, who out of insecurity manufactured a public ego that was unattractive, an intriguer incapable of telling the truth'. Lord McGregor, even as he praised Laski's constant capacity to help, acknowledged, using independently Frida's phrase, that Laski 'loved centre stage'. His constant love of good talk and gossip, which appealed to most, bothered some who found him too judgemental with a ready opinion on anything and everything. 'He's a very viewy person,' Beatrice Webb wrote in 1930. Years later R. H. Tawney noted that Laski did not believe in the homily 'Blessed are the discreet' and lacked in his 'impetuousness' a certain 'self-regarding prudence'.

Not unaware of this trait, Laski described himself to Frida as 'rash and impulsive', but though he 'barks a lot', he 'doesn't bite very much'. But he could be snappy and arrogant, or, as one former student put it, 'such an arrogant, cocky, always right bastard'. Laski once replied to a questioner at a public meeting who had asked what kind of socialism allows a large differential between workers' salaries and Labour Cabinet member salaries, 'My friend, what you know about socialism would go into a nutshell and even then it would rattle.' George Thomas, a former Speaker of the House of Commons and eventually Viscount Tonypandy, recalled an election rally in Cardiff when an elderly woman asked a rather simple question and an annoyed Laski answered, 'Madam, you need to buy a sixpenny book on logic.' Laski was, in fact, an aggressive speaker and writer, who tended to speak and write as if someone had just attacked him an hour earlier, and the speech or essay was often less than judicious and prudent. Typically, however, Laski was open about his own vanity. To an American friend Laski once wrote, 'I'm not coming to America, for there are things to do here which vanity makes me feel I can do better than the next man.'

Even the harshest critics of his character had trouble dismissing him totally, however. George Catlin, fellow academic and Labour Party insider, wrote of Laski's 'waspishness, vindictiveness and treachery towards rivals', of his passion for 'intrigue', his 'jealousy of near-equals', and his 'incapacity to speak the exact truth'. Yet Catlin also noted that Laski 'was the most brilliant conversationalist that I have known' and that his 'was a brilliant spirit, a bitter spirit, but for all that not an ungenerous spirit. I wish he were still around to talk to.' While Isaiah Berlin, the Oxford political theorist, dismissed Laski as 'superficial' and full of 'a certain vulgar boastfulness', a man 'too showy, too glittering, too smart', and someone 'difficult to see in a room by himself without an audience to show off for', he could also admit that few people he had known were 'as good, decent, kindly and not nasty'.

But the character flaw most persistently observed in Laski was his reputation for romancing, the telling of self-enhancing stories about himself, his 'mythomania' as Ralph Miliband called it. Beatrice Webb referred to Laski's 'imaginary conversations', which she added were 'never malicious or mischievous', Malcolm Muggeridge used the same phrase, claiming that 'nearly all he says is imaginary'. Lord Soper remembered that 'you couldn't mention anyone he had not met the previous night'. Margaret Cole, no great friend, noted that 'the tall tales were practically never malicious', and the standard joke in some circles when Laski became Chairman of the Labour Party in 1945 was that he was finally famous enough to get to know some of the people he had known all his life. This reputation for exaggeration was enhanced dramatically by the posthumous publication in 1953 of his correspondence with Holmes: as the historian Robert Blake remarked in his review in the *Evening Standard*, Laski presented himself 'as the hidden hand which guided the faltering step of British statesmen in nearly every crisis from 1920 onwards'.

Friends and admirers accepted this problem as almost endearing. Holmes himself once responded to a Laski anecdote by noting that 'I find it hard not to suspect you of embroidering – but they make bully stories.' Edmund Wilson indicated that the *New Republic* crowd knew that many of Laski's stories were apocryphal but that his fabled talk still made him a favourite dinner guest whenever he came to America. Some of his friends saw it as a kind of addiction and not only humoured him, but pulled his leg a bit. The Harvard legal scholar T. R. Powell, for example, wrote to Laski at the time of the abdication crisis: 'I assume that you have had personal, private, and intimate conversations with all the principals, and that everything will be revealed.'

Some of the time he was, in fact, not romancing or weaving myths: the problem is to distinguish when. Some have tried to quantify the issue. Rebecca West suggested in 1946 that he 'exaggerates by about 50 per cent, but only in areas where it does no harm'. John Saville thinks that between 85 and 90 per cent of Laski's stories or myths are true. His veracity quotient may not be quite that high, but charges that Laski always exaggerated are themselves exaggerated. The American reviewer of the Holmes–Laski correspondence in the *Saturday Review*, for example, questioned the many 'weekends and teas, and dinners with Shaw and Wells, with Lord Asquith and Winston'. Yet Laski did indeed have such a vigorous social life in the 1920s. His claims of a long friendship with Churchill in light of their wartime and 1945 election animosity seem far-fetched unless one knows, as few did, of the family connection. Many of his apparently questionable stories of being at the centre of events, such as the General Strike of 1926, the Passfield White Paper on Palestine in 1929, negotiations with Gandhi in 1931, were, as we shall see, deeply grounded in fact, if slightly exaggerated, to be sure. When he wrote to Frankfurter in 1931 about 'drafting an election manifesto by night', one can find in Hugh Dalton's *Memoirs* the corroborative evidence that 'the NEC met on 7 October and approved an election manifesto drafted by Laski'. Many doubted his frequent 'FDR said to me' and 'When I was at the White House', yet the Roosevelt Presidential Archives at Hyde Park have handwritten comments scrawled by Roosevelt on Laski letters informing him of visits to Washington that read 'Must see him next week, please arrange' or 'I want him at Hyde Park.'

Sometimes, however, it is clear that he not only exaggerated but totally fabricated. Holmes certainly caught him up on his President Wilson inconsistencies, and the editor of the Holmes–Laski correspondence mordantly notes that the distinguished German medievalist Von Below, whom Laski informed Holmes he had recently spent a day with in Germany, had in fact been dead three years when Laski wrote his letter. There is also no doubt that most of those lunches with Molotov, Churchill and Baldwin just before the 2.00 p.m. LSE seminar were mythological, as was without doubt his claim in a 1947 letter to Frankfurter that Attlee wanted him in the House of Lords as Lord Privy Seal to work as his deputy. Some of his stories, on the other hand, can probably never be proved or disproved: did MacDonald offer him a Cabinet post? Less weighty, but more intriguing perhaps, did Laski really play the American tennis champion Maurice McLoughlin, let alone beat him? The story of the Laski–McLoughlin tennis game made the rounds over the years. Laski told Holmes, who told Pollock, and Harvard students must have heard it from Laski since it was tucked into the *Lampoon* attacks. Walter Lippmann, Edmund Wilson and Michael Straight remember it being described by Laski in great detail at various *New Republic* dinners, and decades later Lionel Trilling mentioned the match. McLoughlin did play in England in

1913 on a visit that included exhibitions at Oxford, but was it vintage Laski myth-making – who knows? It was a good story, in any case. Part of why Laski was such a myth-maker is certainly that he was a born story-teller, a performer, an actor. He was a natural mimic and his stories were full of parody and impersonation. His close friend and colleague Lance Beales suggested as much in an article in 1945.

> Sometimes his desire to dramatize a good story leads him to an over-artistic arrangement of its incidentals. He knows he has this little foible of the actor, so he plays on it, and with much virtuosity. The stage lost a grand actor, a brilliant mimic, when he became a professor.

Others see behind Laski's 'mythomania' a profound insecurity and a desperate psychological need to be an insider, to be accepted, to be noticed, to be, and to be seen as, important. The anonymous *Times Literary Supplement* reviewer of Kingsley Martin's book on Laski suggested Laski's story-telling may have been a 'defence mechanism for a racial sense of disadvantage'. No matter that Laski dined with important people, but as a Jew in the alien English Establishment it wasn't enough. Others, like his friend Dr Alfred Cohn, link Laski's romancing to his size and suggest that the stories 'enlarged' Laski, figuratively enhancing his stature and 'heightening' his significance. Was Laski's mythomania, then, part of a never-ending quest to impress his father, to make tall Nathan as proud or prouder of him than of tall Neville? One can have little confidence that any of these efforts at explanation are sufficient. All that is certain is the universal acknowledgement that Laski told tales and that it was a crucial aspect of his personality.

Mention of Laski's father and childhood bring us to one final aspect of his personality and character: his sense of himself as Jewish. In few areas is there as wide a gap between the perception of Laski by students, friends and acquaintances and what Laski's own letters reveal. The former suggest that in their knowledge of Laski his Jewishness seemed irrelevant and inconsequential, with the possible exception of a heightened consciousness shaped by Nazism. His letters, on the other hand, point to Jewishness as a most meaningful, if troublesome, part of his make-up.

The England to which Laski returned was still uncomfortable with Jews. The anti-alien, anti-Semitic urge continued in the 1920s with the ascendancy of the old Manchester nemesis, Sir William Joynson-Hicks (Jix), to power in the Tory Party. Indeed, the very year after Laski's arrival saw many

English Jews offended that the 'Grave of the Unknown Warrior' in
Westminster Abbey, intended to honour all the fallen from the First World
War bore the inscription 'In Christ shall be made alive', when fifteen
hundred British Jewish soldiers had been slain. There were, of course, a few
visible Jews in British politics. Herbert Samuels was Home Secretary in
Lloyd George's 1916 Cabinet, Rufus Isaac, later Lord Reading, was Lord
Chief Justice in 1913 and Viceroy to India in 1921, much to Nathan Laski's
delight. Edwin Montague was a Secretary of State for India, and eventually
Hore-Belisha, from Manchester, would be National Liberal Minister of
Transport and Minister of War. None the less, even the political establishment had problems with the presence of Jews, as on the day in June 1923,
for example, when Sir George Hamilton, Tory MP, screamed out 'Jew'
from the government benches as Emmanuel Shinwell, Labour MP, rose to
speak in the House. The Jewish presence in British politics, to the extent it
existed, was principally in the Liberal Party. With the exception of Leonard
Woolf, Laski was the only important Jew in the Labour Party brain-trust
for decades. The Webbs, on the other hand, felt no remorse over the open
racism and anti-Semitism of their earlier eugenics pieces, and even as
unconventional and iconoclastic a devotee of the left as the Red Countess
of Warwick could put in her memoirs the somewhat double-edged
stereotypical observation that

> We resented the introduction of the Jews into the social set of the Prince of
> Wales, not because we disliked them individually, for some of them were
> charming, as well as brilliant, but because they had brains and understood
> finance. As a class, we did not like brains. As for money, our only understand-
> ing of it lay in the spending, not in the making it.

Laski faced as much trouble with his Jewishness from socialists as from
reactionary Tories. British socialism, so untheoretical and so tied to the
trade-union movement, was unlike the socialist movements of Europe
where Jewish intellectuals and revolutionaries played an important role.
Laski was clearly an outsider in the church of English socialism with its
cleric-like intellectuals and leaders both invoking the new day of Christian
brotherhood. His former friend Mosley in the 1930s, and the Beaverbrook
press in the 1940s, were not the only ones to use Laski's Jewishness in their
attacks on him. Laski would also have to deal with the bullying anti-
Semitism of Ernest Bevin and the more cultivated sarcasm of the economics

don Hugh Dalton, who became a force in socialist politics and persistently referred to his fellow socialist Laski as the 'under-sized Semite' while also ridiculing his far-left 'yideology'.

If, as Frankfurter once defined it, 'a Jew is a person whom non-Jews regard as a Jew', then Laski was certainly a Jew. Beatrice Webb, in her first diary notation referring to Laski in 1922, added after her reference to his brilliance that 'he has a strong Jewish racial feeling and his scoffing little sceptic of a wife has become a Jew to bridge over the displeasure of the family at his marriage to a Gentile'. Fellow Jews also clearly perceived Laski as Jewish. Moshe Shertok (Sharrett), his student in 1921, painted a fascinating portrait of Laski as the best and most impressive of his teachers at the LSE, and he added:

> He is an Anglo-American Jew, a young man, as thin and dark as a Yeshiva student ... His erudition knows no bounds and is almost a riddle when his age is considered ... He is the supreme example of the perspicacious Jew, always negating and criticizing. He knows no pity and nothing is sacred to him. He destroys but does not build anew. He is no socialist, no Jewish nationalist, just a plain Jew whose Jewish bitterness is spilling over.

Laski was a Jew not only in the eyes of others, but by his own testimony as well. His letters to Holmes are full of references to his Jewishness. He is concerned, for example, that too much clerical control over endowments at Oxford worked to keep many Jews out. Several times after pulling off a particularly good deal in his buying and selling of books, he jokes that 'Jewish blood will out'. Of Christmas 1923 he wrote that he 'had done my duty by Xmas as a good Jew should'. The American playwright S. N. Behrman's story of being saved from the Kishinev pogrom moved Laski to tears. In one letter Laski responded at length to Holmes's reference to a comment by Justice White that all Jews were selfish. Laski countered that Jews varied in character, like other people. Their mutual Jewish friends, he suggested to Holmes – Felix Frankfurter, Morris Cohen, Julian Mack – 'don't fit into any box'. He concluded the letter with his one 'difficulty with Jews', their resistance to assimilation, 'their pride in being different, their excessive sensibilities, their intellectual hubris. But I should certainly not accuse them of being selfish in any ordinary sense.' Over and over again he repeats his opposition to Zionism, insisting that he abominated it and that a 'neo-Jew like me' was 'wholly assimilationist in temper'.

Worldly and secular assimilationist Laski might see himself, but there were occasions when his Jewish soul burst forth. One occurred on a visit to Morris Cohen's elderly parents in New York. They were 'two old Russian Jews well in the eighties. Neither speaks English and they live in a tiny three-room apartment on the East Side.' When Laski told Mrs Cohen how impressed he was with her son's work, she beamed and in broken English blessed America 'for making me the richest woman in the world'. Laski was deeply moved and wrote to Holmes, 'Do you mind if I envied America that?' Another such moment occurred on a visit he made to Manchester for the Jewish New Year. His letter to Frida began with the expected cynicism: 'Synagogue this morning. Now and again a prayer – but mostly the hum of business talk interlarded with loud and impressive amens.' But he tells Frida of

> a walk with Father to another synagogue where there was a beautiful musical service that moved me immensely. It was really moving – a dirty smelly hall, poor wearied-looking men and a man with a voice like a god who seemed to sing the whole history of a tragic race.

Laski's sense of Jewishness played a part in his slowly evolving estrangement from Walter Lippmann. Lippmann's move from the *New Republic* to the *New York World* and ultimately the *Herald Tribune*, accompanied, as Laski put it, by his 'becoming the rich man's pet', helped split apart the old trio of Frankfurter, Laski and Lippmann. But equally significant were Lippmann's efforts to renounce or hide his Judaism. Laski was dismayed by Lippmann's endorsement of the effort in 1922 by President Lowell to establish a quota for Jewish students at Harvard and his accompanying statement describing certain 'distressing personal and social habits' of Jews, including their reluctance to 'cleanse their bodies', as the real source of anti-Semitism. The final and definitive end to Laski's friendship with Lippmann would not come until 1933 when, added to his republican *laissez-faire* politics, was a newspaper column he wrote suggesting Hitler's was 'the authentic voice of a civilized people'. But a clear shift in attitude was already apparent after the Harvard episode. Part of Lippmann's rightward odyssey was, it seemed to Laski, his rejection of the dirt in his past, be it his people or the poor in general. Writing to Frankfurter about Lippmann in 1927, Laski commented that 'I loathe people who put on gloves to shake hands with the working class'. Laski's tone was colder several years later when he noted after a visit with Lippmann that 'I left feeling that it was not my world ... I sat there feeling like a poor relation listening to the advice of the really successful man of the world.'

However complicated Laski's sense of himself as Jewish may have been, Frida's conversion cleared the air for 'his people'. One can only imagine the pride in Smedley House on 5 March 1926 when they opened their copy of the *Jewish Chronicle*, Britain's national Jewish weekly newspaper that was read in virtually every Jewish household in the country, and turned to the lead-news page. There they discovered as the third item 'Singular Honours to Mr Harold Laski, appointed Professor at the LSE to succeed Graham Wallas'. The story went on:

Laski, the son of Nathan Laski, JP of Manchester, is little more than in his teens. He has had a brilliant scientific career and has made himself a name in economics which is equalled by few. Our hearty congratulations go out to him as well as to his parents, Mr Laski, JP, and Mrs Laski, upon an appointment that brings credit to the whole of the community.

CHAPTER NINE

Centre Stage: The Labour Party, India and The Grammar of Politics

'We have won an amazing victory . . . a Labour ministry will be in power for the first time in English history,' Laski exuberantly wrote to Holmes on 13 December 1923. Letters quickly followed to Frankfurter, Pound, Brandeis and Firuski about how 'we are luxuriating in the prospect of our new government . . . it won't last long, but at least it will be the parent of a great tradition'. Laski took delight in noting that 'the rentier is in despair, the trade unionist holds his head a little higher'. The *English Review*, meanwhile, expressed its apocalyptic fears in historical terms.

> We stand now at a moment when the sun of England seems menaced with final eclipse. For the first time in her history the party of revolution approach their hands to the helm of the state, not only, as in the seventeenth century, for the purpose of overthrowing the Crown, or of altering the Constitution, but with the design of destroying the very basis of civilized life.

Strong words for a minority government that Laski had noted, as had everyone else, 'won't last long'. Labour had won 191 seats, up from its 142 in 1922, the Liberals 159, better than its previous 117, and the Tories were the big losers with 259 seats, a loss of nearly 100. Since Stanley Baldwin, the Tory Prime Minister who had replaced the gravely ill Bonar Law, had fought the election seeking a protectionist-Empire preference mandate and been so soundly defeated, it was assumed by all that Labour would run a minority government supported by the Liberal Party, now headed by Asquith.

Laski clearly identified with the moderate centre of the Labour Party in 1923 and the tale of the next ten years is about how and why he moved leftwards. He spoke in sixteen constituencies and at more than forty election rallies during the three-week campaign. At one giant rally alone he and George Bernard Shaw spoke to some 4,000 people. It was less an electoral victory for socialism, however, than for free trade and a balanced budget, both of which the Labour Party promised. Laski's favourite quip on the hustings that year was that the electors had a choice between Adam Smith and Lord Birkenhead and that he himself preferred 'the old Adam'. His appeal at election rallies was not, however, in his following the party line: it was his professorial freedom, iconoclasm and lack of inhibition that won over audiences, especially working-class audiences. While the Labour Party leadership in 1924 tried, as it would for the next two decades, to present itself as responsible, sober and 'fit to govern', Laski's speeches held nothing back in attacking property and privilege. Trade-union audiences loved his ritualistic apologies for being born rich or his standard disclaimer that he was 'trained at Oxford University and I haven't recovered from it yet', or, as he sometimes added, 'in the process of recovery, I have discovered that the university of the office, the factory, the shop and even the field breeds more wisdom than the university of the mind'. But whatever the passion and militancy of his stump speaking, Laski knew full well that, as he put it in an election article for the American *Nation*, the minority Labour government would be unable 'to attempt any heroic measures'. It would, however, 'accustom the country to the idea of a Labour government'.

Labour's moderation was dictated not only by electoral numbers, but by the personality and predisposition of its leadership. Ramsay MacDonald was elected leader of the parliamentary party, replacing Henderson who had filled in since 1914 and defeating J. H. Clynes in a close vote of 61 to 52 with the strong support of a group of ten militant Labour MPs from Glasgow, the 'Clydesiders'. MacDonald seemed to them very much a man of the left as he was still frowned on by the respectable for his pacifism in the recent war. But what really made MacDonald leader was his bearing. Beatrice Webb had seen this as early as 1914 when she wrote that 'with his romantic figure, charming voice and clever dialectics he is more than a match for all those underbred and undertrained workmen'. One of the Glasgow militants was also impressed with MacDonald's 'magnificent presence, full resonant voice and splendid dignity'. Strikingly tall and good-looking, MacDonald often acted autocratically. He shocked his fellow Labour supporters by his failure to include Lansbury in his 1924 Cabinet, raising fears that he was unworried about his hold on the rank and file.

Even his ostensibly closest colleague, Snowden, wrote in 1924 of his 'colossal conceit'. There were even questions as to whether he was really still a socialist. After MacDonald's legendary 'treachery' to the labour movement in 1931, there would be a scramble by many to suggest that they had doubts about him all along. Laski was no exception. In an article in February 1950 summarizing the first fifty years of the Labour Party for the *Nation*, Laski wrote that

> MacDonald was in fact an ambitious charlatan who clothed all his opinions in a mass of metaphysical rhetoric; he disliked the left, feared opposition, and was far too timid even to dream of embarking upon a determined programme of socialist legislation. He was vain beyond words and easily captured by the glamour of society in London. His government lasted just over ten months.

But that was not Laski's view during the early 1920s, when Laski was actually an avid enthusiast for MacDonald. He wrote to Frankfurter in November 1922 that 'it is a great thing to have Ramsay as leader. He's eloquent, quick and imperturbable with the personal magnetism that Clynes always lacked.' On the eve of MacDonald's first tenure as Prime Minister, Laski even commented that 'I respect MacDonald more and more.' MacDonald accepted his call to Downing Street, Laski wrote, 'with soberness and dignity and with a full sense of the arduous work involved. And he has a reading mind. He sees the significance of things like research and inquiry, and he will use the non-political expert.'

This praise could well be reciprocation for MacDonald's consulting with Laski. Laski made ample reference in his letters to America about 'spending much time with "JRM" and Webb developing policy', of dinners with Webb and 'JRM' to discuss Cabinet appointments. 'I've had three long talks with him about things and there is a job he wants me to take, non-political of course,' he told Frankfurter. He seems to have passed on to MacDonald notes from Frankfurter and Brandeis about American attitudes on foreign policy and Zionism. Even if we apply Rebecca West's more rigorous rule of roughly 50 per cent accuracy in Laski's claims as insider and power-broker instead of Saville's more generous 85–90 per cent, it is likely that at least some of Laski's claims are true, since two of the most powerful people among the few to whom MacDonald had to pay some attention were strong patrons of Laski, Sidney Webb and the new Labour government's Lord Chancellor, Lord Haldane.

Laski's influential Fabian tract No. 210, *The Position of the Two Parties and the Right of Dissolution*, published in March 1924, played an important role in sorting through the constitutional confusion created by the minority government. The pressing question was what would happen if MacDonald's majority fell because the Liberals deserted him. Could the King reject MacDonald's call for the dissolution of Parliament and the call of a new election, or could he on his own ask Asquith to form a Liberal government? Laski strongly argued that no precedent for the latter existed and, moreover, that such a step would be a devastating blow to the notion of the monarch's constitutional neutrality. Laski's stock as Labour's constitutional expert soared in October, when the Liberals withdrew their support and the King agreed to MacDonald's call for a new election.

MacDonald did not introduce 'bold socialist measures', as some Labourites proposed, because he felt an obligation to 'show the country that we were not under the domination of the wild men'. He would prove that Labour's concerns were 'national well-being', not pushing solutions for working-class grievances. Lansbury, not in the Cabinet, had the luxury of first proclaiming what would become the Labour left's lament at Labour governments' moderation. 'I think,' he told the House of Commons, 'one of the faults of the system under which affairs are managed in this House is that men, when they accept office, are expected immediately to change their attitude towards great public questions.' In fact, doubts existed about the depth of MacDonald's socialist zeal. Nor, for that matter, did the Labour Party as a whole in the 1920s, with the exception of the small group of ILP MPs, have any real coherent economic policy beyond the vague 1918 pledge to socialism. Not until after 1931, with the emergence of Dalton and Morrison's policy committees in the party's National Executive Committee, did such policy agendas emerge. What the first Labour government did accomplish in its ten months was a successful housing expansion presided over by Frida's nemesis on birth control, J. H. Wheatley at the Ministry of Health, and the diplomatic recognition of and the beginning of trade negotiations with the Soviet Union.

Laski began to see in 1924, and much more clearly between 1929 and 1931, what he and Beatrice Webb called 'the aristocratic embrace', the insidious taming of Labour not by power and force but by inclusion in aristocratic dinner parties and country-house weekends. Labour ministers, Laski would suggest in 1933, saw their acceptance by the aristocracy as 'itself a proof that they were equally entitled with it to rule the country. They did not realize the truth of the famous aphorism of Molière that one embraces one's rival better to strangle him.' While this passage also bears the stamp of his greater anger and militancy of the early 1930s, Laski was already thinking about the ease of being bought off. He described Snowden in 1924 as 'an intolerable snob'. Laski told Holmes that J. H. Thomas, the railway union official who served as Colonial Secretary, 'likes nothing so much as to be seen about with royalty ... He is becoming a younger brother to the Albert Memorial.' Ever practical, Beatrice Webb had her own strategies to combat the embrace of the ruling class. She organized a salon that year to upgrade the social skills of Labour Party MPs' wives so that they would not be overly impressed by the etiquette of their social betters. In March 1924 she refused to attend a reception at Buckingham Palace and urged her group of Labour wives 'not to be dragged into smart society'. Most significant of all was her refusal, when her husband was elevated to the House of Lords by MacDonald as Lord Passfield, to accept her title as Lady Passfield, an act widely misread as a feminist statement instead of the anti-snobbishness that it really was.

It was difficult to resist the trappings of power and remain an angry outsider. One of the militant Clydesiders wrote that before he entered the House of Commons he knew little of 'the Great Ones, the Powerful Ones, the Lordly Ones', but felt in his soul that 'they and the world they represented were crushing my fellows down into poverty, misery, despair and death'. When he became an elected MP at Westminster, he was 'full of wonder. I had to shake myself occasionally as I found myself moving and talking with men whose names were household words. More strange was it to find them all so simple and unaffected and friendly.' A bit of Laski's fondness for the socially mobile America of his friends Cohen and Frankfurter must have vied with his concerns over Thomas's conversion as he read in The Times on 8 March 1924 Thomas's claim that 'a Constitution which enables an engine-cleaner of yesterday to be a Secretary of State today is a great Constitution'. No one, however, seems to have been as caught up in the glittering spectacles of wealth and power as MacDonald. He revelled in the pomp of courtly and parliamentary ceremony. He insisted that all his ministers wear morning suits and top hats (rented from Moss Brothers) when presenting themselves to King George V to receive their seals of office. The handsome MacDonald, a widower since 1911, became a great hit with society ladies, and Laski and the Webbs both noted the endless set of garden parties he attended that summer, in addition to the braces of pheasants the King sent him. In September 1924 it was also revealed that MacDonald accepted a Daimler car and a £30,000 block of shares from a wealthy biscuit manufacturer, Sir Alexander Grant, of McVitie & Price, who shortly thereafter received a baronetcy.

While Beatrice Webb was writing in her diary that 'deep down in his heart' MacDonald 'prefers the company of Tory aristocrats and Liberal capitalists to that of trade-union officials and the ILP agitators', Laski buried his concerns about aristocratic embrace and continued to laud 'JRM'. He told American readers of the *Nation* in March that his friendship with the Prime Minister 'makes judgement a matter of difficulty', but still he thought it fair to say he 'is a national asset . . . he has vision and courage . . . a sense of his mission, a power to measure his responsibilities . . . his judgement is cool, his mind a balanced mind'. Laski even suggested that MacDonald had a rare 'love of humble men and the happiness of humble men'. Laski lunched with MacDonald several times and went to several dinners with the Prime Minister, the Webbs and Haldane. Laski himself hosted a dinner at Warwick Gardens for a large number of academics to meet the Prime Minister and the Lord Chancellor.

By October MacDonald's government, so careful not to appear radical, fell in a flurry of claims that it was too sympathetic to Russian Bolshevism and to communism at home. The trade treaty with the Soviet Union and its loan guarantee was attacked by the Liberal Party, who withdrew support; MacDonald resigned and an election was called for 29 October. Laski spoke at two or three meetings a night during the abbreviated campaign and he thought: 'We will do well.' Five days before polling date, the Foreign Office published the Zinoviev Letter, purporting to be an exhortation from the Soviet President of the Third International to English workers to spread Leninism in England. The letter, subsequently proved to be a hoax, added to the mood of Red hysteria, and the Tories scored a dramatic victory, winning 415 parliamentary seats. Labour lost 40, leaving it with 151 MPs, while the major casualty was the Liberal Party, whose representation dropped from 158 to 42. Laski noted, however, that there was a silver lining. Labour was now effectively the opposition party. 'We have wiped out the Liberal Party . . . so I remain incurably optimistic about the future,' he wrote to Holmes. Besides, there seemed a good deal of relief in going back into opposition and 'at dinner last night', Laski reported, Webb made it clear he looked forward to writing books again with 'unconcealed joy'. In fact, Laski seemed less worried about the new Tory government headed by Baldwin than he did about Coolidge as the new American President, who represented 'complacent mediocrity' and was no more than 'a natural churchwarden in a rural parish, who has by accident strayed into great affairs'.

After the election an effort was launched by Bevin and Snowden to replace MacDonald as leader of the party with Arthur Henderson. Henderson rejected the overtures, noting that with all his faults MacDonald was 'the only man with the parliamentary skill and public prestige to lead the party back to recovery'. This saved MacDonald; he was, as Beatrice Webb succinctly put it, 'the best man we've got to put into our shop window'. Though she noted that 'he is no longer intent on social reform', no longer indignant at the distribution of wealth, comfortable only in 'non-political aristocratic society', he was still 'unique in the inner circle of the Labour Party made up, as it is, of fanatics, faddists, refined and self-effacing intellectuals and the dull mediocrities of the trade-union move-ment'. Laski agreed. He wrote in July 1925 in the *New Republic* that 'Mr MacDonald is, at the moment, the only possible leader for the party.' He also wrote reassuringly to MacDonald that the thought of five years in opposition might appear bleak, but 'historically this is a necessary prelude to the greater drama'. He predicted a slow but inevitable transition from the 'epoch of Lloyd George' to 'the epoch of Ramsay MacDonald'. 'Realize that we all care deeply about you, that we have confidence and hope because you stand directly by us.' Publicly he was only slightly more guarded. MacDonald, he wrote in the *New Republic*, had to decide whether he was to address the concerns of his supporters or only 'win over the timid elector by rose-water socialism'. He did the latter extremely well, Laski noted, but he should on occasion 'immerse himself in the hopes of the rank and file'. Still, the bottom line for Laski in 1925 was Beatrice Webb's, that 'no one in the labour movement can rival Mr MacDonald in the gifts which make a leader'.

Another reason why Laski continued to support MacDonald was that he was not on the best of terms with the ostensible replacement, Henderson. For all his faults, MacDonald was for Laski still a man of books and ideas, the author of *Socialism and Society* (1905), *Socialism* (1907) and *Socialism and*

Government (1909), books which had sought to link socialism and liberalism. His home and office had large numbers of books about, and as aloof and uncomfortable as he was even with intellectuals he respected them none the less. A former Methodist preacher and trade-union official, Henderson had skills in managing the party organization, but Laski thought him 'stupid and a bully' and Henderson, for his part, saw 'Laski one more of the uppish young Oxford men who fancied they could walk straight into a constituency without any previous work'. Matters came to a head in 1924 when Laski suggested in a speech that the Labour Party would be better off without men like Henderson, 'who discouraged young intellectuals from joining it'. Summoned by the older, avuncular party secretary, actually called Uncle Arthur by the party faithful, Laski visited Henderson, who held out an olive branch to the party intellectuals, whom he claimed to value greatly. He was good to his word and it is a measure of Laski's increasing ease with a party not dominated by Fabian intellectuals that after MacDonald's 'betrayal' in 1931, when Henderson became temporary party leader, Laski was constantly with him in the election campaign that autumn. Even more significantly, Uncle Arthur did indeed become the party patron of the left intellectuals in the late 1920s and early 1930s, sponsoring and supporting their research efforts. Always the shrewdest of party managers, Henderson once told Dalton, one of his young protégés, why he 'took trouble' with socialist intellectuals.

> I think that I am the only one who knows how to handle these chaps. I get them to come and see me and have a talk. And then I ask them to write me a memorandum. That pleases them and keeps them quiet for a time. And I often learn quite a lot from what they write.

As he was trying to sort out in 1924 and 1925 his exact relationship to Labour, Laski offered a penetrating analysis of the party to his American audience. His *New Republic* piece of July 1925, for example, criticized Labour for its lack of a 'coherent and concrete policy'. It was simply a 'coherence of groups rather than a fighting unit'. He discerned three tendencies in the party. On its right were J.H. Thomas and Snowden, who were good nineteenth-century Liberals. In the middle 'is the Fabian socialism of Webb (still the main source of ideas that count) and the vague idealism of MacDonald'. On the left were the Clydesiders and the ILPs 'with whom George Lansbury and the East London members mainly work'. He was attracted to the 'charm and enthusiasm' of this last group, but 'they make, in general, for heat rather than for light'. For now, Laski was Webb's disciple, calling for light and complaining that 'the party has too many catchwords, and too few detailed proposals.' What the party needed was 'far more research' on industrial and financial questions, instead of 'its tendency . . . to have these examined not by the expert but by the able amateur at the centre of the party machine'.

Laski's political moderation in the mid-1920s is further illustrated by his friendship with Stanley Baldwin, the Tory Prime Minister. MacDonald and Baldwin were good friends, so Laski's close connection with Baldwin may be more understandable. When reading about Laski frequently dining with Baldwin, Holmes sensed Laski's need to be at the centre of events: 'You certainly seem to wiggle in wherever you want to,' he wrote to Laski, 'and I'm glad to believe that men in power know a good thing when they see it.' Less cynically, it was clear that Laski admired Baldwin, no doubt because far from declaring war on the Labour Party as subverters of the Constitution he brought the Tory Party around to accepting Labour in Westminster. In 1922, speaking for the Tory government, Baldwin referred in a House of Commons speech to '*when* the Labour Party sits on these benches', suggesting clearly that one day it would govern. Most important of all was his famous speech of 11 February 1924, when he told the Conservatives that Labour's strength was its promise to ordinary people of 'more equality of opportunity . . . more education and more of the good things of life – a perfectly genuine and altruistic feeling'. Until the Tories devised policies that confronted that feeling, Baldwin concluded, 'we are fighting with one hand tied behind our backs'. Laski felt that the 'New Conservatism' of Baldwin appreciated Labour's moral message and it augured that, once accepted into Parliament and working within the constitutional process, Labour would move the ruling class of Britain to make the concessions and the reforms that Macaulay had said were the necessary antidote to extra-parliamentary, revolutionary politics.

Laski not only admired Baldwin for his parliamentary response to Labour, but he liked him as a person as well, and this, for better or for worse, would be the source of a good deal of his political loyalties throughout his career. He was 'shrewd, practical and direct', one of the 'best souls who ever breathed', he told Frankfurter. He was 'not profound, or big on intelligence', he wrote to Holmes, but a 'man of quiet simplicity' who 'doesn't set himself up to be a great man'; a 'simple, straightforward man', 'the cleanest fighter I ever met in politics'; an ordinary man 'with his pig and pipe and his detective story', who spoke the common English of his steel-master family and embodied the ordinary virtues of decent Englishmen. Laski could have virtually lifted these observations from *The Times*, which noted in 1925 that Baldwin 'brought into public life the fragrance of the fields, the flavour of apple and hazelnut . . . all the unpretentious, simple, wholesome, homely but essential qualities, suggestions and traditions of England'.

Laski wrote to Baldwin in 1923 suggesting that there were 'things in you which make me wish that you were in my party'. When factions within the Tory Party sought to oust Baldwin from the party leadership, Laski wrote to him

> that outside the Conservative ranks, there are many socialists who, like myself, not only feel grateful for the quality of the human directness you bring to our political life, but also recognize gladly that the spirit you represent has made the peacefu¹ evolution of English politics much more certain than it would otherwise have been.

When Baldwin triumphed, Laski congratulated him on a victory 'for the forces of sheer decency in public life'. Before the nightmare events of 1931 Baldwin seemed the best Tory hope to Laski. He was the very model of the decent, fair Englishman who might prod the ruling class 'to make the sacrifices of no small kind' necessary for social peace. All Laski's ambivalence about the Great and the Good is here in his hopeful portrait.

> He is nothing so much as the cultivated country gentleman who wants to see the tenants on his estate happy and contented. He knows that an England divided into rich and poor cannot prosper. He is aware that the rich must make sacrifices if we are to recover our industrial position.

But Laski was no fool. He also knew that Baldwin did not represent prevailing sentiment in capitalist Britain. In the same article praising Baldwin, he assumed that the Prime Minister had to answer to Tories whose social theory consisted of 'longer hours and shorter wages', and that Baldwin's strategy for social amelioration was nothing more than a humane cry of 'peace, peace when the terms of the problem as he states it, make inevitable the continuation of war'.

Baldwin's concern for India also impressed Laski. In the 1920s Baldwin tried unsuccessfully to set the Tory Party on a more progressive policy to India, contemplating even some form of modified home rule. In pursuing this strategy Baldwin awoke the tumultuous fury of Churchill, recently returned to the Tory fold, and the issue died as a Tory priority. Laski had himself become deeply interested in India and it came about in the most unpredictable of ways: he was called to jury service. For five weeks from 1 May to 6 June 1924, and for five hours a day, Laski was one of twelve special jurors in the notorious libel case *O'Dwyer* v. *Nair*. Sir Michael O'Dwyer had been the civilian Lieutenant-Governor of the Punjab in 1919 when General R. E. H. Dyer ordered British troops to fire on 10,000 non-violent civilians gathered by Gandhi in the town of Amritsar. In ten minutes 379 people were killed. A book published in 1922, *Gandhi and Anarchy*, by Sir Sankaran Nair, an eminent Indian jurist and critic of Gandhi's methods, accused O'Dwyer of terrorism in the events leading up to the massacre and of being responsible for atrocities committed by the civil government. O'Dwyer sued Nair for libel and the trial reopened the whole Amritsar affair with the 'diehards' of the Tory right-wing led by Joynson-Hicks (Jix) seeking vindication for O'Dwyer.

Laski could not sit passively in a jury box for five weeks, and in an almost unprecedented spectacle he interjected himself with questions and comments to witnesses, counsel and the judge. Laski did his homework, too, reading up on the duties of an administrator under martial law. He interrupted eight times during the trial, twice to make jokes, which did, indeed, evoke laughter, and six times to ask witnesses or counsel serious questions. One such request was for greater details about rules for flogging, and another asked General Dyer if he would apply the same type of punishment for similar offences in an English city. Dyer answered that Indians could be whipped and made to crawl down streets on hands and knees, when such actions would 'not be suitable' for Englishmen. Laski confessed to Holmes, 'I am having the happiest of times in making the judge pronounce *dicta* on cases that have long interested and puzzled me.'

The tone of the trial, despite Laski's interventions, was embarrassingly supportive of British repression in India as well as utterly insensitive to Indian institutions and values. Counsel and witnesses for O'Dwyer and the judge joked about Indian life and behaviour. In his summing-up for the jury, Judge McCardie opined that General Dyer had been 'wrongly punished by the Secretary of State for India since grave evils may sometimes demand grave remedies'. He repeated his personal view that 'General Dyer, in the grave and exceptional circumstances, acted rightly'. With such a charge the jury, after deliberating for two hours and twenty-five minutes, returned to say, as *The Times* described it, 'that they were unable to agree on a verdict. The parties then agreed to accept the verdict of the majority, and the foreman announced that 11 jurors were in favour of the plaintiff.' Pollock, writing to his friend Holmes about the trial several days later, noted that 'one juryman dissented. The juryman was, if you please, H. Laski.' Pollock added that 'people here say he is a communist, which I can hardly believe considering his historical learning'. As for Pollock's own thoughts on the trial, he confided to Holmes that Laski 'was daft. I don't understand in what school he learned to give a verdict dead against the evidence.'

Laski had harsh comments about his fellow jury members. They were influenced 'less by the weight of facts than by a kind of composite total impression gained from watching what I might call the flow of the drama'. Although they were 'the most decent persons imaginable', he wrote, the average jury was 'quite incapable of appreciating the technique of evidence' and was 'moved by curiously irrelevant things, e.g. the appearance of the counsel'. What bothered Laski most was his fellow juryman's 'intense servility. He literally cannot grasp the fact that an official can lie', and in this case assumed 'the ultimate direction of the judge'.

The legacy of *O'Dwyer* v. *Nair* endured. Indians would not forget the outcome, and sixteen years later, in March 1940, Sir Michael O'Dwyer was assassinated by an Indian nationalist. It also had a profound effect on Laski, introducing him, he wrote, 'to the depth of colour-prejudice', an introduction furthered by his reading of E. M. Forster's *A Passage to India*, published in the week of the verdict. Laski was deeply moved by the book's 'exquisite' treatment of 'the problem of racial context'. Claiming it to be 'one of the great novels of our time', he urged Holmes and Frankfurter to read it. Forster himself followed the trial with fury, his biographer notes, 'and as it happened, he got an inside view of proceedings, for Harold Laski, whom he knew slightly, was on the jury'. Laski told Forster that many on the jury wanted to award O'Dwyer £20,000, which was ultimately brought down to £500, and that several jurors had threatened him, one saying, 'I am sorry for your poor wife and hope she will never speak to you again.' Forster's view of the verdict was closer to Laski's than to Pollock's. 'God I have been enraged,' he wrote, 'a dirty political manoeuvre.' *O'Dwyer* v. *Nair* set Laski on a path that he would tread outspokenly for the next twenty years. He wrote to Frankfurter on the day of the verdict:

> The truth is, dear Felix, that we ought not to stay in India. Literally and simply, we are not morally fit for the job ... I add my grave doubts whether the Indians can govern themselves. But it is better for them to make the effort than to have this running sore at the heart of things. If they fail, let it be their failure. Our success (if it were not too late) would only deepen their sense of inferiority.

Not that Laski had been uninterested in the India question or in issues of colonialism and racism before *O'Dwyer* v. *Nair*. At Oxford he had written to Frida about his involvement in combating anti-Indian bigotry at the university. Two years later in Montreal he told Huebsch, who had asked him to look at a manuscript on India, that while the British had done much good for India – irrigation, abolition of suttee, better judicial administration, acting as a check 'on the disgusting rapacity of the native princes' – there was only one final verdict on British rule: 'I hate it and I personally favour our withdrawal from there.' Back in England he had joined Bertrand and Dora Russell in speaking at election rallies for Shaphuiji Saklatvala, the Indian MP for Battersea, who was not only a communist but, more importantly, the most outspoken and vigorous public critic of British rule in India. Laski was concerned with African issues as well. In November 1923 he addressed 400 delegates to the Pan-African Congress meeting in London, and W. E. B. Dubois, the distinguished American black educator and activist, for one, was deeply impressed: he wrote in the *New Republic* of Laski's 'striking suggestions' that the League of Nations send each mandated territory in Africa 'an accredited minister of the League' who was a trained anthropologist and who would 'have the right to investigate conditions and report to the League'. Laski's proposal, Dubois urged, would help bring to bear 'the force of world public opinion' on the outrages committed by the European powers in Africa.

It was *O'Dwyer* v. *Nair*, however, which formalized Laski's views and marked the real beginning of his commitment to the cause of Indian independence. In the next twenty-five years Laski's connection with India, a country which he, unlike his father, never visited, was second only to his involvement with America. Many of the legions of Indian students who came to study with Laski at the LSE did so partly because of *O'Dwyer* v. *Nair*. Amritsar had itself turned Gandhi and Nehru into revolutionaries and no Indian nationalist failed to forget the one person out of twelve who stood fast for justice and decency. Thirty years later, on 15 August 1954, in opening the Harold Laski Institute of Political Science in Ahmedabad, the Foreign Minister of India, Krishna Menon, noted that 'since the days that he sat on a jury in the Michael O'Dwyer case, Professor Laski became one of us'.

Menon knew of what he spoke, for in 1925 he had become a student of Laski's at the LSE, graduating with a first class degree in 1927, and for two decades in London while he worked as a lawyer, in publishing, and running the pro-independence India League, he and Laski collaborated closely. Menon learned his socialism from Laski. He once suggested that 'Laski was a very great man', and that it would 'take one hundred years to realize the profundity of his thought'. Menon had more than the gratitude of the pupil: he 'learned to love and respect him in a way that I treasure very preciously. He had been a profound influence on my own life.' Their relationship was much closer than simply that of teacher–student. Laski took a domestic interest in the frail, handsome, depression-prone ascetic, who seemed to survive on tea and buns. In turn, Menon was apparently a constant presence in the Laski home after 1925. 'The telephone in the house,' Frida wrote, 'belonged to him. At nine every morning there would be a ring and I used to say, "That must be Krishna," and sure enough it was.' The Laskis sometimes helped Menon with money and he was a frequent attendee at Sunday open-house. At a particularly suicidal moment during his years in London it was the visit of Laski and Frida to his garret room in St Pancras that, according to Menon's biographer, 'put him on the road to recovery'. Through Menon, secretary to the India League, Laski met Gandhi and Nehru on their visits to Britain, and he in turn became the advocate for India's cause that Menon could always call upon, whether it was to lecture Indian students, speak to India League rallies or lobby with the Labour Party. In his absorbing commitment to the cause of Indian independence in the 1930s and 1940s, Laski ironically combated the very economic dependency that was the source of his father's wealth and power, although the more immediate stimulus for his interest was the impact of

O'Dwyer v. *Nair* in 1924 and the long association with the indefatigable Krishna Menon which began in 1925. Speaking to the Indian Independence anniversary celebration in London in 1949, Laski commented:

> I do not know how many times I have gone to meetings that I did not want to attend, have made speeches that I did not want to make, have written articles that I had no time to write, because I was under the grim control of this irrepressible embodiment of the will of India to be free, and I look back and what I owe Krishna Menon for having made me attend as a member of his army is a debt that I can never repay.

Another already prominent international figure that Laski became involved with in late 1924 and early 1925 was Emma Goldman. Though it would be a brief episode and not lead to a longer association as Menon's would, it provides an interesting illustration of Laski's quest for political respectability and moderation in the 1920s. Goldman, the Russian-born anarchist and feminist who had spent most of her early years in America, had been deported on one of Attorney-General Palmer's sweeps through American radicals after the war. The *Harvard Lampoon* issue devoted to attacking Laski in January 1920 had suggested that he join her on the next 'Soviet Ark' that Palmer launched. Goldman was appalled at the police and party repression she found in Russia and was especially disturbed by the Bolshevik imprisonment and torture of dissident anarchist elements, called 'the politicals'. After leaving the Soviet Union she settled for several years in London, during which time she tried to enlist Laski and his friends in a public campaign to denounce the Bolshevik government.

Their mutual friend Roger Baldwin of the American Civil Liberties Union had written to Goldman in London suggesting that Laski might be supportive, given the pronounced anarchist antipathy to the state in his writings. Well might she have anticipated Laski's support. He had, in fact, recently written to Holmes about having heard Goldman lecture in late November, and that 'for sheer torrential eloquence I have heard nothing like it in years'. When Goldman first met Laski in mid-December 1924, she was encouraged. She told Baldwin that 'both he and his wife showed so much interest that I went away elated, thinking that at last I have found people who love the truth above political consideration'. The Laskis agreed to invite thirty-five people, including the Russells and H. W. Nevinson, to tea on 21 December. Goldman asked Laksi's guests to support a public campaign denouncing the Bolsheviks, which she was going to launch with a large meeting on 29 January at South Place Institute, and also to convince the Labour Party to endorse her efforts. She was cruelly disappointed.

Eight days after the tea, Laski wrote to her of his canvass of those who had been present and the result of having had 'the opportunity of talking over your proposed meeting with a variety of people from every group in the Labour Party'. People, himself included, were willing to support demands for decent treatment of the 'politicals' and other prisoners, but virtually no one would sign on to a general assault on the Bolshevik government. He did 'not think you would be willing to limit yourself to speaking at your meeting solely upon the facts of prison treatment; I gather that you want to trace it to the inherent nature of Bolshevism'. That being the case, Laski suggested that Goldman should hold the meeting 'under your own and your friends' auspices'. Behind Laski's assessment was the reality that neither the Labour Party nor the trade unions would have any formal part in a general attack on the Soviet government only weeks after the defeat of MacDonald in a rampant Red scare campaign. It would smack too blatantly of political opportunism.

Particularly upsetting to Goldman was that Laski's letter relied heavily on Bertrand Russell's lack of interest in doing anything more than signing letters for the better treatment of prisoners. She held high hopes for his support, since the book he had written upon his return from Russia, *The Practice and Theory of Bolshevism*, was a passionate indictment of the ruthless dictatorship and repression practised by the Soviet regime. Russell had also played an important role in obtaining a visa for her to enter Britain in 1922. Russell, who still fancied a parliamentary seat with Labour, was worried about the merits of a frontal attack on Bolshevism and, as Laski reported, 'while disliking the Soviets intensely, does not see any alternative government and doubts whether your propaganda would be effective'.

Goldman was also upset by what she took to be Laski's too fine distinctions, and she could not understand 'how any man with some logic can expect to discuss the politicals without going into the background and the forces which made them'. She also felt that Laski had misled her on the occasion of their first conversation, when he had seemed to share her anarchist-based critique of the new Soviet order. 'You, dear Professor, were willing to concede on the evening when I first called on you that the ideas of Bakunin and Kropotkin have been quite vindicated by the Russian experiment.' As for Laski's account of Russell's views, they were 'illogical and inconsistent for any group who claim sympathy with labour and strong socialistic leanings'. In her petulant letter to Baldwin berating him for the very suggestion that she seek out Laski, Goldman grasped quite intuitively the transformation that had come over Laski from when Baldwin knew him in Cambridge and New York, though she underestimated the real ambivalence that people like Laski felt about the Bolsheviks. Laski's scholarly writings were one thing, she felt, but in the world of British political action and party politics moderation and respectability seemed essential. Evidently, to share a platform with Emma Goldman was more dangerous even than bashing Bolsheviks.

> I was a little amused at your announcement that you had written Laski that he and others should avail themselves of my services on the lecture platform. You are so naive, dear Roger. What do you think these political people would want with Emma Goldman, the anarchist? These people neither want the truth nor can they stand it when it is being told them, and they know full well as you will see by Laski's letter that it is not advisable to ally oneself with such an outspoken person as E.G. I really believe that it is the principal reason for the refusal on the part of Laski and the rest of working with me for the political prisoners.

Goldman was right in one respect. Laski was compartmentalizing his life, reserving his outspoken radicalism for his writing. Just days before the initial call from Goldman, Laski had finished a book that he hoped would say new 'and also practical things'. Seven months later, in June 1925, *The Grammar of Politics* was published, one of the largest, most ambitious and best known of all Laski's books. A future Labour Prime Minister, James Callaghan, would point to it as the book that turned him into a socialist. Dedicated to 'the London School of Economics and Political Science and to Sidney and Beatrice Webb, its founders', it was a persuasive and uncompromising statement of socialist ideals, all the more surprising since at the time he wrote it Laski was leading the most respectable of social and political lives. In the thirties the gap between the militancy of his writings and his insider's role as a political operative would be much greater, but it is characteristically there in 1925 as well.

Laski had been working on *The Grammar of Politics* on and off for nine years, and steadily since 1921. With the book he sought to offer no less than, as its opening sentence declares, 'a new political philosophy' for a world which had 'lost confidence in the simplicity of the earlier thinkers'. His book would replace the writings of Bentham, Hegel, Rousseau and Marx, all of whom had been unable to deal with the complexity of modern industrial society. Frankfurter had advised his friend in March 1924 to make his *magnum opus* less dependent on 'your erudite learning' and more direct and accessible. Laski took his advice, and while the book is deeply repetitive it is much freer of intertextual debate and historical digressions than his earlier books. It is, as virtually all his future books would be, principally concerned with the politics of the moment filtered through the insights of a historically sensitive student of institutions and ideas who was deeply partisan, yet never willing to give up the voice and the distance of the scholar.

In *The Grammar of Politics* Laski continued his discussions of the state, further distancing himself from guild socialism and the extremes of his earlier pluralism. The state was now, as befits a book dedicated to the Webbs, depicted in a much more favourable light. It was where citizens met to realize themselves whether 'they are barristers or miners, Catholics or Protestants, employers or workers'. Only in the state could the interests of consumers and producers be reconciled and therefore, while functional sub-units deserved as much autonomy and self-determination as possible, the territorial control of the larger, all-inclusive state remained as the necessary and desirable coordinating unit in political life. But even as Laski conceded the inevitable importance of the state, he still acknowledged that it was 'very largely an institution dominated by the owners of private property', who used its power primarily 'to protect the property of the rich from invasion by the poor. It comes to think of order as the final virtue.' To combat this, Laski, in a dramatic about-face, called upon the earlier moral vision of the state articulated by T. H. Green and his followers, the vision which saw the state making it possible for each citizen to 'be his best self' by 'mitigating the inequalities of social opportunity'.

Laski's pluralism persisted, none the less. His new appreciation of the state did not replace his earlier convictions about the primacy of as-sociational life and the value of decentralization, federalism and localism; it was placed on top of it. His hope for the state was layered above his lingering pluralist suspicion of that very state, an integration of pluralism and statism which gives the book its truly original quality. Laski offered a

new conception of the state, with consultative, advisory bodies at every
level involving the autonomous associations – unions, professors, employers,
and so on – which were closer to people's lives and experiences than the
abstract distant world of civil servants and politicians. The state's power
would be decentralized and democratized, its unitary will shared with the
interests affected by its decisions. The state, then, would merely ratify the
will of the interested parties who had been consulted. The Whitley Councils
and the wartime experience of the co-optation of interests by the state lay
behind Laski's new vision. Enlarging its sphere into the industrial realm, it
would paradoxically undermine its own centrality. As the first major
theorist of the corporate state, whereby state power would be shared with
affected interests, Laski was, unlike other corporatists, still driven by the
motive of undercutting state power. It was necessary, Laski wrote, 'to
surround the central government in particular with bodies it is compelled
to consult', to compel 'organized and prior consultation of all interests
which are affected by a decision it is proposed to make'. Miners, teachers
or the cotton industry virtually would acquire part of the power of the
state, choosing their own representatives to serve on its advisory bodies:

> The groups we encounter in social and industrial life need to be federally
> related to the government if the decisions of the latter are to be wise. That
> means giving to those groups the means of prior and organic influence with
> government before it pronounces upon the problem of coordination. It
> means weighing their opinions, seeking their criticism, meeting their special
> needs. It means, further, allowing them responsibility in their own life.

Laski expected these consultative bodies of owners and workers to take
on an independent life of their own and to work out policy autonomously
for their own area of enterprise. The mining industry, for example, could
establish between its employees and management a pension scheme different
from a national policy, as well as be involved in larger state decisions on
the economy: 'It means making the mining industry a unit of administration
in the same sense as Lancashire.' This would involve less direct administration by the state and leave organized interests more power over their own
affairs. But it would succeed only if workers and the life experiences they
represented were given as much power in decision-making as employers.
Laski's corporatist view of the state was distinctly non-Marxist, however,
in its assumption that it could cease to be the tool of the ruling few and be

made to represent all citizens. Class war would give way to a process of consultation, compromise and concession among reasonable people. The state would no longer be an intangible entity acting out of a 'partial and inadequate glimpse of the total volume of social experience'. Through what Laski called the 'principle of organized consultation' the sovereign state of earlier philosophical theory would finally be demystified and made part of the real experiences of 'everyday life'.

The major new emphasis in *The Grammar of Politics* was Laski's long discussion of Fabian socialism and his suggested reorganization of British industrial life to reflect those ideals. 'The state,' he wrote, 'must control industrial power in the interests of its citizens', or 'industrial power will control the state in the interests of its possessors'. Laski catalogued the evils of a British capitalist system where production was carried on wastefully and without adequate planning, where 'picture palaces' were built when houses were needed, where 'we spend on battleships what is wanted for schools', where the rich 'spend the weekly wage of a workman on a single dinner, while the workman cannot send his children adequately fed to school', and where the rich débutante spends 'on an evening frock more than the annual income of the workers who have made it'. Laski did not recommend total equality or sameness of results, nor did he recommend perpetual public provision regardless of personal effort. His ideal was a revival of the older Fabian principle of a 'civic minimum', the provision by the state of a sufficient share of the primary material wants – food, shelter, health, education and employment – 'which, when unsatisfied, prevent the realization of personality'. His concern was to eliminate special privilege and to provide true equality of opportunity.

Laski's discussion of economic equality set forth a theme he repeated in each of his subsequent books and which anticipated the treatment of distributive justice by the contemporary social philosopher John Rawls. Inequality was morally acceptable to Laski as long as the differential enhanced the good of all, not simply the beneficiary of the inequality, and there existed a prior floor of equality attained by the community as a whole. Once this minimum was met, advantages attained by one's own efforts were legitimate. 'One man,' he wrote, 'is not entitled to a house of twenty rooms until all people are adequately housed'; 'I have no right to cake if my neighbour, because of that right, is compelled to go without bread.' Once primary needs for all were dealt with, society might set a return proportionate to services performed for the community, the surgeon's versus the bricklayer's.

Laski proposed that industries essential to the life of the community be brought under public control. Future generations would find as unthinkable that an 'army of the state should be left to private hands' as that coal, electric power, transport, banking, the supply of meat and the provision of houses 'shall be left to the hazards of private enterprise'. The state was interested only in the provision of 'urgencies', and Laski was adamant that the necessary 'nationalization' need not take a specific form like the Post Office: 'There is room, and to spare, for experiment in the nature of government in nationalized industry.' In the second level of production, items that were desirable but not necessarily urgent, 'the less room there is for private profit, the better', and he suggested that the appropriate organizing principle be consumer cooperatives. A large third component of the economy, 'cosmetic' or non-urgently needed products, should be left free except for governmental maintenance of standards in wages, hours of labour, and so on. He did not, therefore, 'envisage anything like the disappearance of private enterprise'. People would still be able to make fortunes, though they would of course be subject to heavier income and inheritance taxes.

In an important new emphasis Laski also suggested the need for a different ethos in industry, whether it was in a socialized public sector or in the remaining private sector: 'Industry, in fact, must be made a profession. It needs to be informed by a principle of public service.' Like lawyers and doctors, businessmen should seek to enrich 'the public in enriching themselves'. Professionalization of industry involved introducing qualifications and standards for businessmen who would not have jobs merely through inheritance, favouritism or family connections. Greater use of research and scientific expertise by businessmen would be part of a more professional industrial order, including perhaps the requirement of university training. Laski pointed to the Harvard Business School as a healthy sign of the professionalization of industry. Here, too, Laski layered the new on the old, as his socialism retained beneath it a layer of his earlier scientific progressivism.

Laski's pluralist, decentralizing urge operated in the industrial sphere as well. Large-scale industry could not return to a William Morris individual craftsman-cum-artist economy, but Laski urged a 'decentralization of the factory group' built around a notion of 'teamwork' and 'self-government' by small groups of workers, which would allow 'pride and self-sacrifice and initiative' to flourish and enable the worker to 'feel that he is directly related to the centre of control'. Laski's earlier guild-socialist and syndicalist inclinations persist, and in their own way anticipated what much later would seem to be so innovative in Swedish and Japanese industrial practice. In 1925 Laski wrote of decentralized factory team groups as enhancing 'self-respect' and producing a 'new atmosphere of equality' which would translate 'into a new dignity and a new creativeness'.

How might these fundamental transformations of the economy occur? Certainly not by revolution, or 'catastrophic nationalization', which is how he characterized forced confiscation of industrial power. Instead, legislation, achieved through traditional constitutional channels, would initiate a process that 'proceeds piecemeal and by stages' to purchase from and compensate fairly the owners of industries rendered public. 'Nothing,' Laski insisted, 'is so likely to poison the spirit of the body politic than the sudden disappointment of financial expectation,' so compensation had to be certain and just. 'In the transference to a new system,' he added, 'the more good-will we have, the greater is the augury of its success.' His ideas, Laski acknowledged, lacked 'the logic of inevitable catastrophe' and anticipated 'the disappearance of that class war which now lies at the root of the social structure'. Since he also assumed it was 'possible to harmonize the interests of those who are parties to the industrial relation', and he even refused to contemplate the 'complete disappearance of the capitalist system', his proposals must, he suggested, appear 'timid and conservative' to the communist. But so be it, Laski replied. Revolutions seldom achieve the ends for which they aimed, 'and the weapons of which they are driven to make use destroy by their character the prospects they have in view'. Violence was a weapon of the last resort, to be used only when parliamentary-authorized fundamental change was itself resisted by violence.

Having rejected the path of revolutionary communism, Laski also rejected the opposite alternative of maintaining the *laissez-faire* ideal. Indeed, insistence on a pure regime of economic capitalism, he suggested, would itself inevitably lead to revolution 'and there will then be precipitated exactly the situation predicted in the communist analysis'. Laski characteristically positioned himself in the middle. Unless the owners of capital made substantial 'concessions', there would be catastrophic revolution, which would create a world 'probably incompatible with the maintenance of civilized life'. Laski firmly believed in 1925 that the ruling class, following Macaulay's advice, would choose concession and join the emerging consensus that Laski described in the penultimate paragraph of the book.

> There is in the world a growing impatience at the exploitation of man by man. There is a fuller sense, more widespread and more deeply felt, that the inheritance of the world is not the possession of a few, and that for the others life is merely an endless toil. We have discovered the significance of equality; and its demands upon us are not likely to be less than the demands we have known in the name of freedom.

There is one thoroughly new area of concern in Laski's *Grammar of Politics*, international affairs and the world legal order. If the Webbs stood behind much of his domestic agenda, Leonard Woolf was clearly the Labour colleague who initially turned Laski to international issues. The League of Nations and the interdependent world capitalist economy both marked for Laski 'the disappearance of the sovereign nation-state'. No nation-state was any longer self-sufficient, and when England made a decision that directly affected France 'the area of intersecting activity must give rise to a situation jointly planned by England and France'. Laski had high hopes for the League of Nations. Perhaps it would foreclose the 'glamour of war' which, Laski movingly wrote, 'exists only in the experience of those who have not known its deadly furies. For the few to whom there comes the accession of chivalrous exploit, there are millions to whom it means death and disease and maimed lives.' But, remaining true to his pluralist, decentralized instincts, Laski did not see the League as a new super-sovereign state. The nation-state or the League did not exhaust 'the varied groupings of mankind'. The future world order, he suggested, might well be built around all kinds of functional associations of an intermediate regional nature based on economic, transport or communication patterns.

The Grammar of Politics, like all of Laski's writings, combined grandiose political vision with micro-specific suggestions for immediate tinkering with the existing order, not surprisingly reproducing the general tension within his own persona of being both a major social and political theorist and an everyday player in the nitty-gritty of party politics. As would often be the case, almost as much attention and talk were generated from his book by his specific proposals as by his higher-level theorizing. Not only, for example, did he want to overcome amateurism in industry, but he wanted to professionalize politics as well, so he proposed that no one serve as a Member of Parliament who had not had three years of service in a local public authority. He repeated the proposal that Dubois had liked about the League of Nations placing ministerial observers in every territory and colony to see to the interests of the native population. As part of the larger vision of a 'consultative state' he proposed that the general parliamentary committee structure be changed to the American style of specialized committees and that these committees be required to hold public hearings. All government ministries would have formal advisory bodies, paid out of government funds, attached to them to represent the various interests they dealt with, and the memberships of these bodies would be chosen not by the ministers but by the interests themselves. Laski would also introduce pay for service in local government, unheard of in Britain, to encourage localism and decentralization. Another suggestion fleetingly put forth in *The Grammar* was that private firms reserve one half of the seats on their board of directors for the workers and management of the firm. Finally, Laski suggested the elimination of special juries chosen on property qualifications for libel cases, and in a further reflection on *O'Dwyer* v. *Nair* he suggested that 'an average London jury looks upon a libel very differently when the defendant is a Conservative magnate from its views when he is a radical trade unionist.'

Sidney Webb wrote to Laski that he had celebrated his birthday, on 13 July 1925, by 'another read at your great book'. He added, 'I was told that the book was (unlike your conversation) dull, but I have not found it so. On the contrary, I think you have been very successful in overcoming the inherent dullness of the subject.' The *Nation*, under its new management, had problems with 'certain bad habits of thinking and of writing which definitely deprecate the value of his work'. The *New Statesman* found it 'full of luminous comment and useful suggestion, even if it was often slow and tedious reading'. *The Times Literary Supplement*, having problems with its meta-message, suggested that Laski 'is at his best when he leaves considerations of high theory and busies himself with practical suggestion'. In America, where it was published by Yale University Press, the book was reviewed by Charles Beard for the *New Republic*, who, not surprisingly, found it 'a landmark that shows how far we have come from the realm of Herbert Spencer'.

Oliver Wendell Holmes, on the other hand, wrote to Laski that 'it does not command my sympathy and I hate to have any words but praise for you'. He admitted that he had 'never read so penetrating a socialist book', but he didn't share Laski's premises or 'sympathize very greatly with your dream'. Laski reminded him of the abolitionists of his youth with his 'martyr spirit'. Concerned that he had 'not hurt my friend', he confessed to Laski that he had serious problems with the construction of utopian schemes, especially if they were based on a 'passion for equality', which he found an 'ignoble aspiration since it suggests some people aren't intrinsically more talented than others'. Astutely referring to a passage from the book, Holmes added that he saw 'no right in my neighbour to share my bread'. Laski wrote back to Holmes that 'friendship goes deeper than all these things'. Nor did Laski accept the criticism as the last word. America, he told Holmes, was a country where 'the career is still wholly open to the talented', whereas in England 'there is too much social stratification to make the talented easily find their careers'. He returned to Holmes's description of equality as an 'ignoble ideal', and insisted that he had no problem with a Justice of the Supreme Court being more highly regarded than the court's door-keeper, but 'I do not want the judge to have ten times the door-keeper's salary unless and until the door-keeper is paid at a level which assures him social adequacy'.

The most outspoken and devastating American critic of The Grammar of Politics was William Yandell Elliott, Jr, a Harvard Professor of Government, raised in the American South and trained at Balliol College, Oxford. Elliott remained a fierce critic of Laski's writings, his politics and what he took to be his undeserved influence over American academics for the next twenty-five years. Linking Laski's Grammar, appropriately so, to the author's earlier pluralist and pragmatic inclinations, Elliott saw it as symptomatic of what he called 'the pragmatic revolt in politics', an unhealthy and dangerous tendency to stress action and moral relativism at the expense of the metaphysical theory of the unity of the moral state. This criticism had its ironic side, for Elliott featured prominently in the southern Fugitive school and its agrarian rejection of the American nation-state. In the 1930s he would, in fact, author a proposal to break up the unified and sovereign American state into a decentralized collection of autonomous regional 'commonwealths', quite compatible with the dreaded and dangerous pluralist reflex of his opponent Laski.

In his *Grammar of Politics* Laski continued his libertarian defence of the rights of individuals against state authority, the side of him which had prompted Goldman to seek him out. Laski's rhetoric here was vintage John Stuart Mill liberalism, another of the layers he built upon with his socialist ideals. He praised the 'ultimate uniqueness and, therefore, isolation of the individual as the basic starting point of social theory'. One's duty was to conscience first and to the state only if 'I discover moral adequacy'. Disobedience and the forfeit of allegiance were extreme cases to be undertaken rarely, whereas much more significant and ordinary was the sacred libertarian and individualistic commitment to free speech which Laski trumpeted in *The Grammar*. An individual cannot contribute his judgement to the public good 'if a penalty is attached to the expression of his thought'. Citing American constitutional principles, Laski suggested that only overt acts, not speech, should ever be restricted. The libertarian Laski insisted that

> the citizen must be left unfettered to express either individually, or in consent with others, any opinions he happens to hold. He may preach the complete inadequacy of the social order . . . He is entitled to speak without hindrance of any kind. He is entitled, further, to use all the ordinary means of publication to make his views known . . . He may give them in the form of a lecture; he may announce them at a public meeting. To be able to do any or all of these things, with the full protection of the state in so doing, is a right that lies at the basis of freedom.

With these ringing phrases *The Grammar of Politics* was published in June 1925. Several months later Laski turned these civil liberties concerns on a real world issue. The Tory Home Secretary, the old Laski family nemesis, Jix, had moved from his support of General Dyer and Sir Michael O'Dwyer in 1924 to his new crusade, Red-baiting. Now, as Laski informed *New Republic* readers, Jix was 'fulminating against the Communist Party (all 4,000 of them) as a gigantic conspiracy which is shattering the foundations of the British Empire'. It was also clear that Jix saw Bolsheviks behind the renewed coal-miners' agitation which would lead in a few months to the General Strike. On 14 October 1925 Jix arrested twelve British communists for 'seditious conspiracy', including Harry Pollitt, the party's chairman since its founding in 1921, an affable boiler-maker from Lancashire, and Palme Rajani Dutt, a graduate from Balliol and the austere

Eurasian Party theoretician. The trial, the only political trial in Britain in the inter-war years, was set for December while the men were released on surety bail provided by George Bernard Shaw and the Red Countess of Warwick. These two were joined by Laski, C. P. Scott, editor of the *Manchester Guardian*, Professor L. T. Hobhouse of the LSE, H. G. Wells and Bertrand Russell in launching a vigorous defence of freedom of speech and freedom of association. 'I hate their doctrines but they are as harmless as men could be,' Laski wrote to Holmes. During the trial the group organized large demonstrations across the country, culminating in a giant rally in Queen's Hall, London, where Laski thought 'Bertie Russell was even better than I'. Despite his posture of moderation, Laski (nor Russell) showed none of the reluctance to speak out in this case that he had in response to Goldman's plea about the Russians.

In December the jury took twenty minutes to return a guilty verdict for 'seditious conspiracy'. In a bizarre twist the trial judge, Justice Swift, offered to let the defendants off with only a caution if they would publicly renounce their political opinions. The men refused and went to jail, one of the few times in modern British history when someone was imprisoned for their beliefs and speech. In addition to speaking at public demonstrations, Laski made two other interventions. On 23 October he sent Sir Henry Slesser, the leading counsel for the defendants, a learned brief on the history of search warrants, since a search of the party headquarters was one of the issues at the trial. More importantly, on 12 December he wrote a piece for the *Manchester Guardian* entitled 'What is Sedition?' In it he called upon Members of Parliament to support legislation that narrowed the grounds for sedition from the 'impossibly wide standard', including any adverse criticism or comment about the government or the Constitution, which totally inhibited free speech. Seditious speech or publications should be only what a jury held to be 'calculated to lead directly to public disorder'. He urged Parliament to adopt Justice Holmes's principle that there needed to be a clear and present danger of 'definitive and immediate possibility of action' if speech were to be restricted.

Laski was no more successful in persuading Parliament to adopt this principle than Holmes had been in winning over a majority of his fellow Supreme Court justices in the Abrams case. The House of Commons voted 351 to 171 against a motion to censure the government on the proceedings against the communists and to initiate new language in the sedition law.

Laski clearly sympathized more with Holmes's libertarian dream than Holmes did with Laski's socialist vision. But that was no surprise; it had been so since they had met and forged their special Anglo-American relationship. Nor was their common defeat in the cause of free speech unexpected, given the mood of Britain and America after the First World War and the Russian Revolution.

CHAPTER TEN

The General Strike, the LSE and Communism

After six years of absence Laski visited America in April 1926. He wrote to Holmes in January that cynical friends had suggested that Coolidge's State Department might not give him a visa. In fact there was no trouble, and Laski spent three weeks in America: one in Cambridge, one in Washington and one in New York City. In Cambridge Laski stayed with the Frankfurters. He assiduously avoided Harvard and spent his time seeing his old friends David Niles, Zachariah Chafee, Jr, and Pound, and speaking only at the Ford Hall Forum. Most of the time was spent in long late-night talks with Frankfurter.

In Washington Laski had several lunches with Holmes, now eighty-five years old, who was delighted to see him. Laski, in turn, had 'no words to tell you what those days in Washington meant to me . . . my old homage and affection [were] made deeper and more intense by a new richness'. Laski saw Brandeis on three successive days in Washington and, as Brandeis wrote to Frankfurter, 'we have had much talk. It is cheering to find him substantially in agreement with you and me on American problems.' Brandeis's sense of the closeness of the trio was indicated by his aside to Frankfurter about 'unserer Bunde des Dritte' ('our band of three'). While Laski was with Brandeis, he met Sidney Hillman, the President of the Amalgamated Clothing Workers. Laski remained in touch with Hillman and always wrote of him as the most enlightened and progressive American trade-union leader, especially after he led dissident unions out of the American Federation of Labor and into the more militant Congress of Industrial Organizations.

New York was a week-long treat for Laski. Former students took him to dinner at the Harvard Club, and having been brought back into the *New Republic* fold the previous winter, Laski was fêted at a *New Republic* dinner. Laski was renewed in his appreciation of Croly, 'a big fellow, patient, curious, sincere and penetrating'. People like him, he assured Holmes, augured well for the future of America. He had 'a great evening' with Morris Cohen, the acerbic interlocutor who sent students into terror, but who, according to Laski, had mellowed greatly. He also made two new friends in New York. Judge Julian Mack introduced Laski to Benjamin Cardoza, then Judge of the New York Court of Appeals, destined in 1932 to be appointed to replace Holmes, and thus the third New Yorker and the second Jew on a court of nine. Though the two men liked each other initially, no real friendship would develop. Alfred Cohn was another story. One of Frankfurter's closest personal friends and about the same age, Cohn was a distinguished cardiologist attached to the Rockefeller Medical Foundation. Born in America, he wanted to be a rabbi, but at Columbia he became a scientist who would still always love history, philosophy and literature. He wrote three books: an autobiography, a set of essays on the history of medicine, and reflections on tradition and dissent in American letters. Cohn was a sympathizer with leftist causes in politics, interested in the politics of education, and a Zionist compatriot of Frankfurter's. In the early 1930s he worked closely with the Institute of International Education in New York and its director Stephen Duggan, whose assistant Edward R. Murrow ran the emergency committee seeking to help academic victims of Nazism. Eventually Cohn would become second only to Frankfurter as Laski's dearest American friend.

What Laski thought about America can be reconstructed from a talk he gave while there and from an article he wrote for the *New Republic* on his return. In his talk 'An Appeal to America', Laski discerned in the United States 'a fear of innovation, a distrust of doubt . . . a persecuting temper'. Governing Coolidge's America was 'a system of dogmas, narrow and ignorant and crude, preached with all the fierce intensity of a medieval superstition; men are asked to bow down before it'. The heart of this worship to which all was sacrificed was 'the Moloch of property'. American businessmen had not yet even 'learned the elementary significance of the trade unions', let alone anything about the inevitability of 'democratic control in industry'. All the American businessmen believed in was 'a gospel of simple material success'. There was, to be sure, much to praise in America – her architects led the world; in legal and psychological science they did work of the highest distinction; her engineers and medical men were at the forefront of combating waste and inefficiency and in championing preventive medicine. But this vitality paled, Laski suggested, beside the 'economic individualism which distinguishes private and public life from New York to San Francisco'.

Caught up immediately after his return to London in the maelstrom of the General Strike, Laski still had not written up his thoughts when in August 1927 the Sacco–Vanzetti executions took place. Laski stood by his closest friends, Frankfurter and his old Boston mentor Glendower Evans, in his condemnation of what they had worked so tirelessly to prevent. 'The whole world revolts at this execution,' he wrote. President Lowell, appointed to lead a committee which found nothing amiss in the proceedings, was the principal villain. 'Loyalty to his class has transcended his ideas of logic and justice.'

From this visit on, Americans listened to what Laski wrote and said about them. Laski's articles would be read regularly in the *New Republic*, the *Nation* or *Harper's*. As an important foreigner with distinguished American friends, Laski's thoughts about America were also picked up by editorial writers, especially at the *New York Times*. Four times, for example, between the appearance of his *New Republic* piece in January 1928 and his next visit to America in the spring of 1931, *New York Times* editorials discussed pieces Laski had published elsewhere in American periodicals, referring to him as a 'distinguished foreign observer on the American scene needing to be taken seriously'. Were Americans, as he suggested, 'unhappy people'? one *New York Times* editorial asked. Another wondered whether Laski was correct in his *Harper's* claim that America should replace its checks and balances with the British parliamentary fusion of legislative and executive power. Laski had become and would remain a familiar name in some American households.

Laski returned to London on 28 April with fifty books purchased in New York City and, as he wrote to Holmes, he 'came back to find Frida and Diana both very fit; but we tremble on the verge of terrible events here and I do not know what will happen'. What happened was the General Strike, the most dramatic episode in British industrial relations in the twentieth century. For eight days from 4 May to 12 May 1926, the whole of Britain ground to a halt as railwaymen, transport workers, builders, chemical workers, gas and electricity workers, engineers, shipyard workers, miners and taxi drivers went on strike. The unions had agreed that workers engaged in health, sanitary and food services should stay at work.

Troops kept power stations active and helmeted soldiers accompanied food convoys into the main cities. Hyde Park was closed to the public and used as a vast milk depot. Students and volunteers tried to run buses, trains and lorries, or unload ships. Some meagre public transport service did function, and by the eighth day volunteers had restored the central London Underground to an almost normal service.

The General Strike was not a coordinated deed of direct action intended to undermine the capitalist state; it was a vast sympathy strike to show solidarity with the miners. Coal was the largest single industry in Britain, employing more than a million workers, and it had been continually in crisis since 1921. Management demands in the summer of 1925 for longer hours and less pay had led to a strike call for 31 July. Because of this, Baldwin committed the government to a Royal Commission to study the mines and to a subsidy to maintain miners' wages during its deliberations to last until 1 May 1926. 'Black Friday' of 1921 had been redeemed by what the *Daily Herald* called 'Red Friday' of 1925. It was only a buying of time, however, for in March 1926 the Royal Commission issued its report accepting the owners' position of reduced wages and a longer day and calling for an end to subsidies. The owners then demanded a reduction of 13 per cent in the standard wages of the miners and an extension of the workday for a trial period of three years. The Miners' Federation announced it would fight even the smallest wage cut, and soon it and other unions took up the slogan 'Not a minute on the day; not a penny off the pay'. The Trades Union Congress (TUC) took over from the miners and voted for a general work stoppage from midnight 3 May in solidarity with the miners, with Ernest Bevin as chairman of the strike committee. The government, meanwhile, prepared troops and a vast volunteer organization to weather the strike.

Baldwin's conciliatory instincts were pushed to the side as management of the strike in the Cabinet gravitated to Jix, the 'diehard' Home Secretary, and, most importantly, to Churchill, the bellicose Bolshevik-baiting Chancellor of the Exchequer. Churchill took charge for the government and realized that with all the newspapers closed by striking printers, control of news and opinions would be essential, so on 5 May he set up and edited a government-funded daily, the *British Gazette*, printed by blackleg printers. Its position was clear: The strike was not an industrial dispute, but an effort to overthrow the parliamentary system, 'a direct challenge to ordered government'. The British government 'found itself challenged with an alternative government. This alternative government – this soviet – is a small group of trade-union leaders.' Churchill also realized the impact on public opinion of radio, still in its infancy. In 1926 there were two million regular listeners (one in twenty of the population), but its reach was wider than that of the *British Gazette*. Churchill put five strike bulletins each day on the government-controlled BBC and got Baldwin, with his reassuring voice, to make frequent speeches. The TUC was not allowed access to the BBC, nor were Ramsay MacDonald or even the Archbishop of Canterbury, Randall Davidson, who wanted to make an appeal for peace negotiations.

The strikers had only the *British Worker*, a daily single-sheet paper printed in the *Daily Herald* offices by the TUC, in response to the *British Gazette*. Its circulation was about a million. The *British Worker* insisted that the strike was an industrial dispute called to secure a decent wage for the miners: 'there is no constitutional crisis'. It asked all union members 'to be exemplary in their conduct' and to avoid provoking police interference. There was, in fact, amazingly little violence. Rocks were thrown at blackleg lorries, and amateur train- and bus-drivers were responsible for several accidental deaths, but no firearms were ever used and no one was killed on either side in any of the clashes between crowds and the police or troops. An almost eerie tone of life-as-usual was manufactured by Churchill and Baldwin's crucial decision to allow sports and entertainments to go on. The theatres were reopened by government order on 5 May and the tour of the Australian cricket team was allowed to continue. To many people's even greater amazement, on 9 May a team of strikers defeated a team of local police by two goals in a soccer match before several thousand spectators at Plymouth.

The evident failure of the strike to bring the country to its knees – the result of the months of advance planning by Churchill and the government – convinced the TUC to call an end to the strike on 12 May. It claimed to have Baldwin's assurance that he would work quickly to settle some of the miners' grievances. When the miners discovered that the Prime Minister had made no specific promises to the TUC, they remained on strike. While for most people life began to return to normal in mid-May, the miners stayed out until November, when they accepted a settlement no better than the original offer of a 13 per cent reduction and the loss of their seven-hour day.

Laski's role in the General Strike provides perhaps the paradigmatic case-study with which to evaluate his 'mythomania'. Reviews of the *Holmes–Laski Letters* in 1953, whether by political enemies in the British and American press or by old friends like Edmund Wilson in the *New Yorker*, had trouble with Laski's claims of having played an important role behind the scenes. In one letter he wrote of 'those in high places with whom it was my business to deal', in another of 'as I told the Prime Minister' and of carrying out 'private negotiations with the government on behalf of the unions', and finally of the ultimate settlement being based 'upon a draft I had written'. Well might one suspect fabrication, since he added to Holmes that 'this is strictly between ourselves; I have not even written it to Felix'. Yet enough corroboration exists to suggest that, as was so often the case, while exaggeration exists, especially with respect to the final claim, a good deal of the boasts have some factual basis.

Harold and Frida spent most of the strike at the headquarters of the TUC in Eccleston Square. Middle-class socialists with cars were critically useful to the TUC, since only private cars could move about. Frida had the responsibility throughout the strike of driving Arthur Pugh, the General Secretary of the Iron and Steel Federation who was then serving as the Chairman of the TUC, from meeting to meeting. She and Laski also helped to 'look after' Herbert Smith, the head of the Miners' Federation. Laski was also deeply involved in editing the *British Worker*. According to Thomas Jones, the Deputy Secretary to the Cabinet and confidant of Baldwin, Laski did in fact 'negotiate' with the government. On 8 May between 4.45 and 5.45 Jones took notes as Laski reported on the attitudes of Pugh, Smith and Bevin.

> Laski then produced a written scheme for a settlement, signed by himself, but one with the general lines of which he felt sure Pugh was in accord. I went through it carefully, discussing it clause by clause, and putting what I deemed would be the government's objection.

Laski's proposal, according to Jones, called for a conditional end to the strike with mandatory arbitration on all issues and 'the decision of the arbitrator to be enforced on the parties by the government'. Jones proceeded to edit the proposal and 'told him I would show the document if he liked as thus amended to the PM (this I did within an hour)'. Jones's diary notes a meeting with Baldwin at 5.45: '. . . told him also the substance of the Laski interview'.

Other, more powerful, people, Sir Herbert Samuels among them, were drafting memoranda and volunteering as intermediaries, so it is difficult to assess the relative significance of Laski's contribution. None the less, on 13 May, the day after the TUC called an end to the General Strike, Jones devoted an entire page of his diary to reproducing verbatim a letter from Laski with advice for the Prime Minister. Laski's concern was that Baldwin should not be vindictive and that he offer the miners 'the square deal of which he spoke on Sunday'. According to Jones, Baldwin was receiving very different advice from some in his Cabinet 'who were very nervous of the PM showing undue magnanimity'. Jones told Baldwin of the letter from Laski on the way to the House. One can never know the impact of Laski's letter on Baldwin, but that night the Prime Minister's older concilia-tory nature did in fact win out. In Jones's words, 'It would have been perfectly easy to inflame the passions of both sides, but the PM in half a dozen sentences calmed the whole House, saying, "I have always urged that the occasion calls neither for malice, nor for recrimination, nor for triumph."'

In his own public actions Laski was less conciliatory. The very month of the General Strike, Laski was chosen to be Chairman of the Fabian Society's Executive Committee, and on its behalf he issued a statement of 'full sympathy with the Miners' Federation'. In mid-June, when the General Strike was over but the miners were still out, Laski put forward an urgent motion at the Fabian Society annual meeting 'condemning without reserva-tion the government's proposals for settlement'. Privately, on the other hand, he was writing to Frankfurter that 'the miners were impossible. They never budged an inch throughout. They have no plans.' Even if the miners were reluctant to confront economic reality, he was moved and impressed by their courage, and after their final surrender in November Laski wrote to Brandeis of 'the ghastly end of the coal struggle' which he suggested augured a 'vaster tragedy than we have ever known'.

Laski was a principal reporter and interpreter of the General Strike to Americans, writing pieces in the Nation, the New Republic and Survey. He insisted that no one sought 'any political or constitutional change'; it was simply 'a sympathetic strike on a peculiarly massive scale'. He backed this up not only with data about the refusal to curtail food and hospital services but with anecdotes about its orderly and peaceful nature, including, of course, a description of the Plymouth soccer match. He drew distinctions between Baldwin, a man of 'humanity, shrewdness and insight', and his colleagues Joynson-Hicks and Churchill, 'both of them pinchbeck Mussolinis by temperament'. In interpreting the strike for Americans, Laski saw it as proof of what he had written in his American books on pluralism some ten years earlier. The government erroneously assumed that all citizens automatically felt a moral obligation to come to its support. 'It insisted, that is, that allegiance is monistic. In fact, the trade unionist felt that in the given case his allegiance was more rightly due to the trade union than to the government.' Strong stuff for the America of Calvin Coolidge, and strong stuff even for Britain, where on Sunday 9 May in the middle of the strike Cardinal Bourne declared at High Mass in Westminster Cathedral that 'the strike was a sin against the obedience which we owe to God. All are bound to uphold and assist the government, which is the lawfully constituted authority of the country and represents therefore in its own appointed sphere the authority of God himself.' So much for Laski's former Catholic allies in the pluralist critique of the state.

The year of the General Strike saw Laski's personal situation change dramatically. In February he wrote to Holmes that he had been given Wallas's Chair and was now the LSE's Professor of Political Science, one of only two in Britain, the other at Oxford. By March the *Jewish Chronicle* had told everyone of the honour. Laski's letters of recommendation for the Chair had come from Ernest Barker, H. A. L. Fisher, Haldane, A. D. Lindsay and Joseph Redlich, two distinguished political scholars, and Roscoe Pound. Laski's inaugural lecture, delivered on 22 October, was entitled 'On the Study of Politics', which, when it was published as a pamphlet, was dedicated to 'my friend Mr Justice Sankey with enduring affection'. His old tutor Ernest Barker chaired the event, and Haldane and Beveridge, the LSE's Director, both made short speeches. Laski's salary rose to £1,000 per annum. That autumn Laski bought his house at Addison Bridge Place.

At the time of Laski's appointment, the LSE was growing in numbers and prestige. In the early 1920s it had about 2,500 students, one-third full-time and two-thirds part-time. That ratio would be reversed in a decade. Of the total an average of slightly more than 300 were foreign and colonial students, of whom about 130 were Indians. The Webbs in creating and Haldane in supporting the school saw its students as 'the sons and daughters of households of limited means and strenuous lives'. The school's founding memorandum had stipulated that 'it cannot, like Oxford and Cambridge, set itself to skim from the surface of society, the topmost layer of rich men's sons and scholarship winners'. It always had distinguished women scholars on its faculty and from its beginning was open to women and men students; a larger number than usual, sometimes over 20 per cent, were women. In its graduate teaching of economics, politics and anthropology, the school sought to be no less than 'the foremost postgraduate centre in the intellectual world', and over the next several decades many would think it had achieved this. H. G. Wells, perhaps not the most disinterested observer, felt that the LSE was 'the most efficient centre of modern social, political and economic thought in the world'. As for its politics, it tilted slightly to the left, though it was never as leftist as it was perceived to be then or in the 1930s. Laski told a correspondent for America's *Century Magazine* in a 1928 interview that the faculty's politics was much like the students, which he divided as about 800 Conservatives, 1,100 Labour and 600 Liberal.

Shortly after his return in 1920 Laski had written to Frankfurter that the LSE 'is really admirable and I am in love with it'. What he particularly loved was the feel of being near the heart of things, a walking distance to the City, Whitehall and Westminster, enabling one to have government ministers to class or make it back from Soho lunches for the 2.00 p.m. seminar. Oxbridge, on the other hand, was 'cloistered from the world' and their 'dons too removed from life'. Not that Laski wasn't pleased in 1922 to be offered the Special Visiting Lectureship in Political Science at Magdalene College, Cambridge, that Wallas had held for years. For three years, then, 1922–5, Laski also taught at Cambridge for two days a week, with rooms in college.

Ever the object of faculty Red-watchers, in Britain as well as America, Laski was attacked by a group of the school's businessmen governors in 1923 when he was being considered for promotion to a readership. The Director replied that Laski's political beliefs were irrelevant and that the appointment was based purely on 'the technical eminence of the teacher concerned'. Beveridge defended Laski again that year from a woman from Hampstead, M. A. Clay, whose letter criticizing Laski along with others attested to the general 'visibility' he'd achieved since his return. She complained to the Director that the LSE had too much of 'a distinctly socialist influence', which she had heard 'turns out young people with revolutionary ideas'. She mentioned perfunctorily 'Mr Tawney's books' and 'Prof. Dalton's on the Capital Levy' and then zeroed in on her real prey. She had 'learned a good deal about Mr Laski and I cannot help asking you whether it is right that such an important subject as Political Ideas should be dealt with in a London university by a foreigner?' Beveridge assured Mrs Clay that 'Mr Laski was not a foreigner' and that politics was taught at the school by people of widely divergent political attitudes.

More hurtful to Laski than charges that he was a Red were claims from school governors in the City and from Webb that Laski's extra-college activities might be leaving him too little time for the school. The governors emphasized his party politics and his partisan journalism while Webb saw too much time going to adult education trips, BIAE administration, and politics in general. Webb was, of course, uninterested in reprimanding or sacking Laski but wished to propose a possible part-time appointment, perhaps as part of his often expressed desire to get Laski to run for the House of Commons. Beveridge called Laski to see him and suggested that perhaps he wasn't giving enough time to the LSE. An angry Laski wrote back to Beveridge that such charges were unfair. He was at the school '4 to 5 hours a day, every day except Friday and Saturday when I am in Cambridge'. He described seeing and advising students every day and 'entertaining them at my house constantly'. Beveridge wrote back to apologize for the misperceptions and admitted 'I accept it may be wrong.' Neither the businessmen nor Webb got their way: Laski remained at the LSE full-time and, of course, never ran for Parliament. Ten years later Beveridge would not back down so graciously, and his dispute with Laski would be the talk of London.

For thirty years Laski taught at the LSE, and one would expect that some of his closest friends would come from among his faculty colleagues. In fact he developed close relationships with few of them. The initial flurry of friendship with Wallas never developed. Their differences in background and age – Wallas was the son of an Anglican priest and thirty-five years older – didn't seem to matter when Wallas was arranging Laski's position at the LSE. Wallas had also, after all, abandoned belief for a rationalist anti-clerical socialism much like Shaw's, and Laski also had little trouble befriending older men. The Laski who had written that 'if one were to assess the progress of social theory in the last ten or fifteen years, I think no small part of what it has gained would have to be traced to Mr Wallas' soon became much less appreciative of Wallas. 'My main disappointment is Graham Wallas,' he wrote to Holme. 'He is very lovable and charming, but he seems to me totally without the creative instinct.' Wallas's writings in the twilight of his career were 'mere elegant trifling' and, even worse, when Laski succeeded him he claimed that Wallas had left the administrative affairs of the department in a shambles. It is tempting to read Laski's cooling towards Wallas as proof of his self-serving nature, that when he no longer needed his assistance, candour replaced sycophancy. On the other hand, Laski was moving away intellectually from his earlier enthusiasm for the Wallas tendency to imbue politics with psychological theory, speaking critically against such an enterprise for the first time in his inaugural lecture in 1926. Still, when Wallas died in 1932, Laski gave him his due credit, noting that 'all over the world there are first-rate people in the social sciences who owe their original impulse to work to him; and I don't think a man could wish for a finer epitaph'.

Among LSE colleagues closer to his own age, the one he would work with the longest was R. H. Tawney. They were closest in the 1920s. Laski worked hard campaigning for Tawney in several unsuccessful bids for Parliament, and in 1922, when Tawney was extremely ill, Laski described him to Holmes as one of his dearest friends. They were involved in similar Labour Party enterprises, both, for example, helping draft the party manifesto in 1927 and 1928. They shared a common passion for worker education, with Tawney, indeed, surpassing even Laski in the time and writing he devoted to it. Laski thought highly of Tawney's work. In a 1925 review article on 'Political Science in Great Britain' written for the *American Political Science Review*, Laski described 'Tawney's *Acquisitive Society* the most influential English book of the last fifteen years', and the following year Laski helped to get the last chapter of Tawney's new book, *Religion and the Rise of Capitalism*, published for an American audience in the *New Republic*. Tawney also passed the ultimate litmus test for people Laski called his friends, dedicating his 1930 *The Danger of Obedience and Other Essays* to Tawney. On the other hand, Tawney's biographer suggests that Laski in general 'thought more of Tawney than Tawney thought of Laski'.

Tawney and Laski were, indeed, never really close, and by the 1930s they had little to do with each other outside the college. When Laski moved dramatically to the left within the Labour Party, Tawney became the intellectual guru to the mainstream, centrist policy-making apparatus in the party presided over by Hugh Dalton and the younger economists Evan Durbin and Hugh Gaitskell, who were especially influenced by Tawney's last important book, *Equality*, published in 1931. But much more important than party politics is that they were so utterly unlike each other. Tawney was everyone's 'socialist saint'. His Anglican religiosity and humility made him loved, respected and even worshipped. For Hugh Gaitskell he was 'one of the greatest living Englishmen', for Kingsley Martin 'one of the very best men alive'. Tawney's socialism was grounded in a vision of Christian love and Christian fellowship. He saw the British class system as a violation of God's will that all people were equal in his sight. His socialism was personal and moral as well as religious. Socialism for him was not efficiency and abundance, but just and equal social relationships built on fellowship and brotherhood. Laski also tapped into this vast stream of ethical socialism, usually via William Morris, but Tawney's overt and heartfelt religiosity always distanced Laski from the 'scholar saint', as Beatrice Webb described Tawney. Anne Bohm, who knew them both, summed it up: 'Tawney's Christianity never did go down well with Harold.'

Tawney and Laski were polar opposites in temperament as well. Tawney was a quiet man with the retiring and reserved nature of the upper-middle-class Englishman he was. A wizard with the written word, he was awkward at casual conversation as well as public speaking and sought to stay out of the limelight. He was rather stiff and impersonal and came across as slightly aloof. Wise, erudite, morally intense, but also absent-minded, forgetful of names, untidy, and sloppily dressed with cigarette ash and cat hair on his clothes, Tawney seldom fraternized with his students. Though they lived in Tavistock Square in Bloomsbury, the Tawneys seldom saw other intellectuals socially, preferring, for example, William Temple, who would one day be the Archbishop of Canterbury. Tawney's wife, Annette, was another obstacle to a Laski–Tawney relationship. She was the sister of William Beveridge, the LSE's Director, and by the early 1930s Laski and Beveridge were bitter enemies. Even more important, she seems to have been universally disliked, with contemporaries describing her as boring, untidy and acquisitive.

In noting Laski's lack of any real friendship with his colleagues of so many years, one is led outside the LSE to his relationship with the third member of the socialist intellectual trinity between the wars, G. D. H.

Cole. With Cole there was no religiosity barrier, and the two men shared a
similar intellectual move from an anti-statist group socialism around the
First World War to a full-blown acceptance of Fabian statist socialism by
the 1930s. As Tawney outdid Laski in his worker education involvement,
Cole in the 1930s almost single-handedly created or revived Fabian political
and research groups to the extent that he and his wife, Margaret, became
the Webbs' successors as Mr and Mrs Fabianism. While Tawney had pulled
back from much of his Labour Party involvement in the 1930s, Cole, like
Laski, continued to exert great influence in the party for years as an
intellectual behind the scenes. Even their scholarship overlapped; while
Cole was particularly interested in the social history of the labour movement, he also wrote occasionally on political philosophy.

Nor were their temperaments that dissimilar. Cole was as much a
workaholic as Laski, sometimes writing three or more books a year as well
as numbers of articles, and he was always as ready as Laski to volunteer for
a committee or a research project for the labour movement. In addition, he
wrote nearly three dozen detective stories, sometimes three or four a year,
often co-written with his wife. Like Laski, Cole was fastidious in his dress
and appearance. He liked the elegance of college life, and his Oxford house
had large grounds and tennis courts. Unlike Laski, however, he did not
exude geniality and sociability; he was much more reserved. He was slim,
handsome and apparently more interested in young men like Hugh Gaitskell
than in his wife after their marriage. He was an aesthete, a socialist who
was a connoisseur of Bohemian glass and fine wine and who, if he could
manage it, seldom if ever went to industrial England on either lecture trips
or worker education weekends.

Laski and Cole had their differences over the years. In the 1920s Laski
overemphasized his problems with Cole's guild socialism as part of his
enthusiastic embrace of the Webbs, even as Cole himself was abandoning
his earlier views. In the 1930s Cole managed to stay on better terms with
Bevin and the trade-union wing of the Labour Party than Laski did. As late
as November 1939, much to Laski's anger, Cole was still calling for
negotiations with Hitler's Germany and criticizing the Labour Party for
rallying behind the government in the name of national unity. But behind
these intellectual and policy differences there was a much deeper divide
between Cole and Laski. They actively disliked each other. In a biography
of her husband, Margaret Cole describes 'the curious lifelong antagonism'

between Cole and Laski 'which was always present and was well known to their friends'. She suggested, quite perceptively, that it was partly a rivalry over who would be the oracle or intellectual leader of the generations of young socialists they were teaching and who would have more influence on the labour movement for which they both worked so tirelessly. Her husband, Margaret Cole suggests, 'cherished a considerable contempt for certain aspects of Laski', his enjoyment of mingling in important circles and 'his telling of tall stories which he expected to be believed'. For his part, Laski characteristically had trouble with anyone who sought to emulate what he was doing as a political and social theorist, insider and *éminence grise*, teacher and confidant of decision-makers.

It is difficult to recapture the hold over the mind of the left between the wars exercised by the socialist trinity of Cole, Laski and Tawney. A survey of Labour MPs in 1962 asked: 'What books or authors have had the greatest influence on your political beliefs?' The answers revealed that after Shaw, Wells and Marx, the next were Cole, Tawney and Laski. A similar survey in 1975 found Tawney and Laski in the top eight influential authors, but Cole had dropped out. Of the three, Tawney was and remains the most influential scholar, even if he wrote little after 1931. He was the best writer of the three, though he wrote much less than they did. He was the most restrained and his fewer books have survived longer. He alone of the three was elected a fellow of the British Academy. Cole was the most politically influential of the three, not only in Fabian politics, but also behind the scenes in the Labour Party. He was less locked into a partisan corner than Laski in the 1930s and 1940s, and through his students Gaitskell, Douglas Jay and Evan Durbin he had a tremendous impact on the evolution of Labour policy in the 1930s. Laski, on the other hand, was the most well-known and publicly visible of the three. Cole and Tawney were less flamboyant. They seldom left Britain and had much less of a following in America and Europe than Laski. In comparison, Laski was a more universal socialist educator, the popular symbol of Labour intellectuals both for Labour constituency parties and for the public at large.

If Laski never became friends with either Tawney or Cole, there were other possibilities among his LSE colleagues in the 1920s. Laski never warmed to the great anthropologist Malinowski, who seems to have actively disliked him. Among the sociologists, Laski overlapped for a few years with the elderly L. T. Hobhouse, whom he respected for his writings on liberalism and the state and for his friendship with Haldane. Laski and Morris Ginsberg, the new Professor of Sociology, got along, but they never became close friends. In economics there was Hugh Dalton, six years Laski's senior, the son of the Canon of St George's Royal Chapel at Windsor Castle, who had come to the LSE in 1919. He wrote three important books on socialist public finance between 1920 and 1923, and in 1924 was elected to Parliament for Labour. He remained on the teaching staff at the LSE part-time until 1935, when he emerged as a mighty power in the Labour Party. Dalton was a physically overbearing man with a powerful booming voice that exuded arrogance and dripped with sarcasm. He was recognized and respected for his grasp of financial policy, limitless energy and drive, and he was feared for his public viciousness and brutal personal attacks. As one Labour colleague put it, Dalton's eyes were 'deep green pools of insincerity'.

Laski apparently tried to get along with Dalton, and indeed he campaigned for Dalton in his successful bid for Parliament in 1924. But during their thirty-year relationship, they never became friends partly because no one seems to have ever lasted as a friend of Dalton's, but also because Dalton took particular delight as he evolved into a major player in the Labour Party in brutalizing the party's left-wing intellectuals. He clearly had Cole and Laski in mind when writing several years later of intellectuals in the Labour Party that 'we have too many and too talkative and too scribblish . . . these semi-crocks, diabetics and undersized Semites'.

Unlike Dalton, Lionel Robbins, an economist at the LSE, had a relationship with Laski that was an interesting blend of ideological conflict combined with personal respect and even affection. He studied the history of political ideas with Laski, though his major intellectual influence was Dalton. After teaching at New College, Oxford, Robbins joined the LSE as a lecturer in 1925, and in the 1930s he emerged along with his new colleague, Friedrich Hayek, as a defender of the free market and an opponent of state intervention, and as such was the frequent target of Laski's writing. After the Second World War Robbins became a pillar of the Establishment, a life peer, Chairman of the *Financial Times* and author of the report that lay behind the great university expansion of the 1960s, remaining on the staff of the LSE intil forced to leave through illness.

Robbins always had problems with Laski's 'parlour Marxism' and his 'superficial and tedious' observations. Even as a student Robbins recorded in his diary that Laski's phraseology was 'synthetic and so superlative', and he saw behind Laski's acute analytical apparatus 'an almost juvenile personality – a lack of emotional balance that is nearly painful . . . he is still as imitative as a child'. For all his professed collectivism, Laski was 'one of the most individualistic men I have ever met'. 'He will always be a lonely figure surrounded by friends,' Robbins predicted, 'an *enfant terrible* amidst admiring onlookers.' Robbins was deeply hurt by Laski's flippancy in describing his paper, critical of nationalization of the mines, as 'reactionary', and wrote: 'What did this spoilt child of fortune and intellectual fashion know of the ardours and endurances of my intellectual and spiritual pilgrimage?' Despite their mutual complaints over the years about the other being a propagandist with students and their frequent criticism of each other in print, they maintained a cordial relationship at the LSE, though they saw little of each other outside. Robbins was also a book collector and they often exchanged news on their finds. More significantly, Robbins, like Laski, was an outspoken critic in the 1930s of Beveridge's dictatorial methods as Director of the School. Nor could Robbins deny that Laski was 'kindly . . . compassionate, and a lively and entertaining companion'. By adult standards, Robbins insisted, Laski often did things that were inexcusable. 'Judged as a very precocious boy with the bewildering mixture of good and bad impulses which usually go with precocity, he had much in him that was positively lovable.' But what lay at the heart of their friendship at the School was, according to Robbins,

that quick apprehension and sense of fun that so often when we were on committees together, even at times of considerable dissension, would cause our eyes to meet in mutual relish at the absurdity of some pompous colleague or some preposterous academic formality.

Laski's friend Kingsley Martin was also a colleague at the LSE for a time in the 1920s. When Martin first met Laski at Magdalene College, Cambridge, he 'was stunned, as most young men were, by this man who seemed to know everything about all the subjects that interested me', by his comprehensive library of books 'and by his endless stream of anecdotes about all the famous men of our day'. Martin was not unaware of suspect qualities of Laski, writing in his diary about a socialist weekend that year that 'Laski is getting a reputation as a charlatan'. When Martin went to Princeton in 1922 on a fellowship, Laski gave him introductions to Holmes,

Frankfurter, Brandeis, Lippmann and Croly, and when he returned to England Laski helped to arrange a job for him as lecturer in politics at the LSE. They became fast friends, with Martin accompanying Laski on book-buying jaunts to Paris, coming by in the evenings, and even dutifully sitting in daily at the Amritsar libel trial. Martin left the LSE in 1927, worked for the *Manchester Guardian* and then in 1931 was chosen by Keynes to edit the newly combined *New Statesman* and *Nation*, a job he held for thirty years, turning the magazine into the premier socialist weekly in English. For the next two decades there was always room in the weekly for a piece by Martin's friend Laski. On numerous occasions he even let Laski do the 'London Diary', the editor's personal page of reflections. Through the *New Statesman and Nation*, both Kingsley Martin and Laski acquired a reputation in the 1930s and 1940s as world-wide publicists (the weekly was widely read in Africa and Asia) for a kind of democratic socialism associated with Fabianism and the LSE.

Laski, the dependable voice on the Labour Party's left, did not appear as regular Saturday morning reading in the *New Statesman* until the 1930s. The years immediately after the General Strike found him still a voice of moderation, taking no part in attacks on the party leadership from the left. In 1925 the 'Clydesider' James Maxton had become Chairman of the ILP and along with Lansbury's new journal, *Lansbury's Labour Weekly*, attacked MacDonald mercilessly. The ILP produced its own more radical socialist vision in 1926, published as *The Living Wage*, which called for a legally guaranteed minimum wage, a state-run system of family allowances funded by taxation, and public ownership of banks, credit institutions, coal, electricity, transport and land. The Labour Party's leadership, loath to commit a future Labour government to an excessively detailed agenda, disassociated itself from *The Living Wage*.

Laski cast his lot with the leadership in this dispute. In 1927 and 1928, as we have noted, he helped to draft the official Labour Party manifesto, which was much less specific than the ILP document. In July 1926 Laski, along with Herbert Morrison, the powerful London Labour Party leader, visited Neville Chamberlain, the Minister of Health, to make a presentation on the effects of a proposed reform of the Poor Laws. Laski continued to see Baldwin occasionally, who he told Holmes in 1928 had offered him a post as secretary of a research committee of the Cabinet, which he turned down, and he even had no problem seeing Churchill frequently after the

General Strike. Laski had met him again after many years on a trip to his father's summer-house, where Churchill was visiting. He then saw him in London for occasional dinners and lunches, finding him 'amusing and brilliant', one who 'talks electrically'. In May 1927 Laski brought Churchill to dinner at the LSE to meet Beveridge and some of the younger faculty. According to Laski, 'he was like a great actor playing a part. He did it supremely well, and, I think, enchanted them ... He is a good fellow, incurably romantic and an arresting mind.'

In 1927 Laski worked closely with Citrine, the leader of the TUC, and the Parliamentary Labour Party in opposing the Tory government's revenge for the General Strike, the Trade Disputes and Trade Union Act. Laski was one of six people appointed by the TUC to a Bureau of Advisers on Legal and Constitutional Questions whose main purpose was to fight the legislation intended by the Tories to prevent future general strikes, the first legislation since 1825 to interfere with the freedom of workers. The legislation declared sympathetic strikes by strikers from different industries illegal. It also made it obligatory for workers to 'contract in' if they wished to have a part of their union dues go to the political levy as opposed to an automatic reduction unless they 'contracted out', as allowed by the Liberal legislation of 1913. Finally, the Bill outlawed civil servants from belonging to a trade union to which anyone else belonged.

Laski not only worked closely with the TUC in a public and legal campaign against the Bill, he was also chosen to make Labour's case against the legislation in a pamphlet published in a popular series on important public issues, the 'Present Day Papers'. The defence of the Bill in the series was written by Sir Ernest Benn, the Liberal publisher, who was cast in the awkward role of advocating state legislative interference in the market-place in the service of ostensibly *laissez-faire* ideals. Laski's attack was a ringing and passionate endorsement of trade unions, reminiscent of his earlier writings. Not only was this 'the worst blow aimed at industrial peace in the lifetime of the present generation', it was an effort to destroy 'the main safeguard of labour against the more reactionary elements on the capitalist side'. Laski noted that the legislation required court actions for violators and that 'trade unionists do not believe that they will get a fair trial in the courts', with perhaps only 800 of the 10,000 magistrates who sat on the Bench coming from labour. The Bill only breeds 'suspicion and

antagonism'. Instead of a common search for improvements in industrial
relations, it makes abundantly clear 'that the interests of capital and labour
are permanently incompatible'. Laski used his space in this widely read
pamphlet to call upon earlier themes developed in his less accessible
academic books. He wrote:

> Strikes are not prevented by prohibitory legislation; to prevent strikes the
> only adequate way is to remove their cause. The root of strikes lies in
> economic injustice, and the root of sympathetic strikes lies in that solidarity
> of feeling among the working class the expression of which cannot be
> prevented by law. For when men feel passionately that a certain cause of
> action is demanded by justice, they will pursue the course of action; and if
> the law stands in the way, they will break the law.

While he worked closely with the Labour Party and trade-union leadership, dined with the Chancellor who had led the fight against the General
Strike and eschewed any formal links with the left's criticism of the
leadership, Laski was not totally out of tune with their message. He did on
occasion criticize the labour movement, but, as was often the case in the
1920s, he felt more at ease (or less in jeopardy) in voicing his concerns to an
American audience. In the *New Republic* he dissented from the 'determined
moderation' of the Labour Party conference in 1926. MacDonald, he
wrote, 'has largely ceased to be interested in ideas.' 'Picturesque, vivid and
eloquent,' MacDonald's mind was 'episodic and timid, and he is well
behind the majority of his followers'. After the 1927 party conference Laski
recited the same litany for the *New Republic*. 'Mr MacDonald himself has
something like a horror of ideas . . . Mr Snowden has largely ceased to be a
socialist . . . and Mr Thomas never was a socialist.' Laski had noticed the
re-emergence of Lloyd George after Asquith's resignation in 1926 and his
attraction to Keynesian ideas about public expenditure on public works.
Labour's lack of interest in a 'more audacious policy', he joked, 'makes Mr
Lloyd George look like a reckless Bolshevist'. Intimations of Laski in the
1930s could be heard in his attack on the party's leadership for American
consumption in the very months he was busily doing its bidding in
Westminster.

> If it [the Labour Party] is merely to become the alternative to the
> Conservative Party with a philosophy that is as related to socialism as a
> jerry-built house to Westminster Abbey, it will not continue to attract

those who still venture to dream of a new world built by high courage and arduous effort.

But Laski was riddled with paradoxes. The other side of his passionate defence of trade unions in 1927 and their right to strike was his hope for industrial cooperation in the wake of the General Strike and which he had outlined in his *Grammar of Politics*. Bevin, Citrine and the TUC Chairman in 1927–8, Ben Turner, envisioned the creation of formal machinery patterned on the Whitley Report of 1917 in which discussion and negotiations would be established through industrial councils in different industries. In response, Sir Alfred Mond, the head of Imperial Chemicals, convened a joint committee of employers and TUC officials in 1927 to discuss approaches to industrial collaboration. These Mond–Turner talks, as they were called, produced nothing concrete, but Bevin and Citrine were impressed at the prospect for some kind of agreements among workers, employers and the state to control industrial production as well as industrial relations. Sympathetic to the TUC's revived interest in the Whitley Council principle, Laski applauded Citrine in late 1927 in the *New Republic* as a man who 'has a philosophic grasp of the industrial problem, rare, indeed, in the history of trade unionism', but cautioned the TUC to realize as it embarked on 'conferences with employers out of which might evolve an epoch of peace in industry' that labour and capital do not necessarily mean the same thing by 'industrial peace'. 'To capital it means no strikes and an increased output for slightly higher wages.' To labour, and to the author of *The Grammar of Politics* 'it means elevation to the rank of joint adviser on every aspect of industrial policy'.

As if Labour Party work, along with his teaching, writing and worker education, wasn't enough to keep him busy, Laski in the autumn of 1926 was appointed an arbitrator on the Industrial Court, a position he retained for the next twenty-four years. The Industrial Court had been established in 1919 as part of the same 'reconstruction' of industrial relations which had produced the Whitley Councils in 1917. The Ministry of Labour under the Industrial Courts Act had the power to appoint arbitrators to settle disputes that employers and employees jointly agreed to take to the court. The arbitration panels followed the Whitley principle of an independent chairman, one representative chosen by the employers and one by the workers. In the period between 1917 and 1919 over 180 Whitley Councils had been established in various industries. By 1926, however, most of the industry-wide Whitley Councils had vanished, leaving little work for the Industrial Court. Only the Second World War would see a revival of the Whitley councils. In one important area, the civil service, however, the Whitley Council flourished throughout the inter-war period and so did the recourse to the arbitration services of the Industrial Court. Technically, then, Laski was appointed in October 1926 to the Civil Service Arbitration Tribunal of the Industrial Court, chosen by the staff side.

Laski sat on about ten cases a year, though in some years the number was much higher. A case could take an afternoon in London or could involve days out of town taking testimony and deliberating. 'It's perfectly fascinating work,' Laski wrote to Frankfurter, 'but it requires more time than I thought likely when I took the appointment.' Laski had to master the most minute details about different occupations, work-loads and salaries, and combine this with sensitivity to witnesses. He did it extremely well and soon found himself on a panel of the National Conciliation Board of the Co-operative Society and as an arbitrator in non-civil service disputes. In a letter to Holmes Laski boasted that 'I shall for the next month be able to recite backwards the wages and hours of the boot and shoe operatives of England.' While he found it difficult, as he put it, to sit for eight or nine hours and 'make no observation that indicates your view' or to 'keep a tight grip on your head lest your heart run away with you', Laski derived immense satisfaction from his work on the settlements which gave milkmen a six-day week, postmen ten days' sick leave, government typists twenty-two shillings more a week, or dairy workers, 'who in the past had not even Christmas Day as a holiday', a week's holiday with pay. In the midst of a letter to Frankfurter devoted mainly to musings on Hitler in 1936, Laski turned suddenly to his latest case and noted that 'to my surprise, after a grim fight, my two colleagues collapsed and agreed to £70 per annum increase for 2,500 men immediately and for another 7,000 later'.

Laski's many years of service on the Industrial Court speak to his heartfelt sympathy for the working class, but most significantly they are testimony to his amazing capacity to compartmentalize his life. He was at once the meta-theorist of social change which envisioned fundamentally transforming the lives of the British working class, perhaps even of the world's proletariat, and the micro-manager of the wages or paid holidays of 300 civil servants in Aberdeen. To arbitrate over twenty-two shillings was to accept the existing economic system; it raised no questions about ownership and control of industry or property. Just as he would flail the Great and the Good while at the same time cultivating them, so he would invoke the demise of capitalism and yet devote so much of his time to fine-tuning it.

Laski's Industrial Court career had at least one profound effect on the future course of British politics. Impressed in 1938 with the presentation made to his court by a young trade-union official, Laski took the young Jim Callaghan under his wing and set him a course of reading at the LSE library. As the future Prime Minister later described it, 'He kept in touch with me in the years that followed, using his good offices to put my name forward as a potential parliamentary candidate . . . I remain grateful to his memory, for the trouble he took to help an unknown and rather prickly young man.'

Involvement with the Industrial Court represented Laski's micro-involvement in post-General Strike Britain. His macro-speculations of those years are best found in his 1927 book *Communism*, a little book for H. A. L. Fisher and Gilbert Murray's Home University Library series, which captured public attention. Dedicated to his colleagues L. T. Hobhouse and M. Ginsberg, it sold 40,000 copies in three printings in 1927 alone, while arming a generation of the British left with arguments about what was wrong with communism and why they were socialists. Michael Foot remembers that when he went to Oxford several years later, 'we all had read Laski's *Communism*, the first real book on communism by an English critic'. It also led many Tories, like Baldwin, to see Laski as the major intellectual influence on the Labour Party.

Labour's attitude to communism was a pressing practical issue as well. The Communist Party of Great Britain (CPGB) in these years was seeking to affiliate itself to the Labour Party. In his journalism Laski was of two minds on the issue. British communists, he wrote in the *New Republic*, 'lie, they intrigue, they falsify, they distort, they indulge in vile personal abuse, and then express astonishment that a fraternal hand is not extended to them'. On the other hand, he regretted their exclusion, because 'they are among the most energetic of the labour ranks'. He was especially taken with Harry Pollitt, recently released from prison. But, ultimately, like the Labour leadership, Laski concluded that the communists' tendency to 'regard all differences from themselves as proof of moral obliquity' made their exclusion from Labour necessary and inevitable.

Laski's *Communism* was a meticulous study of Marxist ideas, Bolshevik practice and the appeal of communism. Descriptions in minute detail of how party cells infiltrate institutions in capitalist countries read like J. Edgar Hoover's exposé of 'the enemy within'. Laski described vividly the 'iron dictatorship' imposed by Lenin and the Bolsheviks, which suppressed opposition and manipulated elections. In an anticipation of the 1930s reality, Laski suggested that the poor and frustrated around the world saw in Russia not its tyranny but its affirmation of a society at the service of ordinary workers. Laski distinguished between the laudable ideal of communism, its vision of a classless society and common ownership, and its methods, social revolution and the dictatorship of the proletariat, which socialists should reject. Against the 'prophetic aspect of communism', its belief in the inevitable unfolding of historical tendencies and laws, there was in history always, Laski cautioned, 'the novel and the unexpected'. More to the point, he could not convince himself that capitalism was incapable of transforming itself into socialism by peaceful and parliamentary methods. Unless, he wrote, there is 'considerable and continued effort for social improvement' there would be pressure for revolution. Laski insisted that no violent upheaval could achieve the aims of a just social order in an age of chemical and aerial warfare. Armed revolution might have worked in 1640, 1789, 1871, and even in Russia in 1917, but not, Laski argued, in 'the modern states of the West'. The communist theory of a secret armed minority seizing power in a single stroke was 'unthinkable in the modern state if the army and navy are loyal to the government'. Violence unleashed savagery and 'makes the generous impulses of an ideal communist society hopeless'. Laski doubted that 'the method of violence is ever the midwife of justice', or that any regime built on hate, fear and violence 'can give birth to an order rooted in fraternity'. Better than communist violence, Laski suggested, is socialist politics. In an age of universal suffrage one might capture power at the polls and 'throw upon the capitalist the onus of revolt against a socialist democracy'. One would then have as allies the army and navy as well as all those who believed in constitutionalism.

What gave the book its enduring influence was Laski's brilliant and counter-intuitive assessment of communism's appeal. 'Communism has made its way,' Laski wrote in a sentence that was forever quoted, 'by its idealism and not its realism, by its spiritual promise, not its materialistic prospect.' The appeal of communism, according to Laski, was its moral and ethical fervour and its vision of spiritual regeneration. The Marxist convinced of the primacy of matter in the universe might react in horror, but his message moved people not through historical objectivity but through ethical and spiritual longing for a moral and just world. In developing this interpretation Laski offered a full-blown analysis of communism as a religion. The year before, Keynes had written 'What is the Communist Faith?' and Bertrand Russell had addressed 'religious Bolshevism', but neither had developed the analogy as fully as Laski did. He depicted the Bolsheviks as Jesuits convinced of 'religious certitude'. There was the same rigorous and unyielding set of dogmas and iron discipline. There was the same passionate loyalty and unlimited self-confidence. Ambitions were set aside; both were the servants of a great idea, whose knowledge of the rightness of ends entitled them to use any means to achieve them. 'Communism is a new religion,' Laski wrote, and like all true believers the Bolsheviks were impatient and intolerant of criticism and dissent. The Communist International, Laski observed, was like the Roman Catholic Church and allegiance to Moscow was as obligatory as to Rome.

Comparisons of communism with religion would become so commonplace in the years to come that one easily forgets that Laski was the first to make this extended argument. It is also easy to forget that he made the case, not to dismiss communism, but to understand its appeal, and to convince socialists that they must match that spiritual message and fervour in democratic politics. To counter communist 'seduction', socialists had to convince everyone to undertake 'an alteration of the present social order by concessions larger in scope and profundity than any ruling class has so far been willing to make by voluntary act'.

Even his frequent critic George Catlin described Laski's *Communism* as 'a book of brilliant lucidity' in the *Nation*, and the *New Statesman* deemed it 'unquestionably the best book Laski has written'. The Communist Party of Great Britain, on the other hand, published *A Defence of Communism in Reply to H. J. Laski* by Ralph Fox to rebut 'the extraordinary and amazing distortions of facts' from the 'professor at the service of capitalism' with the 'halo of labour on his head'. As for Marxism as religion, Fox could only call it 'condescending nonsense' and 'highly-coloured rot'. Brilliance, distortion or rot, Laski's message was also heard in America. *Communism* was published there in 1927 and the following year when the magazine *Current*

History devoted its entire October issue to the topic 'Marxism Today',
Laski's 'The Value and Defects of the Marxist Philosophy' was one of three
articles used. In this new piece Laski repeated that Marxism was a 'faith
held by its adherents with an intensity as passionate as ever moved the
protagonists of a religious creed'. For all its errors of prediction and
interpretation, it was responding to something fundamental in the hearts of
people. Laski drew the lesson for his American magazine readers.

> When the communist draws Utopia upon his map he is human enough to
> have faith in his direction. We shall not answer Marx by telling him that it is
> intellectual error to pursue that road. Our task is rather the proof that the hill
> can be breasted by a different and easier path.

CHAPTER ELEVEN

The Labour Government, Palestine and 'Real Political Influence'

By the end of the 1920s Laski had 'made it' in England. He moved easily in political circles and his writings were widely read by the cultural and governing elite. He was also actively involved with a wide circle of leftist intellectuals in various publishing and organizational ventures. The magazine the *Realist*, conceived and edited principally by his sometime rival George Catlin and with which Laski was associated in 1929, brought him together with a sparkling group of scientific and literary socialists. Catlin had received money for the venture initially from Sir Alfred Mond as well as from H. G. Wells, and when he needed more he asked Laski to join his *New Republic* connections to Catlin's own Cornell University links in a request to Dorothy Straight and Leonard Elmhirst for financial help. The *Realist's* intent was indicated by its subtitle, *A Journal of Scientific Humanism*, and to its organizing meetings, monthly lunches, social evenings and editorial sessions flocked the brightest young intellectuals interested in science, rationalism and humanism. Laski was on the editorial board, as was his New College classmate J. B. S. Haldane. Other scientists included Julian and Aldous Huxley and Richard Gregory, the editor of *Nature*. H. G. Wells was an important presence, as was Leonard Woolf, Herbert Read, the distinguished art critic, and the novelist Arnold Bennett. Laski's *Realist* circle also included four accomplished women, the writer Rebecca West and the academic Eileen Power, both of whom Laski knew already, and Naomi Mitchison, J. B. S. Haldane's sister, later an important Labour Party figure and novelist, and Vera Brittain, Catlin's wife, feminist and future author of *Testament of Youth*. As impressive as the *Realist's* editors were, nothing could save the monthly from the Depression, and it folded in 1930.

A literary connection that Laski also maintained in these years was with the poet Sigfried Sassoon. Frida described the two as devoted pranksters who shared with each other witty and satiric attacks on contemporary figures which they would, of course, never publish. Sassoon often left his humorous creations in the letter-box at Devon Lodge, much to the dismay of the postman. Another friend acquired and maintained through Laski's puckish sense of humour was David Low, who became well known during the General Strike and from 1927 to 1949 was the fabled political cartoonist for Beaverbrook's *Evening Standard*. He also did portrait caricatures for the *New Statesman*, Low often poking fun at Laski with his pen.

Laski's connections with the *Realist* and its creed of 'scientific humanism' overlapped with another circle he moved in during these years, the anti-religious ethical humanists or, as they referred to themselves, the rationalists. The organizational focus of the group was the Rationalist Press Association (RPA), which had been founded in 1899 to foster 'free-thinking'. Laski was chosen President of the RPA in June 1930. J. B. S. Haldane, Wells and Julian Huxley were also active in the RPA. The exception was Catlin himself, who was a convert to Catholicism. The RPA's founding creed announced that it took 'science seriously' and 'accepted the consequences of its methods in all departments of thought and life'. Any claims to derive superior knowledge 'either from intuition or sacred writings are unaccept-able'. Man's fate is in his own hands, 'he must expect no miracles'. Scientific knowledge can either 'increase human happiness and well-being which is the rationalist way', or be used 'for destruction in the service of fanaticism and bigotry'. In telling Holmes of his election as President of the RPA, Laski referred to himself as a 'Voltairean' who believed 'religion more harmful to civilization than any other single factor in history'. A good sense of how Laski appeared to contemporaries in 1930 is found in the RPA's annual newsletter description of their new president.

We in the rationalist movement know that the 'best of causes' has in him a devoted servant, one who by voice and pen is ready and willing to do yeoman's service in its behalf. Those who have heard him speak will remember his bold and clear-cut pronouncements, the easy flow of well-chosen words, the deliberate, perfectly audible enunciation; those who have read his articles in the *Literary Guide*, the *Rationalist Annual* and elsewhere will not need to be reminded of his interest in the more important humane movements of the day – that for the reform of the divorce laws, for instance, and birth control; the latter a cause very dear, too, to the heart of Mrs Laski, who has, I believe, toured the country in its advocacy.

There is a certain East-coast town that every summer is advertised by a famous poster as being 'so bracing'. It seems to me that the term is peculiarly applicable to Mr Laski. It is impossible to imagine any of his students dropping off to sleep when he is lecturing on Hegel or Marx . . .

Every movement has need of such men – men filled with the vigour and enthusiasm of youth, possessed of the wisdom and knowledge usually accorded only to old age.

Laski took several public positions in these years that expressed his rationalist convictions. In February 1929, for example, he spoke out against the Lateran Treaty between the Pope and Mussolini, which granted the Vatican its claim of political sovereignty and which made Roman Catholicism the sole religion of the state. 'Permanently and impenitently anti-clerical', Laski was appalled that marriage questions in Italy would go to ecclesiastical courts and that there would be religious education in all the schools. Laski invoked Voltaire again in his conviction 'that there will be really no peace in the world until the last king has been strangled in the bowels of the last priest'. In November 1929 Laski also visited the Home Secretary to propose legislation repealing Britain's ancient blasphemy laws. The Labour minister J. H. Clynes, finding no time on the legislative calendar, pledged, however, that he would not allow any proceedings under the laws to take place. Several months later a Private Member's Bill implementing Laski's proposal was defeated and the blasphemy laws remain on the statute books to this day. All of these actions sat uneasily with many English socialists. William Temple, for example, the left-leaning Archbishop of York, wrote of Laski in 1931 that though he wanted the Church to help the Labour government, 'he dislikes the Church intensely, and his net is spread too visibly in the sight of the birds'.

There was one issue during this period when Laski the Voltairean rationalist was, in fact, a strong defender of the Anglican Church and the efforts of Archbishop Temple. In 1927 and 1928 one of the most divisive issues Parliament dealt with was the revision of the Anglican Prayer Book. The heart of the controversy lay in the tendency of the new edition to give greater latitude in the Prayer Book to higher-church Anglo-Catholic practices and doctrines. Lower-church Anglicans, especially the evangelical wing, Scots Presbyterians and other dissenters, as well as unbelieving humanists, combined twice in the House of Commons to reject the revisions, led almost single-handedly by the ever-present, conspiracy-prone government minister Jix, a devout Evangelical who, unable to impugn the revisions as a conspiracy wrought by Jewish aliens or Bolsheviks, condemned them as a papist plot, which had older resonance in Westminster. Laski supported the revisions, purely out of consistency with his pluralist notions of associational autonomy and independence. If the Church of England wanted to revise its Prayer Book, he held, it was none of the state's business. Frankfurter, who disagreed with Laski on this issue, couldn't resist noting that 'it was rather amusing to have these two Jews have this fight across the Atlantic that so divided English opinion'.

Within the same intellectual circles that intersected the *Realist* and the rationalists Laski was involved in two other schemes in these years. H. G. Wells convinced Laski, the Huxleys, Rebecca West, Leonard Woolf, Kingsley Martin and Bertrand Russell to join him as sponsors of a new world-wide organization called the Federation of Progressive Societies and Individuals. The federation was committed to establishing a common creed among all left-wing movements in the world, centring on public ownership replacing private property, the creation of a world monetary system, treaties to control armament, vast educational initiatives, and guaranteed rights of free speech, publication and movement. The idea floundered and despite its impressive list of sponsors never came to anything. The much more successful intellectual venture of these years was Laski's participation in founding the *Political Quarterly* in 1930, one of Britain's most distinguished journals devoted to politics. The idea came out of a small group of LSE faculty that included Laski, William Robson, Tawney, Kingsley Martin and, from outside the school, Leonard Woolf. The school had its own quite technical journal, *Economica*, founded in 1921 by its three editors, Beveridge, Dalton and Laski, which split off in 1934 into two journals, the second, *Politica*, handling politics until it died at the outbreak of the war in 1939. What the group sought in 1927 and 1928 was a general political quarterly on the order of the great nineteenth-century Victorian journals of ideas. In December 1928, with talk of Laski and Hammond as co-editors, Shaw and Keynes helped put up the money and Harold Macmillian agreed to be the publisher. Wells, meanwhile, complained in 1929 that the contemplated publication would hurt the *Realist*, which in fact it did. The *Political Quarterly* appeared finally in January 1930 with Kingsley Martin and Leonard Woolf as co-editors, and with a small editorial committee of nine that included Laski and Keynes. Martin left almost immediately for the *New Statesman* and Leonard Woolf edited *Political Quarterly* jointly with William Robson from 1931 to 1958.

Laski's affiliation and support in these ventures were especially valuable, for with the accession of Labour to office in June 1929, albeit again as a minority governing party, Laski finally achieved some of the 'real political influence' he had mentioned to Holmes in 1920 as one of his reasons for returning to England. The general election of 1929 was fought over no single issue: the five years of Baldwin's Tory government had elapsed and there had to be a new election. The election focused on the personalities of the would-be prime ministers: the avuncular pipe-smoking confidence of Baldwin; the still widely distrusted Lloyd George, surrounded, to be sure, by powerful intellects like Keynes; and the elegant and eloquent Ramsay MacDonald. In the first election held under truly universal suffrage, with some five million women voting for the first time (the voting age for women was dropped from thirty to twenty-one in 1924), and the first and last meaningful three-party election, Labour nearly doubled its number of seats to 289, just twenty short of an absolute majority. The Tories had 266 and the Liberals fifty-nine. Laski campaigned in over thirty constituencies, and as Beatrice Webb noted in her diary for 1 June 1929, 'Sidney and I sat up with the Laskis, listening to the flowing tide of Labour victories – almost hysterical at the prospect of Labour being in a majority in the House.' The majority never quite materialized, but Baldwin, who loathed Lloyd George, resigned rather than seek Liberal support to remain in power. Once again Labour was in office but not in power, and on 4 June a huge victory celebration was held at Albert Hall with Ramsay MacDonald showing up in white tie and tails on his way to Buckingham Palace.

Laski played an important role in MacDonald's own campaign in the Prime Minister's coal-mining constituency of Seaham, near Durham. The CPGB, which ran twenty-five candidates but won no seats, had singled out MacDonald's constituency with the hope of pulling enough votes from MacDonald to elect his Liberal opponent and thus embarrass Labour and create a leadership crisis. MacDonald asked Laski if he 'could help me up there, especially by a meeting or two on the subject of communism. They say that Pollitt is living on the doorstep in Seaham areas which are in industrial trouble at present, and my [election] agent wants a very good reply.' The reputation Laski had made with *Communism* and the appeal of his fiery campaign oratory to workers made him MacDonald's obvious choice. 'Needless to say, if you could do this,' MacDonald concluded, 'you would be putting me under a great personal obligation to you and I should be most grateful.'

That MacDonald made this request of Laski was itself quite surprising. A year and a half earlier he had taken great offence at Laski's portrait of him in the *New Republic*, with its suggestion that he had a horror of ideas and only wanted power. He had written to Laski in November 1927 with what would be the first of a string of rebukes from Labour Party leaders over the years of Laski's loose tongue, especially to foreign audiences. MacDonald disputed much of what Laski had said in the article. 'Not only are your facts very wrong and your selection of them most imperfect, but your logic is all at fault.' Even worse, he added, 'it is a pity that foreign papers should be used for these criticisms'. MacDonald's criticism had not chastened Laski: he continued to write of MacDonald as a 'brilliant, jealous prima donna' or as 'vain, aloof, reserved and theatrical', simply 'not big enough'. Less surprising, perhaps, was Laski's agreeing to MacDonald's request, and in a letter to Frida he wrote:

> Dearest, the enclosed letter from Ramsay Mac explains itself – I thought that in the circumstances I ought not to say no, especially as we may sometime need something from him . . . I felt that if we *do* form a government, I want to sit on commissions and things and I better have MacDonald in my debt.

Laski campaigned in Seaham for two days and Labour won a majority from the miners of 28,000.

MacDonald served as Prime Minister of this Labour government for slightly over two years. On the Labour benches trade-union officials were now a minority and there were over sixty Fabians with seats. MacDonald's Cabinet included Snowden as Chancellor again, Henderson as Foreign Secretary and Sidney Webb, elevated to the peerage as Lord Passfield, as Colonial Secretary. Laski's friend Sankey was made Lord Chancellor. The only figure from the party's left in the Cabinet was Lansbury, this time not overlooked, who was Minister of Works in charge of parks and palaces. The Labour Cabinet had not even one Etonian. Made up mainly of men of humble origins and the first woman Cabinet Minister, Margaret Bondfield, Minister of Labour, it was also clear that the Cabinet was composed overwhelmingly of the right wing of the party.

One pressing issue dominated the politics of the next two years as it would the entire next decade: unemployment. When MacDonald took office the unemployment rate was already 11 per cent, representing 1,216,000 people out of work, and by 1931 at the beginning of the world-wide depression the rate had risen to 21·5 per cent and the numbers to 2,630,000. Governing with a minority and with the sufferance of the Liberal Party, Labour could not respond with socialist programmes, but its leadership, in any case, was far from committed to destroying British capitalism. Only Lloyd George, who had been converted by Keynes, called for increased public expenditure to put people back to work. Snowden and MacDonald were adamant about balanced budgets, agreeing with Treasury officials and the Bank of England that public works were useless and inflationary. Snowden's Victorian penny-pinching creed was proclaimed in a speech to the House of Commons.

> It is no part of my job as Chancellor of the Exchequer to put before the House of Commons proposals for the expenditure of public money. The function of the Chancellor of the Exchequer, as I understand it, is to resist all demands for expenditure made by his colleagues and, when he can no longer resist, to limit the concession to the barest point of acceptance.

Labour could not even deliver on non-socialist issues like the repeal of the 1927 Trades Dispute Act, which the Liberals did not support. Lloyd George might have been converted to pump-priming, but many in his party were moving to the right, at least away from the pro-trade-union stance of their own party which in 1913 had passed the legislation that Labour now wanted to restore. The Commons votes reveal how difficult it would have been for the Labour leadership to deal more aggressively with the economy. When in April 1930 Snowden introduced a modest increase in income tax, all hell broke loose. Tories like Churchill, Laski informed Holmes, acted 'like a man who had heard that London has fallen', and Lady Astor, the rich American Tory MP, 'was acting like a woman who has just heard that a defaulting solicitor has run off with all her money'. Laski, who reckoned that he might have to pay 'about a hundred dollars' more a year in taxes, could not 'understand why men are so anxious to die for the state and so angry if they are asked to give money to it'.

In addition to these private observations for Holmes, Laski once again became the public interpreter of British politics for a much wider American audience. 'England in 1929' appeared in the *Yale Review*, 'The New Test for British Labour' in *Foreign Affairs* and a lengthy essay on Philip Snowden in *Harper's*. There was no consistent line in his reporting. The moderates in the Labour Party, he admitted, had very modest aspiration; yet he also stressed the parliamentary obstacles to any fundamental change. He moved from suggesting that MacDonald might with a real majority seek 'immediate alteration of the existing social system' to lamenting the lack of real socialism in the party leadership. He suggested that Snowden could become 'one of the pre-eminent Chancellors in British financial history' because of his 'integrity, sincerity, and obstinacy', and relied perhaps on the *double entendre* hidden in his conclusion that 'so long as he is there, the middle class of England will feel that the Labour Party is not a danger to its existence'. Laski alerted readers, moreover, to Mosley as a possible successor to MacDonald, yet he never described the Mosley Memorandum, which would have committed Labour to public control of banking and imports, to an increase in pensions and other allowances, 'rationalization' of industry and increased public works expenditure. Nor did he describe the memorandum's repudiation by Snowden and MacDonald and Mosley's resignation from the government.

Laski's deep involvement with the MacDonald government is the major reason why he shrank from criticizing it. Good things had, indeed, come Laski's way in return for his help at Seaham. He was appointed to a royal commission to study ministers' powers and delegated legislation, and to a departmental committee on local government officials. We have no way of knowing, alas, if MacDonald offered Laski a peerage, as he claimed to Holmes and the Webbs in December 1929. Beatrice Webb had the impression from Laski that he would accept a peerage, which pleased her since, as she wrote to Sidney, 'Laski would be useful in the House [of Lords] and can probably afford to go there'. Laski, however, told Holmes he had turned it down because he couldn't afford it and wanted his independence. He was a scholar, not a politician, he insisted.

Despite his frail health, Laski was incredibly busy even by his own standards as the decade drew to a close. He had been appointed a member of the education committee of the London County Council in March 1928, which for years often took a day or an evening of his week, and still did occasional work for the TUC, as in April 1929 when he wrote part of their May Day manifesto. The MacDonald government added not only the very detailed work of a royal commission but, as we shall see, extensive behind-the-scenes activities with Webb and Sankey on Palestine, India and other colonial issues. Sankey also asked Laski for constitutional and political advice on MacDonald's plan for an economic advisory council to the Cabinet. Laski had written critically of such an idea in his *Grammar of Politics* and took time now to repeat his objections in a detailed memorandum. Neither Sankey nor MacDonald took his advice and the council, with Bevin, Keynes, Tawney and Macmillan as members, was established.

Laski's most time-consuming and most public involvement with this minority Labour government was his service on the Donoughmore Commission, an activity which forced him to postpone his plans to spend the spring semester of 1930 teaching at the Yale Law School. Serving on the royal commission appointed by Sankey to study whether the rise of delegated legislation was undermining 'the sovereignty of Parliament and the supremacy of the law' was particularly appropriate for Laski, the learned student of British history and political institutions, but his excitement over the appointment also points to the unique standing of the royal commission in British public life. Controversial and important issues are often removed from the rush and apparent partisanship of the parliamentary calendar and given to the more leisurely, reasoned and less partisan consideration of a small collection of eminent and esteemed aristocrats, politicians, civil servants, scholars, lawyers and judges whose recommendations are usually deferred to by the government and parliamentary parties. Laski's wish 'to sit on commissions and things' implies that such an appointment was almost the defining feature of stature as one of the Great and the Good. After consulting MacDonald, Sankey appointed in addition to Laski the Earl of Donoughmore, the Duchess of Atholl and the Earl of Clarendon. Three of the group were Tory ex-Cabinet members, six were distinguished lawyers and six were Members of Parliament. The commission also included two good friends of Holmes – Sir Leslie Scott, an eminent Tory lawyer, and Sir William Holdsworth, the Oxford legal historian - and Sir John Anderson, already an important civil servant, and Ellen Wilkinson, the Labour MP for Jarrow.

The immediate background to the Donoughmore Commission was the unusual action taken by the Lord Chief Justice, Gordon Hewart, in publishing early in 1929 a series of newspaper articles (later collected in *The New Despotism*) denouncing Parliament for delegating rule-making power to bureaucrats and civil servants. A despotic power, Hewart worried, now resided in government departments, which were outside the sovereignty of Parliament and beyond the jurisdiction of the courts. Bureaucrats had been given discretionary and decision-making authority in complex areas like housing, education, unemployment and health. An unredeemed advocate of *laissez-faire* individualism, Hewart was hailed by critics of the 'New Liberalism' and Fabian socialism who welcomed his thinly veiled attack on the state-interventionist policies that gave rise to *The New Despotism*. Before Hayek and his neo-Conservative disciples, Hewart was claiming in this undeservedly forgotten book that the very officials who had professional and personal interests at stake were the great champions of these public programmes. Sounding like a neo-conservative of the 1970s and 1980s, Hewart presciently wrote in 1929 that it was 'the officials in the departments concerned who initiate the legislation by which the arbitrary powers are conferred upon them'.

Laski had himself been interested in this same issue and, not surprisingly, he came down on a different side. In his *Grammar of Politics* he approved of how 'the growing area of state activity has transformed the major part of legislation from detailed and exhaustive statutes into skeleton acts, the details of which are, in various ways, filled in by the departments concerned'. In fact he suggested that delegated legislation and administrative decision-making had outdistanced the 'law-making directly due to the legislative assembly'. This tendency could not be reversed, he argued, since state-interventionist policies involved both details and complexities which Parliament had neither the time nor the expertise to deal with. Not that Laski was unmindful of potential problems. It was, he wrote in 1925, 'increasingly necessary to protect the public against bureaucratic abuse of these powers'.

In the first edition of the *Political Quarterly* Laski had anonymously reviewed *The New Despotism* using the signature 'XYZ'. He noted both the ideological animus behind the article as well as the professional interests of the legal profession who saw themselves excluded from the domain of administrative decision-making. But Laski, as was the left traditionally, was also concerned about the biases of the civil service. If increased rule-making authority that affected the well-being of the great mass of the people were to be given to upper civil servants, how well would these Eton and Winchester graduates of Oxford and Cambridge understand the life experiences of those affected by their decisions? So Laski, albeit in ways different from Hewart, worried too about the 'new despotism'. Still, he dismissed Hewart's essays as a 'rearguard action that has been fought for many years now against a phantom army of bureaucrats lusting for power which has never had any experience outside the imagination of those who warn us of impending doom and disaster'.

In his characteristic way Laski worked energetically on the Donoughmore Commission, preparing briefs for his colleagues about the history of delegated legislation from the reign of Henry VIII and about the inappropriateness of seeing executive (administrative) encroachment on legislative authority in a system like Britain's which had no real separation of powers as the United States did. His single-minded, tireless work for the commission paid off. The commission's report tended to reflect his views, declaring that the practice of delegating legislative and judicial powers to administrative organs was inevitable and necessary. It saw no grounds 'for a belief that our constitutional machinery is developing in directions which are fundamentally wrong' and suggested that if safeguards were taken against possible abuse, 'there is no ground for public fear'. Leading the list of these precautionary steps, the commission suggested, was a standing parliamentary committee whose sole function would be to scrutinize every rule and regulation made by a department in the exercise of delegated legislation. Laski's imprint was clear on every page, but he could not resist appending a personal 'note' as an annex to the report. Exasperated with the lawyers and jurists on the panel, Laski's memorandum repudiated what he took to be their misguided and naïve view of the judge as the purely impartial arbiter in disputes over the interpretation of statute law. If he had learned anything from his legal realist friends in American jurisprudence, it was that it was time 'to end this humbug of the judge as a soulless automaton whose mind and heart are silent when he performs his operations'.

Royal commission service was the public face of Laski's 'real political influence'. The more private face was his intense behind-the-scenes involvement in the great Palestine crisis. Laski's claims of an important role in what Lord Passfield (Sidney Webb), the Colonial Secretary, called his 'Jewish hurricane' have been dismissed by sceptics as yet another example of his fondness for exaggeration. But even more clearly than in the General Strike there is independent evidence that Laski did indeed play a significant part in the drama of the Passfield White Paper. For nearly two years he would be caught up in the conflict created by a sense of loyalty to his American friends, Frankfurter and Brandeis, who were urging him to influence his British friends and allies, Webb, MacDonald and Henderson. Hovering over it all were the towering presence of Chaim Weizmann, memories of his childhood and his own complicated attitudes to Zionism and Jews.

That he was destined to play a crucial role of international middleman was augured by Frankfurter, the consummate insider, already announcing an agenda before Labour's victory. Frankfurter wanted Laski to convince MacDonald to meet Henry Stimson, Secretary of State, to talk over Anglo-American foreign policy issues. Could Laski induce MacDonald to write to Frankfurter suggesting he convince Stimson to join him for talks? In June Frankfurter proposed that these talks would proceed better if MacDonald could pledge on behalf of the British government the dismantling of British fortifications in the Caribbean. Laski wrote back after the election with word that MacDonald planned an autumn visit to Washington and that he would certainly see Stimson. Could Felix, Laski asked, in preparation for the visit, send him 'at length please, the private idiosyncrasies of Stimson', which he would pass on to MacDonald? Laski also informed Frankfurter that he had given MacDonald what he had written about the Caribbean and that he had received a response from MacDonald which read: 'Quite understand, have called for an immediate report.'

But all of this was a mere prelude to Laski's dramatic involvement in the fuss over Palestine. The chain of events began in late August 1929 when Palestine was rocked by the bloody 'Wailing Wall' riots. A group of youths, contravening the orders of the Jewish leadership, had marched to the Western Wall, unfurled a Zionist flag and made fiery speeches. Arabs, in turn, harassed Jewish worshippers at the wall and on Friday 23 August bands of armed Arabs began attacking Jews in Jerusalem; the violence soon spread throughout the country. Troops were flown in from Cairo and after a week the British put an end to the violence, but not before 133 Jews and 116 Arabs died, most of whom were killed by the security forces. On 13 September Passfield announced the establishment of an investigative commission headed by Sir Walter Shaw to visit Palestine and 'enquire into the immediate causes which led to the recent outbreak in Palestine and to make recommendations as to the steps necessary to avoid a recurrence'. The commission was not intended to look at broader questions about the nature of the mandate or the Balfour Declaration.

Requests to Laski came immediately from his American Zionist friends. At Brandeis's suggestion Frankfurter sent a copy of Prince Faisal's 1919 Versailles letter, pledging Arab cooperation, which Laski passed on to Passfield. When the Prime Minister visited Washington in October, Laski arranged a cordial tea at the British embassy, where MacDonald and Brandeis talked about Palestine. Laski wrote to Holmes that when MacDonald returned to London he told him that he was more impressed with Brandeis than with anyone else he met in America. This bit of gossip could well have played an unexpected role in the unfolding events of the next few months, for it might have led Brandeis to overestimate his potential influence with MacDonald. Holmes passed on Laski's comment to Brandeis, who in passing it on to Frankfurter added 'that opinion of me may be of some service hereafter'.

The Shaw Commission issued its report in March 1930, attributing the underlying cause of the riots to Arab fear that their livelihood and political independence were threatened by Jewish immigration and land purchases. With this in mind the commission recommended a decrease in both. Going beyond its charge, the commission also suggested that Palestine envisioned as a national Jewish homeland exceeded the League mandate under which Britain ruled. Labour was, in fact, less wedded to Zionism than either the Conservative or Liberal governments who in coalition had sponsored the Balfour Declaration, but MacDonald, worried that Zionist outrage at the report would jeopardize an American loan he hoped to negotiate, decided not to propose any immediate cessation of immigration or settlement. Instead, he sent Sir John Hope Simpson, a civil servant in India and member of the League of Nations Commission for resettlement of Greek refugees, as a government commissioner to Palestine to conduct an evaluation of the entire Palestine situation.

Zionist leaders in America and Britain kept up their pressure on MacDonald and Passfield throughout the summer of 1930. 'I do not want to lose my patience with the Zionists but really they try it greatly,' MacDonald complained. Brandeis urged Frankfurter in June to go to London to make clear that the British could not suspend immigration permits. Laski, mindful of MacDonald's anger, sent Frankfurter a telegram on 12 June: 'Imperative you should not intervene in the situation here until the Hope Simpson report is made.' There was a 'very real danger', Laski told his friend, that 'Zionists will do grave harm by calling in too many people to exercise pressure. This pertains particularly to the Americans. They are the great weapons of last influence. I don't want a temperamental person like the PM irritated by what looks like nagging.' If the Simpson report were unfavourable, he added, 'that is the time to play the American card. Not before then.' In essence, Laski was cautioning Frankfurter not to be the stereotypical 'pushy Jew': 'In my talks with the PM and others the unfailing criticism of the Zionists has always been that they never cease opening doors to try indirect influence even when it is known where they stand.' That Brandeis didn't recognize the potential for embarrassment of premature interference, as Frankfurter did, revealed one of his 'blind spots', Laski told Holmes.

That summer Laski saw and stayed in close touch with Weizmann, who was himself holding back his fire. Weizmann retained a deep reservoir of faith in British good-will towards Zionism and also paid heed to MacDonald's warnings that pressure was inappropriate while Simpson was in Palestine. Brandeis, on the other hand, took matters into his own hands and in late June met Sir Ronald Lindsey, the British ambassador to America, for three hours in a Boston hotel room. Brandeis lectured the ambassador on the power of Jews in American politics and what a turnabout in British attitudes to Zionism might mean for cooperation between the United States and Great Britain. When he heard about this, Laski complained to Frankfurter that 'the Zionists have done themselves serious hurt with JRM and Webb by their policy of pulling strings, and everyone who has taken part in it has gravely injured his influence'.

The next and most tumultuous act of the Palestine drama began to unfold in late September. MacDonald had left it to Passfield to evaluate the Hope Simpson report and prepare for the Cabinet the government's policy in light of its recommendations. Passfield's intentions were hinted at in a letter to his wife in which he worried 'whether we can anyhow avoid a shriek of anguish from all Jewry I don't know!' On Saturday 18 October Laski brought an advanced copy of the Passfield White Paper to Weizmann and the two decided to urge MacDonald to delay publication in order to provide time for Frankfurter and Felix Warburg, the American Jewish banker and Zionist, to come from America to try to persuade Passfield to change his mind. They failed. The Passfield White Paper was published on 21 October. It recommended that Jewish immigration to Palestine as well as land purchases virtually cease, since they threatened Arab employment and the general economic well-being of the Arab community in violation of 'Article 6 of the mandate, which directs that the rights and position of the other [non-Jewish] sections of the population shall not be prejudiced by Jewish immigration'.

Passfield wrote to Beatrice the next day that 'the Jewish hurricane continues . . . they seem to go wild with excitement and rage'. Attacked for his misplaced trust in the British government, Weizmann resigned his positions as President of the World Zionist Organization and President of the British-run Jewish Agency. The industrialist Alfred Mond, now Lord Melchett, the Chairman of the Jewish Agency Council, also resigned, as did Felix Warburg, the Chairman of the agency's Administrative Committee. Brandeis met President Hoover on 28 October for an hour to urge American intervention. On 3 November 20,000 Jews attended a rally at Madison Square Gardens to protest against the Passfield White Paper. *The Times* account reported 'all traffic in the district at a complete standstill' and 'cheers at the name of Lord Balfour and howls at the name of Lord Passfield'. Frankfurter chaired the meeting and speeches were given by New York Senator Robert Wagner and Felix Warburg. Jimmy Walker, the Mayor of New York, told the crowd that 'there are more Jews in New York City than in any other city in the world, and the message the Mayor of that City sends to Downing Street is that . . . I wish we had twice as many'. Franklin Roosevelt, Governor of New York, sent a message of support that was read to the meeting. *The Times* concluded drily that 'similar meetings were held in Philadelphia, Boston and Cincinnati'. There were also sharp letters to *The Times* from the Tory Lord Hailsham and the Liberal Sir John Simon, who insisted that the White Paper did not comply with Britain's obligation under the mandate to encourage Jewish settlement in Palestine and to help establish a Jewish national home. Other important political figures joined the critics, among them Baldwin, Lloyd George and Churchill.

Laski was caught in the middle. He had urged restraint until a decision was made, and now there seemed no time between the decision and its implementation. He had received a frantic transatlantic phone call from Frankfurter on 18 November which had prompted him to seek a postponement. The next day he saw MacDonald, who was 'very official and very hard'. It was impossible, the Prime Minister reported, to reconsider at this late hour. MacDonald claimed he was 'trying to hold the scales even between Jew and Arab', and could not 'submit a policy to alien strangers for comment before publication'. Laski reminded MacDonald that this had in fact been done in 1918 when Brandeis had been shown a draft of the Balfour Declaration before publication and predicted a devastating impact on Jewish opinion and Anglo-American relations. MacDonald replied that Laski exaggerated: 'He was convinced that Jews would realize the *bona-fides* of the government.'

At the same time his friends in the Cabinet urged Laski to help them to mollify their Jewish critics, especially in America. Passfield hoped that Laski could 'dispel the extraordinary Jewish misconceptions of our statement of policy' and drafted a telegram for Laski to send 'as from yourself, to your American friends'. Laski never did send the telegram. When Henderson, the Foreign Secretary, asked Laski to help to 'assuage feelings', Laski replied that he 'could do nothing'. And when the Prime Minister requested that Laski 'assure my American friends that the Cabinet would do all in its power to act justly', Laski reminded MacDonald that he 'had treated my views with contempt . . . nothing could be done now unless he sacked Webb or withdrew the Declaration'. When MacDonald expressed surprise at the bitterness of a man who was not even a Zionist, Laski explained:

> My views on Zionism had not changed, but that as a Jew I resented a policy
> which surrendered Jewish interests, in spite of a pledged word, to the authors
> of an unjustifiable massacre. No doubt when the Arabs killed the next lot of
> Jews, Webb would be allowed to expel all Jews from Palestine.

Far from doing the bidding of his friends in the government, an angry Laski now told Frankfurter that it was '*fundamental for you all to take nothing short of a withdrawal of the Declaration*' (his italics). Laski's involvement in the effort to reverse the White Paper was apparent to the Zionist leader Berl Katznelson, who wrote to colleagues in Palestine that 'even a man like Laski, who boasted of his anti-Zionism, is now eager to speak for us'. Katznelson may have known that Laski was the author of the article 'The New Palestine Policy' that appeared in the *Week-End Review* on 25 October. Under the cloak of anonymity, Laski branded the White Paper a 'breach of faith with the Jewish people' which rewarded the Arab rebellion, while turning the 'development of the country' into 'reproaches' against the Jews. The basic fault lay in the 'incompetent and vain' personnel of the British government, the article claimed. Only Parliament could 'redress this vicious error'.

Webb couldn't believe the fury of 'the Jewish hurricane'. Finding 'nothing in the White Paper of October to which the Jews can honestly object', he saw a plot whipped up by Weizmann 'to stir the emotions of world Jewry in order to revive the flow of donations . . . fallen off owing to the American slump'. Beatrice Webb asked: 'Why is it that everyone who has dealings with Jewry ends by being prejudiced against the Jews?' Sidney, she noted disingenuously, 'began with a great admiration for the Jew', but now found 'even many accomplished and cultivated Jews intolerable as negotiators and colleagues'. She offered a socialist reading of the policy shift, describing the Arabs as natives and the Jews as exploiters with 'superior wealth', but she was not above crude anti-Semitism either, noting the irony of her husband's White Paper reversing the process by which the Holy Land had been handed over 'to the representatives of those who crucified Jesus of Nazareth and have continued, down all the ages, to deny that He is the Son of God!'

As Passfield wrote that 'some ministers would have resigned rather than stand what I have had to stand since last October', the whole issue was taken out of his hands. After a meeting with Weizmann, MacDonald, who was more concerned about Anglo-American relations and projected loans than Passfield, announced that a new Cabinet committee would consider the situation in Palestine jointly with Zionist leaders. Speaking for American Zionists, Brandeis authorized Laski to join the committee as their 'observer'. The Cabinet committee was presided over by Henderson, who had been away in Geneva on the day the White Paper had initially been discussed and approved by the Cabinet. Four Cabinet ministers – Passfield, Henderson, the First Lord of the Admiralty and the Secretary of State for War – and Norman MacDonald, the Prime Minister's son, represented the government. On the Jewish side sat Weizmann, James de Rothschild, Harry Sacher, a lawyer and journalist for the *Manchester Guardian*, Selig Brodetsky, a mathematician at the University of Leeds (and later the President of the Hebrew University), Lewis Namier, the distinguished historian, and Leonard Stein, the long-time Secretary of the World Zionist

Organization. Representing the interests of American Zionist leaders were Harold Laski and Maurice Beck Hexter, an American official with the Jewish Agency who happened to be in London.

Laski played a critical role on the committee. Once the deliberations began it became clear, as Weizmann later wrote, that while the government was amenable to his suggestions for a revised document, pressure was coming from America 'in telegrams, solely of a negative nature', from Brandeis, Frankfurter and Warburg. Laski told Holmes that the Prime Minister asked him through his son to act as 'the honest broker' between 'Webb's pedantic obstinacy and ambiguities' on the one hand, and 'Felix and Brandeis's immovability' on the other. He told Holmes that 'I have spent a fortune in telegrams to New York'. By January Laski also noted with appropriate exaggeration that his work had 'meant three hours a day for six weeks and I hope that I shall have peace from Palestine for the next ten years'. The source of the pressure from America was Brandeis's anger at Weizmann's willingness to allow MacDonald to announce his revisions in a published letter and not in a new White Paper. Brandeis wanted Laski to hold out for that formality. If the government resisted, Brandeis warned, American and British Jews would withdraw their money from British banks. Laski again urged Frankfurter that 'the Americans not overplay their hands and make negotiations difficult by an attitude which might alienate our friends here'. Laski told Holmes that since the negotiations with the British government began, Brandeis had bombarded him with instructions and 'I cannot remember one telegram of his which has been really helpful'. 'Brandeis is a very difficult person,' Laski confided to Holmes.

> He is intransigent and dominating, and unnecessarily prone to read evil motives into obvious actions. Felix is like clay in his hands, and if it were not for my deep affection for them both, I think I would have told them long ago to go to hell and see what they could accomplish without my intervention.

In addition to his role as American broker, for which he asked Frankfurter in late January if the American Zionists could reimburse him £17 for all the telegrams he had sent, Laski was his own person at the Anglo-Jewish conference. He suggested that the British use the Trans-Jordan for Arab settlement and that the mandate be transferred from the Colonial Office to the Foreign Office, pointing to the poor quality and pro-Arab bias of British officialdom in Palestine. In general, however, he thought the government was in 'earnest in trying to make a document as good as possible'. He passed on to Frankfurter some doubts about the British Zionist leadership on the committee. Weizmann was 'of course a genius, but very unstable and chaotic'; Lewis Namier was 'clever of course but an intolerable egoist'; Stein was too legalistic, Sacher too truculent, and Brodetsky, alas, 'the worst type of East End Jew'.

Concluded in mid-January, the negotiations, as Laski wrote to Holmes, 'ought to satisfy every decent aspiration to which they [the Jews] are entitled'. The 'Jewish hurricane' officially blew over on 13 February 1931 when the Prime Minister read to the House of Commons the letter he had written to Chaim Weizmann. To the end the government declined to issue another White Paper, and the Jewish delegates had agreed only if MacDonald read the letter into the parliamentary record with its opening sentence offering therein 'the authoritative interpretation of the White Paper on the matters with which this letter deals'. MacDonald reaffirmed that 'to facilitate Jewish immigration and to encourage close settlement by Jews on the land remains a positive obligation of the mandate'. The only limits to immigration would be 'the economic absorptive capacity of Palestine'. Weizmann, who had drafted most of the language, saw the letter as restoring the *status quo ante* and the Americans grudgingly agreed, through no small effort by Laski who had here, at least, a small taste of 'real political influence'.

He was very pleased with himself. Beatrice Webb noted in her diary that Laski 'is bubbling over with delight at his own importance'. The 'Jewish hurricane' did not interfere with the friendship of the Laskis and Webbs. In fact, on Beatrice's seventy-third birthday she and Sidney spent the evening in their flat with the Laskis. Two years later Laski asserted in print (and not anonymously) that the Palestine policy of the second Labour government had been produced not by anti-Semitism, but by an overworked Cabinet not reading a document carefully. On the night of Beatrice Webb's birthday Laski was particularly full of himself. His sense of importance, she wrote, took the form of

graphic and amusing stories, some true and others invented, about his dealings with the Zionists, especially the American Zionists, and with the

Indians ... He is a devotee of Sankey's and has been used by the great man as an assistant negotiator running between various groups of Indians, Mohammedan and Hindu.

She suspected that much of his conversation was imaginary, 'but it is all very good fun; he is never malicious or mischievous'. She did worry, however, that 'all these personal comings and goings' which were so stimulating 'to his great fault – personal vanity' might be dissipating his commitment to scholarship and his powers of thought.

In his 'personal comings and goings' Laski was indeed working for Sankey on India. He had been ever since Sankey had been appointed Lord Chancellor in June 1929. There was, of course, a long tradition in British politics of academics assisting government ministers with research and writing, but seldom with the intensity and regularity of Laski, who one day a week worked on Sankey's correspondence, read Cabinet papers for him, wrote memoranda and suggested sources of study. Sankey relied upon Laski in discussions of territorial or constitutional drafting. Laski worked on Kenya and other African territories, and in spring 1930 Sankey asked him to help plan the forthcoming Indian round-table, which would deal with the principles of a federal constitution, a subject on which Laski was an expert. Sankey also knew Laski's standing with Indian activists in Britain like Krishna Menon and his London-based India League.

Much like Palestine, India preoccupied MacDonald's Labour government. Lord Irwin (later Lord Halifax), Viceroy of India, made it clear in October 1929 that India would some day have dominion status. Gandhi responded by demanding it immediately and began 1930 with a dramatic new campaign of civil disobedience, marching across India and defying the British salt monopoly by extracting and using crystals of untaxed salt. He and 50,000 of his followers were jailed. MacDonald then decided to speed up the process and called the first India round-table conference for November 1930. Neither Gandhi nor his India Congress Party attended.

Laski prepared memoranda on constitutional history for Sankey, and when the delegates arrived he briefed them on the history of federalism as well as its practice in Europe and America. He was struck by the enormity of the problem, the good-will of people like Irwin and MacDonald confronting bitter religious strife between Hindu and Moslem. 'We can't govern it and it really is not fit to govern itself,' he wrote, wondering whether Britain was not about to face 'the biggest crisis in our colonial affairs since 1776'. Laski's greatest fear was that 'India will become the Ireland of the next generation – a prospect to me of unmitigated horror'. What worried him was the analogous role of religion, for his meetings with the Indians convinced him that 'the depths of their religious fervour makes any plan for effective justice between them a matter of extraordinary difficulty'. The first round-table ended on an optimistic note, the Indian princes in attendance agreeing in principle to a future Indian federation. Laski had been a good teacher and Sankey wrote appreciatively to him on Christmas Day thanking him for his 'wise counsel and advice'. Some of the hopes for an easy settlement were dimmed during the great parliamentary debate on India held on 22 January 1931 when, with Baldwin and the Tory leadership supporting the government's India policy, Churchill announced his implacable opposition to dominion status and to any conciliation of Indian nationalism. He spoke of 'warrior races' and 'the grandeur of the British Empire' as he resigned from the Conservative Shadow Cabinet, beginning the long years of isolation from Tory leadership circles that would end only with the outbreak of the Second World War.

When the second round-table met later that year, Gandhi and the Congress Party came. Gandhi lived in Kingsley Hall, a settlement house in the East End, where he had his goat's milk and spun on his spinning-wheel daily. Krishna Menon, the Secretary of the India League, brought Gandhi, the man Churchill labelled 'a naked fakir', to meet Laski. Involved closely in the second negotiations, especially on constitutional questions related to political control of a contemplated federal Indian army, Laski also worked on a criminal code and its implementation through the various levels of the projected federal structure. Sankey asked Laski to confer with both the Aga Khan and Gandhi on the future constitutional status of religion in India and the likelihood of Moslem acceptance of secular institutions. Laski had little luck with the Moslem spiritual leader: 'It was like talking to a wall. His religion was ultimate truth,' Laski wrote. Nor did the general talks go well, and after the first few weeks Gandhi resented having come. The different tone of this conference was attributed by Laski to the late-summer change in government after MacDonald's 'betrayal' in which the new National government had a Tory Secretary of State for India, Sir Samuel Hoare, who was sympathetic to Churchill's position. Laski even suspected that some Tories were backing the Moslems behind the scenes to wreck the talks.

Gandhi was not a socialist. He had joined the Fabian Society when he lived in England in 1920, but resigned four years later. By 1931 he had adopted his traditional posture eschewing modernity and industrialism and, unlike Menon and Nehru, he would never be converted to the secular socialism of Laski and the *New Statesman* or see it as the model for an independent India. Still, he admired Laski's commitment to India's freedom and he often recommended students to study with Laski. Laski, in turn, was fascinated by the theatrical 'wizened little man with the whole power of the Empire against him'. 'The crowd goes out to see him arrive in his loincloth and blanket as they might want to see Charlie Chaplin,' Laski wrote to Holmes. He suggested that Gandhi's 'secret' was akin to the Quaker's inner light, 'a power of internal self-confidence which having established its principles is completely impervious to reason. At bottom it is an incredible egoism ... the arrogance of humility.' Laski was struck by how Gandhi's followers 'hang on his words, he who has neither eloquence nor the gift of verbal artistry'. It helped him to understand 'why Christianity in the first century appealed to the poor and the oppressed. Through Gandhi the Indian ryot feels himself exalted, he embodies for them their own impulse to self-affirmation.'

The second Indian round-table broke up in utter failure on 1 December, and Gandhi told Laski he would return to India 'helpless, homeless and empty-handed'. For Laski the débâcle was the inevitable result of Sir Samuel Hoare's belief that 'the white man ought not to be asked to give way to the black' and Gandhi's 'haunting fear that the white man in India will always take a yard for each inch of compromise'. Laski predicted 'an India in flames for the next few years and out of that tragedies too vast even to think of'. Gandhi left London, travelled through Europe, arrived in India and immediately renewed his campaign of passive resistance.

The evening before he left London, Gandhi met with a group of Labour Party sympathizers that included Kingsley Martin, Leonard Woolf, H. W. Nevinson, H. N. Brailsford and Laski. Gandhi asked the group what course he should follow on his return to India. He asked each person in the room to tell him how they read the break-up of negotiations and what he should do. Leonard Woolf's account of what then happened provides a fascinating contemporary portrait of Gandhi's 'friend Harold Laski'.

When we had all said our say, there followed one of the most brilliant intellectual pyrotechnic displays which I have ever listened to. Gandhi thanked us and said that it would greatly help him if his friend Harold Laski, who was one of us, would try to sum up the various lines of judgement and advice which had emerged. Harold then stood up in front of the fireplace and gave the most lucid, faultless summary of the complicated, diverse expositions of ten or fifteen people to which he had been listening in the previous hour and a half. He spoke for about twenty minutes; he gave a perfect sketch of the pattern into which the various statements and opinions logically composed themselves; he never hesitated for a word or a thought, and, as far as I could see, he never missed a point. There was a kind of beauty in his exposition, a flawless certainty and simplicity which one feels in some works of art.

Even with all his 'comings and goings', Laski published three books in 1930 and 1931. The first, *The Danger of Obedience and Other Essays*, dedicated to Tawney, brought together many of the essays Laski had published in American magazines. The title essay lamented the decline of liberty while 'the world runs to meet its chains' and the citizen 'is powerless because he is unconscious of his power'. He lumped together Britain under Jix, America and Sacco–Vanzetti, Italy and Mussolini, and the Soviet Union, where 'a dominant party seeks to impress a particular creed upon every aspect of life it controls'. In every part of the world he found only a 'standardized mind' and he urged that it be met everywhere with 'widespread and consistent scepticism of the canons upon which power insists'.

Later in 1930 Laski's *Liberty in the Modern State* was published, dedicated to Frida and Diana. One of Laski's most enduring publications, reprinted and revised in 1937 as his first Penguin paperback and then reprinted in both Britain and America in 1948 and 1949, it is his most fervent libertarian plea for novelty, experiment, curiosity and scepticism in the face of 'those who possess power to prohibit ideas and conduct which may disturb them in their possession'. He again equated America and the Soviet Union as places where 'always the effort is to insist upon an artificial unity, the maintenance of which is necessary to the desires of those who hold power'. In America, he wrote, 'the suppression of liberty is called the inhibition of licence; in a dictatorship like Moscow it is termed resistance to the

admission of incorrect bourgeois notions.' It was the liberal face of Laski at
its most passionate, his anti-statism angrily and indifferently directed at any
regime that restricted the freedom of the mind. In its review *The New York
Times* wrote that 'Professor Laski has written a brilliant defense of liberty.
Not since John Stuart Mill published his famous essay has any English
writer offered so searchingly an analysis of the nature of political liberty or
pleaded so earnestly and, on the whole, convincingly for its largest practical
application.'

An Introduction to Politics appeared in the spring of 1931 and was
dedicated to Jan and Tonia, the Laskis' Belgian friends. It was an attempt to
popularize *Grammar of Politics* for 'the average interested reader', taking up,
in a little over a hundred pages and without any technical apparatus, a
discussion of the nature of the state, its place in society, its organization and
its relationship to the international order. It succeeded, for it was reprinted
nine times in the next twenty years. The book repeated his plea for an
interventionist state introducing redistributive measures of social justice
while transferring parts of the economy to public hands. The book also
retained his pluralist insistence on a decentralized, federal state where
power was widely dispersed and interests participated in ruling by membership on formal governmental advisory bodies. Laski persisted in *An Introduction to Politics* in maintaining his Marxist indictment of the existing state as
reflecting the interests of those who dominate the economic system
alongside his non-Marxist faith that well-meaning, prudent reforms using
the parliamentary process would allow the state to serve the interests of the
whole community.

However many times *An Introduction to Politics* was reprinted and however wide its appeal, it could hardly compare in its impact and reach to the
new vehicle for his opinions that Laski acquired in April 1930. He had
truly 'made it' when he was read weekly in over a million homes in the
new, incredibly successful *Daily Herald*. Since 1922 the paper had been
owned jointly by the TUC and the National Executive Committee
(NEC) of the Labour Party in a deal arranged by Ernest Bevin. It lost
money throughout the 1920s, however, and in 1929 Julius Salter Elias (later
Viscount Southwood) of Odhams Press purchased the paper. Elias agreed
in writing that the editorial policy would remain in accord with the
decisions of the annual conference of the Labour Party and the annual
congress of the TUC. When the first edition of the revitalized *Daily Herald*

was printed in March 1930, the circulation rapidly jumped from its 1920s level of 275,000 to over a million a day. By 1933 the *Daily Herald*, with its new northern edition published in Manchester, became the first newspaper in the world to sell two million copies a day, and Laski's weekly 'Pen Portrait', a short character-sketch of important political personalities, was an important part of its success. His pieces were breezy and chatty, full of the anecdotes and personal details that endeared him as a story-teller to his friends. To everything else he was doing Laski now joined popular journalism for the masses. He was a visible and important figure not only in the academy, in Labour Party circles and in the columns of leftist weeklies, but in a million households as well.

He was on people's radios too. In May and June 1928 he did six talks on the BBC Home Service on 'Why We Obey the State' and 'How We Judge the State'. In November he spoke on 'How Laws are Made'. Two months later he gave a talk on 'The Greatest Man Since Milton' to commemorate the 200th anniversary of Edmund Burke's birth. He also did a book review of Lord Haldane's posthumously published autobiography, a talk on local government and a debate with a biologist on the role of heredity and environment. The BBC must have been pleased with Laski's articulateness and his lack of professorial pomposity. But there was also some political concern, for in the BBC archives a note dated 18 April 1928, approving his first series of talks, reads: 'A lecturer of left-wing tendencies – a Labour candidate for Parliament – therefore he will need careful vetting. But this synopsis is quite innocuous.'

Laski was everywhere. He was on royal commissions, at state dinners at 10 Downing Street, in the popular press and on the radio. His *Communism* enabled many in the Labour Party to differentiate themselves from their more revolutionary comrades. As he set sail on 18 February 1931 on the *Aquitania* for his postponed semester at Yale, he must have known he had made it, that he had achieved the real political influence he could only hope for in his letter to Holmes nearly eleven years earlier. He had played the game, and now if he wanted to he could really speak out; he could be the bad boy, the rebel on the left thundering against the leaders of the labour movement even as they wined and dined him or called upon his generously granted time, energy, voice and pen. One could much more easily and securely be the *enfant terrible* from 'centre stage'.

PART III

THE 'AGE OF LASKI':

THE 1930s

CHAPTER TWELVE

MacDonald's 'Betrayal' and the Socialist League

'I stand with the left of Labour and, if necessary, I go to the extreme left,' Laski wrote to Frankfurter on 6 September 1931 in the wake of the financial crisis which brought down the Labour government and ushered in nearly a decade of Conservative-dominated National government coalitions. Laski was true to his word. Throughout the 'pink decade', which saw catastrophic unemployment, the rise of fascism, the Spanish Civil War and the romance with Russian communism, Laski became, in the words of the historian Carl Becker, an 'omnipresent and omnivocal' force on the Anglo-American left. Through his scholarly writings, his journalism, teaching, lecturing, radio talks and political activism, Laski so dominated the 1930s that it was almost, as the Oxford scholar Max Beloff labelled it, 'the Age of Laski'.

Laski had arrived in America late in February, for his longest stay since 1920, just months before this letter to Frankfurter and the momentous redirection of his politics that it announced. He stayed until the middle of June, moving around the East Coast, Midwest and South by train and, for the first time in his life, by plane, giving scores of university lectures and talks to sympathetic organizations, and, of course, seeing old friends and students. Throughout it all there was not the slightest hint of any dramatic shift in his politics. His base was New Haven, Connecticut, where he taught jurisprudence and administrative law at the Yale Law School and two courses on political theory at Yale College and the Graduate School. On Tuesday evenings he took the train to New York City, where he lectured at the New School, now presided over by his old *New Republic* friend Alvin Johnson, and in the sixteen weeks he was there Laski also managed to fit in lectures at thirteen other universities. Lest Frida be too dismayed at this schedule, Laski told her that he had turned down even more invitations to lecture at Vassar, the University of Pittsburgh, Rochester, Kentucky, Michigan, Iowa and Johns Hopkins.

Laski also wrote to Frida about how lucrative speaking engagements were, ticking off the $100 for the talk to the Foreign Policy Association and the $200 for the lectures at Minnesota, etc. Money was still an issue for Laski, determined not to take any from his family, and it seems to have been as important an incentive for him to speak and write as the attention they brought him. His concern with money sometimes pushed sentiment to the side as when he wrote to Frida that 'the Yale students applauded my last lecture, but, much more serious, about sixty bought my book and I signed them and I look forward to my royalties at the end of the year'. Money seems to have vied with self-promotion in his cultivation of American editors and publishers. He wrote to Frida of seeing the *New York Times* people, Hitchcock of Macmillan, Wilber Cross of the *Yale Review*, the *Nation* and *New Republic* people, Canby of the *Saturday Review* and Tommy Wells of *Harper's*. 'It was worthwhile to come to America. It reinforces my connection with these people and it ought to be worth a steady $300 a year, which is pretty good.' Of course, Laski assured his wife, he had also lectured for free to 'socialist working men of New Haven'.

Laski's lectures and articles were widely reported and sometimes controversial. A talk at the elite Foreign Policy Association was covered by the *New York Times*, which cited Laski's attack on businessmen as the 'real powers behind the governments of today'. At a talk that Laski gave at a luncheon sponsored by the League for Industrial Democracy, *The Times* quoted his claim that 'a higher degree of justice is commanded by the wealthy than by the poor'. *The New York Times* also reported the stir caused in Washington 'political and official quarters' by the arrival in April of copies of a 'Pen Portrait' Laski had done on President Hoover for the *Daily Herald*. The article, 'Hoover, the World's Greatest Failure', had, according to *The Times*, upset the White House with passages like 'Mr Hoover is a Rip Van Winkle in ideas' and that 'viewed either as a thinker or as a leader of men, it is difficult not to conclude that he has been a sorry failure'. Three weeks later *The Times* also ran a story on the fuss created by another of Laski's 'Pen Portraits'. 'Professor Laski follows his recent attacks on President Hoover with equally candid opinions of Henry Ford', who, according to Laski, 'is the embodiment of what is most dangerous in American civilization'.

One group that eagerly sought out Laski was the American Zionist community. Two days after his arrival Laski lunched in New York with

Felix Warburg, Julian Mack and others on the Zionists of America executive board, where he told them the whole story of the rescinding of the White Paper. They had a poor opinion of British Zionists and 'want far more than they are likely to get'. That wasn't the end, however. Pestered by the Zionist press in New York for interviews and speeches, Laski 'gave them short shrift'. Invitations to speak at synagogues 'and one from the Jewish Maidens' Club of New York to a tea' in fact led Laski to suggest to Frida that 'the Jews here deserve a study all to themselves; it's a more complicated issue than I realize and I should have guessed that Zionism has done them harm rather than good by making them less integrally a part of America'.

In addition to his new friend Alfred Cohn, Laski also spent time with his old friends Firuski, the bookseller, and Ben Huebsch, then the publisher of Viking Press. He saw Catlin and in New York he dined with Charles Beard, Roger Baldwin – 'as sweet and as mad as ever' – and with Judge Cardoza. He saw Morris and Bessie Cohen on several occasions, had breakfast at Dorothy Straight's New York flat, which, he wrote to Frida, was 'like a palace', and saw a trio of people with whom he would stay in touch whenever he came to America or they to Britain. The brothers Ben and Abe Flexner were friends of Brandeis from Louisville. Ben was an active Zionist official and Abe a medical scholar who would soon be appointed the first director of the Institute for Advanced Study at Princeton. Eugene Meyer, Jr, was also a friend of Brandeis and a Washington insider who after 1933 was the publisher of the *Washington Post*. Several times on this trip Laski also saw his old acquaintance Dean Acheson, who had studied with Frankfurter while Laski was at Harvard and gone on to be Brandeis's law clerk from 1919 to 1921.

In Washington Laski visited both Brandeis and Holmes. It was his good fortune to be there on 8 March, the ninetieth birthday celebration of Holmes, for which Laski published in the *Yale Law Journal* a piece on his political philosophy, as well as the foreword to a special collection of *Representative Opinions of Mr Justice Holmes*. In honour of the birthday a special commemorative radio programme was broadcast live from Holmes's living-room. President Hoover attended, as did all the other Supreme Court justices. Laski stayed that night as Holmes's guest and he wrote to Frida that the maid told him that all week the justice was saying, 'My boy will be here Saturday' and that 'he patted me on the head every so often, he was so happy to see me.'

Just as happy to see Laski was Frankfurter, with whom Laski spent several weekends in Cambridge, where meals were arranged with his Harvard friends McIlwain, Samuel Elliot Morrison, Zachariah Chaffee, Jr, and Roscoe Pound. Laski again spoke at Ford Hall Forum but not at Harvard. He had been asked by Arthur Holcombe to speak to his first-year government students at the college, but Laski declined, explaining to Frankfurter that 'I did not want even indirectly to be obliged to Lowell for any courtesies.' Convinced that Lowell had vetoed a government department offer of a Godkin lectureship, Laski missed no opportunity to get back at him. He had, for example, begun a review of Lowell's book *Public Opinion in War and Peace* with 'This is a very disappointing book', and in 1933 he would write to Frankfurter to suggest that he tell his friend Roosevelt, the new President, it would be a disaster to send Lowell as America's ambassador to Great Britain, which was then being rumoured. Laski must have taken deep pleasure, then, on this trip when his old defenders against the *Lampoon*, the *Harvard Crimson*, invited him to their annual banquet as their guest of honour and after-dinner speaker. Seated next to him at the head table was A. Lawrence Lowell, who, he wrote to Frida, 'was cold as an iceberg until after I had spoken. Then he treated me as an eminent stranger.'

Laski was struck in America by the signs of the depression. He saw long lines of unemployed people selling things on the street, and bankruptcy signs everywhere. Yet wherever he travelled he also noticed the luxuriousness of his hosts' homes, possessions and amenities. In America, even middle-class academics lived in great comfort, he wrote. Eighteen months before the election of Roosevelt Laski worried that there wasn't 'a dog's chance of anything really liberal for years . . . the power of wealth and the volume of corruption here is unspeakable'. But everywhere he spoke the radical professors came to hear him, he told Frida, and the students were thrilled because 'he was willing to speak out'.

Laski shared with Frida his sense that he was a great success on the American campus. Faculty and students couldn't get over his lecturing without notes, he reported, and he passed on that he had been told in Minnesota that 'they never had such a stimulating lecturer' who had 'lifted them off their seats'. In Chapel Hill, North Carolina, someone said that 'he had the largest crowd ever for a lecture'. The *Yale Daily News*, complimenting the Thursday afternoon discussion sessions held in his college rooms, as well as his close rapport with students, editorialized that Yale should try to hire Laski permanently. Laski asked Frida to send the copy of the editorial along with a favourable piece about him from the LSE student publication *Clare Market Review* of April 1931 to his people in Manchester, adding, 'I think it will give them pleasure.'

The night before he sailed back to England on 16 June, Laski was guest of honour at a *New Republic* dinner in New York. Matthew Josephson, the journalist and historian, then a junior editor of the magazine, described the evening vividly in a memoir of the 1930s. After dinner 'this small, thin, pale, owlish young professor' who 'appeared fabulous to us', spoke. Laski had a fine glow about him, 'the spiritual fire of his ancestors who were rabbis, but he was invariably quick of thought and close-gripping in argument'. Laski's speech was about 'the accomplishments of the British Labourites' and he ardently defended the government for bringing security to the unemployed, raising taxes on the rich and transforming British society. When Edmund Wilson, the magazine's literary editor, asked, with his nervous stutter, some sceptical questions, Laski held his ground and 'was quite carried away with his vision'. There would be in Britain 'a bloodless social revolution' with none of the crude measures of the Bolsheviks. This was the message he left the *New Republic* diners, albeit one he seldom articulated to others in this period, and one rendered all the more poignantly naïve by the crisis to which he returned.

Behind the crisis lay Labour's inability to deal with unemployment. Its most popular election poster in 1929 had read 'The Pits are Closed, but the Ballot Box is Open', yet in two years the number of unemployed had grown more than twofold from 1,164,000 to 2,880,000, putting tremendous pressure on the budget by decreasing revenues and increasing dramatically the outflow of unemployment benefits. By 1931 the international liquidity crisis was putting pressure on the pound. The government got economic advice from two committees, the Economic Advisory Council, whose creation Laski had opposed and whose members included Bevin, Citrine, Cole, Tawney and Keynes, and another chaired by Lord Hugh Macmillan, which also included Keynes and Bevin. On both committees Keynes pushed for an expansionary policy to increase purchasing power by getting people to work and to consume more by using the state to launch schemes of capital development. Keynes also suggested a revenue tariff and devaluation of the pound as alternative ways to increase revenues. Snowden, the

Chancellor of the Exchequer, and Montague Norman, the head of the Bank of England, rejected these suggestions as dangerously inflationary and a heretical assault on the sacred doctrine of free trade. The instinctive response of Snowden, whose economic vision began and ended with thrift, was to reduce government expenditure, and in February 1931 he appointed a committee headed by Sir George May, the Chairman of the Prudential Assurance Company, to advise the government on where to cut.

The May Committee report painted a gloomy picture of a British economy on the verge of bankruptcy with an immediate deficit of £120 million. The businessmen majority of five on the committee recommended that £24 million of the deficit be met by increased taxation and £96 million by drastic cuts, £66 million of which would be at the expense of the unemployed, whose benefits were to be cut by 20 per cent. The minority of two Labour men dissented and advocated more government spending. A furious Keynes wrote to MacDonald that to follow May's recommendations would result in a 'most gross perversion of justice'. Any prospect of compromise seemed doomed, however, by the new turn the crisis took when lack of confidence in the British economy led foreign investors to sell sterling. The Bank of England was instructed by Snowden to defend sterling and to borrow heavily from France and the United States. MacDonald was called back from holiday on 11 August and told of the run on the pound. Some American bankers, moreover, would not consider an £80 million loan unless certain political steps were taken. The cause of the trouble, MacDonald's advisers insisted, was not 'financial, but political, and lay in the complete want of confidence in HMG existing among foreigners'. New York insisted that the budget be balanced along the lines urged by the May Committee, though it would accept a mere 10 per cent cut in unemployment relief to restore its confidence.

MacDonald called his Cabinet back to London on 19 August and for four hot days Cabinet members came and went from 10 Downing Street. The Cabinet agreed on drastic cuts in salary for all state employees, 10 per cent from government ministers, judges and those in the military. Police wages were to be cut by 5 per cent and teachers' by 15 per cent. But no agreement was reached on unemployment benefits. Bevin, the head of a TUC group, told the Cabinet's economy committee that the unions would not accept that indignity, the heart of the demands from the American bankers. In a confrontation with Snowden, Bevin proposed new taxation on securities and a revenue tariff. The appeal by the TUC delegation split the Cabinet and on the night of 23 August the crisis came to a head with nine Cabinet ministers – a group including Henderson, Clynes, Greenwood and Lansbury – voting against the unemployment cut, and eleven for it.

MacDonald decided the minority was too large for him to continue in office, so he went to Buckingham Palace that night, leaving his Labour colleagues with the impression that he intended to resign. The next day Britain woke to discover that instead of the Tories, by far the next largest party, an all-party National government had been formed. MacDonald was Prime Minister, the Tory Stanley Baldwin was the Lord President, and the Liberal Sir Herbert Samuels was Home Secretary. Snowden as Chancellor of the Exchequer, J. H. Thomas as Dominion Secretary and Sankey as Lord Chancellor were the only other Labour members of the Cabinet. MacDonald's explanation to his stunned party colleagues was that as soon as the crisis was dealt with 'the political parties would resume their respective positions'. But for now the King had invited 'certain individuals as individuals to take upon their shoulders the burden of the government'.

Labourites were used to MacDonald's aloofness, but jettisoning the party to govern in a collection of individuals was too much. MacDonald was labelled a traitor, 'the great betrayer' of the party and the movement. When the Parliamentary Labour Party met on 28 August to vote on Labour's participation in the National government, only twelve of 288 MP's agreed to side with MacDonald. Labour went into opposition, choosing Arthur Henderson, General Secretary since 1911 and stolidly resistant to the 'aristocratic embrace', as the party's parliamentary leader. The humiliated Prime Minister was drummed out of the party. The Labour Party in Hampstead, where MacDonald lived, 'expelled' him on 31 August and around the country in hundreds of Labour Party constituency offices MacDonald's picture was turned to the wall or destroyed. In New York, on the other hand, bankers came up with an £80 million loan after the Commons voted with a majority of fifty to cut unemployment relief by 10 per cent, 276 Labour MPs voting against the government.

No one on the British left played a larger role than Laski in shaping how MacDonald's 'betrayal' was perceived by the labour movement. Within eight months he had published three important analyses. In late 1931 he contributed 'Some Implications of the Crisis' to a *Political Quarterly* issue completely devoted to the problem, which also included pieces by George Bernard Shaw, Leonard Woolf and Kingsley Martin. In February 1932 he published in Leonard and Virginia Woolf's Hogarth Press series of 'Day to Day Pamphlets' a long study, *The Crisis and the Constitution: 1931 and After*, and three months later a 'Portrait of Ramsay MacDonald' for *Harper's*. In these pieces Laski was at his best, integrating scholarly analysis and historical context within a strongly partisan, interpretive framework that commended itself to the puzzled yet interested observer. He looked at the crisis on three levels: the personal, the constitutional and the political.

MacDonald's actions had to be read, Laski insisted, as the personal betrayal of a man seduced by the 'aristocratic embrace'. Added to his complaints about MacDonald's lack of incisiveness of mind, his jealousy and his lack of collegiality was Laski's conviction that MacDonald had estranged himself from ordinary men and women. He had become a member of London society 'and its standard of values seemed increasingly his own'. He lived on 'a word of praise from the highest quarters', which was meat and drink to him. 'Just as on his American visit he saw nothing of the socialists of New York, so in London his essential contacts were with the aristocracy which has the wealth to make life a thing of grace'. Uncomfortable with the uncouth, the ordinary, the stuff of everyday life, Laski wrote, MacDonald 'is in the seventh heaven. He is leading the gentlemen of England, and there is no price he would not pay for that . . . he is convinced that he has saved the nation. The King tells him so, and nothing else matters to him.'

MacDonald was so angry at the *Harper's* portrait that he told Sankey he would never speak to Laski again. Feelings were deeply frayed. When the Laskis were invited for a weekend in November 1931 by Clifford Allen, a Labour Party friend of long standing who had stuck by MacDonald, Frida wrote explaining why they couldn't possibly come. 'We can't get ourselves up to the point of coming into the enemy's camp . . . in our present spirit you both would hate us and we should be more than embarrassed.' Allen, in turn, was so enraged at Laski's attack that he wrote an article for the *New York Herald Tribune* in praise of the Prime Minister, which he told MacDonald's son was 'a reply to a scandalous attack upon the PM by Harold Laski'. Meanwhile, MacDonald had written to Allen asking him if he would like to be a lord. Allen accepted, which led Laski to observe that he now looked on Allen 'as an early Christian might speak of Judas Iscariot'.

Many young people on the left, among them Michael Foot at Wadham College, Oxford, first discovered Laski in 1931 and 1932 through his 'furious attacks on Ramsay MacDonald' and his critique of the role of George V in the crisis. 'The new Cabinet was born of a palace revolution,' Laski argued, and the 'crown influence has rarely exerted so profound an influence in modern times'. Laski recognized that the financial crisis made dissolution of Parliament and a new election impossible, but George V should have asked Baldwin to try to form a Tory-led government. 'In modern times no man has become Prime Minister merely as a person,' Laski wrote; 'it is to his position as a party leader that he owes his premiership.' MacDonald had no party behind him, so he was an inappropriate and unconstitutional choice to lead the government. By this precedent, Laski worried, the King might in the future be 'a factor of first-class importance in any political crisis where the direction of events is uncertain'.

Buckingham Palace noticed Laski's claim that 'Mr MacDonald was as much the personal choice of George V as Lord Bute was the personal choice of George III'. The King's private secretary, Sir Clive Wigram, requested an interview and Laski kept notes of their meeting, which he described as most cordial. After Sir Clive had begun by saying that Laski seemed 'to have a down on the King', they carried on a serious talk about the monarch's role in a constitutional democracy. Wigram was less interested in rehearsing what had happened than in assuring Laski that the Crown exercised 'due care to keep itself above politics'. It would use its prerogative only 'to save the country from catastrophe'. When Laski replied that even 'this was going into and not keeping above politics', Sir Clive had the last word: the people would approve the King's actions because they trusted his motives.

In several books over the next two decades Laski persisted in referring to the 'Palace revolution'. He held to this view even after Sidney Webb argued in 1932 that the King had simply responded to a proposal made by Baldwin and Samuels. Constitutional scholar Sir Ivor Jennings agreed that there was 'no evidence that the King acted otherwise than with due propriety'. The debate over the King's role endured, however. The most vitriolic critique of Laski's position appeared in 1958 with Reginald Bassett's book *Nineteen Thirty-One: Political Crisis*. Bassett exonerated George V from Laski's charges and sought to rescue MacDonald from nearly three decades of Labour Party accusations of betrayal by arguing that he reacted in the national interest. As recently as 1983, the biographer of George V, Kenneth Rose, felt obliged to refute Laski, who in his words 'epitomizes this long-standing hostility' which saw Labour 'betrayed as much by the King as by MacDonald'. Rose granted that King George personally preferred a National government to cope with the crisis, 'but Laski's accusation that he acted unconstitutionally is entirely misplaced'.

By far the most important aspect of Laski's response to the events of August 1931 was his influential political reading of their significance. 'Is policy to be made by the elected government or by financial interests outside? If the latter, clearly socialism cannot be obtained constitutionally and the Bolsheviks are right,' Laski wrote to Frankfurter in early September 1931. The crisis was, he added, 'the biggest gift communism has had in our lifetime, for it throws the whole foundation of parliamentary government into jeopardy'. The bankers had sabotaged the Constitution, and much of Laski's writings and political involvement in the next decade involved a tortuous effort to prove wrong the apparent inexorable logic and lesson of the crisis which he outlined in the *Political Quarterly*:

> That a party which may command the assent of an electoral majority cannot carry its principles into effect out of fear of what the investing public may do . . . This is an announcement that finance-capital will not permit the ordinary assumptions to work if these operate to its disadvantage. Socialist measures, in a word, are not obtainable by constitutional means. Whenever a party in office seeks by legislative action to alter seriously the distribution of wealth, finance-capital will not accept the rule of parliamentary government. I do not know whether Mr MacDonald and his colleagues have considered the consequences of this implication. To me it seems tantamount to an insistence that if socialists wish to secure a state built with the principles of their faith, they can do so only by revolutionary means.

Laski knew full well that MacDonald's Labour government, his hearty praise of it at the clubby *New Republic* dinner notwithstanding, had not been interested in introducing socialism. His letters to Frankfurter in 1930 and 1931 repeatedly confessed that Labour 'has really done nothing at all' and might be better in opposition. Laski also knew that Labour ministers had accepted most of the cuts demanded by the May Committee and Snowden; only the trade unionist Bevin and the Liberal Keynes had spoken out. If, then, finance-capital could act so powerfully on the minor issue of the level of the dole, what would it do if a duly elected government truly sought to introduce socialism? How, then, could British socialism persist in repudiating Harry Pollitt's and Palme Dutt's communist ridicule of parliamentary politics as the road to socialism if real power in British society lay in the extra-parliamentary hands of capital? This was the issue for Laski in the 1930s – a tug of war in his political soul between this logic and his scholarly and activist instincts that preferred social transformation through constitutional parliamentary processes.

Laski detected one ray of hope – a very important one, to be sure – in the débâcle of MacDonald's betrayal. In its wake the Labour Party might 'purge itself of the liberal elements characteristic of its efforts under Mr MacDonald's leadership', who 'sought merely to extend the boundaries of social reform', and turn from how to treat the unemployed and other cash concessions to the underdog to the fundamental reconstruction of industrial organizations. It could emphasize 'the central principles of its philosophy and not its temporary expedients'. It could develop programmes for the socialization of banking, the national ownership and control of coal, transport and electricity, and the social direction of investment. A party of committed socialists would win parliamentary power from the electorate and transform Britain. After 1931, however, this optimistic scenario always coexisted with a suspicion that entrenched capitalist interests might not sit idly by as their power was being undermined. As Laski put it, 'The Constitution counts for nothing if property were at stake.'

Characteristically, Laski's will, if not his intellect, remained perennially optimistic and he threw himself into parliamentary party politics in the 1930s. In the programme of the Socialist League he would even try to craft parliamentary solutions to lay to rest the potential for extra-parliamentary sabotage by the forces of capitalism. However, Laski's assumption that out of the ashes of August 1931 the Labour Party emerged a purged party of ideological purity was widely off the mark. A consensus on 'the central principles of its philosophy' of socialism did not emerge. Indeed, for most of the 1930s Laski would spend more time fighting colleagues within the Labour Party than he would capitalism.

The stage for these years of bitter internecine struggle within the Labour Party was set by the general election of October 1931, the second Labour débâcle within eight weeks, and in this one Laski played a central role. Henderson, the new head of the party, recruited Laski as his right-hand man in the brief run-up to the election, their past tensions forgotten. 'I work day and night with Uncle Arthur,' Laski wrote to Frankfurter. At the party conference in Scarborough he was always at Henderson's side, and the NEC, according to Dalton, 'approved an election manifesto drafted by Laski, good of its kind, but a bit too literary for some taste'.

Labour's programme, in fact, had little that was new in it. It was still committed to a balanced budget, and although it attacked MacDonald the party itself had done nothing about unemployment for the previous two years. MacDonald and Snowden, in turn, asked for a 'doctor's mandate' to enable their National government team to do whatever was necessary to deal with 'the ills of the economy'. It was a particularly vicious campaign with attacks by Labour on the 'traitors' and with MacDonald and Snowden fanning the fear of the 'Post Office-Savings Scare'. Days before the election, rumours circulated that, if elected, Labour would pay added unemployment benefits from the £300 million deposited in the Post Office Savings Bank. A totally fabricated story, millions of people nevertheless feared for their meagre savings; its memory would haunt the Labour Party for years. Radio was extensively used by the National government to make its case and on the eve of the election Snowden labelled the rather moderate Labour policy as 'Bolshevism run mad', which would 'plunge the country into irretrievable ruin'. The election's results were disastrous for Labour. The greatest landslide in British political history saw Labour reduced from 288 seats to fifty-two while the National government had 554 supporters. Laski, who had spoken in many constituencies, tried to convince himself that the election furthered the Labour Party's purification. He wrote to Frankfurter:

Well, the electorate has certainly done it with a vengeance and we have to settle down to five grim years. It exceeded anything one could have even dimly guessed. Panic, a turgid patriotism, the press, the manipulation of the wireless, business terrorism, all these things explain a good deal of it . . . At least we shall never be weighed down with JRM or Snowden again! The next time we are in, it means socialism, and I take comfort from that.

The electoral massacre of October 1931 had profound and long-lasting effects on the distribution of power in the Labour Party and within the larger labour movement. Of the party leaders Henderson, Dalton and Morrison were defeated; only Lansbury was reelected. Lansbury was chosen to be Chairman of the Parliamentary Labour Party and the party leader in 1932. Also reelected were two younger radical MPs who assisted Lansbury in the leadership of the small Labour group in the House of Commons, Stafford Cripps and Clement Attlee. Henderson would be returned to the House in a by-election in 1933, but Dalton and Morrison would sit out the entire life of the Parliament, not to return until the 1935 general election. With a decidedly more militant parliamentary party, Dalton and Morrison turned to Labour's NEC as a countervailing moderate influence in the party structure. They would also make common cause with Bevin and Citrine of the TUC in resisting the more radical direction that Cripps and Laski were bent on taking the labour movement in 1932 and 1933.

Laski was by now a highly visible figure in labour circles. In addition to his 'Pen Portraits', he was a regular contributor to another of Bevin's journalistic ventures. Seeking to produce a 'plain man's' *New Statesman*, Bevin and the TUC purchased Blatchford's *Clarion*, rechristened it the *New Clarion* and published it for twenty-one months until its modest circulation of 35,000 made it necessary to cease publication. In that period Laski wrote twenty-seven articles for the new magazine. By far the most important indication of Laski's standing in the movement, however, was his emergence in 1931 as a major vote-getter in the annual elections for the Labour Party's NEC. At the Scarborough party conference that year, Laski finished third with 500,000 votes behind Fred Jowett and T. E. Williams for the one seat on the NEC allocated to the Division III category of cooperative and other socialist societies. His vote totals rose each year in the early 1930s, and by 1933 he was a solid second for the seat, something he repeated in 1934 and 1935. Pleased that the radical Laski didn't make it on to the NEC, Dalton described these results as defeats for 'yideology'. Though not elected to the NEC, Laski was appointed to its constitutional sub-Committee in 1933, whose mandate was to study the legal powers necessary to implement socialism when Labour next took office. Laski was also a delegate to the Labour Party conferences in 1933 and 1934. Each of the affiliated socialist societies, the Fabians, the Socialist Medical Association, the Socialist League, the Socialist Christian League, the National Association of Labour Teachers and the University Labour Federation, sent one delegate to the annual conference to speak for and cast the particular society's small number of votes. After 1933 Laski usually represented and cast the votes for the Fabian Society.

Although estranged from the National government, Laski continued to
see Sankey and he did agree to help on rounds two and three of the India
round-table conference in late December 1931 and December 1932 and to
sit on a royal commission on legal education in 1932. By and large,
however, Laski had no other involvements with government ministries or
Downing Street in the 1930s. Yet it would be these very years when Laski
was most visible in the labour movement and with the British public in
general. When Labour was out of office, his importance in the labour
movement was at its greatest. His ideological passion found strong support
in sections of the party and his constant willingness to work, write and
speak for the party gave him visibility and importance second to none of
the party's parliamentary leaders. Once Labour returned in 1940 to the
wartime governing coalition, or in 1945 to governing itself, Labour Party
and trade-union leaders became ministers of state and Laski would be
shunted aside as the professorial gadfly and outsider. His ideological fervour
would find much less favour then than it had in the 1930s. He would be
replaced in prominence by the more realistic and pragmatic orientation of
Labour colleagues involved in the day-to-day processes of governing and
making decisions.

A major part of Laski's public importance in the 1930s came from his
emergence along with Cripps as a leader in the Socialist League, a movement which sought to take the Labour Party dramatically to the left and
which, in turn, led to the intense efforts of Dalton, Morrison and Bevin to
craft a more moderate party. Cripps was the principal organizer and
parliamentary leader of the Socialist League and Laski its preeminent
publicist and intellectual spokesman. The league, its name a self-conscious
evocation of the earlier more militant vision of William Morris, never
had a membership of more than 3,000, less than the ILP or the CPGB
but it played a major role in labour movement politics during that
decade.

The Socialist League emerged out of the inveterate disposition on the left
to form new groups to meet old problems, a tendency aggravated by the
uneasiness with MacDonald just before and after his 'betrayal'. In late 1930
Margaret Cole, G. D. H. Cole and Lance Beales had brought together a
group of Labour intellectuals dissatisfied with the lack of interest in real
socialism by the Labour Party under MacDonald. After three weekend
meetings at the Countess of Warwick's Easton Lodge, they formed the

Society for Socialist Inquiry and Propaganda (SSIP). G. D. H. Cole, who was keen to reach out to the trade unions, brought in Bevin, whom he had come to know on MacDonald's economic advisory council. Bevin impressed the intellectuals, and when the society took formal shape he was made its chairman. The SSIP intended to operate as a 'ginger group' prodding the party to a more vigorous socialist stance. Beales, a lecturer in economic history at the LSE, had become, after Kingsley Martin's departure, Laski's closest friend at the college and through him Laski became actively involved in the SSIP.

The SSIP wasn't the only new group rethinking the future of socialism, however. Cole had established the New Fabian Research Bureau (NFRB) in March 1931, also at Lady Warwick's hospitable Easton Lodge, hoping to revive the moribund research activities of the Fabian Society and make the results available to a post-MacDonald Labour Party. Laski sat on this group's executive board and was chairman of its political committee, but he left both committees in 1933 when he was appointed to the NEC's constitutional sub-committee. Margaret Cole suggested that work on the NFRB was 'not spectacular enough for Harold', and, indeed, he may well have dropped it for a more spectacularly public effort at moving Labour leftwards in the wake of the events of 1931.

Dissatisfied with Labour, the ILP decided to leave the party in 1932, but a group of dissident members led by E. F. Wise merged with the SSIP to form the Socialist League, a new society affiliated to the Labour Party. In the course of the merger the former ILP members insisted that Wise be the Chairman of the league; Cole urged that it be Bevin, but to no avail. It was an insult that Bevin would never forget, convincing him that intellectuals would, if given the chance, stab working-class leaders in the back. Wise died the following year and was succeeded as Chairman by Stafford Cripps. The league, Beatrice Webb wrote in her diary, was the only ray of hope cutting through the 'deep depression' of the 'dreary' Labour Party, and, in fact, as Laski and Cripps proceeded in the next few years to use the league to liven up the Labour Party, there would be nothing dreary about it.

In the fascinating cast of characters in the drama of British socialism in the inter-war years Cripps stands out as unique. A nephew of Beatrice Webb and son of Lord Parmoor, a Labour peer, Cripps was a former scientist also trained in the law whose phenomenal career in patent law made him, at the age of twenty-six, England's youngest King's Counsel, and one of its richest men at the bar. Tall and thin, a deeply austere and ascetic Christian, Cripps was a cartoonist's and columnist's delight. With his diet of raw vegetables and his religiosity he acquired the label 'Christ and Carrots Cripps'. His wealth and forty-room house, on the other hand, led the *Daily Express* always to refer to him as the 'Red Squire'. Most of his wealth went to support the Socialist League in the early 1930s and the *Tribune* in later years. He continued as counsel to Britain's great corporations throughout the 1930s, and Labour meetings were often delayed until after 4.30 p.m. when the Law Courts closed. Cripps was a favoured speaker for the Socialist League all over Britain for his inspiring, albeit lawyer-like, presentations and because he paid for the travel expenses himself. Aloof and distant, a gentleman always in stiff collars, Cripps was visibly ill at ease with the comradeship of politics. His self-righteous manner with its combination of socialist militancy and Messianic Christianity prompted Churchill to remark of him, 'There but for the grace of God goes God.'

Despite their political collaboration throughout the 1930s, Laski and Cripps were never personally close. Nor was their socialist crusade ever that consciously orchestrated. Cripps was the parliamentary and party spokesman for the league and its administrative manager, organizing its lectures, research, conferences and weekend schools. Laski was its publicist. For both of them the league embodied a mood and a message. Its mood was socialist militancy; it talked of class struggle and criticized socialism as reform. Its message was the need to convert the Labour Party into a truly socialist party, get it elected, anticipate and thwart efforts by the ruling capitalist class to prevent the peaceful transformation to socialism. It was their controversial pronouncements about the latter which tended to capture public attention.

A shift to a more militant mood was clear by 1932 in Laski's private letters. In February he wrote to Frankfurter that they were living through 'the twilight of the old world'. 'In the long run,' he added, 'one cannot overturn what this society is without a surgical operation.' Two months later he expressed doubts that socialism could be established in Britain 'within the framework of existing conditions. The dice are too loaded.' Laski confided to Carl Becker, the Cornell historian, that the Labour Party was too legalistic, not aware enough 'that power needs at some point to be used adventurously and inventively'. These private reflections, however, were consistent with a view that socialists should not initiate violence but a duly elected socialist government seeking fundamental change might have to take defensive measures to thwart reactionary resistance. But long before that unfortunate possibility could occur, Labour had first to be converted to socialism.

In numerous speeches for the Socialist League Laski pleaded that 'socialism should take first place, not second place to trade unionism.' Many in the Labour Party, he suggested, 'would make good Conservatives' and should have left the party with MacDonald, Snowden and Thomas. In Lincoln in February 1933, he asked for 'a Labour Party where every member is a socialist'. In Coventry, he asserted 'that two Labour governments had shown that we could not patch up the superstructure of the present system; we must fight on the issue of transforming foundations'. It would be 'a disaster to the socialist movement if Labour were returned in 1935', Laski warned in Manchester, 'not in terms of the positive conviction that they wanted socialism and nothing but socialism, but liberalism as in 1929'.

Laski wrote official pamphlets for the Socialist League with this same central message. The average worker, he feared, was politically indifferent, and may even have supported MacDonald after the betrayal. If the Labour Party, he wrote, were 'seriously to consolidate a possible victory in the future, the conversion of the trade unions to socialism is the essential task that confronts it'. Since socialism could be achieved 'only by the making of eager socialists', the party must abandon its 'characteristic indifference to doctrine' and develop 'the kind of religious enthusiasm for its ends which Russian communism displays'. Laski envisioned an important new political role for a trade-union movement won over from moderate reformism to militant socialism. It would be 'a contingently revolutionary force', ready to be called upon to be 'the protective rampart of the Labour Party' should any extra-constitutional tactics be employed by capitalist interests. The naked power-play of the bankers in 1931 suggested to Socialist League members the likelihood that capitalists would not watch passively as a democratically elected Parliament assaulted their privileges and power. Laski frequently paraphrased Shaw to make this point. When their wealth was challenged, the normally generous, humane and cultivated British governing class would 'batter in the doors of their fellow-men, sell them up, sweat them in fetid dens, shoot, stab, hang, imprison, sink, burn and destroy them in the name of law and order'.

In his league pamphlet *The Labour Party and the Constitution* Laski laid out the legislative programme which Cripps was simultaneously pushing in the small parliamentary party and at annual party conferences. The platform included the immediate socialization of essential industrial enterprise and the financial system, but equally imperative were legislative strategies to confront capitalist obstructionism. An Emergency Powers Act would give Parliament authority to take all necessary steps to deal with an emergency financial crisis or panic through ministerial Orders in Council. The government would not need parliamentary approval, for example, to prohibit the export of capital or foreign exchange dealings. A socialist Labour Party would also require assurances from the King that he would create 'sufficient peers to carry out its policy without delay'. Labour could not allow its programme to be checked by the upper chamber, so it would ultimately move to abolish the House of Lords 'as being completely inconsistent with the character of a democratic and socialist society'. Of these, its two most controversial proposals, Cripps was identified with the need for the emergency powers and Laski with the House of Lords. When Lord Salisbury proposed in 1932 that no more than twelve peers could be created in one year, Laski and the league had a portent of what a socialist Labour Party would have to face when elected.

For Dalton, Morrison and Bevin, the party's moderates, talk of 'emergency powers' and of abolishing the House of Lords smelled of the Marxist 'temporary dictatorship of the proletariat'. Cripps and Laski, on the other hand, saw a fundamental difference in that a Labour Party wielding this extraordinary power, unlike the Marxist proletariat, would have been democratically elected. As the majority party it would have a legitimate mandate to transform the economy, the electorate having been kept well informed about the party's intentions in the course of the election. 'The large principles and main details of socialist schemes should be firmly outlined before the party takes office,' Laski wrote, so there would be no surprises, nothing arbitrary. Other aspects of the league's programme as urged by Laski also contributed to its 'revolutionary' image, however. A truly socialist Labour government, he wrote in *The Labour Party and the Constitution*, would abolish all titles of distinction, curtail all parliamentary discussion of private members' motions and bills, proceed by a rigid timetable and 'transform the character of legislation' by a 'large-scale development of delegated legislation'. Lord Hewart's Tory nightmare, which had prompted the Donoughmore Commission, would be realized as the league saw Parliament affirming general principles and powers with 'the detailed application of those powers to particular objects to be made by way of Orders in Council or departmental regulation'. Finally, a Labour Party converted to real socialism, Laski insisted, would abolish all private schooling, the foundation of the British class structure.

In his Socialist League pamphlet *The Roosevelt Experiment*, Laski even enlisted the new American President for his militant arguments. Only in the Soviet Union, Laski argued, was any statesman undertaking 'an experiment which even approaches in magnitude or significance' Roosevelt's efforts 'to lay the foundations of a new social order'. Laski's Roosevelt sought 'to socialize the profit-making motive by making its operation subordinate to a body of ethical principles'. Roosevelt was intending nothing short of 'a revolution by consent' through leadership that was creative, courageous, audacious and exhilarating. The final lesson from Roosevelt's experiment was his pressuring Congress 'into granting him wide powers which have given him the chance of rapid action'.

In *Democracy in Crisis*, which he completed in October 1932, Laski tried to put the case for the Socialist League in a larger theoretical and historical framework. 'The most creative book I have ever written,' in Laski's opinion, *Democracy in Crisis* reversed the balance in his writings between scholarship and partisanship. Until now Laski had packaged his books principally as academic monographs, with no efforts to disguise the political passion, but this, the first of his 'agitative books', dedicated to the Faculty of Yale University Law School, was principally and powerfully political, though some effort was still made to provide a scholarly framework. The book assumed the demise of capitalism, 'an old regime which is dying and a new one which is seeking to be born'. Crucial in this transition had been the events of 1931, which had moved the Labour Party to a realization 'that compromise with capitalism was impossible'. Labour, Laski insisted, was united now on the need for a direct assault on the foundations of capitalist economic power through national ownership and control of major industries. The 'grim fact', however, was that an electoral victory by this truly socialist party would precipitate a 'crisis of parliamentary democracy' where the men in power would 'choose to fight rather than abdicate' and would utilize the courts, the press, the educational system, the army and the bureaucracy to preserve their rule. Since Laski doubted that 'the possessing class' would 'meekly abdicate', he revisited and endorsed in this book the Socialist League's arguments for emergency powers to deal with 'financial or economic sabotage' and a recalcitrant House of Lords. Laski also introduced a new possibility of a Labour government's 'suspension of the Constitution', which could well lead to a civil war. He even speculated that should the governing class resist the duly elected socialist government the armed forces would probably side with the government in the name of constitutional continuity.

In *Democracy in Crisis* Laski freed himself from his pluralist past. No improvement in citizenship or democracy could flow from 'improvements in institutional forms' of the state, such as functional representation, decentralization, federalism or territorial devolution. Such solutions he now labelled 'specious' and ineffective in a society riven by class conflict, where the two rival faiths, socialism and capitalism, good and evil, prepared for the final struggle. There was no longer room for compromise as Laski repudiated the Whitley principle and all other 'attempts, more or less sincerely made, to find intermediate terms between a capitalist and a socialist society'. There could no more be peace in a society, Laski insisted, 'between the motives of private profit and public service than it can continue half slave and half free'.

In Laski's pessimistic prophecy, as socialist parties won democratic elections the commitment of capitalism to democracy would erode. For capitalists to cooperate in their own extinction would be 'something entirely new in historic experience'. The issue, then, was not the socialists' commitment to peaceful methods, but the capitalists'. Laski's commitment to democratic means paralleled his socialist passions, however, and mitigated his pessimism. A socialist Labour Party had fully to acquaint the electorate with its revolutionary plans before it ever took office, and then had to act prudently when in power and 'pay reasonable tribute to the established expectations of vested interests'. It must be willing 'to discuss, negotiate, conciliate, that it may attain the maximum possible agreement to its plans; for solutions made by consent are usually better than those which are imposed'.

Although hailed as 'a book destined to be a classic', *Democracy in Crisis* must have confused many readers. Pessimistic Laski made a powerful case for the likely emergence of extra-parliamentary, non-democratic methods to resist socialism, while optimistic Laski assumed the ruling class could be persuaded through prudent negotiations to relinquish their rule in the higher name of democratic and constitutional ideals. Moreover, Laski used the word 'revolution' in two totally different ways in *Democracy in Crisis*: 'revolution' through constitutional terms, or by consent, referred to a degree of economic change which was fundamental and transformative, from capitalist principles of self-interest to socialist principles of fellowship; but 'revolution' was also used to describe a method of change that involved violence and bullets, not ballots. Alongside the hoped-for 'revolution by consent' was the lamented 'revolution, [which] like war, is infinite tragedy, since in its very nature, it means pain and suffering and the tragic confusion of means with ends'. Revolution in this sense meant that 'hate and fear rule the destinies of us all'.

The leadership of the small parliamentary Labour Party in opposition was openly sympathetic to the Socialist League and the views articulated in Laski's *Democracy in Crisis*. Lansbury, Laski's first patron, thrust by circumstances into the leadership, revelled in the league's militant socialist rhetoric. Cripps was, of course, the major force in the league, along with Laski, and Attlee, who had served as Postmaster-General in the Labour government, was a supporter of the league while never its leader. Indeed, few would have imagined that this shy, self-effacing middle-class leftist, schooled in economics at Oxford and in Christian service at Toynbee Hall, had the leadership qualities to one day be His Majesty's Prime Minister. He wrote easily, though, and his pen was at the service of the league, with calls to action such as his insistence that 'the moment to strike is the moment of taking power when the government is freshly elected and assured of its support. The blow struck must be a fatal one and not merely designed to wound and to turn a sullen and obstructive opponent into an active and deadly enemy.'

The more moderate wing of the Labour Party, on the other hand, was unwilling to subscribe to the inevitability of a final apocalyptic struggle, even if only at the ballot box, between the forces of capitalism and socialism or to the impossibility of some merger of capitalism and socialism. Dalton and Morrison energetically developed the party's NEC as an alternative power-base committed to more moderate politics. Dalton, in particular, sponsored a series of policy sub-committees on the NEC, enlisting young moderate economists like Hugh Gaitskell, Evan Durbin and Douglas Jay, who worked out a socialist vision coloured by Keynesianism that would eventually dominate party planning. Morrison, the son of a London policeman, headed the Reorganization of Industry and the Local Government and Social Services committees, which produced some of the social programmes ultimately at the heart of Labour's postwar 'welfare state'. Since 1915 Morrison had assiduously worked to broaden the London Labour Party's electoral base by reaching out to lower-middle-class teachers, civil servants and professionals, and in March 1934 his work was rewarded with a Labour majority in the London County Council (LCC). Both he and Dalton saw the Socialist League as a fundamental threat to the future of the Labour Party. Laski, meanwhile, dismissed them as interested only in power, not ideology.

> The right wing (Dalton, Morrison, etc.) are determined to make a party which will win Liberal votes at any cost. Nothing matters to them except the election of 1936. They will sacrifice everything and anybody to that. In the long run it is going to mean the break-up of the Labour Party.

Bevin and Citrine were also busy beefing up the TUC as a moderate power-base in the Labour Party. They established an Economic Committee in the TUC as a focus for the discussion of economic policy questions and, even more importantly, in the winter of 1931 and 1932 they reconstituted the National Joint Council of Labour, which had three delegates from the Parliamentary Labour Party, three from the Labour Party NEC and seven from the TUC. With a built-in trade-union majority, the National Council claimed to speak for the labour movement as a whole. Bevin, who joined the council in late 1933, used it as his power-base for the rest of the decade and turned it into what one historian has called 'the most authoritative body in the labour movement in formulating policy'. The National Joint Council wasted no time and in 1933 published *Dictatorship Versus Democracy*, which equated the Socialist League's demand for emergency powers with the dictatorship of the proletariat and fascism.

A direct confrontation between Citrine, the General Secretary of the TUC, and the Socialist League took place in June 1933. Citrine characterized a speech by Cripps at a Socialist League conference as 'irresponsible drivel'. Discussion of emergency powers represented a 'very grave electoral handicap upon the Labour Party', Citrine wrote in Bevin's *New Clarion*, which placed 'a weapon in the hands of Labour's enemies which they are only too willing to use'. 'This sort of wild talk is far more likely to produce an atmosphere favourable to dictatorship than anything else.' A summit meeting was arranged by Arthur Pugh, the unions' emissary to Labour's intellectuals, between Citrine and a group of league intellectuals that included Laski, Cripps, Attlee, Tawney and Kingsley Martin. At the meeting – held, interestingly enough, at the LSE – Citrine stuck to his views, adding for good measure that the league's claim that a socialist government with an electoral mandate 'could do as it thinks fit' made it difficult for Labour to criticize Hitlerism. The emergency powers, Laski explained, 'would be like the extra constitutional powers taken by President Roosevelt', but Citrine concluded the meeting by saying he had come 'to discuss practical politics', not 'ultimate socialist objectives of a theoretical character'. Nor was he willing 'to waste my time further in doing so'.

The battle over the League filled the pages of Bevin's *New Clarion*. Herbert Morrison took the offensive in an article of 30 September 1933, suggesting that Laski was using 'the loud pedal' in condemning fascist dictatorships and 'the soft pedal' in condemning communist dictatorships. The insistence on special powers and revised parliamentary procedures, he added, 'would destroy constitutional government'. The following week Laski denied flatly that he or Cripps had ever sought to persuade Labour to overthrow the Constitution. He had not dealt differently in his criticism of fascist or communist dictatorships, but he insisted that there was a difference between a dictatorship which deliberately overthrew democratic and constitutional government and one which 'whatever its faults, crimes and blunders' was born of war and tyranny and sought 'to realize the well-being of all citizens upon the basis of equality'. Their fundamental difference, Laski maintained, was that Morrison 'merely proposed to patch up the worst results of capitalism', whereas he sought 'to win an election for thorough-going socialism'. Deeply hurt at Morrison's charge that his writings and speeches embarrassed the Labour Party, the first of many such claims made by the party leadership over the next fifteen years, Laski used a defence he would have recourse to in the future.

Our members are profoundly anxious to discuss the methods of obtaining socialism as well as the measures in which it is to consist. I assume they are entitled to a frank discussion of the position even if telling what I (and my friends) conceive to be the truth is 'embarrassing'. I have served the labour movement for twenty years, and its victory means more to me than life . . . I should be a poor servant of it indeed if I sought to conceal from it the facts I believe it must face; and it would be a poor sort of movement if it did not affirm its faith in the need for all its members to say forthrightly what is in their minds ... It may be 'embarrassing', though I do not think the sober confrontation of reality is ever embarrassing in the long run; but it is certainly the only honourable thing to do.

By far the largest inter-party furore over the league occurred, however, in the wake of Cripps's 'Buckingham Palace' speech on 6 January 1934. Speaking at Nottingham, Cripps outlined the potential sources of resistance to a truly socialist Labour government. When Labour came to power, he insisted, 'we must act rapidly and it will be necessary to deal with the House of Lords and the influence of the City of London. There is no doubt we shall have to overcome opposition from Buckingham Palace and other places as well.' Barely a month earlier Laski had himself written in the *New Clarion* that 'any reconstructed House of Lords is a deliberate invitation to revolution ... we must make it equally plain in Buckingham Palace as in Downing Street'. Laski's reference to the Palace went unnoticed; Cripps's speech was picked up by the press, however, and its implied criticism of the King provoked a storm of protest. Dalton was furious and ten days later at a regularly scheduled meeting of the Constitutional Sub-Committee of the NEC, he attacked Cripps as someone who 'seems to think that only he and his cronies know what socialism is'. Attlee and Laski defended Cripps and Dalton made 'a violent – perhaps too violent – speech – asking that this stream of oratorical ineptitudes should now cease ... it is the number of such gaffes which is so appalling. Our candidates [in by-elections] are being stabbed in the back and pushed on to the defensive. Tory HQ regard him as their greatest electoral asset.' The meeting then turned to a discussion of whether the Labour Party should publish a list of statements it considered out of line with party policy. Laski objected to any reference to individual statements and, Dalton noted, 'ended with a polysyllabic threat to diminish his interest in the work of the party, if such a repudiation were issued'. The matter was tabled and several days later Cripps assured an audience in Glasgow 'that he was in favour of constitutional monarchy'.

Some years later Dalton wrote of a dream in which he found himself at a Labour Party conference 'moving a resolution to nationalize the solar system'. Many in the dream saw it as a brilliant idea, but near the end of the conference debate 'a Socialist Leaguer got up at the back of the hall and moved an amendment to add the words "and the Milky Way".' The reality was not unlike Dalton's dream. The Labour Party conferences were annual battlegrounds, with the league winning the first few skirmishes. The most spectacular victory occurred immediately after its creation in October 1932 at Leicester, when the league sponsored a resolution urging a future Labour government to 'introduce at once, before attempting remedial measures of any other kind, great socialist measures'. Henderson, speaking for the NEC, argued that the resolution would tie the party's hands. Attlee countered that a socialist Labour government 'had to strike while the iron was hot and before their supporters and the voters had been scared'. The resolution carried. Then at the same conference, almost as in his dream, Dalton's resolution for the NEC to nationalize the Bank of England was amended by Wise and Cripps to include nationalization of the joint-stock banks. Dalton and Bevin opposed the amendment as electoral suicide, guaranteed to anger millions of small depositors, but the amendment carried by a close vote.

The Socialist League did well at the 1933 Labour Party conference at Hastings as well. As a result of Socialist League pressure, the NEC, for example, agreed to a resolution pledging the party to resist war by a series of tactics which could even include a general strike. Cripps later asked in a resolution that the NEC 'specify the means to be adopted by the next Labour government for a rapid and complete conversion of the capitalist to the socialist system'. His resolution listed as the means the immediate abolition of the House of Lords, an Emergency Powers Act and revision of House of Commons procedures 'so that a rapid transition to socialism may be carried through constitutionally and dictatorship avoided'. The NEC decided to study Cripps's resolution and report to the next conference, though Bevin spoke bitterly against Cripps's ideas in the general debate, with Attlee supporting them.

At the party conference in October 1934 at Southport, the NEC proposed the adoption of its new policy statement *For Socialism and Peace*, which subtly eroded the Socialist League position. It spoke of potential abolition of the House of Lords, of minor reforms to House of Commons procedures to speed up the legislative process and of greater use of delegated legislation. But it also delineated emergency powers that were strictly limited in scope and defined for specific narrow purposes. The manifesto noted, moreover, that the party 'sees no reason why a people who, first in the world, achieved through parliamentary institutions their political and religious freedoms should not, by the same means, achieve their economic emancipation'. Cripps and the Socialist League read these statements, quite rightly, as signs of the party's willingness to moderate its programme in order to win the votes of progressive non-socialists and radicals, and offered seventy-five amendments to the NEC's document. The most fundamental change the league suggested was the addition of a Programme of Action committing the party to seek an electoral mandate to make 'a decisive advance within five years towards a socialist Britain'. The league lost on this proposed change by over a million votes to 200,000 and it lost on every other amendment as well. The work of Bevin and Citrine, with their huge union block votes, and of Dalton and Morrison on the NEC had paid off. The party had been recaptured by its extra-parliamentary moderates, who were even clever enough to have Cripps elected to the NEC, an acknowledgement of the validity of the *Manchester Guardian*'s observation that 'when a man is a nuisance the best way to make him behave properly is to burden him with responsibility'.

At the Southport party conference Laski himself was the centre of a floor dispute between the NEC and party dissidents on the left. The former proposed to expel from the Labour Party anyone who remained connected with 'the Relief Committee for the Victims of German and Austrian Fascism', which it had declared that summer to be a communist front organization. The delegates knew this meant expulsion of three people who were prominent in the party: Lord Marley, a Labour peer who chaired the committee; Ellen Wilkinson, the MP from Jarrow; and Harold Laski. Morrison argued that affiliation with a committee financed by communists was inappropriate for a Labour Party member. Motivated not by 'a desire for heresy hunting' but rather to preserve 'the good name of the Labour Party', Morrison told the conference:

> I do not say that Harold Laski goes into these activities to lead our people 'up the garden', No one questions his absolute sincerity, least of all me, but I say that he is being unduly innocent, and others are being unduly innocent, in being used by these people for their own political ends, and it is about time that they were rescued.

The fiery Aneurin Bevan, a Labour MP since 1929, attacked the resolution for compelling members 'not [to] undertake any propaganda on their own initiative without first of all getting the permission of the party executive'. This was an egregious assault on their freedom. In turn, Ernest Bevin defended the application of party discipline and linked the issue to resentment of the Socialist League. Referring clearly to Laski, he noted that the case involved someone who belonged to that section of our movement which was 'always telling us we do not go fast enough, who claim a liberty in their own conduct almost amounting to licence'. Such men, he went on, forget that the trade unions formed this party and that insisting on party discipline 'entitles the party itself to recognize their responsibility to these great organized bodies'.

Laski, delegate for the Fabian Society, spoke to the conference on his own behalf. He did not care who funded the relief committee or what ulterior political motives they had, because he was interested 'in a purely philanthropic way for the assistance of such victims – many of them members of my own race in Germany and elsewhere'. He resented any suggestion that his association with the committee called into question his fundamental loyalty to the Labour Party. Had he not for fifteen years answered every call for help from the party's leaders and from the TUC? Unable to contain his penchant for sarcasm he urged the conference to ask 'the High Archbishop of Orthodoxy in this Movement – Mr Herbert Morrison' whether or not there had been an election since 1922 when he, Laski, had not answered Morrison's call to speak at a Labour election rally. He pleaded with the delegates not to grant the NEC 'power to expel me from this movement, because in the spirit of everything that this movement has ever stood for, I propose in my charitable work to follow the lines of my conscience'. Laski lost. On matters of party discipline the trade unions with their tradition of solidarity always voted as a solid block in support of the leadership. The vote was 1,347,000 in favour of the NEC's recommendation and 195,000 against. Rather than be expelled, Laski (Wilkinson and Marley, too) resigned from the Relief Committee three weeks after Southport.

Laski's concern for the victims of Hitler's 'brutal, beastly and belligerent New Germany', as he described it to Holmes, of course continued. Deeply involved as early as March 1933, the beginning of Hitler's rule, Laski was crucial in organizing efforts to find university posts for exiled scholars and financial support for refugee students. The LSE faculty, he wrote to

Frankfurter, had pledged 5 per cent of their salaries to help academic victims of fascism, and he himself had got 'some ten appointments in English universities'. Laski mobilized the academic community, with the help of his former New College mentor Gilbert Murray, to protest against the German persecution of scholars to the Foreign Office. In August 1933, in a letter to the *Manchester Guardian*, Laski urged the British government to make it clear at the next meeting of the League of Nations that the German rulers' actions were 'a wanton defiance of the decent opinion of mankind'. At public rallies Laski denounced 'the perpetual nightmare' where 'a whole people luxuriates in sadism'. In private, Laski ripped up the letter he had received from the Professor of Political Theory Carl Schmitt, and sent the little pieces back in an envelope to the well-known Nazi supporter.

Frequent letters appeared in *The Times* in 1933 and 1934 about the plight of Jews in Germany from Laski's brother, Neville, who had become President of the Board of Deputies of British Jews early in 1933. In his characteristic preference for the more militant, Laski found his brother's public utterances too mild and too 'weak and indecisive'. The Jewish community, he wrote to Frankfurter, should do more than stand 'at the back door of foreign offices'. One letter in particular from his brother to *The Times* annoyed him: in it Neville assured the British people that Jewish refugees would neither be a charge on public funds, which the Anglo-Jewish community would guarantee, nor fleeing German communists, as some on the British right were charging. Laski felt that Neville, as well as the Labour Party, was too obsessed with avoiding communist contamination.

Not that Laski wasn't himself on the receiving end from British communists, who had never forgiven him for his 1927 book. In the immensely popular apologia for communism, *The Coming Struggle for Power*, published in 1933, John Strachey dismissed Laski as an 'English liberal'. As painful as it was for a socialist to be so cursed, Laski agreed with Strachey that Western civilization was drifting chaotically to its destruction, though he saw 'no reason why there should necessarily be a communist victory'. Much more likely to result from the breakdown, according to Laski, was 'a dark age of dictatorship without principles'. The Socialist League and Laski sought a revolutionary change in the British economy and social structure, but not as those to their left, like Strachey, advocated through a proletarian uprising. Although the popular Tory press helped to convince many that the league was bent Lenin-like on violent revolution and dictatorship (which lots of labourites accepted as well), nowhere in the league's or Laski's literature is there the least suggestion of anything other than Parliament as the arena of political and social change. The struggle was confined to particular measures of parliamentary legislation. No effort was made by the Labour left to develop a socialist strategy that called upon industrial action or mass support beyond Westminster.

Although not always apparent at the time, a consensus on 'parliamentary socialism' was virtually all that unified the otherwise divided intellectual and trade-union wings of Labour. Laski and Cripps made little effort to root the Socialist League in any mass base, and they, just as much as Bevin, were responsible for the huge gulf separating the wings of the party in the 1930s. There seemed to be either Citrine's interest in 'practical politics' or his LSE hosts' concern for 'socialist objectives of a theoretical character'. And the rhetoric on both sides scarcely helped. Bevin saw either the 'trade unionist who has to ... deliver the goods to our members' or the people who join the party for the 'folly of putting up programmes that are not likely to be realized'; 'the intelligentsia's conception of our work' he thought was a 'libel on trade unions'. In turn, the *Socialist League* complained that at party conferences 'the anti-intellectual attack got an automatic cheer'.

Laski, of course, was the intellectual incarnate. One learns a good deal about the politics of the Labour left in the thirties from a speech he gave to a conference in Manchester, called to discuss libraries, literature and the labour movement. Laski's point, according to the *Manchester Guardian*, was that 'Labour must become a literate movement'. Blissfully unaware that he might offend anyone, he suggested that if 'one tenth of the enthusiasm spent on football, on movies, on Derbys, on drink were devoted to studying and understanding the position Labour occupied, Labour would long ago have been master in the country'. Only when every member of the Labour Party joined a public library and used his influence to include Labour literature in that library would victory come to socialism.

CHAPTER THIRTEEN

The London School of Economics and the 'Dangerous Teacher'

When he was the American ambassador to the United Nations, Daniel Patrick Moynihan wrote that the London School of Economics was 'the most important institution of higher education in Asia and Africa'. In its classrooms, Moynihan added, 'Harold Laski once moulded the minds of so many future leaders of the new majority' of unaligned Third World nations at the UN. Moynihan's feelings about the LSE – not uncommon – were set indelibly in the 1930s when its location and perceived politics gave it the nickname 'Red Houghton Street'. No matter that its Director was a Liberal, that it was heavily funded by American foundations and that its Economics Department contained the two most influential *laissez-faire* theorists in Britain. It was, nevertheless, 'the place where Laski teaches', largely because he was a much more recognizable public presence than Hayek and Robbins on the right or Tawney, Power and Beales on the left. As political actor in the Labour Party, as journalist, radio speaker and a socialist, Laski was always 'the professor from the LSE'. When for the second time in his life Laski became a public *cause célèbre* in 1934, Laski, the LSE and socialism became inextricably linked as he once again tested the limits of academic freedom.

Behind the events of 1934 lay years of friction between Laski and the LSE's Director, Beveridge. In 1924 Laski thought that Beveridge was 'an awkward, shy person' with 'a first-rate mind', but over the years he became convinced that he was an autocrat who one day sought to make statistics a mandatory subject and the next sold out to capitalist-sponsored research. In turn, Beveridge originally regarded Laski as a great asset to the school, given the vogue of *The Grammar of Politics* and *Communism* and his connections with prominent and wealthy Americans. By the early 1930s, however, Beveridge's 'vehement objection to Laski's propagandist activities' had become an 'obsession', according to Beatrice Webb. Beveridge saw

Laski as a grave threat to the LSE's strong support in City financial and business circles, presided over by Sir Arthur Steel-Maitland, the Tory MP, Baldwin's Secretary of Labour during the General Strike, Chairman of the Conservative Party and Head of LSE's Board of Governors.

In his impetuous way Laski threatened Beveridge's master plan for the school's continued growth. Beginning in 1923 Beveridge had negotiated nearly £500,000 of grants from the Rockefeller Foundation, then committed to fostering social science, which allowed the school to expand its library, increase its space, develop new fields of teaching and provide for faculty research. Laski wrote to Frankfurter in 1928 that Beveridge 'has been corrupted by Rockefeller into a stunt merchant', and Kingsley Martin was telling Beatrice Webb that Beveridge returned from his frequent visits to America 'with the autocratic manner of the representative of the USA millionaires'. On one of his visits to America in 1928 Beveridge was horrified to discover from the Rockefeller Foundation staff that Laski had just written an attack on capitalist university philanthropy in Harper's. In 'Foundations, Universities, and Research' Laski wrote, presciently in his own case, that when the university 'has to sell itself to the sources of economic power, the "dangerous" teacher is undesirable'. What is studied and what is taught will be affected by the attitudes of donors, Laski warned, and foundations will set the direction of expansion. What, Laski asked, were the chances for promotion if one 'pursues a path of solitary inquiry in a world ... competing for the substantial crumbs which fall from the foundation's table?' Laski sensed that he himself was a victim of the new influence of foundations in university life. Lesser men than he were being invited to lecture in America, he wrote to Morris Cohen in 1928, because American foundations 'just want safe people'.

Despite the denunciation of foundations in Harper's, Laski was not above a practical and opportunistic pursuit himself of their favours. When he taught at Yale in 1931 he met with Raymond Fosdick, an officer of the Rockefeller Foundation, and he pushed increased general endowment for the LSE and 'for help with all the things I care about, buildings, library and research professorships and not what I dislike'. Convinced that he had succeeded because 'they were so concerned to remove the impression I have given in my writings on the foundations', Laski met again in New York City with members of the staff of the Rockefeller Foundation and invited its Director, Edmund Ezra Day, to New Haven to talk about the future of universities. Laski wrote to Frida that his tactics gave him 'pull with Rockefeller which in view of the situation at the school it is most useful to have'. The strategy seemed to work, for he received a 'sweet' letter from Mrs Mair, Beveridge's secretary and principal assistant, which he attributed to their both knowing that he was seeing Day. They see 'that I stand here with Rockefeller on equal footing with W. H. B. and have a great deal of influence with them.'

Jessie Mair was herself a large part of the problem at the LSE. Married to a cousin of Beveridge, she had come to the school as secretary to the director in 1922 and they were inseparable. She fast emerged as a domineering partner in what Beatrice Webb referred to as 'the Beveridge–Mair dictatorship'. The two would ultimately marry after they left the LSE. According to Frida, 'Mrs Mair was a dragon who bullied the staff and hated Harold.' Faculty would literally stop talking when Mair, Beveridge's spy, approached, and virtually none of the teaching staff ever joined Beveridge and Mair at lunch. In a place run 'on a policy of favouritism and benevolent autocracy', Laski told Beatrice Webb, the result would be 'an explosion somewhere'.

These tensions became all the more apparent amidst the heightened political conflicts in the school in the 1930s. A member of the school governors, Frank Pick, Chairman of the London Passenger Transport Board, suggested to Beveridge in 1930 that the school exercise greater control over teaching faculty. Beveridge brushed the request aside, even though Laski's flamboyant socialism troubled him. In February of that year Beveridge had recorded in his diary that Laski had made 'a rather savage speech' critical of the school at a student dinner. By the following year Beveridge was required to give background information on Laski when negotiating grants from industrial sources. City interests seemed reluctant to subscribe to appeals for an enlargement of the Commerce Department because of Laski and the school's reputation for socialism. In response, Beveridge bullied the school's Professorial Council in 1931 into adopting a resolution which recognized the faculty's 'absolute freedom in both speaking and writing' but declared that 'they should nevertheless regard it as a personal duty to preserve in such writings or speeches a proper regard for the reputation of the school as an academic centre of scientific teaching and research'.

After 1931 the more strident ideological conflict throughout British politics was mirrored on the LSE faculty, fuelled by the arrival of Friedrich August von Hayek in the Economics Department. As quiet and retiring as Laski was brash and outspoken, Hayek was a match for Laski in his ideological passion, ever critical of the socialist bias he saw in the school's teaching and in certain faculties' 'emotional aversion to capitalism'. Beveridge himself was abandoning in these years the New Liberal politics that had earlier made him an important ally of the Webbs and turning more to the free market orientation of his Economics Department. By 1933 Beatrice Webb noted in her diary that civil interaction had virtually ceased between the economic individualists, Robbins and Hayek, and the socialists in the Political Science Department. 'Apparently the lively and brilliant Laski,' she observed, 'is feeling the cold winds of intolerance blowing – even in his direction.' In March 1934 the trouble at the school got worse, with Beveridge citing Laski 'as the centre of the mischief' and Laski denouncing 'Robbins and his group of fanatical individualists'. Beveridge urged the faculty to desist from any partisan discussion of topical issues 'as inconsistent with the scientific outlook', but both sides ignored the Director's warnings.

The show-down of 1934 was ignited by an outburst of student protest at the school which Beveridge attributed, in part, to Laski's influence. The *Student Vanguard*, a Marxist undergraduate newspaper, published an article in late February accusing a faculty member by name of spying on Indian students for the Colonial Office. Beveridge banned the sale of the paper, holding it to be libellous, but six students led by the President of the LSE Student Union, a Marxist American graduate student named Frank Meyer, continued to sell the paper. Beveridge, they held, had no authority in a student matter. Beveridge expelled the students, which produced throughout early March daily rallies with LSE students marching around the Aldwych and the Strand shouting 'Down with Beveridge' and 'Bring Back Frank Meyer'. The *Daily Herald* covered the story on its front page, even to its denouement with Beveridge succeeding, with a word to the Home Secretary, John Simon, in having Meyer deported back to America.

No one on the teaching staff supported the students' defiance of Beveridge's ban on distributing the paper. Indeed, Beatrice Webb applauded the way the Director had dealt with the irresponsible actions of 'a knot of Marxists led by an odious American Jew'. Laski had called the publication of the faculty name libellous and he criticized the students' insistence on defying Beveridge as 'indefensible from any angle'. He had, however, urged clemency with respect to the expulsion. Beveridge saw Laski's hand all over the affair, especially when he heard that Laski had, in fact, met with the students after they were expelled. He wrote to Laski demanding an explanation. Laski replied that he had told the students 'that the completeness with which they were in the wrong was beyond discussion and that the whole staff was united behind you in thinking so' and suggested they apologize to Beveridge, making clear that the apology would have no bearing on how they would be treated. Beveridge was not mollified. He accused Laski of 'dictating' the student apology, putting himself 'without consultation with me into the position of an adviser of the students'. He was upset enough to add that if there were any more 'independent interventions in such matters, I shall feel that there was no advantage in my continuing as Director'. Laski denied 'dictating' an apology. He had only suggested an apology, he wrote, and had no idea when the students left his office whether they were going to write one. Beveridge accepted the correction and the matter was dropped. There was no clemency and Meyer was sent back to Chicago, where he would become a leader of the Young Communist League and then an anti-communist informer to the House Un-American Activities Committee and finally the literary editor of William Buckley's conservative journal, the National Review.

The Beveridge–Laski truce was short-lived because in the course of their discussions over the Meyer affair Beveridge raised the more sensitive issue of Laski's writings for the Daily Herald. Beveridge's concern, he later claimed, was strictly technical. Laski's large amount of outside writing raised salary equity issues. He was being paid on a higher scale and should have asked permission from the governors before undertaking a large amount of outside work. In fact, Beveridge was really concerned with the effects of Laski's political visibility on the school. He wrote to Laski on 18 April that he might be violating the Professorial Council's 1931 resolution. He was, he wrote, 'sure that the reputation of the school as an academic centre of scientific teaching and research, and your own reputation also, are being damaged and in the nature of the case must be damaged by the continued stream of articles of an ephemeral or partisan character appearing over your name'.

It is difficult to believe that Beveridge really considered Laski's weekly 'Pen Portraits' dangerous. When the flap arose in April 1934, Laski had authored 192 weekly pieces for the *Daily Herald*. About two thirds of them were gossipy, anecdotal sketches of British public figures from politics, unions, the civil service and the business world. The others were either about intellectuals, scientists, writers, historical figures or foreign political figures. If they were partisan, the message was informal and chatty, never didactic or deep excursions into Laski's ideological preferences. If they offended, it was done with the light and witty touch that Laski's former Yale student Henry Luce was popularizing in *Time* magazine. Laski was often surprisingly kind to Tories in his profiles, describing Anthony Eden in 1933, for example, as 'the English gentleman at his best'. To be sure, a handful of the 'Pen Portraits' had caused some fuss. The Herbert Hoover sketch had bothered many Americans, as had the piece on Henry Ford. Some people were disturbed by his fondness for flattering sketches of foreign colonial rebels like Gandhi and Nehru. Although his sketches of British politicians were generally lively and inoffensive, one in particular, his sketch of Lady Astor, annoyed many people. With tongue in cheek, Laski had portrayed a woman whose only claim to be in the House of Commons was that her rich husband had freed a seat when made a lord and who contributed nothing to English politics except to run grand parties at her estate, Cliveden, where socialists like Shaw and Americans like Henry Ford took tea with the aristocracy. 'The Pollyanna of the political world', according to Laski, had no imagination, no brains, and 'her entrance into British politics was America's revenge for George III'. That the Astors had friends on the Board of Governors and that Cliveden was a centre for American influence in London concerned Beveridge, but even this piece pales in partisanship when placed against Laski's articles for the *New Clarion*.

Laski was stunned by Beveridge's desire to pursue the issue with the LSE's governors, and by the evidence of 'how profound had become your personal antagonism towards me', which 'came upon me with all the force of an unexpected blow'. To Sir Arthur Steel-Maitland, the governor to whom Beveridge had referred the matter about salary, Laski defended himself in a six-page handwritten letter. In a typical week he was at the LSE 'from Monday until Friday, from ten o'clock until five'. He listed twenty-two books and essays he had written or edited since he had come to the school in 1920. How then, he asked, could the Director suggest that 'my articles prevent my giving full time service to the school?' The 'Pen

Portraits' took but 'two hours of my leisure each week', and the annual fees (£200) went to pay a secretary and as gifts to students. As for whether his activities injured the institution, Laski recited the long list of honours, distinctions and invitations he had garnered which enhanced the prestige of the school. His outside activities helped his teaching, for, unlike Beveridge, he believed that 'full contact with practical affairs is one of the best ways of understanding the academic problems of politics'. It was no surprise, Laski concluded, that 'the views I hold in politics should provoke strong dissent', but he assumed the school and even the resolution of 1931 'left teachers free to express views of an unorthodox kind'. If, on the other hand, the Board of Governors shared the Director's view, Laski would 'of course, accept its decision at once', though he would have to tell friends like Lansbury, Henderson and Citrine 'why I must cease to continue work in which they have been kind enough to show some interest'.

Steel-Maitland's correspondence with Beveridge indicates that he saw the issues as more complicated than the Director did. After all, Laski himself served as a governor, having been chosen by the faculty to occupy one of the three seats reserved for the professoriate. There was the even more serious issue of timing. Steel-Maitland picked up Laski's hint and spoke to Citrine, who advised that action be delayed until a decent interval had elapsed after the Meyer affair. Steel-Maitland agreed and wrote to Beveridge in May that the matter would have to be put on hold until he returned in early summer from a trip to America. By then, however, everything had changed, for the question of the relationship between Laski's politics and the LSE was eclipsed by the much larger crisis over academic freedom generated by Laski's lectures in Moscow.

Laski went to the Soviet Union in late May with Frida. He gave three lectures to his hosts at the Institute of Soviet Law, which were essentially summaries of *Democracy in Crisis*. The lectures were interrupted continually by hecklers, according to the American journalist Louis Fischer, then on assignment in Moscow. This, it turned out, would be the least of Laski's problems, for on 6 July the *Daily Telegraph* ran a story about Laski's third lecture given in June under the headline: 'Professor Laski's Pestilent Talk of Class War'. It was an outrage, the *Telegraph* intoned, 'that a Professor of London University should parade his pestilent programme for producing civil strife or civil war in England for the delectation of a communist academy in Moscow'. Phrases about anarchy and financial panic after a socialist election victory were cited, as were intimations of capitalist resistance to a socialist programme. 'The ordinary, decent Englishman would blush to talk thus in a foreign capital,' the article concluded, 'but Mr Laski is a cosmopolitan socialist.' The next day the *Morning Post* and the *Evening Standard* picked up the story and made much of what they saw as a particularly offensive passage from the *Telegraph* account, the suggestion that 'when the rules of the game prove unsuitable for victory the gentlemen of England change the rules of the game'.

Two weeks earlier the *Manchester Guardian* had written a totally different account of the same Moscow lecture, emphasizing that 'for the first time in sixteen years a public speaker in the Soviet capital made a spirited defence of a socialist party outside the hallowed ranks of the Communist International.' The *Guardian*'s account described Laski as having criticized the Communist Party of Great Britain (CPGB) and its non-parliamentary revolutionary assumptions as well as defending the Labour Party in his speech, even though he referred to the problems it might encounter as it transformed Britain into a socialist society. The *Guardian*'s story stressed that Laski's official respondents, Mr Boris Reinstein and Professor Pashukanis, denounced the speaker, along with other well-known figures of the Labour Party, as 'betrayers of the working class'. It also recounted Laski's comment that 'what had distressed him more than anything else in Moscow . . . was the dogmatic certitude of the communist mind'. A well-known foreign writer, long resident in Moscow, was quoted as being amazed at the entire exchange: 'It sounded as if free speech had suddenly come to Russia.'

Laski immediately wrote a letter to the *Daily Telegraph* claiming that 'all the quotations in your leading article are torn from their context. With one exception they are part of a summary of the communist position which I sought to set out in order that I might expose what I conceive to be its weakness.' The exception was the phrase about the 'gentlemen of England', which he stood by. The *Daily Telegraph*'s editor appended a note to Laski's letter defending the accuracy of their report and noting that 'in any case, Professor Laski's admitted references in a Moscow lecture to the "gentlemen of England" will continue to cause astonishment here'.

It did, indeed. On Wednesday 11 July Parliamentary Question Time was taken up with Laski. Sir John Simon, the Foreign Secretary, was asked if Laski had a special permit to go to Russia. Had he said he was going to give such a talk? He had a passport and no special permission was necessary, Simon replied. Captain P. MacDonald asked the Chancellor of the Exchequer, Duff Cooper, if government funding went to the LSE, adding, 'Is it not the fact that this Professor Laski is an avowed communist as well as being of alien origin?' Cooper answered that the funds came to the LSE from the University of London block grant, not directly from the government. Attlee came to Laski's defence, albeit with slight exaggeration, pointing out that the talk was really 'a defence of parliamentary government, and that it was followed by a five-hour attack on Professor Laski'. Cripps also spoke for Laski, reminding his colleagues that the LSE charter provided professors with complete freedom 'to express their political opinions outside the school'.

Officials at the University of London were worried, and the next day a letter appeared in the Daily Telegraph, The Times and the Manchester Guardian from the Vice-Chancellor and Principal. It would be improper before all the facts were known 'for the university to express an opinion on Professor Laski's action', they pointed out. Rather ominously, however, they suggested the likelihood of a future 'inquiry by the appropriate body' and if it were true that he had said what the Daily Telegraph reported, the university, of course, could in no way 'accept responsibility for personal expressions of opinion by any of its professors'. Kingsley Martin later suggested that this letter was written in obvious panic in response to the intervention of King George V, no friend of Laski's, who as Visitor to London University, had personally intervened with an inquiry to university officials about Laski's activities. This was all too much for the Manchester Guardian, which ran an editorial on 13 July in response to the 'ludicrous' questions asked in Parliament about Laski and the 'chilling' letter from the Vice-Chancellor and the Principal of the University of London. It repeated its earlier version of the Moscow lectures, adding how odd it was that when these same lectures were given the previous autumn at Lady Margaret Hall, Oxford, there hadn't been a word of protest. Laski's argument about possible capitalist sabotage of a socialist government in Britain, the Guardian suggested, was probably mistaken. Indeed, it went on, 'most of us will probably think his imagination a little lurid – but it is a legitimate point of view. Apparently it is one thing to express it in socialist pamphlets in this country and another to express it in Moscow.' As for the University of London, the newspaper asked, 'Since when have universities felt it necessary to comment on the published political views of their staff?'

Enter at this point the MP for the University of London, Sir Ernest Graham-Little, who wrote to the *Daily Telegraph* on 14 July. The letter from university officials, which he read as 'an official repudiation of the sentiments which Professor Laski is reported to have expressed', wasn't enough. There needed to be real 'disciplinary correction of objectionable activities by a member of the staff of a college'. The problem, according to Graham-Little, was that 'the London School of Economics, where Professor Laski functions, has long been regarded as a hotbed of communist teaching, and such action by the governing body is consequently unlikely'. The only solution, then, was for the University of London, the parent body, to punish the LSE for 'this regrettable outburst by one of its teachers' by reducing the financial allocation it made to the LSE.

On the same day, with the appearance on the stands of the *New Statesman*, Laski's defenders began to be heard, wondering 'why is it particularly wicked for an English professor who is also a socialist to defend democratic government and to attack communism in Moscow?' Three days later George Bernard Shaw wrote to the *Daily Telegraph* in praise of Laski's talk and its honest discussion of British politics. He deserved great credit for 'not talking British electioneering bunk in Moscow'. And five LSE professors (Chorley, Gregory, Power, Tawney and Webster) in a letter to *The Times* deemed it 'highly regrettable' and 'a menace to academic freedom' for a university to 'conduct an inquiry into expressions of opinions by its teachers on matters of public interest'. In the next Saturday's issue of the *New Statesman* John Maynard Keynes wrote a scathing letter denouncing both the university officials and Graham-Little for interfering 'with the liberty of speech of one of their professors'. Surely it was 'well established in England, as distinguished from Moscow or Berlin, that a professor is entitled to the unfettered expression of his opinions and that no one but himself has any responsibility in this matter'. Keynes's harshest words were reserved, however, for the 'monstrous suggestion' of Graham-Little to apply financial pressure to the LSE. 'Inquisition into opinions,' Keynes concluded, would ultimately 'destroy civilization'.

Beveridge, too, was concerned about Graham-Little and he asked the LSE's solicitors to advise the school on the potential for a libel suit. When a University of London Professor of Political Economy wrote to the *Daily Telegraph* to label Graham-Little's charge that the LSE was a hotbed of communist teaching, 'a fanatic and erroneous idea' in light of the presence and influence of Hayek and Robbins, Beveridge wrote him a note of thanks. Beveridge was still convinced, however, of 'the necessity of tackling head-on the Laski problem'. The Russian speech episode and Graham-Little's attack on the school had in fact reinforced Beveridge's desire to muzzle Laski. Not even a letter to the *Manchester Guardian* from someone who compared the attacks on Laski to Hitler's attacks on German universities gave him pause.

Beveridge visited Laski at Addison Bridge Place, only to be told, 'My attitude is simple. I will not submit to any investigation by the university as that would imply my admission of its right to define the limits of permissible opinion.' Beveridge told Laski that he, too, would oppose such an investigation but that he intended, none the less, to go ahead with his request to the governors to clarify Laski's obligations to the school when engaged in outside activities. Laski was thankful for the former and repeated his assurances that he would abide by the governor's decision on the latter. The Emergency Committee of the school's governors met on 19 July and agreed to support Beveridge's recommendations, writing to Laski that his *Daily Herald* column violated the rule that outside work for more than £50 needed the consent of the school. Much more significant, however, was 'the sense of the meeting' that:

> The development of public opinion concerning Professor Laski's recent more popular utterances is, as a fact, rightly or wrongly, against the best interests of the school, and ought now to be taken by him into account in deciding upon 'personal duty' under the Professorial Council Resolution of 1931. The committee, therefore, welcomed Professor Laski's willingness to keep his future writing and speaking in character within limits likely to counter that development.

In a letter to Beveridge on 25 July Laski agreed to stop his weekly columns for the *Daily Herald*, explaining later to Frankfurter that even though this meant giving up a secretary, it was prudent to clear away questions of financial obligations and ties from the larger issues of academic freedom. Laski also wrote to Beveridge that 'as far as speeches are concerned' he regarded himself 'free to make occasional speeches on political topics, especially at such times as general elections'. He assumed the committee raised no question about his right to write articles for periodicals 'so long as these do not imply any continuous relation with a particular journal'.

In reconstructing the events for Frankfurter several weeks later, Laski suggested that behind it all was the governors' concern that 'no indiscretion should arrest their plans for university development'. As for Beveridge, 'he could not have been a bigger swine', because he was consulted about the letter from the university spokesman before it was sent to press 'but did not raise a finger to criticize publication, wanting to use it with the governors to prove that I was a disturbing influence in the university'. Laski also told Frankfurter that he had received sixty-two threatening letters over the row, many signed 'Gentleman of England'. 'I suppose,' Laski wrote, 'one must pay for one's convictions.' His sentiments were echoed by Justice Brandeis, who wrote to Frankfurter on 8 August that 'the Laski incident shows that even in England and the University of London eternal vigilance is the price of liberty'.

As much as Laski liked the limelight, he was clearly shaken by once again being at the centre of a public squabble over academic freedom. This was not supposed to happen in Britain, only in America. He had written in 1922 to the American novelist Upton Sinclair, who was then working on an exposé of American universities, about the 'freedom of the English academic atmosphere and the illiberalism of America'. Despite the fact that businessmen predominated on the LSE's governing body, 'interference is never dreamed of'. In America one always felt 'hampered by the sense of control outside', Laski told Sinclair, whereas 'in England you never feel that it is necessary to watch your tongue. No ox treads upon it.' Now, twelve years later, Laski felt deeply embittered about the LSE to which, he told Frankfurter, he had given 'fourteen years of devotion'. He no longer felt 'inclined to put it first when I get nothing from Beveridge but meanness'. He pulled back from involvement with the school, its commit-tees, its governors, its plans for the future. 'The only duties the teacher owes to the university,' Laski wrote several months later, 'are the duties to think hard, to think freely and to think independently.' The teacher's principal obligation was to students who were at university to have their 'minds turned upside down, to be driven back, by continuous questioning, against difficulties they either did not know or sought to avoid – this is the real path of intellectual discipline'. This could only be done, Laski suggested, when the teacher 'makes his pupils his friends, for no teaching work is really successful which remains on a purely official plane'. So it would, in fact, be for legions of students who, as Frankfurter put it, had 'the fires of their minds and souls lit by Harold Laski . . . one of the great teachers of our time'.

'His lectures are the most popular and the most well-attended,' Joan Phillips, an American student, wrote in 1936. Students came to Laski's lectures for the performance. One knew he was lecturing when every five minutes or so a great burst of laughter could be heard through the rest of the building. Richard Pankhurst, Sylvia's son, remembered that many postgraduate students of other subjects, like himself, used to go to Laski's lectures 'when we wished to relax, almost as we might go to a cinema or theatre for relaxation'. Part of his appeal, Rufus Davis, an Australian student and colleague of Laski's, remarked, was that 'he never left you in doubt how important he was'. Pankhurst agreed: 'We felt in listening to him that we were actually inside the corridors of power because his anecdotes were so lively and absorbingly interesting.'

It wasn't only his stories that won him his adoring following; it was also his infectious enthusiasm. Davis remembered how bold, colourful and immensely dramatic Laski was in an academic setting that seemed to privilege the grey, the equivocal, the retiring and the judicious. There was a pyrotechnic, dazzling quality of being with Laski. He was so learned, so eloquent, yet his eyes twinkled and his personal magnetism overwhelmed the student. It was, Davis claimed, 'a mesmeric experience to be in his office for twenty minutes'. Students remembered Laski's personal kindness and warmth, as well. Pankhurst noted that Laski was 'always approachable, never aloof. Students could go to him with their problems and felt they were approaching a friend.' The door to Laski's office, Room 105, was always open if he was at the school. He never kept formal office hours and there was usually 'a queue long enough for a cinema outside his door waiting for advice he was always ready to give'.

Teaching, for Laski, was 'beyond words a joyous adventure', largely because 'students are really adorable, as interesting as flowers'. Watching a student discover the glories of Hobbes was an 'undiluted joy'. But teaching was not intended to produce disciples. Robert McKenzie, the LSE political scientist and popular British television commentator, wrote that 'Laski relished it when students disagreed with him'. He loved nothing more than pushing his Marxist students, or playing devil's advocate with democratic socialists. His object as a teacher, Laski stated, was not to create followers who 'go forth to preach the particular and peculiar doctrines I happen to

1. Sarah with Harold on her knee and Mabel standing, Manchester, 1895. (Courtesy of Pat and Roger Mathewson.)

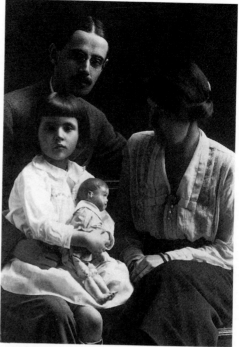

2. Harold and Frida with Diana in Boston, 1920, during their time at Harvard. (Courtesy of Harvard Law School.)

3. Frida Kerry in 1907, two years before she met Harold. (Courtesy of Elzeke de Saedeeler.)

4. The Laski family in Manchester in the 1920s. From left to right; back row: Cissie, Neville, Mabel, Harold and Frida; middle row: Sarah and Nathan; bottom row: Philip, Marghanita, Diana and Pamela. (Courtesy of Manchester Jewish Museum.)

5. Harold at the seaside with a Belgian couple who were friends, 1923. (Courtesy of Andrew Mathewson.)

6. Harold, always a sharp dresser, 'relaxing' with Frida and friends on holiday in 1932. (Courtesy of Andrew Mathewson.)

7. Harold with Diana (to his right) and Frida leaving for New York in 1938. (Courtesy of Topham.)

8. Harold speaking to Hugh Dalton at Labour's Southport conference in 1934. (Courtesy of the National Museum of Labour History.)

9. Harold with other members of the Labour Party's National Executive on their visit to Moscow to see Stalin in1946. From left to right: Harold Laski, Harold Clay (Official of theTGWU), Morgan Phillips (Party Secretary) and Alice Bacon (MP). (Courtesy of Hammersmith and Fulham Archives and Local History Centre.)

10. Labour leaders hold their first press conference at Transport House after the general election victory of 1945. (Courtesy of Hammersmith and Fulham Local History Centre.)

11. Harold conferring with Morgan Phillips during a Cabinet weekend
conference, February 1949. (Courtesy of Press Association/Topham.)

12. Harold with Herbert Morrison in Shanklin, Isle of Wight, 1949.
(Courtesy of Associated Press/Topham.)

13. Harold meets students at Roosevelt College, Chicago, USA, in 1948. Second from left is Harold Washington, later to become the first black Mayor of Chicago. (Courtesy of Roosevelt College.)

14. Harold with Senator Robert Taft ('Mr Republican') of Ohio at Kenyon College, USA, in 1946. (Courtesy of Kenyon College Archives.)

15. Harold at home in his study at Addison
Bridge Place, London. (Courtesy of Andrew Mathewson.)

16. Harold in a reflective mood, with ever-present
cigarette in hand. (Courtesy of Harvard Law School.)

hold'. But the teacher, on the other hand, need not pretend neutrality: his responsibility was 'less to avoid his bias than consciously to assert its presence and to warn his hearers against it; above all, to be open-minded about the difficulties it involves and honest in his attempt to meet them'.

Laski's socialism and fame, as well as his uncharacteristically English warmth, attracted large numbers of foreign students to him. At the beginning of term one year he described for Holmes his 'whirl of new students, black, brown, yellow and white – the Hindu, the Chinaman, the American from Iowa'. Isaiah Berlin suggested that foreign students and Indians, in particular, loved Laski because in their innocence they drank up everything he said about his contacts and influence, whereas British students more easily saw through him. Others have suggested, on the other hand, that Laski appealed to Third World students for the very mundane reason that his phenomenal memory enabled him to remember their names unlike his more absent-minded colleagues. More likely, Laski's appeal to the Indian students that Krishna Menon kept sending him, as well as to other students from the colonial world, lay in what he was saying and writing. His support for independence and his world-view, with its socialist reading of imperialism as generated by the capitalist search for markets, provided an explanation and a solution to their grievous sense of exploitation and oppression.

Over the years Laski also had a stream of students from Canada, like Robert McKenzie, and the United States with whom he loved to gossip about politics back home. His involvement with three North American students in 1934 reveals a great deal about different facets of Laski the teacher. Joseph Kennedy, Jr, then nineteen, was spending a year abroad before entering Harvard. His father, Joseph Kennedy, Sr, who had made a fortune on Wall Street and in Hollywood and was appointed the first head of the Securities and Exchange Commission, worked closely with Felix Frankfurter. Frankfurter, spending the academic year 1933–4 at Oxford, suggested that young Joe Kennedy spend his year studying with Laski. Rose Kennedy, as she later put it, was 'taken aback by the choice'. She had given in on the Protestant preparatory school, but a socialist professor whose wife was an ardent leader of the birth-control movement seemed 'a little wild and a little dangerous'. Joseph Kennedy, Sr, thought Laski was 'a nut and a crank' and 'disagreed with everything he wrote', but he wanted his oldest son, for whom he had high hopes, even the presidency, to know the enemy, to learn what the anti-capitalist mind was like. His sons, he made clear, 'are going to have a little money when they get older, and they should know what the "have-nots" are thinking and planning . . . they should be exposed to someone of intelligence and vitality on the other side'.

Joseph Kennedy, Jr, had a busy year at the LSE, taking virtually all of Laski's courses, totalling about seven hours a week, and writing a weekly essay for him. To stay in touch with Real Truth he also sat in on Robbins's lectures. He became a regular at Laski's Sunday teas, and with his connections with Frankfurter and Roosevelt, his openness and enthusiasm, and his unabashed announcement of his intention to be America's first Catholic President, he became a Laski favourite. Laski was struck by young Kennedy's 'keen satisfaction and obvious affection' for the socialists and Jews from East London who were his classmates. 'With a smile that was pure magic' and a zest for argument, Kennedy would tackle political topics in class or at tea, usually taking the Conservative viewpoint. With his roommate Aubrey Whitelaw, also Laski's student, Kennedy talked endlessly about the professor, his classes and his politics. Whitelaw, who became a businessman in Connecticut, wrote in 1959 that Laski was the 'greatest teacher of our time'.

Kennedy also spent weekends that year with the British aristocracy, had an audience with the Pope and visited Hitler's new Germany, but Laski was always on his mind. His letters home from Germany, for example, reveal how impressed he was with the Nazis and even how he played off his favourable impressions of the Nazis against what he had heard at Laski's teas 'of the frequent brutalities in Germany', and he decided that he would not share his admiration for Hitler with Laski, for 'it might hurt his feelings. Laski would probably give me examples which might change me back again.' Laski tried to do just that by inviting young Kennedy to travel with him and Frida to the Soviet Union when term was over. Strikingly self-confident, Kennedy accepted.

Writing to his father from the SS *Rykov*, Kennedy wondered whether he had made a mistake in accompanying the Laskis: 'Everybody is either a Bolshevist or a communist and I'm all alone.' The conversations were enlightening, he admitted, and 'Laski is very amusing and some other people are screams, so it's darn good fun'. Frida later recalled Kennedy's 'RC reactions at the museum of anti-religion. I can see him to this day in all amazement.' Kennedy family lore has it that the trip affected him deeply, just as Laski had intended. Rose Kennedy remembered that her son 'put on a good show of having absorbed Laski's teaching, and some of us asked him whether he'd be willing to give up his boat if he had to share the wealth. He decided that just his boat wouldn't make that much difference.'

After Kennedy's tragic death in the Second World War, Laski wrote a piece in 1945 for Jack Kennedy's privately printed book *As We Remember Joe*. It was a time, Laski wrote, when Joe's 'mind was only just beginning to discover the enchantment of thought. His essays were written with great care and he took criticism with a disarming friendliness. He never stopped asking questions.' He was popular with his fellow students, who teased him about his American frankness and openness. 'He was always anxious to know. He repaid one's efforts with a fidelity of heart that was deeply moving.'

Kennedy was not the only son of rich American parents who sought out Laski in 1934. Michael Straight, the youngest son of Dorothy Straight, was then seventeen and living with his mother and her husband of eight years, Leonard Elmhirst, at their progressive school, Dartington Hall. With a year before Cambridge to fill, Straight also sought advice from Frankfurter, a family friend, who again suggested a year with Laski at the LSE. In his autobiography Straight described visiting Laski, 'a man despised by the right wing in Britain as a socialist, an intellectual and a Jew', to talk about spending the year at the LSE. Over some port, 'the last of old Haldane's', Laski allayed Straight's concern that he might not be admitted; he would arrange it. Straight lived with his brother Whitney in P. G. Wodehouse's elegant house in Mayfair for the year while studying with Laski, befriending Krishna Menon and participating actively with Frank Meyer in the Marxist anti-Beveridge unrest of March 1934. Laski kept Frankfurter informed about Straight, writing that he was 'a nice lad who has been brought up softly in the past and has too much money now. At seventeen one shouldn't keep a taxi waiting while you talk for forty minutes, or am I excessively ascetic?' When Straight went to Cambridge after his year at the LSE, he consulted Laski about a speech he had to give at the Cambridge Union on proposed legislation forbidding political demonstrations by extremist groups. Laski provided him with a detailed memo on the differences between Mosley's British Union of Fascists and Pollitt's Communist Party. Laski and Straight remained in touch during the 1940s, when

Straight had returned to America and was working for the *New Republic*, but Laski was long dead when it was learned in 1981 that Michael Straight had revealed to American and British intelligence agents in 1964 that his old Cambridge friend Sir Anthony Blunt was the 'fourth man' in the Burgess–Maclean–Philby espionage ring.

Kennedy and Straight illustrate one side of Laski the teacher, his capacity to win favour with important people by teaching their children. But the dominant side of Laski was his legendary role as socialist mentor to countless young people with neither wealth nor famous parents. One such student who worked with Laski at the LSE in 1934 was Crawford Brough MacPherson, a Canadian who would become, along with John Saville, the economic historian, and Ralph Miliband, the socialist theorist, one of Laski's most important leftist disciples in academia. He came to study with Laski in the academic year 1933–4 at the urging of his professor at the University of Toronto, Otto B. Van der Sprenkel, who had himself been a student of Laski's at the LSE. MacPherson's masters thesis written under Laski, 'Voluntary Associations within the State 1900–1934, with Special Reference to the Place of Trade Unions in Relation to the State in Great Britain', clearly reflects his teacher's own scholarly interest.

MacPherson kept a diary during the winter of 1933 and the spring of 1934 which provides a wonderful picture of Laski the teacher. After his first class with Laski, MacPherson noted that 'he promises well though his humour has a tinge of stereotypical cleverness about it, and he seems to be developing a high-and-mighty pose'. He was surprised by how young Laski was, given all the books he had written. Soon MacPherson was going to Laski's teas. One diary entry reads: 'Quite a large group there, Laski rather fond of holding the centre of the stage but did it well. Talked about Bernard Shaw (who had been no good since about 1920 but was a great man up till then), the Indian White Paper, H. G. Wells and so on, L. throwing in personal anecdotes about them.' In November, MacPherson attended a Fabian lecture where Laski's introductory remarks as chairman were 'exquisite wit uttered with a polished and studied brilliance'. A decade later another young Canadian, Pierre Trudeau, came to study with Laski and was even more 'impressed'. Laski was, Trudeau would write, 'a superb teacher'.

Laski not only gave as a teacher, but he received as well. The obvious adulation of his students clearly flattered and excited him. It provided a satisfying sense of power and importance as well as gratifying opportunities to play out a fatherly role. The theatre of teaching with its dramatic lectures, its opportunities to tell stories and to mimic world leaders, the recognition and reverence of his devoted followers, must have appealed to Laski as much as the magical joy and heartfelt responsibility of helping to mould the minds and values of the young people who, with any luck, might themselves build Jerusalem in England or in their native lands. In 1935 Laski was the first faculty member ever to be elected honorary President of the LSE's Student Union, with the students noting that their action was a tribute to their teacher 'and their answer to the university action of last July'. At the very same time the faculty were uniting in opposition to the Director, with Robbins joining Laski in an alliance against Beveridge after he announced that only he would set the scales of professors' salaries. The general lack of consultation led the faculty to push for and get from the University of London a change in the school's constitution which shifted power from the Director to the senior teaching staff and the Professorial Council. The Robbins–Laski coalition had done its work, even winning over the Rockefeller Foundation. On a visit to the school, Foundation inspectors were convinced by the faculty that, as Laski put it, 'the school was effectively a despotism occasionally tempered by benevolence'.

Sensing the changed balance of power, Beveridge sought to make peace. He 'tries assiduously to cultivate me and I keep him at arm's length', Laski wrote to Frankfurter. Beveridge also approved all of Laski's requests for speaking trips away from the school as well as the *Daily Herald*'s invitation in 1936 for a three-month resumption of the biographical sketches. But it was to no avail, and the final crisis came in 1936 when Beveridge insisted that Mrs Mair, who had reached the mandatory retirement age, be re-appointed for five years or he would resign. The faculty united to denounce an extension and threatened to resign *en masse* if she were retained. Beveridge resigned and in 1937 was replaced as Director by Alexander Carr-Saunders, a demographer and Professor of Social Science at Liverpool University. Beveridge assumed the Mastership of University College, Oxford, and then his historic role during the Second World War as a principal architect of the welfare state. Laski went on to nearly a decade and a half of devoted and much happier service to the LSE on 'Red Houghton Street'.

CHAPTER FOURTEEN

Workers, Kings and Fascists

The range of Laski's interests and activities was breath-taking. If he were not engaged in Labour Party or LSE politics, or not teaching, he might be writing on the Marxist theory of the state, religious toleration in the eighteenth century, or the American Democratic Party. Then there were the days each month that he travelled around Britain to lecture workers or to sit on cases for the Industrial Court. In late 1934 Laski entered an entirely new area of involvement, local government. A certain symmetry was at work. Just as in his writings where he could move from the heights of abstract speculation about fundamental social transformation to the nitty-gritty practical essay on the committee structure of the House of Commons, so too in his political activism he could move from playing the highly visible shaker and maker on the national scene to the much less noticed and undramatic world, far from centre stage, of local politics.

The municipal elections in 1934 saw Labour victories around the country. In Laski's own London borough, Fulham, where there had been no Labour representatives since the war, twenty-seven of the forty council seats went to Labour, and in November he was appointed alderman. Frida was elected to the council and Harold was co-opted by the new Labour majority. They both remained on the council for eleven years, she re-elected, he reappointed, devoting an average of four or five evenings a month to council work. Most of their time was spent on committee work. Over the years Frida chaired or worked on the Public Health Committee, Maternity and Child Welfare Committee, and the Housing Committee. She was involved in building 700 new flats and rehousing over 2,000 people, in establishing a midwife service and in starting up a birth-control clinic, a maternity home and a welfare clinic for children. Laski told Frankfurter that 'she really makes me feel damned humble. I do the talking and she does the doing.'

He was doing too. He served on three different committees; Law and

Planning, Staff, and Library. For many of these years Laski was Chairman of the Library Committee and he was principally responsible for building the Fulham Children's Library and in developing the borough's general library services into one of the best in London. He introduced a survey which asked readers what books to stock the library with. When the preference was detective fiction, he ordered that more be purchased. He saw his library work as part of his ongoing commitment to worker education and he got the borough council 'to agree to doubling the Tory estimate for libraries next year'. He took particular interest in developing strategies to make the libraries more hospitable to those unfamiliar with them. He proudly informed Frankfurter in December 1937 that 'we have now (a) doubled the circulation of books and (b) nearly halved the maternity mortality rate. We feel noble people.'

Laski became professionally involved with the British Library Association, speaking to their annual meeting in September 1935 and writing papers on 'The Use of the Public Library' (1935) and 'The Library in the Post-War World' (1944). In general, during his years of work with the Fulham Library and in local government service, practice met theory for Laski. His writings on localism, decentralization of political authority and the experience of citizenship became real. He described such service in an article on local government in 1935 as 'a nursery of local statesmanship' and 'a means of fertilizing Westminster with the results of local experience'. Even as he was advocating central planning and a much larger role for government in the nation's economic life, Laski was praising 'the committee system in English local government' as a crucial 'safeguard against the easy tendency to centralization which is the paralysis of effective self-government'.

In a similar way Laski, who was being pilloried for calling for 'dictatorial' emergency powers, was in fact devoting much of his apparently inexhaustible energy to a vigorous championship of civil rights. The National Council of Civil Liberties was established in February 1934 and Laski was one of its founders. The context which produced the council was a series of hunger marches which punctuated the 'red decade', bringing large numbers of unemployed workers into London to capture sympathy and public attention for the depressed areas of Britain. One of the 'economies' in the wake of the 1931 crisis was the detested means test, which allowed government officials to visit the homes of those out of work in order to investigate exact details of all domestic income. Resentment at the indignity of these intrusions produced angry demonstrations against the means test, which often merged with the hunger marches. Edward, the Prince of Wales, was known to be sympathetic to those marches, but the official leadership of the TUC and the Labour Party kept their distance because the National Unemployed Workers' Movement, which organized the marches, was communist-led. Neither the Labour Party nor the TUC had anything to do with even the most famous of the marches which saw 200 men walk 300 miles from Jarrow to London in October 1936 accompanied by their MP, 'Red' Ellen Wilkinson, Laski's former colleague on the Donoughmore Commission. But it was an earlier hunger march, in February 1934, that had led Laski and others to form what would become the National Council of Civil Liberties.

The Home Secretary, Sir John Gilmour, in anticipation of the marchers' arrival in London, sought to blunt the embarrassment to the government by portraying the marchers as threats to public order. Parents were told to keep their children off the streets for fear of violent hungry men; shopkeepers were urged to board their windows because of 'possible bloodshed'; and students at school were warned of the approaching danger 'before prayers'. Rumours abounded that the police intended to use *agents provocateurs* to create trouble and justify arrests. A group of fifteen prominent progressives and leftists announced in a letter to *The Times* and the *Manchester Guardian* the creation of a Council of Civil Liberties which would 'maintain a vigilant observation of the proceedings of the next few days'. Among the signatories were Laski, Nevinson, Edith Summerskill, Attlee, Vera Brittain, Kingsley Martin and H. G. Wells, though on Sunday 25 February only Wells, Laski, Nevinson and Brittain were actual observers at Hyde Park. There was, in fact, no violence, the *Daily Herald* observing that 'the marchers have shamed their detractors by their dignity and surprised those who know their grievances best by their restraint'. Apparently the police were held back by the presence of well-known people on the watch, which then became a common practice at working-class demonstrations.

The fledgling council was soon caught up in a crisis over free speech, generated by the passage of the Incitement to Disaffection Act, popularly known as the Sedition Bill. For the first time since John Wilkes and 1765, the Bill granted police the power to search on suspicion with a general warrant obtained from a justice of the peace, in this case to find socialist or pacifist literature likely to seduce members of the military from their duty to King and Country. The National Council of Civil Liberties organized public meetings and demonstrations around the country. At the largest rally in April at Kingsway Hall in London, Laski spoke, as did Wells, E. M. Forster and Dora Russell. Laski called the legislation 'the most dangerous attack upon public freedom introduced within a hundred years of English history'. The agitation against the legislation got it modified in important respects and led to little use being made of the power.

The council and Laski also became deeply involved in monitoring police activity surrounding meetings and rallies of the British Union of Fascists, the organization founded and headed by Laski's old leftist friend, Sir Oswald Mosley, who had turned dramatically to the right in the 1930s. The Public Order Act of 1936, which prohibited wearing political uniforms at demonstrations and gave the police the authority to ban political processions, was used more often by the police to detain communist or Jewish anti-fascist protestors than it was against Mosley's followers. Two incidents found Laski as spokesman for the council. He wrote the preface for its report on police singling out anti-fascist protestors at the disturbance in Thurloe Square, South Kensington, in March 1936; and in January 1937 he wrote a long critique in the *Manchester Guardian* of the trial of thirty-one anti-fascist protestors whom police had arrested at Tonypandy while letting the fascists go free. He noted that central to the conviction of the anti-fascists were the police accounts not of their actions but of their political views. The police had to realize that 'in this country, as yet, no political views, however extreme, are a crime!'

In another case in 1937 Laski was more successful. An elderly woman, Mrs Ercourt, who sold the *Daily Worker* outside the Golders Green tube station, had been arrested for causing an obstruction and molesting passers-by. Laski led a sub-committee investigation for the National Council of Civil Liberties, which argued that the police's real concern was the sale of the communist paper. Laski's group was able to obtain £50 damages for Mrs Ercourt plus all the costs of the proceedings and a police letter of apology which appeared in newspapers around Britain. In an essay entitled 'The Outlook for Civil Liberties' Laski was particularly outspoken about the 'curious helplessness of the police' in the face of 'the assaults, intimidations, picketing of shops, threats of murder and arson' visited upon East

End Jews by Mosley and his followers. Civil liberties, he argued, were in danger because the governing class believed that its privileges were threatened by the mere prospect of a truly socialist government. To maintain freedom, Laski suggested, 'where differences are keen, and passions profound, is the most difficult exercise in the act of government. Few things are so easy as to reply to grievance by repression.' He warned that 'unless we can maintain in Great Britain an ample atmosphere of free discussion . . . our fate will be no different from that of Russia or Spain'.

His Workers' Educational Association lecturing enabled Laski to see at first hand the depths of unemployment which fuelled the grievances which so divided the British in the 'red decade'. While lecturing in south Wales Laski stayed with a miner who had been unemployed for seven years. On his street there were nine families with a total of 190 years' unemployment between them. The visit taught him 'grimly what public assistance means. They had a leg of mutton in my honour, so four neighbouring families were invited in to share. As there were only four chairs in the house, the extra guests brought their own chairs and plates. One family had not had a day's holiday in nine years.' Many, like these miners, Laski wrote, were being diverted from the woes of unemployment and hunger marches by the bread and circuses of royalty, and even Laski would be swept up in the grand drama of monarchy to play his small but important role.

When the Silver Jubilee of the reign of King George V and Queen Mary was celebrated in May 1935, the government used the occasion to trumpet loyalty to the Crown as an antidote to the divisions that rent British society. 'The Jubilee business,' Laski wrote to Frankfurter, 'is ghastly in appearance but not, I think, much more to the masses than an extra Christmas celebration.' The occasion was marked by a special honours list which included Citrine, who accepted a knighthood. Intellectuals like Laski and Tawney were shocked: instead of converting the public to Labour's vision of a Britain transformed into an egalitarian fellowship, leaders like Citrine 'sit up, like poodles in a drawing-room, wag their tails when patted, and lick their lips at the social sugar-plums tossed them by their masters'. Eight months later King George was dead, succeeded by Edward, the 40-year-old Prince of Wales. The monarchy once again pushed the news of unemployment and Hitler off the front page. Laski wrote to Frankfurter that 'we, as you can imagine, are literally drowned in an ocean of sentiment about the King'. But all of this was a mere prelude to the riveting attention the Crown would shortly command.

The British press were finally allowed in December 1936 to carry the story the world's press had been running for months: Edward's intention to marry the American Wallis Simpson, a divorcée. Churchill, still a backbencher, championed the marriage as did the Beaverbrook press and Mosley's British Union of Fascists. Edward had supporters on the left as well, especially when, as a compromise, the Palace announced he intended to marry Simpson without her becoming Queen. The *New Statesman* supported this as did George Lansbury, who saw Edward, the supporter of the hunger marchers and unemployed miners, as a 'democratic King'. Cripps and others on the far left supported the King in hopes that it would precipitate a parliamentary crisis that would bring down the National government. Leonard Woolf described Edward as a victim of puritanical Victorian morality. But many in Britain were shocked by Edward's intentions. The most powerful critics were Stanley Baldwin, who had replaced MacDonald as Prime Minister in June 1935, and his Cabinet. What was not at all clear, however, was how Labour, the official opposition party, would respond to Baldwin's strong stand, given the divergence of views in the party.

Enter Laski. On his own initiative he wrote an article for Labour's official newspaper, the *Daily Herald*, supporting Baldwin's position and insisting that profound constitutional issues were at stake: 'The King must act on the advice of his ministers. The place where issues of policy are decided is and must be the House of Commons.' Five days later Laski wrote a second article entitled 'This is the Real Issue', in which he warned of the grave dangers of personal rule undermining democratic government. If the King and his supporters succeeded, 'a blow would have been struck at the root of Parliament's authority from which it would not easily recover'. Perfectly consistent with his writings after 1931, Laski feared that the royal authority would once again become a source of independent political power in the state. Thomas Jones, Baldwin's Cabinet Secretary, noted in his diary on 8 December that Laski's articles 'had a stabilizing effect on Labour' and helped to settle the Labour Party's support of Baldwin. Laski dispatched a copy of his first *Herald* piece to the *New York Times*, which published it on the front page over his byline on 7 December with the headline 'Labour Fears King Might Seize Reins'. Two weeks later he had a piece about the crisis in the *Nation* as well. Edward abdicated his throne on 10 December rather than accept his ministers' advice about the marriage. The next day Laski wrote to an American friend in St Louis about Edward.

> Don't believe the nonsense you hear that he's a socialist. He is no more a socialist than J. D. Rockefeller or any other rich man who has occasional prickings of conscience. I don't care at all who he marries since I am for the British Republic anyway. The intellectuals were for him and they had no sense that his right to choose his own wife had other connotations beside the denial of the sexual standards of the Anglican Church – one more proof that popular instinct is a better guide to wise government than the refined insights of Bloomsbury and Chelsea.

The Labour Party let Laski be its spokesman on the constitutional issue of King Edward's relationship to Parliament, but on little else. The triumvirate of Dalton, Morrison and Bevin gave the party during these years a strongly moderate cast in outright repudiation of what was seen as the extremism of Laski and the Socialist League. Between 1932 and 1935, for example, Morrison fought off the league in the party's great debate over the place of 'worker control' in future nationalized industries. While the league, on this issue with some trade-union support, saw an important role for worker self-management, Morrison envisioned the nationalized industry as a public corporation, free from parliamentary control and run by expert managers dedicated to efficiency and economic planning. For Morrison and subsequently the party, nationalizing industry was not intended to reconstruct the position, function or power of workers in an industrial society, an older syndicalist objective which characterized the position of Laski and the league. Industrial democracy and worker participation were incompatible with planning, which was fast becoming the central value to the party's moderate leadership. At most, Morrison would concede places reserved for trade-union leaders on the autonomous boards of a nationalized industry. The Fabian reflex was alive and well in the party's leadership.

Few were more responsible for defeating Laski's efforts in the 1930s to move Labour left than Hugh Dalton, who in his position on the National Executive Committee dominated the party's policy-making process. Under his patronage young Oxford economists like Hugh Gaitskell, Evan Durbin and Douglas Jay were busy in NEC committees, in the New Fabian Research Bureau and in the XYZ Club, which brought together Labour intellectuals and City radical sympathizers, formulating the alternative vision of socialism focused on state management of a still largely capitalist economy where a public sector dominated, but run by experts not by workers. Like Keynes, these new Fabians tended to be more interested with fine-tuning prosperity than in crafting a new society based on new social, economic and, ultimately, human relationships.

Laski was their nemesis: he was as much the foil of Dalton and his experts as were capitalists. In turn, Laski described Dalton as 'the Devil in the Labour Party'. In their preoccupation with Labour's need to attract middle-class votes, Dalton and Morrison denounced all inflammatory rhetoric and what they considered to be irresponsible resolutions at party conferences. Dalton ridiculed the Socialist League and its leaders as 'officers without a rank and file, better known to each other than to the general public, moving in select circles, carrying almost no electoral weight'. Laski with his 'yideology' just 'doesn't understand the English', Dalton wrote in his *Memoirs* in 1934. His socialism was based on 'thin, theoretical, tinny tintinnabulation'. Dalton's own more moderate socialist vision was laid out in his 1935 book *Practical Socialism for Britain* with an approach he described as 'very British' in its 'distrust of logic and distaste for doctrine' and self-consciously aimed against 'our melodramatists of the Socialist League'. Laski was clearly on his mind as Dalton rejected talk of 'inevitable crises and all theoretical nightmares of violent head-on collisions, wrecking the train of democracy'. The book immediately earned Dalton praise from the press as 'the intellectual dynamo of the party executive'. Evan Durbin wrote a glowing review of his patron's book in which he also stressed its rebuke to Laski's 'use of a half-baked Marxian jargon' and the general 'sickening intellectual spectacle' of the Socialist League.

By far the bitterest attack on Laski from within the Labour Party in these years was Reg Bassett's *Essentials of Parliamentary Democracy*, a defence of 'labour gradualism' against those who 'advocate immediate, far-reaching and simultaneous changes affecting the entire social system'. He defended a socialism that was produced in stages and which acknowledged that much of capitalism would remain, though tempered by small doses of socialism. Bassett, like his close friend Durbin a colleague of Laski's at the LSE, rejected Laski's picture of British political parties as rigidly ideological at heart and uninterested in parliamentary compromises, as well as his understanding of politics as a battle to the death between 'mutual and exclusive opposites between which there is no prospect of final adjustment', a titanic struggle between 'private profit and public service'. Bassett reserved his deepest scorn for what he considered to be Laski's paradoxical urging of socialist militancy on Labour, while fearing that if such a strategy were successful a crisis in democracy would result. Laski was, in fact, to be thanked, for in making this case he actually reinforced the hand of the moderates. In 'drawing attention . . . to the implications of the abandonment of gradualism . . . the less likelihood will there be of the Labour Party adhering to (his) "revolutionary policy" and the less likelihood, therefore, of a breakdown in British parliamentary government'.

The Labour Party was almost as deeply split on foreign policy issues in the mid-1930s as it was on the party's commitment to socialism, and the battle lines were usually the same though confusion and inconsistency plagued Labour in this area throughout the decade no less than it did the Conservatives. The context for much of the debate was the complicated intersection of a strong pacifist mood in Britain with the evident failure of the League of Nations and 'collective security' to curb aggression by Japan in the Far East and by Italy and Germany in Europe. A revulsion against war, fuelled by the publication in the late 1920s and early 1930s of a large number of novels, plays and memoirs bitterly depicting the 1914–18 war, influenced a vote in February 1933 by the Oxford Union that 'this House would not fight for King and Country'. Eight months later a pacifist Labour candidate won a stunning upset in the East Fulham by-election. In 1935 millions voted in a peace ballot which showed overwhelming public preference for the use of economic and non-military League of Nations sanctions rather than force against aggressors. Laski was carried along with the pacifist tide. In a Socialist League speech at Enfield he opposed increased funding for an air force while nothing was being given to education and unemployment, and he criticized the National government for giving lip service to the League of Nations while it was blessing a delegation of British businessmen off to Manchuria, 'a move which recognizes the Japanese infamy the League condemned'. When the government announced in March 1935 its first serious, albeit tentative, move to introduce rearmament, Laski criticized the decision in a *Daily Herald* article.

In the dramatic debate at the 1935 Labour Party conference in Brighton over supporting League sanctions against Italy after its invasion of Abyssinia,

Laski distanced himself from both the pacifists and his fellow Socialist Leaguers. Cripps opposed sanctions against Mussolini because he saw the League of Nations as simply an arena of antagonism between capitalist and imperialist powers, and he would have no part in supporting sanctions which might further strengthen the capitalist states. Lansbury, the leader of the Labour Party, told the conference that his Christian pacifism would not allow him to support sanctions. Laski supported the party leadership on the vote, agreeing with the NEC that it was essential to speak out against fascist aggression, whatever the consequences, and especially since the party had previously denounced the government's refusal to act in the Sino-Japanese dispute. Since the Soviet Union and all the socialist parties of Europe were in favour of sanctions, 'this could not be legitimately regarded as an imperialist war'.

However, Laski did not participate in or approve the action by which this conference is most remembered, the public humiliation of his first patron and the godfather of his daughter, George Lansbury. In a savage attack Bevin said he was tired of the party leader taking his 'conscience round from body to body asking to be told what you ought to do with it'. Bevin was booed for his brutality, but he was unrepentant, saying to friends that 'Lansbury has been going about in saint's clothes for years waiting for martyrdom. I set fire to the faggots.' The sanctions vote was carried overwhelmingly despite Bevin's incivility. Lansbury resigned the leadership of the Parliamentary Labour Party, being replaced by Attlee as acting leader, and Cripps resigned his recently acquired seat on the NEC. Laski, who approved the vote, still worried that the league's principal capitalist members would hesitate to apply sanctions to each other if to do so would 'destroy the countries which they regard as bulwarks against communism. They regret the ambitions of Italy and Germany. But they think their satisfaction a lesser evil than a policy in which England becomes an instrument of anti-fascism.' It was a fear he would return to frequently after the Hoare–Laval plan granting Mussolini most of Abyssinia seemed to validate it and as the decade wore depressingly on.

Exactly one year after Laski's support of the leadership and his common cause with Bevin's union block vote over Abyssinia, he found himself at odds with both over Spain. Franco's revolt against the five-year-old Spanish republic in July 1936 had been followed in August by an agreement not to intervene in the civil war; it was signed by Britain, Italy, Germany and the Soviet Union, an arrangement which bypassed League of Nations authority. Despite signs that Hitler and Mussolini were violating the 'non-intervention' treaty by shipping arms to Franco, the British government stood fast in its resolve not to send arms to the republican forces. At the October Labour Party conference in Edinburgh, the Labour leadership also supported non-intervention against strong opposition from the Socialist League and others on the far left, appalled that all Labour would do was offer 'their sympathy accompanied by bandages and cigarettes'. Bevin would not budge because the small Communist Party had made the issue its cause, and he led the union vote in favour of the leadership's position. Laski was furious: the party's decision, he wrote to Frankfurter,

> goes so directly the road of German social democracy that it turns my hair grey. After a long fight, those blasted trade-union leaders decided on non-intervention though they knew this meant a sure rebel victory in Spain . . . They made the foreign debates at Edinburgh the worst mess since 1931 . . . I have never seen such blindness in a body of leaders since I began to be interested in politics.

Added to Laski's anger was his sense that there was, as he wrote to Frankfurter, 'a profound pro-Hitler movement among the elect here, and its basic desire is at all costs to come to terms with Hitler in the West so if he turns on the East, it's not our concern; it means the risk of a Russian–German war'.

The Labour Party's divisions over foreign policy had earlier taken an unexpected toll on its fortunes, because two weeks after Bevin's humiliation of Lansbury at Brighton, Baldwin had called a general election for 14 November 1935. While the timing was ostensibly intended to secure a popular mandate for his modest rearmament proposals, Baldwin knew full well that unemployment had just declined marginally, production had slightly improved and, most importantly, that Labour's leadership was in a shambles. Attlee was widely believed to be only a temporary appointment as leader and Baldwin assumed that an electorate not knowing definitely who the alternative Prime Minister might be would stick with him.

Dalton drafted most of Labour's election manifesto, noting in his diary that 'this is much better than farming it out to the likes of little Laski'. Despite the rebuff, Laski threw himself into campaigning, delivering forty-one speeches in twenty-seven constituencies in sixteen days, to the amazement of the American correspondent Louis Fischer, who accompanied him. Laski spoke particularly for younger Labour candidates, whatever their place in the party's ideological spectrum. Gaitskell, for example, asked Laski to be one of his speakers, and was amazed when he 'gave the best speech of the lot', winning over the crowd with his familiar definition of socialism 'that there shall be bread for everybody before there is cake for anybody'. A less sympathetic account of a Laski election speech appeared four days before the polling in the *Morning Post*, which is worth quoting at length for what it reveals about Laski as well as his critics.

PROFESSOR ON ALL FOURS
MR LASKI FLIRTS WITH MINERS
SO SORRY HE WAS BORN RICH
BRILLIANT PERFORMANCE IN CINEMA

BY ALAN BELL
DURHAM, SUNDAY

To watch a son of Oxford and a university professor endearing himself to a crowd of miners by apologizing for his parents and upbringing is an absorbing and choice spectacle.

Mr Harold J. Laski, Professor of Political Science at the University of London, must have had a good deal of practice among rough audiences. He addresses them on all fours. At Wingate today, a small colliery village in Mr MacDonald's division, Uriah Heep would not have done better.

A large and tough assembly shouldered into the village cinema to observe this spearhead of the intelligentsia.

As soon as a brass band grouped in the stalls had let off a stirring overture (the trombones standing so as not to imperil the row in front), the curtain whisked up to reveal Professor Laski against hangings of pastel blue . . . unquestionably the academy soothsayer

Enter the Professor

So it proved, for in a moment the Chairman, with simple pride, called on 'the University Professor'. But Mr Laski soon set that right.

'I resent being introduced as a university professor,' he pleaded. 'I do not really know what a university professor is. I come here as a member of the rank and file of the Labour Party to talk to my fellow members.' (Suspicious cheers.)

At intervals in his intellectual harangue Professor Laski threw to the groundlings large sops of self-deprecation. Whatever he may be in the lecture hall, at a political meeting he is peerless at ingratiation . . .

He . . . apologized for being born the son of rich parents. 'I was the accident of an accident,' Professor Laski confidentially assured the miners . . .

He spoke, also, of much else, but there is enough here to illustrate the professorial method. The peroration broke into peals of applause for Russia, where not a soul was unemployed, and ended with luscious flattery of the audience who might fairly have gathered that as soon as socialism has nationalized everything they will one and all be leading men.

'They say I am an evil-minded left-wing socialist and that my opinions are not entitled to respect,' said Professor Laski humbly, in the course of his speech.

If 'they' had been at Wingate the judgement would not for a moment have been shaken.

The election was much more significant than anyone could have anticipated, for the outbreak of war four years later made this the last general election for ten years. The new Parliament, with Baldwin's majority of 246, would sit, refreshed by the occasional by-election, until the great postwar election of July 1945. Labour could take some solace in having done much better than in 1931, its ranks increased from fifty-six to 154. Dalton and Morrison were also finally returned to the House. On the other hand, the party took no joy in discovering that many unemployed workers had voted for Baldwin's government in the hope that rearmament would create jobs. The Liberal Party was virtually finished: despite Lloyd George's preaching a New Deal and quoting Keynes, they were able to run only 150 candidates for the 615 seats, winning only twenty. The Tory Party, itself divided between Harold Macmillan's youngish centrist group talking about the 'middle way' of a mixed economy and the traditional leadership of Baldwin and Neville Chamberlain, would dominate the new National government and British politics for years. Laski saw 'five grim years' ahead for the country, and on 23 November he wrote to Frankfurter with an extraordinary prescience of things to come. 'I even find myself eager for Winston to be in the government. He would be the one person solidly set against an Anglo-German understanding. Without him I fear that gravely.'

Several weeks after the election Laski wrote his customary analysis for American readers in the *Nation*. Victory had been produced, he explained, by the slight economic upturn, the 'absence of definite leadership in the

Labour Party', distrust of the unions and their apparent dominance of the Labour Party, and 'the personality of Mr Baldwin'. He drew the Socialist League lesson from Labour's defeat. The party, he wrote, 'has got to make up its mind whether it is going to be a "social reform" party or a "socialist party"': if the former, it would 'continue to be essentially trade-union in complexion'; if the latter, it had to make a 'frontal attack on capitalism' and 'find a philosophy and fit its scheme of legislative priorities to that philosophy'. The only philosophy, Laski suggested, 'that suits this alternative is Marxism'. The party must also reject the Liberals flocking to it 'now that Liberalism offers no constructive opportunities'. His choice would be to seek 'a rapid transformation of the basic principles of our society' and to educate 'the electorate to an understanding of socialism'.

By the time Laski's piece in the *Nation* was published, the newly elected Labour MPs had met to choose their leader. The contest was between Attlee and Morrison. Attlee had left the Socialist League and for some time had been the principal broker between party militants and moderates. Morrison was the more flamboyant, the leader of London labour, who had emerged in recent years, according to Beatrice Webb, as 'dictator of policy' in the Labour Party. He was supported by Dalton, whose booming voice and high-handed pressure may have done Morrison more harm than good, as well as by the young, the middle class and the intellectuals. He seemed like a strong leader with practical experience in planning and implementing social programmes in London. Illustrating his own 'practical' side, Laski told his *Nation* readers that he supported Morrison, because the party needed a leader who could become a national figure and had 'the more interesting personality'. What Attlee had was the fewest enemies of anyone on Labour's front bench; he threatened no one. He also had Bevin. Though he could not vote, since he was not an MP, Bevin had tremendous influence over trade-union-sponsored MPs and, though not a supporter of worker control, he had not forgiven Morrison for having to be dragged into conceding union representation on future nationalized industry boards during Labour Party conference debates.

There also was the matter of the two candidates' earlier war records. Morrison had sat out the war, considering it purely a rivalry between capitalist and imperialist powers. Attlee, on the other hand, had been an officer and seriously wounded and his union supporters had taken to calling him 'Major Attlee', as incongruously as that sat on the shy economist.

Attlee won on the second ballot eighty-eight to forty-eight because, Laski thought, he 'was the man in possession and trade unionists never do a man out of a job'. He also suggested that Morrison had overplayed his hand by 'getting support from the Tories as the "obvious" leader, making him look too conservative for the rank and file'. There was little joy in the party, as Beatrice Webb noted in her diary that day: 'the irreproachable and colourless Attlee elected Chairman of the Parliamentary Labour Party and leader of His Majesty's Opposition . . . a somewhat diminutive and meaningless figure to represent the British labour movement in the House of Commons'. Dalton agreed: 'a wretched disheartening result . . . and a little mouse shall lead them'. The Parliamentary Labour Party chose as its leader the public-school, Oxford-educated son of the upper-middle class over the seventh child of a London policeman who had left school at the age of ten, and it was done by the votes of the trade union MPs.

The next year Laski and his brother Neville turned for help to Morrison, the 'Prime Minister of London', in resolving an ugly conflict between Mosley's British Union of Fascists (BUF) and London's East End Jews. Founded in 1932, the BUF was presided over by Mosley, 6th Baronet, dressed from throat to toe in tight black clothes. Its mass rallies invariably led to violence between his followers and Jews who were supported by small bands of British communists. Its membership in the mid-1930s hovered between thirty and forty thousand, but its impact was widespread. Otherwise rational people at dinner parties debated whether Jews should be castrated or deported to Madagascar; a four-year-old Jewish child was thrown by a blackshirt through a plate-glass window in the East End and no charges were brought; and the Secretary of State for Home Affairs, Sir John Simon, felt it necessary to publish his ancestry in the press to repudiate rumours that he was of Jewish descent.

Laski condemned 'the complete refusal of the Jews here to adopt a fighting attitude' towards Mosley, attributing the caution to fear of being seen as collaborating with communists. Laski had himself been criticized for his denunciation of Hitler in the 1 April 1933 issue of Mosley's weekly *Blackshirt* and been labelled 'the little Jewish professor'. On 5 August the *Blackshirt* returned to him, noting that 'because we don't like little Laski, there is no reason to suppose we don't like all Jews'. Laski, in turn, drew attention to the 'unspeakably vile' attitude of the BUF. He debated with Major Francis Yeats Brown, a spokesman for British fascism, in April 1934 at Millicent Fawcett Hall, Westminster. That same month in a speech at the Labour College in Manchester, Laski criticized worker support of Mosley as 'ignorant, tragic and fed by misery'; and later that year he warned the Anglo-Palestine Club that anti-Semitism could be as bad as in Germany and that 'Jews could not save themselves by pretending to be more English than the English'.

Laski worried that even the most unrelated incident could fuel anti-Semitism in Britain. When a budget leak occurred in May 1936 involving the father of a partner in the Jewish-owned company Belishares, Laski wrote to Frankfurter, 'I hope to God that it is untrue, for it will have a bad effect on the Jews here if a firm like Belisha's is caught in a scandal of this magnitude.' American visitors to London, like the New York Times future publisher C. L. Sulzberger, wrote that Laski 'suspected fascists everywhere'. Laski insisted that 'they were in the officer class of London's Metropolitan Police . . . in the government itself. That's where you find the gentlemanly kind of fascism.' But Laski was not as mad as he seemed to the young American foreign correspondent. Early in 1936 he sent Churchill, the one vocal critic of fascism, a book 'in the production of which I have had some part' in the hope that 'different as are our political views' Churchill would say some words about it that could be used for publication, which would help to alert people to the potential menace of British fascism. The book, The Yellow Spot, was a documentation of anti-Jewish measures in Germany from 1933 to 1935, and the first widely circulated publication to claim that thirty-four Jews had been murdered in Dachau concentration camp.

The immediate cause of Laski's meeting with Morrison was 'the Battle of Cable Street' on 4 October 1936. After months of unprovoked attacks on Jewish shopkeepers and the desecration of cemeteries and synagogues by fascist hooligans, Jewish communists organized more than 100,000 people to block a march through the East End by Mosley and about 2,000 supporters. The two groups met at Cable Street and in the ensuing mêlée the police used truncheons and mounted forces primarily against the anti-fascist counter-demonstrators. Neville Laski, as President of the Board of Deputies of British Jews, met Morrison on 13 October to urge him 'to instruct his people' to keep away from fascist demonstrations, since Mosley thrived on the publicity the confrontations produced. When Morrison replied that it was crucial to get the communists to agree too, Neville suggested a meeting with Harry Pollitt, the General Secretary of the

CPGB. Neville asked his brother, who knew all the parties, to arrange a private meeting at his home, since Morrison could not be seen publicly with Pollitt. The four men met at 8.00 p.m. on 14 October at Laski's home in Addison Bridge Place, where Pollitt angrily proclaimed that the communists 'would not surrender the streets to the fascists'.

There then ensued a long discussion about 'the East End and the Jewish position' which Neville described in his notes as being characterized by 'good feeling' all around, an extraordinary comment in its revelation of attitudes to anti-Semitism. Neville, Pollitt and Morrison seemed to agree that the Jews stimulated anti-Semitism themselves and that a solution was possible if Jewish merchants stopped violating the Sunday closing laws and underpricing competitors; if Jewish employers ceased using sweated labour; and if Jewish landlords took better care of their houses. 'Jews ought to be super-correct in their economic conduct,' Morrison said, '100 per cent correct, indeed more than 100 per cent if they could.' In East End politics 'Jews play too prominent a part. They should keep in the background . . . and leave it to the Gentiles to fight for them.' Laski took a different position, urging instead an educational campaign to correct popular misconceptions that people held about Jews. To make his point he told of a recent incident, which Neville recorded in his notes.

> He had been in the tube and overheard three workers talking, one of whom was carrying the *Daily Herald*. Their conversation showed that they had been at a Mosley meeting, and they were making derogatory remarks about Jews. One remark was about the million Jews in this country. My brother interrupted and told them who he was and was immediately received with open arms, and was able to deal with a great many of the points which had been made for them very attractively by Mosley at his meeting.

But Morrison and Neville still felt self-criticism by the victims was more useful. 'If the East End could be got to talking about the way the Jews reacted to their own Jews and the improvements we were trying to make in the things the Christians talked about . . . much more good would be done than by all the meetings and literature.'

Laski kept no secrets from Frankfurter, especially on Jewish topics, and his letter four days later described the evening for him, 'entre nous'. 'It is heart-breaking,' he wrote, 'that the three spokesmen could not agree on a public campaign of meetings and literature jointly sponsored by their organizations to counteract the well-organized gangsterism' and the 'beatings-up of Jews, including children every night' which 'will one day mean minor pogroms.' Morrison was afraid of joint action with Pollitt and 'Neville is afraid of an appeal to the CP and its effect on the rich Jews'. Laski's final comment about his brother was uncharacteristically bitter and didactic for his gossipy letters to Frankfurter.

> My dear Felix, make up your mind that there is nothing a business civilization will not do to keep its property. Even rich Jews will risk fascism in the hope of buying themselves off rather than strengthen the working-class cause.

On other Jewish matters in the 1930s, even with Neville sitting as President of the Board of Deputies of British Jews, Frankfurter had less reason to call upon Laski's services because Labour was out of office for the entire decade. Not that Neville's position would have helped, since he was an avid anti-Zionist who throughout his term in office from 1933 to 1939 covertly reported to the Colonial Office about the politics and plans of the Jewish Agency and British Zionists in general. When Britain succumbed to Arab pressure in 1934 and proposed a Legislative Council for Palestine which would have had an Arab majority, Neville tried to impede the efforts of British Zionists to mobilize Jewish opinion against the it. Laski was brought into the effort to block the council not by Frankfurter, however, but by his former student Moshe Sharett (Shertok), intellectual and head of the Political Department of the Jewish Agency in Palestine since 1933. Sharett knew that his old professor was not a Zionist, but he also knew he was well connected, loyal to old friends and students, and sympathetic to Jewish causes. Sharett arranged for his brother-in-law, Dov Hoz, to visit Laski along with other political figures to present Jewish fears that an indigenous Arab majority would use the council to stifle Jewish immigration. As busy as he was with his LSE troubles, Laski did call on Cunliffe-Lister, the Colonial Secretary, to make the case against the council, and in fact the Colonial Office dropped the idea in 1935. Hoz's assistant, Zalman Aran, reported back to Palestine that Laski was very interested in Palestinian affairs and that the Jewish Agency could 'always approach him and get his attention'. None the less, the Zionists knew Laski's limitations: 'He is a central intellectual power in Labour politics', but should Labour win the next election, Aran wrote, 'Laski will not get an important position because he is Jewish'.

Though Laski had none of the access to government offices he had in 1929, Frankfurter asked for information and assistance in thwarting the proposal by the Peel Commission in 1937 to partition Palestine into an Arab and a Jewish state. The American Zionists were furious at having been ignored by British policy-makers and saw the scheme as a British manoeuvre to deprive the Jews of their access to the whole of Palestine. Once again they were angry with Weizmann, this time for accepting a Jewish state that contained only 1,500 square miles, 22 per cent of the area of Palestine, and did not even include Jerusalem or Haifa, as better than no state at all. Laski sided with the Americans. While still proclaiming his opposition to Zionism as a solution to the Jewish question, he insisted that given the exodus from Hitler 'the right of the Jews to a refuge in Palestine cannot be whittled down'. In the *New Statesman*, Laski asserted that 'some, at least, of our officials in Palestine are known to be anti-Jewish in outlook'. Laski urged Frankfurter that 'on publication [of the Peel proposal] there should be an immediate American explosion'. He even suggested that Frankfurter, Brandeis and Stephen Wise, a new important Zionist figure in America, 'play the Irish analogy privately for all you are worth'.

When Ben-Gurion, the Secretary of the Histadrut, arrived from Palestine in May 1937 to talk with National government officials and with Weizmann, Laski introduced him to Attlee and other Labour Party officials. Ben-Gurion, like Jabotinsky, the militant nationalist, was initially opposed to the partition, but to Laski's dismay he was converted to it by Weizmann. Laski accused Weizmann of seeing himself the President of the new state and by late summer 1937 he was deeply fearful for the fate of Jews in Eastern Europe. He told Frankfurter that nearly half a million Jews 'have no hope for the future save in a revolutionary overturn in Poland, Rumania, etc.' Laski saw British anti-Jewish bias behind the government's policy. He placed little significance in any Arab national aspirations exemplified by the Arab general strike of April 1936 or the guerrilla war attacks on the British and the Jews by the Moslem fundamentalist Sheikh Izzal-Din al-Qassam and his followers. 'I frankly don't believe,' he wrote to Frankfurter, 'in Arab nationalism. HMG only wants to preserve its lines of communication and get rid of its Jewish obligation.' Laski tried to put the issue in socialist terms. The way out, he wrote, 'is effective land settlement of the Arab proletariat by breaking up the large estates and a revised educational system'. For the most part, however, his friendship with Frankfurter and his increasing concern for Jews fleeing fascism determined his position. It was imperative that the Americans be emphatic. The time had come 'for a wholesale indictment in public of the British administration in Palestine. It is no use arguing with the British government on one's knees.'

On the issue of partition, Laski and Neville stood on the same side, though for different reasons. Ever cautious, Neville was less interested in the effect of a small state on the flow of refugees from Hitler than he was in the very idea of a Jewish state, which he saw raising grave problems of dual loyalty for British Jews. As President of the Board of Deputies he met in July 1937, two days after the publication of the Peel report, the heads of the Anglo-Jewish elite families – Rothschilds, Montagues, Montefiores and Cohens. The Jewish notables and Neville announced their misgivings about 'the effect of the establishment of a Jewish state on the political position of the Jews in the countries of their birth'. Jewish nationalism was 'a surrender by the Jews to their enemies and an admission that emancipation had failed'. By December 1937 the British government had in fact repudiated its partition proposal, less from the kind of pressure brought by the two Laskis than from American insistence and Arab anger at the two-state solution.

In May 1939 Chamberlain's government, responding to Arab anger at the rising tide of immigration from Jews fleeing continental Europe, published what Laski referred to as 'the notorious White Paper which deprived the mandate of all its meaning'. It restricted Jewish immigration to 10,000 people a year, one sixth of the number who entered Palestine in 1936. When the Jewish Agency helped refugees to arrive illegally, the Colonial Secretary suspended all immigration for ten months. If nothing else, this pro-Arab policy cleared the air. The Labour Party moved a vote of censure in the House of Commons, with Morrison describing the White Paper as 'a breach of British honour'. In a dramatic act of defiance a small group of Tories joined the attack on the White Paper, with Churchill calling it a 'base petition in moral bankruptcy'. Laski was in America on sabbatical leave when the White Paper was published. It was exactly what he had feared most, the anti-Jewish Colonial Office consigning thousands of Jews to Hitler's horrors, the true dimensions of which not even he could know. One member of the Laski family did speak out in the spring of 1939. Nathan wrote to Churchill the day after his attack in the Commons on the White Paper.

May I congratulate you upon the great and statesmanlike speech you made on the Palestine question last night. I think it is not exaggerating to say that you will get the blessings of millions of Jews all over the world . . . As an old man, I ask myself what is the matter with the English people that they sit down to allow a man like Chamberlain keep out of the Cabinet a great statesman, without any flattery, that you are . . . I can only hope that the time is not far distant when England will recognize that we have in you a man who can take charge of the affairs of this country and successfully overcome the blunders that others have made.

Churchill had originally been ostracized to the back-benches for his 'die-hard' views on India, on which he remained in fundamental disagreement with Laski. While Churchill regarded the Indian Raj as the 'Crown Jewel' in the glorious British empire, it was for Laski 'the slum of empire'. After the collapse of the round-table conferences on India, Laski remained an outspoken advocate of Indian independence. He protested the cycle of arrests and repression in India while becoming himself increasingly dismayed by the complications created to the quest for independence by the hardening position taken by Jinnah and the Muslim League. In lectures for Menon's India League in London, Laski always lamented the absurdity of the British teaching Indian students the ideas of Milton, Locke and Mill and then sending them to be second-class citizens in their own country. Laski ridiculed what he saw as Churchill's nostalgic fantasy of Victoria's empire. 'We hold India,' Laski wrote, 'not by the quality of our rule, not by a reciprocal interest born of mutual good-will; we hold India by the sword . . . no country is held by good-will when fifty thousand people have to be sent to jail.' The British were unwilling to recognize that 'Indian nationalism is part of a basic revolt of the East against Western tutelage, to which there is no answer save that of freedom.' It was a lesson that should have been learned from America and Ireland. But it was also 'a lesson that an imperial race can understand only when it is too late. That is the price of empire.'

As was so often the case with Laski, his politics got wrapped up with friendships, and during the 1930s his commitment to Indian independence was intensified by his relationship with Nehru. Three years older than Laski, educated at Harrow and Cambridge, Nehru, who saw Laski on his visits to England in 1935 and 1938, was much more compatible with Laski than Gandhi was. A secular intellectual, Nehru had a vision for a free India that was socialist, where national planning and economic modernization would end centuries of poverty and traditional institutions like child marriage. Nehru adopted Menon's worshipful respect for Laski, who had stood so bravely in the Amritsar trial, who took such interest in Indian students, who spoke out so forcefully for independence, and whose writings outlined the political and economic pattern of India's future. When Nehru's daughter, Indira Gandhi, came to England for school and then Oxford in 1936, Nehru urged her to seek out Laski for advice on books to read. Nehru's admiration for Laski was matched by Laski's for him. What he particularly admired was that Nehru was fighting not only for India's right to govern itself, but also for a fundamental transformation in who would rule. He told his weekly *Daily Herald* readers that Nehru 'wants not merely a political revolution, which would free India from foreign domination; he wants also a social revolution, which would effect a complete change in India's economic system'. Even more revealing was Laski's private assessment. In a letter of 1938 Laski told Frankfurter that 'Nehru I regard as one of the few really great people I have ever met – worlds above Gandhi in strength of character and insight'.

India, like Palestine, preoccupied Laski throughout his career. In 1937 he also became briefly involved with the short-lived China Campaign Committee, organized to oppose the Japanese invasion of the Chinese mainland. Inveterate joiner that he was, Laski became the vice-president of the campaign, working hard, but unsuccessfully, to get dockers to boycott cargoes bound for Japan. The members of the campaign were all intellectuals and, not surprisingly, their other initiative was to produce a book, *China – Body and Soul*, edited by Gilbert Murray, to raise funds for China relief. The book included essays on Chinese painting, poetry, philosophy and politics. Laski's essay placed Japan's invasion in the context of other acts of naked aggression 'by the brutality and barbarism of fascist imperialism'. With uncharacteristic self-restraint, Laski informed the readers of the collection that the cause was so urgent that 'I have sought in these pages to refrain deliberately from the use of any word to which people who do not share my own political faith could take exception'.

This could not be said of Laski's major writings in the mid-1930s. In 1935 he published *The State in Theory and Practice*, which he described to Frankfurter as 'strong medicine – the kind of thing Yandell Elliott thinks communism – but it says plainly things I think ought to be said . . .

whether I shall long survive its publication I don't know'. Dedicated to Marion Denman Frankfurter, whom the Laskis had seen a great deal of in 1934 when she and Felix were at Oxford, it was a deeply theoretical book, fundamentally Marxist in orientation, and worlds apart from the reformist and electoral politics of Labour Party conferences, general elections or Fulham council meetings. The book was a reading of the state which for the first time in Laski's writings used specific Marxist analytical concepts. The state was not, he wrote, an autonomous neutral entity but part of the institutional superstructure built on the economic 'bedrock'. Since the Industrial Revolution the state was 'biased in favour of the owners of the instruments of production as against those who have nothing but their labour power to sell'. Government acted 'as the executive committee of the class which dominates, economically, the system of production by which society lives'. Only when the instruments of production were communally owned 'could the power of the state be devoted to the unbiased protection of the interests of each member of society'. In offering this Marxist reading, Laski took his swipes at Hayek and Robbins, who saw the state as the enemy and wanted its influence to be minimal when, according to Laski, the state and its coercive institutions were the crucial factor in maintaining the rule of the capitalist.

Laski's linkage of the state to the historical dynamic of expanding and contracting capitalism attracted attention, because it led to the characteristic 1930s Marxist explanation of the rise of fascism. When the capitalist economy expanded in the nineteenth and early twentieth centuries, Laski argued, capitalists could give democratic political rights to participation in elections and liberal civil rights of tolerance, free speech and free thought. Democracy led the masses to use their political power to seek higher wages, better working conditions and more social services. This pattern could persist, Laski contended, as long as the capitalist economy continued to thrive and expand. When, as in the 1930s, capitalism contracted, the ruling class had to choose between capitalism and democracy. Enter fascism, which, according to Laski, was the use of state power to abrogate democracy in a contracting economy in order to preserve the privileges of the capitalist ruling class.

After 1935 Laski, virtually unique in this respect among senior British academics, referred to himself as a Marxist. In 1939 he wrote in the *Nation* 'Why I am a Marxist'. But, difficult as these distinctions might be for ordinary people to fathom, Laski was adamant that he was a Marxist socialist and not a Marxist communist, by which he meant a Leninist or Stalinist. To be a Marxist, on the one hand, was, for Laski, to be a real socialist as opposed to a social reformer. It meant that one believed class struggle dominated social life. It meant that one sought a total collective transformation of society in which neither a mixed economy nor the profit motive survived. On the other hand, in Laski's tortuous balancing act, to be a Marxist was not to advocate or belong to a party that wanted violent political change brought by a small group of conspirators, but to believe in parliamentary and electoral processes. To be a Marxist was still to be a civil libertarian committed to the individual's right to think and speak freely, uncoerced by party line, unquestioned dogma or proletarian dictatorship. Consistent with these distinctions, *The State in Theory and Practice* repudiated Keynesianism and the New Deal on the one hand, and the CPGB on the other. In a democracy, Laski insisted, every constitutional means for change must be exhausted before any resort to violence could be made. He conceded that the example of Hitler suggested that the ruling class would itself suspend the democratic process in the face of the Marxist transformation he advocated through parliamentary methods, but there was still in Laski the optimistic, very un-Marxist belief that the British ruling class was different. Generations of rhetorical worship at the shrine of parliamentary democracy, which the historian Laski knew full well was not the case in Germany, Italy or the Soviet Union, would lead the British elite to accept even real socialist transformation, he hoped against hope.

Laski could be utterly inconsistent in this respect. In one chapter he emphasized the unlikelihood of a ruling class ever voluntarily abdicating its power and privilege; in another, he thought it could be done and advised a radical party 'to maintain as long as it can a constitutional order which permits it openly to recruit its strength'. A constitutional party advocating real socialism, Laski suggested, should guarantee the owners of the means of production 'the continuance of the privileges such ownership entails for a period at least long enough to reconcile them to the new social order'. There must not be 'the kind of confiscation which would provoke a possessing class to conflict; it is amply worth while to pay a considerable price for their willing acceptance of a new social order'. Not, of course, that any of this scenario seemed that relevant to the real world of 1935, which was itself unpredictable during the 'red decade'.

If Laski knew of the apparently surprising endorsement given to his *The State in Theory and Practice* by *The Christian Century*, a liberal American church journal, he must have found it amusing, for clergymen were next only to capitalist businessmen in his ranking of most despised people. This, indeed, would be a central theme of *The Rise of European Liberalism*, published in 1936 and dedicated to his new American friends Ruth and Alfred Cohn. A historical study of the triumph of secular liberal ideas in the seventeenth- and eighteenth-century Enlightenment, it has schooled generations of leftist scholars on the ideology of liberalism, and through its influence on the writings of C. B. MacPherson, who was working with Laski when the lectures which make up the book were originally given, these ideas have had a vigorous second life. The argument of the book pivots on what Laski referred to as his 'crypto-Marxist' conviction that the liberal theory of the Rights of Man found in English and French political thought between the English Revolution in 1640 and the French Revolution in 1789 meant not the universal rights of all men but the rights of the limited class of men who owned property. The liberal tradition, then, was forged by the bourgeoisie as part of its assault on the feudal and Catholic old order.

Ideas, Laski argued, like the state, reflected economic class interests. The liberal values of free expression, tolerance and individual rights were born to serve the interests of the middle class in their battle to overturn the hierarchical world of aristocratic privilege. The book was thus a historical companion to his essay on the state of the previous year. If liberal ideas were temporally bound to the interests of the middle class in its assault on the *ancien régime*, then when the property-owning middle class felt that its hard-won power and privilege were attacked, as was clearly the case in the 1930s, it would abandon these liberal values, which is what the fascists were doing. Unfortunately, Laski's 'crypto-Marxism' and its assumption of the relativity of ideas competed with his own abiding conviction that these liberal ideals were autonomous, desirable and enduring. Secularism, tolerance, free speech and science may well have served the interests of the revolutionary bourgeoisie, but they were also eternal verities for Laski.

Laski was very much an eighteenth-century man. A secular Jew, he dismissed religious belief as superstition and fanaticism. He was fiercely anti-clerical, as were his secular rationalist idols, Voltaire and Paine. There was no form of cruelty that organized religion couldn't live with, he once observed. Religion, he wrote to Holmes in 1933, was 'the permanent enemy of all that is decent in civilization'. Like the Enlightenment philosophers, Laski also saw science as the antidote to religion. From his earliest worship of Darwin, whose picture hung in his New College room, Laski regarded science as both the death-knell for religion and the source of progress and all that was good. In a socialist society, Laski wrote, scientists freed from bondage to the profit motive would play a heroic role in providing abundance for all through the exercise of human power and reason over nature. Appropriately enough, Laski dedicated *The Rise of European Liberalism* to the only scientist in his circle of close friends, and some months after the book appeared Laski joined a group of distinguished leftist scientists who in a twenty-page supplement to the magazine *Nature* proposed the establishment of a Society for the Study of Social Relations of Science. Many of the group had been involved years earlier in the *Realist* and were joined now by the Marxists Needham and Bernal. Nothing came of the society, but its manifesto in *Nature* reads like the same lyrical hymn to progress and social amelioration found in the *Encyclopedia* produced by the eighteenth-century French Enlightenment.

The review of *The Rise of European Liberalism* in the *Nation*, written by Laski's American friend Max Lerner, captured Laski's ambivalence between the class-based origins of the ideals of liberty and individualism, and his sense of them as timeless and autonomous values. Laski, Lerner noted, seems 'to be of a divided mind in the matter. Liberalism as the garment of the capitalist ideal he handles with a mercilessly ironic detachment. But liberalism is today also one of the principal hurdles in the path of fascist barbarism. And this liberalism Mr Laski cannot despise or abandon.' This balancing act by Laski between Marxism and a commitment to liberal individual rights, as well as between social transformation and the 'practical' life of everyday politics, would be seen writ large in one of the most ambitious projects of his career, the Left Book Club.

CHAPTER FIFTEEN

The Left Book Club, the United Front and Soviet Russia

Between the outbreak of the Spanish Civil War in 1936 and the Hitler–Stalin Pact in 1939 the mood of the ideological left in Britain was expressed most influentially by the Left Book Club run by Victor Gollancz, John Strachey and Harold Laski, who were dubbed along with Kingsley Martin 'the four pink horsemen of the socialist apocalypse' by Beaverbrook's *Sunday Express*. The idea was Gollancz's. Laski's classmate and fellow radical at New College had gone on to a career in publishing, establishing in 1928, with the help of Dorothy Sayers's Peter Wimsey novels, an extremely profitable enterprise. Like Laski, Gollancz retained his Oxford activism. He had abandoned Judaism for an almost mystical Christian socialism and, like Cripps, had managed to combine his earnings and aristocratic habits, such as always travelling first class, with a serious flirtation with Marxism. Gollancz had been involved for some time in publishing cheap books on serious political subjects, usually of a leftist bent. Before he set up his own company he had created a 'sixpenny library' for the publisher Ernest Benn. Inexpensive and easily available radical books were an important feature of England's 'red decade'. Krishna Menon, who had gone into publishing, was himself editing low-priced serious political books at the firm of Bodley Head. In 1935 he and another Bodley Head editor, Allen Lane, set up their own firm under the name of Penguin, with Lane editing inexpensive paperback works of fiction and Menon looking after the radical non-fiction paperbacks called Pelicans. Lane bought out Menon later in the decade, who then devoted himself exclusively to the India League, but the paperback revolution was born, with radical politics a key element.

Gollancz's commercial innovation was to line up subscribers to a book club in sufficient numbers to guarantee inexpensive pricing of hardbacks. The monthly books were to be the same size and format, all with orange-reddish covers. The criterion for selecting the 'Left Book of the Month' was its contribution to the anti-fascist cause in Europe or to the creation of true socialism in Britain. To help to choose the books and to run the club and its monthly magazine, *Left Book News*, Gollancz turned to Strachey, whose *The Coming Struggle for Power* his firm had published in 1932, and to Laski. The venture was launched in May 1936 with the obligatory monthly selection costing half a crown. After its first year the club offered a second book each month as well, not as an alternative but as a supplement to the required purchase. Each month the magazine, which came free to the subscribers, appeared with an editorial by Gollancz, an article by Strachey and a review of the selection by Laski.

The club was a phenomenal success. After one month it had 12,000 members and twelve study groups. By April 1939 at its peak it had grown to nearly 60,000 members with 1,200 affiliated study and discussion groups. The readership of some of its books approached 250,000 and in its first three years of existence nearly one and a half million of its books were in circulation. Its fortunes declined sharply after the Hitler–Stalin Pact; it managed to survive the war but died a quiet death in 1948. The significance of the club lay in more than simply its sales and membership numbers, however, for it spawned a veritable mass social movement between 1936 and 1939, almost a way of life. Gollancz hired the Reverend John Lewis, a Nonconformist clergyman convinced that Marxism was the heir to the Christian tradition, as full-time organizer of the club's affiliated discussion groups and activities. Local study groups were organized all over Britain (and abroad). There were study groups for accountants, taxi-drivers, scientists, architects, teachers, journalists, poets, musicians, actors and even cyclists. The club organized poetry readings by Stephen Spender and C. Day Lewis and science lectures by J. D. Bernal and J. B. S. Haldane. Over 250 amateur theatre groups were affiliated to the club, each committed to the production of proletarian drama. Russian language classes and tourist trips to the Soviet Union were organized. The club sponsored coffee bars, social evenings and dances, and even football matches for its overwhelmingly white-collar and professional middle-class membership. Its members, usually the non-trade-unionist workhorses of local constituency Labour parties, were convinced, as one left-labour publication put it, that 'even games, songs and recreation can, indeed should, reflect an awakened left-wing attitude to things', and that 'walks, tennis, golf and swimming are quite different when your companions are comrades on the left'. Behind the dances, rallies and poetry readings was always the discussion of that month's book, chosen by the club's eminent three-man selection committee. The hard work, as well as the profits, were Gollancz's, but the notice and veneration were shared. A poem in a bookseller's window read:

> Forced to make the choice themselves,
> our rude forefathers loaded shelves
> with Tennyson and Walter Scott
> and Meredith and Lord knows what!
> But we don't have to hum and ha,
> *nous avons changé tout cela* –
> our books are chosen for us – thanks
> to Strachey, Laski and Gollancz!

Because the Left Book Club self-consciously sought to unite the left, it had no misgivings about its openness to communists. Gollancz had chosen Strachey, he wrote in the first issue of *Left Book News*, because he 'is in broad sympathy with the aims of the Communist Party', and Laski because 'he is a member of the Labour Party'. Gollancz was himself in these years quite close to the International Communist line in its forceful anti-fascist posture, though he did not go as far as Strachey in sharing the British party's conviction that a seizure of power was necessary. He had no problems writing an article for the *Daily Worker* in May 1937, which the communist paper then used in its publicity material, on 'Why I Read the *Daily Worker*.' Laski himself had written three articles for the CPGB's intellectual journal *Labour Monthly*, edited by Palme Dutt, although like Gollancz he wrote principally about the Soviet Union as the leader of anti-fascist forces. Surprisingly enough, the journal allowed him to use its pages to criticize the Moscow domination of the CPGB.

Though he had no problem sharing platforms with Strachey or Harry Pollitt, who spoke frequently at club rallies, Laski did on several occasions have strong disagreements with the more overt pro-communist tilt of his colleagues over pieces in the *Left Book News* or over monthly selections. Gollancz, for example, apologized to Palme Dutt for Laski's 'deplorable review' of Dutt's book *World Politics*, which appeared in the July 1936 *Left Book News*. In 1937 Gollancz would accept *Why Capitalism Means War* only if H. N. Brailsford toned down his criticism of the Soviet Union as a totalitarian dictatorship, which Gollancz labelled a 'violent anti-Soviet tirade'. Laski argued for publishing the book as originally written. When Gollancz insisted on the changes, Laski notified him that he would feel obliged to resign from the selection committee if it were not published. Gollancz gave in, fearful of the adverse publicity from Laski's resignation. A similar fuss about the Soviet Union split the selection board over *Barbarians at the Gate* in 1937, in which Leonard Woolf chastised Stalin and the communists almost as much as Hitler and the Nazis. Strachey was dead set against publication. Laski suggested that Woolf tone down the critique of Stalin, and Gollancz wanted to 'postpone indefinitely' its appearance. Woolf was astonished at the editorial interference and demanded that the contractual obligation to publish be kept. With Strachey adamant, Laski sided with Gollancz in finally agreeing to publish it without changes, while also agreeing that Strachey should review it for the *Left Book News*.

One of George Orwell's books posed a particular problem for the club's editorial committee. When *The Road to Wigan Pier*, Orwell's observations on the impact of unemployment on miners, appeared as the club's selection for March 1937, it made Orwell famous, selling nearly 50,000 copies, but it also created a fundamental row on the left. Orwell had divided the book into two parts: the first a moving social documentary; the second, general thoughts about justice and socialism. Everyone on the left was taken by Orwell's indignant depiction of exploitation and suffering, but many like Gollancz and Laski were upset by Orwell's suggestion in the second part that ordinary British people were diverted from even thinking about socialist doctrine, favourably or unfavourably, by disgust with the cranks who were its messengers, 'all that dreary tribe of high-minded women and sandal-wearers and bearded fruit-juice drinkers who come flocking towards the smell of "progress" like bluebottles to a dead cat'. Instead of cosmopolitan intellectuals praising the Soviet Union with scientific socialist images of society as a well-run machine, Orwell urged a native non-intellectual socialism based on the older ethical ideals of 'liberty, equality, fraternity and justice'.

Gollancz took the unusual step of writing a lengthy foreword to the club edition of the book in which he criticized its naïve and vague humanitarianism and insisted that 'emotional socialism must become scientific socialism'. In his review of the book for the March 1937 *Left News* (the club monthly magazine had shortened its name in December 1936) Laski took the same path. The first part of the book was comparable, he suggested, to Dickens,

Zola and Balzac in its personalization of 'living and suffering men and women', but the second part was both seriously flawed and dangerous.

> Having very ably depicted a disease, Mr Orwell does what so many well-meaning people do: needing a remedy (he knows it is socialism) he offers an incantation instead. He thinks that an appeal to 'liberty and justice' will, on the basis of facts such as he has described, bring people tumbling over one another into the socialist party. People, he seems to say, who have seen ugliness as he has seen it, will become socialist if only they can be made to understand that socialists are not 'cranks' but people like themselves.

Socialism, would not come, Laski countered, 'merely on an appeal to the better feelings of people'. All that would produce was 'a little social amelioration here and there'. In place of an 'emotional plea for socialism addressed to comfortable people', Laski offered a defence of the socialist as intellectual and as the disciplined scientific student of society, political economy and history. Orwell's socialism, Laski wrote, 'ignores all that is implied in the urgent reality of class antagonisms. It refuses to confront the grave problem of the state. It has no sense of the historic movement of the economic process.'

Orwell, on the other hand, would eventually have his own day with Laski. In the 1940s he wrote devastating reviews of several of Laski's books, and in his 1946 essay 'Politics and the English Language' Orwell used a paragraph of Laski's prose as the first of his five examples of 'ugly and inaccurate ... written English ... full of bad habits which spread by imitation and which can be avoided if one is willing to take the necessary trouble'. Not surprisingly, that same year, Gollancz turned down Orwell's *Homage to Catalonia* with its descriptions of communists murdering anarchists in Spain, without even showing it to Laski. More to the taste of the club's selectors on Spain was *The Spanish Testament* by Arthur Koestler, who, like Orwell, was first made a bestseller by the Left Book Club. The club also introduced Mao Tse-tung to the English left in Edgar Snow's extremely popular *Red Star over China*.

Gollancz sought to do more than publish important leftist books for thousands of people to discuss monthly; he also saw the club as the centre of a political movement. Huge rallies were held in 1937 and 1938 at the Albert Hall and in 1939 at Earl's Court in addition to numerous meetings in provincial cities. The platform speakers exemplified the unified left that the club sought to represent. There would be Strachey or Pollitt; Cripps or Laski; Sir Richard Acland, the Liberal Party Whip; the Dean of Canterbury, Hewlett Johnson, intoning 'God Bless the Left Book Club'; and the black American leftist Paul Robeson singing Negro spirituals. At the April 1939 rally after Munich and before the Hitler–Stalin Pact, the venerable Lloyd George described the club 'as one of the most remarkable movements in the political field in two generations'. He was there, he told the Earl's Court crowd, because 'this method you have inaugurated – instruction and enlightenment – is the only way you can save civilization'.

Laski was out of the country for this 1939 'Popular Front' rally, and for the 1938 Albert Hall rally as well. In February 1937, however, Laski addressed the 7,000 people in the Albert Hall, probably the largest live audience of his career. He praised Gollancz's organizing genius before passing on to a bitter attack on the leadership of the Labour Party who, 'like the ancient House of Bourbon, learn nothing and forget nothing'. More important than party leaders, he suggested, were the rank and file who tramped to London on hunger marches, the brave men and women in the East End who told Mosley and his fascists 'You shall not pass,' and the men of the International Brigade in Spain. But the club, Laski insisted, was about books, not rank-and-file actions. Everything had its place and the Left Book Club would always be a minority intellectual movement. A month before his review of Orwell appeared, Laski gave the Albert Hall crowd a ringing endorsement of the club as designed to produce socialist intellectuals. Out of their movement would 'come the inspiration that makes knowledge, that makes organized intelligence, that makes scientific understanding, the hallmarks of whatever is significant in the labour and socialist movements of this country'.

Needless to say, the Labour Party leadership was not pleased with the Left Book Club. Its incessant demands for the party to back intervention in Spain and the constant praise of the Soviet Union as the bulwark of anti-fascism annoyed Dalton and Morrison almost as much as the willingness of Laski and Gollancz to feature Harry Pollitt as a speaker at club rallies. It didn't help when Laski referred to this criticism in his Albert Hall speech, asking how different appearing with Pollitt was from Walter Citrine of the TUC sharing a platform with Winston Churchill, or when he commented that he attracted crowds larger than any the Labour Party could mount. Anger rose with the publication in *Left Book News* of Laski's outspoken article, 'On the Strategy of Socialism', in September 1936. In one of his bitterest attacks of the decade on the Labour Party, Laski pleaded that it must not choose 'a policy of half-measures . . . to placate opponents and doubters . . . to win the votes of Liberals and pacifists'. This, he wrote, would produce a victory only for social reform, not for socialism, and a social reform government would 'come to terms with individual ownership . . . and retain the structure of a class society'. The Labour Party, he urged, must tell the electorate 'plainly and unmistakably . . . that every vote for the Labour Party is a vote for the full socialist transformation of our economic system'. Only then would all Britain's evils be redressed, including the problem of empire, for 'until we abolish the private ownership of the means of production, the white man's burden will continue to be borne by the black'.

When attacks in Left Book publications like this seemed to produce by-election results which worried party leaders, they struck back. The attack didn't come from Attlee, the parliamentary leader, who had in fact referred to the club's success 'as a most encouraging sign', but from Bevin, Dalton and Morrison. A widely circulated NEC memo noted that fifteen of the first twenty-seven club selections were written by communists or open fellow-travellers. Morrison and Bevin attacked the club in the press as a communist front, claiming 'it had become a political movement with substantial money behind it' and that it sought to manipulate and control local Labour parties. It was described as a 'dangerous type of vermin' and accused of making membership in it 'incompatible with membership of the Labour Party'.

Laski tried to bring peace between the club and the Labour Party. He convinced Gollancz in the summer of 1937 to offer the Labour Party two special issues of *Left News* which would then serve as the focus for monthly discussion groups. In response, Dalton, Chairman of the NEC in 1937, suggested that a regular monthly space be set aside in *Left News* for 'official' Labour views, that the book selections keep a closer balance between 'left' and 'official' Labour views, and, finally, that the selection committee running the club be opened up to more people, like himself, sympathetic to 'official' Labour. Laski and Gollancz accepted Dalton's first condition, agreeing grudgingly to give the NEC a monthly platform. The second request did not seem a real issue: Attlee and Noel-Baker had done books for the club, and Morrison had been asked, they countered. Dalton's third proposal was flatly rejected, with Laski explaining in a letter to the *New Statesman* that 'it was plain from the whole character of the discussion on this proposal that Dr Dalton had in view giving to the club a kind of semi-official character'. To do this, Laski added, would fundamentally alter the club's independence.

In 1938 Labour tried to set up a rival Social Democratic Book Club whose books were to be selected by Tawney, Citrine, Dalton and Cole. When it collapsed, a more modest Labour Book Service was created. Not to be undone, a Right Book Club was also launched, all of which led David Low to run a cartoon in the *Evening Standard*, 'The Book Club War', its caption reading: 'A fierce battle is now taking place on the reading front, the Blimp Book Club advancing strongly against the left. Heavy casualties are reported including 29 unconscious and General Gollancz's spectacles blown up.' A. J. P. Taylor couldn't understand the Labour Party's fears. Far from being a threat, Taylor suggested, the Left Book Club was a safety-valve. Reading became 'a substitute for action, not a prelude to it'. Members of the club, he suggested, 'worked off their rebelliousness by plodding through yet another orange-coloured volume'.

The 'respectable' Labour leadership may have overreacted in branding the Left Book Club subversive, but it was quite accurate in its sense of how important the club was in the nexus of forces urging a United Front on the party. The bitter battle waged since 1932 between the Labour left and the party moderates came to a head in 1937 over the left's Unity Campaign. The idea for a United Front of working-class-oriented parties which would include the ILP, Labour and the CPGB had been championed by Pollitt. With the rise of Hitler, Moscow joined the League of Nations in an effort to combat fascism and instructed national communist leaders to cooperate with their social democratic counterparts. Dutifully, then, Pollitt sought affiliation (an affiliation he had spurned from 1928 to 1933) of his Party, then about 11,000 strong, to the Labour Party in late 1935. The NEC replied to Pollitt in early 1936 that the 'fundamental difference between the democratic policy and practice of the Labour Party and the policy of dictatorship which the Communist Party had been created to promote was irreconcilable'. The NEC further suggested that the CPGB was really intent on taking over the Labour Party. The party conference at Edinburgh endorsed the NEC's stand by 1,728,000 votes to 592,000. Laski took a middle position on the party's action. He agreed that the CPGB was too dependent on Moscow's instructions to be taken seriously as an indigenous and autonomous socialist society; yet he lamented the loss of the energy, hard work and ideological commitment of its individual members to the Labour Party.

After this rebuff, Pollitt was more successful with Cripps, Laski and the Socialist League, which in January 1937 agreed to launch a 'Unity Campaign' with the CPGB and the ILP. In a 'Unity Manifesto', signed by the leaders of these three groups and a tiny group of Labour Party figures that included Laski, Aneurin Bevan, Brailsford and G. R. Strauss, a call was made for 'unity of all sections of the working-class movement . . . in the struggle against fascism, reaction and war, and against the National government . . . and the return of a Labour government as the next stage in the advance to working-class power'. The manifesto also announced opposition to the government's rearmament programme because the weapons would be used 'in support of fascism, of imperialist war, of reaction and of colonial suppression'.

The Labour Party wasted no time in announcing its response; on 27 January the Socialist League was disaffiliated from the Labour Party. The NEC ordered that any person who appeared on a public platform with members of the ILP or the CPGB would automatically cease to be a member of the Labour Party. It was a dramatic and effective counter-strike. Spokesmen for the Unity Campaign, who in February and March had launched a series of rallies and public meetings throughout Britain, were forced to advocate the unity of the three parties from separate platforms, occasionally in the same hall.

Even with the Labour Party playing tough, ordering, for example, the trade unions to sabotage a booking of the Albert Hall in April for speeches by Cripps and Laski to a United Front rally, Laski thought the campaign was going well. He wrote to Frankfurter that he and Stafford had spoken to three huge Unity meetings, one at Hull before 500 people. At Peterborough he spoke a week after Dalton, who 'had 180 people in a hall of 800. I had a packed meeting.' It was clear, Laski wrote, that Labour's 'leaders are much more anxious to attack their own left than they are to fight the government. There is no thinking in the party and no conviction.' At a Unity demonstration in Glasgow, Laski told the crowd that 'our labour movement is going to live or die according to whether it is a militant movement or a respectable movement'.

In its zeal for respectability, in February 1937 the party contemplated expelling Cripps, Bevan, Brailsford, Strauss and Laski. Laski told Frankfurter that he would be 'sorry to be thrown out, but I certainly can no more allow the party to control my political affiliations (when the right wing goes its own way, e.g. Citrine) than I can allow the university to control my ideas'. Anticipating the decision which was scheduled for the NEC meeting at the end of February, Laski asked Attlee to intervene. Attlee answered that he would do all in his power to oppose expulsion, though he worried, just as Morrison had in the 1934 party conference discussion of Laski, that 'the offenders against party discipline are prominent and for the most part middle-class people' who shouldn't be treated any differently than rank-and-file members. Nor could he resist tweaking Laski and his errant colleagues. 'I fight all the time against heresy hunting,' he reminded Laski, 'but the heretics seem to seek martyrdom.'

Attlee appears to have held the day, though a brilliant speech by Cripps in the House of Commons attacking a government report on a mine disaster delivered the day before the NEC vote probably helped even more. The NEC postponed a decision on expulsion, but it continued its scorched-earth policy, ruling at its March meeting that mere membership in the Socialist League would disqualify anyone from Labour Party membership after 1 June. This worked, for Cripps dissolved the Socialist League in May, claiming that since its purpose had always been to influence the Labour Party its expulsion gave it no more reason to exist. Dalton cynically suggested to the *Manchester Guardian* that Cripps was getting tired of paying to keep the league alive. The Unity Campaign was by no means dead, however, for Cripps found a new Labour left outlet for his lucrative legal fees and Laski found yet another newspaper, the *Tribune*, to write for.

Founded in January 1939 to provide an alternative to the *Daily Herald*, which was felt to be too trade-union-oriented and too captive to the party machine, the *Tribune* would long outlive the Unity Campaign, which had inspired it, to remain the platform of the Labour left. The money for the new venture was provided mainly by Cripps with the help of the equally wealthy Labour militant G. R. Strauss. 'Cripps's Chronicle', as it was derisively labelled, had a small sponsoring editorial board that consisted of Cripps, Wilkinson, Strauss, Bevan, Laski and William Mellor. Mellor, former Secretary of the Socialist League and a former editor at the *Herald*, was the paper's first editor. On its original staff, also fresh from the

Socialist League, were Barbara Castle (then Barbara Betts) and Michael
Foot, both of whom would remain ideologically and personally close to
Bevan, who wrote a weekly parliamentary column for the *Tribune*. Laski
was both a founder of the twopenny weekly and a frequent contributor to
it. Of more than 100 articles he published in its pages over the next twelve
years, thirty appeared in 1937 and 1938. Frida, too, wrote several pieces for
the new paper that focused on demands for an enhanced role for women in
the Labour Party.

Laski's *Tribune* articles in 1937 concentrated on the Spanish Civil War
abroad and the United Front at home. He hammered away at Britain's
passivity before Mussolini's and Hitler's active role in the Spanish war,
while popularizing his own Marxist reading of fascism. Attributing to the
Labour Party theoretical positions it had not officially accepted, Laski
wrote that 'the Labour Party . . . sees in the aggression of the fascist powers
the logical outcome of capitalism at the stage of decay where it can no
longer admit democratic institutions'. It was in writing for the Unity
Campaign, however, that Laski was most prominently featured in early
issues of the *Tribune*. The boldly displayed titles of his articles announced
his commitment: 'WHAT IS THIS CRIME OF UNITY?'; 'A POLICY FOR
LABOUR: WIN PEACE, BREAD, SECURITY BY UNITY IN ACTION'; 'THIS
BOGEY OF COMMUNISM, FEARS THAT ARE WRONGLY BASED WEAKEN
LABOUR'S POWERS.' His message was clear. 'We have to choose between a
fascism, which grows daily nearer, and working-class unity. To the degree
that the latter is impaired, to that degree, also, the chances of a fascist
victory are strengthened.' Only replacing the National government with a
truly socialist Labour government forged by working-class unity would
stem the tide of reaction at home and abroad. Meanwhile, the Labour
Party was spending so much of its energy 'fighting its own left wing that it
can hardly be easy for the voter to be sure whether the main enemy of
Labour is the National government or the socialist critics of the National
Executive'. What is the sin of associating with communists, Laski asked,
why is it heresy?

> Is it that they have been guilty of grave errors in the past? I think they have.
> But I think, also, that they recognize these errors now. I conclude that the
> cooperation with them on subjects we have in common is more important
> now than working-class disunity because they have made mistakes.

Tension over collaboration with communists and talk of heresy hunting was exacerbated in May 1937 when the London bus strike dragged on for weeks. Bevin for the TUC and Arthur Deakin for the Transport Workers' Union accused communists within the union of exploiting the strike and urged that several rank-and-file strike leaders be expelled as members of a subversive organization. Laski sharply criticized Bevin in the *Tribune*, suggesting that 'every visible sign of militancy (witness the London bus strike) is frowned on as proof of communist agitation'. Bevin's hand was strengthened and the Unity Campaign's undercut by the fact that the strike coincided with celebrations of the coronation of George VI. With his fine eye for irony, Laski wrote it all up for his American audience in the *Nation* in an article entitled 'Kings and Bus Drivers', in which he criticized both the union leadership's foot-dragging over wage demands of a few shillings and the 'unnecessary pomp and luxury' of a monarchy that had been demystified by the abdication of 'Edward VIII, a fairy prince one day and an exile a week later'. It was vintage 'red decade' Laski who speculated that 'the sense that the monarchy is, at bottom, a reserve power in the hands of capitalist interests is more widespread than at any time for fifty years'.

The summer after the coronation was particularly worrisome for Laski. Bevin had triumphed in the bus strike and Baldwin, who made at least some effort to take Labour seriously, retired to the House of Lords, replaced as Prime Minister by Neville Chamberlain, who seemed a more hard-line Tory. Most troublesome of all was the prospect of heresy hunting at the Bournemouth Labour Party conference in the autumn with talk of trouble in store for Cripps, Laski and others in the Unity Campaign, and a full fledged debate did occur on Thursday 5 October. The issue was conference reaffirmation of the NEC's condemnation of the United Front and its threat to expel Labour Party members who appeared on platforms with Communist Party members. Seconded by Laski, Cripps moved that the NEC's recommendation be tabled. 'I stand here to plead for tolerance and for generosity', for the right to speak opinions freely, Laski told the delegates. He announced proudly that 'if I have to choose between appearing upon a platform in the pursuance of our common aims with Mr Harry Pollitt or with Winston Churchill, I have no doubt at all that my proper place is with Mr Harry Pollitt'. Demanding a 'mechanical uniformity of outlook' was, after all, the vice of the CPGB. Laski concluded by urging the conference to tell the NEC with its vote that they were uninterested in heresy hunting or in the question of 'wings': their only interest was 'in the flight and in the direction of the bird'.

In speaking for the NEC against the Cripps–Laski motion, Morrison insisted that the party 'cannot have disunity spread ... in the name of unity', nor could it allow rank-and-file members to be disciplined by their local parties while 'people of prominence and of higher standing' were treated differently. He urged the leaders of the Unity Campaign to return to the fold. 'They have had a good run for their money. They have conducted a great agitation' and now should 'drop it ... practise unity' and accept the conference's decision. He was convinced that the communists' real motive in pursuing the United Front was to create internal dissension within the Labour Party – indeed, 'openly to capture the party for the Communist Party'. In making this case Morrison enlisted Laski himself. Laski had gone to Seaham in 1929 to help MacDonald fight Pollitt, he told the delegates, and 'Mr Laski gave Mr Pollitt what for and he was quite right'. With theatrical flourish, Morrison then held up a copy of Laski's *Communism* and read: 'The tactic of the United Front is then a Machiavellian manoeuvre dictated by the necessities of the international situation; it is the policy which the French socialist Longuet not ineptly described in the famous line of Racine, "I will embrace my rival, but it is the better to choke him."' That book, Morrison concluded, 'was published before the Left Book Club'. The delegates laughed.

More heat than light was generated by the debate. None of the parties discussed whether the world situation in 1937 might not lead many in the small CPGB genuinely to make common cause with Labour while having no interest in seizing control of the party for Moscow. On the other hand, no one asked whether Labour's fears weren't justified given conspiratorial actions still evident in CPGB circles. In any case, the card vote on the Cripps–Laski motion to refer the issue back was 331,000 for and 2,116,000 against. The Unity Campaign was over.

Cripps and Laski returned to the fold. At the very same conference, indeed on the very next day, the two were ushered into the inner sanctum of the Labour Party, the National Executive Committee. A constituency party reform movement, begun in 1932, succeeded when Dalton and Morrison, with Bevin much less enthusiastic, agreed in 1937 that the constituency party group on the NEC would be enlarged from five to seven members and that the vote for them would be taken at the conference exclusively from the constituency party membership. Dalton's biographer suggests that he championed the reform in order to enhance his own popularity and power in the party, strongly rooted as it was in the 700 constituency parties. Nor did Dalton seem to mind that in July Laski and Cripps had announced their intention to stand for the NEC. On 5 October the election was held at Bournemouth for the seven constituency seats. Morrison came in first with nearly 350,000 votes and Dalton second with just over 300,000. Laski was third with 276,000, followed by Noel-Baker, Cripps, Dallas and D. W. Pritt, in that order.

That three members of the Labour left – Laski, Cripps and Pritt, a radical lawyer – were elected along with Wilkinson, in the women's division, did not trouble Dalton or Morrison. Giving them official positions in the party would soften the hurt of those defeated over Unity while making the insurgents part of a larger body of twenty-five, where their radicalism could be expressed and then nullified. They were safer within the NEC than without. Laski, of course, saw it differently. He had told Frankfurter in July that 'if we get on, at least we can do something to create trouble in the machine', and he wrote in the *Nation* in November that the election 'was an unmistakable victory for the left'. Dalton, meanwhile, wrote to Laski that he was 'looking forward to a great cooperative venture by this new executive of all talents'. For the next twelve years Laski would fight for the Labour left within the party's most powerful non-parliamentary body. It made him no less outspoken, no more moderate, however. Unlike Cripps, Gollancz, Strachey and Wilkinson, Laski would not move to the centre in the 1940s. It did mean even more hard work, however. Many weeks during the political season Laski gave three afternoons to party business and his work-day was often sixteen hours long. But the rewards were high. Laski could now 'create trouble' literally on 'centre stage', since one of the privileges of NEC membership was a seat on the stage during Labour Party conferences. As a trouble-maker Laski emerged the darling of the constituency parties, soon eclipsing even Dalton and Morrison in his votes for the NEC. There was no party conference in 1938 as the party shifted from autumn to spring meetings, but in the NEC elections of 1939 and 1940 Laski decisively topped the list of the seven returned to the committee. He fast became, as Kingsley Martin told the BBC in 1962, 'the most popular independent figure not in Parliament in the Labour Party'.

In addition to his Left Book Club activity, Laski undertook in the winter of 1937 a new series in the *Daily Herald*. 'People and Politics' consisted of five or six short paragraphs on different topics in the news or, as the *Herald* described it, 'a new Monday feature in which a brilliant commentator will review the week in politics at home and abroad'. Laski balanced this work for the party's paper with continued writing for the *Tribune* in which he frequently attacked the party. His special stature on the left was indicated by the *Tribune*'s editorial introduction to one of his articles in 1938.

> No name is more widely known throughout the labour movement of this country than that of Professor Harold Laski. Over many years he has had a unique position as a foremost political philosopher and expositor among British socialists.

If Laski, as he wrote to Frankfurter, had trouble understanding the turn of events at the Bournemouth conference, where 'the big battalions attacked us with fury, and then put us emphatically on the Executive', then his Labour Party colleagues must have been just as puzzled at the apparent about-turn in his actions. Just eleven months earlier Laski had written in the *Nation* that if the Labour Party did not openly embrace the 'socialist faith', then people like himself should leave it. Several days before the conference Laski had attacked Bevin for his corporatist suggestion that the trade-union movement had become 'an integral part of the state'. Did Bevin not know that the state was not interested in 'the well-being of all classes' but concerned only with protecting the interests of the owners of the instruments of production? 'Mr Bevin,' Laski wrote, 'has become a liberal social reformer whose principles are not really distinguishable from those of Lord Baldwin or Mr Lloyd George.' Laski was working through the dilemma that haunts all radicals. Will more be accomplished by working from within an organization or by battering it from without? Laski's solution was to do both. He would work cooperatively within and accept the defeats when they came, but he felt free to continue venting his anger at the party's leadership outside in the most public manner, a strategy which most of his colleagues found hard to live with.

Laski threw himself into NEC activity. There was a flurry of uncontroversial work for the various sub-committees to which he was assigned: Policy; Research and Local Government; Organizational; International; Press, Publicity and Campaign. He learned things about the party leaders that he had only suspected before: 'TU hatred of Morrison, Attlee counting for almost nothing ... All except three of the TU members make William Green [American labour leader] look like a Bolshevik.' He was most impressed with Morrison, 'the best of them all – a superb committee-man'. Laski won respect from his colleagues for his willingness to work hard, do research, write countless background papers and give speeches. In his first three months on the Executive Laski spoke in Edinburgh, Bristol, Glasgow and Cardiff on behalf of the party's 'Spanish Campaign', another concession to the militants made at Bournemouth. He proposed resolutions that were usually unanimously endorsed – for example, putting the party on record as protesting against the treatment of Jews in Romania and Germany.

Laski was less successful when his NEC activity touched controversy. In January 1938 his proposal that the party sponsor a trade-union boycott of Japanese ships was defeated by fourteen votes to eight on the grounds that it was trade-union business. 'Of course the TUC won't act,' Laski wrote to Frankfurter; 'Citrine and Bevin on this are to the right of the government.' He lost again in the summer of 1938 when he suggested that a special party conference be held in the autumn to discuss 'the rape of Austria, the intensification of foreign intervention in Spain, fascist attacks on Czechoslovakia and China, the deliberate abandonment of the League by Chamberlain'. The first time he put this proposal to the conference, the NEC vote was eighteen against and five for, and the second and final time fourteen to eleven. Dalton and Morrison were firmly opposed, Laski told Frankfurter, and that killed it.

Laski was turning more and more of his attention to European politics in 1937 and 1938, and here too he was at odds with the party leadership. Bevin, now Chairman of the TUC, told his own union, the transport workers, in March 1937 that it was time for the labour movement to drop its opposition to British rearmament. 'I cannot see any way of stopping Hitler and the other dictators except by force.' Dalton joined Bevin in pushing the Parliamentary Labour Party (PLP) to drop its strong traditions of anti-militarism. He succeeded in July 1937 in persuading the PLP to abstain in the crucial vote to increase armament expenditures, and since the previous year the PLP had voted against the service estimates the abstention was read as Labour's grudging recognition of the need for rearmament.

Laski opposed this reversal, fearing the great profits reaped from rearmament and arguing:

> No one on the left who is not an absolute pacifist denies the need for arms against the menace of fascism. What we say is that this government is not seeking arms for that purpose. It is seeking them only to safeguard imperial interests ... so long as a capitalist government is in power it will fight for capitalist interests.

Laski stuck to this ideological opposition to rearmament throughout the winter of 1937 and spring of 1938 despite his opposition to fascism and his increasing concern about the possibility of British willingness to let Hitler have his way as a prelude to his hoped-for turning on Russia. He knew that Baldwin had told a group of parliamentarians in July 1936 that 'if there is any fighting to be done in Europe, I should like to see the Bolsheviks and Nazis doing it'. Chamberlain's willingness to talk about Danzig, Austria and Czechoslovakia with Hitler, his exchange of friendly letters with Mussolini over *de jure* recognition of the Italian empire in Abyssinia and his visit to Italy, which led in February 1938 to Anthony Eden's resignation as Foreign Secretary, all seemed part of a government strategy to buy peace through concessions. These developments, however, only intensified Laski's opposition to rearmament. He was convinced that the government's request was merely part of a competitive national armaments policy whose only beneficiaries would be weapons merchants.

At an emergency meeting of the NEC called after Eden's resignation, Laski helped to draft a Labour demand for a general election over whether Chamberlain had any right to talk with Mussolini, but what he truly wanted was for the non-fascist powers of Europe to unite and not 'permit the fascist dictatorships the right to alter the map of the world in their unfettered discretion'. The alternative, Laski wrote to an American friend in December 1937, was Hitler's 'attack on Spain today, tomorrow it may be Prague, and the day after will be Armageddon. But if we said "no" now he would, like every bully, retreat ... To give Hitler piecemeal victories is to refresh his prestige. The more he is refreshed, the more he demands.' Sentiments such as these joined Laski to the few, like Churchill, Bevin and Dalton, who were arguing against appeasement. Where he differed dramatically from them was his reluctance until late 1938 to see rearmament as essential in giving credibility to any government's saying 'no further'.

In a series of ten weekly articles, entitled 'Whither Liberty?', which ran in the *Tribune* from 14 January to 18 March 1938, Laski tried to place the frightening developments in Europe in the larger context of nineteenth- and twentieth-century historical development. The series was, in fact, the new introduction he had written for his 1930 book *Liberty in the Modern State*, which was being reprinted in late 1937 as one of the earliest Pelican paperbacks by Laski's disciple and friend Krishna Menon. The 'crisis' of 1931, Laski's dramatic turn to the left and the spectre of fascism were combined in a thirty-seven-page chapter that was grafted on to the 1930 book. Hovering over the new introduction was the premonition 'that mankind is about to enter a new dark age'. According to this gloomy foreboding, the ruling class would end the century-long series of progressive concessions it had made in economic and political rights. Lumping together America and Britain, Laski warned that the Tory-led National government, as well as Mr Ford and Mr Hearst, have concluded that 'if democracy will not tolerate much longer the poverty and unemployment . . . which Mr Keynes has told is "rightly associated with present-day capitalistic individualism", then they are prepared for the destruction of democracy'. Nor did Laski spare the Labour Party. Even as he joined the NEC, he condemned the party's assumption 'that respectable behaviour on their part will eventually bring them to power'. All that respectability does, Laski suggested, was to 'confirm their opponents in their belief of socialist weakness'.

Several months later Laski published the fourth edition of his *magnum opus*, *The Grammar of Politics*. Laski again used a lengthy new introduction to repeat his argument about the crisis of democracy in a contracting capitalist economy and its linkage to the rise of fascism, but also to repudiate his earlier pluralism, which remained, quite schizophrenically, in the text. Although much has been made of this repudiation, the fact is that Laski never completely discarded pluralism. He acknowledged his failure sufficiently to realize the nature of the state as an expression of class relations, but still maintained that a classless society would realize the pluralist vision of eliminating the vast apparatus of state coercion. Then, Laski wrote, authority could be truly plural in form and expression. His earlier use of Proudhon's syndicalism was joined to the Marxist theory of the state, as Laski explained to his scholarly readers that

I now recognize that the pluralist attitude to the state and law was a stage on the road to an acceptance of the Marxian attitude to them. Only by means of Marxism can I explain phenomena like the state as it appears in fascist countries. That state seeks the total absorption of the individual within the framework of its coercive apparatus precisely because it is there, nakedly and without shame, what the state, covertly and apologetically is in capitalist democracies like Great Britain or the United States. To limit its power, as the pluralist sought to limit its power, we must destroy the class-structure of society.

Much more likely to have been read by his colleagues on the NEC and his Left Book Club following was Laski's new book published in 1938, *Parliamentary Government in England*, which Leonard Woolf called 'brilliant and full of truth and wisdom'. Published simultaneously in London by Allen & Unwin and in America by his friend Ben Huebsch's Viking Press, it was dedicated to his new American friend, the scholar and journalist Max Lerner. Ostensibly packaged as a textbook survey of the party system, House of Lords, House of Commons, Cabinet, Civil Service, monarchy and judiciary, the book was really in the same mould as *Democracy in Crisis* and *The State in Theory and Practice*, an 'agitative' Marxist commentary on British politics in 1938. Repetitive as were all his books, what was particularly valuable in *Parliamentary Government in England* was Laski's effort to spell out more clearly what he meant by revolution. Marxist democratic socialists, like himself, he wrote, used revolution to mean a fundamental transformation of the economy from capitalist to socialist, which was achieved through parliamentary election and parliamentary majorities. Marxist communists, however, used revolution to mean both a fundamental change in the economic system as well as its achievement through conspiratorial and violent methods. Laski insisted that when he sometimes wrote that the revolutionary transformation of capitalism to socialism might involve violence, he meant extra-parliamentary violent means used by the right to resist the parliamentary-sponsored transformation sought by the left. In the British system the electorate, through Parliament, was supreme, and nothing, not even the collectivization of the means of production, was beyond its legislative power.

Parliamentary Government in England repeated Laski's non-Marxist commitment to tolerance, liberty, free speech, free press and freedom of association, not simply as rooted in bourgeois history and experience or serving as bourgeois ruses, but as essential trans-historical values. They had an easier time of it, to be sure, in an expanding capitalist era or when there was a consensus on capitalism, and they were extremely vulnerable in periods of conflict and class war; but Laski was adamant. Sounding much like Rosa Luxemburg, he insisted that these were crucial values in the future socialist society. He never envisioned, as many Marxists did, an end to politics once socialism and a classless society were achieved. He did not see a truly socialist society as conflict-free under harmony's reign with one truthful ideology engraved in the hearts of all, making traditional liberal rights and freedoms superfluous. There would be conflict, Laski assumed, in the socialist state over issues of personality, personal power and the directions socialism should take. Freedom of the press, of association, of belief and of speech, just as much as democratic political institutions, would be just as necessary after Jerusalem was built in England's green and pleasant land. *Parliamentary Government in England* was, then, the quintessential statement of Laski's liberal Marxism, for he was convinced that no one would agree how Jerusalem was to be governed, who should govern it and what Jerusalem's government ought to achieve.

Laski's balancing act between Marxism and liberalism was displayed vividly in his attitude towards the Soviet Union. Some analysts have suggested that Laski was one of the many naïve apologists for Stalin and the 'workers' paradise', citing his oft-proclaimed embrace of Marxism, his championing of the United Front and his willingness to forge alliances with Harry Pollitt and the CPGB. The Left Book Club powerfully reinforced Laski's image as a 'fellow-traveller', with its frequent selection of books written by communists and about the Soviet Union. Laski even announced in *Left News* that while the club would welcome 'reasoned criticism' of the Soviet Union, it would not publish 'Trotskyite attacks' which were nothing more than 'a declaration of war on that country'. *Left News* also devoted pages to verbatim accounts of the speeches of Ivan Maisky, the Soviet ambassador to Britain from 1932 to 1943 and a good friend of Laski. Finally, had Laski not visited the Moscow Mecca with pleasure?

Laski's fellow-traveller status is much more complicated than this simple recital suggests. The pilgrimage to Moscow was by itself no sign of membership in the faithful. Everyone went: Lady Astor had gone with her friend George Bernard Shaw; H. G. Wells, R. H. Tawney and Walter

Citrine had gone; and so had Lord Lothian, the Webbs, and Beatrice's
nephew Malcolm Muggeridge. When Hugh Dalton visited, he commented
on his return that 'most of the Russians I saw looked better fed than my
unemployed Durham miners and their families'. Nor was there a lack of
books like *Russia's Iron Age* by the *Christian Science Monitor*'s long-time
correspondent in Moscow, W. H. Chamberlain, praising Russia and Stalin.
Even Walter Citrine's *I Search for Truth in Russia* offered a fairly flattering
picture of Stalin, as did the phenomenally successful *Inside Europe* by the
American journalist John Gunther. In a decade when even Tories like
Harold Macmillan thought capitalism was dying, the appeal of the Soviet
Union was not surprising. While the West reeled under unprecedented
depression, the Soviets were launching five-year plans. In place of the
'despairing apathy' or 'cynical listlessness' of the capitalist world, Beatrice
Webb saw only the 'enthusiasm and devoted service on the part of millions
of workers in Soviet Russia'.

Added to this, of course, was the Soviet posture in world affairs after
1934 as the solid core of international opposition to fascism, especially as
the events of 1937 and 1938 revealed Britain and France as willing to
bargain for a Hitler of modest ambitions. The worsening of the international
situation and the sense that appeasement really cloaked pro-fascist and anti-
red attitudes blinded many on the British left to the nightmarish horrors of
the Soviet treason trials between 1936 and 1938. The executions were
opposed by some: in America by John Dewey, who called them 'frame-
ups'; and in Britain by the *Manchester Guardian*, Walter Citrine, Leonard
Woolf and H. N. Brailsford. For the most part, however, the Labour left,
as Michael Foot has written, kept quiet because 'we were engaged in a
Unity Campaign with the communists on the supreme issue of Spain and
the international crisis'. And the American ambassador in Moscow
throughout the trials, Joseph E. Davies, was himself convinced of the trials'
validity and the guilt of the accused.

Laski's views on Soviet Russia were no less confused and conflicting
than were his contemporaries'. He announced in his first 1934 lecture in
Moscow, according to the not always reliable *Daily Worker*, that 'all my
life socialism has been a dream to me. Here in Soviet Russia it has become
a reality. For twenty years I have been a teacher, but I have come here not
to teach but, as the devout Moslem goes to Mecca, to learn.' This was then
corrected by a Russian critic of Laski, who interposed with, 'But, Laski,

good Moslems go to Mecca not to learn, but to repent.' Laski returned 'in a state of exhilaration about the hope and adventure, the social equality and universal activity in the land of the Soviets', according to Beatrice Webb's diary. Her entry captured his ambivalence as well, for she reported his being smitten with Russia 'so long as Laski may argue in favour of Communism, or against it, in London or Moscow'.

Laski shared his reflections in two 'Leningrad Letters' published in the *Nation* in July 1934. Like everything he wrote on Soviet Russia in the 1930s, they were characterized by an 'on the one hand, on the other hand' approach. It was a land of hope with a mood 'of intense exhilaration, of a buoyant and optimistic faith I have never before encountered'. There was unprecedented social mobility: men who before the revolution were simple working men were now factory managers, engineers, administrators, judges and generals. Enlightened prisons, the judicial system, the educational system, the passion for research, factory democracy, 'deserve all the eulogies that have been heaped upon them'. Yet, 'on the other hand', it was no paradise. The people on the streets were shabby, there was overcrowding, and Laski, unlike Dalton, was in 'doubt whether an unemployed English worker on the dole has a standard of life as low as the lower-paid categories of Russian workers in full employment'. Wherever he went, Laski saw 'the real and omnipresent fact of dictatorship', which ruthlessly and relentlessly suppressed all hostile opinion. The Communist Party was 'dogmatic, intolerant and incapable of scepticism'. Its discipline was iron, it was suspicious of everyone, and it presided over 'a regime of deliberate and organized repression'. The party and its members revered every utterance of Stalin 'not as a thesis to be discussed but as an argument that ended the matter'. Laski's summary assessment captured his ambivalence. The Russian experiment

> obviously makes possible, even for the humblest, an exhilarating fulfilment of personality such as Wordsworth caught in his first enthusiasm for the French Revolution. For the spirit which doubts, however, it means profound discomfort; for the spirit which denies, it means imprisonment and possibly death.

The new Soviet constitution of 1936 left Laski hopeful in one of his 'London Diary' entries for the *New Statesman*. It provided freedom of association and expression, while, of course, 'it is true that the dominance of the Communist Party is maintained'. Still, the gains in individual freedom were impressive and 'politically inconceivable in Germany or Italy'. If only, Laski speculated, the Soviets would now grant 'a generous amnesty to their political opponents', they would enhance their prestige in the Western world. A year later Laski returned to a discussion of Soviet Russia in his introduction to *Liberty in the Modern State*, and the same even-handed assessment was offered. The achievements had been immense: no unemployment, end of illiteracy, growing productivity versus scarcity in the West, application of science to industry and agriculture, democratization of culture, enlightened treatment of criminals, conquest of racial prejudice and the provision of opportunity to individuals. But there was still what Laski labelled, 'the grim logic of Leninism'. Soviet Russia remained after twenty years a ruthless dictatorship with no liberty to criticize the regime, found alternative parties, publish alternative opinions or hold meetings. The fear of foreign attack, while legitimate, given the experience immediately after the Revolution and the spectre of Hitler, did not, Laski insisted, justify executions and the autocratic rule of Stalin and the party, which 'causes grief and disappointment to those who care for freedom'. He was hopeful, none the less, that the 'process of coercion' would give way to 'the process of consent', which is 'a potential revitalization of freedom not possible in the fascist dictatorships'.

By far the most courageous statement by Laski about Soviet Russia occurred in his unexpected criticism of the Webbs, the venerable icons of British socialism (and of the LSE). Originally critics of the Bolsheviks as some strange combination of anarchists and guild socialists, the Webbs were converted by their visit in 1932 to the fervent worship of Soviet communism, a planned, scientific bureaucratic society run by expert managers. At the age of seventy-six (Sidney) and seventy-seven (Beatrice), they published in 1935 a massive two-volume apologia, *Soviet Communism: A New Civilization?*, which sold over 20,000 copies in Britain in its first year alone. The book's last sentence conveyed the spirit of their conversion.

> Will this new civilization with its abandon of the incentive of profit-making, its extinction of unemployment, its planned production for community consumption, and the consequent liquidation of the landlord and the capitalist, spread to other countries? Our reply is 'Yes, it will.' But how, when, where, with what modifications, and whether through revolution, or by peaceful penetration, or even by conscious imitation, we cannot answer.

The problem with the Webbs' book, Laski felt, was their virtual indifference to the repressive face of this new civilization and he said so publicly. He reviewed the book on 7 March 1936 in the American literary weekly the *Saturday Review*, and after a paragraph in which he agreed with the Webbs' conclusion 'that the salvation of mankind depends upon its adoption of the principles of Russian social organization', Laski devoted the remainder of the review to the 'body of evidence' the Webbs had taken 'far too lightly' that 'ideological differences have been penalized with a drastic severity it is impossible to defend'. He then methodically criticized the 'uniformity of thought' in Russia and Stalin's falsification of history to magnify his role and diminish Trotsky's. Laski also described the exile of political prisoners, some Zionists and some social democrats. With uncharacteristic bitterness Laski wrote of the 'disservice' the Webbs did by ignoring Soviet inquisitions. 'They seem,' Laski wrote, 'to have no conception either of the price mankind has had to pay for such liberty of thought as it has won or of the cost its suppression has always involved.' Laski asked whether he could limit his own protests to German and Italian brutality to Jews and communists

> when without any trial, hundreds of Russians, none of whom is guilty of any act against the Soviet government, have been imprisoned not less relentlessly there? Mr and Mrs Webb have no answer to this problem. It is one which makes their denial of a dictatorship in Russia futile; for if Russia were not a dictatorship it would not need methods of this kind to assure its authority.

In late 1937, and after much news about the Soviet treason trials, the Webbs published a second edition of their *Soviet Communism: A New Civilization*, but without the question mark in the title. The only other change was a seventy-page epilogue in which they surveyed the events between 1935 and 1937. The Webbs did not discuss the general history of Soviet denial of civil liberties and seemed to issue an endorsement of the Moscow trials. The new edition so enraged Laski that he wrote to Leonard Woolf, editor of the *Political Quarterly* and the most persistent critic of the Soviet Union among Labour intellectuals, offering to review it. He was, he told Woolf, 'distressed beyond words' that people with their reputations and influence had written thus, since it would confirm for the Soviet leaders that they could neglect foreign opinion. Laski told Woolf:

I have talked till I am sick with people like Maisky and they are not even willing to forward letters to the Soviet Union which might do something to call attention to our own sense of disturbance at persecution.

Laski's *Political Quarterly* review was even harsher than the first one. Laski wrote that he had come to realize the rights provisions of the 1936 Soviet Constitution were sham and 'with great respect to Mr and Mrs Webb ... I cannot take so easily as they do the large guarantee of civil liberties that it contains'. His greatest ire was reserved for the Webbs' suggestion that 'the guilt of the prisoners is so clear that there is no point in the elaborate (British) farce of a plea of not guilty'. The trials, for Laski, involved the identification of 'independent-thinking with treason or Trotskyism'. Tolerance and free thought would come to Soviet Russia, whose immense material progress under Stalin Laski joined the Webbs in applauding, only when people with the authority and influence of the Webbs 'urgently protest against any action that is arbitrary and unexplained'. Laski asked:

> Are not Mr and Mrs Webb disturbed (a) at the wholesale character of the purges that have taken place; (b) at the sense of fear at their possible repercussions that afflict some of even the most eminent Soviet officials so that they will not undertake the most elementary enquiries into the fate of arrested persons; and (c) whether creative work of an intellectual kind can be achieved in a civilization in which an 'ideological deviation' may so easily be identified with treason? I think these are important questions.

In her diary entry for 5 January 1938, Beatrice Webb took 'Laski's hostile review' as a sign of the swing away from the Soviet Union on the part of younger left intellectuals, who found 'the old Webbs' distinctly out of favour. But she was 'delightfully appreciative', several weeks later on her eightieth birthday, to see a worshipful letter to the *New Statesman* from Laski in her honour. One does not know what to make, however, of an entry eight months later when Laski came by on 1 September for 'a five-hour talk' before he went to America for nine months. He was, she wrote, now completely convinced that she and Sidney were right in finding the Soviet trials and executions 'necessary to save the revolution from counter-revolution, a change-over from his critical review of our postscript to the second edition'. Laski's 'change-over' may have been a generous and sentimental gesture from a man feeling guilty over a very public attack on people he deeply respected and, since Sidney had recently had a stroke, people he thought he might never see again. Perhaps, on the other hand, it reveals a Laski who was worried that excesses of his public voice jeopardized his private access to important people, and that if he were to remain the consummate insider he had to backtrack. It is possible, of course, that Beatrice Webb simply misheard or wanted to hear what she heard, or that Laski did in fact 'change over' in a private moment of anger and frustration in response to the announcement that Chamberlain planned later that month to meet with Herr Hitler in Munich.

CHAPTER SIXTEEN

America, the Popular Front and Britain Goes to War

Laski went to America in September 1938 for his longest stay since he had left Harvard. It was his seventh visit in nine years, the first on which Frida accompanied him, to his second home, where in the judgement of the historian Arthur Schlesinger, Jr, Laski influenced 'left-wing thought in the 1930s' far more than 'any native Marxist'. For many Americans Laski played the archetypal role of 'socialist:' he was foreign, an intellectual and Jewish. After teaching at Yale Law School in 1931, Laski came to America for five short visits to see his friends, to make money and to be lionized by former students and American leftists, usually in universities, hungry for unabashed Marxist rhetoric publicly professed. The characteristic pattern of his month-long visits in 1933, 1935, 1936, 1937 and spring 1938 was a set of lectures at the New School in New York City, with occasional forays to Cambridge, Washington and the usual spots on the university lecture circuit.

Laski was newsworthy in America. Always a presence in the respectable American press for his reflections about British politics, he became even more so on his visits as American newspapers watched closely the comings and goings of their 'socialist professor'. Laski was still a favourite of the *New York Times*, so openly and uninhibitedly a socialist, so perfect for the paper's 'Quotation Marks' section, next to its editorials. Sometimes Laski's comments became the focus for its lead editorials, one rebutting his view that capitalism in its contracting phase was an inveterate enemy of democracy, another upset by his suggestion that judges were mere agents serving the interests of the privileged. But in March 1933, when the newspaper wanted an article for its widely distributed subsidiary magazine *Current History* to mark the fiftieth anniversary of the death of Karl Marx, it turned to Laski, as it did a year and a half later for a piece on the fiftieth anniversary of the Fabian Society.

Laski usually provided good copy for the American reporters who followed him around. At the thirtieth anniversary dinner of the leftist League for Industrial Democracy he prescribed 'socialism as the only solution to the world's problems'. He told an association of college teachers that unionization was necessary for them to achieve their goals, and advised a conference of librarians on their obligations to shape a new society. Laski debated with his former student, A. A. Berle, Jr, Law Professor and Roosevelt insider, who called for an 'emphatic return to individualism', while Laski grimly predicted the sacrifice of democracy by fearful capitalists. At a speech to the National Institute of Public Affairs in Washington, Congressman Fred Davenport interrupted Laski with a question about why social welfare programmes never seemed to accomplish their intended purpose. Laski replied:

> Precisely because of people like you. You Republican conservatives try in every way to kill a good social reform by massive propaganda against it. Then you kill it with kindness when its passage is inevitable by loading it up with so many devices to protect the private interests you represent that it becomes an operational nightmare.

With his apparently limitless energy, Laski seemed to be everywhere in America, just as in Britain, and often with pillars of the Establishment. Lunches were often organized for New York lawyers and businessmen to meet Laski, 'the English Socialist'. Laski testified before the Senate Judiciary Committee, calling upon his experiences on the Donoughmore Commission, as it discussed legislation to create a special Administrative Court of Appeals to expedite cases in which the government or its agencies were a party. He also proposed in 1936 the creation of a commission to consider amendments to the United States Constitution.

A minor furore was stirred up by Laski's 1935 suggestion in *Harper's*, which he repeated in numerous talks, that American lawyers, 'the annex of the millionaire class', be 'decommercialized' by reorganizing the profession as 'a great corporation under government control, the members of which should work for the public on a fixed salary at fixed charges'. The President of the American Bar Association assailed this vision of 'socialized lawyers in a socialist state' at the December 1935 annual dinner of the New York County Lawyers' Association; on the other hand, William L. Ranson told the assembled lawyers that Laski's proposal 'excites laughter and seems absurd, but in reality it is in full harmony with the social philosophies which we hear advocated from high places in the United States today'. But even the critics of the New Deal invoked Laski, so widespread was his reputation, so protean his appeal. In a famous speech attacking a planned economy given to the Ohio Bankers' Association in November 1937, Henry Luce, publisher of *Time* and *Life*, enlisted the wisdom of his former teacher at Yale. 'The essential character of liberty,' he explained to the bankers, 'was identified with brilliant simplicity by Harold Laski. He wrote that in any state where men possess unlimited political power, even if re-elected, those men whom they rule are not free.'

The same unabashed espousal of socialism that made Laski such good copy in America made him a great favourite at college campuses. The faculty, often his former students, had read his books. Students, like James Wechsler, then at Columbia and later the progressive editor of the *New York Post*, remembered Laski undercutting 'the infantilism of fraternity life', where students 'were expected to devote themselves to love and liquor'. Everywhere he went, students fondly recalled that he stayed long after the formal lecture to talk with them about American politics and the prospects for socialism. In these appearances Laski suffered no illusions about the likelihood of socialism in America. He repeated the arguments he had made in a *Redbook Magazine* debate he had with John Maynard Keynes in 1934. Each had answered the question posed by the popular American woman's magazine, 'Can America Spend its Way into Recovery?' 'Yes,' Keynes wrote, 'a course of behaviour which might make a single individual poor can make a nation wealthy.' Laski's 'No' was premised not on a critique of Keynesianism, but on the realities of American politics. Greatly increased government expenditure and movement to a planned society, he wrote, would 'outrage' the leaders of American capital who would chafe at 'the burden of taxation'. The only solution for America was fully fledged 'public ownership of the means of production', and he conceded that 'it is to avoid this end that the United States has embarked upon its present experiment'. He captivated American leftist students, none the less, because he pushed for more than the New Deal, which he read as designed simply to rescue capitalism. At the same time he came across as the political realist who saw little prospect on the American left for the evolution of a meaningful socialism. No wonder, then, that his appearances on American campuses in the 1930s led to the long talk sessions remembered so fondly by students.

Laski did not reach out only to Americans on the left. Twice, in 1935 and 1937, he wrote articles in *Harper's*, 'A Word to the Republicans' and 'A Formula for Conservatives', to plead with Americans on the right to abandon their opposition to collective bargaining and 'their blind hostility to trade unionism'. He invoked his storehouse of quotations from Burke and Macaulay on prudential concessions as essential for those who would preserve their power. He also advised Americans in these articles to stop enshrining businessmen and the quest for profits as the American ideal and to replace them with a caring paternalistic elite committed to public service. Although Laski savagely criticized America's ruthless capitalism on the lecture circuit and in print, he saw in Roosevelt and the New Deal a vital experimental mood utterly lacking in Britain. His 'Formula for Conservatives' ended with an evocation of Tom Paine: 'America has an opportunity to renew the springtime of the world.' Unlike most English left-wing intellectuals – Tawney and Cole come to mind – Laski loved America and often repeated that Britain could learn from it, from her schools, her industry, even her hotels and trains. Laski often complained that his fellow socialists only knew America as the materialistic home of Rockefeller and Ford and not as the more egalitarian, less rigid class society he saw. Like Frankfurter, he was taken with the 'American dream' and he berated the British left for not giving America the credit it deserved.

One of the reasons Laski loved America, of course, was his extensive network of American friends. On every visit he saw as many as he could. He saw Firuski in Connecticut and Ben Huebsch, Roger Baldwin and Morris Cohen in New York. He had the obligatory dinner at the *New Republic* and always visited Freda Kirchwey at the *Nation*. He usually managed to see the people in the Brandeis–Frankfurter circle like Abe and Ben Flexner, Samuel Rosensohn, Eugene Meyer at the *Washington Post*, Judge Mack and David Niles. He met the younger New Dealers like Acheson and Benjamin Cohen. He saw Holmes for the last time during his spring visit of 1933, for the great jurist died the month before Laski's arrival in 1935. Laski wrote to Frankfurter after receiving his telegram with the news that 'I feel as though a limb of mine has been cut off.'

His friendship with Brandeis continued throughout this period and Laski visited him whenever he went to Washington. Laski dedicated his 1932 *Studies in Law and Politics* to Brandeis, but he also wrote a long, moving article for *Harper's* in May 1934 that surveyed the justice's legal career, his contributions to the Court, as well as his personality. 'No one can see him in action,' Laski suggested, 'without a new understanding of the Hebraic gift of moral vision. It is not for nothing that he is of the people from whom Isaiah and Maimonides and Spinoza were born.' Brandeis was moved by Laski's praise and wrote to Frankfurter that 'we have also heard from many persons great commendations of Harold's article'. Having made use of Laski's putative power in British politics, Brandeis was convinced that he wielded influence in America as well, at least in shaping public opinion. At a time when he was angry with Roosevelt, Brandeis suggested to the editor of the *Atlantic Monthly* that he ask Laski to write an article on the concentration of power in the presidency. Laski, of course, no longer shared Brandeis's convictions about the curse of bigness, and at least a part of him advocated the very central planning that estranged Brandeis from many in the New Deal. He wrote in 1935 that Brandeis's 'noble passion' was 'like the pronouncement of a believer in the Ptolemaic astronomy that the new Copernican world will not do', and three years later, according to Harold Ickes, Roosevelt's Secretary of the Interior, Laski said he had 'worshipped at his [Brandeis] feet for a good many years, but that he thought he ought to resign so that Frankfurter could be appointed in his place'.

Of the remaining friends from his Harvard days, Roscoe Pound went the way of Lippmann. He seemed to Laski to have become a snob bent on making Harvard Law School a grand palace for the legal establishment and, moreover, was insensitive to anti-Semitism at a time of great peril to Jews. On his return from a trip to Germany in 1934, Pound told a newspaper interviewer that he saw no military presence in the country, no tension, little persecution, and that Hitler was saving Europe from 'agitators'. To make matters worse, Pound received an honorary degree that autumn from the University of Berlin presented to him by the German ambassador to the United States at a Harvard Law School ceremony. Frankfurter refused to attend and complained to James Bryant Conant, Harvard's new President. Frankfurter told this to Laski and the two had little more to do with Pound.

The Jewish question also figured in Laski's estrangement from another friend of Harvard days, the American historian Samuel Elliot Morrison, who saw nothing wrong with the controversial Charles Howard Warren bequest in 1936 to Yale University, which provided scholarships to the 'sons of white Christian parents of Anglo-Saxon, Scandinavian or Teutonic descent'. When Frankfurter protested that Yale had been 'bought for Nazism', Morrison wrote to him that 'we Yankees whose fathers reclaimed this country from the wilderness are being hustled and shoved from every side, politically, mainly by the Irish; economically, by the Jews. Let us at least save some places at mother Yale for our boys.' Frankfurter also passed this on to Laski and another relationship became cool.

Even as Frankfurter's politics settled on New Deal reformism and Laski's moved into Marxism, the two remained the closest of friends. Since Felix had a friend in the White House, it was inevitable that the Laski–Frankfurter connection would generate right-wing criticism of the New Deal. As early as the autumn of 1934 Laski was visited by someone who claimed to be doing a story on how Felix had operated in England 'as a private agent for Roosevelt to make contact with left-wing socialist opinion on his behalf'. A year later Laski speculated to Frankfurter that the Hearst press 'has hit on you as a symbol to be used for attacking the Jewish radical intellectual'. Laski and Frankfurter were also targets of Gerald B. Winrod, travelling evangelist, senatorial candidate from Kansas, and head of the Defenders of the Christian Faith. Winrod was convinced that behind the 'Jew Deal' were Frankfurter, Laski and a President whose real name was Rosenfeld. To prove the existence of a 'Jew Deal', Winrod often used part of a speech where Laski worried about a backlash because of the number of eminent American Jews involved in the New Deal. One of Winrod's associates, Mrs Elizabeth Dilling of Chicago, made the same point in describing who was behind the subversion of America: 'Harold Laski, the little half-pint Jewish Atheist Communistic counterpart of his close friend Felix Frankfurter, the Austrian-born miniature-sized Red Rasputin of the Jew Deal'. Meanwhile Congressman J. Thorkelson of Montana had excerpts from a British book, *The Alien Menace*, read into the House of Representatives' *Congressional Record*, listing one Harold J. Laski of the LSE as one of 'the men of alien race' who was undermining the British way of life. Americans be warned.

Laski made some new American friends during this period. Max Lerner was one. In the early 1930s Lerner wrote several iconoclastic and neo-Marxist *Law Review* pieces on the Supreme Court and on legal realism which caught Laski's attention. He wrote to Lerner and they met when he next came to New York. Enamoured of Holmes – indeed, writing a book about him – Lerner was a lot like Laski. Jewish, short and verbally combative to the core, Lerner was set on a career that combined university teaching and scholarly writing on political philosophy with popular journalism and political influence, all informed by an ideological perspective distinctly to the left of the New Deal. Laski helped to advance Lerner's career, singling him out in a *New Republic* piece as the great hope for a renaissance in creative political thinking in American letters. In the late 1930s Lerner became political editor of the *Nation* and then a columnist, first for the *New York Sun* and then the *New York Post*. He taught at Williams College and then for many years at Brandeis University. Laski and Lerner corresponded frequently and warmly, and assisted each other through book reviews and publishing contacts. Lerner always held a dinner party in his East End Avenue home for Laski to preside over whenever he came to New York, and he always remembered Laski's passion for chocolate sundaes. When Laski suggested that Lerner edit the Holmes–Laski correspondence for Harvard, Lerner was touched, for 'there are no two people in the world I would want more to be associated with'. But it did not come to pass. After Laski's early death, Frankfurter gave the letters to Harvard Law School and its own professor, Mark DeWolfe Howe, became the editor.

Alfred Cohn and Laski had met in 1926 and they saw a great deal of each other throughout the 1930s. While Cohn worked in New York to relocate Jewish academics displaced from German universities as a member of the Executive Board of the Institute of International Education, Laski was doing the same at the LSE and whenever he visited America this activity provided a reason to get together, usually at Cohn's Central Park West apartment. Through his friendship with the cardiologist and research scientist Cohn, Laski met Edward R. Murrow, then the assistant to Stephen Duggan, founder of the Carnegie Endowment for Peace's Institute of International Education, who was in charge of placing refugee German scholars in American universities. Laski gave some of his fees from *Harper's* and speaking, about $100, to Murrow's emergency committee. They also met socially at Iron Hill Farm, Cohn's country place in Connecticut, where, as Murrow's biographer puts it, young Murrow loved the evenings of serious talk with Cohn, Frankfurter and Laski about 'the nature of democracy and the heart of truth – the deep, unfrivolous subjects of conversation that Ed loved'.

Murrow was appointed the European head of CBS Radio News in 1937, and Laski happened to be a fellow passenger on Murrow's Atlantic crossing in April. The two men played ping-pong all day and Laski invited the Murrows to visit his new country place in Little Bardfield, Essex. They did and the two men became friends. Impressed by Laski's erudition and his politics, Murrow also admired his feel for America, including his knowledge of baseball, the blues and even Mormon saints. Laski saw in Murrow the quintessential American, open, forthright, unpretentious and determined to set the world right. When Murrow told Laski he wanted to bring everyday Britons to the American radio audience, Laski took him to the Spread Eagle, the pub in Little Bardfield, because pubs were 'the only democratic institution left in England'. Laski introduced Murrow to the son of the local squire, who was playing darts with a tenant farmer, and when a local character, Uppy Andrews, burst into a chorus of 'The Cat Came Back', Laski followed with 'My Old Kentucky Home' with Murrow joining in for the chorus. A month later Murrow returned to the Spread Eagle with his radio crew for the first-ever live overseas broadcast of the pub conversation and Uppy Andrews's songs. Murrow also met other Englishmen through Laski, important people in public life who came to Laski's Sunday teas.

In the 1930s Laski got to know fairly well two more justices on the Supreme Court. With Harlan Fiske Stone, appointed to the Court in 1925 by President Coolidge, Laski had an interesting exchange in the middle of the decade over the future of America's lawyers. In the spring of 1934 Stone had given an important address critical of lawyers forsaking their role as guardians of the common welfare in order to become spokesmen for industrial finance and private interests. In a *Harper's* piece on Stone's call for a renewal of the profession's dedication to the public interest, Laski asserted that, short of socialized law, the legal profession in America would remain a 'dependency of the business empire'. Laski's plan to detach lawyers from the profit motive, Stone replied, was 'almost the counsel of despair'. He was still optimistic that the law schools could train 'men for the bar who will place the moral and intellectual values in life above greed'.

An episode in Laski's relationship with Stone reveals the danger of Laski's unfortunate capacity to alter the record of events. Laski told him that Holmes's letters to him included numerous flattering comments about

Stone. Stone pestered Laski for examples and finally, in January 1938, Laski sent him a collection of 'extracts'. Stone was thrilled: 'I do not know when I have been so touched,' he wrote back to Laski. But when the Holmes–Laski correspondence was published after Stone and Laski were dead, not a single one of the excerpts appeared in the book. Laski, it turned out, had manufactured a string of compliments for Stone's satisfaction.

Laski was much closer to Senator Hugo Black, whom Roosevelt appointed to the Supreme Court in August 1937. Several weeks after the appointment Black visited Europe and at Roosevelt's suggestion met Laski. While he was in England, the news of Black's youthful Ku-Klux-Klan membership was made public and Black spent two weeks with Laski partly to avoid the press. Laski wrote to Frankfurter that Black's 'brief connection with the Klan doesn't persuade me that he is not now an excellent fellow. He is straight and honest, not very able but a fellow with all the right impulses.' In 1939 Laski dedicated a collection of his essays, *The Danger of Being a Gentleman*, 'to Hugo and Josephine Black', but their friendship, never that intense, waned during the war when Laski was unable to visit America. They exchanged no more than an occasional formal note, book or article after the war, even though Laski wrote to Lerner that he was drawn to Black's judicial activism and vigorous defence of free speech as an absolute right more than to the judicial self-restraint preached by Frankfurter.

By far the most important new friend Laski made in America in the 1930s was Franklin D. Roosevelt. Frankfurter and Roosevelt had been contemporaries at Harvard, but their friendship began in Washington during the war when Roosevelt, then Assistant Secretary of the Navy, had an office on the same floor as Frankfurter. Roosevelt offered Frankfurter the post of Solicitor-General in 1933, but he turned it down, preferring to remain behind the scenes as one of the President's 'brain-trusters'. Frankfurter arranged the first meeting of Roosevelt and Laski at the White House in the spring of 1935, writing to the President's personal secretary, Miss Lehand, that 'the President would find Laski delightful and stimulating'. He assured her that if the President were free in the evening 'for a long, leisurely talk on the present European, and more particularly English situation, Laski would be most informing.'

Laski's reputation for exaggeration haunts his friendship with Roosevelt. Memories of his many apocryphal stories about President Wilson make one suspicious of his frequent claims to have 'just seen the President', 'just visited the White House' or 'just got a letter from Frank Roosevelt'. Laski was certainly not always to be believed, but in the case of Roosevelt he was, in fact, not 'romancing'. The Roosevelt archives at Hyde Park, New York, contain extensive correspondence between the two men from 1935 to 1945. More important still is the clear evidence that Roosevelt enjoyed Laski's company. After their initial meeting in 1935, Laski wrote to Miss Lehand prior to each of his American visits informing her of his schedule and possible dates he could meet the President. On these letters are pencil scrawls written by the President: 'I want to see Laski, get hold of him somehow'; 'Get word to FF to tell HL as soon as he arrives that I shall be glad to see him when he comes to Washington'; 'Will you call HL this morning and ask him for lunch tomorrow'; and 'I want HL at H Park next week'.

As early as 1933 Frankfurter had been passing on to Roosevelt information from Laski. He began by providing an analysis of Ramsay MacDonald as a negotiator, along with a description of his mental habits obtained 'from a trusted friend of mine of great discernment'. In the next few years Frankfurter sent Roosevelt several books and articles by Laski and others chosen by Laski. Frankfurter, for example, made a particular point of seeing to it that Roosevelt saw Laski's *Daily Herald* articles on the abdication crisis. After 1936 Laski himself sent the President his pieces from the *Manchester Guardian* and the *Daily Herald* (but not the *Tribune*) in which he sought to explain the New Deal to the British. His letters to Roosevelt tended to focus on Labour Party politics and positions. When Labour was out of power throughout the decade, there were no defined channels for the dissemination of information about the Opposition, so the information was useful, albeit on occasion unreliable. Although Roosevelt complained jokingly that he needed a magnifying glass to read Laski's letters, he obviously took him seriously enough to invoke his authority. At a Cabinet meeting in January 1936, the President used a statement by Laski to make the point that the Supreme Court's decisions on New Deal legislation were grounded neither in law nor in the Constitution.

Laski's putative influence in the Oval Office prompted Brandeis to ask Laski in 1938 to speak against the British plan for partition in Palestine and urge the President to ask Ambassador Kennedy to intercede with Chamberlain. Benjamin Cohen, one of Roosevelt's brain-trusters, who had been a Frankfurter student, wrote to Laski in February 1938 asking him to write to the President supporting Frankfurter for Brandeis's seat on the Court. Laski's access to the White House was not lost on the British, either. In August 1939 Laski urged the President not to give in to the Japanese on the currency question and added, 'My colleagues on the NEC have, therefore, asked me to tell you this and to express the eager hope that you will put all the pressure on the Foreign Office to this end.'

Despite his conviction that the New Deal was a reformist effort to shore up capitalism with a more benevolent face, Laski thought highly of Roosevelt. The more practical Laski, keenly in tune with the deeper political realities in America, applauded the New Deal as a vigorous effort to bring about a more humane and just America. Roosevelt's willingness to take on Wall Street impressed Laski. In 1935 he praised Roosevelt as 'having the gift of leadership as no man save Lenin in my time'. Fifteen months later he thought 'Roosevelt is the best thing to happen to the USA since Lincoln was at the White House'. In October 1936 Laski told Frankfurter that he got 250 businessmen at the American Chamber of Commerce in London to cheer for Roosevelt. 'Different as his philosophy is from mine,' Laski told them, 'moderate and mild as his measures are, he has done more to maintain the faith of Western civilization in democratic government than any figure of our time.'

Laski wrote a good deal about Roosevelt for American audiences. In the *New Republic* he supported the President's extremely controversial plan to pack the Supreme Court with new justices sympathetic to the New Deal, which explains his desire to have Frankfurter replace Brandeis, who vigorously opposed the scheme. It was warranted, Laski wrote, so that 'the people of the United States shall have the assurance that the next four years of the New Deal shall not be stricken by the Supreme Court into impotence'. He also provided arguments from British and American political history which could be used by the President's supporters in Congress and in the press. For a different kind of audience Laski wrote in 1938 a review of 'The Public Papers and Addresses of Franklin D. Roosevelt' in the *University of Chicago Law Review*. By no means a revolutionary or a socialist, Roosevelt, according to Laski, sought 'to reform in order to preserve'. For Laski, Roosevelt, like Holmes, was a paternalistic patrician taming America's business class. Roosevelt had an 'aristocrat's compassion for the little man battling against economic forces beyond his control', but he had no doubts about the inherent adequacy of American economic institutions to adapt themselves to the crisis. Roosevelt saw America's problems produced by 'the malpractices of evil men', which filled him with indignation and disgust, never with the sense that what was wrong was the system itself. He saw the need for state action, however, to counter social and economic hardship, whatever its source, and he offered America an enhanced sense of community in place of rugged individualism.

Laski impressed on his American readers how different a European in 1938 found the mood of America from that of Europe in the grip of fear and despair. Roosevelt exuded courage, energy, imagination, humour, generosity, self-confidence and an eager willingness to experiment. By bringing to Washington legions 'of young men with ideas', Roosevelt had given the 'intellectual . . . a qualitatively different place in American life from anything previously known'. America under Roosevelt, Laski concluded, was a model to the world of a democracy not in doubt, not slow to meet crises. The Roosevelt experiment showed that there was still great vitality in 'the principle of responsible and democratic self-government'. When Roosevelt received a reprint from Laski of this article, he wrote to Laski that he wished 'it could be reprinted in some magazine with a million circulation'.

Caught up in Roosevelt's activist conception of the Presidency, Laski conceived the idea of writing a book which would provide both historical comparison with Roosevelt and a platform for his view of the office. Laski developed the argument in a series of lectures at the University of Indiana, and when it was ready for publication he tactfully asked Roosevelt if 'it would embarrass you if the book were dedicated to you? Please tell me frankly if it would.' Serenely unworried about any political risks, Roosevelt replied, 'Dear Harold, of course I shall be honoured and happy to have you dedicate the little book to me.' *The American Presidency*, dedicated 'to FDR with deep affection and respect', was Laski's bestselling book in America, in part because it was the July 1940 selection of the Book-of-the-Month Club, which had made sure, of course, that the blurb for the *Book-of-the-Month Club News* noted that the work was 'undisturbed by the Marxist interpretation of some of Laski's other books'. Apologia for Roosevelt and the New Deal it was, but *The American Presidency* was free of ideological pleading for socialism. As such, it has endured to this day as a seminal study of the Presidency, receiving canonical citation in the *New York Times Book Review* on the Sunday before George Bush's inauguration in 1988. Perhaps the classic polemic for a strong Presidency, it was a plea for the exercise of Presidential leadership against the competing claims of Congress. The Presidency, according to Laski, was 'the essential keystone of the political arch'; Congress, incapable of constructive leadership, was useful only for 'criticism and investigations'. Though Americans with their commitment to checks and balances were suspicious of concentrated power, 'the modern state requires a strong executive'. Once the champion of American federalism, with its grant of vast power to the individual states, and of localism and sectionalism, Laski now pronounced federalism 'obsolescent'. Only the central government and national power could deal with economic crisis, and at the heart of a powerful central government was a vigorous and strong President, embodied in Franklin Roosevelt, the very model of a modern President.

The American Presidency was well received in Britain and America. It was 'as thought-provoking an evaluation of American political practices as has been published in the United States in recent decades', according to the *American Political Science Review*; indeed, 'it takes its place along with the work of de Tocqueville and Bryce as an acute analysis of American political institutions by foreigners'. The *Manchester Guardian* wrote that 'as a piece of living political analysis, Mr Laski has done nothing better', and the *New Statesman* found it 'one of the best books ever written about the institutions of another country by a foreign observer'. It was already 'a classic in a field which boasts few classics', the *New Yorker* claimed, and the *Saturday Review of Literature* felt that 'Mr Laski has never written a more readable book . . . and since our unhappy outlook is for larger and more numerous crises, his prescription of a stronger Presidential leadership – a more continuous Presidential pioneering – is likely to remain sound for the indefinite future'.

However, there were criticisms aplenty of the book from the opponents of the New Deal and those who didn't share Laski's contempt for the impotence of a Congress without executive leadership. But *The American Presidency* also raised controversy because of dramatic plagiarism charges. In a letter to the *New Republic*, Stewart Alsop, then an editor of Doubleday, claimed that 'one of the strangest things about this new book is the extent to which Mr Laski depended upon W. E. Binkley's *Powers of the President* (1937) without any citing of it'. Alsop, who had worked as an editor on

Binkley's book, proceeded to list twenty-eight footnote citations that he suggested were lifted from Binkley, as well as various 'interpretations and conclusions' which were 'uncredited appropriations' by Laski. Laski replied that he had indeed read Binkley's book, though he didn't own it, and he might well have appropriated, given his agile memory, some of Binkley's themes and historical examples. He apologized for not being more explicit in his attribution. On the other hand, he insisted that Binkley surely had no copyright on commonplace conclusions about which President, for example, did or did not get along well with Congress. On six or seven occasions, in fact, the anecdotal or historical evaluations the two authors cited did overlap, and if Laski had been led to them by Binkley's book, courtesy would have suggested some acknowledgement. Since this was out of hundreds of such references and since the store of Presidential historical and anecdotal data is well known to scholars, Alsop's charges were, however, grossly exaggerated.

His book on the Presidency was a product of Laski's extended stay in America between September 1938 and May 1939. His time in America was full. In the autumn he taught in New York City at the Teachers' College of Columbia University, managing also in late October and early November to squeeze in some lectures at Radcliffe. In January Laski and Frida crossed the continent to the University of Washington, where he taught for three months. In April they returned to the East with a week of lecturing at the University of Denver, one lecture at the University of Wisconsin, a week at the University of Illinois and then the Presidency lectures at the University of Indiana. Once on the East Coast, Laski lectured at William and Mary College in Williamsburg, Virginia, before sailing from New York on 17 May 1939.

Diana, meanwhile, was studying at Radcliffe. After graduating from St Paul's School, she had gone in 1935 to Lady Margaret Hall, Oxford, where she obtained a third class degree. At Oxford she had met the shy and retiring Robin Mathewson, a classicist at Trinity, who graduated in 1938 with first class honours. Laski had found a position for the academic year 1938–9 for Robin to tutor classics at Harvard. Diana enrolled at Radcliffe for the year to study politics, which pleased Laski no end, since as he noted, 'she had been wheeled about the campus in a perambulator'. When Laski returned to Cambridge in late October to give a set of overflow lectures, his joy was undercut by discovering that Diana was unhappy with her studies. She was on a course with Laski's nemesis, William Yandell Elliott, who also disliked Frankfurter, Diana's very visible protector in Cambridge that autumn, all of which seemed to distress her. She apparently also resented 'being greeted as my daughter, everywhere, instead of being accepted on her own terms'. Laski wrote to Ada Comstock, the Radcliffe President. He added that Diana was also concerned about her relationship with 'young Mathewson', sensing that he and Frida were also perhaps cool towards him. In an impetuous act, not unlike that of her parents years earlier, Diana waited until they had sailed for England and then married Robin in Cambridge on 29 May. It was clearly an act of defiance, since Frida and Harold, their own example notwithstanding, felt that marriage to 'young Mathewson' was premature.

The Frankfurters were not at the wedding either, nor had they been in Cambridge at all that spring, because on 5 January 1939 Felix was nominated to serve as a justice on the Supreme Court. Laski was teaching at the University of Washington when the announcement was made. According to the *New York Times* story the next day, 'Professor Laski of London let out a shout of joy today when he learnt Felix Frankfurter had been named to the Supreme Court. Laski was jubilant.' He joined Frankfurter's Harvard Law School colleagues who were contributing money to buy his justice's robe. The cost was $89 and Laski's share $3, but before Frankfurter could don the robe there was the hurdle of the Senate Judiciary Committee's confirmation hearings and the problem of Frankfurter's radical reputation during the war, his association with the Sacco–Vanzetti case and his role as a New Deal brain-truster. Laski didn't help matters by the utter serendipity of timing by which his 'Why I am a Marxist' article reached the news-stands on 12 January, the second day of the nomination hearings.

When Frankfurter testified that day, Senator Pat McCarran, a conservative Nevada Democrat, asked him: 'Are you acquainted with Harold Laski?' 'Oh yes, very well,' Frankfurter replied, and he proceeded to tell how they met and what good friends they were. McCarran then asked if Frankfurter had read any of Laski's publications and when he answered, 'Oh, certainly,' the Senator asked if he agreed with his doctrine. Frankfurter replied, 'I trust you will not deem me boastful if I say I have many friends who have written many books, and I shouldn't want to be charged with all the views in books by all my friends.' McCarran pressed for a simpler answer and the nominee responded that Laski had written 'twelve or fifteen or twenty books'; he was extraordinarily prolific and it was impossible to say one agreed with his doctrine when it wasn't clear he had a doctrine. Having had enough evasion, McCarran held up a copy of *Communism* and asked if Frankfurter subscribed to his doctrine as expressed there. Frankfurter turned the tables and asked if McCarran had read the book. 'Casually glanced at it,' was the Senator's answer. 'What would you say is its doctrine, Senator?' McCarran answered, 'The doctrine is the advocacy of communism' to which Frankfurter shot back, 'You see, we could debate all day on whether that is in fact the doctrine of that book.' McCarran, not at all deterred, switched to, 'If it advocates the doctrine of Marxism, would you agree with it?' Frankfurter's passionate answer to this question moved the audience to cheers and the committee to unanimous approval of the nomination.

> Senator, I do not believe that you have ever taken an oath to support the Constitution of the United States with fewer reservations than I have or would now. Nor do I believe you are more attached to the theories and practice of Americanism than I am. I rest my answer on that statement.

'Why I am a Marxist' created a huge stir at the University of Washington. Laski's appointment for ten weeks as a lecturer at a fee of $5,000 had been bitterly opposed the previous autumn when it was announced by the University's Political Science Department Chairman. The President of the University of Washington stood by the department's choice and Laski came, the student newspaper applauding his arrival with the headline AT LONG LASKI. The preliminary opposition was tame compared to the furore generated by Laski's article. The local chapter of the Daughters of the American Revolution, a national conservative group of women who claimed connection to the founders of America, demanded that the Washington State legislature investigate communist activities at the university. 'Professor Laski is a scholar,' their spokesman declared, 'but we can find men with just as high scholastic attainment here in the United States who are thorough Americans.' Several state legislators proposed an investigation of Laski's appointment and a resolution denouncing him was prepared by the Republican leader of the state's House of Representatives, though it never came to a vote. The legislature did, however, reject by sixty-four to thirty-two a counter-resolution to invite Laski to speak to a joint session of the body. Only a group of CIO trade unions in Seattle endorsed Laski's appearance at the university. Roosevelt, who had had his own political problems over the years with the Daughters of the American Revolution, and whose own daughter was living in Seattle at the time, was devilish in his response to the fracas. He wrote to Laski:

> A delightful description has come from Anna telling of the furore you have caused at the women's clubs, golf courses, pink tea-parties and university circles. May the furore increase in furiosity. Come and see me as soon as you get back.

In his reply Laski noted that he was doing good by Roosevelt in his speeches, pointing out 'to these red-necked lumber millionaires' that 'the man in the White House is a moderate compared to me'. Laski took his message to Seattle businessmen, to newspaper publishers, to 400 school teachers, and to over 200 men and women at the First Christian Church. His public lectures at the university – on Spain, Labour Party policies and nationalism – were attended by thousands of people. Students were captivated by the celebrity who 'invited all of us to drop in to his office'. The university daily paper noted that as Laski spoke,

> visitors were crowding through the doors, squeezing themselves along the walls and even on the speaker's platform in their anxiety to hear the lecture. Regular students found strangers occupying their seats. Laski has found every lecture hall jammed to capacity so far. Applause, rare in the classroom, frequently follows his remarks.

Frida also got into the act. She spoke to the Seattle Women's Club, and when Laski's ever-recurring sore throat and flu put him in bed for over a week she was interviewed repeatedly by the papers. She felt like a rare specimen, a socialist exhibit in the great American Northwest, who puzzled people unfamiliar with the species. She made no bones about her own Marxism and confessed that she couldn't understand American political vocabulary: 'Everything that is bad you call communism.' The New Deal, which many at the Women's Club called socialist, was 'our 1906 liberalism'. Always the austere, self-denying leftist, Frida insisted that she and her husband were 'not socialists on the platform and capitalists at home . . . We have given up golf. We don't play bridge and we don't drink. If there is nothing to do in the evening, we go to bed and get some sleep.' If these species peculiarities were not sufficiently damning and un-American, then she must have convinced her listeners by noting that she had had enough of people complaining about her husband's stipend of $5,000 from the foundation sponsoring his visit. With the money Laski had made so far in America, she told the *Seattle Times*, 'He's been able to send $11,000 for refugees in Spain and he's been able to get out of Germany I don't know how many refugees.'

After this rare variety of Marxist socialists made their slow way back to London, Laski wrote his almost obligatory observations of his visit. Two articles appeared in the *New Republic* in July 1939. Laski was effusive in praise of the New Deal, which 'brought a remarkable host of able men to Washington' and taught the ordinary American that 'the state is, for good or ill, a positive instrument by whose activities the contours of his life are set'. There was a new vitality in American letters and culture, he wrote, with Dos Passos, Steinbeck, MacLeish, Edmund Wilson, O'Neill and Odets. The universities pleased him less, though he did single out Max Lerner and the historian Louis Hacker for praise. The division in the labour movement between the CIO and the AFL troubled him and he made it clear he sided with John L. Lewis and the CIO. His problems with the Washington State legislature and his new conviction that federalism was obsolescent made self-evident 'the unfitness of the states as units of American government'. Businessmen were still the principal villains in American life: resenting Roosevelt for betraying his class, they were 'as blind to the needs of their time as the French nobility before 1789'. Returning, however, to the grim realities of Europe, Laski had only praise for America:

> To travel through America today is to be conscious that, in a significant way, humanity is on the march. There is a potential renaissance on the American horizon. There is the prospect, if it has the chance of fruition, that America may come to count spiritually in the twentieth century as it counted in the last generation of the eighteenth. It may become the inspiration of the oppressed and the disinherited all over the world. What people could ask for a nobler destiny?

Laski told *New Republic* readers that he had left America with 'its immense energy and exhilaration' to return to a Britain which 'seems strained and fatigued' as its statesmen tried to avoid war. While Laski was away, the Labour Party leadership had resoundingly repudiated the Popular

Front, the idea that Laski, Cripps and others on the Labour left had developed after the demise of the United Front in the wake of the worsening international situation, Hitler's annexation of Austria in March 1938, Nazi pressure on Czechoslovakia and Chamberlain's apparent willingness to forsake the League of Nations and collective security with a policy of appeasement. In the Popular Front the Labour Party would have joined with Liberals and disaffected Tories like Churchill, Eden and Amery to oppose Chamberlain in Parliament and in an electoral pact to choose a candidate to contest Chamberlain's followers in each constituency. It was a dramatic about-face for Laski, Cripps and the Labour left, since they now suggested that the achievement of true socialism had to be put aside in a 'democratic alliance for peace'.

Lloyd George and his small group of radical Liberals supported the idea, which explains his enthusiastic support of the Left Book Club at its 1939 rally. Macmillan's 'middle way' group of Tories seemed interested; but most important of all, after Munich, Churchill and Eden made overtures for an electoral alliance with Labour. Dalton and Attlee for the official Labour leadership were initially willing to talk, but the trade unions were adamantly opposed to a Popular Front, not least because the CPGB was strongly in favour of it. The leadership also had to buck a tradition entrenched since 1931 that set the party against 'weakening of party policy to accommodate other political elements'. Nor was the leadership above capitalizing on the Labour left's 180-degree turn. Attlee drove this home in the *Daily Herald*:

> The swing ... from the advocacy of a rigid and exclusive unity of the working classes to a demand for an alliance with the capitalists, and from insistence on the need for a government carrying out a socialist policy to an appeal to put socialism into cold storage for the duration of the international crisis, is a remarkable phenomenon ...

Laski used the *Nation* in April 1938 to outline his support of the Popular Front. 'The British government is confused and fumbling,' he wrote, 'its habits aid, consciously or unconsciously, the policy of the dictators at every turn.' Only an alliance could reverse the course in Parliament and most decisively at the next election, even if 'Mr Lloyd George and Mr Churchill, notably, are simply British imperialists whose anti-fascism is much more a recognition that the dictators are a threat to the British Empire than a recognition of the bankruptcy of capitalism'. Laski added a final thought, which was exactly the kind of argument that kept official Labour from supporting the initiative. He insisted that inclusion of the CPGB be part of the scheme, because 'to any sort of Popular Front against fascism (and Chamberlain) the United Front of working-class parties is a necessary prelude'.

A month later Laski, Cripps, Pritt and Wilkinson submitted a lengthy memorandum advocating a Popular Front to the party's National Executive Committee. The NEC met on 5 May and rejected the memorandum by seventeen votes to four, with only the four drafters of the proposal voting for it. None the less, the Labour left continued the Popular Front campaign in earnest. The Left Book Club made it a centrepiece of rallies, discussion groups and *Left News*. In addition, the August 1938 virtual take-over of *Tribune* by the Left Book Club, which placed Laski and Gollancz on the *Tribune*'s board of directors, provided the Popular Front with another platform.

The abandonment of Czechoslovakia in late September 1938 gave the Popular Front an even greater urgency. With Laski in America, Cripps resubmitted the memo drafted the previous year to the NEC in January 1939 only to see it again rejected by seventeen votes to three. Undeterred, Cripps circulated the memorandum to Labour MPs and constituency parties. The NEC ordered him to stop, and when he persisted they expelled him. Only Wilkinson dissented; Pritt was sick and Laski was in Seattle. Unwilling to go along with Cripps's defiant disregard for party discipline, however, they did not leave the party in protest. When criticized for not returning to fight for Cripps, Laski replied that he had been given leave of absence by the NEC, was 6,000 miles away and that he in fact did not approve of Cripps's refusal to accept collective committee responsibility when he continued to circulate the memorandum after its defeat. Laski saw greater harm in leaving the party than in accepting its discipline, and despite his admiration for Cripps he worried about 'his Messianic complex ... He badly needs the discipline of teamwork,' Laski wrote to Frankfurter.

Cripps turned next to a national 'Petition Campaign' at the constituency party level. People were asked, non-Labourites as well, to sign a six-point petition calling upon 'parties of progress to act together' to organize a peace alliance with the Soviet Union and France to oppose fascism, and an electoral alliance 'to drive the National government from office'. Liberals like Acland, Keynes and Lloyd George supported Cripps's campaign, but the trade unions were shocked at his flagrant disregard for party discipline. One TUC member derided the 'Bloomsbury revolutionaries', and another trade unionist, sounding much like Orwell, pleaded, 'Away with those senseless females and those ladylike young gentlemen who waste their time advocating everything from the establishment of nudist colonies to pensions for indigent cats.' When two MPs, Bevan and Strauss, accompanied Cripps on a national speaking tour for the 'Petition Campaign', the NEC gave them seven days to desist from the campaign or be expelled from the party. On 30 March Bevan and Strauss were expelled.

Laski was ill and unable to attend the party conference in late May. Cripps, Bevan and Strauss sat in the visitors' gallery. Cripps was allowed to speak; but not about the Popular Front, only on the issue of his expulsion from the party. Speaking for the NEC to justify its actions was Dalton, who in the course of his remarks surprised the delegates by offering 'a tribute to my comrade Harold Laski'. He, like Cripps, had fought for the Popular Front at the NEC in May 1938 but had accepted the principle of majority rule, and not only 'did he loyally accept the decision once given', he even cooperated in the drafting of the executive's statement explaining its vote, which gave both sides of the case. When the card vote was taken, the expulsion of Cripps and the others was reaffirmed by 2,100,000 against 402,000. Three weeks later Laski seconded an NEC motion, which was defeated by twenty to four, to readmit the three expelled MPs. Morrison's alternative motion to reject their admission was defeated thirteen to twelve, and a sub-committee was appointed to decide the issue. Laski was on the sub-committee and he crafted the recommendation of readmission requiring the rebels to agree to three conditions: an expression of regret; a promise not to campaign against the party; and a declaration that they accepted the constitution, programme, principles and policy of the party. Bevan and Strauss eventually agreed to a slightly modified statement of contrition; Cripps refused. He would remain an independent member of Parliament until the next election in 1945.

That same month, July 1939, Laski wrote forcefully about the need for party unity in Left News. With the prospect of an election not far off, if there were no war, the overriding urgency of defeating Chamberlain meant that 'we need all the unity we can mobilize', Laski wrote. 'A party is as strong as its discipline. It cannot fight effectively unless its members cheerfully accept majority decisions and assist in implementing them.' While he accepted the majority view on the NEC and in the party, Laski insisted that he would still work hard to convert the party to his perspective. Labour, he reiterated, would win elections only if it were committed to a real socialist alternative. The party had to replace its Fabian faith in a neutral state seeking the interests of the whole community with an understanding of the reality of class conflict. The Left Book Club, he urged, must educate the labour movement so that it 'really understands socialism'.

Munich had finally galvanized Labour unity on the international question. All segments opposed the government's acquiescence to Hitler's threats of force as the party roles since 1935 were reversed, Labour speaking out for national resistance and the Conservatives in the National government talking about peace and conciliation. Even as huge crowds and virtually all the press cheered Chamberlain for snatching peace from the jaws of war, Labour leaders from Citrine on the right to Laski on the left indignantly denounced Chamberlain's appeasement, worked out, they claimed, by the Astors' pro-German Cliveden set.

Laski heard the news of Munich shortly after his arrival in America. He had warned, before Chamberlain's trips, that 'the future integrity of Czechoslovakia depended on whether France and England would stand firm and resist aggression by force if necessary'. When Chamberlain flew to Munich a second time in September, an American reporter wrote that Laski said of the venture: 'If at first you didn't concede, fly, fly again.' Laski was in Cambridge, Massachusetts, the very day that Chamberlain announced 'Peace in our time', and when a friend asked what he thought, Laski replied, 'If you will forgive the language, I'd like to hang the bastard high as Haman.' In a speech at the Canadian Club of Montreal that December, Laski blasted what he took to be Chamberlain's concern that resisting fascism would benefit only Bolshevism. At the University of Washington Laski repeatedly told his students that if Britain and France had joined with the Soviet Union and threatened to meet dismemberment of Czechoslovakia by force with force, Hitler would have backed down.

Unlike others in the Labour Party and the few disaffected Tories, Laski's public indignation over appeasement was strongly informed by his fears over the fate of European Jewry. In an article in the *Tribune* with an uncannily chilling historical prescience, Laski wrote: '5 MILLION PEOPLE

FACE LIVING DEATH'. Failure to stop Hitler, he wrote, threatened not only
the Jews in Germany and Austria, but the large Jewish communities in
Poland and Romania. He was horrified at the indifference to this probable
consequence of concessions to Hitler. 'The change in temper among people
who realize the brutality the Jews in Central Europe daily confront is
tragic. We have reached a stage where man's inhumanity to man is taken
for granted. We remain silent and ineffective.'

His most detailed analysis of appeasement appeared in an article he wrote
for *Left News* several months after his return from America. He
acknowledged the popular desire for peace and the sense that the grave
injustices done to the Germans at Versailles might explain some of their
demands. But none of this justified yielding to Hitler in Czechoslovakia.
Chamberlain had 'enormously strengthened the Nazi dictatorship. On any
showing he has weakened all the influences in Germany which might have
made for moderation.' Laski repeated the line of the Labour left.
Chamberlain, Halifax and most of the British elite saw no sacrifice to
Hitler as too great if war meant social revolution and the overthrow of the
capitalist system. 'So long as British capitalism is left alone, Hitler's assault
on democratic institutions is not their concern.' Moreover, Laski contended,
behind Munich lay the hope that Hitler's ambitions lay eastwards.

In August 1939, when Britain finally guaranteed the Poles it would fight
if Hitler attacked, pressure mounted in Britain for talks with Russia about
an alliance. The British dragged their feet and the Russians assumed that in
fact Britain feared a Soviet victory against Germany more than a German
move on them. This was the background for the utterly unexpected news
of 22 August that Soviet Russia, the 1930s' leading anti-fascist regime, had
signed a non-aggression pact with Hitler. Laski wasted no time in announcing what he thought of it. The very next day he requested an emergency
meeting of the NEC to deal with the 'betrayal of democracy and peace'.

Germany invaded Poland on 1 September and on 3 September Britain
declared war on Germany. That day Harry Pollitt drafted and circulated a
pamphlet 'How to Win the War', in which he declared that the 'British
Communist Party supports the war, believing it to be a just war supported by
the whole working class and all friends of democracy in Britain'. Radio
Moscow, however announced on 14 September that 'this war is an imperialist and predatory war for a new redivision of the world'. The Central
Committee of the CPGB met on 3 October, with Palme Dutt supporting

the Moscow line and Pollitt dissenting. After a vote of twenty-one to three, Dutt replaced Pollitt as General Secretary. In a supportive letter to Pollitt, Laski wrote, 'I had hoped in early August for such an Anglo-Soviet policy as meant the unity of all anti-fascist forces against Hitler. Now I cannot understand the Stalin line. The only line I can take is that in the interests of the workers all over the world we must destroy fascism.' To Alfred Cohn, Laski wrote, 'the communists here show an irresponsibility that is beneath contempt. Strachey says to me it's more important to destroy Chamberlain than Hitler. It is the raving of a lunatic.' Laski wrote to Roosevelt that Russia's action left America as the only hope for freedom in the world. He urged the President to keep America out of the war, for it was

> more than ever vital to go on full steam ahead with the New Deal. The more the US can now show successful results in the working of democracy, the greater the part it can play in the making of a new orientation of world direction. I cannot think of a greater contribution to peace than this, the greater because the Soviet Union has, I fear, committed one of the supreme psychological blunders of history. I understand its distress, but it has thrown away an initiative which would have enabled it to share in the moral leadership of the world. Now I see no prospect of trust in its good faith for a long period of time.

The Hitler–Stalin Pact and the position of the CPGB was fought over in the pages of the *Left News* with the opposing sides immediately clear. A full-scale debate between Laski and Strachey appeared in the December 1939 issue. Laski wrote with an uncharacteristic fiery passion in criticizing the CPGB's discovery in October that Chamberlain, in deciding at long last to stand up to Hitler, was waging an imperialist war. Nothing in Nazism had changed since 1933, Laski wrote, except the intensification of the rule of the Gestapo and the concentration camp. Trade-union suppression, terrorism and the six-year pogrom against the Jews continued unabated, so why now oppose a war against the brutal, inhumane Nazi murderers? Strachey argued that a victory for Britain 'would result in a world of oppression and reaction ... a world of fundamentally the same character as would the victory of the German government'. A negotiated peace with Germany was the proper course of action. Large numbers of letters to the editor, many of them critical of Laski, poured in, and Laski responded in March, incredulous that so many in the Left Book Club believed that 'the Soviet Union can do no wrong'.

Laski wrote a long letter to the *New York Times* in early October explaining why Labour supported the war. The party had no sympathy for British imperialism and it realized that Chamberlain 'was largely responsible' for the 'disastrous decision' of the Soviet Union to conclude a pact with Hitler. But that didn't make Chamberlain more the enemy than Hitler. The Labour Party, even its far left, supported the war, he told the Americans, 'because our purposes cannot exist in the jackboot, concentration-camp world of Hitlerism'.

Laski's immense reputation on the Labour left prompted the party leadership to enlist him for its official publications describing its support of the war. They wanted Laski specifically to combat the communist line which they feared would cut into working-class support of the war. Laski obliged, and in the pamphlet *Is This an Imperialist War?* he went to the heart of the matter: 'Critical though the Labour Party has always been of the incompleteness of British democracy, it has never doubted that, with all its limitations, this democracy is infinitely preferable to the slavery of the Nazi system.' He rejected claims that a working-class party could not support a war waged by a capitalist government and should call for an immediate peace conference. The crucial point, he wrote, was that this was not a war as in 1914 between similar kinds of states. Socialists had to distinguish in any historical situation between the progressive and reactionary elements. Laski ridiculed those who claimed that Britain was itself a fascist state, no different from Germany; the very unimpeded activity of the CPGB in opposing the war, he noted, gave the lie to that. Laski then introduced for the first time a theme that would become his trademark during the war years. Labour would cooperate with the war effort, but it saw the war's objectives differently from Chamberlain. The Prime Minister was interested only in the defeat of an enemy and sought to exclude social issues from war aims. Labour, on the other hand, Laski wrote, would keep raising the ideological nature of the war and of the need for socialism to replace capitalism, so there would be no more wars. Meanwhile, one had to choose the lesser evil and the choice was clear.

The Labour Party . . . must support Mr Chamberlain in so far as it is his clear purpose to defeat Hitler . . . For in destroying the menace of Hitler, socialists are not seeking to save British imperialism at the expense of the German worker. They are seeking at once to liberate the German worker from a tyranny which threatens our lives as well, and to maintain the opportunity of liberating the British worker also from the bonds of capitalism in this country.

Labour supported the war and it applauded Chamberlain's decision to bring Churchill and Eden into the War Cabinet in September, but it refused to join the National government while it was led by Chamberlain. During the eight months from the declaration of war until Hitler's invasion of Holland and Belgium in May 1940, the 'phoney war' as it was called, life went on in its normal routines in Britain, even with the evacuations of over a million and a half people, mainly women and young children, from the industrial areas. Laski was ill throughout this winter with more than his usual share of respiratory ailments. Though he seldom wrote about his health, he did confide to Cohn, his doctor friend, that 'I have not been well all winter. Still, I have made efforts to do all I must do. It has made for rather an exceptional strain.' All he 'must do' involved his customary over-extended schedule that included, in addition to teaching, answering the communist critics of Labour's support of the war, interminable discussions on the NEC about Labour's war aims and, as always, substantial writing for the party.

Throughout the winter Laski urged the NEC to make Labour publish its own war aims, especially since the conflict postponed indefinitely a general election. Laski's motives were overtly ideological, to commit Labour to a vision of a postwar socialist European order as well as to the evolution, even during the war, of a socialist Britain. His more moderate colleagues on the NEC insisted, therefore, on multi-committee vetting of all documents Laski worked on and of constant review by Attlee, Dalton and Morrison. Laski persisted in his efforts, despite his poor health. Without parliamentary obligations and with his ready and facile pen, he moved drafts back and forth from the International Affairs Sub-Committee to the Press, Publicity and Campaign Committee, and to the whole Executive. He sometimes lost on specific issues, such as the rejection of including a lengthy discussion of Indian independence in the war aims. A resolution he offered suggesting Labour open exploratory talks to see if Soviet Russia could be talked out of the alliance with Germany was defeated by a vote of thirteen to two.

Laski was much more successful in shaping the written material produced by the NEC, often doing much of it himself. He published a pamphlet in November 1939, *The Labour Party, the War and the Future*, which explained that Labour's commitment to remove the causes which brought Hitler to power, deeply rooted in the economic and social system, ruled out joining Chamberlain's government. He played a central role in writing another Labour pamphlet *Labour, the War and Peace*, which appeared in February 1940, condemning the Russian invasion of Finland and committing Labour to fight the war to victory and to the birth of a new Germany as part of 'a peaceful commonwealth of free peoples'. In a further indication of the use the Executive was making of him, Laski presented the party's 'Home Policy' for the Bournemouth party conference in May 1940. Even in this dark hour the party was committed, he told the conference, to economic planning, industrial reorganization, a fairer distribution of wealth and improved health, housing and education. The last sentences of the 'Home Policy' statement were vintage Laski prose and a theme he would constantly return to over the next five years.

> War never leaves a nation where it found it, and it can never be justified save as it elevates the conscience of a nation to new and nobler purposes. If it is a grave catastrophe, it also holds a supreme opportunity. If, before it is once more too late, we can summon to our aid the vision and the courage, we may yet use this war to lay the foundations of a juster and more generous life.

By the time Laski addressed the party conference on 13 May, fundamental changes had occurred in British politics. Three days earlier Chamberlain had stepped down as Prime Minister, replaced by Winston Churchill. The dramatic turn of events had begun on 6 May, when the Commons began a two-day debate on the failure of British forces in their first engagement with Hitler's troops in Norway. Labour pushed for a vote of no confidence in Chamberlain's conduct of the war and was joined by forty Tories with another forty abstaining. The years of anger and frustration burst forth from the small band of his own party's critics as L. S. Amery, quoting Oliver Cromwell's dismissal of the Long Parliament, shouted at the Prime Minister: 'You have sat too long here for any good you have been doing. Depart, I say, and let us have done with you. In the name of God, go.' Chamberlain gave way to Churchill, even though as

First Lord of the Admiralty he bore some responsibility for the Norwegian fiasco. Churchill's speeches in the Commons since he had joined the Cabinet the previous September had stirred Westminster and the country. Convinced that the proper execution of the war required the cooperative participation of the labour movement, Churchill asked the Labour Party to join his War Cabinet as equal partners, and they agreed. The day that Churchill became Prime Minister, the 'phoney war' came to an end as Hitler's troops invaded Belgium, Holland and Luxemburg. In his first speech to the Commons as head of the government on 13 May, the same day that Laski spoke for the NEC to the Labour Party conference, Churchill told the House, 'I have nothing to offer but blood, toil, tears and sweat.'

The man Laski's father had rescued thirty-five years earlier at a desperate moment at the start of his career, the man the thirteen-year-old Laski had accompanied around Manchester as he gave the speeches the boy had watched him practise before the mirrors at Smedley House, was now in charge of defending civilized values against Hitler's barbarism. Laski was pleased. Some months earlier he had written in the weekly *Time and Tide* that the times called for Churchill, who, despite his obvious defects, which included his occasional 'lapses from balance in judgement' and his 'naturally rhetorical mind', had in the past five years 'been recognized by the whole democratic world as its pre-eminent spokesman seeking to free Europe from the Gestapo and the concentration camp'. Laski was more emotional about Churchill in a letter to Alfred Cohn that spring.

> It is an evil thing we are fighting. I hate British imperialism, I admit the gravest faults in British policy, I loathe the inequalities and snobberies of British life. When all is said against them that can be said, I think anyone not engaged in this conflict and prepared to take a judicial view would have honestly to say that a world in which we are a powerful nation is less ugly and less brutal than one in which Hitler's Germany is victorious. And so my choice is made; and when I listened as yesterday to Churchill in the House saying that we would sink every German ship in the sea . . . I cheered and felt that I was right to cheer.

PART IV

DISILLUSION:

THE 1940s

CHAPTER SEVENTEEN

War and 'Revolution by Consent'

Throughout the war years, when Laski worked so hard and unsuccessfully to convince Britain that the purpose of the struggle was more than the defeat of fascism, he and Frida spent most of the week apart. The LSE had moved to Cambridge in late 1939 after its buildings on Houghton Street were taken over by the Ministry of Economic Warfare. Because of his NEC work Laski spent part of the week in Cambridge, part in London and part in Little Bardfield in Essex, where Frida spent most of the war. His weekly regimen, always lived at a hectic pace, now seemed frantic. He continued his industrial court work, and to the workers' education lecturing he added almost weekly talks to army and RAF camps, American air bases and local Labour Party conferences and meetings. He also continued to write, adding to the books and usual journals and newspapers even more commitments to write weekly pieces for the *New Statesman*, the *Glasgow Forward* and *Reynolds News*. He also intensified his BBC appearances. This schedule was managed with no secretary and with the uncertainty of interminable train rides (during which much of the journalism was written) whose duration was always unpredictable given bombings, track damage or the need to make way for troop transit.

The LSE was given space by Peterhouse, Cambridge's oldest college, and Laski usually came up on Wednesday night or Thursday morning to teach his classes, see his graduate students and leave after a lecture on Saturday morning. He stayed at a rooming house run by Lance Beales's wife, Taffy. If no rooms were available there Laski went to the Peterhouse porter's home. The small close-knit community of LSE students and faculty who spent the war at Cambridge saw a good deal more of each other than they ever did in London. The school had eating privileges at Peterhouse, but after Laski once went to High Table and was treated poorly by a resident don, he declined to return. He had a tiny office across from King's College above a chemist's shop. It was bare but for a picture of Frida and a desk and two chairs. On the days that he was there, he lectured for about four hours and saw students for two or three hours. The LSE lectures were open to Cambridge students as well, and his Saturday morning class was immensely popular. Laski, too outspoken to be brought into the wartime civil service like Tawney, was the most senior LSE faculty member during the war. Walking or riding his bike with his long black overcoat and his shapeless black hat, stopping invariably to talk to American GIs in town from the nearby air base, he was again a student favourite. They remember him queuing up for coffee and making jokes; with the arrival of the tiny frail figure, any stuffy, dreary room came to life.

In his constant comings and goings Laski had several close calls. His train was once strafed by machine-gun fire from a low-flying plane, and on a speaking trip to the north-east his hotel was bombed and he fell through three floors, amazingly unhurt. In London, especially during the blitz, he often went to his basement or to a shelter he had built in the garden where he would 'read a little, sleep a little and often manage to write a little'. Twice, in July and August 1944, his London house was hit by a German doodle-bug and made uninhabitable. When this was reported in the *New York Times*, anxious letters arrived from Huebsch, Cohn, Justice Black and Frankfurter, who were all assured that Laski was 'as right as rain' and that miraculously 'all my books are safe'. The general dislocations of the war and Laski's sense that his letters were being opened curtailed his correspondence with his American friends, so when one received a letter he passed it around, as Huebsch did in 1943 when Laski wrote how 'unbearable it is to see one's students go to war one by one and then suddenly to find their name in a casualty list'. His American friends sent food parcels to the Laskis during the war and Frankfurter, Cohn, Morris Cohen, Eugene Meyer, Huebsch and Lerner usually remembered to send chocolates for Laski with the sugar, cheese and tinned food. With her characteristic austerity, Frida told Huebsch that 'we ought not to get parcels that others don't have from the USA. It's all "fare alike now", and none too soon either.'

Frida came to London occasionally for her Fulham Council work and after 1942 for her magistrate's duties as an appointed Justice of the Peace. She was an air-raid warden in Essex and an organizer of activities for the large number of evacuees who were resettled in Little Bardfield. Laski wrote to Justice Black that 'Frida more or less runs the village, organizer of the things that keep relations human'. Throughout the war two cockney boys, evacuees from Whitechapel, lived with the Laskis in their country cottage, forced to endure Harold's efforts to teach them not to drop their h's.

Through the tumult of war Laski continued to have 'at homes' in London, though by no means weekly, and to invite people to Little Bardfield. In Cambridge he often had American GIs to the crowded rooming house for an evening, and in London he invited Harvard friends like the historian Crane Brinton, his former student, and the great scholar of American Puritanism, Perry Miller, both of whom were working for Intelligence at the US embassy. Through Edward R. Murrow Laski befriended a large group of American reporters and radio people which included Clifton Daniels of the *New York Times* and Eric Sevareid of CBS News. Sevareid actually sat in on some of Laski's lectures and later wrote that he 'electrified me' and 'brought me alive intellectually'.

Cutting the grimness of the war was the Laskis' joy at becoming grandparents. Diana and Robin had a son, Christopher, in June 1941 and Frida and Harold saw a good deal of mother and child. Robin was in the services, stationed in Britain throughout the war but seldom able to get home. Laski loved to have Christopher at Little Bardfield, though he would get quite cross when his hidden cache of chocolate was uncovered and raided. Diana was close to both her parents, but there was some distance between Harold and Robin, who after the war taught classics at St Paul's school and then at Exeter University. In spite of Robin's double first and his extremely good looks, Laski found him too urbane, preciously elegant and aloof, as well as academically lazy. Robin, in turn, though initially somewhat in awe of Laski, came to regard him as an egotist who always wanted people around him, hanging on his every word. Robin's Tory politics also drove a wedge between them. Diana was herself generally apolitical, but she became quite religious. Confirmed in the Church of England, she devoted much of her time to Christian charity work.

Diana lived in Oxford throughout the war in order to be closer to Robin's army base. For a while she shared a cottage with her cousin, Neville's daughter Marghanita, and for a while she even lived with Neville and his wife, Cissie, who had a house in Oxford. She then acquired her own flat to which Robin came when on leave. The rivalry of Neville and

Laski seems to have survived unto the next generation, since Laski wrote to Frida in 1944 from a visit to Manchester that 'Neville "the great man" was here full of Marghanita's book', in a tone indicating a wistful inability to make such claims of distinction for Diana. Marghanita would eventually become a prominent postwar literary and TV personality, while Diana devoted herself to her four sons and church work. Laski was also capable of generous solicitude for his niece, especially if it were at the expense of his brother. Several years before, Laski had written a note to Frankfurter the bitterness of which indicated the reopening of old wounds.

> The KC's daughter is engaged to a CHRISTIAN. He writes, 'We cannot, of course, approve the match, but we shall endeavour to do our duty just as though it was a normal marriage.' Can you bear that? . . . I wrote a note to my people telling them to be nice to the child, but I received no answer. These are the people who feel strongly about persecution.

Nathan Laski died on 24 October 1941. Still at seventy-eight a strong, tall and healthy man, he was knocked down crossing the street by a motor car and died shortly afterwards in his own beloved Manchester Jewish Hospital. Laski went straight to Manchester and spent the ritual mourning week with his mother, Mabel, and Neville. As sad as he was, he was pleased, he wrote to Frida, that 'the happy refusal of mother to have any prayers here in the house has made it less distressing than I feared'. Laski wrote to Frankfurter shortly after the death that despite all his limitations, Nathan was 'a grand person in that he did really live to fight for other people and, unlike so many English Jews, did not fear to insist to eminent Englishmen that the Jew ought not to have to go cap in hand to them for his rights'. A week after Nathan's death, Laski received a personal note from the Prime Minister, who had not forgotten.

> I know how much you and your brother will feel his loss. It is for you the severance of a link with childhood which can never be replaced. He was a very good man whose heart overflowed with human feeling and whose energies were tirelessly used for other people and large causes. I feel I have lost a friend, and all my memories of Manchester and Cheetham are veiled in mourning.

The elder Laski had lived long enough to see his name, or at least his son's, cleared in the High Court of Justice. In August 1940 the right-wing and anti-Semitic magazine *Truth* ran an article called 'Contrast in Patriotism' in which the editor reflected about the official list of casualties during the Battle of France. He noted the names of the Duke of Northumberland, the Earl of Aylesford, the Earl of Coventry and Lord Frederick Cambridge, all killed in action, but did not see 'any names like Gollancz, Laski and Strauss'. Perhaps, he concluded, 'what happened in the last war is being repeated in this'. The ancient families of Britain, the hated ruling class of the left-wing diatribes, were sacrificing their sons to keep these families safe in their homes 'which in the last war they did not don uniforms to defend'.

G. R. Strauss, Laski's left-wing Labour colleague and son of a well-to-do Tory MP businessman, had been seventeen at the end of the previous war and sued for libel, recovering substantial damages. Gollancz had been in the war, though never at the front, and he demanded and received a published apology from *Truth*. Harold, of course, had been in Canada and America during the war, so he did nothing. Neville, on the other hand, sued for libel and in August 1941 was awarded £525 in damages. The defence offered by *Truth* was that in fact Neville was not the intended Laski reference, because 'anybody who knows you and your brother would at once realize that the person who was being attacked in *Truth* was your brother, Professor Harold Laski. He has not brought an action against anyone. He has not, but I could give the reason why.' Neville did help his brother by pointing out to the court that Harold had tried to enlist in the First World War, but had been rejected as medically unfit. Neville's comment was uncharacteristically charitable to Laski, for the tension that had existed since childhood burst into open animosity after their father's death. Neville was convinced that Laski's political infamy had ruined his chances for judicial preferment. When a Tory Party leader once suggested that Neville contest a parliamentary seat, Neville reportedly replied, 'Hasn't the Laski family done enough for the Tories? Why do you need another?' A Laski student remembers sharing a platform with Neville in 1942 and being told, 'You are, I gather, a protégé of my brother, you unfortunate young man. If you haven't found him out yet as a phoney, then you never will.'

Laski's move to Canada in 1914 haunted him during the Second World War. A Tory MP told the House of Commons in February 1943 that Laski should be kept off the BBC because in the last war he had run away to America to evade military service. Laski responded in a letter to the

Manchester Guardian in March citing three different dates, 1914, 1915 and 1917, and certificates when he was rejected from enlisting on medical grounds in Britain, Canada, and the United States. The Tory MP, Wing Commander James, apologized to the House of Commons nine months later for his 'most mischievous, misleading and wholly untrue statement'. All the same, he still 'disliked his political outlook intensely and in every respect'.

The challenge to Laski's patriotism in 1943 illustrates how deeply ideological tensions persisted beneath the façade of English wartime unity and how profoundly Laski irritated the British Establishment, despite his early and eloquent defence of the war. Throughout the bleak year marked by Dunkirk in late May 1940, the fall of France the next month, the Battle of Britain in August and the incessant German bombing until the spring of 1941, Laski wrote a series of inspirational essays and books in support of the war effort. His words have not endured as have Churchill's ringing phrases, but their political importance was immense in signifying the solidarity of the left in the struggle against fascism as well as in their influence on American opinion.

Laski repeatedly spoke out against the Communist Party's assertion that Churchill's war was only an imperialist war. A London rally sponsored by the CPGB in January 1941, dubbed the 'People's Convention', particularly infuriated Laski, who fired off a long piece to the *Nation* entitled 'British Communists Help Hitler'. In London he joined Gollancz in publishing *The Betrayal of the Left* for the Left Book Club, which included essays by Orwell and Gollancz and a preface by Laski. Laski lashed out at the message of 'revolutionary defeatism' which the communists urged on British workers. 'A heavy indictment can no doubt be made against British imperialism,' he wrote, 'but it is literally fantastic to argue that its habits even remotely resemble those of its fascist enemies.'

His most moving defence of the war appeared in a slim volume published in late 1940 for Penguin, *Where Do We Go From Here?*, which made its way to the Democratic National Committee in America for its use in that autumn's Presidential campaign. It was quoted everywhere in America and Britain; the Carnegie Foundation purchased a thousand copies for distribution and it appeared in an abridged form in the popular periodical *Omni Book*. Roosevelt wrote to Laski that he found the book inspiring. Particularly moving was Laski's chapter 'What Fascism Is', in which his earlier reading of fascism as simply capitalism in decline was dropped for a subtler inquiry into the relationship of ideology and psychology. The forces of privilege were now depicted as having been as deceived in their acceptance of fascism as had been the masses who supported it. Laski now emphasized fascist unreason, thuggery, terror and power-lust more than economic motives. The fascists were 'racketeers', 'gangsters', 'outlaws' and 'madmen', not capitalists or the privileged class. Laski warned that a fascist victory meant a barbaric new 'Iron Age' of incivility.

Less noted, especially in America, was the second theme in *Where Do We Go From Here?* The war, Laski wrote, was indeed a war against dictators, but to make it truly a people's war, to ask in justice for their sacrifices, it was essential that these should not be used merely to preserve the economic and social status quo. If a democracy were to wage total war, it had to commit itself to end economic and social privilege as the reward for the people's sacrifices, and as the price of victory. 'When the leaders of a nation ask the masses to die for a dream,' Laski wrote, 'the men who risk their lives are entitled to know on whose behalf those leaders dream.' If the war sought to set the winds of democratic doctrine blowing through Europe, 'we must first set them in play in Great Britain'. Laski meant, as he would soon make abundantly clear, that fundamental socialist economic changes had to occur in Britain during the war, but he also zeroed in on minor inegalitarian irritants that revealed an elitist Britain at war. Why, he asked, in articles in the *Tribune* and in his war pamphlet 'Rights of Man', were not basements of big homes and estates used as shelters for homeless evacuees, why were the vast grounds of country houses and golf courses exempted from war service? Why weren't the schools of the poor moved to the country as were those of the middle class? Why was all the 'commanding' in local domestic defence units always done by the 'local bigwigs' and all the 'obeying' done by ordinary people? Why didn't the government realize 'that a woman who has spent years running efficiently the local cooperative guild will be at least as good as the local squire's wife on one or another of the adventures needing to be organized'? Why was the suffering and the sacrificing falling more on the poor than on the well-to-do?

During that first grim year of the war Laski sought to inform Americans about the world historic defence of civilized values in which the British were engaged. He no longer hoped America would stay out of the war in order to serve as some future mediator. In several long letters to the *New York Times* in 1940 and 1941, his *Nation* pieces and an article in *Look* magazine, he urged America to help to defy and defeat Hitler. When he received letters from Lerner and Frankfurter indicating that American college students seemed uninterested in 'Europe's war', Laski dashed off a book in the summer of 1941, *The Strategy of Freedom: An Open Letter to American Youth*. In it Laski meticulously countered arguments across the political spectrum against American involvement, from anti-Semites like Father Coughlin, Lindberg and the Christian Front, to the Western isolationist senators, to John L. Lewis's CIO, reactionary Republicans, Irish Democrats, and pacifist and anti-war socialists. Laski knew full well that he was also writing for Roosevelt, if not to convince him, then certainly to help to generate support for more interventionist policies. His message was as clear to leftists like Robert Hutchins who feared that total war would threaten American democracy and the reign of human rights, as to proto-German sympathizers like Lindberg and Joseph Kennedy. 'It cannot be a matter of indifference to America,' Laski wrote, 'that half the civilized world stands on the brink of an enforced subordination.' Were Britain to fall, 'What safety would remain for the American way of life?' His message to American students and leaders was the same. 'Men are either for or against the Nazi tyranny, and if they declare their indifference to it they are already its allies.' A letter Laski wrote two days after the fall of France containing the same message so moved Frankfurter that he passed it on to Roosevelt.

The full weight of the German attack will fall on us . . . who of us lives if England dies? I beg you to stimulate every American you can to realize fully the measure of the evil things we are fighting. Make them see the need to organize in time. Make them settle all internal quarrels and find the resources that alone give victory. Make them learn the lesson a million of us are going to die for, because Chamberlain would not learn it. There is little you should not be ready to sacrifice to kill this thing . . . Tell the President to explain to his people that fascism is so literally the enemy of mankind that there is no price you can pay for its destruction that is too high . . . If you do not get ready now, you will have your Dunkirk too; and were that to come, there would be no prospect for the sons of men . . . Either you or Hitler makes the future. You will have to fight for the right to make it. I beg you to realize the need to be ready for the conflict.

Very different messages were coming to Roosevelt in 1940 from his ambassador to London, Joseph Kennedy. Laski had taken a keen interest in the Kennedys ever since Joe, Jr, had studied with him in 1934. The following year Jack Kennedy had come to the LSE, also for a year with Laski before Harvard. In October 1935, however, the future President fell ill and returned to America. The family patriarch arrived in 1938 as Roosevelt's ambassador to Britain and immediately moved into the fashionable life of the Cliveden set. Laski was shocked by Kennedy's ambition and 'the degree to which he is anti-liberal'. Kennedy's speeches belittling the threat of Hitler, Laski informed Roosevelt, were being 'turned to the service of the worst elements of reaction in Great Britain' as well as giving people the impression that Roosevelt was solidly behind Chamberlain's policies. Nor did it help that Father Coughlin's Jew-baiting weekly, *Social Justice*, declared Joe Kennedy 'the Man of the Week' in February 1939.

Kennedy and Laski openly clashed in 1940 and 1941, and the cause was not politics, but a proud father's request for a favour. Joe Kennedy had persuaded Jack to turn his Harvard senior honours thesis, a study of Britain's response to Hitler, into a book. He arranged interviews with British officials in London, and Arthur Krock of the *New York Times*, a Kennedy confidant, was encouraged to 'rework' the manuscript and to find a publisher; Henry Luce wrote a foreword to the book. In August 1940, when Kennedy received two advance copies of the book by air mail, he sent one to Churchill and one to Laski, with a note that 'the reviews have been swell. If you feel like writing him a line, I know he would be delighted to hear from you.' Laski, used to playing courtier to the Great and the Good, told the ambassador with brutal candour what he thought of *Why England Slept*.

While it is the book of a lad with brains, it is very immature, it has no real structure, and it dwells almost wholly on the surface of things. In a good university, half a hundred seniors do books like this as part of their normal work in their final year. But they don't publish them for the good reason that their importance lies solely in what they get out of doing them and not in what they have to say. I don't honestly think any publisher would have looked at that book of Jack's if he had not been your son, and if you had not been ambassador. And those are not the right grounds for publication.

I care a lot about your boys. I don't want them to be spoiled as rich men's sons are so easily spoiled. Thinking is a hard business, and you have to pay the price for admission to it. Do believe that these hard sayings from me represent much more real friendship than the easy praise of 'yes-men' like Arthur Krock.

While Jack Kennedy, according to Frida, later told Laski that 'you were quite right about my book', the ambassador would not forget the harsh criticism. In October, two months after Laski's chastisement, Kennedy was recalled to Washington and dismissed from his post. In an interview he gave to the *Boston Globe* after his return, Kennedy claimed, 'I'm willing to spend all I've got left to keep us out of the war.' Democracy was done for in Britain now that Labour was sharing power, and if America went to war, it too might stumble into national socialism. When the reporter asked about the lyrical praise of Britain's democratic fighting spirit in Laski's writings, Kennedy snorted, 'Laski is greatly overrated here . . . He doesn't represent anything.' Five months later, in April 1941, Laski replied with 'British Democracy and Mr Kennedy' in *Harper's*. British democracy was alive and well, he reassured Americans. Individual rights, civil liberties, freedom of the press and freedom of speech flourished despite the immense wartime powers of the government. Parliament had prolonged its own life, to be sure, and the general election was postponed, but vigorous parliamentary politics and open debate were still the order of the day. Laski suspected that Kennedy disliked 'wartime controls in Britain for the same reasons that he grew increasingly cool towards the New Deal'. To Kennedy's suggestion that Labour was an anti-democratic party, Laski retorted that it sought to reconstruct the British social and economic system only 'on its ability to win a majority in the House of Commons for its views; so long as it cannot obtain that majority, it agrees that its socialist principles cannot be translated into action. It abides, that is, by the judgement of the people.' Kennedy, Laski charged, had no idea about the true spirit of Britain; he knew only peers, bankers, editors and important politicians. If he had gone beyond these comfortable circles, he would have seen that democracy was far from finished in Britain and 'that we shall emerge, no doubt, from this conflict scarred and crippled; at least, as victory comes, we shall emerge from it as free men'.

Kennedy had the last word, however, several times over. In 1943 he orchestrated an anti-Semitic and anti-red attack on Frankfurter and Laski. Two years later FBI agents reported to J. Edgar Hoover that Kennedy insisted that after six months with Laski his son was 'a completely devout communist on his way to Spain to fight for the Spanish loyalists'. The agents added that Kennedy claimed that after he became ambassador he felt obliged to invite Laski to dinners because 'he could not avoid inviting the man who had written a number of speeches for the President of the United States'. In his speech to the Illinois Junior Chamber of Commerce in 1946, Kennedy asserted that there was no difference between British socialism and Russian communism. According to the *New York Times*, 'Mr Kennedy specifically singled out Prof. Harold Laski with this declaration. I know Laski, and I have before this referred to his habitual attacks upon what he calls our rotten, decadent capitalistic system.'

Laski never wrote speeches for Roosevelt but he wrote many for Kennedy's successor as ambassador in London, John G. Winant. With roots in the American labour movement, Winant, a good friend of Frankfurter, served as Governor of New Hampshire and Chairman of the Social Security Board. A shy man with few intellectual pretensions, Winant's instincts were egalitarian and humane. His visits to areas devastated by bombing and to war plants, his concern for the sacrifices of ordinary men and women, endeared Winant to the British people. To Laski, Winant personified the American 'common man'. Laski saw a great deal of Winant from 1941 to 1943, usually having regularly scheduled dinners when he was in London. He also arranged periodic meetings for some of Labour's NEC members with the ambassador. A peculiar chemistry brought the two into a close friendship, and Laski volunteered to write speeches for Winant, an offer Winant gladly accepted. It was a characteristic Laski move. It fed his sense of being an intimate influential friend doing favours behind the scenes for the eminent, who themselves had powerful friends and sponsors like Presidents and Supreme Court justices. Perhaps most important of all, he could now send his letters to his American friends through the ambassador's diplomatic pouch.

Kennedy had been dismissed in large measure because his support of appeasement did not sit well with the blitzing of British civilians. Laski, ironically, became involved in the early years of the war with the opposite, rather delicate, problem of exonerating the German people from charges that barbarism was an essential aspect of the German character. The major indicter of the German psyche was Sir Robert Vansittart, the permanent civil servant in charge of the Foreign Office, who in a series of seven radio broadcasts in 1940 traced what he saw as Germany's war-like tendencies to its medieval past. The Germans were all 'butcher birds' preying on other 'sparrows' and 'songbirds'. When Vansittart's talks were published as *The Black Record: Germany's Past and Present*, Laski answered in a pamphlet published by the Left Book Club, *The Germans – Are They Human?* The Germans, Laski wrote, were not a uniquely inhumane people. There was no evidence that 'the national character of a people is a fixed and unchanging thing'. Ten thousand gangsters had brutalized Germany, and their unlimited power and ability to manipulate the German people were the result of a particular historical situation produced by specific political, economic and psychological factors. Laski was worried about the fate in Britain of refugee German socialists, even German Jews, against whom Vansittart's arguments were being used to justify expulsion or internment. He was also concerned that 'Vansittartism' might lead to a punitive postwar policy that would make a socialist rebuilding of Europe impossible.

Vansittartism split the left. H. G. Wells and A. L. Rowse sided with the 'butcher birds' thesis. The Labour Party's major advocate of Vansittartism was William Gillies, chief of the party's International Department and Secretary to the NEC's Sub-committee on International Affairs. In October 1941 Gillies argued that the Labour Party could put no faith in German socialists in its planning for the future of Europe, since all Germans were untrustworthy and power-hungry. Gillies had a powerful patron on the NEC, Hugh Dalton, who supported an anti-German Labour group called 'Fight for Freedom'. Convinced that Germans, not the Nazi Party, were responsible for the war, Gillies and Dalton endorsed the total destruction of German postwar industrial potential. Their proposal, Laski insisted, was 'nonsense which seeks to make the German national character the vital factor in the emergence of Hitlerism'.

If the war was not being fought against Germans, what was its purpose? Laski's anti-Vansittart writings seemed at first to offer victory over ten thousand outlaws of the Nazi Party. By 1941, however, Laski turned to an overt socialist reading of the war which he had always provided in his far-left *Tribune* articles, but which he now published even in more mainstream progressive journals like the *Daily Herald* and the *Nation*. As soon as Chamberlain had been replaced by Churchill and Labour had joined the coalition, Laski wrote regularly in the *Tribune* about the contradiction between defeating Hitler and 'leaving unchanged the vital aspects of the property system'. He had no illusion that Churchill's government 'is going to take us into the socialist state', but he assumed that it would 'understand that the price of victory is the rejection of plutodemocracy'. Social and economic reconstruction starting 'in the very midst of war' would quieten doubts and strengthen faith, Laski wrote. The Churchill government had 'aroused vast hopes of a new day among the multitude' and it had to deliver. The crucial mainstream statement insisting that the war was really about the arrival of socialism was his widely discussed March 1941 *Nation* article, 'Revolution by Consent', which became Laski's wartime manifesto.

The war, he now wrote, marked a declaration of bankruptcy on the part of capitalist civilization and its agents of privilege. Fascism was now depicted as the ruling class using the outlaw to defend itself 'against the demand of the masses for justice' in the period of contracting capitalism. A European socialist revolution marking 'an epoch of creative liberation' was the objective in defeating the fascist armies, and in Britain the beginning of a socialist transformation by consent was the price to be paid for the sacrifices of the poor. Britain would 'have to pay the bills' for the heroic endurance of the common people. If this was a war for democracy and freedom, there was no better way to show it 'than to broaden and deepen in the midst of war the democracy and freedom we have'. In the face of Churchill's rousing rhetoric of national solidarity, Laski did not hesitate to use the language of class division.

> The masses of Britain will not be content with a victory which leaves the gains of life still to the Westminsters and the Bedfords, while the men and women of London and Coventry and Jarrow have no heritage but its toil. Our problem is whether we can use the dramatic opportunity of war to lay the foundations of a new social order.

'Revolution by Consent' introduced a fundamental Laski theme: producing revolutionary economic changes consensually was easier in wartime when a spirit of sharing, cooperation and community inspired all ranks of society and when crisis broke 'the cake of custom'. War and its spirit of self-sacrifice on the home front and on the battlefield suddenly provided Laski with the way out of his recurring 1930s dilemma. Moved by their appreciation of and debt to the ordinary people of London, Coventry and Jarrow, the ruling class of Britain would finally, as Laski had always hoped, be stirred to make the unprecedented concessions and sacrifices of power and privilege that would usher in without any violent resistance the revolutionary (i.e., fundamental) transition to socialism. With the war the whole country now had, he thought, the inspirational and psychological context in which altruism and selflessness could win out over self-interest and the status quo. All this, assumed, of course, that Churchill, as well as the Labour Party's leadership, seized the historical moment and began the consensual transition to socialism during the war.

The five-year effort to make Churchill, Attlee and Bevin initiate this 'revolution by consent' began with Laski sketching the kind of changes 'which offered hope and exhilaration to the people and safeguards us, in the post-war period, against the danger that the forces of privilege will prefer their vested interests to those changes which are obviously required'. These included the removal from the private sector of credit, coal, electricity, transport and ownership of the land, free secondary education for all, an extension of the public health system, rehousing the population, and a general commitment to economic planning. A transformed Britain, then, not only the overthrow of Hitler and Mussolini, was the war's purpose for Laski.

In urging his 'Revolution by Consent' upon the wartime coalition government, Laski had become the principal spokesman for the Labour left. Cripps had been sent as ambassador to Moscow by Churchill and in 1942 returned to join the War Cabinet, only to launch an unsuccessful assault on Churchill's control of the government. His 1930s militancy was now channelled more into a vision of Christian regeneration, in any case, and, as Laski wrote to Frankfurter, 'Stafford finds me embarrassing.' Strachey had become transformed into an adjutant in the RAF and Gollancz was so embittered by the Hitler–Stalin Pact that even after Germany attacked Russia in June 1941 he remained a less audible voice on the Labour left. In the House of Commons and on the National Executive Committee Emmanuel Shinwell and Bevan were Labour militants, but Laski's consistent capacity to command attention through his writings and his instinct for controversy made him the principal Labour left gadfly. In a remarkable display of this influence, Laski topped the voting for the NEC each year during the war. From 1939 to 1944 he led the seven-man group selected by the constituency parties, and in 1945 he tied for top place with Shinwell. He consistently received more votes than Dalton and Morrison, who were both ministers of state in Churchill's government.

None the less, the leaders of the Labour Party were moving even further from Laski's militancy during the war than they had been in the 1930s. With their power as ministers in the governing coalition, they acquired a more 'responsible' view of public affairs, enhanced by their close working relations under great stress with Tory colleagues and senior civil servants. Attlee as Churchill's Deputy Prime Minister, Bevin as Minister of Labour and National Service, Morrison as Minister of Supply and then Home Secretary, and Dalton as Minister of Economic Warfare were impatient with Laski's visionary insistence on a real socialist party and wartime enactment of socialist measures. The dynamic of Laski's career, set in the 1930s when his fortunes and the Labour Party's alternated in an inverse relationship, continued as the Labour Party shared power during the war and exercised total power after the war. His real influence and importance waxed when Labour was out of power and waned when it had power. Ironically, then, the 1940s would prove to be a period of bitter disillusionment for Laski, because Labour in power revealed even more dramatically the marginality of Laski's ideological leftist vision.

Laski's first dose of disillusion came from Churchill. He actually believed that the spirit of sacrifice generated by the war would so move Churchill, with his romantic and heroic self-image, that he would lead his class to make the concessions required for a 'revolution by consent'. No matter that Churchill's long career in British politics was punctuated by anti-labour and anti-red adventures, Laski now saw him as embodying the historical spirit of the English-speaking peoples who would in their darkest hour reinvigorate the ideals of freedom by moving it to its next logical step – socialism. Laski could be effusive in his praise of Churchill. He wrote of him as 'the greatest war minister this country has known since Chatham', who was bound to be among the greatest of all English statesmen. He embodied 'the will of the nation to live'. His drive, energy and audacity had 'caught the imagination and held the loyalty of the people in a pre-eminent way'. Churchill was indeed, Laski wrote, one of the greatest 'historic personalities in British history'.

Churchill, however, had no intention of doing anything but win the war. 'Everything for the war, whether controversial or not, and nothing controversial that is not needed for the war' was his explanation of why he would not push nationalization of the mines. In a speech delivered on 27 March 1941 Churchill made clear that fulfilling Laski's expectations was the furthest thing from his mind. He was interested only in non-partisan national unity which contributed to the common victory. He would offer no catalogue of war aims since, he was convinced, 'everyone knows quite well what we are fighting about'. To do otherwise would disturb the unified national resolve and have us 'descend into the arena of heated controversy'. Some disagreed with this strategy, he acknowledged, clearly having Laski in mind.

> Anyone in any party who falls below the level of the high spirit of national unity which alone can give national salvation is blameworthy. I know it is provoking when speeches are made which seem to suggest that the whole structure of our decent British life and society, which we have built up so slowly and patiently across the centuries, will be swept away for some new order or other, the details of which are largely unannounced.

Laski persisted and made a private appeal to Churchill in early 1942, suggesting that the National government continue after the war with Churchill in charge of a non-partisan reconstruction effort in which the mines, electricity, transport, land and credit were socialized, and education, public health and social insurance reforms undertaken. Only Churchill, Laski assured him, could deliver this programme and 'hold the elements into a cohesive unity which may save the world'. In a remarkable example of an inflated sense of his own influence, Laski wrote to Churchill that if he were to promise 'to lead the nation on this basis, I believe I could carry it through the Labour Executive'. Churchill flatly rejected the proposal asserting that the war had to be won before any talk of reconstruction and post-war policies. 'In a free country,' Churchill insisted, 'the issues of socialism and free enterprise can be fought out in a constitutional manner.' It would be utterly 'undemocratic if anyone were to try to carry socialism during a party truce without a parliamentary majority'.

When he finally realized that Churchill was interested only in winning the war, Laski turned on him in the *Tribune*, the *New Statesman* and the *New Republic*. Laski particularly seized upon Churchill's line from his March 1941 speech about 'the whole structure of our decent British life and society, which we have built up so slowly and patiently across the centuries' not being swept away. He suggested repeatedly that Churchill was fighting to preserve 'traditional Britain', the 'Britain of 3 September 1939'. Traditional Britain, Laski fired back in essay after essay, meant large-scale unemployment, distressed areas and massive inequalities in education. It meant positions of importance in society reserved for members of the middle and upper classes and a quarter of the population inadequately nourished. Surely, Laski wrote, 'the men and women of the working class whose heroism and resolution in these grim days are laying the foundations of victory are entitled to a better deal than they received in the Britain of the pre-war years'.

What else could one expect from Churchill, Laski now insisted, as he rehearsed the litany of Churchill's offences against the working classes, beginning with ordering troops to shoot strikers in 1910? Churchill was nothing but a Whig aristocrat, like his great ancestor Marlborough, a romantic adventurer who knew only how to make war. 'He fights Hitler as Marlborough fought Louis XIV, as Pitt fought Napoleon. The immense social forces which have gone to make this war are outside his consciousness.' Churchill was 'one of the great anachronisms of our time', Laski charged, fighting to preserve an obsolete economic and social system. Laski's watershed attack on Churchill, 'Epitaph on a System', was published in both the *New Statesman* and the *New Republic* in the summer of 1942. Churchill spoke movingly about 'the people's war', but, Laski asked, why did he not assure Britain's working people that it would be followed by a 'people's peace'? He sought victory only for 'an old world that is dying, not for a new world that is struggling to be born'. The problems confronting the railways, the mines and the social services in general, Laski argued, were being postponed because Churchill's desire to win the war was embedded in 'a desire to protect the old way of life'.

This criticism of Churchill shocked many in America, where Churchill was fast on his way to canonization. The *New York Times* first described Laski's attack in a news story and then several days later was moved to write a critical editorial about the essay. Particularly upsetting to Americans was Laski's threat to the war effort, now that America had entered the war, by his raising issues of class conflict. What good would it do to write of 'watching the erosion of a whole culture' or of 'a way of life dying'? How useful was his depiction of Churchill exploiting national unity 'as a plaster with which temporarily to cover up the profound disintegration of the old regime which has in fact occurred'? Laski replied to the *New York Times* criticism in a long letter which restated his *Tribune* and *New Statesman* attacks on Churchill. The war was about more than the overthrow of

Hitlerism, he wrote; it sought to create a world where such counter-revolutions against the masses striving towards freedom and equality would not recur. To permanently destroy fascism, the world needed 'a revolutionary idea ... to arouse hope and exhilaration in the masses'. All Churchill offered the masses was 'the maintenance of the traditional system as the reward for their effort and sacrifice'. Real changes had to be undertaken during the war, since in the previous war all sorts of promises were made about a rebuilt nation fit for heroes which were conveniently later forgotten. How likely, Laski asked in a refrain he would frequently repeat, are the chances for real social change after the war when with the passing of the national crisis 'we resume the differences by which we are divided' if there is so little 'when grave external danger makes us aware of how much we have in common'?

Almost immediately after 'Epitaph on a System' appeared in the *New Statesman*, Churchill retaliated. Cohn and Frankfurter had persuaded Eleanor Roosevelt to invite Laski to Washington in September to address an international meeting of students at the White House. Laski told her that, proud and delighted as he was to come, wartime regulations required him, as a political figure on the NEC, to first receive the Prime Minister's permission to travel. He wrote to Churchill with the request on 2 July. After consulting Lord Halifax, his ambassador to Washington, Churchill decided that Laski's arrival in America during the congressional election period raised the risk of a perception of foreigners giving speeches interfering with American politics. Accordingly, Laski was informed that the Prime Minister 'deprecates your paying a visit to Washington'.

Laski was deeply disappointed by Churchill's decision, he told Winant. He acknowledged that he had 'criticized particulars in his government's policy, but I've also praised him'. For Frankfurter, Laski put on a more stoic face. He had to pay the price, after all, for his criticisms of 'the corroding influence of power' and was not surprised or pained by Churchill's decision. 'An academic Cassandra with gall in his ink could not expect a salute either in Downing Street or Connecticut Avenue, he'd be a fool if he did, but oh! I would have liked to look round the universe with you and Alfred [Cohn] and FDR.' Meanwhile, Churchill confided to Harry Hopkins, Roosevelt's aide, that Laski was 'a considerable nuisance' who had 'attacked me continually and tried to force my hand both in home and war politics'. He hoped the widespread dissemination of Laski's writings would not paint England too red for 'timorous but friendly' Republicans.

Laski fared no better in getting his own Labour Party to push Churchill and the Tories in the coalition to introduce dramatic economic and social change during the war. This failure was even more disillusioning for him, because it created persistent and painful conflicts with the party's leadership and with colleagues on the NEC. His relationship with Attlee began well enough, for when Churchill asked Attlee to be his Deputy Prime Minister Attlee asked Laski to serve as one of his assistants. Laski accepted, although he had written to Cohn just before Chamberlain's departure that 'Attlee hasn't an ounce of leadership in him'. None the less, Laski worked closely with Attlee at his office at No. 11 Downing Street from June 1940 to the spring of 1941, particularly with advice on America, civil liberties, war aims and social legislation. He wrote memoranda for him as well as radio talks and speeches. Their working relationship was doomed, however. Attlee's strength was his capacity for conciliation and compromise, while Laski's every instinct sought to push issues to their extremes. Attlee fitted perfectly into the War Cabinet, writing later that 'it was very seldom that any party issue arose to divide us'. Laski, on the other hand, constantly sought to get Attlee to prod Churchill and the party into a firm commitment to socialist war aims. By late January 1941 Attlee was writing to Laski that their styles were incompatible and that he could not agree on a 'frontal attack with a flourish of trumpets' as the way to proceed in the midst of a desperate war. Two months later Attlee suggested that Laski cease working for him, since 'you wish to continue propaganda of various kinds'.

Attlee had shed whatever Marxist convictions he might have had in the early 1930s and was particularly bothered by the ease with which Laski could summon his. After Russia was invaded in June 1941, Laski, in a Labour Party pamphlet, *Great Britain, Russia and the Labour Party*, warmly welcomed Russia into the alliance against Hitler and offered a detailed Marxist explanation of the Nazi–Soviet pact that almost seemed to vindicate the Russians. Attlee, who wanted a simple acknowledgement that Russia's national interest changed with Hitler's attack, saw in the pamphlet 'an over-emphasis on the importance of the economic factor as the motive for all action which is rather due to theory than to the consideration of the events of the last twenty years'. Nationalism, not communism, Attlee suggested, should have been Laski's theme. Moreover, Attlee contended that the pamphlet was 'written for the intelligentsia rather than for the rank and file of the party. I should prefer something written in more simple and homely language.' Laski, meanwhile, was spreading the word that Attlee was incapable of making decisions, that he lacked 'the drive and imagination' required of a party leader and that 'nature meant for him to be a second lieutenant'.

At various times during the war Laski thought he had found his general. He turned first to Bevin in March 1942 as 'easily the most outstanding figure in the Labour Party'. The party needed a 'fighting leader' who understood 'the urgent needs of the common folk', Laski wrote to Bevin. It was time that 'you become the first man instead of the second'. Bevin's failure even to respond to this proposal indicates how little he thought of Laski. Uninterested in a wartime 'revolution by consent', Bevin talked of 'social security' at home while fascism was defeated abroad, by which he meant not socialism, but employment, good wages and good housing. More significant still was Bevin's basic mistrust of intellectuals who, he felt, had little intuitive sympathy with actual trade unionists. Bevin, for example, vehemently objected to Laski's plea in the *Daily Herald* for a ceiling on the age of Labour Party MPs in which he had matter-of-factly singled out 'unions which regard their title to nominate a prospective candidate as inalienable'. Nor for that matter did Bevin take kindly to Laski's attacks on him as virtual tsar over war production, who urged joint consultation between trade unions and employers' associations while opposing strikes as disruptive of the nation's industrial policy. Whitleyism revisited sat poorly with Laski's 'revolution by consent'.

After the unsuccessful overture to Bevin, Laski turned to Dalton, telling him he was the only possible alternative to 'poor little Attlee'. Dalton suspected that he was insincere, and when Laski predicted that the next party conference would be a scene 'of wild and indignant disorder against the failure of Labour in the government to get any socialism at all', Dalton wrote in his diary that 'this little fool lives in an unreal world of his own making'. And later that year, after a conversation in which Laski had told Dalton that he had lunched with Churchill who sang only Dalton's praises not Attlee's, Dalton wrote in his diary, 'What a little liar.' Dalton had no problem domineering Laski in public as well. In late 1940 Laski offered a memorandum to the NEC's policy sub-committee suggesting that in order to raise the morale of the people, land and the Bank of England should be nationalized. Laski was soundly criticized by trade-union members and by Dalton, who replied that, whatever the arguments for such steps, raising morale was not one. That, Dalton insisted, would be better done by air force victories, full employment and better dependants' allowances. When the motion was defeated, Dalton gloated that Laski 'goes away with his little tail between his little legs'. On another occasion when the NEC was meeting with foreign socialists from the Allied countries, Dalton was angered by a particularly militant comment by Laski and, as he described it in his diary, 'I find this a bit much and tick him off in front of the foreigners, which, I think, will have been no bad thing.' Dalton's response to Laski's party pamphlets was equally critical. 'A long screen of tiresomely written generalities,' he wrote in September 1941, and several months later he lamented that the NEC wasted a meeting in talk about a 'much too long document . . . written in Laski English and very remote and unprofitable'. The only person Dalton browbeat as much as Laski on the NEC was Shinwell, whom he referred to consistently for years as 'Shinbad the Tailor', a not too subtle anti-Semitic reference to Shinwell being the son of a Glasgow tailor.

Morrison was another possible general, and after the spring of 1943 when he ran unsuccessfully against Greenwood for the post of Labour Party Treasurer and was supported by Laski and Dalton, Morrison was the leader to whom Laski was closest. They appeared on platforms together, speaking, for example, to over a thousand members of the Firemen's Union in August 1943. Morrison alone among the leadership was vaguely sympathetic, after 1943, to Laski's insistent calls for a socialist Britain in the near future. In 1945 Laski would try to stage a coup for Morrison.

Laski's relationship with the party leadership during the war was seldom easy, punctuated as it was by recurring fights and threatened or applied rebukes over his crusade to have Labour preach 'revolution by consent'. George Ridley of the NEC thought that since Laski was a professor with nothing to do, he not only became a troublemaker but was 'getting too much influence in the National Executive'. Laski, on the other hand, was convinced that only the party's leadership stood between him and the party faithful who agreed with him about the need for wartime enactment of socialist measures. Serving as Churchill's government ministers turned the leadership to cautious managers, he informed Frankfurter. Power's effects were loathsome, he wrote in 1941: 'Not one of our people . . . has not been harmed by it – its pomp, its need to please, its massive indirection.' He noted that 'Herbert M is the least affected, but even he has a certain tinge of the bureaucrat which is distressing'. Laski was convinced that he played an indispensable role on the NEC as someone who had no public office and who therefore could speak with complete frankness; if he weren't there, 'no one could issue the appropriate warnings against compromise'.

The reality was that Laski was often reprimanded by that very NEC for his attacks on party leaders. The first of these incidents occurred in October 1940. Laski wrote an 'Open letter to the Labour Movement' entitled 'DEMAND WAR AIMS!' for the *Daily Herald*. It was the obligation of the labour movement, he argued, to insist that the Labour Party as coalition partners of Churchill 'secure from the government a precise definition of the purposes of the battle'. A special meeting of the NEC was immediately called for 5 November 'for the purpose of putting little Laski on the mat', as Dalton described it, for his failure to follow the party's position, which was not to urge a new social order on Churchill. After a lengthy discussion Laski told the group, which included Attlee and Dalton, that 'he now felt that probably the publication of the article in the *Daily Herald* was unwise'. The chairman of the meeting then thanked Laski 'for the very free and frank manner in which he had dealt with the matter'.

All Laski actually did was to stop writing this kind of material for the *Daily Herald* and reserve it for the steady stream of *Tribune* articles he wrote in 1941, including one in which he urged Attlee to pressure Churchill, entitled 'DON'T KEEP US WAITING CLEM'. Laski openly attacked Attlee in the *New Statesman* in March 1942 as a Party Leader who 'puts a profession of his socialist faith into his perorations' but 'does not move for their translation into action'. Like Churchill, Attlee accepted that pre-war Britain could win the war 'and that we may turn to the discussion of its future economic shape after victory', Laski wrote. Two weeks later Laski presented a ten-point memorandum, 'The Party and the Future', to the NEC as the basis for a discussion with Attlee. It was, he wrote to Max Lerner, the prelude to a 'show-down' on the issue of wartime socialism. Laski was blunt in his charge to the leadership.

The Labour Party is being dragged at the tail of the Conservative Party; in return for a handful of social reforms, none of them fundamental in character, we are assisting the vested interests of this country to strengthen their hold upon the state-power, and when the war is over, they will be able, as things stand, to preserve their privileges at the expense of the workers.

The response from Attlee to Laski's memorandum came at a full meeting of the NEC on 9 April. He flatly rejected the idea that the Labour Party should 'try to get socialist measures implemented under the guise of winning the war'. There was, he insisted, 'no majority in the House for a socialist policy or for a fundamental change in the economic organization of the country'. Such actions required the mandate of a general election, Attlee reminded the committee, as Laski had written so often in his books. The matter was closed when Attlee pointed out that 'continual decrying' of the government upset opinion in America and in the Dominions, hurt the Labour Party and 'does not help the morale of the civilian population or the fighting forces'.

The party leadership gave Laski what they felt was a harmless platform for his militant ideas at the annual party conference a month later in London. Speaking for the National Executive, he offered a resolution that 'there must be no return after the war to an unplanned competitive society', noting that the pressures of war had already necessitated far-reaching governmental control of industry, central planning of the economy and general subordination of private interests to the common good. In its operative clause the resolution suggested, in vague language to be sure, that these foundations 'had to be maintained after final victory is won' and that the conference urged undertaking without delay 'the necessary preparation for the vital changes here proposed'. The stirring speech with its muted criticism of Churchill and none for the party's members in his Cabinet was more inspirational than operational, as indicated by one delegate who complained that it and the resolution contained 'many admirable general statements, but we do not find any sufficiently clear and definite commitments to do definite things', which explains why the leadership drafted the resolution and chose Laski to present it.

Laski returned in the summer to outright attacks on the Labour Party leadership, choosing this time a series of articles in the Co-operative Society's radical newspaper *Reynolds News*, which would lead to yet another dramatic 'carpeting of Laski', as the *Daily Herald* described it. In July Laski charged that 'no one can point to any serious effort by Mr Attlee to make the ideal of a partnership with the people a conscious part of the

Prime Minister's policy'. When George Ridley a week later in *Reynolds News* chastised Laski for raising matters in public that belonged in the NEC, Laski wrapped himself in the commitments, albeit vague, of the May party conference. Laski's 'LEADERS ARE PARALYSED', published in August, rekindled outrage, especially at his suggestion that 'paralysis seems, alas, to have settled down like a blight on the leaders of the Labour Party in the Cabinet'. A third article in early September, 'WHAT LABOUR MUST TELL THE PREMIER', rounded out Laski's summer offensive.

Trade union members of the NEC, appalled at such open defiance of the leadership, demanded a meeting to consider expelling Laski, which was scheduled for 12 October with Bevin and Attlee invited to attend as well. The two and a half hour 'inquest into the misdemeanours of Laski' was the stuff of high drama. With Attlee and Bevin in the room, Laski admitted that he had recently asked Bevin to run for the leadership against Attlee, and in Dalton's account Laski, 'looking across at me and Bevin, [stated] that he has completely lost confidence in Attlee's leadership and thinks there are only two possible alternatives'. In the general discussion that followed, Bevin characteristically spoke more than Attlee, surveying benefits that had accrued to the working class as a result of the presence of Labour Party members in the Cabinet, as well as insisting on the need for party loyalty. The meeting was adjourned when Bevin and Attlee had to leave for ministerial engagements and the 'inquest' was reconvened on 28 October. In an effort at conciliation, Morrison claimed that no one really wanted to expel or even to muzzle Laski, but that 'his criticism had been made more public than was desirable in the interests of the welfare of the movement'. Laski accepted 'the general views put forward during the debate' on the condition that if he desisted from public criticism, he was still 'entitled to criticize or raise the personal issue of the leadership within the NEC'. A vote of thirteen to four resolved that 'the NEC accepts Mr Laski's explanation and proceeds to the next issue'.

Laski was relatively quiet until the furore over the Beveridge Report broke in December and January. Still Master of University College, Oxford, and working for the government as head of an inter-departmental committee, Beveridge issued a White Paper in December 1942 outlining a system of comprehensive social insurance that in return for a weekly flat-rate contribution would provide a minimum standard of living through children's allowances, a National Health Service and old age pensions. In addition, the government would be committed to the maintenance of full employment. Beveridge had switched again, leaving his 1930s flirtation with economic individualism and returning to his First World War statist New Liberalism. Beveridge's blueprint for the post-war British welfare state was to be discussed by the House of Commons in February 1943. Rumours circulated in January that Churchill and his Chancellor of the Exchequer, Kingsley Wood, were going to oppose any vote that would immediately implement the White Paper. What Churchill's Labour Cabinet ministers would do in that case became the crucial question, and Laski turned up the heat by insisting that this would be the fundamental test for the party leadership.

In an article for *Reynolds News* on 10 January, Laski acknowledged that Beveridge's recommendations were not socialism, but 'merely the completion of that social reform we began to build thirty years ago'. None the less, they were a test of the good faith of the government and especially of its Labour members. If the Cabinet refused to support the White Paper's implementation without delay, 'it ought', he wrote, 'to be a signal to the whole labour movement of the country to insist on the withdrawal of the party from the government'. In keeping with the theme of replaying old-fashioned Liberal reform, Laski turned to Lloyd George. His former enemy, now eighty, still sat in the House of Commons, and Laski urged him to speak out for the Beveridge proposals. 'No authority less than yours,' he wrote, 'will compel this government to face its problems.' He was certain that 'a challenge from you to the Cabinet in the name of the people would light a flame of hope all over the world'. In the meantime, Laski prepared a twenty-three-page memorandum for the NEC on why Labour should leave the government and move into opposition if the Cabinet opposed the White Paper. It was particularly directed at Bevin, so fond of pointing out the many ways the War Cabinet had served the interests of working people. Laski wrote:

Labour leaders are blind indeed who look at the portentous list of Acts of Parliament, of regulations, and Orders in Council and ask for congratulations upon the solidity of the achievement they represent ... a socialist may, I think, be pardoned for the remark that the merit of all this can easily be exaggerated. These are essentially wartime measures; they do not touch any of the fundamental issues of economic power.

Churchill decided to waffle. He announced his support of much of the social insurance and full employment proposals in principle, but he opposed any expenditure of funds to implement the schemes until a general election had provided a popular mandate. The Labour ministers in the Cabinet, concerned about the survival of the coalition and winning the war, decided to support Churchill – Attlee and Morrison reluctantly, and Bevin, who saw many shortcomings for union members in the schemes, less so. Laski had achieved his party revolution. On 18 February the government obtained its majority to postpone indefinitely the implementation of the White Paper. But of the 121 votes cast against the War Cabinet's recommendation, there was the venerable Lloyd George as well as ninety-seven Labour back-benchers voting against the government, and only two Labour MPs supported the party leadership.

Coming as it did only weeks after Sir Anthony Eden's first public revelations to the House of Commons of the horrendous magnitude of the Nazi extermination of Jews, this apparent betrayal by his party's leadership sent Laski into a mood of deep depression. He still spoke out, however. On 5 May, when an NEC vote to continue the electoral truce (i.e., not to contest Tory seats at by-elections, the equivalent to announcing its determination to remain part of Churchill's government) was carried, Laski voted against. Bevin was so furious at Shinwell and Laski for trying both to change the party's leadership and to break up the government that he refused to attend Labour Party meetings from February 1943 to May 1944.

In pamphlets written in May and July for the Fabian Society and for the National Peace Council, Laski intensified his criticism of the Labour Party. In *Marx and Today* Laski returned to older themes, 'the bankruptcy of the traditional horror of principles' which permeated the Labour Party. When in the 1930s the unemployed became uppity 'the Labour Party was almost more embarrassed than the government', and during the war, Laski charged, Labour leaders again mirrored the Conservatives. For Labour, as for the Tories, 'Hitler, however evil, is merely one new figure in the long procession of tyrants whose march to power Britain has checked in each century since the Spanish Armada'. Having rejected Marxism, the party was not even sure about comprehensive social insurance, 'which leaves the masters of our present social order confident about their future'.

In early August the *Daily Telegraph* disclosed that Laski had written an article in America suggesting that the Labour Party knew that to stick with

Attlee in the next election meant defeat, but that it nevertheless clung to an uninspiring and uninteresting leader because it could not decide between Bevin and Morrison. The trade-union movement, Laski had also suggested, was a serious brake on the Labour Party. All hell now broke loose, especially in trade-union circles, and calls were made for a vote of censure. The NEC met on 25 August for another 'Laski inquest'. Laski spoke on his own behalf with a lengthy statement and it was apparent that he was not well. The rebuke was, accordingly, a relatively mild one. The committee voted fifteen to two to dissociate the NEC from these statements 'which constitute an attack on Mr C. R. Attlee, MP, the leader of the Labour Party, and on the leadership of the British trade-union movement.'

While enmeshed in these internecine wars, Laski continued to do his fair share for the Labour Party. From the summer of 1941 onwards he methodically attended as secretary the NEC's Central Committee on Reconstruction Problems, chaired by Shinwell. The original idea of a committee to draw up a plan for the post-war organization of virtually every feature of British life was Laski's, with Dalton and Morrison signing on perhaps to turn the energy of Laski and Shinwell inwards rather than have them confront the party leadership and Churchill. The two rebels were able to do both, as it turned out, though even they tired of the interminable committee meetings involved in drafting the largely ignored report, *The Old World and the New Society*. Dalton, never one to resist an opportunity to ridicule, lampooned the ineffectiveness of the Reconstruction Committee, even if he had agreed to its creation as a means of overwhelming the militants with work. Shinwell and Laski and all the attendant sub-committees, Dalton claimed, produced nothing but a 'litter of committees'. Never, he wrote, 'was so little decided by so many'.

Laski did perform an important service for Labour in speaking out against the new Commonwealth Party in 1942 and 1943, which had self-consciously sought to create a leftist party unrelated to trade unions or any working-class base. Led by Richard Acland, former Liberal and Left Book Club figure, the new party attracted middle-class idealists, progressives, technical workers and intellectuals. It captured public attention when, disregarding the electoral truce, it defeated the Tories in several by-elections. Laski might have frequently depicted the trade unions as a brake on the Labour Party's socialism, but he rejected a non-working-class party of the left. In an important debate with Acland reprinted in the July 1942 *Left*

News, he criticized splitting up or atomizing progressive forces. Laski understood quite intuitively the potential appeal of Acland's 'commonwealth of common ownership' to the membership of the Left Book Club and he warned them against setting themselves up as 'those who seek to teach the working class what the working class ought to know while separating themselves from the masses embodied in the trade unions'. Thirty years of his own ambivalence about the Labour Party lay behind Laski's final observation.

> I know of no country in the world so far in which middle-class idealists, however well-meaning – and I regard myself as a well-meaning middle-class idealist – have been able in any real way to build the foundations of the kind of movement that socialism requires without having their roots essentially and vitally in the working class.

If such service didn't sufficiently impress the leadership, there was always Laski's role as a lightning-conductor catching flashes of Tory ire. Attention to his battles within his own party obscured the frequent public attacks on Laski by the right, especially by those not worried about maintaining the coalition. Beverly Baxter, a Tory back-bencher, caused a stir in 1941 with a sensational *Sunday Graphic* piece, 'THIS MAN LIBELS BRITISH LABOUR', which so bitterly attacked Laski in an *ad hominen* way that Carr-Saunders, the LSE's Director, suggested that Laski might have cause to sue. Laski saw no such need and merely wrote his own reply to Baxter in the *Tribune*. The journal *Truth*, which had been involved in the Gollancz–Laski–Strauss affair, ran an entire article ridiculing a piece, 'Who are the Real Rulers of Britain?', that Laski had published in the *New York Times*. Such public pandering to class hatred, *Truth* believed, was best reserved 'for the seclusion of the Bloomsbury and Hampstead debating societies and study circles'.

One Tory attack on Laski provoked an uncharacteristic show of support for him from NEC members. The right-wing, but ever so respectable, *National Review* had written a scathing and overtly anti-Semitic editorial about Laski's address to the 1942 Labour Party conference. Since Laski had been speaking officially for the National Executive at the time, it sought legal advice as to whether the article was actionable. The article had characterized the resolution on the need for post-war socialist planning as 'unpatriotic', and noted that it had been offered by 'Mr Harold Laski, who comes of a family only recently settled in Britain'. But, after all, the editorial continued, the Labour Party of John Burns, Keir Hardie and J. H. Thomas had passed, and its leaders no longer had anything in common with the working men of Britain. Did not Laski and Shinwell, 'neither of them of our race', receive the greatest number of votes for the party's executive? It was 'a confession of bankruptcy that no Englishman, Scotchman or Welshman received the votes given to these men', the *National Review* sadly concluded. The party decided to take no action, nor did Laski or Shinwell. Perhaps Dalton worried that such a worthy gesture would only get bogged down in a 'litter of committees'.

CHAPTER EIGHTEEN

War and Breakdown

Justice Holmes had worried that Laski in his early twenties was working his frail 'machine' too hard, and just short of thirty years later these fears were realized. In the late summer of 1943 Laski suffered a nervous breakdown. The hectic pace of his life, with his enormous teaching and political commitments, the repeated humiliations of NEC inquests and recantings, and the personal attacks in the British and American press led finally to physical and mental collapse. In addition, there was a serious strain in his relationship with Frankfurter, as well as an increasing absorption with his own Jewishness, especially in the wake of the horrific news of Hitler's Holocaust.

The tension with Frankfurter was long-brewing as their politics moved in different directions in the 1930s, Laski's to Marxist socialism and Frankfurter's to New Deal pragmatic liberalism and then to judicial 'restraint' after his appointment to the Supreme Court. What brought matters to a head in 1943 was Laski's harsh criticism of Roosevelt. In the early years of the war Laski beat the drums loudly for his friend in the White House. After the President's unprecedented third election victory, for example, Laski deemed Roosevelt's triumph 'the voice of the common man speaking above the fears and hates that power and wealth engender, proclaiming he will be free'. In April 1942 Laski wrote another essay on FDR's Papers and Addresses for the *University of Chicago Law Review*, full of praise for the President. Several months later, when Laski asked Roosevelt to send a few words of greeting to a group of émigré French and Belgian scholars recently set up at the New School, the President promptly did Laski the favour. So apparently close was their relationship that Dalton worried that 'he gives the President quite a false impression of what is going on here, and his status in the USA is far higher than in this country'.

Laski did indeed receive widespread notice in the United States. The *New York Times* reported on his major speeches and printed his articles. There were his *Harper's* pieces, as well as essays for the *Nation*, the *New Republic* and Max Lerner's *P.M.* Henry Luce's *Time* and *Life* magazines paid attention to Laski, the latter, in fact, carrying a large picture of him in August 1943 in a piece about the post-war future. There were also Edward R. Murrow's radio broadcasts. Particularly effective in giving Laski an American audience were his almost weekly news articles syndicated in many American newspapers by the Overseas News Agency (ONA). Though they might be abbreviated and presented with different headlines and some political fine-tuning, these ONA pieces tended to reflect quite faithfully Laski's strident views, including his persistent griping at the Labour Party leadership as well as Churchill. The attacks on Churchill particularly bothered Frankfurter. In his diary in February 1943 Frankfurter reflected, 'I thought Harold's strategy in attacking Churchill all wrong, not furthering his aims and making mischief he does not intend.' Frankfurter sent word to Laski that he had cut back on his correspondence because he was convinced their letters were being opened and was worried about comments that might be harmful to the President. Still, he conveyed 'abiding and enveloping affection' for Laski.

However, matters came to a head two months later on 10 April, when Laski unexpectedly lashed out at Roosevelt in 'An Open Letter to President Roosevelt' published in the *New Statesman* and the *New York Times*. Roosevelt, as well as Churchill and his own party's leaders, Laski feared, was blind to the real objectives of the war. The 'Letter' criticized Roosevelt's patronage of right-wing or monarchical regimes in Spain, France and Italy, suggesting that the President accepted a post-war world 'run by the old men for the old purposes'. In America, Laski charged, 'big business had taken over the New Deal', and he wondered aloud about America as he did for Britain – 'for whom and for what the victory is to be won'. An annoyed Roosevelt wrote to Frankfurter the very day the piece appeared, 'He knows not whereof he speaks – and that is bad for Harold and his reputation. He is capable but should stick to his line.' 'Saddened' by Laski's attack, Frankfurter replied that he still felt 'deep affection' for his friend, but 'for some time I have not been able to see eye to eye with Harold on various phases of the war, its conduct and what is beyond'. He assured Roosevelt that 'Harold has known from my silences my disagreement' and he concluded by observing that 'the poor lad is golden-hearted and his ardour is all for the right things. But I'm afraid the road to the Heavenly City is easier for him than for me.'

Winant was not silent, either. While he did not speak or write to Laski, he let his thoughts be known. Laski heard and wrote to the ambassador on 22 April:

> I'm told you are 'furious' with me for my piece in the *New Statesman* . . . I ought to tell you quite frankly that I am completely unrepentant about it. I think Anglo-American policy at present is laying the foundations for a vast betrayal of the common peoples of the world even though it achieves the military defeat of the Axis powers . . . the implications of the last few months have already gone far towards losing the peace . . . I don't regret what I wrote. My regret is that I have no means of making what I said clear to the millions who hope for the four freedoms and will find they are slowly left to drift into a new feudalism.

Winant replied that the 'Letter' weakened Laski's own influence and also that of 'men like Frankfurter and others at home who are deeply sensitive to the issues involved and whose liberalism in the war period is of value to both our countries'. Like others, Winant found it hard to believe that 'the administration would be willing to sacrifice the lives of American soldiers in North Africa or elsewhere in order to set up a fascist or a Nazi regime'. Laski retorted that he had no regrets and that, like Felix, Winant did not understand that equally important as winning the war was 'winning it in the right way for the right ends'. The victory he wanted was the certainty that Hitler would not be replaced by Hitlerism. Though he remained 'unrepentant, even more militant about my sins', he assured Winant that 'I keep for you and FD and Felix a faith and affection that is about as essential a reason as I have for living'. They sought the same end, he suggested, 'even if my road to it is on the left of yours'. Despite the olive branch, Winant had clearly cooled. In November Laski asked, 'Have you thrown me to the dogs?' On another occasion, still concerned about not hearing from Winant, Laski wrote to him that perhaps 'an evil-minded socialist like me is not a fit and proper person to cast his shadow in the American embassy'.

That Frankfurter remained a good friend to Laski is a tribute to his ability to tolerate the embarrassment their relationship created for both him and the President. Roosevelt knew how vulnerable he was on this score. In 1939 Sir Arthur Willert, the long-serving *Times* American correspondent, told the President that while lecturing at Palm Beach he had been asked 'whether I had heard that the New Deal had been invented by a Jewish professor in London'. The President immediately exclaimed 'Harold Laski' and laughed; then, very seriously, 'The fools, cannot they see that I am protecting them from the deluge?' Obviously not, for in June 1941 Congressman Tinkham of Massachusetts read into the *Congressional Record* an indictment of 'the international communistic cabal' whose members were President Roosevelt, Justice Frankfurter, Ambassador Winant, Harold Laski, Harry Hopkins and Benjamin Cohen. Laski was described as 'confidential adviser of Mr Roosevelt, Ambassador Winant and Justice Frankfurter', singled out as the 'communistic cabal's intellectual switchboard' and regarded by Washington insiders 'as having, directly or indirectly, more influence on the President than any one individual with the exception of Justice Frankfurter'. The 'Roosevelt program' was in reality the 'Laski program' and Roosevelt received his orders from Laski via a weekly letter he wrote to Frankfurter. Eleanor Roosevelt was part of the plot as well, since she recommended Laski's books to friends.

Laski's unique influence in America was a remarkable phenomenon and not just grist for paranoid weavers of conspiracy. He was the foreign, Jewish, intellectual radical that Americans could immediately call up in their minds when they envisioned a 'socialist'. Arthur Schlesinger, Jr's assessment of Laski's influence is matched by the equally sober Eric Sevareid of CBS, who wrote that 'through his students like [University of Minnesota Professor] Lippincott, Laski influenced a lot of young American men and women, many out there in the isolationist heartland of this country, some of whom came to positions of considerable influence in the United States'. With a nastier right-wing slant this could come out like the claim in the *Congressional Record* that 'Laski has probably done more than any other man to teach our younger generation disbelief in our economic and political systems and distrust of the Constitution and the way of life it sustains'.

The doyen of right-wing columnists, Westbrook Pegler, went after Laski in October 1942 through Mrs Roosevelt's planned visit to London. The trip was appropriate, Pegler wrote, because Britain was the base 'from which her communistic and social-democratic authorities or feeders are now operating'. Among these 'the most influential' was Harold Laski, 'one of the most potent voices in Washington'. To be sure, 'You don't see Laski around Washington, but his influence is there all the time and it is being imposed on the lives of Americans who never even have heard of him.' Nevertheless, Mrs Roosevelt went out of her way to visit the Laskis when she arrived in Britain, and when Laski wrote glowingly of her for the *New Statesman*'s 'London Diary' she wrote to him about 'how deeply appreciative I am of the very kind things you say.'

By far the most upsetting episode for Frankfurter in being linked to an attack on Laski took place in a fully fledged exchange on the floor of the House of Representatives. On 24 March 1943 Congressman Fred Bradley of Michigan attacked David Niles, long-time political operative for Roosevelt and for nearly thirty years a close friend of Laski and Frankfurter from earliest Harvard days, for being the centre of a communist plot in the White House. Laski, the Congressman noted, was in England, but Frankfurter and Niles were 'the pipelines through which the schemes of foreign radical internationalists flow into Washington'. Bradley described at great length the 'Harvard Frankfurter–Niles–Laski radical clique' which sought 'to regiment every man, woman and child in this country in one huge state-socialistic, communistic, or collectivist, or fascist state, as you will'. In his *Diaries* Frankfurter mused on the difficulty facing him in converting America to both communism and fascism, and then solemnly noted that 'the real animus I had supposed was anti-Semitism and anti-Rooseveltism' and the real source of the attack 'is none other than Joe Kennedy'.

Only a saint, which Frankfurter was not, could have been unaffected by the repeated attacks on him through his friendship with Laski, especially when combined with his sense of Roosevelt's political vulnerability and his own ideological estrangement from Laski. Still, they remained the warmest of friends until Laski's death. Laski, however, was clearly hurt by Frankfurter's silence, which contributed to his mood of deep depression. A new testy tone entered their correspondence when they wrote of political matters, especially on Laski's part. Laski appreciated Frankfurter's efforts, ultimately unsuccessful, to get Roosevelt to approve storing Laski's library, including the Holmes letters, in the American embassy during the war, but he clearly became irritated with his friend's move to the right. He complained to Max Lerner especially about Frankfurter's use on the

Supreme Court of Holmes's doctrine of judicial restraint, which Holmes had enlisted against the Court's reactionaries, and which Frankfurter now turned against the more aggressive civil libertarians Black and Douglas. Laski also wrote to Huebsch about his misgivings.

Laski wrote fewer letters to Frankfurter during the mid-war years, but when he did write they were an unusual combination of personal warmth, endless gossip and political coolness. In one he noted in passing 'that I am not impressed by any of the well-educated Tories for whom you retain your curious penchant'. As he was coming out of his period of dark decline in December 1943, Laski wrote a rambling letter full of personal sentimentality, self-deprecating references to his being a halfpenny academic compared to Felix on his Olympus, and poignant comments about how 'when one has been into the Valley of Death and come out on the other side friendship becomes the final joy of living'. Through the sometimes disjointed prose it was clear that the loss of Frankfurter's support hurt him deeply. He longed to be able to talk it all out and convince Felix that 'the world needs a revolution, while you remain a pragmatist who takes each issue as it comes'. Laski's never-failing optimism was replaced by cynicism, incorporating his views of the actions and aims of his Labour colleagues, Churchill and Roosevelt. But some months later, Laski insisted that he now understood and accepted the deep political differences between himself and Frankfurter, even those over the Court and the war. In a thoughtful insight that only a close friend could offer, Laski noted that 'the basic assumption of all your thinking is that what you are today, this kindly, generous, sprawling America made possible, and you compare it with what might have been your fate if you had lived in Vienna, and you take from it that the contrast justifies America'. They would remain good friends, he hoped, in what he insisted 'is going to be a new world'. They did.

His American friends were always capable of dealing with the two Laskis, the warm, generous friend and the lecturing ideologue. His wartime letters to all of them were full of revolutionary messages, even to such unlikely would-be fellow-travellers as Hugo Black, but none wrote back critically or argumentatively. They wrote of personal and neutral matters or, like Frankfurter, answered with hurtful silence. Their affection for someone whose politics were, even for Lerner, so different from theirs was remarkable. When he become ill in 1943, each of his American correspondents wrote with compassionate concern. When they read on 10

August 1944 that his house had been bombed and heard the next day on
the news that he had escaped unharmed, they wrote to him with gratitude
and love, and Ben Huebsch even sent him a copy of the Jewish prayer for
deliverance from danger.

American Congressmen and Hearst columnists were not the only ones,
though, who worried about Laski's loyalty during the war. Closer to home
there were recurring suspicions at the BBC, at the Ministry of Information,
among politicians and in the press that it was dangerous to allow Laski too
large an audience to inculcate with his subversive views. No wonder Laski
came to feel a lone, ineffective pariah, shunned and boycotted because the
stridency of his message frightened powerful people. Even his tireless
lecturing to troops around the country for the Army Bureau of Current
Affairs was attacked as a misuse of public funds and part of a leftist plot to
persuade many in the army to vote Labour, which in fact they
disproportionately would in 1945.

The BBC, however, proved the great battleground. The government
saw radio as the essential tool in maintaining civilian morale during the
war, and it made great use of Churchill and the King visiting the sites of
severe bombing destruction. Great sensitivity existed in the government
about who had access to the air waves. A talk by Laski in April 1942 on the
American political scene angered Lord Croft, under-secretary at the War
Office, and two months later the Tory back-bench 1922 Committee wrote
to Bracken, the head of the BBC, in protest against the use of Laski on
domestic broadcasts. By early 1943 Laski was effectively blacklisted (along
with J. B. Priestley and Julian Huxley) from giving talks on the BBC's
Home Service. The BBC's archives detail its concern over 'the constant
attacks on us on the grounds that we make too much use of left-wing
speakers', noting specifically that 'the Ministry of Information have always
been nervous about our use of Laski'. There was also concern that 'Laski is
a red rag' to Conservatives and 'they would not like him giving a series of
weekly talks'. Even when the NEC designated Laski as their liaison officer
between the Labour Party and the Ministry of Information, the BBC
resisted Laski's request 'to have working-class interests represented at the
microphone'. Though agreeing with the principle, they wrote to Laski that
'they preferred to have the actual working-class man rather than the
politician representing him'. The blacklisting of Laski applied only to the
Home Service and its domestic programming. Laski was more than

welcome to give broadcasts abroad on European, American and Dominion programming, where, as the BBC's Director-General noted, 'his reputation is of value in certain quarters'. During the war Laski participated as speaker or panellist in a remarkable 108 BBC radio programmes, of which seven were home broadcasts and 101 overseas. When his suggestion of a Home Service broadcast on the 300th anniversary of the publication of Milton's *Areopagitica* was rejected with a note preferring speakers 'less coloured by party politics, for example T. S. Eliot or E. M. Forster', Laski finally had had enough and fired off a letter to the BBC.

> During the years of the war I have ... been used by the BBC only for foreign broadcasts, mainly to the United States; and I think that every proposal for a talk that I have made has been rejected. It seems to me that for the purpose of explaining such views as I have to listeners in this country, I am for all practical purposes 'black-listed' where you allow me to talk with some freedom to the United States, India and Germany. As I do not wish to become what is little more than an alibi for the BBC's enthusiasm for free discussion abroad, while I appear to be carefully excluded from discussion at home, I propose to resign from *Freedom Forum* ... I prefer not to broadcast at all rather than to be used for foreign audiences only.

Most of Laski's foreign broadcasts, seventy-nine of the 101, were as a panellist on *Freedom Forum*, conceived and produced for the BBC by Lanham Titchener and broadcast on its North American service. Laski appeared regularly, along with G. M. Young, the distinguished Tory historian, and Edward R. Murrow of CBS. Each programme was a debate on a controversial political topic such as 'Can we banish the fear of war?', 'Can we achieve a classless society?' or 'Is national sovereignty compatible with world peace?'. Broadcast steadily from 1942 to 1944, *Freedom Forum* intensified Laski's friendship with Murrow. Charles Collingwood of CBS observed that 'Laski fascinated Murrow, simply because of the quickness and virtuosity of his mind, a sort of intellectual swordsmanship, the matching of ideas. Churchill he saw as a great man, "with all his flaws ... whereas he saw Laski as a fascinating individual". In one of Murrow's rare broadcasts to the British over the BBC, he commented that he 'would be willing to trade several squadrons of aircraft, a few hundred tanks if we might have Laski ... in the States for a few years when this war is over'.

What Laski did not know was that there was little governmental 'enthusiasm for free discussion abroad' either. The British Library of Information, 30 Rockefeller Plaza, New York, was trying to decide during these years whether to cease distributing Laski's writings. In an extensive correspondence with the Foreign Office in London, some involving R. A. Butler, Anthony Eden and Lord Halifax, the merits of censorship were debated. T. N. Whitehead of the Foreign Office worried that 'Mr Laski is beloved by all the pink sentimentalists in America'. It might be unwise 'to shut down on Mr Laski too suddenly' given his important friends, he suggested, but 'they should certainly not push him'. Notes were sent from New York about Americans worried that Britain's 'social and economic policy would be guided by Mr Laski and his friends'. Foreign Office officials replied that 'Mr Laski is a far more important person in America than he is in England', referring in fact to 'left-wing Americans' like Frankfurter who were close to Laski and the President. Indeed, the reply added that 'he [Frankfurter] is romantically fond of Mr Laski'.

The decision was to keep Laski's books on the shelves but to let important people know how 'relatively insignificant' he was in Britain. Butler was distressed enough to say that he 'would gradually initiate Winant' about Laski and to suggest that Halifax 'take some convenient opportunity to reassure the President with regard to the position that Laski and his kind hold in this country'. Halifax did just that, telling Roosevelt 'about the trade unions being an essentially conservative affair with us'. He reported that Roosevelt, like so many intelligent Americans, found 'it very difficult to understand how essentially opposed the ordinary Englishman is to abstract ideologies'.

In 1942 and 1943 additional complaints were received at the Foreign Office from British Library of Information officials in New York and Mexico City about Laski's 'gloomy and mean-spirited articles' about the war distributed by the Overseas News Agency, 'a small predominantly Jewish concern', to large numbers of North, Central and South American newspapers. To these complaints from the field of 'this snivelling Hebrew's' efforts 'to damn the Prime Minister', the Foreign Office replied in January 1944 that there 'is nothing we can do about it without taking an unreasonable risk'.

Contributing also to the depression that overtook him in 1943 was Laski's increasing bitterness at a world where educated British officials could describe him as 'a snivelling Hebrew' and fellow socialists could refer to him as an 'undersized Semite' while millions of his fellow Jews were being gassed to death. Despite extensive rumours and documented accounts, the British government labelled talk about the magnitude of Jewish persecution by the Nazis as 'rather wild stories', Jewish Agency 'sob stuff' and the 'Jewish technique of atrocity propaganda'. Only on 17 December 1942 did Anthony Eden announce to a hushed House of Commons and the British public the staggering dimensions of Hitler's 'bestial policy of cold-blooded extermination of the Jewish people in Europe'. On first hearing about Belsen and Buchenwald Laski wrote, 'I now know what it means to sit down and weep by Babylonian waters.'

After a career in which he had rarely made public mention of his Jewishness, Laski became preoccupied with Jewishness in 1943, writing two long explorations of it in the *New Statesman*. Fundamentally an eighteenth-century rationalist steeped in the Enlightenment's conviction that reason would inevitably triumph over darkness and evil, Laski was devastated by the revelation of the Nazi atrocities. But for Laski 1943 was also a deeply felt personal crisis. It was as if his sense of himself as a political and personal outcast took on the historical persona of the Jew as pariah and victim. He accepted, moreover, 'the obligation [one] cannot escape to the helpless millions on the European continent whose fate, but for an accident in historical time, might well be his'. Laski could also feel an identity with Nazi victims, for it was not beyond belief that he could become one himself. The most visible Jew in English political life during the war, he was singled out by William Joyce, the Englishman who fled to Germany and as Lord Haw-Haw became a notorious German propaganda broadcaster. On 15 April 1943 Joyce devoted his entire fifteen-minute broadcast 'to the Jewish publicist Harold Laski'. Using his 'Hebrew mentality', Laski, 'this detestable and wily Jew', was guilty of the most 'flagrant abuse of human credulity . . . the Jewish attempt to convince the British people that Bolshevism is harmless'. Laski's former student the Harvard historian Crane Brinton, working for the OSS at the American embassy, had a copy of Joyce's broadcast sent to Laski. What Laski did not know, however, was that his name was on Himmler's list of prominent persons to be rounded up by the Gestapo after the Nazi occupation of Britain.

As much as Laski attacked Churchill throughout the war, after 1943 he was drawn to the Churchill at least who from Smedley House days had stood virtually alone among public figures as a friend of British Jewry.

Now he seemed to stand between Hitler and those Jews. He knew 'very intimately', Laski wrote to the Prime Minister, 'as I look at the Europe Hitler has devastated, that as an Englishman of Jewish origin I owe you the gift of life itself'. So deeply did he feel this debt that Laski proposed that a Churchill Fund be established after the war to mark the Prime Minister's career-long concern for Jews.

Laski was all the more drawn to Churchill because of his own party's inadequate response to the news of Nazi atrocities. As Home Secretary, Morrison did little to facilitate the entrance of Jewish refugees into Britain, first from Vichy France and then from Central and Eastern Europe, even after Eden revealed what was happening on the continent. Morrison was ostensibly worried that increased immigration would fan English anti-Semitism. 'If there were any substantial increase in the number of Jewish refugees,' Morrison told his Cabinet colleagues, 'we should be in for serious trouble.' At the April 1943 Allied conference on refugees at Bermuda, Morrison reported that his government was prepared to deal only with a 'token entry of Jews', one or two thousand perhaps. Although Laski also deplored Roosevelt's foot-dragging, his own government most embittered Laski, a government which could state in September 1943 that 'from our point of view, fortunately, the German government appears to be intending to persist to the last in their refusal to allow Jews to leave Germany'. As head of the Cabinet committee on Palestine, moreover, Morrison also resisted demands for unlimited immigration of political refugees, agreeing grudgingly only to allow a few hundred children above the numbers authorized in 1939 from Romania and Hungary to be admitted. When Morrison announced that he was trying to find a country for Jews to go to other than Palestine, Laski replied, 'I am not known as an extremist Zionist, but I tell you that no Jew will even consider such a thing and the very broaching of the idea is an insult to us.' Several weeks later Laski poured out his rage, telling Churchill how hurt he was 'that among my own colleagues in your government Dr Goebbels has induced a spirit of caution [on the Jewish refugee problem] when you have so amply shown that audacity is the road to victory'. In the tension between the universalist vision of his socialism and the particularist identification with his Jewishness, Laski in 1943 was being moved to subordinate a revolutionary transformation of society to the simple defeat of Hitler as the defining purpose of the war.

Laski's traditional assumptions were being undermined. The one time he had written at any length on anti-Semitism before the war, he had taken the straightforward line that anti-Semitism was a product only of capitalism and that 'socialism makes the Jew an ordinary and integral part of the general population'. Laski never abandoned his belief that anti-Semitism fed on the exploitation of economic misery, but he began to see darker and more elusive forces at work, too. His *New Statesman* essay on anti-Semitism in 1943 wrote of Jewish victimization by the 'professional man, lawyer, doctor, teacher', by all who saw the Jew invading areas 'where the standards ought not to be of alien making'. He cited the historical curse on the Jew 'as a standing defiance of the Christian revelation'. Anyone who spoke out as a Jew would sooner or later perceive that 'those to whom he appeals have, at bottom, the half-conscious sense that he is, after all, an alien amongst them pleading for aliens whose claims are in no aspects rights'. If he had scripted it himself, Laski could not have done better in proving his point, for two Saturdays later the *New Statesman* printed a letter from a fellow socialist applauding Laski's article, but faulting him for omitting the one factor which produced more anti-Jewish feeling than any other: 'the behaviour of foreign Jews'. They are 'such a noisy minority, these people, that they seem more numerous than they are'. Added beneath this letter from Hampstead was an editor's note from Kingsley Martin that must have made Laski's heart stop.

> We have received several similar letters from people whose opinions deserve serious attention. They are fully alive to the grave political danger of anti-Semitism and are not themselves anti-Semitic. But they charge some sections of the Jewish community with a number of social faults; these, it seems to us, can be summarized by saying that some Jews, particularly in areas where refugees congregate in considerable numbers, have bad, or at least unEnglish, manners, behave inconsiderately and selfishly to their neighbours in shops and buses and generally make themselves unwisely conspicuous. Xenophobia easily spreads in wartime. Similar complaints are made about some Americans in this country.

In the spring of 1943 Laski attended for the first time a meeting of the Poale Zion, the Jewish Socialist Labour Party, an affiliated society within the Labour Party. The members took it as a sign of Laski's return as a Jew to his people, and indeed, at the 1943 Labour Party conference on 17 June,

Laski spoke for the NEC in supporting the resolution moved by the Poale Zion 'expressing horror and indignation with which all civilized mankind witnesses Hitler's bestial campaign of extermination of European Jewry', as well as reaffirming 'the traditional policy of the British Labour Party in favour of building Palestine as the Jewish national home'. From the platform Laski noted in his first sentence that it was 'fitting that a member of the National Executive who is also a Jew' should accept the resolution. He proceeded to make a public declaration of his Jewishness to the delegates: 'I as a Jew in the fullest sense of the word claim absolute equality of status in political, social and economic rights with any other people in the world.' The Jews 'are always selected as the first victims [of reactionaries]. For 2,000 years we have been the victims of persecution of this kind. But we have stood at the grave of every one of our previous oppressors and we shall stand at the grave of our Nazi oppressors, too.'

His former student Sharret saw a good deal of Laski that spring. He had come from Palestine to work on the Labour conference proposal and the talks with the NEC were mediated by Laski. Sharret noticed that the Nazi atrocities and the Warsaw Ghetto uprising had 'awakened a Jewish soul in this assimilated Jew'. Laski had told Sharret, 'I am Jewish. I am part of my people. I could have been on the Struma,' a reference to the ship carrying 769 Jewish refugees which broke down off Istanbul in February 1942. The Turks would not allow the refugees to land and the British ordered the ship back into the Black Sea. When it started up again it sank, with one person surviving.

Laski's most heartfelt exploration of his Judaism came in an article he submitted to the New Statesman in October 1943, 'On a Jewish Soldier's Letter', which was written as he began to recover from his breakdown and when he was still seeing virtually no one. Ostensibly 'an adaptation of a letter to me from an old student too grim to print', the article was Laski's confrontation with Judaism, Hitler and the redemptive significance of Zionism. Stationed at Suez, 'the soldier sees no shame in being a Jew'. He was proud of his people's history and committed 'to fight for his rights as a human being; no one else is likely to fight for them if he is servile and indifferent'. The soldier watched as a boatload of Jewish refugee children arrived on their way to Palestine. 'On their faces was written all the tragedy of all Jewry, of boys and girls who had seen the kind of thing which belongs not to civilization but to the tiger in the jungle when it flings itself upon its prey.' They had watched their parents be buried alive; they had seen 'a whole community of Jews driven to the edge of a common grave into which they fell as they were machine-gunned'. The soldier wondered 'why the British and American governments should look so coolly on the work of rescuing Jews'. He heard the verbal sympathy, but could not understand the lack of action. In Palestine these exiles from Nazi persecution became transformed 'from tragic automata into human beings who learn, within a year, how to laugh and play, who no longer carry in their eyes what seems like the sorrow of all the ages'. Why, then, was the British government unwilling to open this land to 'the hundreds of thousands of orphans whom kindness might similarly transform'? Why did the British worry instead about the Arab landlord, 'the effendi who lives in luxury on his earnings in Cairo and Alexandria and the south of France'? The soldier ended his 'letter' with a plea that the Jewish struggle for survival and freedom was the struggle of all to make it impossible 'for the powerful to oppress the humble, the rich to oppress the poor'. If Jews did not fight themselves, then governments after the war would forget them and Hitler would triumph even as he was overthrown.

Laski sent a copy of 'On a Jewish Soldier's Letter' to Winant along with a letter shorn of Laski's usual gossip and mock-heroic complaints about being socially snubbed by the ambassador. All he wrote was an aggressively phrased request that 'the government of the United States which was the legendary dream of refuge for the oppressed tell our government here that a Jew is not out of place when he is free, and, still less, when he is free in Palestine'. Maintaining his distance, Winant replied perfunctorily, 'Many thanks for the article in the New Statesman and Nation which interested me very much. I do hope you are feeling better.'

Laski was, in fact, just beginning to feel better. Since midsummer he had been inactive. Frida took care of him in London at Addison Bridge Place as he rested from the physical and emotional strain of exhausting travel, estrangement from colleagues and friends, as well as tortured self-exploration. Some effort seems to have been made to hush up the details of the breakdown. Friends remember talk of a minor stroke, and Dalton's diary records that at an NEC meeting in November 1943 Laski looked rather ill and told everyone he had had a heart attack. At the NEC meeting of 22 September, however, the minutes note the absence of Laski, who 'has suffered a serious breakdown', and his LSE personnel file contains a letter from Carr-Saunders to Frida in September about her husband's 'nervous breakdown'.

Frida had anticipated it. She told Carr-Saunders that 'I have watched this come on for months and could not do anything other than warn him and he took little notice. Now the doctor has more influence than I, so I am glad.' She had written to Huebsch earlier that Harold 'was going too hard all the war' and that she had been urging him to give up his weekly *Freedom Forums* on the BBC as 'too trying and too demanding of his time'. She also commented about how 'very much alone' Laski had come to feel about his politics. At the time of his NEC rebuke in October 1942 Laski had written to Frida in Essex about feeling 'a patch of inner misery lately' and how her 'understanding and sympathy helped so these last few days. They were a strain and your patience and sweetness made me able to stand where I had to stand.'

Others saw it coming as well. Laski's occasional black-outs and falls in the spring and summer of 1943 alarmed Kingsley Martin. His repetition of the same lectures worried Lance Beales, who began reminding him that 'last time he had lectured on topic X and this time he was to talk on topic Y'. In the spring of 1943 Laski was often so exhausted in Cambridge that Beales would put him on his bike with his briefcase and push the bike back to the rooming house. His American friends were worried too. He had written to Huebsch in March about being 'rather tired, but one can't live three lives without a certain fatigue'. They noticed that instead of the meticulously neat and precisely controlled tiny straight lines, his script became larger and rambling. Then letters stopped coming. Cohn wrote in November, 'It is months since any word has come from you. I hope nothing is wrong. There are rumours that you have been ill.'

By late October Laski returned to teaching, NEC meetings, writing and correspondence. He wrote to Freda Kirchwey that 'despite the medical solemnity of long names' he had merely suffered from 'a long dose of overwork'. He told Frankfurter in December that 'I am much better indeed, I shall be all right again in the next two or three months' and he informed Lerner that 'I am pretty fit again after having had three rather ugly months which I suspect came from an unhappy mind and a tired body'. Laski's almost immediate resumption of his remarkable range of activities made it seem that nothing had happened. Close friends noted, however – though often in hindsight – that he never totally recovered his vitality, that his lectures were never again as scintillating and that even his magnificent memory now occasionally failed him.

There is scant material to go on in amplifying and interpreting Laski's breakdown. The climate of the time, less sympathetic and less understanding of psychic illness, helps to explain the lack of detail and specificity in the historical and anecdotal records. He was certainly in poor health and there clearly seems to have been physical aspects to the crisis. A chain-smoker, always frail and vulnerable even when not under the strain of exhausting wartime travel, Laski might have suffered a stroke as the talk of passing out and diminished memory suggests. There are abundant contributing causes to psychic trauma, all of which seemed to bring major issues in Laski's life to the foreground. His father's death could well have triggered a crisis over Laski's own sense of mortality as he turned fifty, which was then exacerbated by the horrible news of Jewish deaths on the Continent. His sudden preoccupation with his own Jewishness might have been fraught with his own guilt at his earlier betrayal of his father and his religion, complicated perhaps by watching his own daughter moving rapidly to a life that proudly embraced a devout Christianity. The world was falling apart at the seams with evidence of nightmarish inhumanity, just as his own world seemed to self-destruct. The carefully woven contradiction that constructed his life as the consummate insider friend of the Great and the Good who also thundered from the outside at their power and privilege was unravelling. He was cast as an outsider by party regulars, the press, the BBC and government functionaries. He, in turn, had alienated Churchill, Roosevelt, Attlee, Frankfurter and Winant, who declared limits to what they would tolerate in his thundering, and who might even say, perish the thought, that he was no longer fun to have dinner with. Indeed, in his heart of darkness Laski might have confronted the limits of his life's strategy, the ultimate impossibility of supping with both the mighty and the miners, with both Mr Wigglesworth of the Harvard overseers and the wives of the police strikers.

Excitement over a projected summer trip to the Soviet Union as part of a Labour Party delegation provided Laski with an important lift from his depression in early 1944. Since the summer of 1941 and Hitler's invasion of Russia, Laski had called emphatically for closer ties with the Soviets. He had become a director of Gollancz's Anglo-Soviet Public Relations Committee, and in *New Statesman* and *Daily Herald* articles he praised the Soviet

Union for its resistance to Hitler's armies as well as for its accomplishments in shaping a 'new civilization' marked by universal literacy, large-scale industrialization and the triumph of science and technology. Russia, he wrote, had 'banished the twin enemies of civilized living – unemployment and ignorance'. Beatrice Webb, still vigorous in her eighties, wrote to Laski to say how thrilled she was about his articles on the 'heroic Soviet resistance' and Russian 'scientific humanism'. She asked him to look over the proofs of a new edition of *Soviet Communism*, and just before her death in April 1943 she asked Laski to be one of the executors of her will.

If Laski seemed less concerned in revisiting his 1930s criticism of the Soviet Union and the Webbs' indifference to its autocratic denial of civil liberty, he was in good company during the war. Churchill himself had announced unreserved solidarity with the Soviet Union, commenting that 'if Hitler invaded Hell I would make at least a favourable reference to the Devil in the House of Commons'. Beaverbrook's papers announced a 'Tanks for Russia Week' and throughout 1942 ran constant stories 'Thank[ing] God for Russia' as it bore the brunt of the war against Hitler. In June 1942 a Gallup Poll showed that 62 per cent of the population thought Russia 'more popular with the British' than was the United States. When victory came at Stalingrad, George VI presented the Sword of Stalingrad to the Russian people for the victory which he said had 'turned the tide'.

Although Malcolm Sargent conducted the London Philharmonic in a salute to the twenty-fifth anniversary of the formation of the Red Army, the Labour Party did not change its mind about allowing the CPGB to affiliate in either 1943 or 1944. Moved by the national spirit of empathy with the Soviet resistance and convinced that Stalin's move to dissolve the Communist International broke the tyranny of Moscow over Pollitt's party, Laski was more favourably disposed to affiliation than in the past. He offered a substitute proposal in May 1943, declaring that 'while unable to accept the application for affiliation of the Communist Party', the Labour Party still sought 'to achieve the unity of the working-class movement on the basis of the principles and policy of the Labour Party'. His hope was that the CPGB would agree to accept Labour's perspectives, but his resolution to the NEC to initiate discussions was defeated by fourteen votes to two.

While the Labour Party was saying no to Pollitt, Laski was on his own trying to establish it as the central player in a revitalized world socialist movement. In *Left News* he proposed the creation of a new Socialist International with London as its headquarters and the Soviet Union as one of its many members. The fourteen points of international socialist understanding animating the new organization included 'a resolve to do all in our power, as organized socialist movements, to secure racial and religious equality for all peoples everywhere' as well as 'a resolve to prevent, so far as we can, any attempt by the victorious governments to hinder working-class revolutions, especially by the denials of relief to socialist governments which take power'. An advisory committee with Laski as chairman, which included representatives from émigré socialist groups in London, was created under the banner of the International Socialist Forum. Every month from January 1943 through to the end of the war *Left News* allotted space to the Forum. In November 1944 the Forum published a manifesto calling on socialist parties around the world and especially in the liberated countries to convene an International Socialist Conference 'at the earliest possible date, and on the basis of full equality'.

Buoyed by the experiences of wartime cooperation, Laski assumed that Stalin would in turn shed his fear of the West and join this new Socialist International. He hoped to make this case on his visit to Moscow. Even if Laski had been successful in convincing the NEC to go along with what really was his own initiative, which it was far from clear he could achieve, Stalin's reaction became moot, because the Labour Party's request to Anthony Eden for permission for a delegation to travel to Moscow was denied. Laski's efforts, some two years in the making, were dashed. The War Cabinet decided 'that the visit of a single political party when several parties were represented in government would be liable to misrepresentation and it would be preferable for a parliamentary delegation including representatives of each of the political parties to visit the Supreme Soviet of the USSR'.

The Soviet Union was a central theme in the two books Laski published in this period, his 1943 *Reflections on the Revolution of Our Time* and his 1944 *Faith, Reason and Civilization*. The first of the two was dedicated to Edward R. Murrow and Lanham Titchener, the BBC producer of *Freedom Forum*, though Murrow was singled out for how profoundly 'his faith and trust in our people' had given Britain 'a new power to endure and hope'. Murrow told the journalist William Shirer that he was 'right proud' of the dedication, which had an added advantage: 'It has freed me from the pressure of some Tory dinner invitations.' In *Reflections*, his most radical book, Laski self-consciously used the title of Burke's great book on the French Revolution, for just as Burke was unable to see the outlines of the new world that was struggling to be born, so Churchill, Attlee, Bevin and Roosevelt were, he was convinced, locked into old world ways of thinking.

The Russian Revolution, Laski argued in the *Reflections*, marked the first stage in a fundamental transformation of Western civilization. Despite its 'follies, blunders, and crimes', its restrictions on freedom of movement, its lack of free speech, press or assembly, its arbitrary arrest, imprisonment and execution without trial, and its farcical elections, the Soviet Union since the summer of 1941 had come to represent 'a body of ideas to which every government in the future will have to accommodate itself'. It announced the competence of state power to abolish unemployment, plan production and organize scientific research for social benefit. Cooperation with the West, and a greater sense of its own security which would come from the capitalist world renouncing for ever any intention to attack the Soviet Union, would lead eventually, Laski was convinced, to the decline of Stalin's dictatorship.

But even before that came to pass, Laski insisted, Soviet Russia had much to recommend it. The Russian worker could not criticize Stalin as the British worker could criticize Churchill or the American Roosevelt, but he could criticize his factory manager 'in a way that is not easily open to the British worker'. Communist dictatorship 'may punish with harshness those who seek to escape from the fundamental rules', but it has 'achieved for millions the sense of a capacity for growth ... which enables its possessor to affirm his or her personality and is the very secret of freedom'. Laski called this 'positive' freedom, and in *Reflections* he offered an important and much-copied distinction between 'negative' freedom and 'positive' freedom. 'Negative' freedoms, according to Laski, are state-provided protections of individual rights and privileges against interference, while 'positive' freedom is the organization of opportunities by the state to harmonize individual and social purpose. The objective of socialism, to safeguard personality not property, involved a 'transvaluation of all values, the birth of a new civilization', and Soviet Russia was at the vanguard.

'With all its limitations, in its phase of dictatorship it genuinely seeks to exalt,' Laski wrote, 'and does in fact exalt, the stature of its citizens . . . Freedom in society has begun to operate on a positive plane.'

Accompanying the discovery of 'positive' freedom in Soviet Russia and his plea for an end to Stalinist repression, Laski filled *Reflections* with the arguments he had been making throughout the war about the introduction of socialism in Britain. In every chapter he insisted that 'the favourable moment is now and no other moment' because war broke familiar routines, enhanced social dependence, and created an 'experimental mood'. Laski warned against the siren call back to *laissez-faire* in the attacks on planning offered by Hayek, Robbins and Walter Lippmann (in his 1937 book *The Good Society*), which saw freedom achieved only by the free play of the market. *Reflections* was ultimately an argument for 'revolution by consent'. 'Men who begin with violence as a technique for securing power,' he was convinced, 'move as rulers to the concentration camp and the machine-gun.' It was Laski's recurring refrain. Only if the ruling class aborted peaceful revolutionary change was retaliatory violence legitimate.

> The curse of our social order is its irrational inequalities. Either we must find ourselves able to cooperate in their removal, or we shall move rapidly to conflict about them. Either, that is, the middle class must cooperate with the workers in essential revisions, as the aristocracy was wise enough to do, even if at the eleventh hour, a century ago over the Reform Bill, or violent revolution will be unleashed by means that may well transform the ends either party to the conflict has in view. That is the ultimate choice that lies before us.

Reflections on the Revolution of Our Time was a popular book in both Britain and America, riding the crest of public respect for the Soviet Union. *The Times Literary Supplement* found it a 'scintillating book' that 'everybody will be the better for having read and – still more – having digested it'. But not everyone liked it, by any means. Sir Alexander Cadogan, Permanent Under-Secretary of State at the Foreign Office throughout the war and the first British ambassador to the United Nations, recorded his views in his diary entry of 9 October 1943.

> Read Harold Laski's book. What warped and puny minds these ideologists have! And when they get down to the core of the matter, and try to analyse

it, they take refuge in mumbo-jumbo which of course hasn't any sense, and can't even be read as English ... Ye Gods! What roaring insanity! No – wicked mendacity, and conscious, sinful, unrepentant mendacity. Laski is an ass.

Socialists too were critical. Rebecca West in *Time and Tide* wrote of Laski the 'beloved teacher and beloved friend' whose strength was his hunger for righteousness and whose weakness was 'an impulsiveness which makes him desire to take the kingdom of heaven more quickly than by storm, even by burglary'. Whatever he wrote, she noted, 'Britain is not fighting Germany in order to defend socialism'. Laski's demand that 'socialists should push on their programme now would fail to burst open the doors of the kingdom of heaven', she concluded, and, on the contrary, would 'give Lucifer another lease on life'.

In a review for the *Observer* George Orwell emphasized the problems of Laski as 'a socialist by allegiance and a liberal by temperament'. Still trying to get a publisher for his anti-Soviet *Animal Farm*, he concentrated on what he took to be Laski's 'unwillingness to admit that socialism has totalitarian possibilities'. He faulted Laski, whose 'own instincts are all for liberty', for not realizing that socialism could in fact coexist with hierarchy and the rejection of free thought. Orwell applauded the boldness of Laski's criticism of the Soviet regime which, he suggested, 'will get him into serious trouble with the left', but he found Laski naïve to think that if Russia were safe from foreign aggression, the dictatorship would relax. Had it not grown tighter, Orwell asked, as the USSR grew stronger?

Even more central to his *Faith, Reason and Civilization* was Laski's lyrical hymn to the 'Russian idea' or the 'spirit of Stalingrad'. Dedicated to Winant, and written just before and in the early stages of his breakdown, the book was a rambling and often structureless philosophical meditation on the cultural and spiritual state of modern man desperately in need of a new faith. As Christianity had brought new values which rescued the West from the crisis of Roman decline, so for this generation, Laski argued, the 'Russian idea' offered a new triumphant faith. More than the turning-point in the battles of nations, Stalingrad became Laski's metaphor for the revitalization of the human spirit, marking the twilight of one cultural era, capitalist and Christian, and 'the threshold of an epoch of emancipation', the age of socialism and science. With the end of the profit and class systems, science and knowledge would make humanity the master of all the hostile forces in the universe and provide a saner, more rational world of social equality. The 'Russian idea', Laski argued, would conquer the West as Christianity did. Like early Christianity there was much, he granted, that was ugly, brutal and cruel about the 'spirit of Stalingrad', but 'these are part of the price a society is bound to pay which attempts the transvaluation of all values'.

Faith, Reason and Civilization was the least successful of Laski's many books in the 1930s and 1940s. Its excursions into literary criticism were shallow and its explorations of late classical history and philosophy were inaccessible to the lay reader. Lacking an argumentative base in the political issues of the late war period, it was too abstract to generate partisan controversy. The American reviews by Reinhold Niebuhr in the *Nation* and Norman Thomas in the *Progressive* were highly critical. In Britain, Orwell was even less kind to *Faith, Reason and Civilization* than he had been to *Reflections*, criticizing Laski for turning a blind eye to Russian 'purges, liquidations, the dictatorship of a minority, suppression of criticism and so forth'. Louis Fischer reviewed the book for the American journal *Common Sense* with the title 'Laski Should Know Better'. It wasn't an idea that triumphed at Stalingrad, Fischer complained, it was simply Russian power and courage, cannons and bombs, not values and beliefs. Laski himself seems to have soon regretted the excesses of his own argument. When the editors of *Common Sense* sent a copy of Fischer's review to him asking if he cared to write a rebuttal, the usually combative Laski replied: 'In this case, my friendship for Louis Fischer would make me humbly accept the application of his whip without repining.'

Perhaps Laski thought he had to be more circumspect about what he wrote in rebuttal after the book was published, because he was much more in the public eye than usual. George Ridley, Chairman of the NEC, died suddenly in January, and since positions rotated by seniority in service, Wilkinson became Chairman and Laski became Vice-Chairman. Chuter-Ede, Labour's junior minister at the Board of Education, noted in his diary in horror that 'if the Labour Party can survive these two appointments, it must be indestructible', and Dalton worried how 'deplorably ill-timed' it was that 'little Laski' was ascending to the leadership. In the autumn Wilkinson became ill and Laski began to preside over NEC meetings, writing to Frida that 'I like it'. In December he also served as Chairman of the annual Labour Party conference, which had been postponed from Whitsun because of the D-Day landings and German V-2 attacks on London. As militant as his attacks on the Labour Party leadership had been over the years, as insistent as he was that his concern was not a more expert or compassionate leadership for Britain but a total restructuring of power and authority within society, Laski was always willing to play the game of party politics even if its stakes were at best incremental and ameliorative change. Suddenly, only a few months after his breakdown, Laski was a party leader in his own right. Not that the responsibility stilled him. In the course of the year Laski managed to feud with the trade-unionist base of the party and with Bevin, Dalton and Attlee.

Most of the trade-union members of the NEC did not like Laski. They resented his frequent public calls for an age ceiling on MPs. They read his criticism of 'ancient' men, some 'stone-deaf', as directed at trade-union-sponsored MPs, and they were annoyed by his special pleas that in the next election, whenever it came, the party put up as many servicemen as it could. What brought open warfare, however, was Laski's comment in an American article, repeated in the *Tribune*, that 'there is hardly an aspect of Labour policy today in which trade-union leaders are not a brake on the wheel'. James Walker wrote to Dalton that Laski 'suffers from an overweening vanity in his belief of his own knowledge of men and affairs'. Charles Dukes, General Secretary of the National Union of General and Municipal Workers, felt that 'Laski was not fit to be Chairman of the National Executive next year'. Trade unionists knew socialism from life, Dukes wrote in his union magazine; they knew 'what the Laskis of today will never learn, that you cannot ram theories down the throats of men, no matter how attractive they may sound in the lecture room'. The labour movement, he wrote, was tired of the 'talking-down' attitude of these 'self-appointed mentors of our movement'.

> No, my dear Laski, it is not trade-union leaders who are putting the brakes on our movement, it is the academic people who build up false hopes and drag their followers into the belief that their finely phrased resolutions are capable of practical application.

Ernest Bevin, never one to resist fanning smouldering tension between trade-union members and intellectuals, joined the attack. Fearing any industrial chaos which would hamper the war effort, Bevin had required compulsory arbitration when miners went on strike in early 1944. His most vocal critics were Nye Bevan, Sidney Silverman and Laski on the NEC. Furious that only one third of Labour Party MPs supported his position, Bevin the next day managed to blame the intellectuals and Laski, who, of course, wasn't a Member of Parliament. Nor for that matter were the other two men intellectuals.

> Friends, what has the Labour Party been, what has it done? It is the fashion now for men like Harold Laski, Aneurin Bevan and Silverman, the intelligentsia, of those people who claim to be members of our party, to ridicule us, to denounce us, to say we are slow, to say we are conservative, to say we are reactionary. After all, we are the Labour Party.

Laski, not in the least inhibited by his vice-chairmanship of the NEC, replied in 'A WORD TO MR ERNEST BEVIN', published in the *Tribune* in May. Irritated by Bevin's phrase 'claim to be members' of the Labour Party, which he returned to repeatedly, Laski indicted Bevin, 'always certain that he is right', for dismissing as disloyal, hostile to trade unionism and lacking experience anyone who offered criticism. What Bevin must understand, Laski suggested, was that 'the main body of Labour Party supporters are profoundly dissatisfied' that their leaders made no effort to introduce 'a socialist commonwealth'. 'The allegiance of a socialist,' Laski bluntly concluded, 'is due to socialism first, and to Mr Bevin only as he fights for the achievement of socialism.'

The same week that Laski's rejoinder appeared in the *Tribune* Attlee wrote him a long and thoughtful letter. In four single-spaced typed pages Attlee finally replied in his way, privately and confidentially, to the years of Laski's public criticism of his leadership. Characteristically restrained, Attlee acknowledged that there was a gap between the party's socialist programme and what the wartime government had accomplished. It was unfair, however, for Laski to have expected more. 'We have to work today with the House of Commons which we have got', he argued, but then he was 'only a working politician' whereas 'you are a theorist'. Dramatic changes, moreover, had occurred. The government, not the Bank of England or the City, controlled the financial machine and state planning. There was not yet nationalization of the mines or the railways, Attlee conceded, 'but we cannot get this until we have a House of Commons ready to pass the necessary legislation', which meant a socialist majority after a general election. Meanwhile, many people had been converted to socialism by what they had seen Labour's leaders do in wartime, he asserted, despite Laski's 'mistaken tactics to belittle what has been done' and no matter how often he publicly pointed out that 'I have neither the personality nor the distinction to tempt me to think that I have any value'.

Laski also had troubles with Dalton in 1944. They both served on the NEC sub-committee which was drafting a statement on the post-war international settlement. Laski's illness left Dalton with most of the initial work, but in a series of meetings from November 1943 to April 1944 they addressed their disagreements. Laski had trouble with Dalton's hardline insistence on laying the burden of post-war recovery on the whole of German society and on his failure to encourage post-war development of German socialism or trade unionism. He was also bothered by the document's lack of attention to building a united working class in Europe or in reviving international socialist unity. Laski tried to have the whole document referred back to committee, but lost by nine votes to seven; he was then invited by Dalton to redraft minor parts that displeased him. Laski confined himself to replacing the word 'German' with 'Nazi' in several places.

Dalton was happy to discover that the Palestine paragraph in the draft pleased Laski immensely. It was approved by the December annual party conference, which Laski chaired. Labour was committed 'to let Jews, if they wish, enter this tiny land in such numbers as to become a majority'. The resolution as approved by the conference also included Dalton's controversial sentence, 'Let the Arabs be encouraged to move out as the Jews move in.' On the other sensitive colonial issue that the conference dealt with, India, it was Laski, not Dalton, who took the lead.

Since 1942 many of the leaders of the Indian independence movement had been imprisoned for their refusal to back the British in the war against Japan. Nehru was willing to support the war if self-government were granted, but when the British insisted on postponing action until the war was over and only if it were demanded by a Constituent Assembly, he and Gandhi and the Congress Party turned to passive disobedience and were jailed. Krishna Menon worked throughout the autumn of 1944 with Laski on a strategy for bringing before the conference the India question, which had been sidestepped in Dalton's draft. They persuaded the powerful National Union of Railwaymen (NUR) to move a resolution on the last day of the conference affirming the party's conviction that 'the granting of freedom to the people of India to establish an independent Indian National government will be a decisive factor in the fight against fascism'. The resolution called for the release from prison of all Indian political leaders and the beginnings of negotiations 'with a view to the formation of a responsible National government'. The NUR resolution was carried by a large majority and the Labour Party stood strongly committed to an independent India. It was a sweet victory for Laski, who throughout the war had objected to the party's refusal to push Indian independence as part of its price for sharing power with the adamant foe of independence, Churchill.

It was a good conference from Laski's perspective. Dalton thought Laski as chairman was 'a bit too flippant and ironical in some of his observations', but the mover of the vote of thanks at the end of the conference joked how everyone sympathized with Laski for having to be 'absolutely orderly and restraining himself'. He once again topped the poll for constituency party membership on the NEC and he was re-elected Vice-Chairman through to the next party conference scheduled for May. There were also substantive Labour left triumphs in addition to India. Hugh Dalton's rather vague and Keynesian economic proposal was amended from the floor, after a dramatic speech by Ian Mikardo, to spell out particular industries to be nationalized and then, consistent with its militant mood, there was the conference defeat of Bevin over Greece.

The Germans had withdrawn from Greece in October, and by December in a dramatic dress rehearsal of Cold War politics Churchill ordered full-scale suppression by British troops of the communist forces which had led the struggle against the Nazis. The battle in Greece raged as the Labour Party met in London, and Laski helped to draft an emergency resolution with Dalton, Attlee and Noel-Baker, calling for an armistice and free elections 'in order that the will of the Greek people may be expressed'. Bevin spoke forcefully against the resolution. The actions by the British in Greece were not simply Churchill's decision, he told the delegates: the whole Cabinet had agreed. Sounding like Churchill and the Cold War warrior he would soon become as Labour's Foreign Secretary, Bevin announced that 'the British empire cannot abandon its position in the

Mediterranean. On the settlement of these countries much of the peace of the future world depends.' The conference would have nothing of a traditional Europe, with monarchies once again in Yugoslavia and Greece, even if the messenger was Bevin; the resolution was passed by 2,455,000 votes to 137,000. Not that it changed much. Three weeks later Laski, Greenwood, Griffiths and Bevan visited Churchill on behalf of the NEC to discuss Greece, but to no avail. The fighting continued and, as Dalton recorded in his diary, 'though they don't admit it, he captivated and to a considerable extent persuaded them.'

Two months after the conference Sarah Laski died with Harold and Neville at her bedside. Laski had made many trips to Manchester since the previous spring, when she had become deathly ill, and had written movingly to Frida about Sarah and pathetic Mabel 'lost in bewilderment'. When she died on 24 February 1945, Laski felt it 'rather keenly, more than I can say, and it makes me grateful to have you [Frida] and Diana. I never knew it could hurt so much. I never knew in all these years all you and Diana meant to me until I found myself alone.' Smedley House was given to a charitable organization that ran hostels for young Jewish 'displaced persons', and Mabel was moved to a home. Seven weeks after Sarah's death Roosevelt died, and once again Laski was bereft, writing to Frankfurter that 'it was a blow almost beyond words. If you knew how much I counted on him for the first years of the peace. It is hardly a fortnight since I had a grand and cheerful letter from him. I can hardly bear to think that I shall never see him again.' Diana gave birth to a second son that very day and she gave him the middle name Franklin.

Some weeks after his mother's death, in an address to the Poale Zion, the Manchester Jewish Socialists, Laski proclaimed his conversion to Zionism, which made him feel 'like a prodigal son returning home'. He had been an advocate of assimilation 'who thought that the best service Jews could give to civilization was to lose their identity'. But now he was 'firmly and utterly convinced of the need for the rebirth of the Jewish nation in Palestine . . . No other country but Palestine could have any meaning for them.' In the remainder of his speech, however, Laski set in motion angry letters to the *Jewish Chronicle* from irate rabbis and Jewish lay leaders, though some came from sympathetic secular Jews as well. Laski did not want to be misunderstood. He was returning, he told the Poale Zion, 'to a special kind of home'. He had 'no more interest in the Jewish religion, professed by so many and practised by so few, than in any other creed'; moreover, he wanted his audience to know that 'as a Marxian socialist he held that religion was an opiate for the people'.

Laski never, in fact, returned to his Manchester 'home'. As his parents never fully embraced Zionism, he could not accept their traditional Judaism. He had, indeed, become an outspoken partisan of Palestine and Zionism. During the war, for example, he became close friends with Orde Wingate, the maverick British officer who when stationed in Palestine had embraced Zionism in the 1930s and trained Jewish settlers in commando tactics. Indeed, in late 1944, after Wingate's death, Laski wrote a worshipful speech about him in response to a frenzied request from Winant, which brought Laski back to favour with the ambassador. But religion was another matter. Laski was to his core a secular rationalist and he managed to stir up trouble for his much more spiritually inclined Labour colleagues by his very public wartime criticism of the Lord's Day Observance Society and of compulsory prayers in state schools, let alone by speeches on religion as a mass opiate.

Very much a loose cannon whose combative and controversial nature and views attracted trouble, Laski was not the person one would want to be chairman of the party in an election year. That would be, in Dalton's terms, 'deplorably ill-timed'. But so it was to be, for a week after Laski's Manchester speech, Churchill and his Labour allies brought the wartime coalition to an end and scheduled a general election for July. At the Labour Party's annual party conference held in Blackpool the same week as Churchill's announcement, Laski was chosen in his rightful turn to be Chairman of the Labour Party. Labour would fight the first general election in ten years with the most unlikely of chairmen. No one was more sensitive to the historical ironies than Laski. Indeed, six months earlier he had begun his Chairman's Address at the party conference, as Wilkinson's stand-in, by dramatically drawing attention to them.

Your Chairman today is . . . not one of those who have been able either to influence the course of discussions in the House of Commons or in the great Trade-union movement out of whose aspirations and dreams the Labour Party has so largely sprung. Your Chairman today is an example of that dangerous species who, so far as my knowledge goes, is in our movement rarely trusted and never praised – the species whose professional work is criticism and thought . . . In a party composed of workers by brain as well as workers by hand, I represent something a little different from the past – British by birth, middle class by origin, Jewish by inheritance – as symbolic of the vital fact that the Labour Party knows no boundaries save those which are defined by faith in its principles and policies.

CHAPTER NINETEEN

Labour's Triumph and 'A Period of Silence'

Two days after VE Day Frida worried about Harold who had 'aged ten years and has felt the war more than most'. Three weeks later she felt he was 'in much better shape now with the exhilaration of election work'. Apart from the euphoria of victory over Hitler, there was also the return to some semblance of normalcy which Laski described to a friend in Illinois: 'After six years in the cave, light and no curtains at night and the right to lie awake without the need to listen for an alert is like the forecourt of heaven.' There were clear intimations, however, that the election year with Laski as Chairman of the Labour Party was going to be less than seraphic. The *National Review* had already indicated the tough tone of what was to come, picking up on Laski's Labour Party conference speech.

> Anything less like the British working man than an international Jew could not well be imagined, and yet Mr Harold Laski presided at the big meeting of the Socialist Party on 11 December. It is said that every nation has the Jews it deserves. We do not know what we in England have done to deserve Mr Laski, but there he is, sneering at us and decrying us and our very English Prime Minister, but though he has so much contempt for this country, with no thought of returning to the country, whichever it was, that his parents came from and with no idea about the land he happened to be born in, save to make a revolution in it.

The Labour Party was playing tough politics itself, though at first against itself. A full-scale effort was waged in May to dump Attlee as party leader before the election. Public opinion polls throughout the war showed little support for him as a national leader, and the popular refrain within the party was that he brought to the fierce struggle of politics the tepid enthusiasms of a lazy summer afternoon at a cricket match. In February the

New Statesman had called for Labour 'to elect a popular national leader'. Efforts began in earnest to replace Attlee at the Blackpool conference in mid-May, orchestrated by Wilkinson, the Chairman, Laski, the Vice-Chairman and Maurice Webb, the former parliamentary correspondent for the *Daily Herald*. Cripps, Bevan and Shinwell seemed inclined to replace Attlee, though they couldn't agree on an alternative. The trio of prime conspirators, Wilkinson, Laski and Webb, were pushing for Morrison, largely because he had sided with the Labour left on the NEC – Laski, Shinwell and Bevan – earlier that month in opposing the apparent willingness of Attlee, Bevin and Dalton to stay in Churchill's governing coalition. Also crucial for Laski was the fact that Morrison was his principal ally among the party's leaders. He was the one among them who most liked and respected Laski. In turn, Laski was more likely to listen to him than to others when cautioned to hold his fire at party conferences and NEC meetings. Morrison once even corrected a parliamentary colleague who had criticized Laski as 'just an intellectual'. 'There is a difference,' Morrison chided him, 'between intellectuals who rise with the labour movement and those who rise on it. I object to those who rise on the movement. Laski rose with it.'

Morrison was more than willing to answer the call, but at the party conference the Wilkinson–Laski–Webb 'coup' picked up few recruits. Dalton felt it would be a disastrous sign of Labour indecision and Bevin was furious. Not only would replacing Attlee be an act of consummate disloyalty, but Attlee was just what Bevin thought was needed as party leader, a man who had a gift of holding together a team of clever subordinates. Moreover, Attlee's self-effacing modesty was preferable, Bevin insisted, to the personal leadership of a MacDonald or Churchill. So angered was Bevin at efforts to oust Attlee that he stopped talking to Laski for a time. Meanwhile, the Labour Party Whip, William Whiteley, advised Laski 'to leave matters alone as it would confuse the party if Attlee resigned just before the election as Lansbury did in 1935', but Laski persisted. In a hand-written personal letter to Attlee on 27 May he proposed that for the sake of the party he resign as leader.

> This is a very difficult letter to write . . . I have been made acutely aware for many weeks, especially during the Blackpool conference, of the strong feeling that the continuance of your leadership in the party is a grave

handicap to our hopes of victory in the coming election . . . No one, to my
knowledge, has anything but respect for your character and high integrity
. . . but it is no less strongly agreed that the peculiar personal qualities which
the leader of a party now requires, the sense of the dramatic, the power to
give a lead, the ability to reach the masses, the maintenance of an intimate
relation with your immediate followers, the definition of great issues in a
great way – that these require a different personality from yours. As
Chairman of the party . . . I should be failing in my obligations if I did not
ask you regretfully . . . to draw from this the inference that your resignation
of the leadership would be a great service to the party.

Attlee's reply to Laski was characteristic and brilliant: 'Dear Laski, thank
you for your letter, contents of which have been noted.' The matter was
dropped, or so it seemed.

Churchill set the tone of the election campaign. There were, according
to Beveridge, two Churchills: the 'Great Churchill', the war leader who
spoke to the heart of all Britons; and the 'Little Churchill', who insulted,
sneered and ridiculed his opponents. It was 'Little Churchill' whom the
electorate heard most of the time. Many who revered Churchill were
shocked when in his first campaign broadcast on 4 June he established the
theme of his campaign. He wanted to inform the British, he began, about
'this continental conception of human society called socialism'.

My friends, I must tell you that a socialist policy is abhorrent to the British
ideas of freedom . . . Socialism is inseparably interwoven with totalitarianism
and the object worship of the state . . . It will prescribe for every one . . .
where they are to work, what they are to work at, where they may go and
what they may say; what views they are to hold and within what limits they
may express them. . . . Socialism is an attack on the right to breathe freely
without having a harsh, clumsy, tyrannical hand clasped across the mouth
and nostrils . . . No socialist system can be established without a political
police . . . No socialist government . . . could afford to allow free, sharp, or
violently worded expressions of public discontent. They would have to fall
back on some form of Gestapo, no doubt very humanely directed in the first
instance.

Socialism as an alien 'continental' ideal was difficult enough to accept,
but the reference to the Gestapo so few months after the opening of Belsen
and Buchenwald outraged even *The Times* and the *Economist*, which
described Churchill's speech as 'pernicious nonsense'. Harold Macmillan

later described as an 'outrage the implied attack on colleagues with whom [Churchill] had been working in perfect amity for the last five years – men of moderate opinions such as Attlee, Morrison and, above all, Bevin'. Churchill had a problem about how to run against Attlee, the self-effacing 'sheep in sheep's clothing'. His decision was to run not against the leadership, but against the Labour left. It was not only a tactical decision but a heartfelt one too, for Churchill had recently been moved by Hayek's immensely popular 1944 book *The Road to Serfdom*, in which he had argued that socialist state planning led inexorably to a totalitarian police state. Nazi Germany was itself, Hayek argued, as much a product of socialism and anti-capitalist fervour as a 'mere revolt against reason'. Not surprisingly, since Laski had so consistently criticized Hayek in his writings since the 1930s, Hayek singled out Laski several times in this book, which took the business community in America and Britain by storm. Citing Laski's concern with 'security', Hayek concluded outrageously that Laski was 'employing the very same argument which had perhaps done more than any other to induce the German people to sacrifice their liberty'. Churchill's decision to campaign against socialist planning by equating it with a Gestapo state created the bizarre phenomenon of a general election being fought on one level between the rival doctrines of two LSE professors.

Not all Tories followed Churchill and the ideas contained in *The Road to Serfdom*. Beaverbrook was the principal champion of *laissez-faire*, but 'Tory reformers' like Quintin Hogg, Peter Thorneycroft, Macmillan and Butler wanted to continue on the path of social reform. Still, Churchill's speeches set the theme: socialism meant foreign totalitarianism. Lord Croft, a Churchill camp-follower, accused the Labour Party of wishing 'to impose upon the British people the crude ideas of the German Marx, developed by the German Engels, and regiment our life in a manner not very different from that of National Socialism in Germany'. Admiral of the Fleet Lord Keyes reinforced the alien nature of this socialism by invoking the Labour Party's Chairman: 'I cannot believe,' he protested, 'that the British people could follow a government whose ministers are dominated apparently by an individual with the good old British name of Laski. Vote British, please.' Not that Labour was above pandering to nationalism either. In his radio reply to what came to be called Churchill's 'Gestapo speech', Attlee drew out carefully for criticism Churchill's use of the equally foreign 'second-hand version of the academic views of an Austrian professor Friedrich August von Hayek'.

Laski gave over sixty speeches during the five-week campaign. Despite Frida's fears, they seemed to revivify him. Edmund Wilson accompanied his old *New Republic* colleague to many of the hustings and was impressed with the eloquence, passion and satire. The press loved to write about Laski as 'the brains of the Labour Party' and quote, for example, his characterization of Lord Beaverbrook as 'the first Baron of Baloney'. Churchill, Laski repeated, did not win the war by himself. He was helped by a Cabinet which included Bevin, Morrison and Attlee, by the armed forces, by the civil defence forces and by the workers in the factories. Occasionally Laski had to respond to hecklers. On 24 June someone asked if he were English and on 28 June another inquired, 'Did you write asking Mr Attlee to resign as leader of the Labour Party and are you still of the opinion that he should resign?' Laski answered curtly, 'It is none of your business.' After 15 June things got much nastier, however, because most unexpectedly Laski himself became a central issue in the campaign. The Beaverbrook press had decided to run against Laski, the red professor and *éminence rouge* behind the kindly Attlee and the avuncular Bevin and Morrison.

Beaverbrook and Churchill were handed the Laski issue by Laski himself. On 14 June Churchill had announced that he, Stalin and Truman were to meet in Potsdam on 15 July to discuss the post-war international settlement. He invited Attlee to accompany him since the election results were not to be announced until 26 July, even though polling day was 5 July, because of the time needed to collect the votes of servicemen around the globe. It was important at the conference, Churchill announced in the House of Commons, to show the world that Britain was united. Attlee's presence provided 'an opportunity for saying that although governments may change and parties may quarrel, we stand together on some of the main aspects of foreign policy'. Enter Laski, Labour Chairman and Professor of Political Science, whose profession was making learned points and fine distinctions. He wrote privately to Attlee that night: 'I assume you will take steps to make it clear that neither you nor the party can be regarded as bound by any decisions taken at the meeting, and that you can be present for information and consultation only.' What Laski did not know was that Attlee had already consulted with Labour's parliamentary leaders, who had agreed that he should accept the invitation. Unable to reach Attlee by phone that evening, Laski published a statement in the *Daily Herald* the next morning.

It is, of course, essential that if Mr Attlee attends this gathering he shall do so in the role of observer only. Obviously it is desirable that the leader of the party which may shortly be elected to govern the country should know what is said, discussed, and agreed, at this vitally important meeting. On the other hand, the Labour Party cannot be committed to any decisions arrived at, for the Three Power Conference will be discussing matters which have not been debated either in the Party Executive or at meetings of the Parliamentary Labour Party.

The Tories had their villain. The next day Beaverbrook's *Daily Express* ran as its banner headline OBSCURE LASKI CAUCUS WILL GIVE ORDERS. Laski, the head of the NEC, was the real power in the Labour Party, the dictator of 'the secret party caucus'. Attlee, the paper suggested, was a prisoner to the NEC and Laski his jailer. Would Parliament, the paper asked, be sovereign if Labour won or would its majority party be bound to some final power residing in some little-known committee presided over by 'Gauleiter Laski'?

Laski defended himself in a memorandum to the NEC. He was concerned, he wrote, about Churchill's assumptions about the continuity of foreign policy and the need to make clear that Labour had different views on Greece, a left-wing government in France or Franco. Only Bevan supported Laski's position. The Labour leadership was incensed at what Dalton called Laski's 'silly little intervention' and the public picture it gave of a divided party. Attlee did not publicly rebuke or try to silence Laski, he simply wrote to Churchill immediately in a public letter that 'there seems to be great public advantage in preserving and presenting to the world at this time that unity on foreign policy which was maintained throughout the last five years. I do not anticipate that we shall differ on the main lines of policy which we have discussed together so often.' As for the NEC, it had a right to be consulted about party policy but it had no 'power to challenge the actions and conduct of a Labour Prime Minister'. Sensing the value of a public retreat, Laski issued a statement that 'everything has now been satisfactorily cleared up'. But no one told this to the Tories who now ran against Laski. In his next radio broadcast Churchill told the nation that Labour was a party where 'the tail wagged the dog'.

A new figure has leaped into notoriety. The situation has now been complicated and darkened by the repeated intervention by Professor Laski, chairman of the Socialist Party Executive. He has reminded all of us, including Mr Attlee, that the final determination on all questions of foreign policy rests, so far as the Socialist Party is concerned, with this dominating Socialist Executive.

Professor Laski has declared on several occasions, three at least, that there is no identity of purpose between the coalition foreign policy of the last five years, as continued by the present National government, and the foreign policy of the powerful backroom organizations, over one of which he presides.

My friends, the British people have always hitherto wanted to have their affairs conducted by men they know, and that the men should work under the scrutiny and with the approval of the House of Commons. Now it seems we must refer to an obscure committee and be governed by unrepresentative persons, and that they will share the secrets and give the orders to the so-called responsible Ministers of the Crown, who will appear on the front Socialist bench of Parliament if they are returned and deliver orations upon which they have been instructed not from their own heart and conscience, not even from their constituencies, but from these dim conclaves below.

Attlee vigorously responded to Churchill that 'the new position with which we are confronted exists only in your mind'. 'The Chairman of the Executive Committee of the Labour Party,' he added, 'has not the power to give me instructions, nor do his remarks to a press correspondent constitute the official authoritative and reiterated instructions of the Executive Committee of the Labour Party.' Beaverbrook was not going to let matters rest, however. The *Daily Express* covered the Churchill–Attlee exchange under the headline SOCIALISTS SPLIT: ATTLEE REPUDIATES LASKI ORDER. It ran a front-page picture of Laski accompanied by a quote from his 1930s pamphlet *The Labour Party and the Constitution* which argued that monarchy and social democracy 'are not, in the long run, easily compatible'. Several days later the *Daily Express* ran a long front-page article THIS MAN LASKI – HE IS THE POWER BEHIND THE PARTY AND WHY. The article, a profile of 'the prominent public man of whom least is known by the vast mass of the British public', also featured quotations from Laski critical of the throne and in favour of root-and-branch socialism.

Beaverbrook returned daily to 'Laski-ism', which the *Express* described as the doctrine of not trusting the leader. 'Warn him that he must never make a decision,' read one of its principles, 'until it has been referred back to be approved or rejected by an obscure caucus or junta who are not answerable to the electors.' In a general story on Attlee, the *Express* columnist William Barkley added 'Goody, goody, but Mr Attlee will have to ask Mr Laskee'. In a speech at Streatham Baths on 20 June Beaverbrook told the Conservative faithful that

> in fact the simple issue at this election is – shall foreign policy be decided by the House of Commons or by the Laski Council? I hereby declare that Laski is aiming at the destruction of the parliamentary system of Great Britain and that he hopes to set up in its place the dictatorship of something commonly called the National Executive.

Tory Party hecklers followed Laski to each of his campaign speeches armed with excerpts from his writings and speeches. Their instructions were to ask questions about revolution, hoping to trap Laski into an unguarded slip or ugly anger. It seemed to have worked in Newark, since on 20 June the banner headline in the *Daily Express* read: NEW LASKI SENSATION: SOCIALISM EVEN IF IT MEANS VIOLENCE. Laski had come to Newark on Saturday night, 16 June, to speak for Air Vice-Marshal Hugh Vivian de Crespigny, the unlikely and ultimately unsuccessful local Labour candidate for Parliament. Laski spoke by microphone from the back of a long lorry to about 1,500 people standing in the largest cobbled market square in the country. According to the *Newark Advertiser*, a weekly Beaverbrook paper with a circulation of 10,000, Laski spoke for over an hour, and when most of the crowd had left one man came up to the truck and belligerently asked Laski two questions. Why had he not served in the First World War and (consulting cards or papers he held) why had he openly advocated revolution by violence in speeches at Bishop's Stortford and Bournemouth during the war? The *Newark Advertiser* and the *Daily Express* reported that Laski angrily replied he had been rejected by the army on medical grounds and 'as for violence, he continued, if Labour could not obtain what it needed by general consent, we shall have to use violence even if it means revolution'. The story ended by quoting the moral that the questioner, Mr Wentworth Day, fired back.

> You are precisely the sort of bloodthirsty little man, full of words, who has never smelt a bullet, but is always the first to stir up violence in peace. We expect serious constructive thought from the Chairman of the Labour Party, but since you have consistently attacked everyone and everything from Mr

Churchill to the leaders of your own party and the Constitution of this country, and have been disowned by Mr Attlee only this morning, how can anyone take you seriously? I suggest that you are not an asset to the Labour Party but a liability.

Laski immediately issued writs for libel against the *Newark Advertiser*, the *Nottingham Guardian* and the two multi-million circulation London Beaverbrook papers the *Daily Express* and the *Evening Standard*. He circulated to the Press Association a letter denying that he had advocated violent revolution at Newark or at any other time in his life. It was false and malicious to report that he had said if Labour were not elected 'we shall have to use violence even if it means revolution'. He had said, he claimed, that 'great changes were so urgent in this country that if they were not made by consent they would be made by violence'. In other words, he was warning the electorate to beware the possibility of violence.

The writ for libel made any discussion of the events at Newark *sub judice*. Since the original claims could not be further investigated by a newspaper or reported publicly without incurring the risk of heavy penalties for contempt of court, there was no overt discussion of the charges after 21 June. Churchill asked Lord Kilmuir, his legal adviser, 'how far he could go' in using Laski's Newark remarks and was told to steer clear of it, or he would face contempt charges. Some in the press found ways to keep Newark alive obliquely. The *Daily Mail*, for example, took to referring to Laski as 'the bland bombshell', and 'Candidus' in the *Daily Sketch* accused Laski of not running for Parliament because 'in his heart he despises parliamentary institutions as outmoded and useless for the consummation of the socialist purpose'. Lord Simon, Churchill's Lord Chancellor, suggested that Laski initiated the libel suit only to prevent discussion of the Newark incident during the campaign. He told a Tory meeting at Carshalton, 'I'll bet you that as soon as this election is over you won't hear anything more about these writs.'

The Labour leadership was horrified at the damage Laski was inflicting on the party. One newspaper described 'an atmosphere of confusion amounting almost to despair at Transport House, the party's headquarters'. Dalton reviewed the incident in his diary: 'A further fuss, as to whether the little fool said that in any circumstances we should "use violence" – I always find it rather comic that this contingency should be discussed by this puny, short-sighted, weak-hearted, rabbinical-looking-like chap!' Forbidden by the writ from addressing the details of the Newark incident, Morrison and Attlee denounced 'Tory attempts to divert public attention from the real issues of the election – houses, jobs, social security and food – by stunt-mongering, untruths and scares'. In the tradition of previous scares such as the Zinoviev Letter of 1924 and the Post Office savings affair of 1931, Morrison claimed that 'these bright gentlemen of the Conservative Central Office, aided by their lordship of Fleet Street, have nailed on Professor Laski as their main instrument of electoral diversion and excitement'. It was 'preposterous and absurd' to suggest that the Labour Party or any of its members was in favour of violent revolution, he added. To be a member of the party, both Attlee and Morrison reminded the press, one had to be committed 'to fighting elections in a democratic way'. Meanwhile, Laski had retained G. O. Slade, KC, the country's leading authority on libel law who had represented Neville in his suit against *Truth* magazine five years earlier, and his suit began wending its way through the judicial process.

On election eve the Conservatives still hammered away at Laski, despite evidence that few voters seemed worried by, let alone interested in, 'Gauleiter Laski'. By demanding a joint letter from Attlee and Laski on the powers of the Labour Party Executive, Churchill tried to keep alive the perception that Attlee was merely 'the titular socialist leader'. The *Daily Express* asked in one of its last election headlines, SHALL THE LASKI '25' RULE GREAT BRITAIN? Labour's *Daily Herald*, by contrast, complained that Conservatives 'recklessly exploited the name of Professor Laski because Laski is a foreign-sounding name and because the Party Chairman is a Jew'. If his name were Smith, the paper noted, 'his utterances would never have been so distorted'. The *Manchester Guardian*, in its editorial of 3 July, criticized the Conservative Party for its preoccupation with the 'Laski letter', linking Laski's note to Attlee with the Zinoviev Letter of 1924. And even *The Times* pronounced the 'Laski bogey' exaggerated. 'There is a genuine likelihood that the public will end by treating the whole affair as a diversion.' In his election eve speech in Kensington, Laski light-heartedly congratulated his audience for coming to hear 'the Himmler of the Labour Gestapo' who was about to make 'Ernest Bevin, Clem Attlee and Herbert Morrison dance to the tune I choose to play'. He promised in a day to 'return to the academic obscurity from which I have emerged. I know my place and it was generally known. I only wish Mr Churchill were able to understand it.'

For three weeks no one knew the outcome of the balloting as servicemen's votes were received. Attlee accompanied Churchill and Eden to Potsdam on 15 July, and a recess was declared on 25 July to allow Churchill and Attlee to return to London for the announcement of the election count. Three days later Attlee, the new Prime Minister, and his Foreign Secretary, Ernest Bevin, returned to Potsdam; Churchill and Eden remained in Britain. It had been a stunning Labour victory with a majority in the House of Commons of nearly 150 – accompanied by one last dramatic effort to replace Attlee as party leader and Prime Minister. Churchill had sent a message to Attlee on the afternoon of 26 July conceding victory and telling him that he would be tendering his resignation to the King that evening and also recommending to George VI that he send for Attlee to form a new government. Morrison, Attlee, Bevin and Laski were all at Transport House for the election returns when the concession arrived, and Morrison and Laski urged Attlee to tell the King that forty-eight hours were needed for the newly elected Labour MPs to choose their leader. Morrison gave formal notice that he intended to be a candidate and Laski provided the constitutional rationale. The Labour Party Constitution, he insisted, required the election of a leader at the beginning of each Parliament. Attlee had been elected in 1935 by a Parliamentary Labour Party of 154 members. The new body of 393 Labour MPs now had the responsibility to choose a leader. Bevin was once again the critical figure. People had voted for Labour assuming Attlee would be Prime Minister, he maintained, and even a short delay in assuming power would convey an image of a divided party. Bevin told Attlee to go to the Palace and accept the Prime Ministership as soon as the King's message arrived, which Attlee did. 'If you're invited by the King to form a government, you don't say you can't reply for forty-eight hours,' Attlee wrote later. 'You accept the commission, and you either bring it off successfully or you don't.' The next day Attlee met with the Parliamentary Labour Party, and when Bevin moved that the body register a vote of confidence in the new Prime Minister, there was unanimity. Laski's plot had failed.

Labour's victory was a stunning upset. So great was the expectation that Churchill and his party would be returned that on 27 July the American

Catholic magazine *Commonweal* ran a story by George Catlin bitterly attacking Laski's vanity, ineptitude and desire to be the centre of attraction under the headline THE MAN WHO LOST THE BRITISH ELECTION. Churchill, the great war hero, had been turned out of office, however, by what Dalton called 'the votes of the football crowd'. The service vote of over 1.7 million also went predominantly to Labour. Churchill notwithstanding, the Tories were seen as the party of Munich, and Labour, not as wild revolutionaries but as efficient managers who had proved they could 'get the job done' in their wartime ministries. The forced sharing and mutual suffering of the war had produced a communal climate responsive to Labour's electoral message of a better-planned egalitarian society with full employment and improved social benefits for all. Laski was generous to Churchill in this moment of personal vindication as it fell to him as Party Chairman to speak of the former Prime Minister at the tumultuous Labour victory rally at Central Hall, Westminster, late on the night of 26 July.

> May I, as the temporary head of the Socialist Gestapo, say that not all of us have been treated with generosity in this election. But on the day his rule as Prime Minister draws to a close I want in the name of the British Labour Party to thank Mr Churchill for the great service he has rendered to this nation.

When Attlee returned from Potsdam five days later, Laski made peace with him. In a letter dated 2 August, Laski granted that 'I have often criticized you' but pledged that 'whatever support my loyalty can bring to aiding the government I will give gladly and proudly'. In the next sentence Laski asked Attlee to make him ambassador to Washington. He knew America well, he wrote, and Bryce a half-century earlier had shown that a scholar politician could successfully interpret and represent Great Britain to the United States. He reminded Attlee of his twenty-five years of not insignificant service to the party. He was convinced he 'could do a good job in Washington and I care for that more than for anything else'. The appointment would also let 'the Beaverbrooks and the Brackens know that my own party does not regard me as a leper it would not touch'. A week later Laski asked Dalton to help with the ambassadorship and was told diplomatically that he could do nothing since it was totally up to Attlee and Bevin.

Laski believed he would receive the appointment. He had worked tirelessly for the party, deserved recognition and was perfect for the job. But he had virtually no idea what people in the party really thought about him, or at least he pushed it out of mind. Laski as ambassador to Washington, especially in a period when Britain was clearly going to be financially dependent on America, struck political insiders as ludicrous. In his wartime diary, Sir Bruce Lockhart of the Foreign Office wrote of meeting Richard Crossman in early August, who told him 'that Laski was trying his hardest to be made ambassador to Washington' and that 'he had no chance of getting the job'. A Jew would not be sent to Washington, Crossman told Lockhart, and in any case 'the trouble about dear Harold' is that nobody in the Labour Party 'ever believes more than two per cent of anything that he says'. Of course, nothing came of Laski's request. Attlee never answered the letter of 2 August. He didn't have to, for in the next few weeks Laski so annoyed Attlee that the Prime Minister rebuked him in what became a fabled chapter in British political folklore.

Behind the 'period of silence' lay Laski's failure, as he had promised on election eve, to return to the anonymity of academic life. He had repeated this promise during the three-week wait for the election returns in a *New Statesman* article, 'On Being Suddenly Infamous', where he described being 'whisked back from the front page to that ivory tower in which I could live in that state of wistful coma the universities call research'. These visions of Laski off centre stage presumed, however, Labour's defeat and some attribution of responsibility to him. Being chairman of a victorious party with, for the first time in its history, real power as well as office was another matter, and not surprisingly Laski spoke out frequently about what Labour should do. Bevin knew even at the victory rally that Laski and the Labour left would not quietly let moderate Cabinet ministers govern. To an equally jubilant Kingsley Martin at the Central Hall, Westminster, festivities, Bevin said, "Ullo, oogly! 'ow long before you'll be stabbin' us in the back?' Not long, in fact.

In a series of well-publicized articles, radio talks and foreign trips in the month after the victory, Laski managed to infuriate not only the Tories but the leadership of the new Labour government. Laski's assertion on Edward R. Murrow's radio programme that the socialization of the Bank of England was the first priority of the nationalization schedule sent the London Stock Market into a sharp decline. Speeches to socialist meetings in Europe on Labour's future foreign policy caused Laski the most trouble, however. Well might he think he spoke with some authority on foreign affairs, for in addition to being party chairman he had on 1 August replaced Dalton as Chairman of the NEC's Sub-committee on International Affairs, since Dalton's ministerial duties as Chancellor of the Exchequer gave him too little time for the NEC. In the summer Laski made speeches at socialist meetings in France, Denmark, Norway, Italy and Sweden. He was virtually lionized in European socialist circles, where his kind of secular socialist intellectual was a much more typical presence on the left and where his books and pamphlets were widely reprinted and his articles and speeches widely quoted. In France he had been the friend of Anatole France, and since 1930 the good friend of the literature professor turned politician Léon Blum. There and in Italy he was seen as a towering intellectual figure. Benedetto Croce, for example, made a trip expressly to meet Laski on his visit, and many others regarded him 'as a figure comparable with Marx in the intellectual history of socialism'.

Everywhere Laski went in Europe the British press followed, labelling him 'the peripatetic professor' or 'the wandering minstrel of socialism'. And they reported his every controversial comment. In France he claimed that Labour was committed to 'squeezing Spain' through economic pressure to bring down Franco, which was immediately denied by Bevin. There were reports that he urged an economic union of all Western Europe focused on a unified system of transport, an ideal not far removed from his earlier writings on functional pluralism. He was also quoted as advocating the creation of a unified single state out of the two nations of Britain and France, assuming, that is, that the socialists were victorious in the French elections. In a speech in Italy Laski endorsed the decatholicizing of the state through the abrogation of the concordat between Italy and the Vatican and the establishment of a totally secular system of public education. In Sweden he commented that Britain was a second-class power.

Tory politicians demanded to know who spoke for the government, Laski or Foreign Secretary Bevin and Prime Minister Attlee. Had Churchill and Beaverbrook been correct in their fears about Laski as the real power in the party? All of this emerged dramatically in the parliamentary debate over the King's Speech, the government presentation of its legislative agenda. In the House of Lords Lord Cranborne complained that 'the almost daily declaration of policy made by the Chairman of the Labour Party came in a regular spate'. Were these, he asked, 'Professor Laski's own views or were they the views of His Majesty's Government'? Lord Addison replied that the government 'accepted no responsibility whatever' for Laski's comments. Attention was really riveted on Laski,, however, when Churchill raised the issue in the Commons. 'What precisely,' Churchill asked, 'was Mr Laski's authority for all the statements he was making about our foreign policy?' Was His Majesty's Government going to reverse its policy on Greece, as Laski was claiming? Was there a plan to unite France and Britain in one nation with a common citizenship? Did the government 'contemplate vehement intervention in Spain against General Franco'? Churchill denied he was suggesting that the government 'endeavour to muzzle Mr Laski'. 'Anybody,' he said puckishly, 'in a free country can say anything, however pernicious and nonsensical it may be', but it was essential 'for the government to let us know exactly where they stand with regard to him'.

Replying to Churchill's questions, Attlee suggested to much laughter that, like Churchill, 'Professor Laski had a somewhat ebullient phraseology and at times was apt to be a little impulsive'. On a more serious note he made clear that Laski spoke only for himself 'and as a citizen of this country he had the right to express his views'. As for the policy of the government it was, Attlee assured the House, laid down by no one but the Labour ministers. Others spoke more directly to some of the substantive issues Churchill had raised about Laski. In his 'maiden address' as a new MP, Michael Foot, for example, asked whether suggesting a new attitude towards Greece made Professor Laski 'guilty of some monstrous crime'. Contacted that night at home by the press, Laski reinforced Attlee's answer to Churchill. 'I think he stated the position with the accuracy and precision which are characteristic of him,' Laski told reporters. 'It is quite obvious I was only speaking for myself in Paris . . . The Labour government would obviously speak through the mouth of its Prime Minister.' This was the reasonable public face of the Attlee–Laski rift; but three days later Attlee wrote in private to Laski.

> The constant flow of speeches from and interviews with you are embarrassing. As Chairman of the Labour Party Executive you hold an important office in the party and the position is not well understood abroad. Your utterances are taken to express the views of the government. You have no right whatever to speak on behalf of the government. Foreign affairs are in the capable hands of Ernest Bevin. His task is sufficiently difficult without

the embarrassment of irresponsible statements of the kind you are making. I can assure you there is widespread resentment in the party at your activities and a period of silence on your part would be welcome.

The Tory *Evening Standard* on 22 August applauded the public comments Attlee and Lord Addison had delivered on Laski the 'wandering minstrel', and invoked Lord Samuels's warning to Labour: 'Beware your intellectuals – and one intellectual in particular.' Laski, of course, didn't observe even a small period of silence. He wrote first to Attlee suggesting rather testily that he should not 'accept your friends at the valuation of your enemies', and to a Labour MP who accused him of 'possessing an admirable tactlessness', he replied that he meant to fulfil 'his duty as guardian of the principles of the party'. Attlee wrote again in January, not, as he put it, 'to raise any question of your loyalty' but to 'complain of a lack of judgement and accuracy of statement which is not infrequently embarrassing'. Some of the younger Labour MPs in the House of Commons were in fact not unsympathetic to Laski's message. Michael Foot recalls thinking then that 'a period of silence' was less in order from Laski than 'a period of spokesmanship' and leadership from Attlee. For his part, Laski offered his reflections on his relationship to the party in an October 1945 letter to Max Lerner.

I, and heaven help me, seem to Attlee and Bevin rather like I seem to Westbrook Pegler since I take the view that until the annual conference next May I am the guardian of party policy whatever the government may do, and that I must see that this is stated without fear as a body of socialist doctrine. So it follows that everything I say and write is 'not helpful', and I have had frankly to insist that I am not a member of the government and that I must go on doing my duty even if they are embarrassed, and that their obvious remedy is to ask the Executive to compel me to resign. So far, at least, they have not had the courage to face that issue, and we merely have angry discussions and angrier letters. I, of course, will not be a tame creature of their lack of courage; but it is a hideous situation, when all one's leaders are on the side of one's enemies and one can't even tell the truth to the rank and file. It makes me want to bury myself somewhere so far away that I can't even hear the echo of their noises.

Attlee and Bevin had less reason to worry about the embarrassment

Laski caused in Britain than they did about what Americans thought of him. By a strange twist of fate, it was Laski's reputation and visibility in America in 1945 and 1946, more than the barbs of the Tories, that troubled the Labour government. The context for these fears was Britain's immediate post-war economic dependence on America. Truman had unilaterally suspended lend-lease aid to Britain immediately after the end of hostilities, and in September Keynes was dispatched to America to negotiate a huge loan to keep the British economy afloat. After eleven weeks of deliberations and then months of congressional debate, a loan of $5·4 billion was approved narrowly in the Senate and House of Representatives. The negotiations were complicated by American insistence on the use of British bases around the world, in wrangling over British attitudes to the future of Palestine and in demands for a vigorous anti-communist stance from Westminster. Reservations in America about supporting a socialist government had to be overcome by Keynes and Halifax, still the ambassador, but President Truman and Senator Vandenberg championed the loan as crucial to American self-interest in combating the spread of Soviet ideology. In Britain it was clear to Bevin that Britain's financial weakness 'has necessarily increased the need to coordinate our foreign policy with that of the only country which is able effectively to wield extensive economic influence, namely the United States'. No one seems to have posed a greater threat to Britain's receiving the fruits of that economic influence than Laski. When Richard Crossman, himself on the Labour left, visited America in February 1946 in the middle of the Congressional deliberations, he speculated that the loan's chances of approval were only fifty-fifty and complicating it all was Laski.

> For the average American – and even for the well-informed New Yorker – British Labour means Harold Laski and nothing else. His most insignificant address to a local Labour Party makes the front page. No one fails to ask you about him and what you reply is completely unimportant. America has made up its mind that Laski is the Lenin of the British Reds . . . No one should underrate the effect of this wave of Laski-itis, following on the equally untempered cult of Mr Churchill . . . to this underestimate of our strength is added the myth that the British people voted Churchill out and Laski in.

Socialist-baiting Americans, like Churchill, seemed to have trouble in deciding who governed Britain. Immediately after the vote count, for example, the *New York Mirror* ran the long headline CLEMENT ATTLEE MADE PRIME MINISTER OF ENGLAND AND THE BOSS IS HAROLD LASKI A PRO-RUSSIAN FIGURE. Feature articles by or about Laski appeared in the four great American weekly pictorial magazines, their circulations in the millions. During the war he had written a piece for *Look* on Britain's war aims and in September 1945 he wrote 'Socialism, British Brand' for *Collier's*. It was, however, the long biographical profiles of him, complete with pictures and cartoons, in the *Saturday Evening Post* and *Life* in 1946 that conveyed true celebrity status. The *Post* story, called 'We Beg Him to Insult Us', had as its sub-title 'For some reason beyond human ken, Americans keep on encouraging Red Prof. Laski, a London hot-house brain, to tell us why he doesn't like the way we live'. It was complete with American journalese characterizations like 'a natural-born showman and spiritual seducer, Laski has something of the eternal Sinatra appeal, and one does not need to stretch one's imagination far to visualize the raptly listening girl students in his audience as so many swooning bobby-soxers'. Speaking of his diminutive appearance, the *Post* wrote, 'The world's most brilliantly destructive mind may lurk within, but the exterior is highly unalarming.' *Life*'s treatment was true celebrity stuff. Written by John Chamberlain, one of its editors, it had a full-page photograph of Laski seated in his book-lined study as well as the requisite set of cartoons. Titled HAROLD LASKI, its sub-title was 'Britain's controversial Red professor is not so important in the Labour Party as the US supposes. But his ideas permeate its thinking.'

Laski was everywhere in the American press. Henry Luce's other weekly, *Time*, gave his former teacher an equally large spread immediately after the election. Under the title OFFICIAL PHILOSOPHER there was a detailed biography complete even to a reproduction of the Laski *Lampoon* cover from 1920. The 'March of Time' newsreel shown in 7,000 cinemas had a feature on the 'Chairman of the Labour Party and semi-official government spokesman'. In *Harper's* Rebecca West wrote a thoughtful profile of Laski in 1946, and even the more careful *New York Times*, which informed readers BRITAIN NOT RUN BY INTELLECTUALS: LASKI'S ROLE MINIMIZED, could in another story on another day describe the Labour Party's programme with no mention of Laski in the text yet use as the only picture to accompany the article a picture of Laski. Frequently reported in the

American papers were Laski's criticisms of American businessmen. His
Collier's article, for example, was one long indictment of America as a
business culture. A London speech describing 'big business in America' as
'hard, relentless and grasping' was reported in the *New York Times*, with
the headline LASKI AGAIN RAPS US BIG BUSINESS. No wonder there was
concern about the American loan on both sides of the Atlantic. An article
by the American conservative columnist George Sikolsky in the *New York
Sun*, widely reported in the British press, complained that 'since the
Labourites have come to power Harold Laski has done nothing but talk'. If
Britain wanted to go berserk by spending its own money on Laski's
socialist schemes, so be it, Sikolsky concluded, but America should not be
asked 'to underwrite the profligacy' to the tune of $3–6 billion. The *New
York World Telegraph* wrote in December that 'the Chairman of the Party
now in control of the British government is not thrilling Americans over
the idea of lending that government $4 billion out of the fruits of our
terrible businessman-dominated free enterprise system'. It was unseemly,
the paper added, for representatives of nations 'in the front rank of
panhandlers' to be criticizing America.

Laski, meanwhile, was suggesting in public that American opponents of
the loan were out to sabotage Britain's socialist experiments, just as many
Americans were running out of patience with him. 'If Mr Laski wanted to
wreck the current negotiations,' the *Christian Century* wrote on 26
September, 'he could scarcely have found a more likely method than this
of planting the idea that what the United States is being asked to do is vote
for or against socialism.' If Congress took Laski seriously, 'the negotiations
might indeed run into trouble'. In Attlee's papers at the Bodleian Library
are numerous letters and telegrams written in these months to the Prime
Minister from America about Laski. 'The man is intolerable,' writes one.
Another asked whether Attlee couldn't 'run him out of the Labour Party'
or at least 'prevent him talking quite so much'. A Mr Charles C. Everett
wrote to Attlee that millions of Americans thought that 'loud-mouth Laski
is Prime Minister'. If, he warned the real Prime Minister, 'present negotiations fail, he will be largely responsible. Americans don't like his kind
(Hillman, Dubinski and others) all foreign-born Jews and all very noisy . . .
They and their kind are due for rough treatment.'

The negotiations were not made easier by press leaks revealing that the
two left-wing Labour ministers, Bevan at Health and Shinwell at Fuel and

Power, were (unlike Laski) opposed to the loan. The politics of the loan also made for strange bedfellows: the old Tory appeaser Halifax told Americans in a nationwide broadcast on 25 September that they 'need not fear that the British government is about to plunge into rash economic and social experiments'. Attlee came to America in November and made his own case for the loan in a speech to Congress, but, by and large, Labour was hesitant, fearful of stirring up 'the socialist issue'. When, for example, in February 1946 the American Broadcasting System offered a free fifteen minutes to British Cabinet ministers, the Labour Cabinet declined, prompting ABC's Director to observe that 'the Laskis will always talk and Americans should not be blamed for thinking that the voice of the latter are the real voices of Britain, they hear the real voices so seldom'.

Many Americans were disturbed by Laski's criticism of 'big business'; by his casual acknowledgement on the Murrow broadcast that 'we are revolutionists' (even if he had insisted that change would come not by 'bombs and hand-grenades' but 'through the mechanism of parliamentary government'); and by Laski's speeches about 'the age of capitalism drawing to a close'. But no comment ignited anything like the fire-storm created by a radio statement on 24 September to a rally at Madison Square Garden, New York, sponsored by the Spanish Refugee Appeal, at which the Soviet chargé d'affaires, the Vice-President of the United Auto Workers and the actor José Ferrer spoke. A CIO chorus, augmented by Broadway stars, sang Spanish Republican war songs. In his broadcast to the rally Laski, speaking 'in a purely personal capacity as a private British citizen', demanded that diplomatic recognition of Franco be withdrawn by America and Britain. He ridiculed the idea advanced by the Vatican that the Spanish monarchy could be re-established through the free choice of the Spanish people. Would a Spanish monarchy, he asked, 'prevent the Roman Catholic Church in Spain from remaining a rich monopolist at the expense of mass poverty?' London and Washington were doing nothing, he claimed, because 'they feared the hostility of the Vatican to support of a democratic resurgence in Spain'.

A week later Max Lerner wrote to Laski that this speech, which had been reported on the front page of the New York Times, 'has all the Catholic hierarchy out against you, breathing fire and brimstone thru their nostrils'. Even liberals were a little upset, Lerner added, since many 'still regard the Church as being sacred and immune from all political criticism'.

Two days after the rally the *Manchester Guardian* reported that William Barry, a Democratic Congressman from New York, had sent a telegram to Truman opposing any loan to Britain because of Laski's 'typical communistic smear attack on the Catholic Church and advocacy of the restoration of the so-called Spanish Republic'. As the Vatican press office in Rome denied involvement in any effort to restore the Spanish monarch, a county prosecutor in New Jersey lodged a formal complaint against radio station WJZ for violating a New Jersey statute 'that makes it a misdemeanour for anyone to broadcast an attack on any religion'. Responding to public pressure the ABC radio network, to which WJZ was affiliated, gave free radio time on 8 October for a national broadcast by the Commander of the Catholic War Veterans to reply to Laski. In attacking the Vatican, Commander Edward T. McCaffrey claimed that 'this non-American Laski' was 'insulting millions of God-fearing Americans'.

Columbus Day on 12 October, celebrated in America with Catholic parades and rallies, provided a venue in New York for further attacks on what speaker after speaker referred to as Laski's 'malicious attacks upon the Vatican' and his effort 'to establish a bastion of communism in Spain'. In early November the House Un-American Activities Committee weighed in, announcing that over 5,000 letters protesting against Laski's remarks had been received by the committee 'from Jews as well as Christians'. The committee declared its intention to investigate the affair. It was time, a spokesman stated, 'to determine how far you can go with free speech'. Meanwhile, the Catholic actor Frank Fay asked the actors' union to censure the five Broadway stars who had attended the 'red meeting which condemned religion'. Actors' Equity, the union whose President was then Ronald Reagan, rejected Fay's complaint, and in turn voted by 470 to seventy-two to censure Fay for making public his condemnation of his fellow actors. This led on 11 January to yet another rally at Madison Square Garden, where 20,000 people gathered to protest against the censuring of Fay and, as the meeting's chairman put it, to expose 'communism as a godless philosophy seeking to undermine American democracy'. Only the liberal Catholic weekly *Commonweal* seemed to demur as it insisted that Laski had not assailed religion or Catholicism, only the politics of the Church.

The Laski fire-storm was further fanned by the announcement in the *New York Times* on 7 November that he would be visiting New York City on 3 December to give an address at a dinner sponsored by Freda Kirchwey's *Nation* magazine. The Commander of the New Jersey Catholic War Veterans, calling Laski 'an international trouble-maker', demanded that Secretary of State James Byrnes cancel Laski's visa and give the plane ticket to a GI war bride from Britain who 'would be a definite asset to America as the mother of future American citizens'. American Catholics were not the only ones worrying about Laski's forthcoming trip to America, his first since 1939. J. Edgar Hoover's Federal Bureau of Investigation paid close attention to Laski's movements, but even more concerned was Halifax, the British ambassador, who wired Bevin to try to get him to forbid or postpone the visit.

Foreign Office files reveal the anguished dilemma confronting the British embassy in Washington. 'Professor Laski,' one memorandum noted, 'would very soon start to provide the kind of ammunition for hostile Congressmen' which might torpedo the loan. But if his trip were in any way cancelled or postponed, 'the entire liberal press of America would be filled with fulminations against us'. The advisory minute given to Halifax could not decide 'which is the greater evil from our point of view – to infuriate the conservative and Catholic elements, or the liberals who admire Professor Laski. The Catholics are certainly the more numerous and politically powerful group.' Moreover, because of Ireland, Catholics traditionally exercised anti-British influence in American politics. 'Catholic pressure on Congress is more dangerous' for the fate of the loan, an embassy official wrote, but 'the liberals have considerable nuisance value'.

Halifax telegrammed Bevin on 12 November that 'the visit would be a mistake'. He 'would much prefer the visit not to take place or at least to be postponed so as not to coincide with possible discussion in Congress on the economic and financial agreement'. Throughout this period Laski knew he was being monitored, for he told Max Lerner in late October that whenever he was attacked in the USA 'the busy little bees in the Washington embassy send it all over to London to make Bevin feel I am an evil influence poisoning Anglo-American relations'. Indeed, before Freda Kirchwey's invitation to New York, Laski had assumed that he would not be coming to America for some time, writing to friends that no college president would endorse an invitation to 'public enemy No. 1'. Bevin, however, decided to permit Laski to go, writing on the bottom of his request, 'Make arrangements for him, it will do no harm.' Not only did he then receive top-level clearance, but also promise of passage on a government plane.

His itinerary in America was kept secret by the embassy and the *Nation* as Laski flew to Montreal and then to Washington for a brief visit to Frankfurter before going to New York for the dinner on the night of 3 December. The affair for 2,000 people at the Hotel Astor was the climax of a three-day conference sponsored by the *Nation* to discuss the atomic bomb and the future of atomic energy. Laski, the evening's main speaker, sat at the head table with Kirchwey, Eleanor Roosevelt, the Foreign Minister of Australia and Dr Leo Szilard, one of the scientists who helped to develop the atomic bomb. Hours before the guests arrived, black-robed Catholic priests and nuns began picketing in front of the hotel entrance. They carried banners and signs reading 'Hands off Catholic Spain'. 'Franco saved Spain from Reds, Mr Laski' and 'Oust Laski anti-Catholic hate-monger'. There was no physical disruption when Laski arrived, and when he began his speech he departed from his text to note that he had never 'assailed the Roman Catholic religion . . . nothing could be more fantastic or untrue. My life has been devoted to tolerance. I made a criticism of a state.'

Laski's speech only intensified the furore in America. John Balfour, a career British diplomat then posted in Washington, wrote years later that it was vintage 'firebrand' Laski, 'goading and exasperating Americans by stinging references to the free enterprise system, which he compared to a political and economic concentration camp'. The speech was indeed a diatribe against the 'anarchy of free enterprise'. A society dominated by businessmen, he argued, could not be trusted to create a climate in which atomic energy would be confined to peaceful uses. The world had come to a crucial dividing line: 'there is no middle way. Free enterprise and market economy mean war; socialism and planned economy mean peace.' Turning Hayek on his head, Laski described the American economy as 'the direct road to serfdom'. As for atomic energy, no nation could be trusted with its development, not even the Soviet Union 'where the businessman has ceased to count'. Only a new international order, where national sovereignty had been replaced by 'planned internationalism, economic social and political', could bring peace in the nuclear age.

The reaction was immediate. J. Parnell Thomas, the Republican Congressman from New Jersey and member of the House Un-American Activities Committee, asked on 5 December why the State Department allowed 'red trouble-makers' like Laski to enter the country. His 'rabble-rousing speech' in New York, in which he attacked 'our American way of life', was an insult to all Americans. Why didn't 'bleeding hearts' from Britain mind their own business, Thomas asked, 'instead of demanding loans from America'? In the Senate on 7 December, Homer Capehart of Indiana announced that 'unless the British government denounces the views pronounced by Professor Laski, I cannot and will not support the loan', and on 8 December the Chairman of the Republican Party, Herbert Brownell, declared that Laski would be a central issue in the Congressional elections in 1946. He was thankful for Laski's visit and his speech, since Laski, 'the darling of the left-wing elements' in the Democratic Party, defined the choices the American people faced at the polls. 'If they agree with Mr Laski,' he urged, 'they should vote for the so-called Democratic candidates.' If they disagreed with the 'Laski or left-wing democratic solution', they should vote Republican.

Laski returned to London on 5 December. The day he left, the *New York Herald Tribune*, like Brownell, thanked the editors of the *Nation* for bringing him to America. At long range, 'the beauty of his prose, the extent of his erudition and the weight of his reputation' overwhelmed with their impressiveness. Only getting him there on home ground enabled one 'to realize how silly and intellectually irresponsible he can be'. For his part, Laski told reporters at La Guardia Airport that he had two vivid memories of his brief visit: the size of New York newspapers and the rediscovery of American chocolate ice-cream.

Before the Congressional votes in May and July 1946 finally put to rest the Laski furore there was one more brief episode. In a February House of Commons debate on the funding for the British Information Services in New York, a Tory MP referred to Laski as 'an international problem' who 'the American people thought represented the British Labour government and about 80 per cent of the people as well'. The Labour Under-Secretary for Foreign Affairs agreed with the Conservatives' suggestion that Bevin, whose blunt language the Americans loved, be sent quickly to speak to Americans. He added that since Labour had not yet perfected a Gestapo to enforce its will, the government could do nothing, however, to keep 'wandering minstrels from the London School of Economics at home'.

Laski returned often in early 1946 to the subject of his New York *Nation* speech, repeating in much more highly charged ideological language the plea that Attlee had made to Congress in November that America share the secrets of atomic energy with the world scientific community and that research and development of atomic weapons be under international control. Laski worried that Truman's decision not to share nuclear information with the Allies would revive dormant Soviet suspicions about the West's intentions, and he urged that all stockpiles of atomic bombs be destroyed or put in the possession of an international authority so that one power could not 'compel the submission of another power to its will'. In his zeal, Laski created another international flap in April 1946. The Americans, he said, had bombs so devastating that one or two could destroy the states of Indiana and Illinois, and five could obliterate the whole of the United States below the Mason - Dixon line. 'It was,' he told a Co-operative Party conference, 'an iniquity that three men in a room in the White House should be in the position to determine the fate of mankind.' Major-General Leslie Groves, who had been in charge of the Manhattan project which developed the atomic bomb, immediately replied that 'he could not imagine a bomb of that power' and that the atomic bomb was being discussed 'by so many who know so little about it'. The *New York Daily Mirror* was less diplomatic. Laski's remarks were all 'a big lie' invented by the 'Russian-loving, American-baiting British pip-squeak Laski'. Senator Hart, a member of the Senate Committee on Atomic Energy, insisted that, 'Mr Laski knows nothing whatever concerning the subject on which he talks. Even if he did know. I am quite unable to agree with him that we should teach everybody how to do it.'

'Russian-loving' Laski was actually trying in these months to get the British left to claim leadership of a world-wide socialist community that, while sympathetic to Russia and its interests, would not regard it as an ideological master. Churchill's 'Iron Curtain' speech in Fulton, Missouri, in March 1946 worried Laski because it portended a military alliance of the United States and Britain against Russia which not only might lead, he wrote in the *Glasgow Forward*, to 'Wall Street pressure on England to abandon socialism' but also jeopardize any independent British role in world socialist politics. On his visits to France, Italy and Scandinavia in 1945 Laski pleaded with socialists like the Italian Nenni to avoid 'fusion' with their national communist parties, as Labour had managed to do for decades, and instead to work for the establishment of a Socialist International as the cornerstone of the post-war world order.

In January 1946 Laski and Nenni did indeed announce in London the formation of a new body, the Fifth Socialist International, which would meet formally later in the spring. In the March issue of *Left News* Laski described the proud autonomous history of the socialist parties of Europe. There was no universality to the Bolshevik experience which made Russia a model for socialist politics. 'We deny,' he wrote, 'that Moscow is, as it were, a Mecca where every socialist must go on pilgrimage to be cleansed of the sin of believing that the method of freedom rather than the method of violence is a possible road to power.' Defence of Russia from Western interference yes, but European socialists, Laski insisted, 'should not be compelled to defeat their own movements and to remodel them on a basis that is rarely applicable to their own condition'. It was necessary, of course, to convince the Russians not to be upset by these 'socialist' intentions, so Laski revived his old idea of a Labour Party visit to Moscow and plans were set for a summer trip. Laski would do his best when he met Stalin to counter the old Leninist line which Alexandrov, the chief Soviet propagandist, was now using to criticize Laski, the attack on meddling 'professors in bourgeois society who sell learning to serve the interests of capital and who are ready to utter the most improbable nonsense and unconscionable stupidities and rubbish'. In Laski's advice to European socialists to cooperate but never merge with communists, Alexandrov saw an utterly different Laski than the American press did: he saw him engaged in 'anti-Soviet propaganda' and 'opposing the interests of the working class'.

Nor did the American press pay much attention to Laski's slashing assault on the Communist Party of Great Britain in the very month of his speech on atomic bombs. For the tenth time Harry Pollitt in 1946 asked the Labour Party to allow his party to become an affiliated socialist society. The NEC again rejected the bid and this time Laski volunteered to write a pamphlet explaining the action to ensure party conference endorsement in June. 'Clem thanked me for it,' Laski wrote to Frida. The result was the influential pamphlet *The Secret Battalion*, which allowed Laski to make for Britain the case for socialist autonomy he was making for other European countries and for the world scene *vis-à-vis* Moscow as well. After a thoughtful but blunt contrast between 'authoritarian' and 'democratic socialism', Laski addressed what it would be like to have the CPGB within the Labour Party. He employed themes he had used as early as 1927.

They act like a secret battalion of paratroopers within the brigade whose discipline they have accepted. They meet secretly to propose their own line of action; they have one set of rules to be observed towards those who are not in the battalion . . . the contradiction between the open profession and the secret purpose makes them willing to sacrifice all regard for truth and straight dealing . . . They require from their own members the complete and unquestioning sacrifices of their consciences to the decisions their inner leadership makes.

In terms of reproach similar to those often hurled at him, Laski condemned the CPGB for thinking in 'terms too alien from the historic experience of this country to be valid premises for the political action of the British working class'. The Labour Party, he concluded, intended neither 'to follow the communist road to dependence upon Moscow or the road of dependence upon Washington'. If the members of the CPGB wanted to bring their energy to the working-class tents of the Labour Party, they would be more than welcome as individuals, but the party would be foolhardy 'to admit a Trojan horse within its citadel'.

The pamphlet produced yet another chapter in the long relationship of Laski and Pollitt. Taking great exception to the pamphlet, but especially to Laski's use of an alleged quotation from the Bulgarian communist leader Dimitrov about communist parties seeking to stab social democratic parties in the back, Pollitt wrote a letter to the *Daily Herald* suggesting that Laski was mistaken not only about that quotation but in his entire depiction of CPGB motives. Pollitt then questioned Laski's own motives. 'It is well known in political circles,' he suggested, 'that Professor Laski is trying to work his passage home into the good graces of Transport House so that his turn of office as chairman may end in a blaze of anti-communist glory.' Laski had ulterior motives in writing the pamphlet, to be sure, but they were less to ingratiate himself into Labour Party favour than they were to further his personal initiative to create a unified socialist third force beholden to neither Moscow nor Washington.

Pollitt notwithstanding, Laski had no problems in distancing himself from Labour even as party chairman. He spoke generously about its achievements, often with humour. The nationalization of the Bank of England had 'turned the little old Lady of Threadneedle Street into an honest woman', and the National Health Service meant an end to charitable dependence on 'My Lady Bountiful and My Lord Bountiful'. But most of

the time Laski acknowledged that the party's welfare state vision was not
the socialist commonwealth he dreamed of with, as he liked to insist, a
transvaluation of values and a real transfer of power in society. There was
no swift audacity, no willingness to outrage powerful interests in the
Labour government's actions. He confided to his close friend Lance Beales
that the party felt

> no sense of urgency. There is too much fear of making a mistake, the desire
> to be respected by the officials. Coalition-mindedness has the same result as
> being in a minority . . . and so the favourable moment passes by.

Even in delivering the ritualistic chairman's address at the June conference
in Bournemouth Laski maintained his allegiance to the Labour left. Yes,
the party could be proud of reforms in finance and credit, nationalization,
social insurance and national health. It had finally repealed 'that mean and
ungenerous' Trade Union Bill of 1927. But it was a different vision that
Laski called the party to in his concluding paragraph, using the apocalyptic
language of 'building Jerusalem' favoured by the party's earliest leaders.

> I do not even pretend that our own generation can enter the promised land.
> But I believe, with all my heart, that if all the men and women in this
> movement not only feel about it deeply, but also think about it greatly, we
> can, in the next years, build the foundations of an experiment in the good
> life to which posterity will look back with admiration. I covet for our party,
> even more I covet for our country, the ability to pioneer in a full socialist
> achievement as we pioneered in the definition of socialist principles. If we are
> still hardly out of the Valley of the Shadow of Death, we have begun to
> climb the Mountains of Hope. Let us remember that the more the energy
> with which we advance, the more hope and courage this stricken world will
> find in our example. Let us, therefore, with high hearts and unbreakable
> courage, march on to the socialist commonwealth.

It was a tired and spent Laski who addressed the delegates on 14 June
1946. He had led a gruelling schedule in the twelve months since Blackpool.
Even more painful was the realization that he had little influence in a party
that now governed, compared to former colleagues who ran huge and
powerful departments of state. The beginning of his eclipse was poignantly
symbolized in the constituency party balloting for the NEC, where for the
first time since 1938 he did not receive the most votes, finishing second to
Nye Bevan, the Minister of Health. The London papers on 15 and 16 June

characterized his year as party chairman with phrases like 'annoying genius', and 'blazing indiscretions'. The consensus was that the Labour Party leaders were happy the year had come to an end, because, put most generously, 'the swiftness of his intelligence often outgalloped his judgement'. Laski himself, in the concluding minutes of the conference, turned and thanked the reporters for 'the devoted attention they have given to my activities. Never in the history of mankind have so many followed just one. The skeleton now goes back to the cupboard.'

Exhausted as he was after his remarkable year at centre stage, Laski soon made two tiring trips, first to the Soviet Union and then to the United States. The official Labour Party visit to Russia that Laski had long sought took place between 29 July and 13 August. Laski went with two members of the NEC, Alice Bacon, MP, Harold Clay, an official of the Transport and General Workers' Union, and Morgan Phillips, the party secretary. The group was kept busy visiting Moscow, Leningrad and Stalingrad and meeting daily with Soviet and party officials, as well as making the obligatory visits to factories, hospitals, collective farms and schools. Laski, along with the others, was convinced that the mistrust and misconceptions of the Soviet leaders could be dispelled by personal contact, and they assured their hosts that the British labour movement and the British people strongly desired a real and abiding friendship with the Russian people.

The highlight of the visit was a two-hour private session with Stalin on the evening of 7 August. Much of the talk was about the achievements of the Labour government in its first year in office. Stalin spoke about 'the more roundabout British way' towards socialism, which he contrasted with the 'shorter but more difficult' path trod by the Soviets. When Stalin asked whether industrialists dispossessed by nationalization had offered any resistance, Laski stressed the importance the progressive outlook of intellectuals had on all elements in society, concluding with quotations from Voltaire and Diderot. When Laski finished, Stalin turned towards him and quietly said, 'Ah yes, Mr Laski, but Voltaire and Diderot had no coal mines.' As the four visitors got up from the table, Stalin, according to Laski, whispered to him to leave his umbrella behind, to justify his return, for he wanted to talk to him alone. As Laski tells it, he did, and the next day they had a four-hour chat. The story bears an uncanny resemblance to the hairbrush episode thirty-one years earlier with Holmes, and none of the other three visitors remembered Harold slipping away, although they did disagree on other details. Laski remembered coating his stomach in advance with mineral oil and then being pleased when the Russians exclaimed, 'Mr Laski, for a small man you have quite a capacity.' Alice Bacon, on the other hand, recalls Laski 'getting drunk out of his mind drinking vodka with Russian generals and having to be carried to bed'. Whatever really happened, the assessment of the visit by Foreign Office officials was best captured by one of the translators. 'That evening's neatest piece of wit came from an Englishman, who seeing Laski surrounded by a group of Russians and talking volubly, remarked to me, "There's Laski, casting as usual imitation pearls before real swine."' He also remembered, however, that when a Russian disparaged Churchill's recent 'Iron Curtain' speech, Laski 'insisted that Mr Churchill was a great leader, for whose services in the war the Russians had good cause to be grateful'.

Laski wrote four short articles about his reactions to Russia for the *New Republic*. In 'My Impressions of Stalin' he described the Generalissimo as shrewd, patient, rather quiet and possessed of a 'sly humour'. He respected power, 'the strong state, the strong man, strength in itself'. He was more tolerant, Laski suggested, of 'other possible routes to a socialist society' than most observers assumed. On the other hand, Laski worried 'how much of the stream of thought and ideas outside of Russia penetrates to him'. Sober and generally critical, the articles contained none of the rhapsodic invocation of a new civilization, which had characterized his wartime books. The principal set of observations was about the absence of civil liberties, 'the immense power of the secret police,' and the rigidly hierarchical party apparatus. Laski suggested that the real villain was Molotov, whom he thought less flexible and conciliatory than Stalin, although in a revealing comparison with Churchill he sensed that Molotov did not speak for himself.

> I know, further, that if some of Churchill's speeches must seem deliberate and massive provocation to the Russians, at least they have only his personal responsibility behind them; while some of Molotov's speeches, at least equally deliberate, and equal in their massive provocation, have behind them the great weight of the Russian government.

While in Russia Laski had been unable to discern how policy-makers regarded his plans for a new Socialist International. He was impressed by the apparent acceptance of non-Soviet paths to socialism, but events were fast overtaking his dream of a unified socialist alternative. The Labour Party, preoccupied with its own domestic agenda and rapidly being brought to accept Washington's vision of the world by Bevin, was reluctant to play the institutional sponsoring role that Laski had held out to the European socialist parties. Moscow, for its part, all of Stalin's tolerant talk of multiple paths to socialism notwithstanding, was cracking down on democratic socialist parties in the countries in its orbit, the very parties Laski assumed would play a vital role in the new Socialist International. A second meeting of the new Socialist International had been held in London in June with Laski heading the British delegation and very much in charge. Schumacher, the German socialist leader, declined to come, however, for fear of offending the Soviets, while Nenni, already contemplating an electoral pact with the Italian communists, was losing interest. Laski sensed that his vision of a reconstituted Socialist International to replace the technically dissolved Communist International was doomed, and despite another, even less well-attended, London meeting in the autumn the initiative was bearing no fruit.

It was, then, not only a tired but a sadly disillusioned Laski who arrived in America in late August for two months of well-deserved holiday. He was also worried. Diana was to give birth to a third child while he was in America and his letters to Frida were full of his concern for 'Dikey's' well-being. As in the past, Laski promised Frida that he would not lecture extensively, but this time, even though the invitations poured in, he stuck to his word. It was a time to visit friends. He spent weekends with Ruth and Alfred Cohn in Connecticut and New York City. He saw the Frankfurters several times, and despite their by now very divergent political views he and Felix fell easily into their old joy in each other's talk. He found Marion Frankfurter and her aloofness difficult, writing to Frida that 'she makes me feel like the bourgeois French writer being received by the *grande dame* of the eighteenth century'. There was good talk and good food with Max Lerner both in New York City and on Long Island. In Washington he had a quiet dinner with Mrs Roosevelt, and also saw Justice Black, Dean Acheson and David Niles. Niles, a very close adviser to Truman, wanted to arrange a meeting for Laski with the President, but Laski uncharacteristically declined, writing to Frida that he didn't want Attlee and Bevin to think he was playing politics behind their backs. Laski visited Morris Cohen, who was deathly ill in New York, and when the

Murrows returned from a cross-country motor trip he spent time with
them. There was no lecture at Harvard, but dinners with Perry Miller,
Crane Brinton and Larry Winship of the *Boston Globe*. Laski visited the
New Republic, where he missed Michael Straight, but went to yet another
nostalgic dinner. He saw a good deal of Freda Kirchwey at the *Nation* and
of Huebsch and Harold Guinzburg of Viking Press.

Laski spent a particularly sentimental day with a group of non-famous
New Yorkers, former GIs who had studied with him in London. While
they awaited their return to the States, GIs had been encouraged by the
US army to attend university courses. Over 200 American servicemen
lived in a half-bombed-out hotel in Russell Square. Even while party
chairman, Laski taught full-time at the LSE and he was a particular
favourite with the GIs because he seemed to treat them with more respect
than other faculty did. He in turn loved to talk with them after class and
accepted their invitations to join them for dinner at their mess in London.
He also invited them to his reinstituted evenings at home, impressing them
with his knowledge of and interest in America, several of them remembering in particular his urging them to read Gunnar Myrdal's recently
published book on race relations, *The American Dilemma*. Laski liked to
play up to them by puckishly telling outrageous anecdotes about American
politicians. He loved their vitality, self-confidence and friendliness, and he
eagerly agreed to a reunion of eight GIs from the New York area at the
Volney Hotel, where the talk went on for hours and was followed by a
trip to the theatre.

Coming from the post-war austerity of London, Laski couldn't believe
how full the shops were in America. He bought himself several pairs of
trousers and shirts, dresses for Frida and Diana, a coat for Robin and a train
for young Christopher. Everywhere, he wrote to Frida, there was 'speed,
spending, excitement, the whole background is one of reeling dizziness'.
The British seemed a civilized people alongside this, though 'one has to
hold on to oneself not to feel or read of us as poor, very poor relations'.
Laski sensed a sea change in American politics from what he had known in
the 1930s. It was 'a horror politically . . . the poor liberals like the *Nation*
have just nowhere to go, and hardly anything to do'. America had become
'harsh and acrid, and so conscious of its power and wealth'. Everywhere he
went he found intense hatred of Russia and eagerness to attack the Labour
Party. Britain was still depicted as an 'imperialist' power, skilfully

manoeuvring to use American strength to stage a come-back. Even though Truman seemed to Laski to be 'a nitwit who can't control anyone or anything', the outstanding impression Laski found among Americans was the sense 'of their overwhelming consciousness of power. There runs through it the historic stream of American idealism; put generously, it is the conviction that other people ought to be pitied because they haven't the good fortune to be Americans.' As he talked to Americans, even his good friends, Laski became convinced that he had grown 'very English or very European'.

> I think things blatant they take for normal. I think things fantastically rich which they think poor. I believe they have a picture of America in the world which has very little relation to reality, and a sense of innocence and purity in international affairs which is just moonshine. As a people, they are kind and brutal, quick and slow, honest and slick, certain that the future is on their side, and that they can meet all their issues with ease. And they over-organize, over-eat, over-drink, while they curse the shortages in a way that makes me hold my breath.

While Laski was in America Truman fired Henry Wallace, his Secretary of Commerce and the closest parallel in American politics to Laski in Britain's. On the left fringe of the Democratic Party, Wallace had as Roosevelt's Vice-President in the middle of the war argued for renewed New Deal initiatives to bring about fundamental social and economic change. In fact, in February 1944 a letter had been sent to every member of Roosevelt's Cabinet and to every member of Congress by a Los Angeles attorney which claimed that Henry Wallace's plans for a 'bloodless revolution by consent during the war' had been plagiarized from the writings of 'Laski, an admirer of communist political and economic philosophy'. Wallace's talk of a 'people's revolution' and of the war introducing the 'century of the common man' helped to make Truman Vice-President in 1944. As Secretary of Commerce, Wallace shocked the Truman administration in a September 1946 speech at Madison Square Garden by insisting that the United States was as much to blame as the Russians for the growing tensions between the two superpowers. When Secretary of State Byrnes threatened to resign, Truman fired Wallace and set him on his independent way, which would culminate in a 1948 run for the Presidency as a 'Progressive' Party candidate.

Laski was much too knowledgeable about American politics to support Wallace's bid for the Presidency, though in the next two years their views on the Cold War would develop along remarkably similar lines. Laski knew that only a major party candidate could win and he already had his candidate for 1948. He had become a great admirer of General Eisenhower during the war, met him several times, and much to the astonishment of friends Laski began as early as 1946 talking about Ike as the best candidate for the Democrats. It was not ideological affinity, since Eisenhower had been relatively apolitical, but his decency, honesty and understanding of Europe's suffering that recommended him to Laski. So when Eisenhower's secretary called him in New York in early September to come to Washington and speak to senior army and navy officers at the newly created National War College about his trip to Russia, Laski jumped at the chance. The talk was given no public notice and the press was excluded. Through a leak, however, the *Daily Telegraph* found out and ran a short story about it the next day. Unable to describe what Laski had said, the *Telegraph*'s Washington correspondent wrote that he was led 'to understand that the speech was strongly pro-Russian and much of it, I am informed, was controversial'. He wryly concluded his report by noting that Field Marshal Viscount Montgomery was to speak at the War College the next day.

In fact, a recently discovered transcript of Laski's appearance reveals that he made a rather conventional plea for international understanding in his talk. Laski was introduced by George Kennan, who had been a diplomat in Moscow and was the author in February 1946 of a famous 8,000-word 'telegram' to the State Department about Russian paranoia and policies governed more by ideology than by security interests. Kennan spoke warmly of Laski and told the officers it would be a challenging encounter because 'there is no one in the world who likes a good argument better than he does or is better able to handle himself in one'. Laski began with a moving tribute to the American armed forces, which set the tone of a talk punctuated by light-hearted banter about the aristocratic world of Oxbridge, Harvard and Yale and the democratic spirit American GIs had found at his university. While the substantive part of his talk roamed across the globe with pauses at China, Palestine and Germany, most of it dealt with Russia and his 'four-hour private talk' with Stalin. His theme was that America had to understand 'that Russia is afraid, that Russia knows that she is not in a position to make a major war, and is convinced as she was in 1919 that it is impossible for a socialist power to survive alone in a world of capitalist powers'. Laski suggested that Americans would better understand Russia if they saw her having 'all the aggressiveness of manner which is characteristic of the *nouveaux riches*'. It was afraid of being overlooked 'and can say nothing quietly and can do nothing quietly'.

Laski thought some *modus vivendi* could be reached with the Soviets 'if you don't make every minor incident into a major crisis' and recognize that 'you are not going to convert them to a belief in the American way of life'. Both sides had to listen to and understand each other better. He had urged Stalin, he told the officers, that exchanges with the West would ease fears of foreign encirclement. 'I couldn't convince him that I was right,' he added. Similarly, Americans had to learn more about the Soviet Union. As a country never invaded since 1812, America had to make an effort to 'know the psychology of a country which has been perpetually invaded'. Americans should launch 'real efforts at the university level to begin to understand the Soviet Union'. Too many people studied English history and English literature anyway, he added, breaking the group into laughter with an aside that 'there isn't a remote dead man who was a member of a minor circle gyrating about Dr Johnson who hasn't been the subject of a thesis by some student in America'.

Laski made several other exceptions to the vow of public silence he had made to Frida. Two nights after his Washington talk he appeared on the popular radio programme *Town Meeting of the Air* in a debate with Max Eastman on the topic 'Does Russia Want War?'. It was an occasion not without its historical ironies that spoke volumes to the politics of post-war America. Eastman had been the leading literary Marxist in America for decades. In the *Harvard Lampoon* attack on him in 1920, Laski had been urged to join Eastman on the next available 'Soviet Ark'. After travelling to Russia frequently in the 1930s, Eastman had become disillusioned and moved to the right, becoming a contributing editor of the *Reader's Digest* and then ultimately like Frank Meyer, the LSE Marxist of 1934, he became an associate of William Buckley's on the *National Review*.

His next public occasion put Laski once again on the front page of many American papers. Kenyan College in Gambier, Ohio, ran a conference in October on 'The Heritage of the English-Speaking Peoples and Their Responsibility', and the speakers included 'Mr Republican', Senator Robert

Taft of Ohio. Laski's address on 5 October unspectacularly advocated an Anglo-American-led 'new economics for a new world' that valued 'common welfare above private gain'. What placed the event and Laski on the front page was Senator Taft's unexpected condemnation of the Nuremberg war-crime trials in his talk and the hanging of eleven Nazi war criminals. The entire proceedings, Taft argued, were for an *ex post facto* crime, and hence offensive to Anglo-Saxon justice. When challenged from the floor, Taft backed off a bit and acknowledged that life imprisonment would have been sufficient punishment. Laski made all the newspapers because while still on the platform he challenged Taft. If it were proper judicial procedure to send a man to prison for life in an *ex post facto* proceeding, he argued, it was equally proper to impose a more severe penalty. Much was made in the following weeks of this story, since Taft was a leading contender for the Republican presidential nomination. In the retelling of the story Laski's rebuttal played a crucial part, so much so that the event would soon quite mistakenly be labelled the 'Taft–Laski debate'.

His other major speech in America, at Princeton University's bicentennial celebration, had been the centrepiece around which Laski had planned the entire visit. Laski, the Jewish socialist, was pleased by this summons from America's most aristocratic and still overwhelmingly Christian university. In March he had written to Huebsch of his plans to visit in the autumn with 'my great news that I have been invited to speak at the Princeton, yes Princeton, my dear Ben, bicentennial'. Laski's speech on this prestigious occasion was not about socialism but about war and international government. He depicted the major governments of the world standing as gladiators poised for war. Peace would not come, he was convinced, until a truly successful international government evolved, which required nations to abandon their sovereignty. The speech zeroed in on the veto power granted to the great powers at the United Nations and particularly abused, he noted, by the Soviet Union. 'So long as the veto power remains,' he told his Princeton audience, 'international government is bound to remain interstitial and incomplete'.

On other occasions on his holiday Laski did talk politics. He had dinner, along with Frankfurter and Dalton, at the British embassy with the new ambassador Lord Inverchapel, who had replaced Halifax. The ambassador had previously been posted in Moscow, so there was much talk of Stalin, with Laski insisting that relations with the Russians would go much better if Bevin occasionally said 'a kind word to Molotov'. When the talk turned to Palestine, Dalton noted, 'both the Jews say that Truman isn't just electioneering in his endless repetition of the 100,000', a reference to a request by Truman to Britain that it issue 100,000 certificates for Jewish immigration into Palestine.

In October, at tea with Corlis Lamont, the American humanist and leftist, Laski held sway with a group of people that included a young economist, John Kenneth Galbraith, who had met Laski in London in the late 1930s through their mutual friend Murrow. Galbraith and Laski argued for some time about British policy and the German coal mines in the Ruhr. But if Lamont's notes on the conversation are to be believed, the most remarkable feature of the evening was Laski's optimism about Britain's socialist future, which, he told the group, was well on its way to being transformed into a real socialist commonwealth. Labour would be in power for twenty years, he predicted, during which time it would socialize 85 per cent of the economy, leaving the remainder as cooperatives and privately owned small businesses. He was convinced that land would be socialized and that when the House of Lords opposed it, Labour would move quickly to abolish it. The weeks of rest must have mellowed Laski, who at home was much less pleased with Labour's performance and potential. When he returned to London, however, neither Bevin's demeanour towards Molotov nor the intensity of Labour's commitment to socialism would be his worries, for he would confront almost immediately the personal and public crisis that had lain dormant since that warm evening of 16 June 1945 in Newark market square.

CHAPTER TWENTY

The Trial

Frida was pleased that Laski had spent such a long time in America, because it took Harold's mind off the libel trial which was finally heard on 26 November. The courtroom was 'packed and crowds could not get in' to the opening day of the trial of 'one of the world's most noted historians and philosophers', the *New York Times* correspondent wrote. Reporters and photographers jostled spectators at the entrance to London's High Court of Justice on the Strand to catch a glimpse of Laski and the legal giants assembled for one of London's most sensational trials in years. As in the autumn of 1919, the summer of 1934 and the election campaign in 1945, Laski and his utterances were the focus of widespread public attention.

That he persisted in the libel suit surprised most people. Dalton, for example, thought withdrawing the suit after the election victory could have been presented 'either as a magnanimous or as a contemptuous gesture to those whose arguments, whether true or false, had been so overwhelmingly rejected by the electors'. Laski, however, insisted that the newspaper account was patently false and he saw his reputation libelled. His lifelong commitment to parliamentary socialism, forged after a brief experimentation with direct action, had been questioned, and he demanded vindication. There was also the matter of Sir John Simon's intemperate and unprofessional suggestion during the election campaign that Laski, having taken out the writs to pre-empt having to explain his Newark comment, would drop the action 'as soon as this election is over'. Simon, the Lord Chancellor, had apologized to Laski several days later in a public letter to the press, but the original comments must have weighed heavily on Laski's resolve to proceed. Perhaps Laski also saw the attacks on him during the election as motivated by anti-Semitism and felt it necessary to answer them in this public way. Or maybe he was convinced he was going to win, since he was telling everyone at the LSE that he would endow 'the Beaverbrook Chair of Political Science' with all the damages he would get from the libel action.

The trial was heard by a 'special' jury of five men and two women, selected from a roll of people with higher property holdings than required to be on the list of common jurors. The special jury was usually invoked when either party to a case deemed the material so complicated that jurors of greater intelligence and education (correlated, it was assumed, with higher economic status) were required. When counsel for Beaverbrook invoked this privilege the trial judge, the Lord Chief Justice, Rayner Goddard, agreed. A staunch defender of corporal and capital punishment, the solicitor to Wallis Simpson and a former unsuccessful Tory candidate for Parliament, Goddard had recently been appointed to Britain's highest judicial post as part of Attlee's effort to make it clear that a Labour government ought not to frighten anyone.

The counsel for Laski as plaintiff was G. O. Slade, the country's foremost expert on libel law. Beaverbrook had hired as counsel for his newspapers Sir Patrick Hastings, the leading KC. Hastings had long ago abandoned his socialism of the early 1920s when he had been Labour's Attorney-General and occasionally chaired Fabian meetings at which the likes of Laski spoke. Laski had good reason to be anxious in the months before the trial, because nearly twenty years earlier he had written to Frida that Hastings's examination of Collins in the famous Savage case 'was the most brilliant thing I have ever heard in a court of law'.

The final player with a starring role in the High Court drama was James Wentworth Day, who had been the questioner on 16 June 1945 in Newark market square and whose description of Laski as a 'bloodthirsty little man full of words' had been carried in the Beaverbrook press story about the rally. Just as Laski personified the urban Jewish intellectual of the left, Day embodied the county interests of the Tory squirearchy. A professional journalist by trade, Day had worked for *Country Life*, the *Field*, the *Sunday Express* and *Illustrated Sporting and Dramatic News*. He had been propaganda adviser to the Egyptian government, founder of the Essex Farmers and Countrymen's Association and, in 1945, the public relations adviser to the Conservative candidate for Newark, Sidney Shepherd. A serviceman during the First World War and a war correspondent during the Second World War, he had been married three times and written numerous books with titles like *A Falcon on St Paul's, or the Birds, Beasts, Sports and Games of London, King George V as a Sportsman, Sporting Adventure, The Dog in Sport* and *Farming Adventure.* In his *Who's Who* entry Day listed membership of five London clubs and his recreations as 'taking the left-wing intelligentsia at its own valuation; shooting (especially wild-fowling), riding, fishing, sailing, natural history, books, weapons and old furniture'. In his entry Laski listed one hobby, 'book collecting'. The contrast between Day and Laski was a journalist's dream come true.

The first witness called, Laski was questioned by Slade's assistant, Sir Valentine Holmes, who respectfully elicited from him the credentials by which the jury would know with whom they were dealing. Holmes then devoted the bulk of his questions to what the plaintiff saw as the central issue of the trial, the Newark meeting of 16 June 1945. Laski testified that he had answered Day's inquiry about his avoiding war service and of advocating violent revolution in wartime speeches by saying 'it was quite untrue to allege that I preached revolution'. He had told Day that 'social transformation by agreement was admirable'. If this were not done, there 'might be a slow evolution to revolution and that would be a terrible disaster that we ought to avoid and that we should avoid it by making great social changes now'. Laski flatly denied ever uttering the phrase 'if Labour could not obtain what it needed by general consent, we shall have to use violence, even if it means revolution'.

After devoting most of his questioning to details of the Newark meeting, who stood where, who said what, etc., Sir Valentine Holmes guided Laski to a few general comments about his long career. Was it not the case that never before had he been accused of being a 'person who advocated revolution by violence'? Was it not true that he could not be a member of the Labour Party, in fact, if he were not 'committed to the acceptance of constitutional democracy'? When asked about his 'attitude towards communism', Laski replied that he had been 'a critic of communism ever since 1920'. Asked his views on 'revolution', Laski replied:

I have said, ever since I began to write, that if changes were effected in this country by violence, it would be disastrous, because it would result in the suppression of democratic government and with it all the good things, religious toleration, freedom of speech, the security of the person, and so forth, that are naturally and logically associated with constitutional government ... where you can get the electorate of a national society like Great Britain to agree by the choice they make upon the desirability of great changes and thereby, by true constitutional means, transform the social order towards what I regard as greater social justice, the benefit of change effected by consent of that character is overwhelmingly greater than any benefit that could be secured by coercion.

With these words ringing in the courtroom, Sir Patrick Hastings began his cross-examination of Laski. The great moment of theatre had arrived with the country's most skilful trial lawyer sparring with the brilliant professor. Hastings's strategy became apparent at once. He was not very interested in Newark, nor would he treat Laski with respect or courtesy. For five hours Hastings badgered, baited and ridiculed Laski, referring to him several times in Day's words as the 'bloodthirsty little professor'. His very first question set the tone.

'Mr Laski, do you believe that the use of violence to achieve your political ends is practically inevitable?'

'No.' As Laski began to explain his answer, Hastings interrupted him.

'Keep the answers short. Have you not preached the inevitability of revolution for twenty years? Are you not a public danger?' Efforts by Laski to shape a reply were stopped with, 'Could you just answer yes or no?' Hastings sought in his first moments to paint Laski as a malcontented, unpatriotic, socialist intellectual who for decades had been deluding the loyal British working class with violent fantasies of revolution.

'Have you not continuously been writing that the condition of Britain under capitalism is so bad that capitalism had to go?'

'Yes,' replied Laski, 'that is why I am a socialist.'

'Everything in our system you think is thoroughly bad, do you not?'

'Not at all,' Laski replied.

'What about the legal system, English law and justice? Haven't you written that judges and juries pervert the law to the interest of the rich? Is that offensive, unfair and thoroughly unjust?' Hastings challenged Laski.

As Laski sought to put the charges in a broader context, Hastings constantly interrupted. 'Did you hear my question?' 'If you do not hear any question, please say so, and if you do not understand it, please tell me.' 'Listen to my question, you are a professor of so many things.' 'This is not what I asked you. If you would be good enough to listen to my questions and not try to answer something different, we shall get on very much better. Just listen to the question.'

Having told Laski that he had read 'some twenty, thirty or forty different publications of yours, so I know something about them', Hastings proceeded to take the professor and the jury through carefully chosen excerpts from 'some of your writings which I suggest are the most dangerous'. In the months before the trial Hastings had hired some of Laski's former students to read through Laski's books, articles and speeches to find passages on revolution and violence. At times it seemed that the courtroom had become an LSE classroom as counsel, plaintiff and even, on occasion, the judge debated the precise meaning of concepts like 'the erosion of the capitalist class'. But always there were the jury and debating points to be scored. And there was also the reversal of roles, the professor shorn of authority. The characteristic academic plea by Laski for subtlety and nuance in interpretation was peremptorily put down by the no-nonsense Hastings. 'Mr Laski, I am reading this to a professor in many, many universities all over the world. Do you really mean to say that that does not mean what it says?' To every claim by Laski that 'you do not do justice to my thesis' or 'you do not describe it in a way I would', Hastings would repeat the quote in question and ask rhetorically, 'Can anything in the world be clearer than that what you are saying is ...' Laski's words, drawn from different works over his long career, were, Hastings told the jury, 'dangerous, disgraceful, monstrous'.

Hastings targeted lengthy passages from Laski's 1933 book *Democracy in Crisis*. Laski's argument, Hastings insisted, was that proletarian revolution in Britain was inevitable and desirable and that the destruction of capitalism required non-constitutional actions and violence. Laski denied Hastings's reading and he tried to introduce the book's historical context, the 1931 betrayal of the minority Labour government by Ramsay MacDonald under pressure from world banking interests, but Hastings shot back with his demand for short 'yes' and 'no' replies. To Hastings's suggestion 'that what you have written over and over again is a direct incitement to violence', Laski offered the obvious reply which was, of course, his logical defence. 'What you describe as exhortation,' Laski countered, 'is in fact sober analysis and is in fact not an appeal to do anything.' Thus was introduced the crucial distinction between advocacy and analysis, incitement and description. Hastings's strategy, however, was to obfuscate the distinction, to insist that describing revolution as inevitable involved approval and advocacy. Slade's mistake was to leave Laski alone to try to make this distinction as he confronted a badgering counsel determined to keep his answers short.

Immediately after this first exchange the Lord Chief Justice intervened and made a decision which proved crucial to the outcome of the trial. A somewhat confused Goddard informed Hastings that he was concerned about 'this lengthy inquiry we have embarked upon about the whole of these extracts in order to get clear in my mind to what issue this will go as the pleadings stand'. Hastings insisted that when the time came for the jury to decide if Laski had made the statements attributed to him by the *Newark Advertiser*, they would want to know 'whether they are his beliefs ... The jury will want to know whether it is the sort of thing he has said over and over again.' Goddard now understood and allowed Hastings to pursue this strategy, and in fact indicated that he would instruct the jury that even if it concluded that Laski had not used the words at Newark, they could offer a verdict for the defendant 'on the grounds that Mr Laski had used words of that sort and advocated this sort of conduct on other occasions'. The law of libel would allow this, the Lord Chief Justice concluded, by the 'plea of justification'. Damages need not be awarded if the newspaper could justify what it wrote in the light of a reasonable assumption that Laski had said it. Having said or written it before provided just such a justification.

When Hastings's questioning resumed, the seminar-like inquiry into the political philosophy of Harold Laski continued. Even the judge participated. 'Would you just explain one thing to me,' Goddard asked Laski over one passage, 'does that mean you distinguish between constitutional government and parliamentary government?' Laski was at a distinct disadvantage in the seminar, however; he was obliged to be always the respondent and to answer always with brevity. At one point he pleaded for equal time from the ostensibly impartial seminar leader.

May I ask your Lordship for guidance? What Sir Patrick Hastings is asking me to do is to take a series of sentences and to answer them by 'yes' or 'no' when the significance of those sentences derives from the whole context of the book in which they appear. Were I to answer 'yes' or 'no' to particular extracts that Sir Patrick reads from the book, I should give in the one case or the other a wholly false impression of its purpose. Am I to answer 'yes' or 'no', or am I to explain the context to your Lordship and the jury in which these phrases are set?

Goddard acknowledged the dilemma. 'I think you are entitled to give an explanation,' he answered the uncharacteristically throttled professor, 'but I do not want this case turned into a discussion of the socialist creed.'

Given a rare opportunity to expound at some length, Laski replied in moving terms about his convictions and once again made a distinction between advocacy and scholarship.

> I take the view that the maintenance of social peace and the avoidance of violence is one of the most vital things at which our society can aim. That is why I am a member of the Labour Party and not a member of the Communist Party. This is at no point (nor is any of the material you have so far quoted) exhortation. Every part of the material that you have quoted is careful, and I hope accurate, diagnosis; and I think that you put me in an unfair and an unjustifiable position by asking me to accept diagnosis as exhortation.

Hastings was undaunted, noting that he was concerned only 'to take your own words and to suggest what they mean to an ordinary person reading them'.

Laski having been allowed this once to say more than 'yes' or 'no', Hastings returned to his attack. He left for a moment the issue of inevitable revolution and set out to portray Laski as, in general, an unsavoury and seditious 'bloodthirsty little professor'. He roamed far and wide.

'Didn't you advocate taking machine-guns to more important people if the situation becomes intolerable?'

'No,' answered Laski.

'Did you not attack Mr Churchill in the *Chicago Sun* in 1943 in the middle of the war period?'

'Yes,' Laski replied, 'as did many other people.'

'In one short sentence, which is the most offensive thing ... you have ever said ... in a book I think called *Threat to the Constitution*, or something of that sort, did you not describe religious belief as "rubbish"?' Hastings asked. 'Didn't you suggest that Wesley blackmailed the workers to accept conditions in the old factories by promising them eternal life?'

Laski replied that Hastings's characterization of this 'most offensive' reference was a 'fantastic rhetorical exaggeration'. He had been describing only what 'is well known by all historians', that 'Wesleyism deflected the sense of men's indignation with their conditions in the new factories to religion as a consolation for the sorrows of this life'. Hastings allowed Laski to complete this clarification; he saw no need to demand brevity here.

Hastings would not always be so obliging. One of the sharpest exchanges occurred when Hastings asked Laski whether people of privilege could be found in socialist movements.

Laski began, 'Why, indeed, Sir Patrick, when you were a member.'

Hastings cut him off with a sharp 'Do not be rude . . . It may be difficult for you to be courteous, but do not be rude.' Hastings would not let the matter drop. 'You are rude to everyone, are you not?'

Laski replied, 'I do not think so.'

Hastings came back. 'Of course, when you are rude to other people, Mr Laski, you think it is argument; when people say something about you, you bring action for libel. That is your view of fairness, is it not?'

'Not in the least, Sir Patrick,' was Laski's brief response.

The exchanges between Hastings and Laski alternated between short, badgering interludes and long readings with civilized seminar-like scholarly debates. Hastings read several paragraphs from a Laski book and the professor replied by requesting that a neighbouring paragraph be read. The Lord Chief Justice joined in on occasion. Goddard once interrupted Laski during a description of when violence might occur in society with the observation that 'that really presupposes the government of the day is not supported by popular opinion'. Laski, the professorial discussion leader, linked the comments of the seminar participants. 'No, I do not think so, my Lord. I am arguing, I think in all the passages with which Sir Patrick is concerned, the situation where a Labour government with a majority is in power, and where the will of that Labour government is not accepted by the forces of opposition.'

Hastings conceded that Laski preferred revolution by consent, but he dwelt on Laski's repeated suggestions that it was impossible for the capitalist class to concede power willingly and that, therefore, revolution was inevitable. Laski in turn offered the clarification that while he had held such a view in the 1930s, since the beginning of the war he had seen the potential for a peaceful transition to socialism in Britain. But Hastings had been well prepared. 'Haven't you,' he asked Laski, 'repeatedly insisted that violence is regrettably inevitable in the process of social transformation, but that its use in politics is also justified and desirable on occasion?' Had Laski, 'the bloodthirsty apostle of violence', not argued in *Reflections on the*

Revolution of Our Time that resistance to the law of the land was sometimes appropriate, that violent disobedience to established authority was sometimes justified? Laski, told to answer briefly, said, 'Yes.' Allowed to amplify, Laski noted that Hastings's citations came from passages dealing with Stalin's rule in Russia, and that it was meant to apply also 'to the Germany of Hitler . . . or to the Italy of Mussolini. Even Mr Abraham Lincoln would agree,' Laski insisted.

'Never mind about him. He is not in court. Let us keep to ourselves,' Hastings retorted.

Hastings would not concede here. He turned to Laski's *Liberty in the Modern State*, published in 1930, to develop further for the jury the portrait of Laski the advocate of violence. This required Hastings to make a complete ideological turn. From the picture of Laski as the advocate of collectivist violence and statist tyranny, Hastings moved to Laski the anarchist enemy of state oppression. Laski acknowledged his conviction 'that the individual should refuse submission to the powers-that-be where he is sincerely convinced that he can do no other'. He defended the 'moral obligation to resist' and admitted that this was a 'denial of the sovereignty of the state' before the 'individual conscience'. Laski invoked George Washington and the early Christians as examples of people who thought 'there are times when the law may be rightly disregarded'.

Hastings was unmoved. To encourage resistance to established authority at any time was to preach subversion. He returned to machine-guns. 'Have you not carried this argument so far that you advocate bloody anarchy when you say people may use machine-guns in the street?' Hastings read to the court the offending passage without commenting, of course, on the incompatibility of this line of questioning with the earlier depiction of Laski as the apologist for an oppressive socialist state.

> Obviously enough, we must make our protest proportionate to the event. We need not march out with machine-guns because the income-tax inspector has assessed us wrongly. But if the state to which we are reduced is that of the French peasant in 1789 or the Russian peasant in 1917, it is difficult to see why the wisdom of our ancestors should be dignified by the name of wisdom. Social peace need not be invaded for minutiae, but social peace may well be purchased at too high a price. Order may be disturbed; but there are kinds of order which are closely akin to death. Government is necessary enough in all conscience, but there must be limits to its empire. It is not

enough within a social system to proclaim the supreme desirability of peace until we are satisfied with the purposes for which peace is made. And because the individual is so small, the power of government so vast, we may be certain enough that, in general, organized disobedience is always the price of injustice. Men do not revolt until wrong has driven them to revolt.

When asked by Hastings whether he still agreed with those sentiments, Laski answered, 'Yes.'

'Are you not telling your followers,' Hastings asked, '"Get what you can by consent but you must not think that is the only way to get it"?'

Laski answered, 'I utterly and emphatically deny that is the case.'

'What relevance could such sentiments have, then, for the present, if not a call to violent socialist revolution?'

'Hitler had committed unendurable wrong against the people of Germany, leaving them no alternative but to revolt against the conditions he established.'

Hastings was still undaunted. Could Laski comment on whether insurrectionary violence would be justified in any other cases? he asked. The ensuing exchange defined the parameters of the entire enterprise when ideas and their authors are tried before a jury.

A. That is one of your questions that it is impossible for a professional historian like myself to answer by 'yes' or 'no'.

Q. Forgive me, but for the moment could you forget you are a professional historian, forget everything, and just remember you are an ordinary Englishman and I am asking you a question in ordinary English?

Hastings's dissection of Laski reached its climax in the fifth hour of his questioning when he turned to the election rally at Newark. Laski insisted that he had responded to Wentworth Day by saying that 'great changes were so urgent in this country, and if they were not made by consent they would be made by violence'. Pressed by Hastings and, amazingly enough, the Lord Chief Justice to specify who would initiate violence if change was not brought by consent, Laski became entangled in generalities. It would be 'by the drift of events in the country', he suggested. However, when pushed to be more specific he agreed that it would be 'by the violence of those who believe in socialism', but then he also returned to the 'theme' of his 1930s writings that an extra-parliamentary right-wing resistance might violently overthrow a leftist government seeking fundamental change. Laski also suggested that 'supporters of socialism ... outside the Labour Party', less committed to constitutional methods, might be the ones to use violence.

With Laski reeling after hours of questioning, Hastings asked angrily, 'Where in the world does "If great changes are not made by consent, they would be made by violence" differ from the passage of which you complain in which it is said that "Should great change not occur through consent, we would have to use violence."' In his reply Laski repeated the distinction between exhortation and advocacy, and he gamely tried to explain transitive and intransitive verbs. Hastings cut down each effort. 'I do wish you would try if you could, Mr Laski, to answer my questions a little more shortly'; 'I do wish you would not make speeches, Mr Laski'; and, perhaps the cruellest cut, 'I am sure you are accustomed to making yourself quite plain to your students ... try again.'

Laski sat in the witness chair for a few more minutes under re-examination by Sir Valentine Holmes, who tried to salvage what principles he could from the assault of Hastings's cross-examination. Under Holmes's guidance Laski told the court that any revolution by violence would be a 'disaster to all classes of society' and that whenever he wrote of revolution as nearly inevitable, it was not to encourage revolution but 'in every case to warn against the danger of revolution'. Holmes emphasized for the jury that in Hastings's questions 'never were so many examples of extracts torn from their proper context'. He asked Laski to amplify what his phrase 'erosion of capitalism', made much of by Sir Patrick, meant. How could that be done without violence? Laski responded aptly with Labour Party policy. Nationalization of the mines would transfer ownership to the public sector and require compensating the owners 'under the authority of Parliament; that is what I mean by revolution by consent. The capitalist ownership of the mines is then eroded by such legislation.' Laski's counsel asked him to give his views about Russia and the Bolshevik Revolution. Laski had no hesitation. 'I have always said in all my books that the transformation of Tsarist Russia into Soviet Russia by violent revolution has involved a price in human suffering too high to ask any people to pay.'

Two important exchanges between the Lord Chief Justice and Holmes marked this re-examination. When Holmes asked Laski if he had read *The*

Times Literary Supplement's favourable review of his *Reflections on the Revolution of Our Time*, Goddard objected (Hastings, interestingly enough, did not). Holmes argued that the book had been characterized by Hastings as 'advocating violent revolution' and that it was relevant to have the opinion of independent reviewers. Goddard would not yield; there were too many learned extracts being read in court already. Goddard was also annoyed by Laski's counsel re-reading some of the passages cited by Hastings in an effort to allow Laski time for clarification. He interrupted to ask, 'How far are we getting now by reading more of them?' Hadn't Laski been extremely clear in his answers? Goddard then turned to Laski and by way of apparently clearing the air asked:

> Your thesis has been throughout, Professor, as I understand: 'I am in favour of a revolution in the sense of a complete change of social circumstances. I have never advocated revolution by violent means. I have always suggested the ballot-box rather than the lamp-post?

Laski answered, 'Yes,' and added, 'I have always pointed out the immense danger to society.'

The air was cleared. Laski's counsel had got him to distinguish between his advocacy of peaceful revolution by consent, the nationalization of the mines, and his warnings against violent revolution. The judge had got Laski to distinguish between the kind of revolutions he favoured and those 'he never advocated'. What the jury would do with acknowledgements that he was a kind of revolutionary would remain to be seen. As the Lord Chief Justice concluded this intervention, 'It will be for the jury to form an opinion, and nobody else, as to what the ordinary meaning of the words used is.'

A weary Laski finally sat down. The terrorizer of the lecture and committee room, the indefatigable infighter in Labour Party squabbles, the irascible gadfly of the transatlantic elite went quietly to his seat. One of his students sitting in the gallery remembered him looking 'punch-drunk'. Goddard's clerk thought 'he retired extremely white and shaken . . . Had it not been for his insufferable arrogance, I should have felt very sorry for him at that moment.' What went through Laski's mind as his duel with Hastings came to an end was something he later tried to put to paper in 'My Day in Court', an essay found among his papers after his death.

You are then handed over to that same counsel whose life has so largely been passed in pricking men until they bleed. He performs his war dance about you like a dervish intoxicated by the sheer ecstasy of his skill in his own performance, ardent in his knowledge that, if you trip for one second, his knife is at your throat. He makes a pattern from bits and pieces picked with care from a pattern of life you have been steadily weaving for a quarter of a century to prove either that you never meant what you intended, or that you lacked every element of skill to give the world the sense of your intent. He moves between the lines of sarcasm and insult. It is an effort to tear off, piece by piece, the skin which he declares no more than a mask behind which any man of understanding could have grasped the foulness of your purpose. He treats you not as a human being, but as a surgeon might treat some specimen he is demonstrating to students in a dissecting room.

In addition to Laski, his counsel called ten other witnesses. Their testimony took little time and revealed the narrow strategy that informed the plaintiff's case. Each of these witnesses had been at the Newark rally and offered a recollection of the words Laski had actually used. No witnesses had been planned to rebut Hastings's case, the depiction of Laski as a lifelong advocate of violent revolution. No character witnesses were called from the Labour Party to regale the jury with tales of Laski's indefatigable work in the vineyards of everyday non-violent party politics. No one dazzled the jury with stories of his close friendships with pillars of the Establishment, with American ambassadors, Presidents, Justices of the Supreme Court or the British literary and social elite. No non-socialist intellectuals were called to corroborate Laski's insistence on the differences between exhortation and analysis. The jury was only given eye-witnesses or, more precisely, ear-witnesses.

Of these, only one, the first, was of a social bearing impressive enough to get through the class stereotypes that must have filtered out the trustworthy for the 'special' jury. A novelist could not have conjured up a more unlikely Labour candidate for the parliamentary seat at Newark than Air Vice-Marshal Hugh Vivian de Crespigny, who had returned to testify from his post as Governor of Schleswig-Holstein for the occupation forces in Germany. Asked by Sir Valentine Holmes if at the Newark rally for his unsuccessful candidacy eighteen months earlier he had heard Laski use the words 'if Labour cannot obtain what it needs by general consent, we shall have to use violence even if it means revolution', de Crespigny answered, 'I did not.' He went on, 'I am quite sure that Professor Laski did not make that statement, otherwise I should have paid particular attention to it.' There were no further questions from Sir Valentine. As for Hastings, his one-question cross-examination of the RAF war hero revealed how he would deal with the group of people about to be called to tell what they heard from the back of the lorry that spring night in Newark. Had de Crespigny heard Laski refer to the British army's efforts to organize a mutiny over Irish Home Rule in 1914 in his reply to an earlier question by Day? The court had heard Laski claim that he had used this example of right-wing violence in his response to a question from Day, and Hastings knew the jury would think a military man might have taken particular notice of this controversial Laski claim. To de Crespigny's answer that he had not heard Laski say that, Sir Patrick noted that 'many things may have been said which you did not hear'.

After the unsuccessful candidate a parade of local Labour Party members who had been on or near the platform at Newark were called to testify. One after another they told the court what they had not heard, and just as methodically Hastings elicited from them that they had not heard words that Laski had acknowledged using. Most telling were the denials from three witnesses that Laski had said that 'great changes were so urgent, if they were not made by consent they would be made by violence'. To one of these denials Hastings mockingly replied, 'Dear, oh dear, Mr Laski seems to be so unfortunate. He must have been not very good at hearing himself; he said that is what he did say.' Hastings astutely perceived that many of these witnesses instinctively dissociated themselves from any learned distinctions between exhortation to and analysis of revolution. They could not have heard either from their distinguished party chairman. For the Labour Party faithful any talk of revolution, however qualified, was clearly inappropriate.

On the trial's third day, 29 November, Hastings introduced the case the defendants would make. It was a brief performance with but two main emphases. He would portray for the jury a man who might appear in the courtroom as 'not a very dangerous person', whom they might think no more than 'troublesome and a little tiresome'. But Laski was in fact a man of 'monstrous' views and 'repulsive thoughts'. 'For years past he has been writing about revolution. A big nasty word, revolution,' Hastings told the jury. And then he drummed it in. 'Revolution, revolution, revolution – it

all runs through these long and perhaps not very entertaining books.'
Indeed, Mr Laski had been 'pouring out revolution for the last twenty
years. Sure, he tells us that he would be glad if revolution were peaceful,'
Hastings noted. 'I suppose Lenin would have been too.' Religion was
Hastings's second theme. Religion, in general, seemed to be the issue, but it
was Laski's own religion that was clearly the sub-text.

> We have belief in many things which Mr Laski does not believe in at all. We
> believe in law and justice in England; we believe in fairness; we believe in
> religious beliefs; we do not talk about the myths of future happiness; we do
> believe in them. Look at him . . . He says, 'Away with all your religion.'
> Perhaps he has got none; I do not know; he is entitled to have none. I could
> not help noticing that he took an oath upon the Bible . . . Has he a religion?
> If so, why does he want to go and hurt people by saying things like that?

Hastings's principal witness was Wentworth Day. Hastings began his
examination by getting Day to concede that he was at Newark in the
employ of the Conservative Party, specifically to heckle Laski, and was
armed with extracts from Laski's speeches and writings published by
Conservative Central Office. He had asked Laski the provocative question
about having spent the whole of the last war lecturing in America. He had
asked him why he advocated revolution by violence. He had accused Laski
of being 'the sort of bloodthirsty little man, full of words, who has never
smelt a bullet, but is always the first to stir up violence in peace'. And he
had been successful in baiting the professor, Day told Hastings, for he had
vividly heard Laski's response. 'As for violence, if Labour could not obtain
what is needed by general consent, we shall have to use violence even if it
means revolution.' As he left Day to be cross-examined, Hastings asked
him if he bore any personal animosity to Laski. 'None whatsoever,' Day
replied.

Slade questioned Day at much greater length than had Hastings. He
went over in some detail the facts about Laski's medical deferment in the
First World War, since Day had raised the issue at the Newark meeting.
Day still insisted that the Red Cross would have been a less cowardly
alternative than teaching in Canada and America. Finally, Slade pushed
Day on the critical phrase, and he repeated what he had told Hastings. In
the course of the questioning the Lord Chief Justice interrupted to ask if
Day felt the phrase Laski admitted saying was an incitement to violence.

Day replied that the comment 'great changes were so urgent in this country, and if they were not made by consent they would be made by violence' was an incitement to violence. Slade then asked, 'You really mean that, do you?' to which Day answered 'Yes.' Slade let the matter drop.

Slade tried to undermine Day's assurance to Hastings that he had not 'the slightest animosity against Mr Laski', asking him to confirm some passages about Laski from Day's soon to be published book, *Harvest Adventure*. It was a risky strategy, because in trying to discredit Day as someone carrying on a personal vendetta against Laski, Slade was himself reading to the jury yet another character assassination consistent with that offered by Hastings. Had not Day described Laski in his forthcoming book, Slade asked, as an 'urban-minded and garrulous little petrel of socialist politics' swooping down upon the peaceful rural folk of Newark? Had he not described Laski appearing 'on a sort of French Revolution cart'? Had he not depicted him as 'fitted with a microphone instead of a guillotine, dressed in a tight-fitting, hip-slinky overcoat of the sort that dance-band leaders wear'? Indeed he had, replied Day. None of this was meant to be offensive, he assured Slade, but merely to show how out of place Laski looked in a rural market-place. In following this strategy of discrediting Day's objectivity by showing his hatred of Laski, it would be Slade who then introduced the most anti-Semitic references so far in the trial. He asked whether Day had written of Laski that he

> seemed to find so much solace in the revolutionary standards of less happy countries and so little comfort in the Britain which his ancestors had adopted as a place of profitable residence ... For the better part of an hour he sprayed us with an oleaginous stream of rhetorical oratory ... yes oily ... and the British idea of freedom, with which the little professor did not apparently agree. No doubt it was not in his blood ... his Manchester accent which married so ill with the affectation of Oxford donnishness ...

Day admitted he had written all of that and also acknowledged that he doubted whether the masses in France were justified in the French Revolution, for 'perfectly normal people would never think that violence was justified'. Slade also got Day to admit that this was not the first time 'when it has been suggested against you that you had issued a report of a meeting to the press which is inaccurate'. Yes, Day grudgingly acknowledged, his newspaper account of why he had recently been rejected as a candidate by an Essex Conservative constituency had been criticized in letters to the *Southend Standard*.

The defendant's final witness was their 'man in the market-place'. Bertram James Spinks, who had been at the entire meeting, told the court that he had heard Laski answer Day's question with the comment 'if Labour cannot get power by consent we must use violence to get it, even if it means revolution'. In his cross-examination Slade used the same tactic Hastings had used so effectively on Laski's witnesses and was equally successful, for Spinks claimed that he had not heard the parts of Laski's speech and even of his answer to Day which Laski admitted saying. But when Slade tried to get Spinks to agree that 'revolution by consent' was neither a monstrous nor a repulsive objective, Spinks stood his ground, insisting that to someone like himself, 'a man on the street', the words 'revolution' and 'violence' were 'horrible words to use at any time'. Slade pursued the point. What about revolution by consent? Wasn't that different? The exchange produced a most significant indication of what the jury might be thinking as well.

Q. Do not think I am being in the least unkind, Mr Spinks, but you say, do you not, that whenever you hear the word 'revolution' you picture bloody strife?

A. Exactly, like Mexico and those sorts of places.

Q. I mean it does not matter in what context it appears. If you hear the word 'revolution' you picture the French Revolution of which you have probably read?

A. Yes, I think it is a horrible word, sir.

Should Slade have been so surprised? Just as it is difficult, if not impossible, to carry on a learned debate about abstract concepts in the adversarial context of a jury trial, was it not too much to expect that everyone comprehended the meaning of 'revolution by consent'? Laski was trapped not by Day but by the baggage of language. If his counsel had paired Laski's phrase with 'fundamental change by consent', the message might have been different. Laski had used 'revolution by consent' in his writings, which were addressed principally to an audience that could make such fine distinctions. But for most people the very word 'revolution', however modified, however qualified, was a 'horrible word'. Merely to use it branded one an advocate of violence.

Immediately after the midday adjournment on Friday 29 November, Sir Patrick Hastings gave his closing comments to the jury. It all boiled down, he said, to whether Laski used the words that the newspapers said he did. Not that every word had to be the same, however. Even if 'one word is not quite accurate and another word is not quite accurate', the jury could still find the newspaper's account 'a fair and accurate report'. In deciding whether Laski used these words, the jury should bear in mind that Laski often wrote and thought about revolution: 'He has written about nothing else for thirty years.' They should bear in mind that Laski acknowledged the accuracy of the entire *Newark Advertiser*'s account 'except that one sentence'.

Hastings's presentation reduced any distinction between advocacy and analysis of revolution into mere mention of or reference to revolution. The words Laski complained of in the account of the Newark meeting, he told the jury, 'are what he thinks and what he has said himself over and over again'. Hastings then read to the jury a passage from the testimony where Laski had acknowledged an earlier description of the inevitability of revolution if the condition of the working class were not improved. For Laski this had clearly been scholarly or political analysis, but Hastings did not mention this qualification. Laski had said, according to Hastings, that 'if the condition continued, the relationship between classes would be resolved by force'. Hastings then added, 'I really do not understand the difference between that and what we say he says at the meeting.' Hastings blurred the distinction between 'would' and 'should' just as he had between 'we shall have to use violence' and 'they would be made by violence'. He simply reminded the jury that what 'we say . . . he said' he has been saying for years. No one on the jury, Hastings noted, should think that he and the newspapers he represented 'suggest that the Socialist Party believes in this rubbish'. There were indeed people in the country who, sadly, 'have not got comforts', who live in a state of misfortune. Laski should be ashamed of the 'doctrines he scatters so recklessly' to those unfortunate but good people. Hastings offered the jury the spectre of Laski as the callous, unpatriotic intellectual who actually despised ordinary people.

. . . a man who comes and decries the things they believe in and levels them into the mud. I say he brings these things into the mud by advocating this sort of horror, shouting about Russian Revolution with all the horrors of that, the misery and – Well, I had better not put it too strongly, or I might be carried away myself. He is doing no great good to the cause which he says he supports.

Hastings had one rhetorical flourish left for the jury, Laski was un-English with his repulsive thoughts

because in England we are not like the countries of which Mr Laski speaks so sympathetically ... It may be that we have belief in our parliamentary institutions. We have belief in many things which Mr Laski does not believe in at all. We believe in law and justice in England, we believe in fairness, we believe in religious beliefs; we do not talk the myths of a future happiness.

Laski's later thoughts about Hastings's summing-up vibrate with his sense of public ridicule, of being falsely revealed as the notorious Florentine about whom he himself, the historian of political thought, had written.

You have to sit once more with Buddha-like impassivity while the counsel for your opponent sums up for his client. Here at least, he is simple and direct: he knows precisely the effect he desires to produce on the jury. He assures them that he will make the complex material that has been put before them so simple that their minds can be at ease and confident. He paints your character in a few incisive sentences. You begin to see the outlines of an evil enemy of the realm, clever enough to dress up his long-cherished stratagems in garments skilfully designed to conceal their nefarious purpose. You are in substance like a figure in one of those Elizabethan dramas which Machiavelli influenced; noble men have worked with you, innocent of the ugly ends for which you proposed to use their alliance. You hear attributed to yourself principles you have never held. You find yourself driven by motives you have never known yourself to possess. You become, indeed, the supreme and ardent enemy of the very cause you have sought to serve. But now, he concludes triumphantly, we have torn the mask off the villain; he can no longer disguise himself as an honourable servant of a great movement; he stands revealed before you as one who has striven all his life to undermine the foundations of social peace.

In his summing-up Slade finally turned to his plaintiff's writings and speeches. Never in all his career, Slade told the jury, had Laski ever said that the Labour Party should use violence. Laski was in fact 'warning the populace against the inevitability of it coming from another source'. To consider this advocating violence would be to consider Churchill's 'harping on the danger of war with the Hitler regime' as advocacy of war with Germany. It was a flawed analogy, however. War with Germany came and for most people was patently justified. Slade tried valiantly to clarify Laski's message. If the Tories were elected, Laski was warning, revolution might come spontaneously from the people, led by communists 'who believe in it'. There was but one way to avoid revolution, then: elect a Labour government. Rather than introduce the jury to examples of overt advocacy of revolution by Labour's critics on the revolutionary left, and there were many of them, Slade turned from his general description of Laski's politics to commentary on specific passages introduced earlier by Hastings. His strategy involved repeating some of the passages Hastings had selected as incendiary and pointing out in each case qualifying sentiments and/or clarifications that Hastings had omitted, which Slade then read to the jury. These revealed a different Laski. One such omitted passage, for example, showed Laski insisting that Labour's strategy was 'to discuss, negotiate, conciliate, that it may attain the maximum possible agreement to its plans'. In another, Laski insisted that 'government decisions which are built upon the assent of citizens are better than those which rely upon force'.

Again, Slade was taking risks. This approach required repeating the problematic passages from Laski's writings that Hastings had already presented to the jury, reinforcing Hastings's claim that Laski wrote over and over again about revolution. Slade insisted that Laski always sought peaceful revolution through parliamentary processes, through consent. But here, as throughout the trial, Slade was trapped by the emotive power of the word 'revolution' itself. He concluded his readings from Laski with a passage from *Democracy in Crisis* by way of showing how Hastings had misrepresented Laski's meaning.

> For revolution, like war, is infinite tragedy, since in its very nature it means pain and suffering and the tragic confusion of means with ends. The innocent not less than the guilty are its victims. It is the enemy of Reason and Freedom, the twin goddesses whose triumph gives what of beauty there is in the ultimate texture of men's lives.

In this stirring passage the word 'revolution' stands by itself, however. It is not specified as revolution by violence. What, then, was the jury to make of earlier claims by Laski and his counsel that he was only in favour of 'revolution by consent', and only in that sense was he a revolutionary. As often as Slade repeated that Laski never advocated violence, there was the problem of whether the jury could rise above the powerful linkage in everyday speech of the word 'revolution' with violence.

Slade's performance may well have confused the jury, because with his denials that Laski ever advocated violence he announced to the jury that 'not one single passage in any of Mr Laski's writings has been shown to you which could possibly be construed as an advocacy of revolution'. Yet what about all of his and Laski's painstaking distinctions between seeking 'revolution by consent' and 'revolution by violence'? Such was the power of the word 'revolution' that Slade was himself instinctively distancing his client from the 'horrible word'. There were serious problems with Slade as an explicator and translator of Laski's learned texts. While Hastings self-confidently offered his clear and precise readings of various passages, Slade told the jury at the outset of the trial that he had trouble understanding Laski. Why, then, should they be any better than he in making sense of his distinctions? He had said:

> Now let me come to what Mr Laski's theme is, and I want to do it as pithily as I can as a layman – because I am a complete layman in these matters; my knowledge of history is positively negligible – almost as bad as my knowledge of geography – and if I make silly mistakes, as no doubt I shall, it is merely because Professor Laski's theme is being put before you through the mouth, I am afraid, of a very imperfect medium. But I have done my best, and speaking as a layman, this is how I would, first of all – I have written it down myself – put his theme in just three lines.

In the remainder of his summing-up Slade did not present the jury with a detailed description of the differences between advocacy and analysis, exhortation and prediction. Instead, he moved directly to his final point, a suggestion that Laski deserved exceptional damages not only for the pain of the original libellous account, but for the additional assault on his character during the trial. Slade then reviewed for the jury the questionable tactics pursued by Hastings in the course of the trial which Slade suggested were introduced to 'create prejudice in your mind'. He ticked off questions and discussions by Hastings of Laski's views on religion; his attacks on Churchill;

his criticism of the impartiality of British judges and juries; his passages on the use or non-use of machine-guns. It was a bizarre ending to Slade's presentation. His effort to convince the jury that Hastings's courtroom libelling of Laski merited larger damages led him to recount for the jury what Hastings had refrained from repeating in his own summing-up – those very aspects of Laski that Hastings had earlier sought to convince the jury were 'offensive' and 'repulsive'.

Laski was pleased, none the less, with Slade's address to the jury. In 'My Day in Court' he wrote of the 'great relief' that came from being rescued by Slade from Hastings's depiction of him as 'a Marat or a Robespierre'. With a 'profound psychological comfort' he listened to Slade 'prick the rhetorical bubbles' that Hastings had 'so hastily blown'. He was heartened to think 'that now, at long last, truth will emerge unsheathed from all efforts to twist and contort it'.

There was only the Lord Chief Justice's instruction to the jury left. He seemed to Laski 'a kindly old man, with a winning smile that lights up his eyes'. Laski heard him speak to the jury with 'unemphatic quietness' and had to lean forward to hear what he said 'in an easy, almost conversational tone'. At times during Goddard's description of principles of the freedom of discussion, Laski felt he was 'back in some pleasant lecture room of an Oxford College where an elderly don is retelling the details of some ancient trial decided long ago'. But the spell was soon broken. 'With a sudden gasp', Laski wrote, he realized 'that he is not going to push your case at all. He makes his point . . . but they are always your opponent's points.'

Whatever the jury's verdict, Goddard told them, Laski was clearly irresponsible in his use of words. In a most unusual and questionable line of argument, Goddard noted that 'there is no question at all . . . that he used the word "revolution" or that he used the word "violence"' in his Newark talk. Laski had a responsibility 'to make it very clear what you mean'. As a professor he should know 'that when you are dealing with such highly explosive material as revolution and violence in public speaking it is desirable to make it abundantly clear just what you mean'. More to the point, Goddard reinforced for the jury the centrality of the 'horrible word' revolution and its seemingly inexorable linkage to violence. He made no mention of Laski's references to and defences of 'revolution by consent'. His choice of words reveals that for the Lord Chief Justice revolution was always 'highly explosive material' invariably associated with violence.

Goddard also reviewed the law of libel. If the jury thought that the speech was inaccurately reported, they had to consider whether the newspaper had reason to think it true given their larger 'picture of Mr Laski in his capacity of a political writer, a political pamphleteer and a political speaker'. The newspaper had not libelled if it had reason to think Laski 'a stirrer-up of sedition', a man who had said seditious things in the past, and 'whatever your speech may have said, it is true you are that sort of man'. Goddard did not lecture the jury on the difference between stirring up sedition and analysing or predicting the inevitability of revolution. On the contrary, he paraphrased Laski's defence in terms that virtually accepted Hastings's readings of Laski's arguments.

> Mr Laski says – again I repeat to you, Mr Laski says – that is not what I have written. My theme is something different. I have only said what any political philosopher might say, that there is always a risk of violence if the one side cannot get by general consent that to which the conditions of life in their opinion entitles them.

Goddard assured the jury that it need not worry that if they followed this logic and read Laski as an advocate of revolution, a 'stirrer-up of sedition', they were also saying he was guilty of high treason, for 'it is the birthright of Englishmen to say what they like, to write what they like, to write fearlessly and to write openly'. In a bizarre twist, Goddard wrapped the sanctity of free speech around such a possible jury finding. Laski's views might have been 'unpopular with the multitude ... distasteful ... repugnant', but 'the expression of abstract academic opinion in this country is free'. As long as his views were not offered to an audience in a context which might influence them to 'produce the disorders or crimes or violence imparted', Laski 'is at perfect liberty to do so'. Goddard had shifted the focus from whether Laski, at Newark or in prior writings, did in fact advocate revolution, to his right to have done so. Goddard drove home the presumption that Hastings's case was proven with a further bit of advice. The jury, Goddard allowed, might find such talk about 'rebellions, insurrections, outrages, assassinations ... deplorable', but the principles of 'free speech and free expression' protected Laski from accusations of treason. 'Professor Laski is entitled to state what his political creed is.' With such defenders, Laski needed few critics.

The Lord Chief Justice had one more comment for the jury. Goddard introduced his own critique of Laski's reading of history. 'Speaking only for myself', Goddard told the jury, 'I was a little surprised to hear' him argue that revolutionary violence might come first from 'the capitalists who will fight in defence of their capital and their institutions'. This theme, Goddard argued, made no sense. Surely it is 'the working classes, or labourers, or whatever you like to call it, who will use violence first', the judge offered. It was clear, he informed the jury, that in the French Revolution 'the first violence came from the proletariat in their seizure of the Bastille'. Ironically, as inappropriate as these comments were, they were also factually wrong. First blood in the French Revolution, scholars agree, was drawn by the 'revolt of the nobility' who rose in violent insurrection in Béarn, Brittany and Dauphiné in 1788 against Louis XVI's plans to solve his financial crisis by taxing the privileged classes. But no one expected Lord Goddard, the Lord Chief Justice of England, to be an expert in revolutionary history, or for that matter to speculate on it in his instructions to the jury.

All that mattered to Laski was, as he later put it in 'My Day in Court', that 'the judge not only hates the opinions I hold, but . . . explain[s] to the jury that they are dangerous opinions'. He realized that what was at stake was 'not what was said at some place on a definite occasion', but that he held views 'which both judge and jury are convinced it is bad to hold and worse by far to express'. The legal drama, 'his day in court', had come to an end. 'You know the result of your case', Laski later wrote, before the jury's verdict has been given. 'The actors continue their parts, for the play must be officially closed.'

The jury retired at 3.00 p.m. and returned forty minutes later with their verdict: the report in the Newark Advertiser had been 'a fair and accurate report of a public meeting'. In addition, Goddard ruled, Laski would be required to pay all the court costs. Laski left the court through a side door to avoid the reporters and photographers, fleeing from the 'public hanging' to the safety of his 'own fireside without the stare of a thousand eyes'. The Tories were exultant: it was their first good news since Churchill's defeat at the polls. Congratulatory letters and telegrams poured into the Newark Advertiser, one from a jubilant Alfred Roberts, a local alderman and grocer in nearby Grantham, whose daughter Margaret would one day be Prime Minister. Roberts commended Cyril Parlby, the editor of the Newark Advertiser, and hoped that his 'courage will inspire others to fight these enemies of freedom'.

Laski was devastated. According to Frida, 'he bore up well till he got home and then wept as I have never seen a man weep'. Diana thought 'it broke his heart', and most of his closest friends insisted that Laski never recovered his buoyancy after the verdict and was never really well again. For several weeks after the verdict Laski cancelled his public appearances. He immediately offered to resign from the faculty of the LSE since he had been 'declared a liar'. He also wrote to Philip Noel-Baker, his successor as chairman, suggesting he ought to leave the NEC, which was also rejected. Kingsley Martin and Nye Bevan rang up with warm support and the news that Attlee and Morrison were going to ask Morgan Phillips, the Labour Party secretary, to get the party to raise Laski's court costs by public subscription.

A revolutionary would have expected the verdict and taken it in his stride. But Laski had faith in the system even though twenty-two years earlier he had come away from his own jury experience in *O'Dwyer* v. *Nair* convinced that the average juryman, 'incapable of appreciating the technique of evidence', always deferred to authority. He was demoralized even though he had himself written, as Hastings devilishly pointed out, that 'a London jury is fairly certain to award damages for libel to a Tory Member of Parliament but it is also fairly certain to assume that a Labour sympathizer cannot be libelled'. Hastings had suggested that such a view 'was unfair, stupid and offensive'. Laski took no solace in the verdict having vindicated him in this particular exchange with Hastings. He wrote to Frankfurter that 'my own philosophy ought to have taught me not to expect any other outcome'; still, he had had 'an inner and unjustifiable hope that the worst will not happen'. He was profoundly mistaken and he saw three decades of fifteen-hour days rendered worthless by this 'public entertainment' which left him permanently fixed in the popular mind as 'a regicide about to be beheaded in Tyburn or Tower Hill'. His post-Oxford commitment to the politics of reason and the ballot-box was decreed a public lie by five men and two women of substantial property. The verdict seemed to mark people like him permanently as outsiders. 'The intellectual was a thing apart in our society,' Laski wrote after the trial, 'not exactly a pariah, but perhaps the jackal that accompanies the animal who does the kill.' Hastings knew the system better. In his autobiography he drew from the 'Laski case' a simple principle. 'Very few people have ever embarked upon a libel action without bitterly regretting their adventure.' Edmund

Wilson, writing in the *New Yorker* seven years later, had a different reading of the trial's outcome. He blamed Laski's insularity for his miscalculation of what a jury would do. Laski 'always had the freedom of the classroom and the left intellectual world' and was unaware of 'how much less secure his position was in relation to the general public'.

Particularly stressful to Laski after the trial was his legal obligation to pay the court costs for both sides, estimated initially as somewhere between £15,000 and £20,000. Living on an LSE salary that had just been raised for the first time in ten years to £1,600 annually, he assumed that he would have to sell his house and his books. He was 'at the end of my tether. I feel like suicide at having to ask Frida to begin at the beginning after all these years.' Laski's friends came through, however. Money poured into Morgan Phillips's 'Laski fund', usually in small sums of ten shillings or one pound from individuals, unions, constituency Labour Parties and co-ops. The meticulously kept account books in Transport House show a total of 5,329 contributors. Not all of Phillips's post contained cheques, alas. Several weeks into the subscription drive he told Ian Mikardo that he had received 'about fifty virulently anti-Semitic letters condemning me for starting the fund'. Apparently Beaverbrook was initially willing to free Laski from having to pay his side's legal costs, but was talked out of his magnanimity by E. J. Robertson, the general manager of his papers, who told him of the rumours that Laski had boasted of founding a Beaverbrook lectureship at the LSE with the damages he expected to receive.

In America $6,306.23 was raised by a committee headed by Max Lerner. When Frida wrote on her own to Cohn asking him to get people to send cables and letters 'to comfort' Laski, Cohn, Frankfurter, Huebsch, Murrow and Kirchwey immediately contacted 'their beloved friend'. The *Nation* and *New Republic* ran stories about the trial and the appeal for funds. The Lerner committee, including Albert Einstein, Alvin Johnson, Stephen S. Wise, Cohn and Kirchwey canvassed for money with a covering letter that reminded people 'how big a force Laski has been in progressive thinking on both sides of the ocean'. One hundred and five people contributed in a matter of weeks. There were gifts from Laski's friends Roger Baldwin, Benjamin Cohen, Alfred Cohn, Freda Kirchwey, Corlis Lamont, Max Lerner, Edward R. Murrow and Michael Straight; from politicians Harold Ickes, Fiorella La Guardia and Henry Wallace; from the labour leader Jacob

Potofsky as well as liberal business leaders Ralph Lazarus, Julius Rosenwald, James Warburg and Mrs Marshall Field. Among the writers, scholars and publishers who contributed were Bruce Bliven, Rupert Emerson, Clifton Fadiman, Merle Fainsod, Laura Hobson, Harry Levin, Helen Lynd, F. O. Mathiessen, S. E. Morrison, Otto Nathan, Linus Pauling, Paul Sweezy and Theodore White. There were contributions from well-known progressives in the arts such as Melvyn Douglas, Elia Kazan and Lillian Hellman. The two largest contributions were $1,000 from Eugene Meyer of the *Washington Post* and $500 from Viking Press.

With the American contributions, Phillips's fund received a total of £14,000, or $52,000, by May 1947. When finally reckoned the court costs totalled only £12,000, and with the surplus of £2,000 the Labour Party began an educational trust fund. Laski himself received nearly 4,000 letters of sympathy in the seven weeks after the verdict, which he answered in a public letter of appreciation in the *Daily Herald*. Earlier he had reserved a special thanks for Frida, writing on Christmas Eve:

> If I tried to put into words what I have felt about your magnanimity to me in these last weeks, I should fail quite utterly. But I do want to tell you that I know what you have done for me, and that I thank you from the bottom of my heart for your generous courage. But for you I could not have faced it, and I could not have borne the burden it seemed to put on me. You have saved my self-respect for me and made me able to face life even before this bitter blow. I know it is only one of an endless series of acts of devotion you have given me over the years. But I must whisper to you alone that it has made me feel, as never before, the depth of love between us. I hope 1947 will be the happiest of all your years.

The 'Laski trial' had an enduring impact on English law, for more than anything else it was responsible for the abolition of special juries. Years earlier in his *Grammar of Politics* Laski had proposed their elimination after his experience in *O'Dwyer* v. *Nair*. After the verdict in his own trial Laski wrote to Frank Soskice, the Solicitor-General, suggesting that Labour do away with the legal anachronism. In early 1949 the Juries Bill introduced by Sir Hartley Shawcross, Labour's Attorney-General, was passed into law, once and for all ending special juries. In other ways, as well, the trial lived on in English political and public memory. It was featured on a BBC programme on famous trials in 1962, and the tactics of Slade and Hastings are extensively cited in Richard du Cann's *The Art of the Advocate*, a leading British legal text on courtroom technique. Its highly charged ideological nature also persisted, even as it receded into history. Thirteen years after the trial Goddard's legal clerk, Arthur Smith, still wrote of Laski as being 'a Polish Jew by origin although he had spent most of his life in England', who was 'evasive, hair-splitting and sometimes plainly offensive' as a witness, with 'no patriotic feelings for any country' and 'sworn allegiance to the Kremlin'. And in 1990 Roger Parlby, the son of Cyril Parlby, publisher of the *Newark Advertiser* in 1946, who is now himself in charge of the paper, suggested that 'Laski got most of his court costs from the Polish Communist Party. It was in the papers then.' Finally, there is the alleged repentance of the Lord Chief Justice. Responding to the *Times* obituary after Goddard's death in 1971, one H. Philip Levy wrote a letter to *The Times* in which he claimed that Neville Laski told him that on 10 June 1965 he had met Goddard, then eighty-eight, in the smoking-room of the Inner Temple. Goddard asked whether 'your brother was very grieved and angry with me for my conduct of his libel action.' To Neville's reply that his brother had indeed been hurt, Goddard was reported to have said:

> The reason I am speaking of this is very important. I have never worried about a case I tried so much as this one. Lately there has been a revival of the case on the wireless and I have received numerous letters, mostly critical – some of which I have answered. I did not agree with the finding of the jury . . . I gravely considered whether there was anything I could do, but as a jury was involved I was helpless. I have been unhappy about the case always and often think about it. I can say that it has been on my conscience. I do want to add that your brother was not a good witness. He could not answer simply 'yes' or 'no' and made long speeches. Slade was no match for Pat Hastings.

CHAPTER TWENTY-ONE

Palestine, the Cold War and America Revisited

In the early months of 1947 Laski went into what he described to Frankfurter as 'a dark cave' from which he emerged only with the aid of Frida and the thousands of people who wrote to him to convince him that 'I was not really a disastrous failure who injured those I loved and all the principles for which I care'. Laski's private hell was matched that winter by the misfortunes of the Labour government, which in 1947 reached the low point of its five years in office.

Dalton called 1947 Labour's '*annus horrendus*' and as Chancellor of the Exchequer he bore much of the blame. Bitter cold and heavy snow persisted through the winter creating a major shortage of coal, the final blow in undermining the confidence of a people tired of war and post-war privations. Laski wrote to Huebsch wryly in February that he couldn't understand why 'America wants bases in the Arctic instead of coming to occupy this country. We can give you the temperature if you will give us the coal.' When the fuel shortage ended with the arrival of summer, a currency convertibility crisis saw the Treasury lose 700 million precious United States dollars in one month, which was followed by cut-backs in public expenditure. Dalton fell from power in 1947, both for his alleged mismanagement of the economy and for an unguarded conversation with a reporter which let slip some details of the budget he was about to present to the House of Commons. He was succeeded as Chancellor of the Exchequer by the former red nemesis of the 1930s, Sir Stafford Cripps, whose Christian Socialist and vegetarian asceticism helped to give these post-war years their label as the 'age of austerity'. In the midst of Dalton's darkest days he received a warm letter of support from Laski, who generously reached out to another traveller through the cave of darkness:

This is merely a word to bid you be of good heart. The dogs bark, but the caravan passes on. I know, I suppose, as well as most people the infamy of political rancour. It does hurt. But it does not matter as long as you retain the confidence of those whom you respect. Be quite sure you have that. And be quite sure that those who, like me, have faith in you, will in their small way, fight your battle. Courage, camarade.

Comrades first at the LSE and then as Labour Party insiders, the two fended off the barking dogs in 1947, but there was an important difference in their fates. Dalton could at least take solace that his vision of the Labour Party was triumphant. Labour in power did not create a centrally planned totalitarian police state but a benign welfare state. It produced neither Jerusalem nor a socialist brotherhood, only a Keynesian-managed capitalist society, with but 20 per cent of the economy in any sense 'collectivized'. The working class clearly benefited from Labour's reforms, with full employment for the first time in peacetime, and social insurance and health provisions for everyone, but Labour left basically untouched the country's capitalist structure and the existing distribution of wealth and power. The Labour government's commitment was to Dalton's *Practical Socialism*, a social-ism of economic efficiency and traditional social reform. Dalton's ideal of a capitalist order made more humane and efficient by socialist and technocratic management triumphed over Laski's vision of a final end to exploitation and injustice in the replacement of a competitive market society by a socialist community. Laski's agenda was not a high priority for Attlee and Bevin either, or, alas, by 1947 for Cripps.

Unlike Cripps, Laski remained on the Labour left. He continued to speak and write about a real socialist transformation of Britain even as most of his energy went into criticisms of Labour's foreign policy. From 1947 to his death, however, Laski was no longer the pre-eminent figure on the Labour left. The trial had clearly undermined his authority with some elements in the party, especially the trade unions, and his membership on the NEC constantly required him to balance charges of party disloyalty against too visible a role in dissent. He was not in Parliament, which further handicapped him, especially with the emergence of a vigorous new group of young left-wing Labour MPs elected in 1945, principally journal-ists and teachers, whose leaders Michael Foot, Ian Mikardo and Richard Crossman established the 'Keep Left' group of MPs in 1947. Laski, tired,

dispirited, somewhat discredited, and still with daily commitments to the
LSE, was no match for Nye Bevan, the party veteran sitting in Cabinet, as
putative leader to the Young Turks. And Laski was mistrusted. In a late
1946 lunch with Sir Bruce Lockhart, for example, Michael Foot praised
Bevan's youth, brains and energy, which made him, according to Foot,
'the rising star in the Labour Party'. According to Lockhart's diary, Foot
had no use for Laski, whom he regarded as a liar who 'has over-written
himself and over-played his hand'.

Michael Foot's dismissal notwithstanding, Laski toiled valiantly for the
Labour left throughout the period Labour governed. The *Left News* and its
sponsoring Left Book Club died a quiet death in 1948, symbolically
ringing down a curtain on the ideological turbulence of the 1930s, but in
its place four other weeklies continued to push the left Labour line and in
them a piece by Laski could invariably be found. The *Tribune*, now edited
by Foot, and Kingsley Martin's *New Statesman* had always published Laski,
and to them were added Emrys Hughes's *Glasgow Forward* and the Co-
operative Society's *Reynolds News*. Laski was openly critical of the National
Health Service for its retention of fee-paying medicine. He argued that all
private practice should be abolished if medicine were to be totally removed
from the market. Like the 'Keep Left' MPs, Laski opposed the party's
abandonment of direct physical planning of the economy through price,
investment and import controls, consumer rationing, manpower movement
and wage controls, an abandonment symbolized by Harold Wilson's
'Bonfire of Controls' when he lifted sixty direct economic regulations on
Guy Fawkes' Day in 1948. In his weekly 'London Letter' in the *Glasgow
Forward* Laski lamented Cripps's shift to a less direct budgetary mode of
planning that used fiscal controls and market mechanisms for the
implementation of economic policy. Laski argued that not only was this
too definitive an acceptance of the Keynesian version of planning, but also
that direct physical planning of the economy was more equitable and more
just. When, however, 'Keep Left' resolutions were presented at the Labour
Party conference, Laski kept quiet, sitting silently on the platform when,
for example, Tom Sargent insisted at the Margate 1947 conference that
'socialist economics mean seeing and dealing with our problems as a whole
in real physical terms, with all the money-juggling, all the manoeuvres for
private profit, all the waste of duplicated effort cut down to a minimum'.

He sat silently the next day too, when Bevin, in a speech rivalling his

1935 brutalization of Lansbury, ridiculed his critics on the left for abstaining the previous autumn on a vote on the King's Speech as a protest against Bevin's emerging Cold War foreign policy. Even if his ire was directed at Crossman, Foot and Mikardo, Bevin could not resist comparing himself to Laski. He was a trade-union man who understood loyalty. He had 'been to Eton one night, Harrow one afternoon . . . and left school when I was ten'. He was so 'unprejudiced' because 'intellectuals like Laski have never got hold of me'. In awe of Bevin's performance, Crossman described Bevin's foes sitting passively on the platform, 'dapper Harold Laski biting hard on his pipe . . . Nye Bevan in sombre mood'. Bevin's voice rose

> to a hoarse roar of righteous indignation. No man is so skilful at handling a working-class audience, mixing the brutal hammer blow with sentimental appeal . . . He did not merely smash his critics, he pulverized them into applauding him.

Bevin's union supporters had good reason to be pleased with his bashing of the 'Keep Left' group and Laski. The trade unions were solidly opposed to any form of direct government control over the movement and compensation of workers which, left Labourites argued, was essential to a truly planned socialist society. Many thought Laski's recent comments about the fuel crisis insensitive to the working class. In the *Daily Herald* of 5 March 1947, Laski advocated drastic cut-backs in luxury consumption – for example, the virtual elimination of the cosmetics industry. Most offensive, however, was his suggestion in the course of supporting higher duties on tobacco that

> we cannot afford to luxuriate either in the expensive escapism of Hollywood films or the pleasant opiate of Virginia tobacco. We cannot waste thousands of workers upon pools and dog racing and mid-week football. We have to test workers' demands by workers' output.

The magnitude of Laski's affront was intensified by editorial cartoonists parodying Laski's advice, emphasizing the intellectual's disdain for working people as well as highlighting Laski's own fondness for the opiate of tobacco. Coal miners were not pleased when Laski insisted that the fate of the socialist experiment rested on their capacity to work harder and increase their productivity. Equally annoying were his frequent calls for worker wage restraint and the need to rethink the place of collective bargaining in a socialist economy. At Buckley, for example, he proclaimed:

'You cannot recklessly ask for higher wages. You have got to alter the whole attitude of the trade unions to industry. They have new functions to perform and nowhere more than in nationalized industries.' Nor was Laski's appointment in July 1948 to a Labour Party sub-committee to study the role of workers in the management of nationalized industries good news for union members, for it too was an issue principally identified with left-wing Labour intellectuals and not, for example, of great concern to the National Union of Mineworkers which did not even advocate workers' control of their own industry.

Laski's general response to the events of 1947 was that they represented not 'a crisis of socialism, but a crisis of capitalism and decay', and would not be remedied in any profound way 'until capitalist society had given way to a socialist commonwealth'. The real culprit haunting the British economy was not the horrendous winter, but the Tory 'inertia of the inter-war years' and 'the even more devastating blizzard of 1939–45'. The coal crisis illustrated starkly how difficult it was 'to build a socialist economy piece by piece within the framework of a capitalist society'. Gaitskell, the Minister of Fuel and Power, might offer practical advice about the coal crisis, telling reporters that less bathing was in order, but Laski's advice was either frighteningly stoical and apolitical ('Let us face it quite frankly. We cannot have two world wars in one generation and expect not to have a hard time.') or openly ideological ('The coal crisis makes a swift progress to socialism not less but more important.').

Despite his radical response to the fuel crisis, it was nevertheless usually a tamer Laski who spoke out on British politics after his trial. He no longer, for example, called for the abolition of the House of Lords, writing now in support of the government's bill to reduce the power of the Lords to delay legislation from two years to one. As his role in the Zilliacus affair reveals, Laski was subdued in part because of his NEC responsibilities. On the far left of the party for decades, Konni Zilliacus had infuriated his colleagues in the House of Commons by associating with a small group of 'crypto-communist' MPs. His prominent attendance at a communist-inspired World Peace Congress in Paris led the NEC, with Laski in the minority, to reject his selection in early 1949 by the Gateshead East constituency Labour Party as their candidate for the next general election. Zilliacus's efforts to appeal the NEC's decision at the party's annual conference that June in Blackpool focused on Laski, who had agreed to open the debate on his behalf. The NEC minutes for the 5 June meeting on the eve of the conference indicate, however, that Laski was persuaded 'to refrain from taking this course'. The NEC had apparently held that its members were bound by majority decisions. Laski had hoped that Michael Foot, newly elected to the NEC, would support him in opposing this blanket prohibition, but when Foot 'did not say a word', Laski proposed to speak merely as a delegate from his local Labour Party but was told he could not because the duly accredited delegate had the vote. A group of 'Keep Left' MPs pleaded with Laski to speak out the next day against this stifling of back-benchers, but in the end Laski said nothing.

On occasion Laski was even useful to the NEC at party conferences. At Margate in 1947 Attlee's reintroduction of the draft created a first-class row in the Parliamentary Labour Party among those who saw it as a Cold War diversion from the real socialist agenda. So widespread was the opposition that Attlee reduced the term of service from eighteen to twelve months in order to get approval. At the conference the former firebrand Laski, speaking for the party, insisted that conscription was regrettable but necessary. The alternative was 'to recruit the army in the old way, the way of hunger, poverty and unemployment'. The resolution critical of the NEC was soundly defeated.

Laski did the NEC's bidding at the 1948 conference as well, requiring him to take a stand about which he certainly felt some ambivalence. Earlier that year he had brought to the attention of the NEC concerns about the revival of fascist and anti-Semitic activities in Britain. The Executive appointed a small committee which met on several occasions with the Lord Chancellor, the Attorney-General and the Home Secretary, Morrison. At the Scarborough party conference in May a resolution calling for criminalization of organizations or publications that propagated religious or racial hatred was opposed by the Executive both on constitutional grounds and because of its implied criticism of Morrison. Laski was selected to make the NEC's case against the proposal. He outlined the pitfalls of restricting free speech and assured the delegates that 'naturally, as myself a member of the Jewish race, I should be watchful of anything likely to undermine the right of the Jew in Great Britain to be treated as an equal citizen with all other citizens'. The resolution was withdrawn. He repeated these assurances the next year, a far cry from the Laski who in the 1930s would have relished the opportunity to embarrass his party's leaders.

It was not, however, simply NEC collegial pressure or post-trial loss of authority that tamed Laski. There was also the realization that perhaps he had expected too much, too quickly from a Labour victory. He now understood better how much less his party was committed to socialism than he was, as opposed to its concern for labour and the interests of workers, but also that he had underestimated the power of circumstances, like a brutal winter, to affect policy plans. Most significant of all, however, was his sense that he had failed to grasp adequately the subtle strategies by which capitalism ensured its perpetuation. In a Fabian lecture in the autumn of 1947 he speculated about how difficult transformative social change was since 'man is a conservative animal, whose ideas are imprisoned within a framework he is not easily persuaded to abandon'. His reading and rereading of Trollope and Burke taught him this. Moreover, in an important insight, not unlike that associated with the Italian Marxist Gramsci, Laski told his audience that the attainment of real socialism was rendered so difficult and slow because

> we are trying to transform a profoundly bourgeois society, in which all the major criteria of social values have been imposed by a long indoctrination for whose aid all the power of church and school, of press and cinema and radio, have been very skilfully mobilized; we have got to transform this bourgeois society into a socialist society with foundations not less secure than those it seeks to renovate. We have, moreover, to accomplish this in a dramatically revolutionary period, in which quite literally millions, afraid of the responsibilities of freedom, yearn to cling to whatever they have, however fragmentary, of a security with which they are familiar.

Laski's new realism helps to explain his preoccupation with foreign policy issues during Labour's rule. The international order operated under more volatile processes with much greater capacity for individuals to effect change, he thought, and much less constraint from the historical or sociological weight of capitalist indoctrination or from the NEC and the leaders of his party.

On at least one important and long-simmering foreign policy issue Laski was at first uncertain about how committed Labour was to keep its pre-election promise, but ultimately he would praise Attlee's statesmanship. In the autumn of 1945, a month after taking office, the Labour government announced a general election for India to help it decide its own future, but the Congress Party, fearful that this was merely a way to postpone real action, decided to put pressure on the government. Krishna Menon organized a massive celebration of Nehru's fifty-sixth birthday on 14 November at St Pancras town hall and invited Laski as the principal speaker. Laski's speech, in the opinion of Menon's biographer, 'must be considered a landmark in the history of India's struggle for freedom'. Every paper in London carried his words.

> Indian freedom is inevitable and inescapable, and what we have to decide is whether that freedom shall come gracefully by British cooperation or, instead, by British hostility ... We have to make up our minds ... A Labour Party which is unwilling to play its full part in the emancipation of India will, sooner or later, be unwilling to play its full part in the emancipation of the British working class. As a movement that is part of the international movement for human emancipation, a Labour Party which fails this test will pass from the historic scene, for the Indian problem is part of a much wider and more vital issue. The end of imperialism everywhere ... Freedom and democracy know no bar of colour, religion, class, or birth.

The strategy worked and Labour quickly set in motion the process by which Earl Mountbatten, the last Viceroy, granted independence to India. Laski, fittingly enough, was the speaker at the London celebration of Indian Independence Day. That same year he was invited by Nehru to visit India and to lecture at various universities in the winter term of 1947–8. Laski anticipated that his request for leave would be denied because of the pressures on the LSE with returning servicemen and colonial students flocking to Houghton Street, and told Nehru that his visit must wait. It would never come to pass, but Laski did see his student Menon become the first ambassador from a free India to the Court of St James nearly a quarter of a century after the Amritsar trial when Laski became, according to Menon, 'one of us'.

Palestine was another matter. What had begun in 1929 as an effort to please Frankfurter and Brandeis, as well as to prove his access to the corridors of power, became after the Second World War a veritable crusade which obsessed Laski. It was almost as if having become the prophetic pariah of the Labour Party intensified his identification with Jewry, the outsiders personified, and almost as if he had finally resolved his insider–outsider ambivalence by willingly accepting the latter. So embittered would Laski become at Labour's 'mean and shameful' handling of the 'Palestine question' that he thought, but for American intervention, Bevin might have filled 'with victims of his angry fury the graves that Hitler had left empty by his defeat'. Behind Labour's retreat from its 1945 party conference commitment to a Jewish national homeland, Laski saw Bevin's anti-Semitism. 'I am not sure EB hates Jews more than communists, it must be a near thing,' he wrote to Max Lerner. In many post-war letters to Frankfurter Laski reiterated his conviction that Bevin was 'quite definitely anti-Semitic in a brutal way'. It was, in fact, their mutual dismay with Bevin and his Palestine policy that helped to maintain the warmth of the Laski–Frankfurter friendship in these years, giving them much to write about other than their disagreements on the Cold War.

Bevin's defenders attribute his position on Palestine to traditional Foreign Office bias towards the Arab world and its oil reserves as well as to fears that a Jewish state would tilt to the communist bloc. If Bevin seemed intemperate on occasion about Zionists and Jews, it was a not unjustified response to the intense pressure put on him. Anti-Zionism or indifference to Jewish pleading, his champions assert, was not itself anti-Semitism. There is evidence, however, to justify the claims for Bevin's anti-Semitism. Gladwyn Jebb, later Lord Gladwyn, who worked closely with Bevin at the Foreign Office in these years, has written that Bevin was 'prejudiced against Jews, Catholics and the lower-middle class'. The writer and journalist Maurice Edelman has even suggested that Bevin 'tended to visualize all Jews as multiplications of Professor Harold Laski . . . voluble, alien and to be patronized'. There is also the 1944 entry in Chuter-Ede's wartime diary of a

> story circulating that Bevin asked the Labour Party Executive to send some members to discuss the future of Britain. Laski, Shinwell and Mrs Ayrton Gould [a member of the NEC since 1929, elected MP in 1945] were chosen. Bevin is supposed to have said he could spend his time better than in discussing Britain's future with three Yids.

The debate over Bevin's anti-Semitism notwithstanding, Laski's hatred of him and his policy developed slowly. In fact, Laski wrote in June 1945 that among those in the party leadership 'Bevin will be good for Palestine', and he stood by him through Labour's first crisis over Palestine. Immediately after Labour took office, President Truman wrote to Attlee asking the British government to absorb 100,000 Jews into Palestine, the estimated number of Jewish refugees in Europe. A Cabinet committee on Palestine had already decided to continue allowing Jewish immigration at the rate of 1,500 per month until a permanent solution to the Palestine problem evolved. Attlee turned down the higher request, citing the difficulty of obtaining Arab consent, fears about the reaction of Moslems in India, and a conviction that other nationals had suffered in concentration camps as well, so that there was no reason why Jews should be put 'at the head of the queue' for resettlement. Trying to contain his fury, Laski arranged for members of the NEC to meet a Jewish delegation consisting of his former student Moshe Sharett and Berl Locker, both officials of the Jewish Agency. For over two hours Locker and Sharett described the appalling conditions under which an estimated 100,000 to 120,000 Jews lived in displaced persons camps in Europe. 'What was happening,' Locker said, 'was a continuation of the extermination policy by other means – it meant the death of tens of thousands of Jews.' Laski then organized a meeting for Sharett, Locker and himself with Attlee, Bevin and George Hall, the Colonial Secretary. The delegation was disappointed to hear that the government would not reconsider its response to Truman and was offended when Bevin suggested that Europe's Jews ought not to abandon their countries of birth and the chance to make a contribution to the rehabilitation of Europe.

Laski wrote to Frankfurter of 'the Attlee–Bevin betrayal of the Jews', but publicly he held his fire because he knew that Bevin had a plan to enlist America in the process. On 15 November the Foreign Secretary announced that President Truman had agreed to the creation of a joint Anglo-American commission of inquiry to re-examine the Palestine issue. Although David Ben-Gurion, the head of the Jewish Agency, saw the plan as yet another stalling tactic to appease Arabs, Laski sent Bevin a private note praising his statement as a 'great success'. Bevin's plan, Laski told the New York Times correspondent Sidney Gruson, opened the way to a long-term solution, though he would have also liked 'immediate relief to the Jews in Germany and United Nations protection to the Jews in Poland where there are now pogroms'. That same day Laski drafted a 'Note on the Palestine Policy of HMG' which was circulated privately to the members of the NEC. In it Laski raised numerous concerns about the fate of the Anglo-American commission, especially about the extent of the Cabinet's commitment to abide by its recommendations. He also proposed that during the commission's deliberations '4,000 Jews monthly be allowed to enter Palestine'. Such a move would make it clear that the notorious 1939 White Paper no longer applied and would help 'calm down the general acerbity of Jewish agitation'. A warning, he added, 'should be given to Hungary, Romania and Poland that the British and American governments will not tolerate the resumption of anti-Semitic activities'.

Laski remained publicly quiet about Palestine throughout most of 1946 as he awaited the report of the Anglo-American commission. However, a series of events that spring and summer moved him in 1947 to widely publicized outbursts against Bevin. In early May the commission recommended that the 100,000 Jewish refugees in camps for displaced persons be allowed to enter Palestine immediately. On 11 May Laski wrote in the *Glasgow Forward* that 'the crucial test of the bona fides of the British government in relation to the future of the Jews' had arrived. Based on 'considerations of mercy and justice', the report had to be implemented by the Labour government. His strategy, he assumed, had worked. While Zionists like Ben-Gurion had railed at the commission, he saw it as providing the authority the government needed to move. Laski was therefore shocked when Attlee and Bevin linked its implementation to American acceptance of full partnership in its implementation and, in effect killing it, to all Arab and Jewish underground organizations being disarmed before the Jews would be allowed to enter.

The Bournemouth party conference on 12 June added insult to injury. Laski's plea in his chairman's address that 100,000 Jews be given swift entrance to Palestine was answered by Bevin, who exacerbated the issue with one sentence that was quoted around the world. The American push for the admission of 100,000 Jews to Palestine, he suggested, 'was proposed with the purest of motives. They did not want too many Jews in New York.' A month later twenty-eight Britons were among the ninety-one killed in the bombing of Jerusalem's King David Hotel, carried out by the terrorist group Irgun, led by Menachim Begin. The British response was to round up and imprison leading Jewish Agency officials, including Sharett. There was picketing at British consulates across America, and the driveway of the Washington embassy was painted with the words 'British Nazis in Palestine'. In several letters to Sharett, Laski asserted that he and others were doing their best to obtain his release.

One experience more than any other moved Laski to a recognition of the tragedy of Britain's Palestine policy, one in which he was personally involved in the unfolding drama of the attempted refugee exodus from

Europe to Palestine. In defiance of British orders the Jewish Agency encouraged Jewish displaced persons to move illegally by ship to Palestine. The British usually intercepted these ships and directed them to Cyprus or, in the much-publicized case of the *Exodus*, ordered it back to France. In the spring of 1946 Laski happened to be visiting the Socialist Party conference in Italy with Frida and Denis Healey when the British asked the Italian authorities not to allow 1,014 Jewish refugees without immigration certificates to sail from La Spezia to Palestine. The refugees went on a hunger strike, and after seventy-four hours the British counsul in Florence and a Jewish Agency official asked Laski, who was in Turin, to speak to them. He agreed, once it was accepted that he personally could promise nothing except consultation with London. When Laski arrived at the pier he said 'shalom aleichem' to the passengers crowded along the railings of the SS *Fede* who cheered loudly. To Laski's request that they call off the hunger strike, the leader responded that the group planned a public suicide of ten people before the pier gate if Britain did not provide the certificates for entrance to Palestine. He agreed, however, to let Laski address the committee who represented all the refugees. By the light of a tiny petrol lamp Laski met with the twenty leaders in a small crowded cabin for an hour and twenty minutes. His words were translated into Yiddish.

> I wish to help you, but you have to help me. I am ready to fight for your case and you know that I am a fighter, but if we fight each other I can do nothing. The cooperation that I ask from you is to call off the hunger strike and to let me negotiate in your name. I wish to be empowered by you. Should my grandfather not have settled in England I would be one of you; I was in the black-list of Hitler and we would not be here if he had reached our isles. It took me a long time to become a Zionist ... You must remain confident and not resort to despair. I appeal to you as one who wishes to be helpful. I am ready to state your case to the Foreign Secretary and to look for a way out which will allow you to proceed to Palestine.

The group leaders agreed to call off the hunger strike for eight days in order to give Laski time to return to London to make their case. Laski was met at the airport in London by a Foreign Office car and taken to Bevin for a two-hour meeting, where Laski made the case for the strikers. When Bevin agreed to make a decision within a few days, the refugees on the SS *Fede* agreed to wait. At the news of their self-imposed deadline, word reached the British embassy in Rome that the Foreign Office had given authority to grant 679 certificates to Jews at La Spezia. Laski sent a wire urging that the refugees accept the offer and that the remainder await a further grant in the next month. Tense negotiations ensued and when the group, refusing to be split, threatened to resume the hunger strike, Laski returned twice more to the Foreign Office for meetings with Bevin. A solution was finally reached by a bureaucratic ruse which allowed the 1,014 refugees to be placed on two ships, one of which would go more slowly to Palestine allowing its passengers to be counted from the next month's allotment. An embarrassment for the government was avoided and Attlee sent Laski a warm letter of thanks. Laski, meanwhile, was all the more convinced of the tragic consequences of the monthly distribution of no more than 1,500 certificates to the survivors of the Nazi nightmare.

It was clearly a socialist and secular Palestine, not a purely Jewish state, that Laski envisioned. 'The Arabs have as much right to be in Palestine as the Jews,' he told a meeting of the Bath Labour Party in July 1946. 'The Jews have a great contribution to make to Palestine, but they can make it without seeking to dominate Palestine any more than the Scottish people have dominated the English since the Act of Union.' A Jordan Valley authority, he suggested, comparable to America's Tennessee Valley authority, would enable Palestine to sustain over four million people. Laski often spoke in class terms as he described the future of Palestine, where Arabs would be liberated from the oppressive semi-feudal rule of a small group of rich, functionless landlords, the effendi, to live in communal collectives run jointly by Arabs and Jews. Free and compulsory education, as well as a national health service, would be available to Arab and Jew, all made possible by state-run economic development enterprises clustered around a regional water-power authority. This vision of a socialist modernizing state in the post-colonial future attracted others on the Labour left like Crossman, Foot and Mikardo to the Zionist cause, which added another element of friction to Bevin's handling of the 'Palestine question'.

Bevin and the Cabinet had come up with a plan in late 1946 that would have divided Palestine into three 'cantons', British, Jewish and Arab, with the Jewish sector by far the smallest, under joint central rule. When the Zionist leadership proposed instead a partition of Palestine into two states, Arab and Jewish, an angry Bevin announced to the House of Commons that Britain was returning the Palestine mandate and the resolution of the whole issue to the United Nations. Zionists saw this as a trick, assuming that the UN would return Palestine to Britain under a trusteeship. In Bevin's speech to Parliament he lashed out at the United States and the Zionist leadership. Truman's motivation for pressuring Britain to meet the Anglo-American commission's recommendation on the refugees was the Congressional elections. 'In international affairs,' Bevin told the House, 'I cannot settle things if my problem is made the subject of local elections.' He also criticized the two-state solution, suggesting that religions are not nations and ought not to be represented in bodies like the United Nations. Nor did he think that private organizations like the Jewish Agency, 'largely financed from America, should determine how many people should come into Palestine and interfere with the economy of the Arabs, who have been there for 2,000 years.' That autumn when, much to the surprise of the Zionists, the United Nations voted to partition Palestine into two states, Britain abstained and the Arab states voted against it.

Laski grudgingly accepted the idea of a separate Jewish state as the only alternative to Bevin's strongly pro-Arab tilt on Palestine. Britain was 'selling the Jews down the river' and 'backing the wrong horse', he wrote in March 1947. 'It is inconceivable folly for socialist Britain to support a group of Arab feudal chiefs who have never shown any interest in the well-being of their unhappy subjects.' Bevin was acting as the 'ally' of Standard Oil. Laski also bristled at the suggestion that Jews had a controlling voice in American elections. Such claims revealed an ignorance of American politics and were 'bound to be used by fascists in support of their anti-Semitic propaganda'. Laski spoke at Jewish meetings in London of Bevin's policy as 'an outrageous blot on the whole labour movement'. Announcing that he spoke 'as a simple Jew' and a socialist, not as a member of the NEC, Laski said he 'knew no socialist experiment that surpassed the results achieved in the Jewish settlements of Palestine'. He was now convinced that a Jewish national home meant a home 'in which Jews played the part of a government. Questions of cantonization and the contemplation of a permanent Arab majority were an insult to the millions of Jewish dead.'

In the autumn of 1947 Laski wrote in the *Nation* that Bevin was supporting 'reactionary feudal Arab interests', some of whom had collaborated with the Nazis, and that Bevin was haunted by the prospect of the Russians filling a vacuum left by the British in the Middle East. Picked up and repeated in virtually every British paper was Laski's claim that 'the breaking by the British Labour Party of every pledge they made to the Jews is one of the best-known examples of the imperialist pattern'. The *Daily Mail* insisted it was once again time for Laski to be quiet, and his old nemesis *Truth* attacked him as unpatriotic and in the hire of 'unscrupulous American Zionists'.

With the establishment of an independent Israel in 1948 Laski turned to an attack on Britain's failure to follow the speedy Russian and American recognition of the new state as well as its tacit support of Arab League military action against Israel. In an address to the biennial convention of the American Jewish Congress in New York, Laski called Bevin the author of 'one of the most cynical betrayals in history', which saw the British government 'sacrifice its honour and the Jews to oil and strategy'. Laski had criticism for everyone, however, as he did a general stock-taking of recent years. He castigated Jewish terrorists in Palestine 'for using indefensible means for an end to which they were never proportionate' and 'Jews of the world' because 'they failed to convince the Arab masses that the development of a Jewish homeland would be an Arab liberation as well as a Jewish achievement'. On his return to London Laski joined two Jewish Labour MPs, Mikardo and Silverman, in a visit to Bevin to urge recognition. The Foreign Secretary, whom Laski had just described to Frankfurter as 'so completely in hatred of all Jews that he enjoys the sensation of combining with the *mufti* for the development of Hitler's uncompleted task', did nothing.

In the summer of 1948 Laski hit upon the idea of trying to get Lord Halifax, a Tory dissenter from the 1939 White Paper, to urge recognition of Israel. To appeal to Halifax Laski cooked up a scheme with his friend Léon Blum, the former French premier. Blum sent to London two Jewish refugee children who were about to leave France for Israel, with the expectation that they would visit Halifax and move him to speak out for recognition. Halifax, however, refused to see the children or to criticize Bevin. The children's visit, meanwhile, turned into a disaster. They were ultra-Orthodox and furious that their hosts did not have kosher food. In fact, the entire episode led Laski to share his worries with Blum about the future of the Jewish state. The children's was a

spirit which does not make for a new humanity in Palestine, but above all a fascist spirit which results in a deformation of their nature which leads them to divide men between Jews and non-Jews – I hope with all my heart that one can correct in them a training which does not prepare in them a great humanist morality . . .

Laski was himself being taken to task about his own identity as a Jew that summer by the eminently respectable Establishment weekly the *Spectator*. In an article for the *Glasgow Forward*, reprinted widely in America, Laski had written that with its failure to recognize Israel immediately 'the British government has done more damage to the honour and prestige of Britain in the past week than our enemies have been able to inflict on us since the evil days of Munich'. For the *Spectator* 'the question is what "our" means. Are these the words of a Jew or an Englishman?' If the latter, what should one make of an Englishman who not only criticized his government at home but did so in American papers when Britain was so dependent on good relations with the United States?. Clearly it had to be that 'Mr Laski is a Jew first and an Englishman second'. He had a perfect right to so order his loyalties, the *Spectator* conceded, 'but if that is his choice, his right place would seem to be Palestine, not England'. In a talk about the revival of anti-Semitism in Britain to the Association of Jewish Ex-Servicemen at the Kingsway synagogue in London, Laski, in essence, answered the *Spectator*.

> Referring to Israel, Professor Laski said that the only ultimate enemies of Israel were the Jews who were ashamed of their Jewishness, afraid of their fellow-Jews, and who thought that their status as Englishmen or Americans or Frenchman was compromised by the establishment of Israel.
>
> . . . Although, by tradition and training, he was in the intellectual climate of this country, and although his legal allegiance was as fully English as that of Mr Bevin, he would feel safer if there was a Jewish government sitting in Tel Aviv with the right to interest itself in the Jews of England, just as the Vatican had the right to interest itself in the Roman Catholics.

After Bevin finally granted *de facto* recognition on 29 January 1949, Laski planned a trip to Israel. He was to give a series of lectures at the Hebrew University in Jerusalem sponsored by *Molah*, the literary magazine of the Histadrut, the Israeli labour movement. The visit, he told a friend, would 'satisfy one of the profoundest inner emotions he possessed'.

Laski's feud with Bevin over Palestine was part of their more fundamental disagreement over foreign policy in general. Laski saw Bevin as the principal architect of Britain's commitment to the Cold War, a development which even more than the failure of Labour to produce real socialism in Britain contributed to the deep disillusionment Laski experienced in these years. Here, too, Laski had originally had high hopes for Bevin. He had saved Soviet Russia from a British-sponsored Polish invasion early in its existence and he knew the importance of cooperation with Russia during the war. Attlee, however, picked Bevin to be Foreign Secretary, largely because he thought he would be tough on the Russians, hardened by decades of fighting communist and fellow-traveller influence in the trade-union movement. Attlee proved a better judge of his man than Laski, who in September 1947 would describe Bevin as 'poisoned by anti-communist hate'.

Increasingly Laski feared that 'communist blindness' and 'American folly' would lead to the 'conflict of two Messianic philosophies'. The Soviet Union was not expansionist, he believed. It sought 'neighbours friendly to herself' to bolster its security, much as America 'has been doing since she became an independent state'. In his address to the 1946 party conference he had pleaded with Bevin and America 'to try friendship' with the Russians. Convinced that Roosevelt would have fostered trust between the West and Russia, Laski labelled Frankfurter's characterization of America's good-will in foreign policy as 'far more generous than accurate'. In fact, America backed 'every counter-revolutionary movement there is in Europe', he told Frankfurter.

> It is a very hard world. I hope I do not need to prove my affection for America, but frankly the State Department does not make recovery easier . . . I know as well as most people how difficult Russia is, but I think the psychological inability of America to understand Russia is almost as disturbing as the political immaturity of Moscow. I know with all the mind I have that Russia cannot make war, does not want to make war, would be broken by war. All that American policy does is to give an even deeper impression of deliberate provocation, of making ideological conflict where there need be none, of a self-righteousness which is almost as infantile as the propaganda of Moscow . . . I am more convinced than ever that you are on the wrong road – that you are creating the need to choose where there need be no choice, and that all this involves deeper suspicions and heavier burdens – and, above all, fear – I wish I could make Bevin understand that you do not overcome thirty years of suspicion by isolating Russia . . . The initiative for peace is being lost, and, as I see it, needlessly lost . . . I cannot believe that ordinary Americans have

any sense of the implications of what is being done in their name. I hope there is still time to revise the disastrous direction which is being given to the shape of the world, but truly this is one of those grim periods in history when time is not on our side . . . After winning a war for peace and freedom we are combining the factors that are bound to destroy them.

Laski acknowledged that the Soviet Union had thrown away the immense fund of good-will at its disposal in 1945. 'Genuinely baffled at the intensity of the refusal of Moscow to cooperate', he thought 'Mr Molotov has grossly underestimated the desire of Mr Attlee and Mr Bevin for peace'. Both *Pravda* and *Izsvestia*, Laski believed, 'combined sheer lying with ignorant invective' in the 'utter and egregious folly with which Mr Attlee and his colleagues are treated as outrageous war-mongers'. Only weeks after peace had come to Europe in 1945, Laski had pointedly asked, 'Why is the formation of an Eastern Bloc by Russia unexceptionable while the formation of a Western Bloc is regarded as a threat to the peace?' In the very same March 1946 article for the *Glasgow Forward* in which he denounced Churchill's 'Iron Curtain' speech, Laski made it equally clear that

> socialists of the left have no more regard for the virtues of the one-party state when Russia imposes it, than when a streamlined model of non-intervention allows its continuance in Spain and Portugal . . . The deep sympathy of socialists with the high aims of the Russian Revolution does not mean a blind admiration for whatever Russia does. But the deep hatred of Mr Churchill for those same high aims ought not to involve in his mind a blind determination to prevent their extension at all costs, even, if necessary, by war.

Behind this criticism of Russia lay the basic disillusion with the hopes for socialist internationalism which both Russia and his own Labour Party in power were doing their best to wreck. By 1948 there was no evidence, Laski wrote, 'to show that socialists, organized as parties, or organized still more as governments, are not nationalists first, making enlightened self-interest, as each conceives it, the first step of action'.

Crucial to the hardening of the Cold War were the events of early 1947, just as Laski was emerging from his 'dark cave'. In February Bevin announced Britain's inability to finance its troops in Greece and Turkey and its plans for their eventual withdrawal. The fear of a communist take-over in Greece prompted Truman to announce America's plans to move military and economic aid into the eastern Mediterranean. America had assumed the burdens of world leadership, and the 'Truman doctrine' of resisting the expansion of Soviet communism anywhere was born. Laski saw Truman's action as 'a threat to peace greater than any since the rise of Hitler'; the Russians, he thought, had good reason 'to regard the Truman doctrine as a direct threat' to them. He would prefer 'that Great Britain pursue the same policy of friendliness to the Soviet Union as it follows to the USA'. Three months later George Marshall announced plans for a massive economic recovery programme for Europe, including even the Soviet Union and the states of Eastern Europe. Laski was deeply ambivalent about the Marshall Plan. He saw no other way to save Europe than by 'this great piece of generosity', yet he worried that it was intended to bring the states receiving aid under the economic and political domination of America, to require them to drop socialist programmes or the nationalization of industries. 'Our domestic life,' he told a Labour meeting in Coulsdon

> is our affair. Interference in the interest of what is called the American way of life is not something that any Labour Party, and, I think, any Labour government is prepared to accept. We are not going to be the junior partner in an American alliance for the purpose of organizing an American hegemony of the world.

Despite these misgivings, Laski hoped Russia would accept aid under the Marshall Plan and would work with the other nations to develop a plan for the distribution of the aid, the acceptance of which would 'be the test of American good faith'. He told Frankfurter that he might be able to get Moscow to assign his old friend Maisky to represent Russia at the Paris meeting that Bevin had arranged to draw up the European response to Marshall's offer. He was unsuccessful. Molotov attended and he denounced the Marshall Plan as a violation of national sovereignty. Soon the East European countries followed suit. This was a colossal mistake, Laski argued, for Russia gave the impression that it was alarmed at the prospect of European recovery through American aid. There was the real likelihood now that the recovery scheme and Molotov's veto 'might divide Europe in twain'.

Laski's last hopes for a socialist Europe free from the superpower conflict and for a post-war renaissance were dashed by the communist take-over in Czechoslovakia in February 1948. It hit Laski particularly hard because he had paid a sentimental visit to Prague in April 1947, visiting his old friends Jan Masaryk and Eduard Beneš, viewing the city's Jewish antiquities and lecturing in Prague to such a large audience that it was broadcast outside the hall. Czechoslovakia represented Europe's potential. When he returned to London he wrote an article for the *Forward* with a three-line banner headline: DEMOCRACY HAS RISEN AGAIN IN CZECHOSLOVAKIA, FREE PEOPLE WITH A SOCIALIST PLAN, WHERE COMMUNISTS, SOCIALISTS AND LIBERALS WORK TOGETHER.

> If I ever saw a really democratic community I saw it in Czechoslovakia . . .
> This . . . is really a free people . . . There is the fullest freedom of discussion
> . . . Religious freedom is complete . . . the mixed government of communists,
> social democrats and national democrats work together surprisingly well . . .
> to see Czechoslovakia intimately today is to have a real hope of European
> renovation.

Less than a year later the non-communist members of the government were gone, the media had been taken over by the state, and Masaryk had jumped from the window of his office. Arriving in America to lecture at Roosevelt College in Chicago, Laski told reporters that 'secretive, dictatorial Russia in a panic' was responsible for the tragic events. Two New York newspapers on 26 March 1948 captured his pain, while revealing in their headlines two American readings of Laski. The *New York Times* thought PROF. LASKI IS 'DEEPLY GRIEVED' BY THE 'GRAVE MISTAKES' OF RUSSIA and the *Daily News* observed PINKO LASKI'S COMMIE ARDOR COOLING DOWN. Laski reported on the events for the *Forward*.

> A democratic community has been placed under the control of a dictatorship
> . . . There are purges in the universities and schools, in the army and civil
> service; newspapers are suppressed; editors are dismissed . . . Even the Boy
> Scouts have been ordered to unite with the communist youth . . . Why has
> this been done? The fear that reactionaries would attack the regime set up in
> 1945 is nonsense . . . It is, I fear, impossible to avoid the conclusion that the
> Czech communists overthrew the democratic freedom of their country at
> the order of Moscow . . . Blind with the fury of fear, they broke a free
> democracy to exhibit to those whom they deemed their enemies, their
> power and their ruthlessness with which should conflict come, they would
> defend themselves.

Laski was heartbroken. Lionel Robbins remembered commenting to him at the LSE that 'these are disquieting events, Harold' and Laski, with tears in his eyes, replied, 'Lionel, don't let's talk about it. I cannot bear it.' John Stonehouse, then an LSE student, wrote that students could see Laski's 'outlook on life visibly change. From being a buoyant, optimistic philosopher he became depressed and cynical.' Students who went to see him for advice reported that 'they had to counsel him.' Czechoslovakia was the symbol for Laski of the despair felt by men and women of reason at the coming clash of fanaticisms. 'I have a feeling,' he wrote to Frankfurter, 'that I am already a ghost in a play that is over.' In a moving tribute to Masaryk Laski assessed the three years since the euphoria of Hitler's defeat.

> If the statesmen will not make an end of this twilight world in which hope is born only to be broken, and victory won only to be thrown away, it is better to finish the fruitless effort of civilization which lacks the wisdom and the magnanimity without which life is indeed an idiot's tale, for all its fury still signifying nothing.

Laski's sadness at this twilight world after his trial and after Prague, and his recognition of how ineffectual he was as a political actor in shaping policy with his own party in power, turned him back to scholarship, writing and teaching. Never one to avoid excess, Laski's intellectual output remained prolific. In a lecture for the Historical Society of Trinity College, Dublin, in March 1947, commemorating the 150th anniversary of the death of Burke, Laski explored his fascination with the traditionalist who had championed the cause of America and India. He closely identified with Burke, the half-Catholic Irish parvenu who established himself among the English political elite by dint of his brains and exquisite prose. Yet Burke finished his life rejected by that very elite, who, according to Laski, 'were unfit, either in moral character or in intellectual power to hold a candle to him'. In another learned piece commemorating the death of Morris Cohen, Laski revealed that Cohen was the intellectual source of his decision to abandon pluralism and his convictions about the real existence of corporate personality after the First World War. Cohen's paper 'Communal Ghosts' emancipated him, he wrote, from 'the dangerous spell woven, above all, by the exquisite charm of Maitland . . . and that bottomless pit of Gierke's learning which so easily overawes the young student'.

This return to scholarship often served his contemporary political concerns as well. In 1947 Laski undertook the editing and annotation of a centenary edition of Marx and Engels's *Communist Manifesto* for publication by the Labour Party. The volume, which endured as one of the most influential and widely used editions of the *Manifesto* over the next several decades, had a lengthy introduction in which Laski took Soviet Marxists to task for misreading the 'dictatorship of the proletariat'. It was not meant to justify the contraction of democratic participation by the autocratic rule of the Communist Party, he wrote, but to expand political participation from the prior narrow 'dictatorship of the bourgeoisie' to the rule of the entire proletariat. Laski returned to this theme in a new introduction he wrote in August 1948 for yet another edition of *Liberty in the Modern World*. Most of the new material outlined the threat to freedom posed by 'the one-party state' which led inexorably, he wrote, to the idolatry of political leaders, represented most frighteningly by the 'mass adulation lavished on Stalin'. Laski also devoted a small section of the new introduction to the danger posed to freedom by the 'hysterical witch-hunts against radicals all over the United States since 1945'.

Symbolic of his turn to writing was Laski's renewed output of Fabian tracts. With Labour in power, the Fabians had adopted a critical stance to the government, and after his stint as Labour Party Chairman Laski served as Chairman of the Fabian Society from 1946 to 1948. To the many tracts he had written over the years, Laski added one offering a critique of the governing style of the Labour Cabinet and another, an internationalist vision of socialism, which denounced both sides in the Cold War. Laski also revisited the 1930s for the Fabians in their publication of his Webb memorial lecture of 1947 when he spoke of 'the Webbs and Soviet communism'. He was vindicated, Laski pointed out, in his critique of their contention that Soviet Russia was a democracy. There were, indeed, elements of economic democracy to be found there, he suggested, with the population not divided into small numbers of rich and large numbers of poor, but there was clearly no democracy in Russia's political life. What the Fabian publication of the talk did not capture was the LSE audience's laughter as Laski insisted that political democracy did not exist unless one could differ vividly from, and even attack, one's rulers as he did frequently with respect to Attlee and Bevin.

Laski was asked in 1947 by UNESCO to be on a small group of international scholars convened to prepare a preamble to the United Nation's Declaration of Human Rights. The group included E. H. Carr and Julian Huxley, Étienne Gilson from France and Jacques Maritain from America. For their meeting in Paris Laski prepared a lengthy paper 'Towards a Universal Declaration of Human Rights', which recommended a truly universal document that went beyond historic Western assumptions that rights belonged only to particular entities, like the middle class, men and colonial rulers. He urged that there be provisions ensuring equality of the sexes, such as equal educational chances, equal pay for equal work, and the right of a woman to a career which was not terminated by marriage or child-bearing, save of her own volition. He also suggested a social justice component recognizing every person's right to have an equal claim upon the resources of the community. If there were to be, as there inevitably would, degrees of differential claim, the test of their moral legitimacy was still the one he had offered years earlier.

> Where there is differentiation ... it must be possible to show, to the satisfaction of those differentiated against, as well as of those in whose favour the differentiation is made, that the decision to make it does in fact lead to an increase in the resources of the community, and that this, in its turn, results in an increase in the standard of well-being for each individual citizen.

In addition to writing large numbers of book reviews after 1947 for the *Tribune* and the *New Statesman*, Laski resumed writing 'thought' pieces for American journals. He wrote a series of articles for the *Nation* on the nature of power politics and the future of Europe and contributed an essay to the twenty-fifth anniversary number of the prestigious journal *Foreign Affairs*. His status as the representative socialist for the American Establishment was seldom better rendered than when his essay 'The Crisis in Our Civilization' appeared next to others by Henry Stimson, Anthony Eden, John J. McCloy, the Earl of Halifax, Sumner Welles and Arnold Toynbee.

Two books by Laski appeared in these years. *Trade Unions in the New Society*, published in 1949 and dedicated to the American union leader Sidney Hillman, comprised the set of lectures he had given in America in March and April 1949. While Laski examined the responsibilities of unions in industrial research, and the non-working lives of members, most of the book was about American trade-union history and Laski's sense of the need to politicize unions. He had gone full circle. His last involvement in American politics met the concerns of his first, the defence of the rights of unions and workers. Laski's three lectures on British political institutions at the University of Manchester in February 1950 were published posthumously in 1951 with no dedication as *Reflections on the Constitution*. Convinced that the world had gone mad with the irrationality of the Cold War, Laski, always an eighteenth-century Enlightenment man, ended these lectures with a hymn to science and a lament on how little interest in it the public had. Here, too, he had come full circle in his career.

By far the most important intellectual production of these his last years was his 1948 book *The American Democracy: A Commentary and an Interpretation*. Published in America by Viking Press and in Britain by Allen and Unwin, it sought in 761 pages nothing less than a comprehensive survey of American politics, society and culture. Dedicated to Frida 'with my love and devotion', the book had separate chapters on American Traditions, Political Institutions, Business, Religion, Education, Culture, Minorities, Professions, The Press, Cinema and Radio. Laski had been working on the manuscript as early as 1937 and on and off during the war, though the bulk of the serious writing was in 1947. It was, he stated in the Preface, 'written out of deep love of America' and of Americans, of Frankfurter, Cohn and Lerner and of anonymous Americans, 'students, taxi-drivers, railroad conductors, lawyers and doctors, engineers and businessmen who have helped me to form the generalizations I have ventured to make here'.

Laski intended *The American Democracy* to be the twentieth century's counterpart to the earlier magisterial studies of America that de Tocqueville and Bryce had written. He moved in the book from meta-speculation, where, for example, he emphasized the seminal significance for American values and institutions of its lack of a feudal past, to the micro-content analysis of a typical issue of *Reader's Digest* or the weekly programming of CBS Radio. If there was a dominant theme in this huge book, it was the central and malevolent role of business values. A civilization wedded to economic individualism stifled the promise of the America that welcomed the world's hungry and huddled masses and had freed the slaves. On the book's penultimate page Laski pleaded that America 'escape from the limitations of traditional Americanism'. Only the American labour movement, with a progressive coalition gathered around it in a new political party, could call America to its best self. On his last page Laski cited Lincoln's famous 'A house divided against itself cannot stand' and wrote that

Americanism must come to mean the same thing for the sharecropper of
Arkansas as for the stockbroker on Park Avenue in New York City, for the
steel worker in Pittsburgh as for the corporation lawyer in Wall Street, for
the Senator from a southern state like Alabama as for a Senator from a
northern state like Vermont if, indeed, the house is to stand.

The American Democracy was poorly received in America. While Max
Lerner wrote glowingly of it and Perry Miller said in the *Nation* that it
could lay serious claim to greatness, most American intellectuals, even
liberals, saw Laski's book as no more than a biased attack on capitalism and
the American way from a fellow-traveller. Young liberal scholars like
Arthur Schlesinger, Jr. (in a front-page review in the *New York Times Book
Review*) and Oscar Handlin (in *Harper's*) joined John Chamberlain (in
Fortune magazine), who was rapidly moving to the right, in complaining
about the reductionism of the conviction that big business totally ran
America. Even Alistair Cooke told his *Manchester Guardian* readers in his
'Letter from America' that the book had the subtlety of a Diego Rivera
painting. Here Laski did not go full circle. The American intellectuals and
journalists of 1948 and 1949 were a different breed from the progressives
who had welcomed him to the *New Republic* thirty-five years earlier.

One distinguished intellectual in America, on the other hand, thought so
highly of Laski's scholarly eminence and even of his politics that he offered
him a university presidency. Albert Einstein was in 1947 a member of a
committee of prominent Jewish businessmen and academics involved in the
founding of Brandeis University, named after the great jurist and intended
to be a Jewish-sponsored institution where Jewish students would be free
from the quotas applied by most American universities to restrict their
admission. Einstein and Otto Nathan, a professor at New York University,
and Ralph Lazarus, President of the Allied Department Stores, had been
asked to find a distinguished Jewish academic to serve as the first President.
They offered the position to Laski in April 1947, with Einstein writing the
letter.

The Board of Trustees has delegated to me the authority of selecting the first
President of the University ... We all feel that among all living Jews you
are the one man who, accepting the great challenge, would be most likely to
succeed. Not only are you familiar with the United States and her academic
institutions more intimately than many American educators, your reputation

as an outstanding scholar is widespread throughout the country. I am writing, therefore, to ask you whether you would be prepared to consider such an invitation.

Assuming Laski might not want to leave Britain for too long, Einstein suggested that the appointment might be for the two- or three-year period of the university's formation. Flattered as he was, Laski declined, pointing to the precariousness of his health and his temperamental unsuitability for such an executive post. One suspects he also had a better grasp than Einstein of the realities of American post-war politics. Indeed, the offer got caught up in the politics of the American Jewish leadership and the new mood of Cold War anti-communism. The Chairman of the Board of Trustees, George Alpert, a Boston lawyer and Jewish philanthropist, told Einstein that a Laski presidency would have totally subverted the raising of funds for the new school. Einstein was so furious at this rebuke, as well as at the committee's invitation to New York's Cardinal Spellman, recently returned from Spain with glowing words for Franco, to deliver the invocation at a New York fund-raiser that he quietly resigned from the committee, along with Nathan and Lazarus. In a pre-emptive strike to blunt any possible damage, Alpert told the *New York Times* that the offer to Laski was 'a colossal mistake', an attempt by Einstein, Nathan and Lazarus, acting alone, to give the new school a 'radical, political orientation'. Einstein

> had surreptitiously made overtures to a thoroughly unacceptable choice as President . . . To establish a Jewish-sponsored university and to place at its head a man utterly alien to American principles of democracy, tarred with the communist brush, would have condemned the university to impotence from the start . . . I had no intent of identifying Laski with communism, but having filed suit and having a British court throw out his suit, Laski projected an image that would hopelessly complicate the problem of a university that was seeking to establish itself . . . I can compromise upon any subject but one. That one is Americanism. So far as I am concerned, there cannot be now, nor can there ever be, the slightest compromise concerning that.

Alpert's comments compelled Einstein to issue a statement to the press insisting that he had the board's authorization to make the offer. Einstein from that point on had nothing to do with the establishment of Brandeis, the university which in 1946 he had modestly declined to have named after him.

Laski now presented serious problems to liberals in America. Lest they give ammunition to the right, many felt under fierce pressure to dissociate themselves from anyone who was even remotely 'tarred with the communist brush'. After the Democrats lost fifty-four seats in the Congressional elections of 1946, Truman implemented on 21 March 1947 'Executive Order 9835', which ordered obligatory loyalty checks by the FBI for over two million federal employees and the establishment of loyalty boards within agencies to investigate fully the cases deemed most suspicious. Truman's Attorney-General, Tom Clark, also produced a list of 159 political and cultural organizations, membership of which was deemed putative proof of disloyalty. In this new America Louis Fischer, Alfred Kazin, Sidney Hook and Edmund Wilson berated Laski for his 'Sovietism'. There were, however, delightfully paradoxical moments in this distancing. Arthur Schlesinger, Jr, for example, in his influential 1949 book *The Vital Center*, which made the liberal anti-communist case, quoted on the same page J. Edgar Hoover and Harold Laski (from his 1946 *Secret Battalion*) on communist fifth-column tactics in taking over organizations.

Laski was concerned even about his closest friends. Once when Laski wrote that he was coming to America, Murrow recommended with tongue in cheek that Laski stay in England so the FBI could observe both of them: 'I suspect that they are currently informed of my own activities and particularly the guests who stop with us.' If there was any lengthy gap in correspondence, Laski grew concerned about being abandoned. In September 1948 he told Ruth Cohn that he had not heard from Alfred or Felix in over three months. 'Have I done anything wrong?' he asked. In December 1948 he complained to Alfred Cohn that he had sent Ed and Janet Murrow *The American Democracy*, a print of J. S. Mill for his office and a present for their new child, yet he had 'heard nothing in ages'. After another long gap between letters in 1949 Laski joked to Cohn, 'Have you been warned by the FBI not to write to me?'

Unlike many on the American left, Laski had not supported the left-leaning candidacy of Henry Wallace for President in 1948. The previous year when Wallace, fired from Truman's Cabinet and working for Michael Straight's *New Republic*, had visited Britain on a trip arranged by Kingsley Martin and others on the Labour left, Laski had been told by Attlee that it would be embarrassing to relations with Truman if a member of Labour's National Executive Committee appeared on the same platform as Wallace. Laski did not need persuasion because he thought a victory for Wallace would give 'strength to all the forces in Russia which hinder a common move to sensible understanding'. His man, as we have seen, was Eisenhower, the President of Columbia University, this 'wise and imaginative' person whose 'great-heartedness' was 'only surpassed by his modesty'. Compared to the 'pip-squeak' Truman, Ike was literate, experienced and a man of stature. When the 'pip-squeak' won an unexpected victory in 1948 Laski proposed that Eisenhower, 'the most respected of Americans', and Earl Mountbatten be sent to Moscow to explain to Stalin that the North Atlantic pact was defensive in nature and 'to find out whether there is any reality behind Russia's endless protestations of peace'. He also hoped that Eisenhower would become the Democratic candidate in 1952.

Laski and Frida spent two months in America in the spring of 1948. A former PhD student at the LSE, Benedict Mayer, invited Laski to give a course of lectures at the predominantly black Roosevelt College in Chicago. Laski was initially dubious about the trip, fearful for his health as was Frida, who also worried that 'after our own austerity I'll come back dissatisfied to my own poor lot'. The decision to come was made easier by a burglary in their London house in which they lost virtually all their possessions except Laski's books and which left them 'in the dumps'. Laski suggested that accepting the Roosevelt invitation gave them a chance to buy clothes to replace their stolen wardrobe. Although Senator Homer Ferguson of Michigan protested against Laski's admission into the United States in a letter to the Commissioner of the Immigration and Naturalization Service and the State Department, they arrived in New York on the *Queen Elizabeth*. After a speech to the American Jewish Congress, the Laskis flew to Chicago and Roosevelt College. Harold was moved by his warm reception and by Roosevelt's commitment to provide quality education to black students, who like young Harold Washington, the future first black mayor of Chicago, packed his lectures along with their faculty. Laski's name was still magic on the American campus.

It had such appeal that in November 1948 the Sidney Hillman Foundation invited him to return to America in 1949 to give a series of lectures on the future of trade unions at American colleges around the country. Although depressed because of his 'horrible health' and the set of nasty reviews his American book had received, Laski accepted, in hopes that the change of scenery would lift his 'bad mood'. This visit to America was overshadowed politically by Laski's entrance into the controversy over Dean Acheson's appointment as Secretary of State. In a newspaper article in January 1949 Laski had defended Acheson, more out of friendship than approval of his politics, from charges that Acheson was the person in the State Department who had shielded Alger Hiss from efforts to uncover his communist affiliations. Acheson was a man of intellect, of 'great integrity and generosity of temper', Laski wrote. No surprise, then, given the hysteria provoked by the Hiss proceedings that two weeks after he arrived for his Hillman lectures Laski was ordered to fill out registration forms designed for foreign agents so that the Department of Justice could decide whether to allow him to remain in the country. Vigorous protest by the Hillman Foundation and personal intervention by numerous friends, including Acheson, finally led to the withdrawal of the order.

Laski's lectures at Columbia, the University of North Carolina, Howard, Roosevelt, Denver and the New School took place without incident. Strong protests by the American Legion and Veterans of Foreign War in Seattle, however, led the University of Washington, which had stood strong ten years earlier, to cancel his speech and protests in California forced President Sproul of the University of California to cancel two scheduled Laski talks there, claiming that 'Laski's presence would not be pleasing to the Board of Regents'. When the Harvard Law School Forum applied to the Cambridge School Committee to rent the Rindge Technical High School Auditorium for Laski's appearance in Cambridge, the request was denied by a vote of four to two after the Mayor, Michael J. Neville, described Laski as 'pro-communist, anti-Catholic and anti-religious'. *Life* Magazine urged in an editorial that Laski should not be prevented from speaking, since it would give plausibility to his charges that American colleges were controlled by businessmen. Laski did finally get to speak at Harvard almost exactly thirty years after his speech to the police strikers' wives. His career had truly come full circle. This time he was questioned after his talk by two Harvard Government Department Professors – warmly by Sam Beer, a friend of Felix Frankfurter's, and hostilely by the critic of his earliest writings on pluralism, William Yandell Elliott. Laski for his part warned that American democracy was in grave peril, not, however, from communists but 'from those who want to destroy the extreme left in order, so they say, to preserve democracy'.

When he returned to Britain, Laski wrote of his thoughts about America for the *Nation*. In one article about anti-communism on the American campus, Laski blasted the FBI Director J. Edgar Hoover: 'As one hears of what the witch-hunters, big and small, are doing, one is tempted to suggest that an investigation of the FBI is overdue.' Three days later a six-page evaluative report on Laski was on Hoover's desk. It included passages from Laski's 1939 essay 'Why I am a Marxist' as well as more recent quotations from his introduction to the *Communist Manifesto*. A passage comparing Marx and Lincoln has on the FBI file copy a comment handwritten by Hoover in the margin: 'certainly blasphemy on Lincoln's good name'. The final assessment for the Director's attention reads simply: 'Laski may not be an orthodox Marxist, but he certainly is not anti-communist.'

The most bizarre chapter in the tale of Laski the enemy of America involved James Forrestal, a leading American Cold Warrior, Secretary of the Navy from 1944 to 1947 and Secretary of Defense from 1947 to 1949. To complement his vision of American foreign policy as a Christian crusade to eliminate the satanic evil that was communism, Forrestal received frequent briefings from Hoover on communist activities in trade unions, peace groups and universities. He collected and meticulously pasted in his notebooks or diaries letters, magazine articles, government reports, documents, pamphlets and excerpts from books concerned with the communist threat to American security. On the verge of a nervous breakdown, he resigned his office in March 1949 and two months later, after telling friends that the Russians were coming to get him, Forrestal jumped to his death from his window at the Bethesda Naval Hospital. Several years later the publication of his diaries revealed that Forrestal's paranoia focused on Laski, who was referred to so frequently that the editor, Walter Millis, referred to Forrestal's 'obsession with Laski'. Although Bevin assured Forrestal that the Labour Party 'had no use for Laski', Forrestal persisted in his belief that Laski was the number one enemy of America and continued carefully collecting Laski's speeches and writings for his notebooks. In 1946 he asked a friend 'to investigate the circumstances under which our friend Mr Laski was invited (in 1920) to separate himself from Harvard', and from 1944 on he set aides the task of analysing Laski's books in memoranda form for him. He was convinced that Laski was the principal foreign intellectual influence on American radicalism. 'America's best thinkers' in all its universities, Forrestal wrote, were 'subservient' to European thought as carried across the ocean by 'Mr Laski and his associated planners'. It was the warmed-over paranoia of the 1930s critics of Roosevelt, who saw Laski as the foreign 'brains' behind the 'Jew Deal'.

The public mood of Britain and America filled Laski with uneasiness after 1947. The joy of receiving an honorary doctorate in May 1947 at the 500th anniversary of the University of Bordeaux was tempered by fights with Labour Party leaders and continued public hounding of him. Tory MPs twice raised the spectre of Laski at Question Time in the House of Commons, once to discover why the press was barred from a lecture he gave to servicemen and another time to inquire about why *Parliamentary Government in England* was required reading for the cadets at the Sandhurst Royal Military Academy. To Laski's despair at the Red Scare in America was added the announcement to the House of Commons by Attlee that civil servants suspected of being communists would no longer be allowed to handle sensitive government documents.

Laski began shedding responsibilities. He returned the chairmanship of the International Sub-committee of the NEC to Dalton, the recently resigned Chancellor, in November 1947. In September 1948 he resigned as Chairman of the Fabian Society. In his two years as Chairman he had reinvigorated the research and publication operations of the society, planning major publications on socialist philosophy, the reform of government machinery and the application of socialism to international questions. He could not maintain the enthusiasm to continue, however, and he resigned to be succeeded by G. D. H. Cole, who had also preceded him. This left only the NEC and if, as Bevin had told Forrestal, the party had no use for Laski, then by late 1948 and early 1949 Laski finally came to have little use for the party, at least for the NEC.

Laski had told Dalton in 1946 during one of his angry fits over Bevin's handling of Palestine that he might resign from the NEC. He didn't. Instead, he sought to carve out a more powerful role in party policy-making for the NEC *vis-à-vis* the party's parliamentary leadership, an initiative which, if successful, would ironically have gone a long way to validating some of Churchill's claims during the 1945 election. Laski tried to get the party constitution changed in order to exclude sitting government ministers from serving on the NEC. Should serious disagreements then develop between a Labour Cabinet and the National Executive, the annual party conference would arbitrate. Laski formally proposed that the NEC set up a special committee to consider relations between it and the government when Labour was in power; it was defeated by ten votes to seven. He continued to push the issue, however. He wrote an article for the *Tribune*, 'Wanted: A New Constitution', a lengthy memorandum in November 1947 on 'Defining the Relationship between the Labour Party and Labour Government', and often addressed the issue at Fabian functions. His initiative produced a fully fledged debate in the party, but only Herbert Morrison among its leaders seemed interested in rethinking the relationship of the NEC and the Cabinet, offering to take himself off the Executive as Laski's initiative suggested. His offer was declined. Reform of the Labour Party constitution would have to wait for another era.

In August 1948 Laski, enraged at his government's refusal still to recognize the state of Israel, decided not to stand for re-election to the NEC at the conference to be held the following June at Blackpool, and considered resigning before then. It would finally free him truly to speak out. 'You can imagine,' he told Max Lerner, 'what I feel after giving half of my life to this party.' Not above vanity, Laski was also concerned that he might not be elected one of the seven constituency members. He had slipped dramatically in the balloting during Labour's rule. His string of six years in leading the tally from 1939 to 1944 was broken by a tie for first with Shinwell in 1945; a second to Bevan in 1946; a fourth behind Bevan, Dalton and Morrison in 1947; and a sixth in 1948 behind Bevan, Dalton, Shinwell, Morrison and Griffith, with only Foot below him. His serious illness during the winter hardened his resolve not to run in June and in March 1949 he told the party about his decision. By doing this, Laski wrote to Cohn, he could in the next general election 'speak my whole mind about Bevin and his supporters without being held to a duty of silence which I literally could not bear'. Although he might not accomplish much, given Bevin's mass support in the trade unions, he would at least 'ease my conscience'.

> I admit that conscience is at best a pretty poor thing, but it is the only thing really one's own, and it is a deep unhappiness when, week by week, you feel that you are pushing its demands into a corner out of a theory of loyalty which merely gives him [Bevin] and his supporters the power to go on doing evil.

The public announcement of Laski's decision not to run again was made on 21 March. To play down inter-party conflict, Laski's poor health was cited as the major reason for his leaving the NEC. He told reporters in New York that after serving for thirteen years he wanted to make way for a younger person and work full-time on a history of the labour movement in Britain. 'I have had strong differences with the Executive over Palestine policy,' he conceded, 'but this is not the reason for my not seeking renomination.' The London press could not be fooled, however, and Beaverbrook's *Evening Standard* wrote that 'no doubt Transport House will seek to cover up the split by blaming Laski's health for his resignation'. Laski's anti-Semitic adversary, *Truth*, found his choosing to make this public while in New York proof that, like the Rothschilds, Laski was 'a rootless cosmopolitan'.

No longer on the NEC, and despite Attlee's drift 'a little to the right', Laski took to the hustings once again when the general election was called for 23 February 1950 and helped Labour to draft an election manifesto. Despite his physical weakness, apparent to all, Laski spoke at over a dozen election rallies, usually to overflowing audiences, often of 1,500 to 2,500 people. He occasionally summoned up his old fire as he advocated national-izing the legal profession or ridiculed the House of Lords as made up of 850-odd members, 'some of them quite incredibly odd, in fact'. Laski made one election speech out of London when he visited his sister Mabel in Manchester and delivered his three Simon lectures at the university. At a Marylebone rally he became ill and left immediately after his speech and before time for questions, and at an election meeting in London's Red Lion Square Laski had difficulty in standing up and his voice was hardly above a whisper. The Tory *Daily Telegraph* could not resist suggesting that Laski's apparent bout with bronchitis and his curtailed appearances were a great relief to the Labour Party, 'for he has not been attracting as much attention in this election as the last'.

Plagued all his life by respiratory ailments, which had never stopped his chain-smoking, Laski sensed that this illness was different. He had been ill, off and on, since late 1948. A combination of asthma, flu and bronchitis had forced him to his bed for six weeks at the end of the year and for most of January. Laski wrote to his doctor friend Cohn in February 1949 that his pre-Christmas bronchitis had led to congestion of the lungs with a touch of pneumonia after leaving him 'with an enlarged heart and too high blood pressure, and the silly position in which any out-of-the-way exertion leaves me flat for the rest of the day, a condition I have never known before'. As bad as he felt, he still visited America for two months in March. Like clockwork, the bronchitis and pneumonia returned in December 1949 and Laski was treated with penicillin. The renewed discomfort fed the general despair he felt after having left the NEC, and he wrote to Frankfurter on 9 December that 'a grey, grim mood has come over me – self-doubt, inner unhappiness and pain'. Nevertheless, in January 1950 he was working feverishly with Max Lerner to arrange another lecture tour for the LSE break in March and April, with lectures at Roosevelt, where he would also debate with Hayek, Arthur Schlesinger, Jr, and Reinhold Niebuhr, as well as at the New School, Yale, the Ford Hall Forum and Brandeis. He was sure he would go, he wrote to Frida from Manchester on 9 February: 'I am not in the least tired, and I think my cough is better, though the weather is foul.' Four days later he informed Lerner that the doctor would not let him come to America. If he were to recover, 'he had to sit down and merely vegetate'. He would go to Bardfield, lie on a couch and read.

He didn't. Instead, he spoke at several London rallies in the ten days left in the election campaign, presided at an Indian League dinner in honour of Krishna Menon, wrote a long essay, 'A Programme to Prevent World War III', for a United Nations journal called *World*, did a short piece for the *Daily Herald* attacking anti-Semitism in the Soviet Union, and attended his classes at the LSE. Finally, however, Laski had worked his machine too hard. On 18 March his doctor diagnosed a touch of pleurisy. While not alarmed, the doctor was concerned about the persistent cough and suggested a specialist. Harold saw a chest specialist as a private patient on Wednesday 22 March, who decided that there had been a dormant infection in Laski's lungs since Christmas 1948 and suggested he take three to six months off work to recover. That night Laski woke at 4 a.m. in great pain, and by that evening he was in St Mary's Hospital with a collapsed left lung. Twenty-four hours later, at 7.30 p.m. on 24 March, he died, with Frida and Diana at his bedside. He had had an abscess in the lung which had burst, causing it to collapse. Conscious until about a quarter of an hour before he died, Laski's last words to Frida were, 'Isn't this incredible?'

His simple funeral took place four days later at the Golders Green crematorium. Krishna Menon made available the Indian embassy's Rolls-Royce. No one spoke at the funeral, which the *Manchester Guardian* described as 'a remarkable gathering of socialists, scholars, and students'.

The Prime Minister and eight other Cabinet members attended. Committal was preceded by the playing of Chopin's 'Funeral March', and then after a moment of meditation the group dispersed.

Over a thousand letters and telegrams poured in to Frida from politicians, civil servants and scholars from all over the world, but even as Attlee praised this 'man of outstanding gifts who had done great work for the Labour and socialist movement, whose brilliant intellect illuminated many of the social and political problems of our time', his detractors did not hold back their fire. *Time* irreverently wrote of the death of 'the Red Professor' and Colonel McCormick, the publisher of the *Chicago Tribune*, noted that 'Mr Laski died at a very early age, in a country with socialized medicine. He wouldn't have died in the US with a good doctor.' The British Conservative monthly the *Statist* described Laski as 'a sinister personage to the normal Englishman'. He was born to a family 'not native to this soil' and this 'difference of racial tradition and training' had 'led him to bring disaster to the very community and system that had housed and nurtured him'. His was 'an alien mind imbued and impregnated with an alien philosophy . . . He literally did not understand the temper and tempo of the English mind.' In death, too, his career had gone full circle, back to the issues and themes that had coloured its beginning.

By far the cruellest blow, however, came from *The Times*, whose cold, impersonal and critical obituary began with 'Laski, it may fairly be said, was not a profound thinker'. His early books were described as having 'a gift of clear if rather graceless and mannered exposition' and his books of the 1940s 'gave evidence of a somewhat tired mind'. Tucked into the lengthy obituary was but one reference to him as a teacher. 'Laski was a very considerable educational influence and a less ponderable influence in Labour Party policy and affairs.' As for his career in British politics, the 'Laski incident' during the 1945 campaign was briefly mentioned, as was his chairmanship of the party conference in 1946 and his tribute to Russia at that time. A group of colleagues at the LSE, led by Lord Chorley and including Lionel Robbins, Dennis Probert and Graham Hutton, were so annoyed that the entire obituary was devoted to a critical discussion of his writings that they sent a second obituary to *The Times*. This piece was published four days later, a virtually unprecedented event at *The Times*. Its intention was 'to convey the personal qualities of the late Professor Harold Laski which endeared him to his many friends' as well as 'those qualities which gave him such a remarkable influence in the labour movement'.

The Times notwithstanding, many moving tributes to Laski did appear in the days after his death, and two stand out. H. N. Brailsford, twenty years Laski's senior, a distinguished socialist activist and a comrade in Laski's Oxford suffragist period, wrote in a private letter to Frida on 26 March:

> That splendid intellect in a frail and sensitive frame did incomparably more in his brief life than any of his longer lived contemporaries . . . Has anyone ever packed so much into fifty-six years – incessant service to mankind, through his books and lectures, his always anxious work for socialism, the inspiration he gave to his students and his always sympathetic and generous help to them and to countless others? He lived and worked at twice the pace of any man I know. So it was not only a packed but in reality a long life, from which thanks to you, we all profited . . . what an enduring achievement Harold accomplished and what an immense volume of gratitude remains among so many of us to the thinker, the fighter, the friend and to you his help-mate.

The second was from Edward R. Murrow, fifteen years Laski's junior, who broadcast his public tribute on his news programme on 24 March, just five hours after Laski's death.

> We report with profound regret the death in London of bronchial pneumonia at the age of fifty-six, of Professor Harold J. Laski. He was a man who believed, with Heywood Broun, that no body politic is healthy until it begins to itch. Laski was a socialist. His writings and his lectures contributed much to the philosophical basis of Britain's Labour Party. He was the chairman of the party in 1945 and one of the principal architects of Labour's victory. He was also the only leader of his party who, on the morning of the victory, had the courage and grace to pay public tribute to the wartime services of Winston Churchill. He cherished his friends, rejoiced in his enemies, and had many of both. His allegiances were fierce, and neutrality was not known to him. Much of his life was spent in controversy; he gloried in it; was almost prepared to admit that he was not always right; and his friendship and assistance were freely given, without any effort to exact agreement upon political and economic issues as a price for that friendship and assistance. More than most professors or pamphleteers, he caused people to think furiously because he believed that it was only through the exercise of the mind that men could remain free. In addition to that, he thought that thinking, causing the body politic to itch, to doubt, to question, to resolve, was good fun.

Laski's Legacy

'No one can teach politics who does not know politics at first hand,' Laski wrote in 1939, and he practised what he preached. Few people in the twentieth century have lived two such totally complete lives as scholar and politician as he did. After his death he was remembered and honoured in both worlds. The Labour Party's annual conference in 1950 approved a resolution remembering 'with gratitude and affection the outstanding service rendered to the labour movement, the cause of international solidarity and human freedom, by the late Harold Laski'. The resolution's mover spoke of his contribution over the years to the formation of socialist policy and his role 'as one of the principal architects of our victory in 1945'. To honour the memory of 'one of the greatest socialists that this movement ever knew', the party's National Executive Committee also established a 'Laski Memorial Travelling Fellowship' from funds raised by local constituency parties. In France the Socialist Party conference in May observed an unprecedented minute's silence 'in the memory of Professor Harold J. Laski'.

Freda Kirchwey wrote in the *Nation* that the world would miss Laski, 'really a wonderful sort of fellow'. Yes, his brilliance could be exhausting, she confessed, and it was easy to be put off by his 'showmanship' or his 'air of near-omniscience', but this kind and essentially modest man, she wrote, had a 'capacity for devotion and hope' which moved not only young students but cynical old-timers like herself. 'He knew and loved America, explained and chastised it.' Six hundred and fifty former students and friends attended a memorial service for Laski in New York on 16 May at the New School for Social Research, presided over by its Director Emeritus, Alvin Johnson. Supreme Court Justice Frankfurter led the tributes to the man who he said had 'probably influenced political thought and political action in both East and West more than any other individual'.

The London School of Economics' student magazine, the *Clare Market Review*, turned its Michaelmas term 1950 issue into a memorial to Laski. Tributes were published by former students who had become colleagues – W. H. Morris-Jones, Ralph Miliband and Norman MacKenzie – and by Eleanor Roosevelt and Frankfurter. A staff collection was organized by Robson and Kingsley Smellie which purchased a sixth-century BC Greek vase for display in the LSE's Founders' Room, bearing the inscription 'In memory of Harold Laski. Given by his colleagues at the School'. Norman MacKenzie and Lord Chorley served as Secretary and Treasurer respectively of a Harold Laski Society founded jointly by the LSE and India House in 1951, with Krishna Menon as Chairman and H. N. Brailsford as President. The society hoped to raise funds for student scholarships and publications, and to establish an international student hostel. After several years, like Laski's reputation, the society faded away.

Laski's library of rare books, lovingly collected since childhood, was ultimately given as a gift to the LSE by Frida after Cohn and Frankfurter had organized an effort in America to raise funds to purchase the library from her in order to facilitate the gift. They enlisted the banker James Warburg to run the appeal and he managed to collect $5,000 of the hoped for $18,000. Some of the people solicited refused to give, thinking the money was for a gift to Frida and not for the purchase of the library. Laski's will, leaving £19,558 to Frida, had surprised many of his friends (and critics) who had not realized how much Laski augmented his LSE salary of £1,600 a year (raised to £2,040 the year he died) by royalties and speaking fees. The sum, however, also included £8,000 of LSE pension benefits and £2,500 of life insurance.

As so often happens to widows, Frida was slowly dropped from the social circles of the LSE. The ideological complexion of the Political Science Department dramatically changed when in addition to appointments of other Conservatives the Cambridge political theorist Michael Oakeshott, a leading Conservative thinker, was chosen in 1951 to replace Laski, making Frida even less inclined to have anything to do with the school. She devoted herself increasingly to Third World causes, the most important of which was War on Want, and travelled to India in the 1950s where she was Nehru's house guest. Frida frequently saw Diana and Robin and her four grandsons, who lived in Exeter, where Robin taught classics at the university. She outlived her daughter, for Diana died suddenly of a heart attack at the age of fifty-three in February 1969. Frida lived alone through the 1970s while virtually blind. In these last years she enjoyed the company of her youngest grandson, Andrew Mathewson, who was studying in London, and of John Saville, the labour historian at Hull who had studied with Laski in the 1930s, and his wife Constance. Frida died in 1978, when she was ninety-three. Frankfurter had stayed in touch with Frida until his death in 1965 at the age of eighty-three, visiting whenever he was in London in the 1950s and sending birthday and Christmas and New Year greetings annually.

Frankfurter wrote to Frida in January 1952 with a special plea that she let him first look at the letters Laski had written to Roosevelt, which were in the Presidential Library at Hyde Park, before she gave permission to Kingsley Martin to use any of them in a biography of Laski. The mood of American politics, with its 'distortion, misrepresentation and plain lying' with regard to FDR and the New Deal, might lead, he feared, to the selective use of Harold's letters in the current 'passionate and poisonous atmosphere'. He may also have been worrying about himself and what use red-baiting zealots like Senator McCarthy of Wisconsin might make of references to him in the correspondence; in any case, Frida allowed him to screen the letters first, lest any 'real mischief' be created by their publication.

His years on the Supreme Court had not dulled Frankfurter's political instincts: Senator McCarthy would, indeed, hit upon Laski in his anti-communist crusade. After Edward R. Murrow's landmark attack on McCarthy and McCarthyism on the CBS television programme *See It Now* in March 1954, the network granted the Senator twenty-five minutes of the programme a month later. McCarthy recited a series of charges against Murrow, which culminated with the question 'and to whom did Harold Laski, admittedly the greatest communist propagandist of our time, dedicate his book *Reflections on the Revolution of Our Time*?' Murrow had prepared a rebuttal, and when he got to the Laski dedication he said, 'Laski was a friend of mine. He is a socialist. I am not.'

The McCarthy incident came on the heels of a flurry of renewed interest in Laski. A manuscript, nearly complete at his death, which was a revision of his 1944 *Faith, Reason and Civilization*, was edited by R. S. Clark and published in 1952 as *The Dilemma of Our Times: An Historical Essay*. Like a voice from the grave it attacked the 'follies', 'stupidity' and 'insecurity and confusion' of our times and parcelled out equal blame to the United States and Soviet Russia. May 1952 saw a Laski memorial meeting held at Conway Hall in London chaired by Lord Chorley, where Ralph Miliband talked of Laski's fondness for students and a London bookseller reminisced about Laski's visits to his shop. James Griffiths, a Labour MP, recalled evenings that Laski spent 'teaching' miners in south Wales, and Kingsley Martin and H. N. Brailsford spoke lovingly of their friend 'who asked nothing for himself and sought only to serve humanity'. Several days later the new headquarters of the West Fulham Labour Party was opened in a converted warehouse and named 'Harold Laski House', with Frida unveiling the commemorative plaque. In 1953 Kingsley Martin's biography and Harvard University Press's two-volume *Holmes–Laski Letters* were published.

And then nothing. The historian Kenneth Morgan wrote in 1987 that 'Laski's name and reputation have gone into almost total eclipse'. It happened quickly, for in 1956 the leading revisionist in Labour Party circles, Anthony Crosland, could already refer in *The Future of Socialism* to Laski's ideas as sounding 'like an echo from another world'. But there were a few occasions when Laski might be mentioned in the decades after his death. Not infrequently he was miscited as Marghanita Laski's father, or whenever Labour-left types made too much noise Attlee's famous put-down, 'a period of silence on your behalf', might be resurrected from the party's or the press's historical memory. There were also, alas, the inevitable references to Laski the myth-maker, the romancer and story-teller in the parade of memoirs and biographies of the inter-war 'Great and Good'.

Not that these charges were always correct. In 1978 Margaret Cole offered as 'proof' that Laski was prone to flaunt being 'in closer touch with more distinguished persons than was really the case' the examples of Churchill early in his career, and of Stanley Baldwin. On the other hand, there is no doubt that Laski could utterly distort the truth. In October 1947, for example, Laski wrote to Frankfurter that Attlee had called him into his office and asked him to serve as his deputy in the office of Lord Privy Seal with a seat in the House of Lords. Laski told Frankfurter that the Prime Minister was shocked when he turned it down. Morrison tells a far different story, one with Laski informing him that if Attlee were to offer him a peerage he would gladly accept it. Respecting Laski's abilities and achievements, Morrison then urged the idea on Attlee, who turned it down. 'Attlee could be a small man,' Morrison noted in his autobiography.

Laski was a consummate embroiderer and romancer. Part of his generosity and warmth found outlet in his love to flatter and drop compliments, telling this one that 'Holmes said of you' or that one that 'the Prime Minister spoke so highly of you', and, of course, people like Justice Stone loved to hear it. Most of the time, however, his exaggerations and myths were harmless, often made privately, like the fantasy about the offer of a peerage in his letter to Frankfurter. Still, it bothered people because it demeaned a man professionally committed to the quest for truth and it violated the code of the English gentlemen which privileges the reticent understatement over the exaggeration or boast. His myth-making sometimes merged with the perception of Laski's 'Jewishness'. A crucial part of the description of Laski as 'Jewish' was his calling attention to himself by his exuberance, his forwardness and his exaggeration of self – all traits 'alien' to the British elite.

Why Laski persisted in his myth-making is another matter. There hovered about Laski a quality of almost perpetual youth, reinforced by his diminutive size. As Kingsley Martin put it, he acted like a schoolboy always showing off, always wanting to be noticed. It is striking how references to Laski as being childlike or boyish, or as a naughty 'schoolboy' or '*enfant terrible*', recur in characterizations of him from people as diverse as Martin, John Strachey, Lionel Robbins, Isaiah Berlin, Lord Soper, Edmund Wilson and Malcolm Muggeridge. As Francis Williams, labour journalist and personal assistant to Attlee put it, Laski 'looked all his life like a precocious Jewish schoolboy', which, of course, he had been. Like a schoolboy he sought to be, as Frida put it, 'centre stage'. Like a child he sought the approval of those with power while angrily resenting their privileges. Like a child he also lived and spoke spontaneously, for the moment. Quite surprisingly for someone so profoundly aware of the inexorable influence of time and historical development, Laski, as Rebecca West noted, wanted to rush every citadel today and hurry every transformation tomorrow. Like a child he saw words as the agent of instant change. A book could convert a ruling class, a speech could break institutions and a newspaper article topple leaders. But like a child, he had, as Rebecca West also noted, 'a heart of gold' and he could be so warm and lovable that Lord McGregor and many others could say 'he was the nicest human being I have ever met'. Frida was perhaps right when she characterized Laski as 'half-man, half-child all his life'.

Laski was admired by those who knew him more as a warm and generous person than as a scholar. They saw a man of engaging charm and electric personality whom they liked to be with even as he told stories they disbelieved or espoused views they opposed. There were some, to be sure, who thought Laski petty and vindictive. Vera Brittain, for example, was convinced that Laski kept her husband, George Catlin, from a position at the LSE from fear of his rivalry. Few people disliked Laski as much as the libertarian novelist Ayn Rand. She saw 'something evil' behind Laski's smile and her creation, the villainous Ellsworth Toohey, was a 'larger-scale' Laski, 'who was a cheap little snide collectivist'. For the most part, however, people liked Laski, but Laski the person, not Laski the writer and scholar. No surprise, then, that few of his books have endured, with perhaps only *The Rise of European Liberalism* found on college syllabuses today. He wrote too much in general and far too much journalism in particular for the academy to take him that seriously. His journalism sparkled, but Laski's scholarly writings were often unimpressive and poorly written. He loved the recondite word and the learned allusion. The speed with which he turned out books and his disinclination to revise first drafts made his prose repetitive or tortured. Most of his books were not that original and one seldom encounters enduring Laski insights. There is one obvious exception, however; his early writings on the pluralist challenge to state sovereignty were original and they remain seminal studies in political philosophy. With the renewed interest generated in pluralism by recent developments in Eastern Europe, these brilliant early works may once again provoke and inform as they did the progressives in the *New Republic* crowd. Still, Bernard Crick, the distinguished scholar, editor and biographer who studied with Laski in his last years was probably right that Laski's 'greatness was as a teacher and preacher, not as a political philosopher'.

One hefty chunk of Laski's writings has quite surprisingly endured to this day. His correspondence with Holmes is still not only pored over by the seemingly never-ending legions of Holmes fans, but the published *Holmes–Laski Letters* has become one of the twentieth century's legendary epistolary collections. Only in 1988, interestingly enough, did it become clear how close these letters came to being destroyed. The editor of the 1963 paperback edition of the *Holmes-Laski Letters*. Alger Hiss, the law clerk to Holmes in 1930 and student and friend of Justice Frankfurter, who after the controversial 'Hiss Trials' in the late 1940s had been imprisoned in the early 1950s, revealed in his autobiography that year that when he was asked to abridge Mark DeWolfe Howe's 1953 Harvard University Press collection of the letters he discovered, while looking through the originals, that several requests in Holmes's letters for Laski to destroy the correspondence had been deleted. Also omitted were Laski's insistence that re-reading Holmes's letters gave him great pleasure and his promise to order that they be destroyed at his (Laski's) death. Hiss, like Howe, deleted discussion of destroying the letters from his edition of the published letters, for fear that Frida Laski, still alive, might be plagued by those critical of her husband's failure to keep his promise to Holmes. Since Frida was dead in 1988. Hiss told the whole story, noting appropriately that Laski's failure to keep his promise had worked 'to the immense benefit of posterity'.

Nothing eclipsed Laski's reputation as a teacher, 'one of the greatest teachers of our time' as Frankfurter noted, and the later success of countless scholars he trained, politicians he inspired and statesmen like Sharett, Menon, and Trudeau whom he sent to public service has kept him alive. In describing Laski's legendary rapport with students, Frida observed that he kept 'not only an open door and an open house, but an open heart'. In the Laski memorial issue of the *Clare Market Review* one student noted that 'he loved us instead of merely tolerating us'. His students loved Laski, because they saw a man who viewed the world as they did, full of hope and expectation. Laski, the perpetual 'half-man, half-child', also saw a part of himself in his students. As Ralph Miliband has written, Laski

> loved students because they were young. Because he had a glowing faith that youth was generous and alive, eager, enthusiastic and fresh. That by helping young people he was helping the future and bringing nearer that brave new world in which he so passionately believed.

In the darkest days of the war in 1943, and only recently recovered from the depths of his own personal despair, Laski wrote to Ben Huebsch that 'if Diana's and your boys get the chance they will give mercy, justice and magnanimity the place in the cosmos that is their due'. Building Jerusalem would be the achievement of youth, not of the legacy of tired elders, which may be the reason Laski so persistently urged age ceilings on Labour candidates and Members of Parliament.

As a political teacher Laski had none of the clout of Dalton whose legion of disciples, 'Dalton's poodles', went on to dominate the Labour Party in the 1950s and 1960s. Laski had his hand in discovering Denis Healey, George Brown and especially James Callaghan, but none were in any sense his ideological disciples. One measure of his impact, however, is that among the Labour MPs elected in the landslide of 1945 sixty-seven had once studied with him as either university students, trade unionists in worker education courses or officers in wartime courses. His political legacy did live on in the Labour left, the Bevanite and the Bennite left. Bevan always spoke warmly of his *Tribune* colleague Laski. One memorable example was at the 1950 party conference where he and others took offence at the platform eulogies, which they saw as emphasizing principally Laski's warmth and friendliness and giving too little place to his ideas. Bevan devoted his talk at a *Tribune* dinner held the next day to a defence of ideas and intellectuals in the labour movement, insisting 'that it was the writings of Laski and the unorthodox political education of the Left Book Club which prepared the way for the 1945 victory'. Three years later Bevan paid Laski the supreme compliment: 'Mr Churchill has been described as the most articulate Englishman of his day,' Bevan wrote in the *Daily Herald*, 'but personally I would give the prize to Harold Laski.' In his *Arguments for Socialism* (1979) and *Arguments for Democracy* (1981), Tony Benn not only praised Laski for insisting that the Marxist heritage was a crucial part of the Labour Party's outlook, but he offered a Laski-like analysis of the British Constitution in pointing to the power of extra-parliamentary non-elected elites.

Nye Bevan's convictions notwithstanding, others saw Laski's excursion into politics as a cautionary tale to prove that intellectuals should remain in their ivory towers. From different political perspectives Trevor-Roper and Margaret Cole both argued that no one with real power who made public policy ever listened to Laski, though they agreed that even in 'the tedious utterances of his middle age' he helped to shape a climate of opinion that ultimately influenced policy. The *Manchester Guardian Weekly* in 1953 noted that while everybody liked Laski the man and the academic, 'most of those who liked him best would shake their heads over his political judgement'. He lacked, the paper argued, the temperament for the 'ideal backroom boy. He had too much zeal and he thought too emotionally.' The laconic Attlee put it even more bluntly in 1960:

People who talk too much soon find themselves up against it. Harold Laski,
for instance. A brilliant chap but he talked too much. A wonderful teacher.
You must be able to talk to teach and we need all the teachers we can get
but he had no political judgement.

What Attlee meant on one level was that even among intellectuals there
were vast variations in attention paid to practical details. While Laski was
writing position papers for the party on the problems created by the
historical evolution of an economy of contraction out of an economy of
abundance, Dalton and his disciples, Gaitskell and Durbin, were writing
about marginal price analysis in a nationalized industry. Laski's lack of
political judgement, it could be argued, operated even on the level of his
meta-speculation, in his inability to recognize, for example, that his preoccupation in the 1930s with how the Establishment, which would resist the
revolutionary transformation sought electorally by Labour, assumed that
the Labour Party sought such a fundamental change. It was difficult to
have it both ways, predicting, a good deal of the time, ruling–class
repression of triumphant socialist militancy and lamenting, some of the
time, the absence of that very militancy. All of these confusions came back
to haunt him at his trial, even though, ironically, he had by then basically
realized what kind of a party Labour really was and grudgingly thrown in
his lot with it.

Opinions vary widely on a final evaluation of Laski's socialism. For
A. L. Rowse, his ideas were nothing more than those of a superficial
political journalist. Arthur Schlesinger, Jr, saw Laski's socialism produced
by a world of political fantasy 'for which the inward expression was faith
and the outward expression rhetoric' and where facts neither interrupted the
rhetoric nor disturbed the faith. Richard Crossman, who rose from the
Labour left to be Leader of the House of Commons in Harold Wilson's
government, came in the late 1960s to regard Laski's ideas as 'bogus,
phoney and sentimental' and Laski himself as 'hopeless at influencing
British politics'. Brailsford, on the other hand, applauded Laski for being
able to reconcile Marx and Engels of the nineteenth century with the
seventeenth and eighteenth-century liberal defenders of individual rights
and free discussion. He was, Brailsford suggested, as did the obituary notice
in the Paris *Monde*, the exemplar for the inter-war generation of this
necessary marriage of 'Marxism of the mind' and 'liberalism of the heart'.

Kenneth Morgan praised Laski for bringing to insular British socialism a refreshing international perspective grounded in French and German scholarship and American friends and experience. Others like Lord Soper and Isaiah Berlin faulted Laski for replacing the inspirational and ethical thrust of British socialism with a continental Marxism, too ideological and too materialistic. On the other hand, the dean of socialist historians, A. J. P. Taylor, never averse to finding fault, had only unabashed praise for Laski's socialist achievements. He wrote in 1953 that

> there are few men of whom one can truthfully say the world would have been a different place without them. Harold Laski was one of those few. His was the most important influence in remaking English social democracy and giving it its present form ... If today in this country there is still no communist movement of any size, if all socialists can still be at home in the Labour Party, we owe it more to Harold Laski than to any other single man.

On one aspect of Laski's legacy there is, however, little debate: his profound impact on India and the Third World. Even as he belittled Laski's ideas and his influence in Britain, Crossman conceded that Laski's ideology influenced 'half the leaders of the colonial revolution' and, unlike Senator Moynihan, Crossman saw this making them 'not passionately anti-British and pro-communist but liberalistic and pro-British'. John Kenneth Galbraith, former American ambassador to India, contended that 'the centre of Nehru's thinking was Laski' and 'India the country most influenced by Laski's ideas'. Nehru, who used to say that he was 'the last Englishman to rule India', saw Laski as the voice of Fabian socialism with its vision of a central role for the state in a managed and planned economy. Nehru remained close to Frida until his death in 1964, having in 1956 agreed to her request to write a short preface to an Indian reprinting of Laski's Grammar of Politics. A Harold Laski Institute of Political Science, established in the city of Ahmedabad in 1954 by G. V. Mavalankar, the first Speaker of the Indian Parliament, whose son had studied at the LSE with Laski, still exists. So widespread was Laski's reputation in India because of his work for independence and his influence on the political elite through Nehru, Menon and the legions of LSE students in the government and the civil service that it was often said that 'there was a vacant chair at every Cabinet meeting in India, reserved for the ghost of Professor Harold Laski'.

Like most important, even revered, historical figures, Laski was riven by contradiction and ambivalence. He was convinced that the power of reason and the human capacity for good-will would lead people to reach compromises and do justice to views they disagreed with. Yet he was also convinced that people were moved independently of their own conscious wills by historical and economic forces, which prevented mutual understanding, tolerance and empathy. He was a collectivist and an individualist, a Marx and a Voltaire. He was fiercely egalitarian yet an intellectual prone to elitism and cultural snobbery. He loved America and fiercely criticized it. He saw Soviet Russia as the harbinger of a new civilization and its crimes broke his heart. He was selfless and generous to a fault and an indefatigable self-promoter. He was an erudite scholar and a mass circulation publicizer. He detested the status quo yet he wanted to dine with those who presided over and benefited from it. He cultivated the posture of the alienated intellectual outsider, thundering at a social order historically doomed, while working the system as a consummate behind-the-scenes insider who influenced everyday events through connections and friendships. He was a cosmopolitan rationalist and a cultural, ultimately Zionist, Jew. The most popular lecture which this state-socialist gave annually at the LSE was on Martin Luther's 'Hier Stehe Ich. Ich Kann Nicht Anders', in which he literally preached that each and every student must, like Luther, follow her or his individual conscience.

Laski was at bottom a mass preacher and public teacher, one of the most widely read and listened-to public intellectuals of this century. He was more interested in teaching people about and ushering in socialism than in his scholarly or political reputation. That reputation has been shaped in large measure by scholars who are by disposition sceptical of political engagement, the focus on the present and future and the blatant political use of the past in an effort to reach the masses. Laski enthusiastically embraced the mission of the ideological popularizer, writing constantly and gearing it for a wide audience. Like most public intellectuals he addressed all levels of the public. He spoke to the few thousands of professional intellectuals who with their exceptional ability and narrow, concentrated interests read specialized books. He also reached out to the few hundreds of thousands who read weeklies like the *New Statesman* or the *Nation* and who listened to sophisticated radio talks, and, finally, he addressed the millions who read the national daily press.

All of Laski's writings, even the most serious scholarship, were informed by political and ideological purpose and was a response to the vicissitudes of contemporary politics. It is not surprising, then, that his reputation has foundered, for the makers of reputations privilege the search and discovery of enduring and transcendent truths. Laski, on the other hand, was a man of the moment who, never quite abandoning the philosophical pragmatism of his earliest writings, assumed the contingent nature of truth and its dependence on the tendencies, constraints and potentials of a particular context. That is why teaching was so central to his life and why the role of teacher and public intellectual helped to resolve the paradox of him as both an elitist and a popularizer. He taught people how to analyse the world of their moment, not how to perceive timeless reality, but to grasp and to act on that moment in order to usher in socialism. He trained leaders in his classroom to be the builders of a new Jerusalem and he prepared the masses with his writings and preaching for the revolutionary redemption of 'the dark Satanic mills' through the ballot-box.

His most faithful followers were in fact from the enlarged inter-war literate professional class, the broadened base of people with intellectual interests and pretensions who, for example, joined the Left Book Club and who, unlike high-table academics, took him very seriously as a thinker and as a seer. As the depression and fascism sent many of these people to the left, his was the most articulate and liveliest voice for socialism they encountered. Bevan was probably right in suggesting that in 1945 it was these very people who were crucial in bringing Labour to power.

And they encountered the voice everywhere, which is the key to Laski's phenomenal influence in his lifetime. As a publicist, a popularizer and a public intellectual, he made his mark not only by his intelligence and his wit but by his incredible energy which made it virtually impossible for his public to go a week without reading or hearing him. No wonder, then, that with his death his reputation declined so rapidly. He was no longer there to interpret and analyse the moment in the weeklies and on the radio, no longer there to respond to each new event with his insistent urging of socialism, true socialism. The price the engaged public intellectual pays is, quite literally, out of sight, out of mind.

Some time after his death Laski's friend Lance Beales confronted the unusual silence.

It may be claimed, soberly, that he did a giant's work. None of us who worked with him can ever forget him. He had a hundred faults – the flamboyant phrase, the over-good stories (and the good ones, too), the self-deception – but what do these things matter? Great teacher and great friend, he lived his full life as selflessly as may be, as generously and as bravely as the best have done. In many countries, in high places and low, in the East and in the West, there are people who are in debt to him – in debt for increased power of mental striving, in debt most of all for the realism of his vision of possible socialism. His work bears fruit in India as in England, in China as in the United States. It is given to few to stir men's thinking as Laski had done, and to bend that thinking to active purpose.

Frida, who had so significantly shaped the mind and the politics of Laski the young prodigy, summarized Laski's life in her characteristically matter-of-fact way in a letter to Alfred Cohn in April 1950. She described how suddenly the end had come and added, 'He lived a full life and we were divinely happy for thirty-nine years and we had a lifetime of adventure and interest and he left his mark.'

Notes

(Full sources are given in the Notes only when the source is not obvious from the text or the Bibliography. Multi-part quotes may extend across more than one page, but the Notes reference is for the first part only.)

p. 1   'saw Laski . . .', Barbara Branden, *The Passion of Ayn Rand* (New York, 1986), p. 139.

p. 1   'Marx or Hitler . . .', *God and Man at Yale* (Chicago, 1951), p. 181.

p. 1   'I shall never . . .', *Mosby's Memoirs* (New York,1968), p. 158.

p. 1   'The Age of Laski', *Fortnightly* 173, NS 167, June 1950, p. 378.

p. 4   'in England's green . . .', 'Jerusalem', 1804.

p. 4   'historians can never . . .', *Books and Bookmen*, February 1978, p. 28.

p. 5   'left traps . . .', *New Yorker*, 16 May 1953, p. 134.

p. 5   'a proper biography . . .', *Labour People* (Oxford, 1987), p. 100.

p. 9   'history's revenge . . .', 3 April 1950.

p. 10   'perhaps more . . .', Bill Williams, *Manchester Jewry*, p. 4.

p. 10   'iron out . . .' and 'turn Polish . . .', quoted in *Manchester Jewry*, p. 21.

p. 11   'if you saw . . .', interview with Manuel Cansino.

p. 11   'a great big . . .' 'scared stiff' and 'couldn't bear . . .', *Harold Laski: A Portrait for Radio*, BBC, 9 March 1962.

p. 12   'Jewry's . . .' and 'lay head of . . .', *Manchester Evening News*, 29 December 1934.

p. 12   'Sit down . . .', 'If you don't . . .' and 'I'll have you reported . . .', interview with Michael Fidler.

p. 14   'the girls attending . . .', 'We must put away . . .' and 'There is nothing', 'Neville Laski Papers' in *Anglo-Jewish Archives*, University of Southampton, AJ 33/39.

p. 15   'something was wrong . . .', interview with Manuel Cansino.

p. 15   'obstinate as a mule . . .', 'a pathetic little . . .' and 'go up and . . .', 'Harold–Frida', 7 September 1921 and 10 February 1945.

p. 16   'At the top . . .', *Daily Herald*, 1 December 1955.

p. 18   'the need for . . .', Mumford, *The Manchester Grammar School*, p. 433.

p. 18   'he looked like . . .', *Trial and Error*, p. 117.

p. 18   'whom I have', 'Holmes', p. 729.

p. 18   'the greatest living . . .', *Felix Frankfurter Reminisces*, p. 257.

p. 19   'Your affection . . .', 'Laski–Hull', n.d. 1931.

p. 19   'a sort of . . .', Alexander, *Philosophical and Literary Pieces*, p. 49.

p. 19   'realize that . . .' and 'at least dimly . . .', *Labour Forum*, January, March 1948, p. 16.

p. 20   'wherever we examine . . .' and 'the Sir Galahad . . .', 79 House of Commons 789, 6 February 1900.

p. 21   'The aliens will . . .' and 'A foreign Jew . . .', quoted in Jehuda Reinharz, *Chaim Weizmann*, p. 213.

p. 21   'how few aliens . . .', 'all the aliens . . .' and 'patriotism at other . . .', Churchill, *Winston S. Churchill*, Vol. II, pp. 81–2.

p. 22   'Churchill received . . .', 'for freedom . . .', 'a body of . . .' and 'I have had . . .', ibid., p. 83.

p. 22   'It would not be . . .', 48 House of Commons 155–6, 803–4; 10 July 1905.

p. 23   'You respect . . .', H. A. Taylor, *Jix, Viscount Brentford*, p. 64.

p. 24   'he was not going . . .', 16 April 1908.

p. 24   'I do not think . . .', R. R. James (ed.), *Winston Spencer Churchill: Complete Speeches* I (New York, 1974), pp. 984–5.

p. 25   'If they liked . . .', *Manchester Guardian*, 18 May 1908.

p. 25   'stood and gaped . . .', 'Frida', p. 61.

p. 25   'with moving . . .', 'he saw no . . .' and 'the superiority of . . .', *Labour Forum*, January–March 1948, pp. 15–17.

p. 26   'our trade . . .', Gilbert, *Winston S. Churchill* V, p. 691.

p. 26   'the great and . . .' and 'I think . . .', ibid., pp. 150–56.

p. 26   'He was a . . .', 'Laski–Hull', 31 October 1941.

p. 28   'I told the gentlemen . . .', *The Letters and Papers of Chaim Weizmann* IV, p. 56.

p. 28   'ignorance, rudeness . . .' and 'The Cheethamites . . .', quoted in Reinharz, *Chaim Weizmann*, pp. 254–5.

p. 30   'the first non-Jewish . . .', 'Frida', p. 20.

p. 31   'You are a . . .', ibid., p. 11.

p. 32   'Just at the right . . .', ibid., p. 16.

p. 32   'costing them a fortune . . .', ibid., p. 17.

p. 32   'from the word . . .', ibid., p. 20.

p. 33   'I remember . . .', ibid., pp. 19–20.

p. 34   'this morning in a . . .' and 'My wonderful boy . . .', Pearson, *The Life, Letters and Labours of Francis Galton* III B, pp. 606, 608.

p. 37   'by now very . . .', 'Frida', p. 21.

p. 38   'as regards recruiting . . .', quoted in *Eugenics and Politics in Britain*, p. 23.

p. 38   'a more virile sentiment . . .', ibid., p. 34.

p. 39   'All this sounds . . .', quoted in C. Shaw, 'Eliminating the Yahoo: Eugenics, Social Darwinism and Five Fabians', *History of Political Thought* Vol. VIII, No. 3 Winter 1987, p. 540.

p. 39   'An organized whole . . .' (London, 1905), p. 46.

p. 39   'degenerate hordes . . .', Fabian Society Tract 69 (London, 1896), p. 6.

p. 39   'the stunted, anaemic . . .', Fabian Society Tract 108 (London, 1901), p. 9.

p. 40   'No consistent eugenicist . . .', *Eugenics Review* II (1910), p. 237.

p. 40   'to insure the . . .', *Nineteenth Century*, September 1901.

p. 40   'We contrive to . . .', ibid., p. 68.

p. 41   'a service to the . . .', 'it must be provided' and 'the state is . . .' *A Modern Utopia* (London, 1905) pp. 187–8, 54, 183–4.

p. 42   'if superior . . .' and 'scientific propagation', quoted in *The Name of Eugenics*, pp. 84, 21.

p. 42   'The question of eugenics . . .', quoted in ibid., p. 87.

p. 43   'always in the . . .', 'the rule of life . . .' and 'nine-tenths . . .' 'Harold–Frida', January–July 1911.

p. 44   'fully up to . . .', *Problem of Alien Immigration into Great Britain* (London, 1925), p. 47.

p. 44   'taken on the . . .', 'personal cleanliness . . .' and '25 per cent higher . . .', ibid., 125, 47, 22.

p. 46   'mere babe in . . .', 'Harold–Frida', January–July 1911.

p. 46   'what a great thing . . .', 'Laski–Hull', n.d.

p. 46   'but I don't mind . . .' et al., 'Harold–Frida', January–July 1911.

p. 46   'at what she . . .', 'Frida', p. 33.

p. 47   'It seems to me . . .', 'Laski–Hull', n.d.

p. 48   'amongst them . . .' and 'I shall come . . .', 'Harold–Frida', n.d., 9 October 1911.

p. 48   'You are now . . .', quoted in K. Martin, *Harold Laski*, pp. 11–12.

p. 49   'to command people . . .', *Introduction to Contemporary Politics* (Seattle, 1939), p. 92.

p. 49   'we fought just . . .', 'Harold–Frida', 2 November 1911.

p. 51   'told me one . . .', ibid., 30 October 1911.

p. 51   'showed him some . . .' and 'show exactly what . . .', ibid., 24 November 1911.

p. 51   'my God, there . . .', ibid., 2 November 1991.

p. 51   'have disposal . . .', 'because I want . . .' and 'This man Haldane . . .', ibid., 29 November 1911.

p. 52   'as K. P.'s wife . . .', ibid., 1 May 1912.

p. 52   a thousand times . . .', ibid., 29 November 1911.

p. 52   'that because of . . .', ibid., 9 October 1911.

p. 53   'Each day I . . .', ibid., 30 October, 15 November 1911.

p. 53   'and there won't . . .', ibid., 25 November 1911.

p. 54   'because I want . . .', ibid., 29 November 1911.

p. 54   'wee book . . .', et al., ibid., n.d., December 1911, n.d., January 1912.

p. 54   'put it away . . .', 'Huebsch', 11 March 1916.

p. 58   'ham-handedness all his . . .', 'Frida', p. 34.

p. 59   'dearest Barker', et al., 'Harold–Frida' n.d. October 1913.

p. 60   'He was just . . .', *Age and Youth*, pp. 74–5.

p. 60   'done his best . . .', 'Harold–Frida', 6 April 1931.

p. 61   'the racial question', et al., ibid., 30 October 1911.

p. 61   'the first and . . .', et al., *Georgian Adventure* (London, 1938), p. 54.

p. 61   'he came round . . .', et al., *My Dear Timothy*, p. 253.

p. 62   'a devastating critic . . .', Martin, *Harold Laski*, p. 13.

p. 62   'that domes of . . .', ibid.

p. 62   'a woman, a . . .', et al., 'Frida', p. 37.

p. 64   'You are beneath . . .', Postgate, *The Life of George Lansbury*, p. 124.

p. 65   'so as not . . .', 'Harold–Frida', n.d. 1914.

p. 65   'we were all . . .', et al., ibid., 2 May 1912, n.d. October 1912.

p. 66   'sweeping away the . . .', *Harper's* (October 1946), p. 328.

p. 68   'wonderfully, almost madly . . .', Harold–Frida', 8 June 1913.

p. 68   'more or less . . .', *Harold Laski*, p. 14.

p. 68   'necessary to give . . .', et al., cited in Rover, *Women's Suffrage*, p. 101.

p. 70   'Harold Laski, still . . .', p. 330.

p. 71   'We loved him . . .', Laski to Evelyn Sharp, 11 November 1941, Bodleian Library, Oxford. Mss. Eng. Lett. d. 280, Folio 105.

p. 74   'We believe in . . .', Holton, *British Syndicalism 1900†1914*, p. 187.

p. 74   'aid from . . .', Rover, *Women's Suffrage*, p. 288.

p. 74   'Liberal England's . . .', *The Strange Death of Liberal England* (London, 1936).

p. 74   'to get Larkin . . .', et al., 'Harold–Frida', n.d. November–December 1913.

p. 75   'the root evil . . .', et al., ibid., n.d. Trinity Term 1914.

p. 75   'it was wonderful . . .', 'Frida', p. 35.

p. 76   'treasonable conspiracy', cited in Feuchtwanger, *Democracy and Empire*, p. 343.

p. 77   'The law is . . .', *Daily Herald*, 23 July 1914.

p. 78   'His parents had . . .', 'Frida', p. 33.

p. 79   'He sensed their . . .', ibid.

p. 79   'Flat feet or . . .', ibid.

p. 82   'attitudes to Jews . . .', et al., 'Huebsch', 28 February 1915.

p. 83   'Harold had to . . .', 'Frida', p. 42.

p. 83   'I shall go . . .', Postgate, *The Life of George Lansbury*, p. 69.

p. 83   'She's too aesthetic . . .', 'Harold–Frida', 1 May 1915.

p. 84   'Joseph Fels was . . .', p. 154.

p. 84   'Looking for a . . .', et al., 'Frida', p. 42.

p. 85   'much struck to . . .', 'Huebsch', 15 November 1915.

p. 85   'really Frida's enthusiasm', 19 November 1914, Lansbury Papers, Vol. 7, 175, LSE.

p. 85   'his best friend . . .', et al., 24 May 1915, ibid., 192.

p. 85   'advocating a definite . . .', et al., ibid.

p. 86   'stood by Professor . . .', *Montreal Star*, 3 September 1934.

p. 86   'stand my colleagues', et al., 'Huebsch', 28 February 1915.

p. 86   'most extraordinary young . . .' and 'Everything that Hapgood . . .', Frankfurter, *Of Law and Men*, p. 218.

p. 87   'wasn't interested in . . .', ibid.

p. 87   'a wonderful man . . .', et al., 'Huebsch', 11 June, 9 July 1915.

p. 87   'There is a . . .' and 'the greatest authority . . .', ibid., 11 June 1915.

p. 88   'By the way . . .', 'Frankfurter', 18 June 1915.

p. 88   'Heaven knows why . . .', 'Huebsch', 5 November 1915.

p. 88   'you will pay . . .', Laski to Pound, 22 January 1916, *Pound Papers*, Harvard Law School.

p. 88   'I am coming . . .', 'Huebsch', 3 February 1916.

p. 90   'revolt against formalism', Morton White, *Social Thought in America*.

p. 90   'The life of . . .' (Boston, 1881), p. 1.

p. 94   'that it was . . .', 'Huebsch', 12 April 1915.

p. 94   'dark and wide-eyed . . .', 'Frida', pp. 42–3.

p. 95   'clearly another Beethoven', et al., 'Frida', p. 43.

p. 95   'the reply in . . .', 'Huebsch', 10 June 1916.

p. 95   'something in the . . .', Paton to Laski, 'Laski–Hull', 5 June 1916.

p. 96   'turn out so much . . .', 'Holmes', pp. 478. 1072.

p. 97   'I've been superbly . . .', Laski to Henry Moore Bates, 14 July 1918, 'Bates Papers', University of Michigan Library.

p. 97   'the money he . . .', et al., 'Frida', p. 44.

p. 97   'of dreams I . . .', et al., 'Laski–Hull', n.d. May 1919.

p. 98   'new way to . . .', 'Frida', p. 46.

p. 99   'one of a half-dozen . . .' and 'entre nous, Justice . . .', Laski to Dorothy Straight, 3 December 1918, 26 February 1917, *Straight Papers*, Cornell University Library.

p. 99   'his mother . . .', Alvin Johnson to Alfred Cohn, 21 May 1952, 'Cohn'.

p. 99   'I am loving . . .', 'Pound Papers', 5 October 1916.

p. 99   'after two years . . .', 'Holmes', p. 25.

p. 100   'I have written . . .', ibid., p. 51.

p. 100   'the eyes of . . .', et al., 'Harold Laski and the Harvard Law Review', 63
         Harvard Law Review 1398–1400, June 1950.

p. 101   'it then struck . . .', B. Russell, *Autobiography*, II, p. 155.

p. 102   'care a damn . . .', 'Holmes', p. 247.

p. 105   'courageous assertion that . . .', et al., *New Republic*, 14 April 1917.

p. 105   'painstaking and rather . . .', July 1917.

p. 106   'brilliant school of . . .', August 1917.

p. 106   'an unduly allusive . . .', *New Republic*, 15 May 1917.

p. 106   'by a certain . . .' and 'his practical teaching . . .', *Education Review*,
         December 1917.

p. 106   'often loose and . . .', 20 September 1917, 'Holmes–Pollock Letters', p. 248.

p. 106   'my anarchist prejudices . . .', et al., 'Holmes', 78, 110.

p. 107   'was influenced and . . .', *For God's Sake, Go*, p. 123.

p. 107   'we must take . . .', 31 May 1919.

p. 108   'when you are . . .', 14 March 1917, 'Straight Papers'.

p. 108   'I don't know . . .', 'Frankfurter', 24 July 1923.

p. 109   'an unimaginable gift . . .', 'Holmes', p. 272.

p. 109   'What else have . . .', 'Holmes', p. 766.

p. 109   'loved Laski as . . .', Freedman, *Roosevelt and Frankfurter*, p. 698.

p. 109   'you have a . . .', 'Frankfurter', 21 April 1929.

p. 110   'There is Harold . . .', ibid., 26 June 1916.

p. 110   'the languorous beauty . . .', ibid., n.d. 1917.

p. 111   'We Arabs, especially . . .', quoted in Urofsky and Levy, *'Half-Brother,
         Half-Son'*, p. 394.

p. 112   'could have contrived . . .', 'Holmes', p. xiv.

p. 112   'Harold Laski, an . . .', 'Holmes–Pollock Letters', 12 July 1916, p. 238.

p. 112   'a wonderful young . . .', quoted in Cosgrove, *Our Lady the Common Law*,
         p. 253.

p. 112   'diabolically clever and . . .', 'Holmes–Pollock Letters', 19 November 1917,
         p. 252.

p. 112   'a paragon who . . .', quoted in *What a Medley of a Man* (Harvard Law
         School, 1991), p. 24.

p. 113   'that I didn't . . .', et al., 'Holmes', pp. 96, 942, 431, 631, 1291, 948.

p. 113   'moderate the excesses . . .', Parrish, *Felix Frankfurter and His Times*, p. 3.

p. 114   'writes books faster . . .' and 'the best correspondent . . .', 'Holmes', pp.
         1246, 1272.

p. 114 'You are a . . .' and 'What a pleasure . . .', ibid., pp. 114, 413.

p. 114 'You and Felix . . .' and 'my son', ibid., pp. 37, 64, 90.

p. 114 'young prophets', ibid., p. 855.

p. 114 'how many of . . .', et al., ibid., pp. 304–5.

p. 115 'to tell you . . .', et al., 'Brandeis', 20 November 1916.

p. 116 'We threw our . . .', 'Frida', p. 46.

p. 117 'kindly and friendly', et al., correspondence from Daniel Rezneck, 25 January 1989.

p. 117 'a thin, sallow . . .' and 'lying on a . . .', 'Eastwood–Hull', 28 May 1974.

p. 117 'he had just . . .', *Boston Globe*, 10 August 1982.

p. 117 'the university requires . . .', 'Eastwood–Hull', Ruth Davis, 21 August 1974.

p. 118 'Listening to her . . .', Sassoon, *Siegfried's Journey*, p. 304.

p. 118 'plenty of money . . .', 'Holmes', p. 182.

p. 119 'not handicapped by . . .', Alvin Johnson, *Pioneer's Progress: An Autobiography* (New York, 1952), p. 172.

p. 119 'Thus a school . . .', *New Republic*, 8 June 1918.

p. 119 'I am authorized . . .' 21 March 1919, 'Pound Papers'.

p. 120 'Organized labour must . . .', *Fifty Years of Boston, A Memorial Volume* (Boston, 1932), p. 220.

p. 122 'end of the . . .', et al., 'Holmes', pp. 117, 206.

p. 123 'a new enthusiasm . . .' and 'anticipated most of . . .', ibid., p. 81.

p. 123 'whose guild socialism . . .', *Yale Review*, July 1920, p. 799.

p. 123 'one of the . . .', introduction to Duguit, *Law in Modern State* (New York, 1919), p. xxv.

p. 124 'its destruction by . . .', 19 May 1920.

p. 124 'fits gloriously into . . .', 'Holmes', p. 82.

p. 124 'is one of . . .', et al., 31 May 1919.

p. 124 'too allusive and . . .', 20 September 1919.

p. 124 'essentially the same . . .', September 1919.

p. 126 'is to take . . .', 'Holmes', p. 113.

p. 127 'seems to me . . .', ibid., p. 220.

p. 127 'Holmes and Brandeis . . .', *The Autobiography of Bertrand Russell*, p. 159.

p. 128 'of the astonishing . . .', et al., 10 May 1918, Radcliffe College Library.

p. 128 'a vicious poisonous . . .', et al., Hall to Paul Tuckerman, 20 November 1919, 13 November 1919, 'Lowell Papers', Harvard University Library.

p. 128 'As Mr Laski . . .', 13 May 1918, Radcliffe College Library.

p. 129 'I find that . . .', *The Autobiography of Bertrand Russell*, p. 158.

p. 129 'Old Boston is . . .', Baker, *Branderis and Frankfurter*, p. 221.

p. 129 'Mr Laski is . . .', 5 March 1919, 'Lowell Papers'.

p. 130 'he is a Polish . . .', et al., 8 March 1919, ibid.

p. 130 'He is a Jew . . .', et al., 'Lowell Papers', pp. 157–9.

p. 130 'I hear that . . .', et al. 'Holmes', pp. 193–4.

p. 130 'You have all . . .', 'Pound Papers', n.d., January 1919.

p. 131 'People in Boston . . .', 'Holmes–Pollock Letters', 5 April 1919, p. 8.

p. 132 'in a time . . .', et al., H. A. Yeomans, *Abbott Lawrence Lowell*, p. 316.

p. 133 'dull, illiterate, stupid . . .', 'Holmes', p. 524.

p. 133 'Russianizing' and 'submit to Soviet . . .' quoted in Russell, *A City in Terror*, p. 81.

p. 133 'to overthrow Americanism', 9 September 1919.

p. 133 'Soviet government by . . .', quoted in Russell, *A City in Terror*, p. 113.

p. 133 'Bolshevism in Boston . . .', et al., 11, 17 September 1919.

p. 134 'who comes of . . .', et al., 'Lowell Papers', 8 October 1919.

p. 135 'the average American . . .', 23 October 1919.

p. 135 'rattlesnake' and 'glorification of Bolshevism', 17 October 1919.

p. 135 'I spoke for . . .', *The Autobiography of Bertrand Russell*, p. 158.

p. 135 'If Mr Laski . . .', 'Lowell Papers', 28 October 1919.

p. 135 'whose ancestors for . . .', ibid., 6 November 1919.

p. 136 'were much impressed,' et al., ibid., 24 October 1919.

p. 136 'Academic freedom, sir . . .' and 'Under its cover . . .', ibid., 28 October 1919.

p. 136 'who encourages any . . .', ibid., 28 October 1919.

p. 136 'a Russian Jew . . .', ibid., 18 October 1919.

p. 136 'no young man . . .', ibid., 9 April 1920.

p. 136 'Laski's treason . . .', ibid., 16 October 1919.

p. 136 'academic freedom is . . .', ibid., 16 October 1919.

p. 136 'reminds me much . . .', ibid., 12 April 1920.

p. 136 'Harvard University was . . .', ibid., 11 October 1919.

p. 137 'the word "Bolshevist" . . .' and 'although you may . . .', ibid., 30 October 1919.

p. 137 'was rather made . . .', et al., ibid., 3 January 1920.

p. 137 'be a very . . .' and 'I hereby threaten . . .', ibid., 26 October 1919.

p. 138 'Why not clean . . .', Morgan, *FDR*, pp. 214–15.

p. 138 'as a foreigner . . .', Lowell to Mr Appleton, 'Lowell Papers', 6 November 1919.

p. 138 'Lowell was magnificent', 'Holmes', p. 218.

p. 138 'not to expect . . .', Laski, *American Democracy*, p. 357.

p. 139 'Harvard inquisition', 'Holmes', p. 952.

p. 139 'Nothing could be . . .', Martin, *Harold Laski*, p. 33.

p. 139 'I believe in . . .', 'Frankfurter', 29 March 1921.

p. 139 'misunderstood and misinterpreted' and 'If the overseers . . .', 'Holmes', pp. 213, 218.

p. 140 'one of the . . .', 28 January 1920.

p. 140 'would not be . . .', 26 January 1920.

p. 141 'have been discourteous . . .', 'Lowell Papers', 3 February 1920.

p. 141 'that you should . . .', ibid., 28 January 1920.

p. 141 'It is disquieting . . .', ibid., 13 February 1920.

p. 141 'will not yield . . .', Lowell to Dear Madam, ibid., 30 January 1920.

p. 141 'was vulgar and . . .', ibid., 14 February 1920.

p. 141 'I cannot fail . . .', ibid., 5 February 1920.

p. 142 'you and Frida . . .', 'Brandeis', 29 February 1920.

p. 142 'to convince him . . .', et al., 'Lowell Papers', 1 February 1920.

p. 142 'would be a . . .', ibid., 2 February 1920.

p. 142 'he is but . . .', 12 May 1920.

p. 142 'I am heartily . . .', op.cit., p. 160.

p. 143 'was eager to . . .', et al., 'Holmes', p. 230.

p. 143 'one day dedicating . . .', 'Gilbert Murray Papers', 17 July 1917.

p. 143 'the first stone . . .', 'Fisher Papers', 20 January 1917.

p. 143 'brings all kinds . . .', 'Zimmern Papers', 8 November 1918.

p. 143 'Laski seems to . . .', 'Holmes–Pollock Letters', 26 May 1919.

p. 144 'rarely met such . . .', 'Zimmern Papers', 22 December 1919.

p. 144 'how Wallas makes . . .', Laski to Richard Strout, 19 November 1919 (private collection).

p. 144 'Wallas is one . . .', 'Holmes', p. 230.

p. 144 'a masterpiece of . . .', June 1920.

p. 144 'no one has . . .', 2 July 1917.

p. 144 'real landmarks in . . .', 'Wallas Papers', 17 May 1917.

p. 145 'the Boston Police . . .', et al., 'Laski–Hull', 19 December 1919.

p. 145 'Wallas pleaded with . . .', Beveridge, *The London School of Economics*, p. 53.

p. 145 'mad excited Indian', 'Wallas Papers', 26 March 1920.

p. 146 'I suppose that . . .', 'Laski–Hull', 15 April 1920.

p. 146 'I think you . . .', 'Holmes', p. 251.

p. 146 'I shall miss . . .', 'Holmes–Pollock Letters', 14 April 1920.

p. 147 'We have concentrated . . .', et al., 18 February 1920.

p. 148 'what I always . . .', et al., *Felix Frankfurter Reminisces*, p. 177.

p. 150 'brings (I dare . . .', 'Holmes', p. 257.

p. 154 'which an ordinary . . .', Bullock, *The Life and Times of Ernest Bevin*, I, p. 128.

p. 155 'a one-sided . . .', Fenchtwanger, *Democracy and Empire*, p. 282.

p. 155 'A fully equipped . . .', E. Halevy, *The Rule of Democracy 1905–1914* (London, 1952), p. 298.

p. 156 'extraordinary confusion and . . .', et al., *The New Machiavelli* (London, 1911), p. 32.

p. 156 'Mrs Webb . . . settling . . .', *The Victorian Age in Literature* (London, 1920), p. 91.

p. 157 'fact-collecting drudges', Cole, *The Life of G. D. H. Cole*, p. 48.

p. 158 'a fresh figure . . .' and 'has a racial . . .', 25 March 1922.

p. 159 'go for the . . .', et al., *The Spirit of Co-operation*, (Manchester, 1936).

p. 160 'the significance of . . .' and 'equality has no . . .', 'Why I am a Marxist', *Nation*, 14 January 1939.

p. 160 'immersion in a . . .' and 'we've had a . . .', 'Huebsch', 2 November 1921.

p. 161 'Mrs Webb as . . .', 'Lowell Papers', 8 March 1921.

p. 161 'if he said . . .', et al., ibid.

p. 161 'informant must have . . .', et al., ibid., 22 March 1921.

p. 162 'to the School . . .' and 'not in my . . .', ibid., 19 April 1921.

p. 162 'by far the . . .', 'Laski–Hull', 1 March 1923.

p. 163 'a new outlook . . .', 'Laski–Hull', 7 April 1920.

p. 163 equality of chance . . .' and 'more and more', Haldane, *Richard Burdon Haldane*, pp. 309, 292.

p. 163 'an insatiable curiosity . . .', Laski to Pound, *Pound Papers*, 28 December 1920.

p. 165 'adjust our institutions . . .', 'Brandeis', 21 September 1921.

p. 166 'beatification of order', et al., 23 February 1922.

p. 166 'indefatigable writer, with . . .', et al., 25 March 1922.

p. 166 'one of the . . .' and 'will become a . . .', 'Sankey Papers', 23 February 1925, 24 September 1925.

p. 166 'since I came . . .', ibid., 17 February 1928.

p. 167 'And a newcomer . . .', *H.H.A.: Letters of the Earl of Oxford and Asquith to a Friend* (London, 1959), 2 February 1921, p. 167.

p. 167 'drive the country . . .' and 'His faults are . . .', 'Holmes', pp. 343, 312–13.

p. 168 'particular brand of . . .', *Downhill All the Way*, p. 93.

p. 168 'I can't tell . . .', in Martin, *Harold Laski*, p. 51.

p. 169 'does not understand . . .', 6 May 1922.

p. 169 'You meet with . . .', 'Hammond Papers', 20 August 1923.

p. 169 'as a subject . . .' and 'Lenin has shown . . .', 8 January, 21, 30 April 1921.

p. 169 'neo-Napoleonic', et al., 'Holmes', pp. 333, 496.

p. 171 'generosity, enthusiasm and . . .' and 'were so willing . . .', 'Holmes', pp. 356, 647.

p. 172 'purged socialism of . . .', '1890–1990: Up From Fabian Socialism', *Society*, January/February 1990.

p. 172   'Laski is the . . .', N. and J. MacKenzie (eds.), *The Diary of Beatrice Webb*, III, p. 399.

p. 172   'had to . . .' and 'we will see . . .', N. MacKenzie (ed.), *The Letters of Sidney and Beatrice Webb*, III, pp. 338, 288.

p. 172   'pricked the bubble . . .', et al., ibid. IV, p. 52.

p. 172   'very eager to . . .', ibid., III, p. 174.

p. 173   'Laski [who] has . . .', ibid., III, p. 294.

p. 175   'the most important', *The Story of Fabian Socialism*, p. 203.

p. 175   'pamphlet on Karl . . .', 'Holmes', p. 350.

p. 176   'the best mind . . .', ibid., p. 161.

p. 176   'Wells is a . . .', Martin, *Harold Laski*, p. 52.

p. 177   'great eighteenth-century . . .', 'Holmes', p. 659.

p. 178   'We count the . . .', ibid., p. 328.

p. 179   'a lamentable indifference . . .', et al., *Survey*, 26 February 1921, 10 October 1921.

p. 179   'derived from service . . .', et al., 9 February 1921.

p. 180   'the idea of . . .', et al., September 1923.

p. 180   'a devil of . . .' and 'a collection of . . .', Cole, *The Story of Fabian Socialism*, p. 197.

p. 180   'We are running . . .', 11 September 1920.

p. 181   'talked each night . . .' and 'the dozen fellows . . .', 'Holmes', pp. 786–7.

p. 182   'If they are . . .', Eastwood, *Harold Laski*, p. 11.

p. 182   'Of course it . . .', interview with Marjorie Hutton.

p. 182   'spiritual and mental . . .', Iremonger, *William Temple*, p. 74.

p. 182   'the spiritual riches . . .', *New Republic*, 11 February 1920.

p. 182   'gave life its . . .', Laski, *Dilemma of Our Times*, p. 129.

p. 182   'Get knowledge, and . . .', *New Republic*, 22 February 1928.

p. 182   'a maximum objectivity . . .' and 'if working class . . .', *Survey*, 1 October 1921.

p. 183   'with that faint . . .', et al., 'Holmes', pp. 380, 428, 479, 611.

p. 184   'colossally ignorant', ibid., p. 995.

p. 184   'obviously a really . . .', ibid., p. 566.

p. 184   'I at least . . .', *Danger of Being a Gentleman*, p. 30.

p. 185   'the golden boy' and 'the black sheep', 'Frida', p. 51.

p. 185   'real eagerness on . . .', 'Holmes', p. 271.

p. 185   'he looks frail . . .', 'Laski–Hull', 14 July 1920.

p. 185   'They've become very . . .', et al., 'Holmes', pp. 278, 271.

p. 185   'fetched from me . . .', et al., ibid., pp. 285, 290.

p. 186   'largely due to . . .', ibid., p. 290.

p. 186 'the family heroine . . .', 2 November 1921.

p. 186 'for which her . . .', Martin, *Harold Laski*, p. 49.

p. 186 'Not having a . . .' and 'dead against it', 'Frida', p. 52.

p. 186 'who received it . . .', ibid., p. 53.

p. 186 'At heart I . . .', ibid.

p. 187 'treated like gods . . .', Martin, *Harold Laski*, p. 49.

p. 187 'my trousers get . . .', 'Holmes', p. 365.

p. 187 'Mummy, is everybody . . .' and 'muttered, "Yes, everybody . . .', 'Frida', p. 52.

p. 187 'the atmosphere is . . .', p. 876.

p. 187 'dull as hell', 'Huebsch', 5 January 1922.

p. 188 'annual week with . . .', 'Holmes', p. 1094.

p. 188 'I don't think . . .', 'Harold–Frida', 10 January 1930.

p. 188 'I love you . . .', ibid., 16 February 1931.

p. 188 'I leave my . . .', ibid., n.d. August 1945.

p. 189 'wee speck intellectually . . .', ibid., 18 October 1911.

p. 189 'You give me . . .', ibid., 15 November 1911.

p. 189 'the element in . . .', ibid., 14 September 1946.

p. 189 'maddeningly dependent on . . .', 'Frida', p. 45.

p. 189 'It seemed that . . .', ibid., p. 48.

p. 190 'acting hostess to . . .', ibid., p. 49.

p. 191 'were neither equipped . . .' and 'a forthright contempt . . .', Dora Russell, *The Tamarisk Tree*, p. 174.

p. 191 'it would be . . .', 'Holmes', p. 1343.

p. 192 'disturbed and dissatisfied . . .', et al., 'Harold–Frida', 27 March 1922, 29 March 1922, 5 April 1929, 30 March 1922.

p. 192 'grand plans' and 'four entertaining rooms . . .', ibid., 8 April 1929.

p. 193 'so much with . . .', unpaged note.

p. 193 'the atmosphere of . . .', 'Harold–Frida', 2 June 1931.

p. 193 'Who were the . . .', et al., 'Holmes', p. 1185.

p. 193 'Of course she . . .', 'Frida', p. 60.

p. 193 'obviously a most . . .', Martin, *Harold Laski*, p. 57.

p. 193 'of one of . . .', 'Frida', p. 63.

p. 193 'luxurious and fast . . .', N. and J. MacKenzie (eds.), *Diary*, IV, p. 224.

p. 194 'abstemiousness from all . . .', *Our Partnership* (London, 1948), p. 340.

p. 194 'an act of . . .', N. and J. MacKenzie, *The First Fabians* (London, 1977), p. 153.

p. 194 'pack the odd . . .', 'Frida', p. 59.

p. 194 'thoroughly inconvenient place . . .', ibid., p. 50.

p. 195 'Harold produced some . . .', ibid., p. 52.

p. 195 'he never played . . .', *Leader*, July 1945.

p. 195 'elfishly small', *New Yorker*, 16 May 1953.

p. 195 'a mousy little . . .', Denis Healey, *The Time of My Life* (London, 1989), p. 79.

p. 195 'the pint-sized . . .' and 'unassuming little Titan', *Labour People*, pp. 91, 100.

p. 196 'looked like a . . .', *Father Figures*, p. 156.

p. 196 'just a trifle . . .', N. and J. MacKenzie (eds.), *Diary*, IV, p. 235.

p. 197 'on the exquisite . . .' and 'the pleasures of . . .', 'Holmes', p. 682.

p. 198 'only thing I . . .', ibid., p. 84.

p. 198 'damn Joyceism or . . .', et al., ibid., pp. 1472, 1390, 1351, 708.

p. 199 'as fast as . . .', *Of Law and Men*, p. 223.

p. 199 'Anne, did I . . .', personal interview.

p. 200 'as lively as . . .', *Memories and Glimpses*, p. 305.

p. 200 'full of vitality', et al., *Harper's*, October 1946.

p. 200 'not put titles . . .', Laski to Henry Moore Bates, 1 August 1934.

p. 200 'in hours he . . .', *Clare Market Review*, Michaelmas term 1950, p. 43.

p. 201 'You mustn't say . . .', et al., personal interviews.

p. 202 'He's a very . . .', N. MacKenzie (ed.), *The Letters of Sidney and Beatriece Webb*, IV, p. 330.

p. 202 'Blessed are the . . .', *Manchester Guardian Weekly*, 30 March 1950.

p. 202 'rash and impulsive', et al., 'Harold–Frida', n.d. October 1942.

p. 202 'such an arrogant . . .', letter from Paul Nash, 'Eastwood–Hull'.

p. 202 'My friend, what . . .', 'Harold–Frida', n.d. September 1929.

p. 202 'Madam, you need . . .', *Mr Speaker: The Memoirs of the Viscount Tonypandy* (London, 1985), p. 50.

p. 202 'I'm not coming . . .', 'Lerner', 29 October 1941.

p. 202 'waspishness, vindictiveness and . . .', et al., *For God's Sake, Go*, pp. 128, 124, 126.

p. 202 'superficial', et al., personal interview.

p. 203 'imaginary conversations' and 'never malicious or . . .', N. and J. MacKenzie (eds.), *Diary* IV, 235.

p. 203 'nearly all he . . .', quoted in Howarth, *Prospect and Reality*, p. 14.

p. 203 'you couldn't mention . . .', personal interview.

p. 203 'the tall tales . . .', *Books and Bookmen*, February 1978, p. 28.

p. 203 'as the hidden . . .', 16 April 1953.

p. 203 'I find it . . .', 'Holmes', p. 1046.

p. 203 'I assume that . . .', 'Powell Papers', 26 January 1937.

p. 203 'exaggerates by about . . .', *Harper's*, October 1946.

p. 204 'weekends and teas . . .', Fred Rodell, 14 March 1953.

p. 204 'drafting an election', 'Frankfurter', 3 October 1931.

p. 204 'the NEC met . . .' (London, 1953), I, p. 293.

p. 205 'Sometimes his desire . . .', *Leader*, July 1945.

p. 205 'a defence mechanism . . .', 30 January 1953.

p. 205 'enlarged' and 'heightening', 'Cohn', draft review of *Holmes–Laski Letters*, n.d. 1953.

p. 206 'We resented the . . .', *Discretions: The Autobiography of the Countess of Warwick* (New York, 1931), p. 43

p. 207 'under-sized Semite . . .', Pimlott, *Hugh Dalton*, p. 251.

p. 207 'yideology', Dalton, *Diary*, I, p. 180.

p. 207 'a Jew is . . .', Parrish, *Felix Frankfurter*, p. 129.

p. 207 'he has a . . .', 14 May 1922, III, p. 399.

p. 207 'He is an . . .', cited in Gorney, 'The Jewishness and Zionism of Harold Laski', *Midstream*, November 1977, p. 77.

p. 207 'Jewish blood will . . .', et al., 'Holmes', pp. 321, 317, 1353, 574, 613, 1022, 1302.

p. 208 'two old Russian . . .', ibid., p. 1311.

p. 208 'Synagogue this morning . . .' and 'a walk with . . .', 'Harold–Frida', n.d., early-mid 1920s.

p. 208 'becoming the rich . . .', 'Frankfurter', 1 March 1931.

p. 208 'distressing personal and . . .' and 'cleanse their bodies', Ronald Steel, *Walter Lippmann*, p. 193.

p. 208 'the authentic voice . . .', *Brandeis and Frankfurter*, pp. 349–50.

p. 208 'I loathe people . . .', 'Frankfurter', 14 December 1927.

p. 209 'I left feeling . . .', ibid., 30 April 1933.

p. 210 'we are luxuriating . . .', 'Frankfurter', 23 December 1923.

p. 210 'the rentier is . . .', 'Holmes', p. 570.

p. 210 'We stand now . . .', quoted in Miliband, *Parliamentary Socialism*, pp. 99–100.

p. 211 'to attempt any . . .', 17 December 1923.

p. 211 'with his romantic . . .', quoted in McKenzie, *British Political Parties*, p. 305.

p. 211 'magnificent presence, full . . .', ibid., p. 352.

p. 212 'colossal conceit', ibid., p. 367.

p. 212 'I respect MacDonald . . .' and 'with soberness and . . .', 'Holmes', p. 572.

p. 212 'spending much time . . .', ibid., p. 569.

p. 212 'I've had three . . .', 'Frankfurter', 23 December 1923.

p. 213 'show the country . . .', 'national well-being' and 'I think . . . one . . .', Miliband, *Parliamentary Socialism*, pp. 101, 105, 111.

p. 213 'itself a proof . . .', *Democracy in Crisis*, p. 117.

p. 214 'an intolerable snob', 'Frankfurter', 12 April 1924.

p. 214 'likes nothing so . . .', 'Holmes', p. 626.

p. 214 'not to be . . .', N. and J. MacKenzie (eds.), *Diary*, IV, 16.

p. 214 'the Great Ones . . .', et al., Miliband, *Parliamentary Socialism*, p. 95.

p. 215 'deep down in . . .', N. and J. MacKenzie (eds.), *Diary*, IV, 17.

p. 215 'makes judgement a . . .', 12 March 1924.

p. 215 'We will do . . .', 'Holmes', p. 667.

p. 215 'We have wiped . . .', et al., ibid., pp. 669, 673.

p. 216 'the only man . . .', quoted in McKenzie, *British Political Parties*, p. 369.

p. 216 'the best man . . .', et al., ibid., p. 375.

p. 216 'historically this is . . .', et al., Morgan, *J. Ramsay MacDonald*, p. 122.

p. 216 'win over the . . .', et al., 8 July 1925.

p. 217 'stupid and a . . .' and 'Laski one more . . .', Hamilton, *Arthur Henderson*, p. 272.

p. 217 'who discouraged young . . .', ibid.

p. 217 'I think that . . .', Dalton, *Memoirs,* I, p. 195.

p. 218 'You certainly seem . . .', 'Holmes', p. 389.

p. 218 '*when* the Labour . . .', Middlemas and Barnes, *Baldwin*, p. 208.

p. 218 'more equality of . . .', Ramsden, *The Age of Balfour and Baldwin*, p. 190.

p. 218 'shrewd, practical and direct' and 'best souls who . . .', 'Frankfurter', 24 July 1923, 6 June 1924.

p. 218 'not profound, or . . .', et al., 'Holmes', pp. 665, 736, 827, 1154.

p. 219 'brought into public . . .', Middlemas and Barnes, *Baldwin*, p. 506.

p. 219 'things in you . . .', 'that outside the . . .' and, 'for the forces . . .', G. M. Young, *Stanley Baldwin*, pp. 54, 151, 155.

p. 219 'to make the . . .' and 'He is nothing . . .', *New Republic*, 8 July 1925.

p. 220 'I am having . . .', 'Holmes', p. 621.

p. 220 'wrongly punished by . . .', *The Times*, 6 June 1924.

p. 221 'one juryman dissented . . .', *Holmes–Pollock Letters*, II, p. 141.

p. 221 'less by the . . .', et al., 'Holmes', pp. 613, 616, 619.

p. 221 'to the depth . . .', et al., 'Holmes', pp. 619, 627; 'Frankfurter', 6 June 1924.

p. 221 'and as it happened . . .', et al., Furbank, *E. M. Forster*, II, pp. 122–3.

p. 222 'on the disgusting . . .' and 'I hate it . . .', 'Huebsch', 19 September 1915.

p. 222 'striking suggestions', et al., 2 January 1924.

p. 223 'since the days . . .', *Laski Institute Review*, December 1956, p. 5.

p. 223 'Laski was a . . .', George, *Krishna Menon*, p. 68.

p. 223 'learned to love . . .', Kutty, *Krishna Menon*, p. 29.

p. 223 'The telephone in . . .', George, *Krishna Menon*, pp. 68–9.

p. 223 'put him on . . .', ibid., p. 113.

p. 224 'I do not . . .', *The Times*, 27 January 1949.

p. 224 'for sheer torrential . . .', 'Holmes', p. 683.

p. 224 'both he and . . .', 'Goldman Papers', 5 January 1925.

p. 225 'the opportunity of . . .', et al., ibid., 29 December 1924.

p. 225 'while disliking the . . .', ibid., 28 December 1924.

p. 225 'how any man . . .', ibid., Goldman to Baldwin, 5 January 1925.

p. 225 'You, dear Professor . . .', ibid., Goldman to Laski, 9 January 1925.

p. 226 'illogical and inconsistent . . .', ibid., Goldman to Baldwin, 5 January 1925.

p. 226 'I was a . . .', ibid.

p. 226 'and also practical . . .', 'Holmes', p. 681.

p. 233 'another read at . . .', N. MacKenzie (ed.), *Letters*, p. 240.

p. 233 'certain bad habits . . .', 22 August 1925.

p. 233 'full of luminous . . .', 24 October 1925.

p. 233 'is at his . . .', 30 July 1925.

p. 233 'a landmark that . . .', 9 December 1925.

p. 234 'it does not . . .', et al., 'Holmes', pp. 768, 762, 772, 776.

p. 235 'fulminating against the . . .', 6 January 1926.

p. 236 'I hate their . . .', 'Holmes', p. 803.

p. 236 'Bertie Russell was . . .', 'Frankfurter', 24 December 1925.

p. 238 'no words to . . .', 'Holmes', p. 835.

p. 238 'we have had . . .', Urofsky and Levy, *'Half-Brother, Half-Son'*, p. 239.

p. 238 'a big fellow . . .', et al., 'Holmes', p. 836.

p. 239 'a fear of . . .', et al., 'Laski Papers', Columbia University Library, n.d.

p. 240 'The whole world . . .' and 'Loyalty to his . . .', 'Holmes', p. 968.

p. 240 'distinguished foreign . . .', et al., 27 January 1928, 10 June 1928, 29 June 1930, 7 December 1930.

p. 240 'came back to . . .', 'Holmes', p. 838.

p. 241 'a direct challenge . . .', Cootes, *The General Strike*, p. 46.

p. 242 'found itself challenged . . .', *Survey*, 1 July 1926.

p. 243 'those in high . . .', et al., 'Holmes', pp. 835, 839. 'Frankfurter', 5 May 1926.

p. 243 'Laski then produced . . .', et al., Thomas Jones, *Whitehall Diary*, II, p. 43.

p. 244 'the square deal . . .', et al., ibid., II, 52–6.

p. 244 'full sympathy with . . .', *Fabian Society Documents*, Executive Committee, 13 May 1926.

p. 244 'condemning without reservation . . .', Cole, *The Story of Fabian Socialism*, p. 196.

p. 244 'the miners were . . .', 'Frankfurter', 24 May 1926.

p. 244 'the ghastly end . . .', 'Brandeis', 17 November 1926.

p. 244 'any political or . . .', *Nation*, 16 June 1926.

p. 245 'humanity, shrewdness and . . .', ibid., 26 May 1926.

p. 245 'It insisted, that . . .', *Survey*, 1 July 1926.

p. 245 'the strike was . . .', Miliband, *Parliamentary Socialism*, p. 138.

p. 245 'the sons and . . .', et al., quoted in unpublished paper by Lord G. R. McGregor, 'The History of the London School of Economics', pp. 8–10.

p. 246 'is really admirable . . .', 'Frankfurter', 18 December 1920.

p. 246 'cloistered from the . . .' and 'dons too removed . . .', 'Holmes', pp. 918, 1363.

p. 246 'the technical eminence . . .', J. Harris, *William Beveridge*, p. 292.

p. 246 'a distinctly socialist . . .', et al., ibid.

p. 247 '4 to 5 hours . . .', et al., *Laski Personnel File, LSE*, Laski to Beveridge, 31 January 1923; Beveridge to Laski, 1 February 1923.

p. 247 'if one were . . .', *Nation*, 8 April 1921.

p. 248 'My main disappointment . . .', et al., 'Holmes', p. 376.

p. 248 'all over the . . .', ibid., p. 1401.

p. 248 'thought more of . . .', Terrill, *R. H. Tawney*, p. 66.

p. 249 'one of the greatest . . .', ibid., p. 79.

p. 249 'one of the very . . .', Martin, *Father Figures*, p. 155.

p. 249 'scholar saint', N. and J. MacKenzie (eds.), *Diary*, IV, p. 360.

p. 249 'Tawney's Christianity never . . .', personal interview.

p. 250 'the curious lifelong . . .', et al., G. D. H. Cole, pp. 201–2.

p. 251 'What books or . . .', *New Society*, 2 December 1976.

p. 252 'deep green pools . . .', Denis Healey, *The Time of My Life* (London, 1989), p. 77.

p. 252 'we have too . . .', Pimlott, *Hugh Dalton*, p. 251.

p. 252 'parlour Marxism', et al., Robbins, *Autobiography of an Economist*, pp. 81–3.

p. 253 'was stunned, as . . .', et al., Martin, *Harold Laski*, p. 42.

p. 255 'amusing and brilliant', et al., 'Holmes', pp. 365, 617, 940.

p. 255 'the worst blow . . .', et al., Laski and Benn, *The Trade Disputes and Trade Unions Bill* (London, 1927).

p. 256 'determined moderation . . .', 'has largely ceased . . .' and 'Picturesque, vivid and . . .', 24 November 1926.

p. 256 'Mr MacDonald himself . . .', et al., 9 November 1927.

p. 257 'has a philosophic . . .', et al., 12 October 1927.

p. 258 'It's perfectly fascinating . . .', 27 May 1927.

p. 258 'I shall for . . .', et al., 'Holmes', pp. 1233, 962, 943, 981.

p. 258 'to my surprise . . .', 18 October 1936.

p. 259 'He kept in . . .', J. Callaghan, *Time and Chance* (London, 1987), p. 45.

p. 259 'we all had . . .', personal interview.

p. 259 'lie, they intrigue . . .', 9 November 1927.

p. 259 'they are among . . .' and 'regard all differences . . .', *New Republic*, 20 November 1926.

p. 261 'a book of . . .' 14 September 1927.

p. 261 'unquestionably the best . . .', 18 June 1927.

p. 264 'science seriously', et al., quoted in Wood, *Communism and British Intellectuals*, p. 148.

p. 264 'Voltairean' and 'religion more harmful . . .', 'Holmes', pp. 1262, 1258.

p. 264 'We in the . . .', *Rationalist Annual*, January 1931.

p. 265 'Permanently and impenitently . . .' and 'that there will . . .', 'Holmes', pp. 1130, 1198.

p. 265 'he dislikes the . . .', F. A. Iremonger, *William Temple, Archbishop of Canterbury*, p. 510.

p. 266 'it was rather . . .', *Felix Frankfurter Reminisces*, pp. 290–91.

p. 267 'Sidney and I . . .', N. and J. MacKenzie (eds.), IV, 172.

p. 267 'could help me . . .', 'Laski–Hull', MacDonald to Laski, 16 April 1929.

p. 268 'Not only are . . .' ibid., 21, 23 November 1927.

p. 268 'brilliant, jealous prima . . .', et al., 'Holmes', p. 981.

p. 269 'Dearest, the enclosed . . .' 'Harold–Frida', 17 April 1929.

p. 269 'It is no . . .', Colin Cross, *Philip Snowden* (London, 1966), p. 207.

p. 269 'like a man . . .', et al., 'Holmes', p. 1242.

p. 270 'immediate alteration of . . .', *Foreign Affairs*, 20 October 1929.

p. 270 'one of the . . .', et al., *Harper's*, April 1930.

p. 270 'Laski would be . . .', N. MacKenzie (ed.), *Letters*, III, 323.

p. 272 'the officials in . . .', quoted in *Political Quarterly*, January 1930.

p. 273 'rearguard action . . .', *Reflections on the Constitution*, p. 42.

p. 273 'for a belief . . .', et al., *Committee on Ministers' Powers – Report* (London, 1932), p. 117.

p. 273 'to end this . . .', 'Holmes', p. 1364.

p. 273 'Jewish hurricane', N. MacKenzie (ed.), *Letters*, p. 334.

p. 274 'at length please', and 'Quite understand, have . . .', 'Frankfurter', 15 June 1929.

p. 275 'that opinion of . . .', ibid., 29 November 1929.

p. 275 'I do not . . .', Gorny, *British Labour Movement*, p. 79.

p. 276 'very real danger', et al., 'Frankfurter', 13 June 1930.

p. 276 'blind spots', 'Holmes', p. 1206.

p. 276 'the Zionists have . . .', 'Frankfurter', 28 July 1930.

p. 276 'whether we can . . .', N. MacKenzie (ed.), *Letters*, III, p. 332.

p. 277 'the Jewish hurricane . . .', ibid., 334.

p. 278 'very official and . . .', et al., 'Frankfurter', 26 October 1930.

p. 278 'dispel the extraordinary . . .' and 'as from yourself . . .', N. MacKenzie (ed.), *Letters*, III, p. 337.

p. 278 'assuage feelings', et al., 'Frankfurter', 1 November 1930.

p. 278 *'fundamental for you . . .'*, ibid., 26 October 1930.

p. 278 'even a man . . .', Gorny, *The British Labour Movement*, p. 98.

p. 279 'nothing in the . . .' and 'to stir the . . .', N. MacKenzie (ed.), *Letters*, III, 345.

p. 279 'Why is it . . .', et al., *Diary*, IV, 231.

p. 279 'some ministers would . . .', *Letters*, III, p.345.

p. 280 'in telegrams, solely . . .', Litvinoff (ed.), *The Letters and Papers of Chaim Weizmann*, XV, p. 611.

p. 280 'the honest broker', et al., 'Holmes', p. 1296.

p. 280 'meant three hours . . .', 'Frankfurter', 19 January 1931.

p. 280 'the Americans not . . .', ibid., 6 December 1930.

p. 280 'I cannot remember . . .', et al., 'Holmes', p. 1301.

p. 281 'earnest in trying . . .', et al., 'Frankfurter', 6 December 1931, 4 January 1931.

p. 281 'ought to satisfy . . .', 'Holmes', p. 1302.

p. 281 'is bubbling over . . .', N. and J. MacKenzie (eds.), *Diary*, IV, p. 235.

p. 281 'graphic and amusing . . .', et al., ibid.

p. 282 'We can't govern . . .', et al., 'Holmes', pp. 1261, 1264, 1301.

p. 283 'wise counsel and . . .', 'Sankey Papers', 25 December 1930.

p. 283 'It was like . . .', 'Holmes', p. 1335.

p. 284 'wizened little man . . .', et al., 'Holmes', p. 1330.

p. 284 'helpless, homeless and . . .', 'Frankfurter', 28 November 1931.

p. 284 'the white man . . .', et al., 'Holmes', p. 1336.

p. 285 'When we had . . .', Woolf, *Downhill All the Way*, p. 229.

p. 286 'Professor Laski has . . .', 30 November 1930.

p. 287 'A lecturer of . . .', *BBC Written Archive Centre*, Laski File.

p. 291 'omnipresent and omnivocal', M. Kammen (ed.), *'What is the Good of History?' Selected Letters of Carl Becker* (Ithaca, 1973), p. 258.

p. 292 'the Yale students . . .', 'Harold–Frida', 25 May 1931.

p. 292 'It was worthwhile . . .', ibid., 20 April 1931.

p. 292 'real powers behind . . .', 29 March 1931.

p. 292 'a higher degree . . .', 22 March 1931.

p. 292 'political and official . . .', et al., 25 April 1931.

p. 292 'Professor Laski follows . . .', 19 May 1931.

p. 293 'want far more . . .' et al., 'Harold–Frida', 24 February 1931, 16 March 1931.

p. 293 'as sweet and . . .', ibid, 2 April 1931.

p. 293 'My boy will . . .' and 'he patted me . . .', ibid, 2 June 1931, 9 March 1931.

p. 294 'I did not . . .' 'Frankfurter', 1 March 1931.

p. 294 'This is a . . .', Nation, 11 April 1927.

p. 294 'was cold as . . .', Harold–Frida', 16 March 1931.

p. 294 'a dog's chance . . .' and 'he was willing . . .', ibid., 12 March 1931.

p. 294 'they never had . . .', et al., ibid., 24 February 1931, 22 March 1931, 16 April 1931.

p. 295 'this small, thin . . .', et al., Infidel in the Temple, pp. 54–5.

p. 296 'most gross perversion . . .', Elizabeth Durbin, New Jerusalem, p. 65.

p. 296 'financial, but political . . .', cited in K. Feiling, Neville Chamberlain (London, 1946), p. 191.

p. 297 'the political parties . . .' and 'certain individuals as . . .', cited in Pimlott, Labour and the Left in the 1930s, p. 12.

p. 298 'and its standard . . .', et al., Harper's, May 1932.

p. 298 'is in the . . .', 'Frankfurter', 4 September 1931.

p. 298 'We can't get . . .' and 'a reply to . . .', Gilbert, Plough My Own Furrow, pp. 211, 277.

p. 298 'as an early . . .', 'Frankfurter', 7 January 1932.

p. 299 'furious attacks on . . .', personal interview.

p. 299 'The new Cabinet . . .', The Crisis and the Constitution, p. 34.

p. 299 'In modern times . . .', et al., Parliamentary Government in England, p. 196.

p. 299 'Mr MacDonald was as . . .', The Crisis and the Constitution, p. 34.

p. 299 'to have a . . .', et al., 'Laski–Hull', 13 November 1932.

p. 299 'no evidence that . . .', Political Quarterly, April–June 1932.

p. 300 'epitomizes this long . . .' King George V (London, 1983), pp. 378–9.

p. 300 'Is policy to . . .', 6 September 1931.

p. 300 'That a party . . .', October–December 1931.

p. 300 'has really done . . .', 22 March 1931.

p. 301 'purge itself of . . .', et al., The Crisis and the Constitution, pp. 42–3.

p. 301 'The Constitution counts . . .', 'Frankfurter', 9 October 1931.

p. 302 'I work day . . .', 27 September 1931.

p. 302 'approved an election . . .', Memoirs, I, 293.

p. 302 'Well, the electorate . . .', 1 November 1931.

p. 303 'yideology', Pimlott (ed.), Diary of Hugh Dalton, I, 180.

p. 305 'not spectacular enough . . .', Durbin, New Jerusalem, p. 80.

p. 305 'deep depression' and 'dreary', N and J. MacKenzie (eds.), IV, 290.

p. 306 'There, but for . . .', Sissons and French, Age of Austerity, p. 179.

p. 306 'the twilight of . . .' and 'within the framework . . .', 'Frankfurter', 11 February 1932, 17 April 1932.

p. 306 'that power needs . . .', 'Becker Papers', 9 April 1934.

p. 307 'socialism should take . . .' and 'would make good . . .', *Manchester Guardian*, 30 April 1932.

p. 307 'a Labour Party . . .', *Daily Herald*, 27 February 1933.

p. 307 'that two Labour . . .', ibid., 26 November 1933.

p. 307 'a disaster to . . .', *Manchester Guardian*, 30 April 1934.

p. 307 'seriously to consolidate . . .', et al., *The Crisis and the Constitution*.

p. 307 'batter in the . . .', *Parliamentary Government in England*, pp. 154–5.

p. 308 'The large principles . . .', *The Labour Party and the Constitution*, p. 21.

p. 309 'into granting him . . .', *New Clarion*, 13 May 1933.

p. 309 'The most creative . . .', 'Frankfurter', 29 October 1932.

p. 309 'agitative books', Miliband interview.

p. 310 'a book destined . . .', George Catlin, *Books*, 16 April 1933.

p. 311 'the moment to . . .', W. Golant, 'The Emergence of C. R. Attlee as Leader of the Parliamentary Labour Party', *Historical Journal*, XIII, 1970, p. 320.

p. 312 'The right wing . . .', 'Frankfurter', 24 September 1934.

p. 312 'the most authoritative . . .', Bullock, *The Life and Times of Ernest Bevin*, I, p. 512.

p. 312 'irresponsible drivel', Citrine, *Men and Work*, p. 293.

p. 312 'a very grave . . .', 24 June 1933.

p. 313 'could do as . . .', et al., Citrine, *Men and Work*, pp. 299–300.

p. 313 'whatever its faults . . .', et al., 7 October 1933.

p. 314 'we must act . . .', Cooke, *The Life of Richard Stafford Cripps*, p. 159.

p. 314 'any reconstructed House . . .', 25 November 1933.

p. 314 seems to think . . .', et al., Pimlott, *Diary of Hugh Dalton*, I, p. 182.

p. 314 'that he was . . .', Cooke, *The Life of Richard Stafford Cripps*, p. 160.

p. 314 'moving a resolution . . .', *Memoirs*, II, pp. 59–60.

p. 315 'introduce at once . . .', et al., *The Labour Party: Report of the Annual Conference* (1932), pp. 204–5.

p. 315 'specify the means . . .' and 'so that a . . .', *The Labour Party: Report of the Annual Conference* (1933), p. 159.

p. 316 'sees no reason . . .', *The Labour Party: Report of the Annual Conference* (1934), p. 36.

p. 316 'a decisive advance . . .', ibid., p. 165.

p. 316 'when a man . . .', 4 October 1934.

p. 316 'a desire for . . .', et al., *The Labour Party: Report of the Annual Conference* (1934), p. 138.

p. 317 'not [to] undertake . . .' et al., ibid.

p. 317 'always telling us . . .', ibid., p. 140.

p. 317 'in a purely . . .', et al., ibid., p. 136.

p. 317 'brutal, beastly and . . .', p. 1358.

p. 318 'some ten appointments . . .', 12 May 1933.

p. 318 'a wanton defiance . . .', 16 August 1933.

p. 318 'the perpetual nightmare' and 'a whole people . . .', 'Holmes', pp. 1458, 1437.

p. 318 'weak and indecisive' and 'at the back . . .', 'Frankfurter', 13 August 1933.

p. 318 'no reason why . . .' and 'a dark age . . .', 'Holmes', p. 1443.

p. 319 'parliamentary socialism', Miliband's phrase.

p. 319 'trade unionist who . . .', et al., *The Labour Party: Report of the Annual Conference* (1933), p. 161.

p. 319 'the anti-intellectual . . .', October–November 1934.

p. 319 'Labour must become . . .' and 'one tenth of . . .', 25 May 1936.

p. 320 'the most important . . .' and 'Harold Laski once . . .', *Commentary*, March 1975.

p. 320 'an awkward, shy . . .', 'Frankfurter', 6 June 1924.

p. 320 'vehement objection to . . .' N. and J. MacKenzie (eds.), *Diary*, VI, p. 361.

p. 321 'has been corrupted . . .', 'Frankfurter', 17 January 1928.

p. 321 'with the autocratic . . .', N. and J. MacKenzie (eds.), *Diary*, IV, p. 115.

p. 321 'has to sell . . .', and 'pursues a path . . .', May 1928.

p. 321 'just want safe . . .', 'Cohen Papers', 21 February 1928.

p. 321 'for help with . . .', et al., 'Harold–Frida', 29 March 1931, 8 April 1931, 8 June 1931, 14 May 1931.

p. 322 'the Beveridge–Mair . . .', N. MacKenzie (ed.), *Letters*, p. 282.

p. 322 'Mrs Mair was . . .', 'Frida', p. 59.

p. 322 'on a policy . . .', N. and J. MacKenzie (eds.), *Diary*, VI, p. 329.

p. 322 'a rather savage . . .', J. Harris, *William Beveridge*, p. 295.

p. 322 'absolute freedom in . . .' and 'they should nevertheless . . .', ibid.

p. 323 'emotional aversion to . . .', quoted in unpublished paper by Lord G. R. McGregor, 'The History of the London School of Economics', p. 21.

p. 323 'Apparently the lively . . .', J. Harris, *William Beveridge*, p. 297.

p. 323 'as the centre . . .', et al., N. and J. MacKenzie (eds.), *Diary*, IV, p. 330.

p. 323 'a knot of . . .' and 'indefensible from any . . .', J. Harris, *William Beveridge*, p. 300.

p. 324 'that the completness . . .', *Laski Personnel File*, Laski to Beveridge, 3 March 1934.

p. 324 'dictating,' et al., ibid., Beveridge to Laski, 3 March 1934.

p. 324 'sure that the . . .', ibid.

p. 325 'the English gentleman . . .', *Daily Herald*, 26 August 1933.

p. 325 'The Pollyanna of . . .', ibid., 19 April 1930.

p. 325 'how profound had . . .', *Laski Personnel File*, Laski to Beveridge, 19 April 1934.

p. 325 'from Monday until . . .', et al., ibid., 19 April 1934.

p. 327 'for the first . . .', 22 June 1934.

p. 327 'all the quotations . . .', et al., 10 July 1934.

p. 329 'a fanatic and . . .', 17 July 1934.

p. 330 'the necessity of . . .', *Laski Personnel File*, Beveridge to Frank Pick, 18 July 1934.

p. 330 'My attitude is . . .', 'Frankfurter', 18 July 1934.

p. 330 'the sense of . . .', *Laski Personnel File*, 19 July 1934.

p. 330 'as far as . . .', et al., ibid., 25 July 1934.

p. 331 'no indiscretion should . . .', et al., 'Frankfurter', 5 August 1934, 8 August 1934.

p. 331 'the Laski incident', Urofsky and Levy, *'Half-Brother, Half-Son'*, p. 552.

p. 331 'freedom of the . . .', et al., Sinclair, *The Goose-Step*, p. 87.

p. 331 'fourteen years of . . .' and 'inclined to put . . .', 'Frankfurter', 24 September 1934.

p. 331 'The only duties . . .', *New Republic*, 23 January 1935.

p. 331 'minds turned upside . . .' and 'makes his pupils . . .', *Dangers of Disobedience*, p. 102.

p. 331 'the fires of . . .', *Of Law and Men*, p. 272.

p. 332 'His lectures are . . .', 'Eastwood–Hull', 30 November 1936.

p. 332 'when we wished . . .' et al., letters to the authors.

p. 332 'he never left . . .', et al., personal interview.

p. 332 'a queue long . . .', Martin, *Father Figures*, p. 157.

p. 332 'beyond words a . . .', 'Frankfurter', 6 June 1924.

p. 332 'students are really . . .' and 'undiluted joy', 'Holmes', p. 664.

p. 332 'Laski relished it . . .', Abse, *My LSE*, p. 87.

p. 332 'go forth to . . .' and 'less to avoid . . .', *Dangers of Disobedience*, pp. 46–7.

p. 333 'whirl of new . . .', 'Holmes', p. 879.

p. 333 'taken aback by . . .', Kennedy, *Times to Remember*, p. 170.

p. 333 'a little wild . . .', Goodwin, *The Fitzgeralds and the Kennedys*, p. 541.

p. 333 'a nut and . . .', et al., Kennedy, *Times to Remember*, p. 271.

p. 334 'keen satisfaction and . . .' and 'with a smile . . .', Laski quoted in Goodwin, *The Fitzgeralds and the Kennedys*, pp. 542, 543.

p. 334 'greatest teacher of . . .', quoted in *Laski Institute Review* (Ahmedabad, India), December 1959.

p. 334 'of the frequent . . .' and 'it might hurt', Goodwin, op. cit., p. 548.

p. 334 'Everybody is either . . .' and 'Laski is very . . .', ibid., p. 550.

p. 334   'RC reactions at . . .', 'Morrison Papers', Frida to S. E. Morrison, 2 April 1962.

p. 335   'put on a . . .', Searls, *The Lost Prince*, p. 70.

p. 335   'mind was only . . .', Kennedy, op.cit., p. 172.

p. 335   'a man despised . . .', *After Long Silence*, p. 47.

p. 336   'a nice lad . . .', 23 December 1933.

p. 336   'he promises well . . .', et al., 'MacPherson Papers', 9 October 1933, 28 October 1933, 9 November 1933, 19 November 1933.

p. 336   'impressed' and 'a superb teacher', letter to authors.

p. 337   'and their answer . . .', 'Frankfurter', 22 June 1935.

p. 337   'the school was . . .', ibid., 23 February 1935.

p. 337   'tries assiduously to . . .', ibid., 3 November 1934.

p. 338   'she really makes . . .', 20 January 1936.

p. 339   'to agree to . . .' and 'we have now . . .', 'Frankfurter', 17 February 1935, 27 December 1937.

p. 339   'a nursery of . . .', et al., *A Century of Municipal Progress* (London, 1935).

p. 340   'maintain a vigilant . . .', Martin, *Editor*, p. 152.

p. 340   'the marchers have . . .', 27 February 1934.

p. 341   'the most dangerous . . .', *Manchester Guardian*, 30 April 1934.

p. 341   'in this country . . .', ibid., 27 January 1937.

p. 341   'curious helplessness of . . .', et al., Bertrand Russell (ed.), *Dare We Look Ahead?* (London, 1938).

p. 342   'grimly what public . . .', 'Frankfurter', 23 November 1936.

p. 342   'The Jubilee business', 11 May 1935.

p. 342   'sit up, like . . .', Tawney in the *New Statesman*, 22 June 1935.

p. 342   'we, as you . . .', 20 January 1936.

p. 343   'The King must . . .', 3 December 1935.

p. 343   'had a stabilizing . . .', Middlemas (ed.), *Thomas Jones*, II, p. 291.

p. 344   'Don't believe the . . .', copy in 'Frankfurter', no name, 11 December 1936.

p. 345   'the Devil in . . .', N. and J. MacKenzie (eds.), *Diary*, IV, p. 331.

p. 345   'officers without a . . .', *Political Quarterly*, October–December 1936.

p. 345   'doesn't understand the . . .', II, p. 42.

p. 345   'thin, theoretical, tinny . . .', Pimlott, *Hugh Dalton*, p. 398.

p. 345   'very British', et al., *Memoirs*, II, pp. 58–9.

p. 345   'use of a . . .', Elizabeth Durbin, *New Jerusalem*, p. 223.

p. 346   'a move which . . .', *Daily Herald*, 27 October 1935.

p. 347   'conscience round from . . .', *The Labour Party: Report of the Annual Conference* (1935), p. 178.

p. 347   'Lansbury has been. . .', Francis Williams, *Ernest Bevin*, p. 196.

p. 347   'destroy the countries . . .', *Nation*, 6 May 1936.

p. 348 'their sympathy accompanied ...', *The Labour Party: Report of the Annual Conference* (1936), p. 123.

p. 348 'goes so directly ...', 18 October 1936.

p. 348 'a profound pro-Hitler ...', 22 June 1936.

p. 348 'this is much ...', I, 190.

p. 349 'gave the best ...', Philip Williams, *Hugh Gaitskell*, p. 74.

p. 349 'that there shall ...', *Daily Herald*, 30 October 1935.

p. 349 'PROFESSOR ON ALL ...', 11 November 1935.

p. 350 'absence of definite ...', 18 December 1935.

p. 351 'dictator of policy', N. and J. MacKenzie (eds.), *Diary*, IV, p. 360.

p. 352 'was the man ...' and 'getting support from ...', 'Frankfurter', 28 December 1935.

p. 352 'the irreproachable and ...', N. and J. MacKenzie (eds.), *Diary*, IV, p. 360.

p. 352 'a wretched disheartening ...', N. and J. MacKenzie (eds.), *Diary*, I, p. 196.

p. 352 'the complete refusal ...', 'Frankfurter', 4 August 1934.

p. 352 'unspeakably vile', *Democracy in Crisis*, p. 190.

p. 353 'ignorant, tragic and ...', *Manchester Guardian*, 30 April 1934.

p. 353 'Jews could not ...', *Jewish Chronicle*, 12 July 1934.

p. 353 'I hope to God ...', 2 May 1936.

p. 353 'suspected fascists everywhere' and 'they were in ...', Sulzberger, *A Long Row of Candles*, p. 24.

p. 353 'in the production ...', Gilbert, *Winston Churchill*, V, p. 68.

p. 353 'to instruct his ...', et al., *N. Laski Papers*, Mocatta Anglo Jewish Library, Southampton University.

p. 354 'entre nous', et al., 18 October 1936.

p. 355 'always approach him ...', et al., *Mapai Archives*, Beith-Berl, Israel, 101/35, 12 December 1935.

p. 356 'the right of ...' and 'some, at least ...', *New Statesman*, 20 June 1936.

p. 356 'on publication [of ...' and 'play the Irish ...', 20 January 1937.

p. 356 'have no hope ...', 17 July 1937.

p. 356 'I frankly don't ...' and 'is effective land ...', 11 August 1937.

p. 357 'for a wholesale ...', ibid.

p. 357 'the effect of ...' and 'a surrender by ...', *Jewish Chronicle*, 27 April 1988.

p. 357 'The notorious White ...', *Reflections on the Constitution*, p. 169.

p. 357 'a breach of ...', 347 House of Commons, 107, 22 May 1939.

p. 357 'base petition in ...', Sissons and French (eds.), *Age of Austerity*, p. 63.

p. 358 'May I congratulate ...', Gilbert, *Winston Churchill*, V, p. 1506.

p. 358 'the slum of ...', *Political Quarterly*, October–December 1938.

p. 358 'We hold India,' et al., *Daily Herald*, 21 April 1934.

p. 359 'wants not merely . . .', ibid.

p. 359 'Nehru I regard . . .', 4 August 1938.

p. 359 'strong medicine – . . .', 3 November 1934, 14 January 1935.

p. 362 'crypto-Marxist', 'Frankfurter', 28 December 1935.

p. 363 'the permanent enemy . . .', 'Holmes', p. 1428.

p. 363 'to be of . . .', et al., 3 October 1936.

p. 364 'the four pink . . .', 11 January 1953.

p. 365 'even games, songs . . .', *Tribune*, 16 June, 7 July 1939.

p. 366 'Forced to make . . .', quoted in Stuart Samuels, 'The Left Book Club', *Journal of Contemporary History*, Vol. I, No. 2, 1966.

p. 366 'is in broad . . .', May 1936.

p. 366 'deplorable review', Thomas, *John Strachey*, p. 156.

p. 367 'violent anti-Soviet . . .', Edwards, *Victor Gollancz*, p. 268.

p. 367 'all that dreary . . .', Crick, *George Orwell*, p. 309.

p. 369 'as one of . . .', quoted in *Left News*, August 1945.

p. 369 'like the ancient . . .', et al., ibid., March 1937.

p. 370 'as a most . . .', Trevor Burridge, *Clement Attlee*, p. 94.

p. 370 'it had become . . .', cited in Stuart Samuels, op.cit., p. 77.

p. 370 'a dangerous type . . .', cited in Pimlott, *Labour and the Left*, p. 161.

p. 370 'incompatible with membership . . .', *Left News*, April 1939.

p. 370 'official', et al., *New Statesman*, 28 August 1937.

p. 370 'it was plain . . .', ibid., 4 September 1937.

p. 371 'A fierce battle . . .', 13 March 1937.

p. 371 'a substitute for . . .', A. J. P. Taylor, *Politicians, Socialism and Historians*, p. 189.

p. 371 'fundamental difference between . . .', *The Labour Party: Report of the Annual Conference* (1936), p. 54.

p. 372 'unity of all . . .', *Tribune*, 22 January 1937.

p. 372 'had 180 people . . .' and 'leaders are much . . .', 17 July 1937, 20 January 1937.

p. 372 'our labour movement . . .', *Daily Herald*, 6 April 1937.

p. 372 'sorry to be . . .', 20 January 1937.

p. 373 'the offenders against . . .', and 'I fight all . . .', 'Laski–Hull', 22 February 1937.

p. 374 'the Labour Party . . .', 29 October 1937.

p. 374 'We have to . . .', 5 February 1937.

p. 374 'fighting its own . . .', 16 July 1937.

p. 374 'Is it that . . .', 5 February 1937.

p. 375 'every visible sign . . .', 16 July 1937.

p. 375 'Kings and Bus . . .', et al., 22 May 1937.

p. 375 'I stand here . . .', et al., *The Labour Party: Report of the Annual Conference* (1937), p. 158.

p. 375 'cannot have disunity . . .', et al., ibid., p. 163.

p. 377 'if we get . . .', 5 July 1937.

p. 377 'was an unmistakable . . .', 20 November 1937.

p. 377 'looking forward to . . .', *Memoirs*, II, p. 146.

p. 377 'a new Monday . . .', 27 November 1937.

p. 378 'No name is . . .', 14 January 1938.

p. 378 'the big battalions . . .', 10 October 1937.

p. 378 'socialist faith', 31 October 1936.

p. 378 'an integral part . . .', et al., *Nation*, 2 October 1937.

p. 378 'TU hatred of . . .' and 'the best of . . .', 'Frankfurter', 11 November 1937.

p. 379 'Of course the . . .', ibid., 30 January 1938.

p. 379 'the rape of . . .', ibid., 5 August 1938.

p. 379 'I cannot see . . .', Bullock, *Ernest Bevin*, I, p. 592.

p. 379 'No one on . . .', *Tribune*, 1 October 1937.

p. 380 'if there is . . .', Middlemas, *Politics in Industrial Society*, p. 241.

p. 380 'permit the fascist . . .', *Manchester Guardian*, 29 June 1936.

p. 380 'attack on Spain . . .', 'Frankfurter', copy to unidentified friend, n.d. December 1939.

p. 382 'brilliant and full . . .', *New Statesman*, 12 November 1938.

p. 383 'reasoned criticism' and 'Trotskyite attacks', September 1937.

p. 383 'most of the . . .', *Memoirs*, II, p. 57.

p. 384 'despairing apathy' et al., N. and J. MacKenzie (eds.), *Diary*, IV, p. 286.

p. 384 'frame-ups', quoted in Callaghan, *Socialism in Britain*, p. 135.

p. 384 'we were engaged . . .' Elizabeth Thomas (ed.), *Tribune 21*, p. 7.

p. 384 'all my life . . .' and 'But, Laski, good . . .', 18 July 1934.

p. 384 'in a state . . .' and 'so long as . . .', N. and J. MacKenzie (eds.), *Diary*, IV, p. 336.

p. 385 'it is true . . .', et al., 20 June 1936.

p. 386 'distressed beyond words' and 'I have talked . . .', 'Woolf Papers', 15 December 1937.

p. 388 'with great respect . . .', et al., *Political Quarterly*, January 1938.

p. 388 'Laski's hostile review', N. and J. MacKenzie (eds.), *Diary*, IV, p. 406.

p. 388 'delightfully appreciative', ibid.

p. 388 'a five-hour talk . . .' and 'necessary to save . . .', ibid., IV, pp. 419–20.

p. 390 'left-wing thought . . .', Schlesinger, *The Age of Roosevelt*, p. 174.

p. 391 'socialism as the . . .', *New York Times*, 3 April 1935.

p. 391 'emphatic return to . . .', ibid., 22 March 1937.

p. 391 'Precisely because of . . .', Eastwood, *Harold Laski*, p. 79.

p. 391 'the annex of . . .', et al., May 1935.

p. 391 'socialized lawyers in . . .', et al., *New York Times*, 15 December 1935.

p. 392 'The essential character . . .', J. K. Jessup (ed.), *The Ideas of Henry Luce* (New York, 1969), p. 232.

p. 392 'the infantilism of . . .', *The Age of Suspicion*, p. 22.

p. 392 'Can America Spend . . .', et al., December 1934.

p. 393 'their blind hostility . . .', September 1937.

p. 393 'America has an . . .', ibid.

p. 393 'I feel as . . .', 8 March 1935.

p. 394 'we have also . . .', Urofsky, '*Half-Brother, Half-Son*', p. 539.

p. 394 'noble passion' and 'like the pronouncement . . .', 'Holmes', p. 1473.

p. 394 'worshipped at his . . .', Ickes, *The Secret Diary*, II, p. 424.

p. 395 'sons of white . . .', et al., Baker, *Brandeis and Frankfurter*, p. 349.

p. 395 'as a private . . .', 'Frankfurter', n.d. December 1934.

p. 395 'has hit on you . . .', 1 October 1935.

p. 395 'Jew Deal', Herzstein, *Roosevelt and Hitler*, passim.

p. 395 'Harold Laski, the . . .', Carlson, *Plotters*, p. 142.

p. 395 'the men of . . .', *Congressional Record*, 7 September 1940.

p. 396 'there are no . . .', 'Lerner', 12 December 1949.

p. 396 'the nature of . . .', Persico, *Edward R. Murrow*, p. 86.

p. 397 'the only democratic . . .', ibid., p. 120.

p. 397 'dependency of the . . .', May 1935.

p. 397 'almost the counsel . . .' and 'men for the . . .', Mason, *Harlan Fiske Stone*, p. 382.

p. 398 'extracts,' et al., ibid., p. 335.

p. 398 'brief connection with . . .', 23 September 1937.

p. 398 'the President would . . .' and 'for a long . . .', *Roosevelt and Frankfurter*, p. 285.

p. 399 'I want to . . .', et al., 'FDR', 17 January 1937, 14 March 1938, 14 April 1938, 15 October 1938.

p. 399 'from a trusted . . .', *Roosevelt and Frankfurter*, p. 125.

p. 400 'My colleagues on . . .', 'FDR', 19 August 1939.

p. 400 'having the gift . . .', 'Frankfurter', 22 December 1935.

p. 400 'Roosevelt is the . . .' and 'Different as his . . .', 27 December 1937, 24 October 1936.

p. 400 'the people of . . .', 3 March 1937.

p. 400 'to reform in . . .', et al., December 1938.

p. 401 'it could be . . .', 'FDR', 31 January 1939.

p. 401 'it would embarrass . . .', ibid., 5 January 1939.

p. 401 'Dear Harold, of . . .', ibid., 10 January 1939.

p. 402 'as thought-provoking . . .' and 'it takes its . . .', December 1940.

p. 402 'as a piece . . .', 7 June 1940.

p. 402 'one of the . . .', 27 April 1940.

p. 402 'a classic in . . .', 3 August 1940.

p. 402 'Mr Laski has . . .', 3 August 1940.

p. 402 'one of the . . .', et al., 18 November 1940.

p. 403 'she had been . . .', et al., Laski to Comstock, 'Radcliffe College Archives', 24 September 1938, 12 March 1939.

p. 404 'Are you acquainted . . .', et al., *The Nomination of Felix Frankfurter, Hearings*, 11 and 12 January 1939, Washington, pp. 124–5.

p. 405 'Professor Laski is . . .', *Daily*, 24 January 1939.

p. 406 'A delightful description . . .', 'FDR', 31 January 1939.

p. 406 'to these rednecked . . .', ibid., 3 February 1939.

p. 406 'invited all of . . .' and 'visitors were crowding . . .', *Daily*, 23 January 1939.

p. 406 'Everything that is . . .', et al., *Seattle Times*, 15 February 1939.

p. 407 'brought a remarkable . . .', et al., 12 July 1939.

p. 408 'weakening of party . . .', cited in Miliband, *Parliamentary Socialism*, p. 257.

p. 409 'The swing . . . from . . .', 22 February 1939.

p. 409 'The British government . . .', et al., 9 April.

p. 409 'his Messianic complex . . .', 14 October 1939.

p. 409 'parties of progress . . .' and 'to drive the . . .', cited in Pimlott, *Labour and the Left*, p. 175.

p. 410 'Bloomsbury revolutionaries' and 'Away with those . . .', ibid., p. 179.

p. 410 'a tribute to . . .' and 'did he loyally . . .', *The Labour Party: Report of the Annual Conference* (1939), p. 229.

p. 410 'the future integrity . . .', *New York Times*, 20 March 1938.

p. 411 'If at first . . .', quoted in L. Lyons, *Boston Herald*, 11 April 1950.

p. 411 'If you will . . .', 'Eastwood–Hull', T. R. Powell to Eastwood, n.d. 1976.

p. 411 '5 MILLION PEOPLE . . .', 15 July 1938.

p. 412 'The change in . . .', ibid.

p. 412 'enormously strengthened the . . .', et al., August 1939.

p. 412 'betrayal of democracy . . .', 'Middleton Papers', Laski to James Middleton, 23 August 1939.

p. 412 'British Communist Party . . .' and 'this war is . . .', cited in Fischer, *Men and Politics*, p. 581.

p. 413 'I had hoped . . .', Mahon, *Harry Pollitt*, p. 253.

p. 413 'the communists here . . .', 'Cohn', 12 April 1940.

p. 413 'more than ever . . .', 'FDR', 5 September 1939.

p. 413 'would result in . . .', December 1939.

p. 414 'was largely responsible', 3 October 1939.

p. 415 'I have not . . .', 'Cohn', 12 April 1940.

p. 416 'War never leaves . . .', *The Labour Party: Report of the Annual Conference* (1940), p. 195.

p. 416 'You have sat . . .', 360 House of Commons 1140–50, 7 May 1940.

p. 417 'lapses from balance . . .', et al., 22 July 1939.

p. 417 'It is an . . .', 'Cohn', 12 April 1940.

p. 422 'read a little . . .', 'Cohn', 29 September 1940.

p. 422 'as right as . . .' and 'all my books . . .', 'Huebsch', 24 August 1944.

p. 422 'unbearable it is . . .', 22 December 1943.

p. 422 'we ought not . . .', 17 May 1940.

p. 423 'Frida more or . . .', 'Black Papers', 17 August 1942.

p. 423 'electrified me' and 'brought me alive . . .', 'Eastwood–Hull', n.d. 1974.

p. 424 'Neville, "the great . . ."', 'Harold–Frida', n.d. 1944.

p. 424 'The KC's daughter . . .', 4 January 1937.

p. 424 'the happy refusal . . .', 'Harold–Frida', 24 October 1941.

p. 424 'a grand person . . .', 24 November 1941.

p. 424 'I know how . . .', Gilbert, *Winston S. Churchill*, V, 859, 31 October 1941.

p. 425 'anybody who knows . . .', *The Times*, 9 August 1941.

p. 425 'Hasn't the Laski . . .', I. Berlin, interview.

p. 425 'You are, I . . .', N. MacKenzie, interview.

p. 426 'most mischievous, misleading . . .', House of Commons debate, 14 December 1943, p. 1503.

p. 426 'British Communists Help . . .', 15 February 1941.

p. 427 'commanding', et al., *Tribune*, 12 July 1940.

p. 428 'The full weight . . .', 10 June 1940.

p. 429 'the degree to . . .', 'Frankfurter', 4 August 1938.

p. 429 'turned to the . . .', 'FDR', 5 January 1939.

p. 429 'the reviews have . . .', 'Laski–Hull', 20 August 1940.

p. 429 'While it is . . .', ibid., 21 August 1940.

p. 430 'you were quite . . .', *New York Times*, 19 August 1970.

p. 430 'I'm willing to . . .', et al., 10 November 1940.

p. 431 'a completely devout . . .' and 'he could not . . .', 'Laski File', US Department of Justice, Federal Bureau of Investigation, 25 November 1945.

p. 431 'Mr Kennedy specifically . . .', 19 May 1946.

p. 432 'nonsense which seeks . . .', cited in Burridge, *British Labour and Hitler's War*, p. 180.

p. 433 'leaving unchanged the . . .', 21 June 1940.

p. 433 'is going to . . .' and 'understand that the . . .', *Tribune*, 14 June 1940.

p. 433 'in the very . . .' and 'aroused vast hopes . . .', ibid., 18 October 1940.

p. 433 'Revolution by Consent', et al., 22 March 1941.

p. 434 'Stafford finds me . . .', 13 September 1942.

p. 435 'the greatest war . . .', et al., *New Statesman*, 31 May 1940, 29 November 1941.

p. 435 'Everything for the . . .', A. J. P. Taylor, *English History*, p. 566.

p. 436 'everyone knows quite . . .', et al., *Speeches of Winston Churchill*, p. 6363.

p. 436 'hold the elements . . .' and 'to lead the . . .', cited in Burridge, 'A Postscript to Potsdam', p. 728.

p. 436 'In a free . . .', ibid., p. 729.

p. 436 'traditional Britain' and 'Britain of 3 . . .', *New Statesman*, 23 October 1943.

p. 437 'the men and . . .', *Tribune*, 4 April 1941.

p. 437 'He fights Hitler . . .' and 'one of the . . .', *New Statesman*, 18 December 1943.

p. 437 'the people's war', et al., 11 July 1942, 24 August 1942.

p. 437 'watching the erosion . . .', et al., ibid.

p. 438 'a revolutionary idea . . .', et al., 30 September 1942.

p. 438 'deprecates your paying . . .', 'Laski–Hull', 18 July 1942.

p. 438 'criticized particulars in . . .', 'Winant Papers', 17 July 1942.

p. 438 'the corroding influence . . .' and 'An academic Cassandra . . .', 16 August 1942.

p. 438 'a considerable nuisance', et al., 'Hopkins Papers', 13 August 1942.

p. 439 'Attlee hasn't an . . .', 'Cohn', 12 April 1940.

p. 439 'it was very . . .', cited in Miliband, *Parliamentary Socialism*, p. 275.

p. 439 'frontal attack with . . .', 'Laski–Hull', 29 January 1941.

p. 439 'you wish to . . .', ibid., 1 April 1941.

p. 439 'an over-emphasis on . . .' and 'written for the . . .', 'Attlee Papers', Attlee to J. Chamberlain, 2 December 1941.

p. 440 'the drive and . . .', Young (ed.), *The Diaries of Sir Robert Bruce Lockhart*, II, p. 560.

p. 440 'nature meant for . . .', 'Frankfurter', 19 April 1941.

p. 440 'easily the most . . .', 'Huebsch', 17 August 1941.

p. 440 'fighting leader', et al., Bullock, *Ernest Bevin*, II, p. 187.

p. 440 'unions which regard . . .', 30 November 1942.

p. 440 'poor little Attlee', et al., II, p. 413.

p. 440 'What a little . . .', II, p. 538.

p. 441 'goes away with . . .', *Diary*, II, p. 74.

p. 441 'I find this . . .', ibid., II, p. 545.

p. 441 'A long screen . . .' and 'much too long . . .', ibid. II, pp. 286, 359.

p. 441 'getting too much . . .', ibid., IV, p. 236.

p. 442 'Not one of . . .' and 'Herbert M is . . .', 2 June 1941.

p. 442 'no one could . . .', 'Berdahl Papers', 3 August 1941.

p. 442 'Open letter to . . .', 21 October 1940.

p. 442 'for the purpose . . .', cited in Burridge, British Labour, p. 54.

p. 442 'he now felt . . .' and 'for the very . . .', NEC Minutes, 5 November 1940.

p. 442 'DON'T KEEP US . . .', 9 May 1941.

p. 442 'puts a profession . . .', et al., 21 March 1942.

p. 442 'show-down', 12 April 1942.

p. 442 'The Labour Party . . .', NEC Minutes, 6 April 1942, pp. 192–4.

p. 443 'try to get . . .', et al., ibid., 9 April 1942, pp. 83–4.

p. 443 'there must be . . .', et al., The Labour Party: Report of the Annual Conference (1942), pp. 110–16.

p. 443 'carpeting of Laski', 12 October 1942.

p. 443 'no one can . . .', Reynolds News, 12 July 1942.

p. 444 'LEADERS ARE PARALYSED', ibid., 9 August 1942.

p. 444 'WHAT LABOUR MUST . . .', ibid., 6 September 1942.

p. 444 'inquest into the . . .', et al., Dalton, Diary, II, pp. 500–1.

p. 444 'his criticism had . . .', et al., NEC Minutes, 28 October 1942, p. 38.

p. 445 'No authority less . . .', et al., 'Lloyd George Papers', 18 December 1942.

p. 445 Labour leaders are . . .', 'Goldstein Papers', n.d.

p. 447 'which constitute an . . .', NEC Minutes, 25 August 1943, p. 486.

p. 447 'litter of committees' and 'was so little . . .', Diary, II, p. 525.

p. 448 'THIS MAN LIBELS . . .', 9 March 1941.

p. 448 'Who are the . . .' and 'for the seclusion . . .', 2 April 1943.

p. 448 'unpatriotic', et al., July 1942.

p. 450 'the voice of . . .', 'Frankfurter', 6 November 1940.

p. 450 'he gives the . . .', Diary, II, p. 149.

p. 451 'I thought Harold's . . .', cited in Lash, From the Diaries of Felix Frankfurter, 26 February 1943, p. 199.

p. 451 'abiding and enveloping . . .', ibid.

p. 451 'He knows not . . .', et al., Freedman, Roosevelt and Frankfurter, p. 697.

p. 452 'I'm told you . . .', 'Winant Papers', 22 April 1943.

p. 452 'men like Frankfurter . . .' and 'the administration would . . .', ibid., 13 May 1943.

p. 452 'winning it in . . .', et al., ibid., 15 May 1943.

p. 452 'Have you thrown . . .', ibid., 30 November 1943.

p. 452 'an evil-minded . . .', ibid., 17 November 1944.

p. 453 'whether I had . . .', et al., Sir Arthur Willert, *Washington and Other Memories*, (Boston, 1972), p. 215.

p. 453 'the international communistic . . .', et al., *Congressional Record*, 24 June 1941, Appendix A 3029–31.

p. 453 'through his students . . .', 'Eastwood–Hull'.

p. 453 'Laski has probably . . .', 24 June 1941, A 3030.

p. 453 'from which her . . .', et al., *New York Daily News*, 26 October 1942.

p. 454 'how deeply appreciative . . .', 'FDR', 31 December 1942.

p. 454 'the pipelines through . . .', et al., *Congressional Record*, p. 2820.

p. 454 'the real animus . . .', Lash, *From the Diaries of Felix Frankfurter*, p. 237.

p. 455 'that I am . . .', 21 March 1942.

p. 455 'when one has . . .', et al., 12 December 1943.

p. 455 'the basic assumption . . .', 6 March 1944.

p. 456 'the constant attacks . . .', et al., BBC Archives, 'Laski Talks File', 18 January 1942, 23 May 1941, 26 July 1940, 12 July 1940, 17 May 1944.

p. 457 'During the years . . .', ibid., 14 July 1944.

p. 457 'Laski fascinated Murrow . . .', Sperber, *Murrow*, p. 275.

p. 457 'would be willing . . .', Persico, *Edward R. Murrow*, p. 202.

p. 458 'Mr Laski is . . .', et al., *Foreign Office Records*, FO 371 Series, Folio 33, 21 March 1941.

p. 458 'relatively insignificant', et al., ibid., 19 March 1941, 3 April 1941, 20 April 1941.

p. 458 'gloomy and mean . . .', et al., ibid., 18 August 1942, 12 January 1944.

p. 459 'rather wild stories', 'sob stuff' and 'Jewish technique of . . .', Kushner, *The Persistence of Prejudice*, p. 158.

p. 459 'bestial policy of . . .', quoted in ibid., p. 159.

p. 459 'I now know . . .', 'Cohen Papers', Laski to Cohen, 8 September 1945.

p. 459 'The obligation [one] . . .', *New Statesman*, 13 February 1943.

p. 459 'to the Jewish . . .', 'Goldstein Papers'.

p. 460 'very intimately', Gilbert, *Winston Churchill*, VII, p. 972.

p. 460 'If there were . . .', 'token entry of . . .' and 'from our point . . .', Cesarani (ed.), *The Making of Modern Anglo-Jewry*, p. 205.

p. 460 'I am not . . .', Gorny, *The British Labour Movement and Zionism*, p. 175.

p. 460 'that among my . . .', cited in B. Wassersten, *Britain and the Jews of Europe 1939–1945* (London, 1979), p. 33.

p. 461 'socialism makes the . . .', *Left News*, August 1938.

p. 461 'professional man, lawyer . . .', et al., 13 February 1943.

p. 461 'the behaviour of . . .', et al., 27 February 1943.

p. 462 'expressing horror and . . .', et al., *The Labour Party: Report of the Annual Conference* (1943), p. 188.

p. 462 'awakened a Jewish . . .', and 'I am Jewish . . .', Mapei Archives, 11/43, 23 April 1943.

p. 462 'an adaptation of . . .', et al., 9 October 1943.

p. 463 'the government of . . .', 'Winant Papers', 8 October 1943.

p. 463 'Many thanks for . . .', ibid., 4 November 1943.

p. 464 'I have watched . . .', 'LSE File', 25 September 1943.

p. 464 'was going too . . .', Martin, *Harold Laski*, p. 129.

p. 464 'a patch of . . .', 'Harold–Frida', 14 October 1942.

p. 464 'last time he . . .', Lord McGregor interview.

p. 464 'rather tired, but . . .', 27 March 1943.

p. 464 'It is months . . .', 8 November 1943.

p. 464 'despite the medical . . .', Martin, *Harold Laski*, p. 128.

p. 464 'I am much . . .', 26 December 1943.

p. 464 'I am pretty . . .', 2 January 1944.

p. 466 'banished the twin . . .', *Daily Herald*, 6 November 1942.

p. 466 'heroic Soviet resistance' and 'scientific humanism', N. MacKenzie (ed.), *Letters*, III, pp. 452, 458.

p. 466 'if Hitler invaded . . .', A. J. P. Taylor, *English History*, p. 528.

p. 466 'while unable to . . .', *NEC Minutes*, 18 May 1943, p. 123.

p. 467 'a resolve to . . .', *Left News*, January 1943.

p. 467 'that the visit . . .', Foreign Office Files, Series 43325, Northern 1944, Folio 52, 10 July 1944.

p. 468 'right proud' and 'It has freed . . .', Sperber, *Murrow*, p. 227.

p. 469 'scintillating book', 18 September 1943.

p. 469 'Read Harold Laski's . . .', David Dilks (ed.), *The Diaries of Sir Alexander Cadogan* (New York, 1972), p. 565.

p. 470 'beloved teacher and . . .', et al., 16 October 1943.

p. 470 'a socialist by . . .', et al., 10 October 1943.

p. 471 'purges, liquidations, the . . .', Crick, *George Orwell*, p. 463.

p. 471 'In this case . . .', Fischer, *The Great Challenge*, p. 209.

p. 471 'if the Labour . . .', Jeffreys (ed.), *Labour and the Wartime Coalition*, p. 166.

p. 471 'deplorably ill-timed', II, p. 579.

p. 471 'I like it', 'Harold–Frida', 22 November 1944.

p. 472 'there is hardly . . .', 2 September 1943.

p. 472 'suffers from an . . .' and 'Laski was not . . .', *Diary*, II, pp. 732, 762.

p. 472 'what the Laskis . . .', et al., *Daily Herald*, 2 September 1943.

p. 473 'Friends, what has . . .', Bullock, *Ernest Bevin*, II, p. 308.

p. 473 'A WORD TO . . .', et al., 5 May 1944.

p. 473 'We have to . . .', et al., 'Laski–Hull', 1 May 1944.

p. 474 'to let Jews . . .', *The Labour Party: Report of the Annual Conference* (1944), p. 9.

p. 475 'the granting of . . .' and 'with a view . . .', ibid., pp. 185–9.

p. 475 'a bit too . . .', *Diary*, II, p. 815.

p. 475 'absolutely orderly and . . .', *The Labour Party: Report of the Annual Conference* (1944), pp. 189–90.

p. 475 'in order that . . .', et al., ibid., pp. 143, 146.

p. 476 'though they don't . . .', II, 823.

p. 476 'lost in bewilderment' and 'it rather keenly . . .', 'Harold–Frida', 19 January 1945, 24 February 1945.

p. 476 'it was a . . .', 14 April 1945.

p. 476 'like a prodigal . . .', et al., *Jewish Chronicle*, 12 May 1945.

p. 477 'Your Chairman today . . .', *The Labour Party: Report of the Annual Conference* (1944), p. 110.

p. 479 'aged ten years . . .', *Hugo Black Papers*, 10 May 1945.

p. 479 'in much better . . .', 'Lerner', 7 June 1945.

p. 479 'After six years . . .', 'Berdahl Papers', 4 October 1945.

p. 479 'Anything less like . . .', January 1945.

p. 480 'to elect a . . .', 24 February 1945.

p. 480 'just an intellectual', Donoughue and Jones, *Herbert Morrison*, p. 340.

p. 480 'to leave matters . . .', *Labour and the Wartime Coalition*, p. 220.

p. 480 'This is a . . .', 'Laski Papers', Labour Party, LP/LAS/38/21.

p. 481 'Dear Laski, thank . . .', 'Laski–Hull', 29 May 1945.

p. 481 'pernicious nonsense', *The Times*, 5 June 1945, *Economist*, 9 June 1945.

p. 482 'outrage the implied . . .', Eastwood, *Harold Laski*, p. 130.

p. 482 'to impose upon . . .' and 'I cannot believe . . .', Fienburgh (ed.), *25 Momentous Years*, pp. 155–6.

p. 482 'Did you write . . .', et al., *Daily Herald*.

p. 483 'an opportunity for . . .', Harris, *Attlee*, p. 127.

p. 483 'I assume you . . .', 'Laski Papers', Labour Party, LP/LAS/38/30.

p. 484 'OBSCURE LASKI CAUCAS . . .', et al., 16 June 1945.

p. 484 'silly little intervention', *Diary*, I, 357.

p. 484 'there seems to . . .' and 'power to challenge . . .', H. Pelling, *The Labour Government*, p. 25.

p. 484 'everything has now . . .', Eastwood, *Harold Laski*, p. 128.

p. 484 'A new figure . . .', 21 June 1945.

p. 485 'the new position . . .', et al., Eastwood, *Harold Laski*, p. 128.

p. 485 'SOCIALISTS SPLIT: ATTLEE . . .', 23 June 1945.

p. 485 'THIS MAN LASKI . . .', et al., 25 June 1945.

p. 485 'Laski-ism', et al., 23 June 1945.

p. 486 'Goody, goody, but . . .', Martin, *Harold Laski*, p. 163.

p. 486 'in fact the . . .', *The Times*, 21 June 1945.

p. 487 'we shall have . . .' and 'great changes were . . .', *Daily Herald*, 21 June 1945.

p. 487 'how far he . . .', *Political Adventure: The Memoirs of the Earl of Kilmuir* (London, 1964), p. 84.

p. 487 'bland bombshell', 21 June 1945.

p. 487 'in his heart . . .', 21 June 1945.

p. 487 'I'll bet you . . .', *The Times*, 5 July 1945.

p. 487 'an atmosphere of . . .', *Daily Mail*, 21 June 1945.

p. 487 'A further fuss . . .', I, 357.

p. 488 'Tory attempts to . . .', et al., *News Chronicle*, 21 June 1945.

p. 488 'the titular socialist . . .', *New York Times*, 3 July 1945.

p. 488 'SHALL THE LASKI . . .', 4 July 1945.

p. 488 'recklessly exploited the . . .', 5 July 1945.

p. 488 'Laski bogey' and 'There is a . . .', 4 July 1945.

p. 488 'the Himmler of . . .', et al., *The Times*, 5 July 1945.

p. 489 'If you're invited . . .', Bullock, *Ernest Bevin*, II, 392.

p. 490 'the votes of . . .', *The Age of Austerity*, p. 19.

p. 490 'May I, as . . .', *The Times*, 27 July 1945.

p. 490 'I have often . . .', et al., Williams (ed.), *Twilight of Empire*, p. 7.

p. 491 'that Laski was . . .', et al., p. 477.

p. 491 'On Being Suddenly . . .', 14 July 1945.

p. 491 ''Ullo, oogly! 'Ow . . .', Rowse, *Memories and Glimpses*, p. 314.

p. 492 'as a figure . . .', Martin, *Harold Laski*, p. 174.

p. 492 'squeezing Spain', *New York Times*, 5 September 1945.

p. 492 'the almost daily . . .', et al., *The Times*, 17 August 1945.

p. 493 'What precisely . . .', et al., House of Commons, 16 August 1945.

p. 493 'I think he . . .', *Daily Telegraph*, 17 August 1945.

p. 493 'The constant flow . . .', 'Laski–Hull;, 20 August 1945.

p. 494 'accept your friends . . .', Pelling, *The Labour Governments*, p. 47.

p. 494 'possessing an admirable . . .' and 'his duty as . . .', *Daily Herald*, 29 October 1945.

p. 494 'to raise any . . .', 'Laski–Hull', 23 January 1946.

p. 494 'I, and heaven . . .', 20 October 1945.

p. 495 'has necessarily increased . . .', Anstey, 'The Projection of British Socialism', p. 418.

p. 495 'For the average . . .', *New Statesman*, 9 February 1946.

p. 496 'CLEMENT ATTLEE MADE . . .', 31 July 1945.

p. 496 'We Beg Him . . .', et al., 18 May 1946.

p. 496 'Britain's controversial Red . . .', 19 August 1946.

p. 497 'BRITAIN NOT RUN . . .', 9 August 1945.

p. 497 'big business in . . .', et al., 6 December 1945.

p. 497 'since the Labourites . . .', 24 September 1945.

p. 498 'the Chairman of . . .', 6 December 1945.

p. 498 'need not fear . . .', Anstey, 'The Projection of British Socialism', p. 429.

p. 498 'the Laskis will . . .', ibid.

p. 498 'we are revolutionists', et al., *Daily Herald*, 2 August 1945.

p. 498 'the age of . . .', *New York Times*, 11 September 1945.

p. 498 in a purely . . .', et al., ibid., 25 September 1945.

p. 498 'has all the . . .', 3 October 1945.

p. 499 'typical communistic smear', 27 September 1945.

p. 499 'that makes it . . .', *New York Times*, 28 September 1945.

p. 499 'this non-American . . .', ibid., 9 October 1945.

p. 499 'malicious attacks upon . . .', ibid., 13 October 1945.

p. 499 'from Jews as . . .', ibid., 7 November 1945.

p. 499 'red meeting which . . .', ibid., 2 October 1945.

p. 499 'communism as a . . .', ibid., 11 January 1945.

p. 500 'an international trouble-maker', *Daily Mail*, 23 November 1945.

p. 500 'Professor Laski would . . .', Foreign Office, FO 371, North American Papers, 13 November 1945.

p. 500 'the visit would . . .', ibid., Telegram No. 7559.

p. 500 'the busy little . . .', 20 October 1945.

p. 500 'public enemy No. . . .', 'Berdahl Papers', 4 October 1945.

p. 500 'Make arrangements for . . .', Foreign Office, Folio 10–14.

p. 501 'Hands off Catholic . . .', et al., *New York Times*, 4 December 1945.

p. 501 'firebrand' and 'goading and exasperating . . .', *Not Too Correct an Aureole: The Reflections of a Diplomat* (London, 1983), pp. 111–13.

p. 501 'anarchy of free . . .', et al., *New York Times*, 4 December 1945.

p. 501 'red troublemakers', et al., *Congressional Record*, p. 11476, 5 December 1945.

p. 502 'unless the British . . .', *Daily Telegraph*, 8 December 1945.

p. 502 'the darling of . . .', et al., *New York Times*, 9 December 1945.

p. 502 'an international problem', et al., *The Times*, 9 February 1946.

p. 503 'compel the submission . . .', ibid., 11 February 1946.

p. 503 'It was an . . .', *Daily Herald*, 22 April 1946.

p. 503 'he could not . . .', *The Times*, 24 April 1946.

p. 503 'a big lie,' 23 April 1946.

p. 503 'Mr Laski knows . . .', ibid.

p. 503 'Wall Street pressure . . .', 16 March 1946.

p. 504 'professors in bourgeois . . .', et al., Martin, *Harold Laski*, p. 185.

p. 504 'Clem thanked me . . .', 'Harold–Frida', 23 April 1946.

p. 505 'to admit a . . .', *Reynolds News*, 2 June 1946.

p. 505 'It is well . . .', 24 April 1946.

p. 505   'turned the little . . .' and 'My Lady Bountiful . . .', *Hertford and Essex Observer*, 8 June 1946.

p. 506   'no sense of . . .', 'Eastwood–Hull', 15 September 1945.

p. 506   'that mean and ungenerous' and 'I do not . . .', *The Labour Party: Report of the Annual Conference* (1946), p. 105.

p. 507   'the swiftness of . . .', *News Chronicle*, 16 June 1946.

p. 507   'the devoted attention . . .', *The Labour Party: Report of the Annual Conference* (1946), p. 213.

p. 507   'the more roundabout . . .', et al., 'Laski Papers', Labour Party, LP/LAS/38/97.

p. 508   'Mr Laski, for . . .', Rosenfield, *Portrait of A Philosopher*, p. 382.

p. 508   'getting drunk out . . .', authors' correspondence.

p. 508   'That evening's neatest . . .', et al., *Daily Telegraph*, 20 January 1953.

p. 508   'My Impressions of . . .', et al., 14 October 1946.

p. 508   'I know, further . . .', 7 October 1946.

p. 509   'she makes me . . .', 'Harold–Frida', 12 September 1946.

p. 510   'speed, spending, excitement . . .', et al., ibid., 27 August, 8 September, 14 September, 12 September, 2 October, 9 September, 8 September 1946.

p. 511   'bloodless revolution by . . .', *Chicago Tribune*, 20 February 1944.

p. 512   'to understand that . . .', 18 September 1946.

p. 512   'there is no . . .', et al., 'Goldstein Papers', 17 September 1946.

p. 514   'new economics for . . .', *New York Times*, 6 October 1946.

p. 514   'my great news . . .', 'Huebsch', 17 March 1946.

p. 514   'So long as . . .', *New York Times*, 12 October 1946.

p. 515   'a kind word . . .' and 'both the Jews . . .', *Diary*, I, 388.

p. 516   'either as a . . .', *Memoirs*, II, 465.

p. 517   'the Beaverbrook Chair . . .', Miliband interview.

p. 517   'was the most . . .', 'Harold–Frida', 17 June 1928.

p. 518   'it was quite . . .', and all other trial excerpts, *The Laski Libel Action, Verbatim Report* (London, *Daily Express*, 1946).

p. 527   'punch-drunk', N. MacKenzie interview.

p. 527   'he retired extremely . . .', Smith, *Lord Goddard*, p. 182.

p. 528   'You are then . . .', *Atlantic Monthly*, November 1952.

p. 534   'You have to . . .', ibid.

p. 539   'courage will inspire . . .', 'Laski Libel Trial Papers', *Newark Advertiser*, 9 December 1946.

p. 540   'he bore up . . .', 'Cohn', 4 December 1946.

p. 540   'it broke his . . .', BBC, 1962.

p. 540   'declared a liar', *LSE Personnel File*, Laski to Carr-Saunders, 2 December 1946.

p. 540 'incapable of appreciating . . .', 'Holmes', p. 625.

p. 540 'my own philosophy . . .', 7 June 1947.

p. 540 'public entertainment', 'a regicide about . . .' and 'The intellectual was . . .', 'My Day in Court', *Atlantic Monthly* (November, 1952).

p. 540 'Very few people . . .', Patrick Hastings, *Cases in Court*, p. 55.

p. 541 'always had the . . .', 16 May 1953.

p. 541 'at the end . . .', 'Frankfurter', 8 December 1946.

p. 541 'about fifty virulently . . .', authors' correspondence from Mikardo.

p. 541 'to comfort', 4 December 1946.

p. 541 'how big a . . .' 'Lerner', n.d. 1947.

p. 542 'If I tried . . .', 'Harold–Frida', 24 December 1946.

p. 543 'a Polish Jew . . .', et al., Smith, *Lord Goddard*, pp. 172–8.

p. 543 'Laski got most . . .', authors' interview.

p. 543 'your brother was' and 'The reason I . . .', 12 June 1971.

p. 544 'a dark cave' and 'I was not . . .', 11 May 1947.

p. 544 '*annus horrendus*', Beer, *British Politics in the Collectivist Age*, p. 192.

p. 544 'America wants bases . . .', 18 February 1947.

p. 545 'This is merely . . .', Dalton, *Memoirs*, III, p. 267, 30 August 1947.

p. 546 'the rising star . . .' and 'has over-written . . .', Young, *The Diaries of Sir Bruce Lockhart*, II, 567.

p. 546 'socialist economics mean . . .', *The Labour Party: Report of the Annual Conference* (1947), p. 138.

p. 547 'been to Eton . . .', et al., ibid., p. 179.

p. 547 'dapper Harold Laski . . .', *Sunday Pictorial*, 1 June 1947.

p. 548 'You cannot recklessly . . .', *Chester Chronicle*, 24 September 1947.

p. 548 'a crisis of . . .', et al., *Kentish Express*, 28 February 1947.

p. 548 'to build a . . .', et al., *Daily Herald*, 5 March 1947.

p. 549 'did not say . . .', Schneer, *Labour's Conscience*, p. 124.

p. 549 'to recruit the . . .', *The Labour Party: Report of the Annual Conference* (1947), p. 112.

p. 549 'naturally, as myself . . .', *The Labour Party: Report of the Annual Conference* (1948), p. 182.

p. 550 'man is a . . .' and 'we are trying . . .', *The Road to Recovery* (London, 1948), pp. 49–50.

p. 551 'must be considered . . .', George, *Krishna Menon*, p. 126.

p. 551 'Indian freedom is . . .', *The Times*, 15 November 1945.

p. 551 'mean and shameful' and 'with victims of . . .', *The Dilemma of Our Times*, p. 222.

p. 552 'I am not . . .', 'Lerner', 16 August 1948.

p. 552 'quite definitely anti-Semitic . . .', 11 May 1947.

p. 552 'prejudiced against Jews . . .', *The Memoirs of Lord Gladwyn* (London, 1972), p. 176.

p. 552 'tended to visualize . . .', M. Edelman, *Ben-Gurion: A Political Biography* (London, 1964), p. 33.

p. 552 'story circulating that . . .', *Labour and the Wartime Coalition*, p. 193.

p. 552 'Bevin will be . . .', 'Frankfurter', 6 June 1945.

p. 553 'at the head . . .', Harris, *Attlee*, p. 391.

p. 553 'What was happening . . .', NEC Minutes, International Sub-Committee, 5 October 1945.

p. 553 'the Attlee–Bevin . . .', 6 October 1945.

p. 553 'great success', Bullock, *Ernest Bevin*, III, 180.

p. 553 'immediate relief to . . .', 15 November 1945.

p. 553 'Note on the . . .', et al., 'Goldstein Papers'.

p. 554 'was proposed with . . .', *The Labour Party: Report of the Annual Conference* (1946), p. 166.

p. 555 'shalom aleichem' and 'I wish to . . .', S. U. Nahun, *The 1,000 Immigrants Detained at La Spezia in 1946: Two Reports to the Zionist Executives* (Jerusalem, 1972), p. 20.

p. 556 'The Arabs have . . .' and 'The Jews have . . .', *Bath Chronicle and Herald*, 5 July 1946.

p. 557 'In international affairs . . .' and 'largely financed from . . .', House of Commons, 25 February 1947.

p. 557 'selling the Jews . . .', et al., *Nation*, 29 March 1947.

p. 557 'bound to be . . .', *Manchester Guardian*, 22 December 1947.

p. 557 'an outrageous blot . . .', et al., *Jewish Chronicle*, 18 April 1947.

p. 557 'reactionary feudal Arab . . .' and 'the breaking by . . .', 10 October 1947.

p. 558 'unscrupulous American Zionists', 15 October 1947.

p. 558 'one of the . . .' et al., *New York Times*, 1 April 1940.

p. 558 'so completely in . . .', 7 May 1948.

p. 558 'spirit which does . . .', 'Léon Blum Papers', 8 August 1948.

p. 559 'the British government . . .', 5 June 1948.

p. 559 'the question is . . .', et al., 11 June 1948.

p. 559 'Referring to Israel . . .', *Jewish Chronicle*, 24 September 1948.

p. 559 'satisfy one of . . .', ibid., 20 March 1950.

p. 560 'poisoned by anti-communist . . .', 'Frankfurter', 27 September 1947.

p. 560 'communist blindness', et al., ibid., 11 May 1947.

p. 560 'neighbours friendly to . . .' and 'has been doing . . .', ibid., 11 September 1947.

p. 560 far more generous . . .', et al., ibid., 16 July 1947.

p. 561 'Genuinely baffled at . . .', *Nation*, 15 June 1946.

p. 561 'combined sheer lying . . .' and 'utter and egregious . . .', *Russia and the West*, National Peace Council, 20 November 1947. p. 6.

p. 561 'Why is the . . .' and 'socialists of the . . .', 16 March 1946.

p. 561 'to show that . . .', cited by I. Mikardo, *Tribune*, 31 March 1950.

p. 562 'a threat to . . .', *Age of Austerity*, p. 108.

p. 562 'to regard the . . .' and 'that Great Britain . . .', *Willesden Chronicle*, 23 January 1948.

p. 562 'this great piece . . .' and 'Our domestic life . . .', *Coulsdon and Purley Times*, 30 January 1948.

p. 562 'be the test . . .', 'Frankfurter', 16 July 1947.

p. 562 'might divide Europe . . .', *Glasgow Forward*, 26 July 1947.

p. 563 'DEMOCRACY HAS RISEN . . .', 10 May 1947.

p. 563 'A democratic community . . .', 6 March, 26 March 1948.

p. 564 'these are disquieting . . .' and 'Lionel, don't let's . . .', Eastwood, *Harold Laski*, p. 166.

p. 564 'outlook on life . . .' and 'they had to . . .', Stonehouse, *Death of an Idealist*, p. 83.

p. 564 'I have a . . .', 27 September 1947.

p. 564 'If the statesmen . . .', *Glasgow Forward*, 26 March 1948.

p. 564 'the dangerous spell . . .', 'Morris Cohen's Approach to Legal Philosophy', *University of Chicago Law Review* (1948), p. 578.

p. 566 'Where there is . . .', J. Maritain (ed.), *Human Rights: Comments and Interpretations* (New York, 1949), p. 90.

p. 568 'The Board of . . .', 'Laski Papers', International Institute for Social History, Amsterdam, 16 April 1947.

p. 569 'a colossal mistake . . .', et al., *New York Times*, 23 June 1947.

p. 570 'Sovietism', E. Wilson, *Letters on Literature and Politics*, p. 523.

p. 570 'I suspect that . . .', Persico, *Edward R. Murrow*, p. 331.

p. 570 'Have I done . . .', ibid., 1 September 1948.

p. 570 'heard nothing in . . .', 'Cohn', 30 December 1948.

p. 570 'Have you been . . .', ibid., 7 November 1949.

p. 571 'strength to all . . .', *New Republic*, 20 December 1948.

p. 571 'wise and imaginative', et al., 'Berdahl Papers', 4 October 1945.

p. 571 'the most respected . . .' and 'to find out . . .', *New Republic*, 20 December 1948.

p. 571 'after our own . . .', 'Berdahl Papers', 13 January 1948.

p. 571 'horrible health' and 'bad mood', ibid., 7 March 1949.

p. 572 'great integrity and . . .', *Glasgow Forward*, 22 January 1949.

p. 572 'Laski's presence would . . .', Michael O'Brien, *McCarthy and McCarthyism in Wisconsin* (Columbia, Missouri, 1980), p. 174.

p. 572 'pro-communist, anti-Catholic . . .', *New York Times*, 6 April 1949.

p. 572 'from those who . . .', ibid., 27 April 1949.

p. 573 'As one hears . . .', 9 July 1949.

p. 573 'certainly blasphemy on . . .', *Laski US Department of Justice, Federal Bureau of Investigation File*, 12 July 1949.

p. 573 'obsession with Laski' and 'had no use . . .', Millis (ed.), *The Forrestal Diaries*, p. 80.

p. 573 'to investigate the . . .', et al., Rogow, *James Forrestal*, pp. 146, 148.

p. 575 'You can imagine . . .', 'Lerner', 18 August 1948.

p. 575 'speak my whole . . .' and 'I admit that . . .', 'Cohn', 6 February 1949.

p. 576 'I have had . . .', *New York Times*, 22 March 1949.

p. 576 'no doubt Transport . . .', 21 March 1949.

p. 576 'a rootless cosmopolitan', 24 March 1949.

p. 576 'a little to . . .', 'Huebsch', 23 December 1949.

p. 576 'some of them . . .', *Stockport Express*, 16 February 1950.

p. 576 'for he has . . .', 15 February 1950.

p. 576 'with an enlarged . . .', 6 February 1949.

p. 577 'Isn't this incredible?', 'Cohn', Frida to Cohn, 9 April 1950.

p. 577 'a remarkable gathering . . .', 28 March 1950.

p. 578 'man of outstanding . . .', *New York Times*, 28 March 1950.

p. 578 'the Red Professor', 3 April 1950.

p. 578 'Mr Laski died . . .', quoted in *Spectator*, 31 March 1950.

p. 578 'a sinister personage . . .', et al., 31 March 1950.

p. 578 'Laski, it may . . .', et al., 25 March 1950.

p. 579 'That splendid intellect . . .', 'Laski–Hull'.

p. 580 No one can . . .', 'Why I am a Marxist', p. 51.

p. 580 'with gratitude and . . .', *The Labour Party: Report of the Annual Conference* (1950) p. 86.

p. 580 'really a wonderful . . .', et al., 1 April 1950.

p. 580 'probably influenced political . . .', *New York Times*, 17 May 1950.

p. 582 'distortion, misrepresentation and . . .', et al., 'Frankfurter', 10 January 1952.

p. 582 'and to whom . . .' and 'Laski was a . . .', Persico, *Edward R. Murrow*, p. 390.

p. 583 'who asked nothing . . .', Eastwood, *Harold Laski*, p. 169.

p. 583 'Laski's name and . . .', *Labour People*, p. 91.

p. 583 'like an echo . . .', p. 66.

p. 583 'in closer touch . . .', 'Red don at large', M. Cole in *Books and Bookmen*, February 1978, p. 28.

p. 583 'Attlee could be . . .', p. 230.

p. 584 'looked all his . . .', *Nothing So Strange* (London, 1970), p. 212.

p. 584 'half-man, half-child . . .', 'Frida', pp. 44–5.

p. 585 'something evil', et al., Barbara Branden, *The Passion of Ayn Rand*, p. 139.

p. 585 'greatness was as . . .', *My LSE*, p. 151.

p. 586 'to the immense . . .', Hiss, *Recollections of a Life*, pp. 196–7.

p. 586 'not only an . . .', 'Frida', p. 66.

p. 586 'loved students because . . .', quoted in Martin, *Harold Laski*, pp. 253–4.

p. 586 'if Diana's and . . .', 'Huebsch', 22 December 1943.

p. 587 that it was . . .', *New Statesman*, 14 October 1950.

p. 587 'Mr Churchill has . . .', 12 January 1953.

p. 587 'the tedious utterances . . .', H. Trevor-Roper, *Sunday Times*, 18 January 1953.

p. 587 'most of those . . .' and 'ideal backroom boy', 25 January 1953.

p. 588 'People who talk . . .', cited in Eastwood, *Harold Laski*, p. 170.

p. 588 'for which the . . .', *New York Times*, 24 July 1955.

p. 588 'bogus, phoney and . . .', *The Diaries of A Cabinet Minister*, III, 377.

p. 588 'Marxism of the . . .' and 'liberalism of the . . .', Brailsford, *Reynolds News*, 19 September 1953.

p. 589 'there are few . . .', *New Statesman*, 17 January 1953.

p. 589 'half the leaders . . .' and 'not passionately anti-British . . .', *The Diaries*, III, 377.

p. 589 'the centre of . . .', et al., authors' interview.

p. 589 'there was a . . .', Eastwood, *Harold Laski*, p. 94.

p. 592 'It may be . . .', 'Eastwood–Hull', Folio 6.

p. 592 'he lived a . . .', 'Cohn', 9 April 1950.

Select Bibliography

MANUSCRIPT COLLECTIONS

'Abbot, George – Papers', University of Chicago Library.

'Attlee, C. R. – Papers', Bodleian Library, Oxford.

'Bates, Henry Moore – Papers', University of Michigan Library.

'Becker, Carl – Papers', Cornell University Library.

'Berdahl, Clarence – Papers', University of Illinois Library.

'Black, Hugo – Papers', Library of Congress.

'Blum, Léon – Papers', Bibliothèque National, Paris.

'Brandeis–Laski Correspondence,' University of Louisville Library. (Cited as 'Brandeis'.)

'Chaffee, Zachariah – Papers', Harvard Law School Library.

'Cockerell Papers', The British Museum.

'Cohen, Morris – Papers', University of Chicago Library.

'Cohn, Alfred E. – Papers', Rockefeller Archive Center. (Cited as 'Cohn'.)

'Curti, Merle – Papers', State Historical Society of Wisconsin.

'Eastwood, Granville – Papers', Hull University Library. (Cited as 'Eastwood–Hull'.)

'FDR', see 'Laski Papers', Franklin Delano Roosevelt Library.

'Fisher, H. A. L. – Papers', Bodleian Library, Oxford.

'Frankfurter, Felix – Papers', Library of Congress. (Cited as 'Frankfurter'.)

'Frida', see 'Laski, Frida'.

'Galton, Francis – Papers', University College, London.

'Garber, Howard J. – Papers', Case Western Reserve University Library.

'Goldman, Emma – Papers', University of Michigan Library. (Cited as 'Goldman Papers'.)

'Goldstein, Joseph – Papers', Yale University Law School.

'Haldane, J. B. S. – Papers', National Library of Scotland.

'Hammond, Barbara and J. C. – Papers', Bodleian Library, Oxford.

'Harold–Frida', see 'Laski–Frida Correspondence'.

'Holmes', see Howe (ed.), Holmes–Laski Letters.

'Hopkins, Harry – Papers', Franklin Delano Roosevelt Library, Hyde Park, NY.

'Howe, Mark DeWolfe – Papers', Harvard Law School Library.

'Huebsch–Laski Correspondence', Library of Congress. (Cited as 'Huebsch'.)

'Jones, Arthur Creech – Papers', Rhodes House Library.

'Labardie Collection', University of Michigan Library.

'Lansbury, George – Papers', London School of Economics Library.

'Laski Family Papers', Anglo-Jewish Archives, Mocatta Library, University of Southampton.

'Laski Family Papers', Manchester Jewish Museum.

'Laski, Frida – Autobiography', A. Mathewson Private Papers. (Cited as 'Frida'.)

'Laski Papers', Franklin Delano Roosevelt Library, Hyde Park, NY. (Cited as 'FDR'.)

'Laski Papers', Hull University Library. (Cited as 'Laski–Hull'.)

'Laski Papers', International Institute for Social History, Amsterdam.

'Laski Papers', Labour Party Archives, Walworth Road, London.

'Laski Papers', London School of Economics.

'Laski Papers', Manchester Reference Library.

'Laski Papers', Radcliffe College Archives.

'Laski Papers', St. Hilda's College Library, Oxford.

'Laski Papers', Syracuse University Library.

'Laski–Frida Correspondence', Hull University Library. (Cited as 'Harold–Frida'.)

'Laski–Hull', see 'Laski Papers'.

'Lerner, Max – Papers', Yale University Library. (Cited as 'Lerner'.)

'Lloyd George – Papers', House of Lords Record Office.

'Lowell, A. L. – Papers', Harvard University Archives.

'MacPherson, C. B. – Papers', University of Toronto Library.

'Mander, Linden – Papers', University of Washington Library.

'Martin, Charles E. – Papers', University of Washington Library.

'Middleton, James – Papers', Ruskin College, Oxford.

'Morrison, Samuel Elliot – Papers', Harvard University Archives.

'Murray, Gilbert – Papers', Bodleian Library, Oxford.

'Pearson, Karl – Papers', University College London.

'Pound, Roscoe – Papers', Harvard Law School Library.

'Powell, T. R. – Papers', Harvard Law School Library.

'Rogers, Lindsey – Papers', Columbia University Library.

'Sankey, John – Papers', Bodleian Library, Oxford. (Cited as 'Sankey Papers'.)

'Schaefler Papers', Columbia University Library.

'Sharp, Evelyn – Papers', Bodleian Library, Oxford.

'Simon, John – Papers', Bodleian Library, Oxford.

'Soskice, Frank – Papers', House of Lords, Record Office.

'Straight, Willard – Papers', Cornell University Library.

'The Chosen People', A. Mathewson Private Papers.

'Winant, J. G. – Papers', Franklin Delano Roosevelt Library, Hyde Park, NY.

'Woolf, Leonard – Papers', Sussex University Library.

'Zimmern, Alfred – Papers', Bodleian Library, Oxford.

DOCUMENTS

Fabian Society Documents, Microfilm.

Fulham Borough Committee Records, Fulham Local History Library.

Harold Laski File, McGill University.

Labour Party, National Executive Committee Minutes.

Laski File, BBC Written Archives Centre, Caversham Park.

Laski File, Foreign Office – North American Papers (Political), Public Record Office.

Laski File, Foreign Office – Soviet Union, Public Record Office.

Laski File, Harvard University Archives.

Laski File, US Department of Justice, Federal Bureau of Investigation.

Laski File, US Department of Justice: Immigration and Naturalization Service.

Laski File, US Government Military Intelligence Reports, War Department.

Laski Personnel File, London School of Economics.

Laski Libel Trial File, Newark Advertiser, Newark.

Student Records, Manchester Grammar School.

The Labour Party: Report of the Annual Conference, 1932–1950.

Warden and Tutors Minutes, New College, Oxford, Archives.

NEWSPAPERS

Daily Herald

Daily Mail

Daily Mirror

Daily Telegraph

Daily Worker

Evening Standar

Glasgow Forward

Jewish Chronicle

Manchester Evening News

Manchester Guardian

News Chronicle

New York Times

Reynolds News

The Times

CORRESPONDENCE

H. W. Arndt; Julian Bach; Alice Bacon; Clarence A. Berdahl; Mervin Block; Jay G. Blumler; Max Brasch; Alexander D. Brooks; Trygve Bull; Shulamit Charney; Elizabeth Crittal; James W. Fesler; Lewis C. Feuer; K. Ruben Gabriel; Vittorio Gabrilli; H. Gilbert; Virginia C. Harland; E. M. Holman; D. M. Howard; H. Montgomery Hyde; Alfred Kazin; Gertrude Langsam; Gertrude Lippincott; Melvin Marcus; Kenneth Aloe Marshall; P. A. W. Merriton; Ian Mikardo; Susan Moser; Eileen O'Connell; Michael O'Connell; Richard Pankhurst; Roy Parsons; Joan Philips; Dale Pontius; Charles Regan; Daniel A. Rezneck; Iris Robbins; A. Rosenthal; Elzeke De Saedeeler; Raymond South; Henry W. Spiegel; Ann Susman; Pierre Trudeau; Bernard Wand; Anthony Weale; Rita Wilson; Nochem S. Winnet.

INTERVIEWS

Geoffrey Alderman; Baroness Bacon; Samuel Beer; Tony Benn; Sir Isaiah Berlin; Anne Bohm; Lord Callaghan; Manuel Cansino; Lord Clinton Davis; Maurice Cowling; Bernard Crick; Rufus Davis; Marjorie Durbin; Granville Eastwood; Michael Fidler; Michael Foot; John Kenneth Galbraith; Joseph Goldstein; Stephen Graubard; Herbert Gurbst; Andrew Hacker; Barabara Hag; Joseph Hamburger; Roy Hattersley; Paul Hirst; Graham and Marjorie Hutton; Baroness Jaeger; Lord Jay; Maurice Jones; Helena Kennedy; John Laski; Philip Laski; Max Lerner; Baron Lever; Norman MacKenzie; Andrew Matthewson; Pat Mathewson; Lord G. R. McGregor; Ralph Miliband; Edmund Morgan; Janet Murrow; Klaus Moser; Roger Parlby; Richard Pear; Baroness Philips; Sir Lew Pliatsky; Ben Roberts; Sir Frank Roberts; John Saville; Daniel H. Schwartz; Peter Shore; Lord Soper; Richard Lee Strout; Frank Untermeyer; Lord Wilson.

BOOKS

Abse, Joan (ed.), *My LSE*, London, Robson, 1977.

Addison, Paul, *The Road to 1945*, London, Cape, 1945.

Ahmed, Mesbahuddin, *The British Labour Party and The Indian Independence Movement 1917–1939*, New Delhi, Sterling, 1987.

Akbar, M. J., *Nehru, The Making of India*, New York, Viking, 1988.

Alderman, Geoffrey, *London Jewry and London Politics 1889–1986*, London Routledge, 1989.

Alexander, Samuel, *Philosophical and Literary Pieces*, London, Macmillan, 1939.

Anderson, Perry and Blackburn, Robin (eds.), *Towards Socialism*, Ithaca, Cornell University Press, 1965.

Armytage, W. H. G., *Sir Richard Gregory, His Life and Work*, London, Macmillan, 1957.

Attlee, C. R., *As It Happened*, New York, Viking, 1954.

Ayling, S. E., *Portraits of Power*, London, Harrap, 1963.

Baker, Leonard, *Brandeis and Frankfurter: A Dual Biography*, New York, Harper and Row, 1984.

Barker, Ernest, *Age and Youth*, Oxford, Oxford University Press, 1953.

Barker, Ernest, *Political Thought in England, From Herbert Spencer to the Present Day*, New York, Henry Holt, n.d.

Barker, Rodney, *Political Ideas in Modern Britain*, London, Methuen, 1978.

Bassett, R., *The Essentials of Parliamentary Democracy*, London, Macmillan, 1935.

Bassett, R., *Nineteen Thirty-One: Political Crisis*, London, Macmillan, 1958.

Bealey, Frank, *The Social and Political Thought of the British Labour Party*, London, Weidenfeld and Nicolson, 1970.

Beer, Samuel H., *British Politics in the Collectivist Age*, New York, Knopf, 1965.

Belloc, Hilaire, *The House of Commons and Monarchy*, London, Allen and Unwin, 1920.

Benn, Tony, *Arguments for Socialism*, London, Jonathan Cape, 1979.

Benn, Tony (ed.), *Writings on the Wall, A Radical and Socialist Anthology 1215–1984*, London, Faber and Faber, 1984.

Benson, John, *The Working Class in Britain, 1850–1939*, London, Longman, 1989.

Bermant, Chaim, *The Cousinhood: The Anglo-Jewish Gentry*, London, Eyre and Spottiswoode, 1971.

Beveridge, William, *The London School of Economics and Its Problems 1919–1937*, London, Allen and Unwin, 1960.

Binkley, W. E., *The Powers of the President*, New York, Doubleday, 1937.

Blake, Robert, *The Conservative Party from Peel to Churchill*, New York, St Martin's, 1970.

Blunden, Margaret, *The Countess of Warwick*, London, Cassell, 1967.

Blythe, Ronald, *The Age of Illusion, Some Glimpses of Britain Between the Wars, 1919–1940*, Oxford, Oxford University Press, 1983.

Boardman, Harry, *The Glory of Parliament*, London, Allen and Unwin, 1960.

Briggs, Asa and Saville, John (eds.), *Essays in Labour History, 1918–1937*, London, Croom Helm, 1977.

Brittain, Vera, *Testament of Experience*, London, Gollancz, 1957.

Brown, Kenneth D., *The English Labour Movement, 1700–1951*, New York, St Martin's, 1982.

Bullock, Alan, *The Life and Times of Ernest Bevin*, 3 Vols., London, Heinemann, 1960–1983.

Burns, C. Delisle, *The Philosophy of Labour*, New York, Oxford University Press, 1925.

Burridge, T. D., *British Labour and Hitler's War*, London, André Deutsch, 1976.

Burridge, Trevor, *Clement Attlee: A Political Biography*, London, Jonathan Cape, 1985.

Butler, David (ed.), *Coalitions in British Politics*, London, Macmillan, 1978.

Callaghan, John, *Socialism in Britain since 1884*, Oxford, Blackwell, 1990.

Carlson, John Roy, *The Plotters*, New York, E. P. Dutton, 1946.

Catlin, George, *For God's Sake, Go! An Autobiography*, Gerrards Cross, Colin Smythe, 1972.

Catlin, John, *Family Quartet*, London, Hamish Hamilton, 1987.

Caute, David, *The Fellow-Travellers*, New Haven, Yale University Press, 1988.

Cecil, Hugh, *Conservatism*, London, Thornton Butterworth, 1928.

Cesarani, David, *The Making of Modern Anglo-Jewry*, Oxford, Blackwell, 1990.

Chaplin, Charles, *My Autobiography*, New York, Simon and Schuster, 1964.

Churchill, Randolph S., *Winston Churchill: Vol. II, Young Statesman*, Boston, Houghton, Mifflin and Co., 1967.

Citrine, Walter, *Men and Work: An Autobiography*, London, Hutchinson, 1964.

Clark, Ronald W., *JBS: The Life and Work of J. B. S. Haldane*, New York, Coward-McCann, 1969.

Clarke, Peter, *Liberals and Social Democrats*, Cambridge, Cambridge University Press, 1978.

Cohen, Michael, J., *Palestine and the Great Powers, 1945–1948*, Princeton, Princeton University Press, 1982.

Cohen, Morris Raphael, *A Dreamer's Journey, The Autobiography of M. R. Cohen*, Boston, Beacon Press, 1949.

Cohen, Stuart, A., *English Zionists and British Jews*, Princeton, Princeton University Press, 1982.

Cohn, Alfred E., *Minerva's Progress, Tradition and Dissent in American Culture*, New York, Harcourt, Brace, 1946.

Cohn, Alfred E., *No Retreat From Reason and Other Essays*, New York, Harcourt Brace, 1931.

Cole, Margaret, *The Life of G. D. H. Cole*, London, Macmillan, 1971.

Cole, Margaret, *The Story of Fabian Socialism*, London, Heinemann, 1961.

Cole, Margaret (ed.), *The Webbs and Their Work*, London, F. Muller, 1949.

Cook, Fred J., *The Nightmare Decade, The Life and Times of Senator Joe McCarthy*, New York, Random House, 1971.

Cooke, Colin, *The Life of Richard Stafford Cripps*, London, Hodder and Stoughton, 1957.

Cootes, R. J., *The General Strike 1926*, Harlow, Longman, 1983.

Corrigan, D. Felicitas, *Siegfried Sassoon: Poet's Pilgrimage*, London, Gollancz, 1973.

Cosgrove, Richard A., *Our Lady the Common Law: An Anglo-American Legal Community 1870–1930*, New York, New York University Press, 1990.

Crick, Bernard, *George Orwell: A Life*, Harmondsworth, Penguin Books, 1980.

Cronin, James E., *Labour and Society in Britain, 1918–1979*, New York, Schocken, 1984.

Crosland, C. A. R., *The Future of Socialism*, London, Jonathan Cape, 1956.

Crossman, R. H. S., *The Charm of Politics and Other Essays in Political Criticism*, New York, Harper and Brothers, 1958.

Crossman, R. H. S., *The Diaries of a Cabinet Minister*, London, Hamish Hamilton and Jonathan Cape, 1977.

Crowther, Anne, *British Social Policy 1914–1939*, London, Macmillan, 1988.

Dahl, Robert A., *Democracy, Liberty, and Equality*, Oslo, Norwegian University Press, 1986.

Dalton, Hugh, *Call Back Yesterday, Memoirs 1887–1931*, London, F. Muller, 1953.

Dalton, Hugh, *The Fateful Years, Memoirs 1931–1935*, London, F. Muller, 1957.

Dalton, Hugh, *High Tide and After, Memoirs 1945–1960*, London, F. Muller, 1962.

Dawson, Nelson L., *Louis D. Brandeis, Felix Frankfurter, and the New Deal*, Hamden, Conn., Archon Books, 1980.

Deane, Herbert A., *The Political Ideas of Harold J. Laski*, New York, Columbia University Press, 1955.

Dennis, Norman and Halsey, A. H., *English Ethical Socialism, Thomas More to R. H. Tawney*, Oxford, Clarendon, 1988.

Diggins, John P., *The American Left in the Twentieth Century*, New York, Harcourt Brace, 1973.

Donoughue, Bernard and Jones, G. W., *Herbert Morrison, Portrait of a Politician*, London, Weidenfeld and Nicolson, 1973.

Du Cann, Richard, *The Art of the Advocate*, Harmondsworth, Penguin Books, 1986.

Dunne, Geralt T., *Hugo Black and the Judicial Revolution*, New York, Simon and Schuster, 1977.

Durbin, E. F. M., *The Politics of Democratic Socialism*, London, Routledge, 1940.

Durbin, Elizabeth, *New Jerusalem: The Labour Party and the Economics of Democratic Socialism*, London, Routledge, 1985.

Eastwood, Granville, *Harold Laski*, London, Mowbrays, 1977.

Edwards, Ruth Dudley, *Victor Gollancz, A Biography*, London, Gollancz, 1987.

Elliott, William Yandell, *The Need for Constitutional Reforms*, New York, McGraw Hill, 1935.

Elliott, William Yandell, *The Pragmatic Revolt in Politics*, New York, Howard Fertig, 1968.

Estorick, Eric, *Stafford Cripps: Prophetic Rebel*, New York, John Day, 1941.

Fels, Mary, *Joseph Fels: His Life-Work*, New York, B. W. Huebsch, 1916.

Feuchtwanger, E. J., *Democracy and Empire, Britain 1865–1914*, London, Edward Arnold, 1984.

Fienburgh, Wilfred (ed.), *25 Momentous Years: A 25th Anniversary in the History of the Daily Herald*, London, Odhams, 1955.

Fischer, Louis, *The Great Challenge*, New York, Duell, Sloan and Pearce, 1946.

Fischer, Louis, *Men and Politics: An Autobiography*, London, Jonathan Cape, 1941.

Fisher, H. A. L., *An Unfinished Autobiography*, Oxford, Oxford University Press, 1940.

Foot, Michael, *Aneurin Bevan: A Biography*, 2 Vols., London, MacGibbon and Kee, 1962.

Foote, Geoffrey, *The Labour Party's Political Thought, A History*, London, Croom Helm, 1985.

Fox, Ralph, *A Defence of Communism in Reply to H. J. Laski*, London, Communist Party, 1927.

Frankel, William (ed.), *Friday Nights: A Jewish Chronicle Anthology*, London, Jewish Chronicle Productions, 1973.

Frankfurter, Felix, *Felix Frankfurter Reminisces*, New York, Reynal, 1960.

Frankfurter, Felix, *Of Law and Life and Other Things That Matter*, Cambridge, Harvard University Press, 1965.

Frankfurter, Felix, *Of Law and Men*, New York, Harcourt, Brace, 1956.

Freedman, Max (ed.), *Roosevelt and Frankfurter, Their Correspondence, 1928–1945*, Boston, Little-Brown, 1967.

Freemantle, Anne, *This Little Band of Prophets: The British Fabians*, New York, Mentor, 1960.

Furbank, P. N., *E. M. Forster: A Life*, London, Secker and Warburg, 1978.

Gandhi, Mahatma, *The Collected Works of Mahatma Gandhi*, New Delhi, Government of India, 1971.

Gannett, Frank E. and Catherwood, B. F. (eds.), *Industrial and Labour Relations in Great Britain*, New York, America's Future, 1939.

George, T. J. S., *Krishna Menon: A Biography*, London, Jonathan Cape, 1964.

Gilbert, Martin, *Plough My Own Furrow: The Story of Lord Allen of Hurtwood*, London, Longmans, 1965.

Gilbert, Martin, *Winston S. Churchill*, Vols. V–VIII, Boston, Houghton Mifflin, 1977–1986.

Glasser, Ralph, *Gorbals Boy at Oxford*, London, Chatto and Windus, 1988.

Golding, Louis, *The World I Knew*, New York, Viking, 1940.

Goldstein, Israel, *Brandeis University: Chapter of Its Founding*, New York, Bloch, 1951.

Gollancz, Victor, *My Dear Timothy: An Autobiographical Letter to His Grandson*, London, Gollancz, 1952.

Gollancz, Victor, *Reminiscences of Affection*, London, Gollancz, 1968.

Goodwin, Doris Kearns, *The Fitzgeralds and The Kennedys*, New York, St Martin's, 1987.

Gorny, Joseph, *The British Labour Movement and Zionism, 1917–1948*, London, Frank Cass, 1983.

Graham, J. A. and Phythian, B. A., *The Manchester Grammar School*, Manchester, Manchester University Press, 1965.

Grimshaw, Eric and Jones, Glyn, *Lord Goddard: His Career and Cases*, London, Allan Wingate, 1958.

Gupta, Ram Chandra, *Harold J. Laski, A Critical Analysis of His Political Ideas*, Agra, Asia Press, 1966.

Haldane, R. B., *Richard Burdon Haldane: An Autobiography*, London, Hodder and Stoughton, 1929.

Hamilton, Mary Agnes, *Arthur Henderson*, London, Heinemann, 1938.

Harris, José, *William Beveridge: A Biography*, Oxford, Clarendon, 1977.

Harris, Kenneth, *Attlee*, New York, Norton, 1982.

Hart-Davis, Rupert (ed.), *Siegfried Sassoon Diaries 1923–1925*, London, Faber, 1985.

Hastings, Patricia, *The Life of Patrick Hastings*, London, Cresset, 1959.

Hastings, Patrick, *Cases in Court*, London, Heinemann, 1949.

Hay, Alice Ivy, *There was a Man of Genius: Orde Wingate*, London, Neville Spearman, 1963.

Hayek, F. A. von, *The Intellectuals and Socialism*, Menlo Park, Institute for Humane Studies, 1978.

Hayek, F. A. von, *The Road to Serfdom*, Chicago, University of Chicago Press, 1944.

Henriques, Robert, *Sir Robert Waley Cohen, 1877–1952*, London, Secker and Warburg, 1966.

Herzstein, Robert Edwin, *Roosevelt and Hitler, Prelude to War*, New York, Paragon, 1989.

Heuston, R. F. V., *Lives of the Lord Chancellors, 1885–1940*, Oxford, Oxford University Press, 1964.

Hirst, Paul Q., *The Pluralist Theory of the State*, London, Routledge, 1989.

Hiss, Alger, *Recollections of a Life*, New York, Henry Holt, 1988.

Hodges, Sheila, *Gollancz: The Story of a Publishing House 1928–1978*, London, Gollancz, 1978.

Hoffinger, David A., *Morris R. Cohen and the Scientific Ideal*, Cambridge, MIT Press, 1975.

Hollander, Paul, *Political Pilgrims*, New York, Oxford University Press, 1981.

Holton, Bob, *British Syndicalism 1900–1914*, London, Pluto Press, 1976.

Howarth, T. E. B., *Prospect and Reality, Great Britain 1945–1955*, London, Collins, 1985.

Howe, Mark DeWolfe (ed.), *Holmes–Laski Letters*, 2 Vols., Cambridge, Harvard University Press, 1953.

Howe, Mark DeWolfe (ed.), *Holmes–Pollock Letters,* Cambridge, Harvard University Press, 1946.

Hubenka, Lloyd J., *Bernard Shaw: Practical Politics*, Lincoln, University of Nebraska, 1976.

Hughes, Emrys, *Keir Hardie*, London, Allen and Unwin, 1956.

Ickes, Harold L., *The Secret Diary of Harold L. Ickes*, 3 Vols., New York, Simon and Schuster, 1954.

Iremonger, F. A., *William Temple, Archbishop of Canterbury*, London, Oxford University Press, 1948.

Jeffreys, Kevin (ed.), *Labour and the Wartime Coalition: From the Diary of James Chuter-Ede, 1941–1945*, London, Historians Press, 1987.

Jenkins, Mark, *Bevanism: Labour's High Tide*, London, Spokesman, 1979.

. Jones, Thomas, *A Diary with Letters: 1931–1950*, London, Oxford University Press, 1954.

Josephson, Matthew, *Infidel in the Temple: A Memoir of the Nineteen-Thirties*, New York, Knopf, 1967.

Jupp, James, *The Radical Left in Britain, 1931–1941*, London, Frank Cass, 1982.

Kellner, Peter and Hitchins, Christopher, *Callaghan: The Road to Number Ten*, London, Cassell, 1976.

Kennedy, Rose Fitzgerald, *Times to Remember*, New York, Doubleday, 1974.

Kevles, Daniel J., *In the Name of Eugenics*, Berkeley, University of California Press, 1986.

Keynes, John Maynard, *Laissez-Faire and Communism*, New York, New Republic, 1926.

Kimche, Jon and David, *The Secret Roads, The 'Illegal' Migration of a People 1938–1948*, New York, Farrar, Strauss and Cudahy, 1955.

Kinnear, Michael, *The British Voter, An Atlas and Survey Since 1885*, Ithaca, Cornell University Press, 1968.

Kloppenberg, James T., *Uncertain Victory: Social Democracy and Progressivism in European and American Thought, 1870–1920*, New York, Oxford University Press, 1985.

Koskoff, David E., *Joseph P. Kennedy: A Life and Times*, Englewood Cliffs, Prentice Hall, 1974.

Koss, Stephen E., *Lord Haldane: Scapegoat for Liberalism*, New York, Columbia University Press, 1969.

Kushner, Tony, *The Persistence of Prejudice: Anti-Semitism in British Society during the Second World War*, Manchester, Manchester University Press, 1989.

Kushner, Tony and Lunn, Kenneth (eds.), *Traditions of Intolerance*, Manchester, Manchester University Press, 1989.

Kutty, V. K. Madhavan, *V. K. Krishna Menon*, New Delhi, Government of India, 1988.

Lansbury, George, *Looking Backwards and Forwards*, London, Blackie and Son, 1935.

Lash, Joseph P., *Dealers and Dreamers: A New Look at the New Deal*, New York, Doubleday, 1988.

Lash, Joseph P. (ed.), *From the Diaries of Felix Frankfurter*, New York, Norton, 1974.

Laski, Harold J., *The American Democracy*, New York, Viking, 1948.

Laski, Harold J., *The American Presidency: An Interpretation*, London, Allen and Unwin, 1940.

Laski, Harold J., *Authority in the Modern State*, New Haven, Yale University Press, 1919.

Laski, Harold J., *Communism*, London, Williams and Norgate, 1927.

Laski, Harold J., *The Danger of Being a Gentleman and Other Essays*, New York, Viking, 1940.

Laski, Harold J., *The Dangers of Disobedience and Other Essays*, New York, Harper and Brothers, 1930.

Laski, Harold J., *Democracy in Crisis*, Chapel Hill, University of North Carolina Press, 1933.

Laski, Harold J., *The Dilemma of Our Times*, London, Allen and Unwin, 1952.

Laski, Harold J., *Faith, Reason and Civilization*, New York, Viking, 1944.

Laski, Harold J., *The Foundations of Sovereignty and Other Essays*, New York, Harcourt, Brace, 1921.

Laski, Harold J., *A Grammar of Politics*, London, Allen and Unwin, 1925.

Laski, Harold J., *An Introduction to Politics*, London, Allen and Unwin, 1931.

Laski, Harold J., *Karl Marx: An Essay*, London, The Fabian Society, n.d.

Laski, Harold J., *Liberty in the Modern State*, Harmondsworth, Penguin Books, 1937.

Laski, Harold J., *Parliamentary Government in England*, New York, Viking, 1938.

Laski, Harold J., *Political Thought In England, Locke to Bentham*, London, Oxford University Press, 1961.

Laski, Harold J., *Reflections on the Revolution of Our Time*, New York, Viking, 1943.

Laski, Harold J., *Reflections on the Constitution*, Manchester, Manchester University Press, 1951.

Laski, Harold J., *The Rise of European Liberalism: An Essay in Interpretation*, London, Allen and Unwin, 1936.

Laski, Harold J., *The State in Theory and Practice*, London, Allen and Unwin, 1935.

Laski, Harold J., *The Strategy of Freedom: An Open Letter to American Youth*, New York, Harper and Brothers, 1941.

Laski, Harold J., *Studies in Law and Politics,* New Haven, Yale University Press, 1932.

Laski, Harold J., *Studies in the Problem of Sovereignty*, New Haven, Yale University Press, 1917.

Laski, Harold J., *Trade Unions in the New Society*, New York, Viking, 1949.

Laski, Harold J., *Where Do We Go From Here?*, Harmondsworth, Penguin Books, 1940.

Lerner, Max, *Ideas for the Ice Age*, New York, Viking, 1941.

Lerner, Max, *The Unfinished Country: A Book of American Symbols*, New York, Simon and Schuster, 1959.

Letwin, Shirley Robin, *The Pursuit of Certainty*, Cambridge, Cambridge University Press, 1965.

Leventhal, F. M., *Arthur Henderson*, Manchester, Manchester University Press, 1989.

Levy, David W., *Herbert Croly of the New Republic*, Princeton, Princeton University Press, 1985.

Lewis, John, *The Left Book Club: An Historical Record*, London, Gollancz, 1970.

Litvinoff, Barnet (ed.), *The Letters and Papers of Chaim Weizmann*, New Brunswick, Transaction Books, 1978.

McCarran, M. Margaret, *Fabianism in the Political Life of Britain, 1919–1931*, Washington, DC, Catholic University Press, 1952.

MacDonald, J. Ramsay, *The Socialist Movement*, New York, Henry Holt, 1911.

MacIntyre, Stuart, *A Proletarian Science: Marxism in Britain, 1917–1933*, London, Lawrence and Wishart, 1986.

MacKenzie, Norman (ed.), *The Letters of Sidney and Beatrice Webb*, Cambridge, Cambridge University Press, 1978.

MacKenzie, Norman and Jeanne, *H. G. Wells*, New York, Simon and Schuster, 1973.

MacKenzie, Norman and Jeanne (eds.), *The Diary of Beatrice Webb*, London, Virago, 1982–5.

McKenzie, R. T., *British Political Parties*, New York, St Martin's, 1955.

Macmillan, Harold, *Winds of Change, 1914–1939*, London, Macmillan, 1966.

Mahon, John, *Harry Pollitt: A Biography*, London, Lawrence and Wishart, 1976.

Mandle, W. F., *Anti-Semitism and the British Union of Fascists*, London, Longmans, 1968.

Mansbridge, Albert, *Fellow Men, A Gallery of England, 1876–1946*, London, Dent, 1948.

Martin, David E. and Rubinstein, David (eds.), *Ideology and the Labour Movement: Essays Presented to John Saville*, London, Croom Helm, 1979.

Martin, Kingsley, *Critic's London Diary*, London, Secker and Warburg, 1960.

Martin, Kingsley, *Editor: A Second Book of Autobiography, 1931–45*, London, Hutchinson, 1968.

Martin, Kingsley, *Father Figures: A First Volume of Autobiography*, London, Hutchinson, 1966.

Martin, Kingsley, *Harold Laski, A Biography*, London, Jonathan Cape, 1969.

Masani, Zareer, *Indira Gandhi, A Biography*, London, Hamish Hamilton, 1975.

Mason, A. T., *Harlan Fiske Stone: Pillar of the Law*, New York, Viking, 1956.

Meehan, Eugene J., *The British Left Wing and Foreign Policy*, New Brunswick, Rutgers University Press, 1960.

Mendelson, Wallace (ed.), *Felix Frankfurter, A Tribute*, New York, Regnal, 1964.

Messinger, Gary S., *Manchester in the Victorian Age*, Manchester, Manchester University Press, 1985.

Middlemass, Keith, *Politics in Industrial Society, The Experience of the British System Since 1911*, London, André Deutsch, 1979.

Middlemass, Keith (ed.), *Thomas Jones: Whitehall Diary Vol. II, 1926–1930*, London, Oxford University Press, 1969.

Middlemass, Keith and Barnes, John, *Baldwin, A Biography*, London, Macmillan, 1969.

Miliband, Ralph, *Capitalist Democracy in Britain*, Oxford, Oxford University Press, 1982.

Miliband, Ralph, *Parliamentary Socialism: A Study in the Politics of Labour*, London, Merlin, 1987.

Millis, Walter (ed.), *The Forrestal Diaries*, New York, Viking, 1951.

Mohan, Anand, *Indira Gandhi, A Personal and Political Biography*, New York, Merideth Press, 1967.

Morgan, Austen, *J. Ramsay MacDonald*, Manchester, Manchester University Press, 1987.

Morgan, Kenneth O., *Labour in Power, 1945–1951*, Oxford, Clarendon, 1984.

Morgan, Kenneth O., *Labour People, Leaders and Lieutenants, Hardie to Kinnock*, Oxford, Oxford University Press, 1987.

Morgan, Ted, *FDR: A Biography*, New York, Simon and Schuster, 1985.

Morris, Margaret, *The General Strike*, Harmondsworth, Penguin Books, 1976.

Morrison, Herbert, *Herbert Morrison, An Autobiography*, London, Odhams, 1960.

Mosley, Oswald, *My Life*, London, Nelson, 1968.

Muggeridge, Kitty and Adam, Ruth, *Beatrice Webb*, Chicago, Academy Chicago, 1983.

Mullally, Frederick, *Fascism Inside England*, London, Claud Morris, 1946.

Mumford, Alfred, A., *The Manchester Grammar School*, London, Longmans Green, 1919.

Nahon, S. U., *The 1,000 Immigrants Detained at La Spezia in 1946*, Jerusalem, Bitfuzot Hagolan, 1972.

Naylor, John F., *Labour's International Policy, the Labour Party in the 1930s*, London, Weidenfeld and Nicolson, 1969.

Nehru, Jawaharlal, *A Bunch of Old Letters*, Bombay, Asia Publishing House, 1958.

Nevinson, H. W., *The English*, London, Routledge, 1929.

Nevinson, H. W., *More Changes, More Chances*, New York, Harcourt Brace, 1925.

Newman, Aubrey, *The Board of Deputies of British Jews 1700–1985*, London, Valentine, Mitchell and Co., 1987.

Newman, Michael, *John Strachey*, Manchester, Manchester University Press, 1989.

Nichols, David, *The Pluralist State*, London, Macmillan, 1975.

Nichols, David, *Three Varieties of Pluralism*, London, Macmillan, 1974.

Ovendale, Ritchie, *Britain, The United States, and the End of the Palestine Mandate 1942–1948*, Woodbridge, Suffolk, Royal Historical Society, 1989.

Oxbury, Harold, *Great Britons, Twentieth-Century Lives*, Oxford, Oxford University Press, 1985.

Panitch, Leo, *Working Class Politics in Crisis*, London, Verso, 1986.

Parker, John, *Father of the House, Fifty Years in Politics*, London, Routledge, 1982.

Parrish, Michael E., *Felix Frankfurter and His Times*, New York, Free Press, 1985.

Pastore, Nicholas, *The Nature–Nurture Controversy*, New York, Columbia University, 1949.

Pearson, Karl, *The Life, Letters and Labours of Francis Galton*, Cambridge, Cambridge University Press, 1930.

Peden, G. C., *Keynes, The Treasury and British Economic Policy*, London, Macmillan, 1988.

Pelling, Henry, *America and the British Left, From Bright to Bevan*, London, Black, 1956.

Pelling, Henry, *The Labour Governments, 1945–1951*, London, Macmillan, 1984.

Perkin, Harold, *The Rise of Professional Society, England Since 1880*, London, Routledge, 1989.

Persico, Joseph E., *Edward R. Murrow, An American Original*, New York, McGraw Hill, 1988.

Phillips, G. A., *The General Strike*, London, Weidenfeld and Nicolson, 1976.

Pierson, Stanley, *British Socialists, The Journey From Fantasy to Politics*, Cambridge, Harvard University Press, 1979.

Pimlott, Ben, *Hugh Dalton*, London, Jonathan Cape, 1985.

Pimlott, Ben, *Labour and the Left in the 1930s*, London, Allen and Unwin, 1986.

Pimlott, Ben (ed.), *The Political Diary of Hugh Dalton*, 2 Vols., London, Jonathan Cape, 1986.

Polenberg, Richard, *Fighting Faiths, The Abrams Case, The Supreme Court, and Free Speech*, New York, Viking, 1987.

Postgate, Raymond, *The Life of George Lansbury*, London, Longmans, Green, 1951.

Potter, E. C., *Kings of the Court, the Story of Lawn Tennis*, New York, A. S. Barnes, 1963.

Provine, William B., *The Origins of Theoretical Population Genetics*, Chicago, University of Chicago, 1971.

Pugh, Patricia, *Educate, Agitate, Organise: 100 Years of Fabian Socialism*, London, Methuen, 1984.

Qualter, Terence H., *Graham Wallas and the Great Society*, New York, St Martin's, 1979.

Radice, Lisanne, *Beatrice and Sidney Webb*, New York, St Martin's, 1984.

Ramsden, John, *The Age of Balfour and Baldwin 1902–1940*, London, Longman, 1978.

Rée, Jonathan, *Proletarian Philosophers, Problems in Socialist Culture in Britain 1900–1940*, Oxford, Clarendon, 1984.

Reed, Bruce and Williams, Geoffrey, *Denis Healey and the Policies of Power*, London, Sidgwick and Jackson, 1971.

Reinharz, Jehuda, *Chaim Weizmann: The Making of a Zionist Leader*, New York, Oxford University Press, 1985.

Robbins, Keith (ed.), *The Blackwell Biographical Dictionary of British Political Life in the Twentieth Century*, Oxford, Blackwell, 1990.

Robbins, Lionel, *Autobiography of An Economist*, London, Macmillan, 1971.

Robson, William A. (ed.), *The Political Quarterly in the Thirties*, London, Penguin Books, 1971.

Rodgers, W. T. and Donoughue, Bernard, *The People into Parliament: An Illustrated History of the Labour Party*, London, Thomas and Hudson, 1966.

Rogow, Arnold A., *James Forrestal: A Study of Personality, Politics and Policy*, New York, Macmillan, 1963.

Rolph, C. H., *Kingsley: The Life, Letters and Diaries of Kingsley Martin*, London, Gollancz, 1973.

Rosen, Andrew, *Rise Up, Women!*, London, Routledge, 1974.

Rosenfield, Leonora Cohen, *Portrait of a Philosopher: Morris R. Cohen in Life and Letters*, New York, Harcourt, Brace and World, 1962.

Rover, Constance, *Women's Suffrage and Party Politics in Britain, 1866–1914*, London, Routledge, 1967.

Rowse, A. L., *Memories and Glimpses*, London, Methuen, 1986.

Russell, Bertrand, *The Autobiography of Bertrand Russell 1914–1944*, Boston, Little, Brown, 1968.

Russell, Dora, *The Tamarisk Tree: My Quest for Liberty and Love*, New York, G. P. Putnam's Sons, 1975.

Russell, Francis, *A City in Terror: 1919, The Boston Police Strike*, New York, Viking, 1975.

Sachar, Abram L., *A Host at Last*, Boston, Little, Brown, 1976.

Sanders, Jane, *Cold War on the Campus*, Seattle, University of Washington Press, 1979.

Sarma, G. N., *The Political Thought of Harold J. Laski*, Bombay, Orient Longmans, 1965.

Sassoon, Siegfried, *Siegfried's Journey: 1916–1920*, New York, Viking, 1946.

Saville, John, *The Labour Movement in Britain*, London, Faber and Faber, 1988.

Schlesinger, Arthur M. Jr, *The Vital Center: The Politics of Freedom*, Boston, Houghton Mifflin, 1949.

Schlesinger, Arthur M., Jr, *The Age of Roosevelt: The Politics of Upheaval*, Boston, Houghton Mifflin, 1988.

Schneer, Jonathan, *Labour's Conscience: The Labour Left 1945–1951*, Boston, Unwin Hyman, 1988.

Schwarz, Jordan A., *Liberal, Adolph A. Berle and the Vision of an American Era*, New York, Free Press, 1987.

Searle, G. R., *Eugenics and Politics in Britain, 1900–1914*, Leyden, Noordhoff, 1976.

Searls, Hank, *The Lost Prince: Young Joe, the Forgotten Kennedy*, New York, New American Library, 1969.

Seideman, David, *The New Republic: A Voice of Modern Liberalism*, New York, Praeger, 1986.

Seton, Marie, *Panditji, A Portrait of Jawaharlal Nehru*, London, Dennis Dobson, 1967.

Seyd, Patrick, *The Rise and Fall of the Labour Left*, New York, St Martin's, 1987.

Shaw, G. B., *Fabian Essays in Socialism*, New York, Doubleday, n.d.

Shinwell, Emmanuel, *The Labour Story*, London, MacDonald, 1963.

Sinclair, Upton, *The Goose-Step, A Study of American Education*, Los Angeles, The Author, 1922.

Sissons, Michael and French, Philip (eds.), *Age of Austerity*, London, Hodder and Stoughton, 1963.

Smith, Arthur, *Lord Goddard: My Years With the Lord Chief Justice*, London, Weidenfeld and Nicolson, 1959.

Smith, David, C., *H. G. Wells, Desperately Mortal*, New Haven, Yale, 1986.

Sommer, Dudley, *Haldane of Cloan: His Life and Times*, London, Allen and Unwin, 1960.

Sperber, A. M., *Murrow, His Life and Times*, New York, Freundlich, 1986.

Stansky, Peter and Abrahams, William, *Orwell: The Transformation*, New York, Knopf, 1980.

Steel, Ronald, *Walter Lippmann and the American Century*, New York, Vintage, 1980.

Stevenson, John, *British Society, 1914–1945*, Harmondsworth, Penguin Books, 1984.

Stocks, Mary, *The Workers' Educational Association; The First Fifty Years*, London, Allen and Unwin, 1953.

Stonehouse, John, *Death of an Idealist*, London, W. H. Allen, 1975.

Strachey, John, *The Coming Struggle for Power*, New York, Covici-Friede, 1933.

Strachey, John, *The Strangled Cry*, New York, W. Sloane, 1962.

Straight, Michael, *After Long Silence*, New York, Norton, 1983.

Strauss, Patricia, *Bevin and Co. The Leaders of British Labour*, New York, G. P. Putnam, 1941.

Strum, Philippa, *Louis D. Brandeis, Justice for the People*, Cambridge, Harvard University Press, 1984.

Sulzberger, C., *A Long Row of Candles: Memoirs and Diaries, 1934–1954*, Toronto, Macmillan, 1969.

Swanberg, W. A., *Luce and His Empire*, New York, Dell, 1972.

Taylor, A. J. P., *English History, 1914–1945*, New York, Oxford University Press, 1965.

Taylor, A. J. P., *Politicians, Socialism and Historians*, New York, Stein and Day, 1982.

Taylor, H. A., *Jix, Viscount Brentford*, London, Stanley Paul and Co., 1933.

Terrill, Ross, *R. H. Tawney and His Times*, Cambridge, Harvard University Press, 1973.

Thomas, Elizabeth (ed.), *Tribune 21*, London, MacGibbon and Kee, 1958.

Thomas, Hugh, *John Strachey*, New York, Harper and Row, 1973.

Thurlow, Richard, *Fascism in Britain: A History, 1918–1985*, Oxford, Blackwell, 1987.

Ulam, Adam B., *Philosophical Foundations of English Socialism*, Cambridge, Harvard University Press, 1951.

Urofsky, Melvin and Levy, David (eds.), *'Half-Brother, Half-Son': The Letters of Louis D. Brandeis to Felix Frankfurter*, Norman, OK, University of Oklahoma Press, 1991.

Vernon, Betty D., *Ellen Wilkinson, 1891–1947*, London, Croom Helm, 1982.

Vernon, Betty D., *Margaret Cole, 1893–1980*, London, Croom Helm, 1986.

Watkins, Ernest, *The Cautious Revolution: Britain Today and Tomorrow*, New York, Farrar, Strauss, 1950.

Webber, G. C., *The Ideology of the British Right 1918–1939*, New York, St Martin's, 1986.

Wechsler, James A., *The Age of Suspicion*, New York, Random House, 1953.

Weiner, Martin J., *Between Two Worlds: The Political Thought of Graham Wallas*, Oxford, Clarendon, 1971.

Weisbord, Robert G., *African Zion*, Philadelphia, The Jewish Publication Society, 1968.

Weizmann, Chaim, *Trial and Error: The Autobiography*, New York, Harper and Brothers, 1949.

Weizmann, Vera, *The Impossible Takes Longer*, London, Hamish Hamilton, 1967.

Werskey, Gary, *The Visible College, The Collective Biography of British Scientific Socialists of the 1930s*, New York, Holt, Rinehart and Winston, 1978.

Wheeler, John Harvey, *The Conservative Crisis: England's Impasse of 1931*, Washington, Public Affairs Press, 1956.

White, Leonard D., *Whitley Councils in the British Civil Service*, Chicago, University of Chicago Press, 1933.

White, Morton, *Social Thought in America, The Revolt Against Formalism*, London, Oxford University Press, 1976.

Williams, Bill, *Manchester Jewry*, Manchester, Archive Publications, 1988.

Williams, Francis, *Ernest Bevin, Portrait of A Great Englishman*, London, Hutchinson, 1952.

Williams, Francis, *A Prime Minister Remembers, Memoirs of Earl Attlee*, London, Heinemann, 1961.

Williams, Francis (ed.), *Twilight of Empire: Memoirs of Prime Minister Clement Attlee*, New York, A. S. Barnes, 1962.

Williams, Philip M., *Hugh Gaitskell: A Political Biography*, London, Jonathan Cape, 1979.

Wilson, Duncan, *Leonard Woolf: A Political Biography*, London, Hogarth Press, 1978.

Wilson, Edmund, *Letters on Literature and Politics 1912–1972*, New York, Farrar, Strauss, and Giroux, 1977.

Wilson, Francis, G. (ed.), *Introduction to Contemporary Politics, Selected Literature by Harold Laski*, Seattle, University of Washington Book Store, 1939.

Winant, John G., *Letters from Grosvenor Square*, Boston, Houghton Mifflin, 1947.

Wood, Neal, *Communism and British Intellectuals*, New York, Columbia University Press, 1959.

Woodcock, George, *The Crystal Spirit: A Study of George Orwell*, Boston, Little Brown, 1966.

Woolf, Leonard, *Downhill All The Way: An Autobiography of the Years 1919–1939*, London, Hogarth Press, 1967.

Woolf, Leonard, *The Journey Not the Arrival Matters: An Autobiography of the Years 1939–1969*, New York, Harcourt Brace, 1969.

Wright, Anthony, *R. H. Tawney*, Manchester, Manchester University Press, 1987.

Yeomans, Henry Aaron, *Abbott Lawrence Lowell 1856–1943*, Cambridge, Harvard University Press, 1948.

Young, G. M. *Stanley Baldwin*, London, Rupert Hart-Davis, 1952.

Young, Kenneth (ed.), *The Diaries of Sir Robert Bruce Lockhart, Vol. II, 1939–1965*, London, Macmillan, 1980.

Zylstra, Bernard, *From Pluralism to Collectivism: The Development of Harold Laski's Political Thought*, Assen, Van Goreum and Co., 1968.

ARTICLES

Anstey, Caroline, 'The Projection of British Socialism: Foreign Office Publicity and American Opinion, 1945–50', *Journal of Contemporary History*, Vol. 19 (1984).

Beloff, Max, 'The Age of Laski', *Fortnightly*, June 1950.

Burridge, T. D., 'A Postscript to Potsdam: The Churchill–Laski Electoral Clash, June 1945', *Journal of Contemporary History*, Vol. 12 (1977).

Burton, David H., 'The Intellectual Kinship of Oliver Wendell Holmes, Jr, Frederick E. Pollock and Harold J. Laski', *Proceedings of the American Philosophical Society*, Vol. 119, (1975).

Chafee, Zachariah, Jr, 'Harold Laski and the Harvard Law Review', 63 *Harvard Law Review* 1398, June 1950.

Cosgrove, Richard, 'Harold Laski and The American Democracy: A Four Decade Perspective', *Mid-America*, April–July 1988.

Ekrich, Arthur A. Jr, 'Harold Laski: The Liberal Manqué or Lost Libertarian?', *Journal of Libertarian Studies*, Vol. 4 (1980).

Feuer, Lewis S., 'The Inventor of Pluralism', *The New Leader*, 4 September 1989.

Gorni, Yosef, 'The Jewishness and Zionism of Harold Laski', Midstream, November 1927.

Grantham, John T., 'Hugh Dalton and the International Post-War Settlement: Labour Party Foreign Policy Formulation, 1943–44', *Journal of Contemporary History*, Vol. 14 (1979).

Greenleaf, W. H., 'Laski and British Socialism', *History of Political Thought*, Vol. 2 (1981).

Hall, John and Higgins, Joan, 'What Influences Today's Labour MPs?', *New Society*, 2 December 1976.

Kampelman, Max, 'Harold Laski; A Current Analysis', *The Journal of Politics*, Vol. 10 (1948).

Moynihan, Daniel P., 'The United States in Opposition', *Commentary*, March 1975.

Neuchierlein, James A., 'The Dream of Scientific Liberalism: The New Republic and American Progressive Thought, 1914–1920', *Review of Politics*, April 1980.

Peretz, Martin, 'Laski Redivivus', *Journal of Contemporary History*, Vol. 1 (1966).

Shaw, Christopher, 'Eliminating the Yahoo: Eugenics, Social Darwinism and Five Fabians,' *History of Political Thought*, Vol. 8 (1987).

Wilson, Edmund, 'Justice Holmes and Harold Laski: Their Relationship', *The New Yorker*, 16 May, 1953.

Winter, J. M., 'The Webbs and the Non-White World: A Case of Socialist Racialism', *Journal of Contemporary History*, Vol. 9 (1974).

Wright, Anthony W., 'Guild Socialism Revisited', *Journal of Contemporary History*, Vol. 9 (1974).

Index

Wechsler, James 392

Weizmann, Chaim 10, 26–9, 276–81, 356

Wells, H. G. 1, 41–2, 66, 89, 156, 158–9, 163, 171, 176–7, 193, 195, 204, 236, 246, 263–4, 266, 336, 340, 341, 383, 432

West, Rebecca 66, 200, 203, 212, 263, 266, 470, 496, 584

Westminster Review 34–7

Wheatley, John 191, 213

White, Morton 90

Whitelaw, Aubrey 334

Whiteley, William 480

Whitley, J. H. 165

Whitley Councils 165, 228, 257–8, 440

Wigram, Clive 299

Wilkinson, Ellen 271, 316, 317, 340, 373, 377, 409, 471, 477, 480

Williams, Francis 584

Wilson, Edmund 5, 114, 168, 195, 204, 243, 295, 407, 483, 540–1, 570, 584

Wilson, Harold 546, 588

Wilson, Woodrow 86, 93, 111, 149, 167, 204

Winant, John G. 431, 438, 452, 458, 463, 465, 477

Wingate, Orde 477

Winrod, Gerald B. 395

Wise, E. F. 305, 315

Wolf, George 200

Woodhull, Victoria 42

Woolf, Leonard 168, 193, 206, 263, 266–7, 284, 298, 343, 367, 384, 387–8

Woolf, Virginia 50, 193, 298

Workers' Birth Control Group 191

World War One 76–9, 85–6, 93, 104–5, 122, 128, 131, 228

World War Two 412–28, 431–9, 442, 445–6, 451–2, 456–7, 458–63, 474, 465–71, 490

XYZ Club 344–5

Yale University 118–19, 145, 291–2, 321, 394–5, 577

Yale University Law School 271, 287, 291, 309, 390

Yale University Press 94, 101, 124, 233

Young, G. M. 457

Zangwill, Israel 27, 84

Zilliacus, Konni 548

Zimmern, Alfred 106, 143

Zinoviev Letter 215, 488

Zionism *see* Palestine